DECENCY AND DISORDER:
THE AGE OF CANT 1789–1837

Making Decent by George Cruikshank, 1822. When the ladies of England subscribed for a memorial statue to the Duke of Wellington and the veterans of Waterloo in Hyde Park, few predicted that it would be a naked Achilles. Some sections of the public were disgusted and petitioned to have the offensive parts of the statue covered up. Mocking the futility of such a campaign, not to say the attention it drew to parts of the statue which most had overlooked, Cruikshank has William Wilberforce hold up his hat to preserve public decency

Decency and Disorder

THE AGE OF CANT 1789–1837

Ben Wilson

faber and faber

by the same author

THE LAUGHTER OF TRIUMPH: William Hone and the Fight for the Free Press

First published in 2007
by Faber and Faber Limited
3 Queen Square London WC1N 3AU

Typeset in Sabon by Faber and Faber
Printed in England by Mackays of Chatham, plc

The frontispiece illustration and those on pages 49 and 318–19 are courtesy of the Trustees of the British Museum; that on page 345 is from the Victoria and Albert Museum and the photograph is copyright Francis Glibbery and John Ingledew; the rest are from private collections

A CIP record for this book
is available from the British Library
ISBN 978–0–571–22468–5
ISBN 0–571–22468–7

2 4 6 8 10 9 7 5 3 1

To MCW

‘My dear friend, clear your mind of cant . . . you may *talk* in this manner; it is the mode of talking in society; but don’t *think* foolishly.’

Dr Johnson

Contents

Introduction: Untaught Feelings

> 'If liberty produces ill-manners and want of taste, she is a very excellent parent with two very disagreeable daughters.'
>
> William Hazlitt[1]

William Palfrey, a recent graduate of Cambridge, paraded naked along the side of a canal on a summer's day in 1818, loudly proclaiming that 'he would not put on his clothes for any man living'. The parish of Camberwell, where the offence took place, had recently stationed constables on the banks of the canal to arrest those who engaged in the 'indecency and immorality' of swimming on Sundays. Palfrey, as he saw it, had started a one-man war against puritanism.

When the case came to court, Palfrey's attorney said that his client was naked for the purpose of swimming: 'men are not to be indicted for a healthful and beneficial amusement because indelicate women pass by'. Palfrey had taken off his clothes not as an early statement of nudism, but to test the boundaries of British liberty. No petty parish official had the authority to dictate morality to the rest of the community. People had always been able to bathe, and until recently no one had complained. He 'conceived that if this squeamishness of seeing naked figures was to be listened to, there would soon be an end of our boasted constitution!'[2]

The crusade failed, and Palfrey was fined one shilling. It was a silly case and it had occurred only because people felt alienated by the fastidious meddling of a minority of self-appointed moral guardians. In 1815 Parliament had discovered that 'a pious fraud' had been played upon it: a clause which effectively banned swimming had been slipped into the Thames Police Act it had passed the year before. Despite the pleas of the evangelical lobby, the House of Commons repealed the clause; one MP said that if a few women were offended they had better stay at home rather than make the lower orders 'suffer for the accommodation of their delicacy'. He told the House that 'this is one of those melancholy evils which result from an itch for legislating which prevails in the subordinate offices of the state'. Since Parliament would not help, local authorities and individuals had taken matters into their own hands; there had been a spate of prosecutions against bathers who had not even been fully naked. A magistrate said of canal bathing that a 'practice more offensive to decency could not well be imagined'.[3]

Palfrey deliberately provoked the law to expose this kind of nonsense. The concern over exposed flesh was seen as something new. A decade before, people had been free to amuse themselves as they liked without being accused of endangering public morals. In August 1803 *The Times* had reported from Brighton on the unashamed and natural habits of the ladies of the fashionable world: 'To-day the bathing has been very numerously and *charmingly* attended, OLD NEPTUNE must have a happy time on't, when such shoals of beauty daily rush to his gelid embraces; and afterwards rise, like so many *Venuses*, glowing with new blushes from his briny bed.' The curious observer might enjoy 'the sportive frolics and various forms of the fair *Nereides*, displayed by their thin bathing costumes'.[4]

But the unrestrained language of *The Times* was out of step with the moral feelings of some very respectable and very sensitive people. The origin of the canal prosecutions lies in a test case of a few years before. In March 1809 a young man called John Crendon found himself summoned to court for a crime which was 'most offensive to common decency'. He had, as fashionable people were wont to do, bathed off Brighton beach. 'Can it be in a civilized country that females are subjected to such an insult?' the Society for the Suppression of Vice asked. 'Can any husband or father endure that the feelings of his wife or daughter shall be thus outraged? Can any youth be willing that the female, on whose domestic virtues he has staked his hopes of connubial happiness, shall be subjected to such insults?'

Some of the townsfolk of the resort had formed a private prosecuting committee, which dug up old laws to put a stop 'to the very indecent and scandalous practice of bathing in public'. The young sportsman had persistently ignored its officious notices warning that bathers who paraded their flesh in front of dwellings were a nuisance and would be prosecuted. Crendon laughed at the prudish vigilantes, claiming that the sea was free and he could do as he pleased. The Brighton Committee prosecuted him for indecent exposure. Crendon and most of the country must have assumed that the case would be laughed out of court.

When he was brought to trial at Horsham, Crendon defended himself on the grounds that the place where he had swum was formerly out of the way of housing; the new dwellings were the 'nuisance', not him. He also said that there was no evidence that he had done anything indecent or exposed any part of his body further than was necessary for the purposes of bathing. But the trial judge declared that 'wherever houses come, decency comes with them'. He recommended those who were offended by others' conduct 'to admonish by handbills, by boards, and by persons appointed to attend the beach, and if any one is obtuse, and will persist after remonstrance, as this young man has done, to bring him here, and ask a jury whether this is to be endured? In my opinion this is a very bad case.'

Crendon was duly found guilty. The moral of the story was that people were not just entitled to form vigilante groups but duty bound to see that the law upheld public manners. As the judge affirmed, 'Every person has a right to prosecute those who commit indecency.'[5]

There was a growing squeamishness about naked flesh, whether real or represented in literature, song or art. People talked of 'false delicacy' and a 'verbal decorum' which was placing taboos on what was previously considered normal. It was not that people were offended, but that they were affecting a claim to virtue by crying loudly against minor infractions; in other words, an insincere and entirely manufactured moral outrage. People were self-conscious, afraid that toleration might be taken as connivance or that indelicate words suggested impure thoughts and deeds. This unease with the body was expressed by the nineteen-year-old Drusilla Way when she encountered the *Venus de Medici*. 'As to the Venus, she looks like what she *is*, and ought to be. *A naked woman thoroughly ashamed of herself! Perfect nudity* I never saw before, and how ladies can stand *looking* and *staring* and *admiring* with gentlemen at it, I cannot conceive and hope I never shall.'[6]

We should not doubt that Miss Way's response was sincere. She was born in a country and a time when anxieties about sex, nudity and bodily functions were mounting. It was a generational change. In her autobiographical jottings, Lady Sarah Lennox mused that, compared to her youth back in 1760, what was permissible now in common parlance was very different. It was 'thought too indelicate' to say 'breeding' or 'with child' by 1818: people preferred to say 'in the family way' or 'in confinement'; 'stomach' became a generic term for any internal organ. Anna Laetitia Barbauld wrote that in the past, when manners were less strict, writers might have used uncouth words, but 'in our more refined age we do not call a *spade* a *spade*'. Modern women were said to 'go into fits at the bare mention of *breeches*, or expire at the dinner-table if you were to name the *thigh* of a chicken', as if to hear such things with equanimity would call into question their modesty and chastity. Lady Sarah was ticked off by her prim grandchildren for saying 'belly'.[7]

Her grandchildren were only following the fashion in verbal niceties. They may not have been more moral than older generations, but they were aware that society expected an exaggerated display of modesty and decorous language in young ladies. This book is about their generation – whatever their class, high, low and middling. They were born in the shadow of the French Revolution and decades of war, cyclical economic depression and aberrations in the climate. They grew up in fear of invasion by the French, domestic revolution, natural disaster and crime. It was a time of anxiety and apocalyptic nightmares; yet they also saw Britain advance in wealth and industry to become the richest country in the world. Many of them lived to celebrate the accession of Queen Victoria in 1837. They imbued their children – 'the Victorians' – with the moral and religious values that had taken root and flourished in the early part of the century. Many looked back on the coarseness and vulgarity of Britain in their youths with horror and prided themselves on having conquered their noxious habits and turbulent emotions. Others pined for a freer, less censorious world.

The journalist Hewson Clarke joked in 1811 that one day society would ban 'every object that seems to bear a *Phallic* outline'; there was a suggestive obelisk on Bridge Street that should be destroyed, while 'rolling pins should be burnt without mercy, and pokers driven from the parlour stove'. No horses but mares and geldings should enter a town. Once the inquisition was complete, and all suggestive artefacts removed, 'not a caterwauling shall be heard, or an unchaste idea enflame the bosom of a single virgin'. Only then could parents sleep easy in their beds, sure that their daughter would not be inflamed to a pitch of lust.[8]

It was a joke at the time, but it was prescient. A decade later

William Cobbett told a story of a gentleman who sued his neighbour, a farmer who kept a bull in the next-door yard which was '*offensive* to his *wife* and *daughters*'. 'If I had been the father of these, at once, *delicate* and *curious* daughters, I would not have been the herald of their purity of mind; and if I had been the suitor of one of them, I would have taken care to give up the suit with all convenient speed; for how could I reasonably have hoped ever to be able to prevail on delicacy *so exquisite*, to commit itself to a pair of bridal sheets?' It was all fake, people like Cobbett believed, a craving to be thought genteel rather than an expression of genuine innocence. People were not true to themselves; they tabooed words and suppressed their desires. 'Cant is so much stronger than the Cunt nowadays,' Byron asserted in a private letter.[9]

'Cant' is a four-letter word we don't use much now. Most people of my generation have never heard of it, let alone used it in conversation. It is a strong word, one that should be used sparingly. To apply it to someone is to accuse them of sloppy thinking, if you are being kind, or, at the very worst, of a total lack of sincerity. In the former sense, cant (or humbug) is a language of borrowed sentiments: 'a substitute for thought' made up of a string of 'lackadaisical common-places and superficial plausibilities'.[10] It is society's clichés which infect the mind like the refrain of a popular song and are repeated without reflection.

The word derives from the Norman French for 'chanting'; in common parlance it was used to mock those who made up for the absence of genuine devotion by parroting formulaic verse. In the sixteenth century it was applied to the fake piety and whining language of beggars, which they were believed to have designed to extort charity from the tender-hearted. (Vagabonds, 'By lies and cants, Would trick us to believe 'em saints'.) In the following century its meaning was extended to the preaching of the myriad new religious sects. Zealots were accused of inventing a private language, delivered with excessive vehemence, to paper over their ignorance and insincerity. Later in the seventeenth century the word also meant the elliptical and excluding terminology used by professions, trades and academics; lawyers, for example, were nicknamed 'the canting tribe'.[11]

Descended from the slang of fraudsters and hypocritical religious sermonising, cant has always been synonymous with insincerity, imposture and meaningless jargon. In the nineteenth century it meant overstrained verbiage that accorded with social convention or a modish theory but was no more authentic than an old counterfeit coin that had been in circulation for years, passed from hand to hand without being glanced at.[12]

We are probably all guilty of that, and it is relatively harmless. Without adopting at least some of our time's commonplace chatter and everyday slang we would become unnecessarily stilted and almost unintelligible. Why then was the word virtually an expletive at this time? It was Byron who dubbed the early nineteenth century 'the age of cant', and many were happy to agree. But surely every age has more than enough humbug, dogma and mind-numbing cliché mercilessly spun by politicians, advertisers, businesses, gurus of all types, self-appointed prophets and everyone who sets up to dazzle and persuade us; what was special about this time that it deserves such an epithet? In part, it came from a fear that Britain was entering a period when the unremitting babble and din of discussion would drown out sense and moderation. As the press began to penetrate the furthest corners of the kingdom, literacy improved, the middle class grew in size and railways reached hitherto impossible speeds, many writers envisaged a world governed by specious sophistry and smooth-talking charlatans. Britain was smaller, and everyone seemed connected to the same metropolitan print culture; like never before, the people read the same news, wore the same clothes and imbibed the same opinions. Used to hearing and speaking clichés, modern man and woman would lose the power of independent thought. Censorship, once decreed by state and Church, would be replaced by the no less intolerant and bigoted fiat of public opinion. The people would be reduced to a standard of bland conformity, mouthing the same stale platitudes.

Of all humbug, the 'cant of virtue' – a kind of moralising verbiage that sounded virtuous but was really empty – was considered the most alarming. People were encouraged to talk the talk of virtue and to judge each other by outward appearances of respectability and public rectitude which had nothing to do with inner morality. The 'mere cant of words' was not just irritating but the manifestation of a deep moral illness: the British were becoming censorious and small-minded, vindictively pursuing people for petty things while letting more serious crimes go unmentioned and unpunished. The lies that society told itself and the jargon that upheld dogma had been in circulation for so long and had become so widely repeated that people had stopped noticing hypocrisy and injustice. Lady Blessington wrote of Byron: 'He on all occasions professed a detestation of what he calls *cant*; says that it will banish from England all that is pure and good; and that while people are looking after the shadow, they lose the substance of goodness.'[13]

Byron was sensitive to such things because he had faced the full force of British moral outrage twice: first when he separated from his wife and again when he published the first two cantos of *Don Juan* in 1819. The hysteria that greeted his poem was taken as a sign of the unthinking prurience and puritanism that were gripping the country. Cant, for him, was threatening to banish truth because the British could not face hard facts and accordingly purged their language and conversation of 'indelicate' words and allusions. The same could be said for the reformation of manners that evangelicals and others were trying to impose on the people by manipulation of the law and aggressive vigilantism. These people were accused of hijacking moral language to bully and coerce the labouring classes into subservience and to deprive them of their more boisterous pastimes and amusements. As Byron wrote in 1821:

> The truth is, the grand '*primum mobile*' of England is *cant*; cant political, cant poetical, cant religious; but always cant, multiplied through all the varieties of life. It is the fashion, and while it lasts will be too powerful for those who can only exist by taking the tone of the time.[14]

The moralising cant of the nineteenth century was considered distinctly *un*British. Those who talked of an 'age of cant' were concerned that national traits were being cleaned up by a breed of repressed, coercive and fastidious puritans. 'Speaking English' was a French slang term in the eighteenth century for being frank to the point of offensive.[15] And well it might, judging by the words and phrases that the compiler of a French–English/English–French dictionary considered indispensable for French and British tourists. The French traveller would hear words and phrases such as 'shittenly' and 'to be very turdy' when he crossed the Channel. When translated, neither of these Anglo-Saxon terms retained their force: the former was rendered '*pitoyablement*' and the latter '*être fort chagrin*'.* But how could a Briton survive without the French for 'shitten girl', 'short-arse' or 'he

*Expressive words did not always reflect well on the supposed robustness of British life. The English slang word 'dangler' (a man who pretends to like women 'but never makes warm love to them') had no possible equivalent in French.

is the crackfart of the nation' when he was abroad? While French civility was knowingly hypocritical – or courtly, to use a more polite word – the British prided themselves on their frankness and candour. The British liked to see themselves as open, honest and free from affectation. The French saw their neighbours as merely coarse.[16]

This self-congratulation was inseparable from British notions of liberty. They, unlike the French, were free because they were frank, sincere and independent-minded. Most took a robust view of the vulgarity of British life. It was a coarse and often brutal country; people of all classes in the eighteenth century were not constrained by niceties of language or deportment on all occasions. They were 'a polite and commercial people', to be sure; but by Victorian standards their manners were loose, their talk licentious and their amusements vulgar.

Politeness, as they understood it, did not conflict with embracing the earthiness of life or relishing the excesses of popular culture. The British were heavy drinkers and fond of bawdy and vulgar entertainments. It was bound up with the national character. This is why attempts to impose a system of manners on the people were so fiercely (and childishly, in the case of Palfrey) resisted and attacked as unpatriotic. Self-restraint and the restraint of others were perceived to be fanatical; many believed that it was preferable 'to practise open looseness of manners because they said it was better than hypocrisy'.[17]

As one lady wrote, 'freedom of manners is the principal point at which the high and the low invariably meet . . . from this influence results a logical disposition to despise all restraint'.[18] It was the Briton's right to spit, swear, take his clothes off, drink to excess and conduct his life as he saw fit. Prince Pückler-Muskau, a German visitor to Britain in 1826, wrote that Mr Punch, he of the famous puppet show *Punch and Judy*, was a perfect symbol of an Englishman. Both were wooden and heartless, that was true; but the puppet, like his public, 'conquers everything by his invincible merriment and humour, laughs at the laws, at men, and at the devil himself'.

In the puppet show, Mr Punch is a bloody-minded sadist – he kills his baby and wife in almost all versions of the story and takes up with his buxom mistress. The public, however, were attracted to another aspect of his character: he brooks no interference with his destructive liberty or sense of privacy. In one version of the show from this time he amuses himself by singing and ringing a bell as loudly as he can. The noise angers his respectable and well-to-do neighbour, who sends a servant to get Punch to stop. Punch responds by increasing the racket and brawling with the officious servant. Next to try and meddle with his recreations is the parish constable, who comes to enforce the rich man's order. 'I don't want constable,' says Mr Punch. 'I can settle my business without constable, I thank you. I don't want you.' He knocks down the constable and celebrates by singing 'Green Grow the Rushes-o'.

'Punch is certainly not a very moral personage,' wrote Pückler-Muskau; 'but then was there ever one more free from hypocrisy?' He has delighted audiences rich, poor and middling, young and old, male and female from the seventeenth century to the twenty-first, and never more so than in this period. It was not a seaside children's show, as it became when the Victorians sanitised some of its worst elements and sentimentalised the rest, but an important part of grown-up popular culture. Its hero was free of hypocrisy and false feeling, but he also had other sterling British qualities: he was proudly anti-authoritarian, he was not debased by cringing deference to his betters and he answered all objections with a blow and a joke. Adult audiences undoubtedly loved Punch for all these reasons: they too had to defend their recreations from busybodies and moral reformers. This is not to say that poor British people were successful in resisting authority or that they were bloodthirsty; the show was a fantasy of vengeance and freedom. Punch was, after all, not British but an Italian immigrant. He punishes the bogeymen of the popular imagination: mothers-in-law, bailiffs, creditors, doctors, parish overseers, officious meddlers. As Pückler-Muskau realised, Mr Punch 'shows in part what the Englishman is, in part what he wishes to be'.[19]

It was rather what he aspired to than what he was. The mass of the people may not have confronted the hand of the state very often; they were, however, subject to control at a local level by overseers, constables and magistrates. They did not submit easily. One writer in the late eighteenth century said that 'the lower sort of people in England, from a romantic notion of liberty, generally reject and oppose every thing that is forced upon them'. There were many of the higher orders who admired the people's sense of freedom. Britain, unlike most other countries, allowed its people an extensive degree of personal responsibility; there was no centralised or preventative police force watching over the people and meddling in trifling matters of drunkenness or antisocial behaviour. It was felt better to put up with a certain level of crime and disorder: it was the price a country had to pay for its liberty.[20]

In 1811 the MP William Frankland rejected the whole notion of a police force. 'We may be so swathed, and swaddled, as not to be able to commit crimes,' he told the House of Commons. 'Destroy the free action of our limbs, put us into leading strings, and give us the go-cart,* we may have few vices and few crimes, and may become a very pretty behaved and contemptible people.' The view that a policeman on the beat would be psychologically damaging was shared by a majority in Parliament and a large portion of the people. Like Mr Punch, they didn't need a constable to sort out their disputes. 'Are we a mean, creeping, overawed people?' asked Frankland. 'I never look at the people without feelings of respect, affection, and admiration, which overcome me.'[21]

That 'pretty' manners were contemptibly servile was a view that was going out of fashion. There had always been those who looked with horror and a good deal of fear at the excesses of popular culture that thrived without hindrance: hard drinking, brutal sports, sexual impropriety and general licentiousness. In the early nineteenth century these activities came under a level of attack which had a precedent in the Puritans of the 1650s who imposed their joyless reformation of manners on the people.

The origin of the word 'cant' (in the sense of social control) became a pun on the earlier usage referring to bogus chanters and mawkish beggars thanks to Andrew Cant, a preacher who thrived in the godly and oppressive mid-seventeenth century. It was associated with obsessive religiosity and bigoted intolerance, with the puritanical coercion and strict enforcement of the laws seen a hundred and fifty years before. Back then, 'canter' was a common equivalent for 'puritan'. Those in the 1800s who sought to curb heavy drinking, enforce observation of the Sabbath, restrain sexual profligacy, cleanse the street of nuisances and take it upon themselves to patrol the boundaries of public morality were associated with the same obnoxious zeal and prurient vigilance. The prolific use, or overuse, of 'cant' in these years made

*A go-cart was a hoop mounted on a wheeled frame, used to teach infants how to walk without letting them fall over; it was used in this period as slang for 'restraint', as was 'leading strings', which are now called reins.

that connection explicit. For contemporaries the word meant the pretext of religion to justify social control.

'Cant' had a resonance in the late eighteenth century that is lost on us now. It had a power as an insult or term of moral opprobrium that could only exist in a society where hypocrisy was regarded as the greatest of evils. The suspicion of moralistic platitudes and mannered language did not just originate from a national relish for plain speaking and coarse pleasures; there was an intense hatred of duplicity. 'It is pretending to feel what we do not feel, to believe what we do not believe, to practise what we do not practise,' William Cobbett wrote, defining hypocrisy. 'It is an odious vice: it is greatly mischievous, because, by assuming the garb of, it reflects, in the hour of detection, disgrace upon, virtue itself: it must be founded on evil design, because it proceeds from cool deliberation and calculation.'[22]

Everyone hates a hypocrite. There is something revolting in the person who is unmasked for preaching or enforcing a thing while secretly indulging it. But what separates us from people in the eighteenth century are the limits in which we circumscribe hypocrisy. Friends who occasionally borrow opinions and thoughts or act one way in public and another in private may be annoying or risible to those who know them intimately; it is not a radical flaw that corrodes the soul. Politicians who overstrain their opinions in the ordinary course of political rhetoric are generally acquitted of bad intentions, unless they advocate an obvious double standard. We might tend to agree with Socrates: 'Be as you would wish to appear to others'; or Machiavelli: 'Appear as you may wish to be.' The desire to put on an act of goodness is evidence of a wish to *be* good whatever your inclinations; it is the quintessence of politeness. 'Hypocrisy is the tax that vice pays to virtue': the act of plausibility at least restrains the impulse to err and, even if not genuine, is productive of a good effect for the individual and society. If that is so, why, as Hannah Arendt asked in 1963, 'should the vice that covered up vices become the vice of vices?'[23]

In the eighteenth century people were more on their guard against any kind of duplicity in themselves and others. Hypocrisy was the greatest of vices, the spring of all other moral failings. This is particularly acute in English literature. Shakespeare's villains are false to themselves and others; from that stems their evil, not the other way round. Iago is corrupted to his very soul by duplicity and cunning: it is innate within him and one act of hypocrisy makes him commit ever greater crimes. A hypocrite is a hypocrite through and through, day and night; a criminal spends but a small portion of his time committing crime. Hypocrisy wrought itself into the soul and stifled virtue. 'The link between the inward and the outward man is indissoluble,' wrote William Godwin; 'and he, that is not bold in speech, will never be ardent and unprejudiced in enquiry. Add to this, that conscious disguise has the worst effect upon temper, and converts virtue, which ought to be frank, social and ingenious, into a solitary, morose and misanthropic principle.'[24]

In Britain's rudeness and suspicion of continental sophistication there was said to be a naturalness which precluded artificiality and hypocrisy. Edmund Burke, in a bravura passage, wrote: 'we have not yet been completely embowelled of our natural entrails; we still feel within us, and we cherish, those inbred sentiments which are . . . the true supporters of all liberal and manly morals. We have not been drawn and trussed, in order that we may be filled, like stuffed birds in a museum, with chaff and rags . . . We preserve the whole of our feelings still native and entire, unsophisticated by pedantry and infidelity. We have real hearts of flesh and blood beating in our bosoms . . . [W]e are generally men of untaught feelings.' Again, in the language of patriotism we find the relish for the earthy and natural, or 'native', over the refined, stilted and artificial. But the lack of artifice did not imply a wild or savage state. For Burke, manners and customs and a reverence for the Church, the Crown and nobility were guardians of public morals, perfectly concordant with the modern world. The British did not need a Voltaire or Rousseau to teach them how to act.[25]

The mass of the people were considered to be more in touch with their natural instincts than the more refined and cultivated classes above them. They were not obliged to learn the arts of politeness and courtly manners; they were free to live simply, untouched by the contrivances of cosmopolitan civilisation. The middling and upper classes did, however, want to reconcile their refinement and manners with natural sincerity. In political life, sincerity and integrity were repeatedly held up as manly traits that contrasted favourably with Machiavellian cunning and mechanical management. While William Pitt was mocked for being stilted, stiff and overprepared, his rival Charles James Fox made sincerity and ardour political virtues. He made no effort to conceal his many private vices, rather flaunting them as evidence of his public probity. His speeches were praised for being spontaneous effusions of the heart, not arid and stale recitations; witnesses of his performances described him as almost in tears as he strove to find adequate words for his sentiments. Pitt held on to power for considerably longer than his opponent, but in his oratory Fox reflected the age's ideal of the gentleman politician.[26]

Politicians like Fox exemplified something that was prized in private life as well. The mania of 'sensibility' from the mid-eighteenth century gave the public display of emotions a noble aspect. It expressed what philosophers called 'the natural language of the heart'. Men and women greeted each other in public with kisses, to the shock of the more restrained French. This was a time when men wept openly, as Fox did in the House of Commons when his mentor and ally Edmund Burke denounced his policies towards revolutionary France, marking the irreversible termination of their long friendship. In daily life, people were reduced to tears by displays of benevolence and charity, touched to the quick by sublime nature and poetry. And they made sure people knew about it. It was called 'moral weeping'. As was said in 1755: 'it may be questioned whether those are properly men, who never weep upon any occasion'.[27]

There was a demand for this to be reflected and vindicated in novels and plays. In *The Liberal American* (1785), for example, the protagonist lays down a book; a friend picks it up and turns to the last marked page. 'It was wet with tears. He regarded me with a look of enquiry, then, pressing the page to his lips, he exclaimed: "Gracious heaven! what enchanting sensibility".' In another novel, a gentleman has to take to his bed at four in the afternoon after a touching incident, lest inferior matters tarnish his exquisite feeling. Sensibility was a refined feeling experienced by people who had a cultivated understanding of the world; its display was the manifestation of innate moral instincts that were uncorrupted by the cynicism of less refined mortals. No one wanted a return to nature; the ideal was to strike a balance between the best of human instincts and the 'duty of politeness' taught by civilisation.[28]

'One cannot be sincere and seem so,' wrote André Gide. In the cold light of the world, a human's attempt to bring forth an inner thought, howsoever altruistic it is, seems nothing less than an attention-seeking and artificial performance. The naturally suspicious human mind ensures that cynicism will always triumph over a faith in perfectly pure intentions; cold reason will hunt out an ulterior motive lurking even in an angel. Trying to be sincere will be taken for the deepest hypocrisy because the very effort of appearing so will seem like a cloak for baseness. Sincerity can only be measured by consistent actions, not sporadic gestures. Godwin wrote that being sincere did not mean that you were obliged to stop all and sundry on the street to inform them of your inner self or be candid to the point of offensive; the only obligation is to not hide anything or pretend to be something you are not. That seems reasonable. Nonetheless, people in the eighteenth century feared that they would be thought cold and heartless if they did not conform to the expectations of fashion.[29]

Looking back at this time, Lady Louisa Stuart said that when she was fourteen she was afraid that she 'should not cry enough to gain the credit of proper sensibility'. People who did not weep on the right occasion were judged to be failures of humanity. The demand that people prove their sincerity encouraged a competitive spirit: he who cried the loudest was the most refined. What was more obvious to reflective minds, however, was that the person who was the most ostentatiously sincere was the greatest actor. As one anonymous author wrote: 'The most candid characters, who value themselves most on their openness, and who delight in indulging their real sentiments, often fall into [dissimulation] unawares and unknown to themselves, in merely endeavouring to conform to the customs of society.'[30]

The reaction against sensibility, when it came, was severe. Hazlitt memorably wrote that the only intimacy which did not sicken him was a purely intellectual one because it had 'none of the cant of candour in it, none of the whine of mawkish sensibility'. The virtue of candour – judging other people's foibles generously and speaking in a frank manner – was fake. People of sensibility indulged fantasies of fine feeling and deceived themselves by savouring the sensations of emotions they could not in reality conjure up. It was narcissistic and self-indulgent. It was a delusion, a con invented by novelists and third-rate poets to sell their syrupy and overwrought books. The 'man of feeling' became increasingly pathetic. Sir William Harrington was once overcome with emotion in a public garden in Bath and felt that there were no words in existence to convey it, so he cast himself face first into a flower bed. Boswell told the story of a man who was overwrought with anxiety about the health of his son, who was away at school. Sensibility dictated that he sit down and unburden himself in an elegy. 'Had not you better take a post-chaise and go and see him?' suggested his more sensible friend. It was no wonder that Hazlitt called the rage of sensibility 'do-me-good, lack-a-daisical, whining make-believe'.[31]

The displaying of emotions may have been easy to satirise and disparage as fake, but it at least showed that the *ideal* of perfect candour was considered a high virtue. The manifestation of sensibility may have been manufactured, but the desire to be free from hypocrisy and false feeling and in touch with noble human instincts was, in most cases, genuine. That might have been so, but what the phenomenon illuminated was that the accomplished charlatan could make himself better than the saint if outward appearances were to be the measure of personal worth. Societies that treasure sincerity this highly are likely to be on their guard against impostors to an obsessive degree. The cult of sensibility, with all its embarrassing performances and obvious confusion of real feeling, made this pertinent in the late eighteenth century. Once you have to define and prove sincerity it ceases to have any real meaning. Everything crumbles to baseness and becomes an object of suspicion.[32]

Negotiating the path between genuine feeling and self-delusion forced people to scrutinise and justify their motives. The period saw an intense religious revival. From 1738 the direct and engaging message of Methodism converted tens of thousands of the lower orders, expanding with even greater velocity in the nineteenth century. The emotional punch of a field meeting and the stirring hymns contrasted with the torpor of the Church of England, which deplored the zeal which John Wesley brought to popular religion. In the 1780s a similar spirit animated a small but powerful group within the established Church and the upper class. William Wilberforce wanted to do in the drawing rooms and chapels of high society what Wesley had done in the field and the meeting house. Methodism was seen as vulgar and appallingly fanatical; Wilberforce's great achievement was to make evangelicalism attractive to the upper and middling classes. He attacked the 'nominal' faith of those whom he called 'professed Christians' – those who treated their spiritual life as a set of formal ceremonies. Evangelicals were stirred by feelings, not by measured rationality. But this was part of the divine plan, not heedless fanaticism. God had given the human mind passions that inspired religious zeal. Christ had not sacrificed himself for mankind's sins on the cross so that polite families could sit sedately in church once a week going through the frigid motions of observance. So-called 'vital religion' should awaken people to their own inherent sin and make them perpetually conscious of Christ's atonement. The Bible enjoined that people love God with their hearts, not their heads. 'Lukewarmness is stated to be the object of God's disgust and aversion,' Wilberforce warned emotionally continent Christians.[33]

Evangelical religion was disparaged in much the same way as sensibility: as the heady effusion of a weak mind intoxicated by rousing hymns and a hectoring preacher. In his book *Religion Without Cant*, the orthodox clergyman Robert Fellowes wrote that evangelicals 'make the *delirium* of sensation a substitute for integrity of character'. Theirs was a profession of belief founded on turbulent emotions, not deep thought; they mistook the excitement of their passions for 'rapture' and imagined that they had experienced an instantaneous and miraculous rebirth, like the conversion of St Paul. As with sensibility, the tyranny of religious emotions was seen as betraying people into hypocrisy and self-deceit. And none knew it better than Wilberforce. He was acutely aware that people would look at evangelicals and accuse them of 'studied hypocrisy'. The fear of insincerity and false feeling was felt most by the evangelicals themselves, who realised just how easily they could lose sight of the truth in the turmoil of their passions. It was traumatic to have to admit to oneself that an intoxicating, delicious moment of spiritual ecstasy might be an illusion created by Satan. Wilberforce and his followers subjected themselves to constant, painful self-scrutiny and proved the purity of their intentions with practical good works to avoid the snare of hypocrisy.[34]

Religious revival and the fashion for sensibility forced society to ask itself searching questions. Was there such a thing as a sincere emotion? How were people to retain their integrity in the refined and artificial modern age, when civilisation had taken them so far from natural simplicity? Were authenticity and modernity reconcilable? Hazlitt wrote that the higher the 'standard of perfection' is set, the more hypocrisy there is perceived to be in the world. This was certainly the case in the late eighteenth century and the beginning of the nineteenth. When integrity and authenticity were elevated to supreme moral goods it became ever harder to live up to them. For that very reason people came to see fraud and charlatanism everywhere, not least in their own souls.

As imposture seemed to be such an easy act in the advanced eighteenth century, it was reasonable to suspect that their society harboured and nurtured polished hypocrites. This anxiety was at the heart of all thinking about society at this time. The plausible pretender, the accomplished seducer and the profit-hungry hypocrite were believed to be active in all sections of society, taking the fruits of civilisation, enlightenment, morality and religion and perverting them for their own bad ends. A person who could act the part and mouth the right words was more dangerous than an out-and-out villain. Cultivation, education and knowledge of the fine arts and science had improved some people, but knowledge had made many more adept actors. As one journalist wrote: 'A cheerful temper, a ready wit, a convivial disposition, and pleasing manners, joined to the knowledge of the world, and an insight into the weakness of human nature, is sufficient to compose a character which may produce . . . abundant mischief.'[35]

Wearing a mask and acting a part were not harmless aspects of modern life; imposture and hypocrisy were things that really threatened modern society. Doctors masqueraded as altruistic experts, but they poisoned the public with deleterious drugs; young men seduced gullible young girls with honeyed words and romantic sentiments only to abandon them to prostitution; unscrupulous journalists plundered scholarship to dress up their specious arguments in layers of plausible jargon; preachers plucked vivid phrases from the Old Testament out of context to work their congregations into a frenzy; moralists spread panic about modern degeneracy in return for fame and a government pension; beggars manipulated the natural generosity of the British with tragic tales and downright lies. The list of artful fraudsters was endless. The unsophisticated and guileless British character stood very little chance against the silver-tongued con man.

'We must acknowledge that there never was an age or any country so favourable to the success of imposture, as this very age and this very England,' wrote Robert Southey. The problem was that the country was advanced and wealthy to an extent unknown in human history; she was in the vanguard of progress and civilisation. Her very success damned her to a host of unprecedented moral diseases. In the civilising process, it was believed, greater riches initially led to sensuality and intemperance. Britain had reached this crisis in the late seventeenth century, when the court of Charles II had encouraged a voluptuous and sensuous culture. But refinement was the process by which the early vices of a modern society were transformed into civilised behaviour. It was the gradual victory of manners and politeness over primitive barbarism, the relics of which still existed in civilised societies. Literature evolved from bawdy Restoration poetry and plays, which were high in artistic standards but low in morals, and was gradually refined into more decorous language without losing the artistic quality. 'More refined pleasures succeed the more gross, which become gradually despised and reprobated as below the dignity of man,' wrote Hugh Murray, a Scottish moral philosopher. Knowledge of the arts improves, conversation becomes less frank and more cultivated, and fashion gilds the rough edges of society; the luxuries, literature and manners of an advanced culture are 'employed in throwing a veil over [society's] grossness'.[36]

'Refinement', for moralists, could be a dirty word. While society looked better, in reality the same old vices lived on – or flourished – behind the pretty facade that civilisation had constructed over its primeval barbarism. The manners of the refined age, the vast cities that came with it, the bustle of life and the speed of communications destroyed the face-to-face, hierarchical society of the past; men and women slipped into anonymity, judging each other by 'reputation' or by external markers like clothes or manners. It was no wonder then that fear of impostors mounted. It was hard to tell the genuine from the plausible once everyone was levelled to the same standards of appearance and deportment. Adam Smith wrote of the 'frequent and often wonderful success' of impostors and quacks of all kinds – medical, religious, political and professional. Their ostentatious success showed how easily 'groundless pretensions' could be transformed into things of worth when supported by little more than fashion and the fiat of the great.[37]

Fashion was called an omnipotent deity and its followers worshippers at its altar. It undoubtedly wielded vast powers. Unlike in many other countries, the difference between the classes in Britain was hard to tell at first sight: the middling were often indistinguishable from the nobility; apprentices on their nights out wore all the finery of a gentleman. It was possible to tell a lord from a labourer, to be sure; but in public areas, especially in towns, there was little to differentiate the classes. In 1819 Captain Phipps, Lord Mulgrave's nephew, arrived in Taunton and impressed the local fashionable set with his rank, dress and demeanour. 'He was therefore received into "the best company". He danced with one party, played cards with another, escorted a third and . . . made proposals of marriage to one young lady.' He patronised local traders, who were more than happy to give him credit to purchase luxury goods, fine clothes and all the trappings of gentility. His intended bride was saved a grievous mistake when he was unmasked as a penniless vagrant.[38]

That might have been an outrageous example of an impostor playing on the snobbishness of a small town, but there were plenty of more subtle ways in which boundaries in society were blurred. Throughout the century the middle class had been able to afford a range of luxury goods; their silverware, porcelain, clocks, heavy furniture, glass and linen resembled those of the elite. Fashion magazines, novels and plays informed them of what was in and what was out; servants transmitted news of their employers' latest styles to people of their own class. Fashion therefore moved fast, the arbiters of style striving to keep ahead of hoi polloi who snapped at their heels.

This levelling principle existed only in Britain. It was harmless enough in itself, but this very visible aspect of life dramatised a serious moral question. Fashion was not just the clothes people wore or artefacts they consumed, but included the opinions and moral standards that were dictated by print culture – a distant, anonymous authority. Might not people change their opinions in politics, religion or ethics as readily as they changed their coat? And if so, what kinds of people had assumed the authority to dictate to the public? As one journal said, 'the opinions most in vogue at the passing moment will tomorrow infallibly be out of date as a stale newspaper'. Accustomed personal influence was dying, replaced by a secretive media, unknown and unaccountable. The accomplished rogue, polished and camouflaged by the arts of refinement, could assume a position of authority as readily as the vagrant could masquerade as a young gentleman. Respectability – the highest virtue in the British mind – was all too often determined by wealth and status rather than anything intrinsic. Gibbon Wakefield pithily said that 'respectability has various meanings in England: with some it means to keep a carriage, with others a gig'. Prescribed manners and fashion levelled everything to uniformity. Differences of social status, moral worth and personal integrity were impossible to determine. Moral writers decried the studied artificiality of 'this boasted age of refinement, when virtue, and vice, like the colours in shot-silk, are so ingeniously interwoven by corrupt artisans, that it is difficult to distinguish the one from the other'.[39]

It wasn't just a concern for moralists who took a lofty view of modernity. It was a live issue in daily life. In this stage of human progress – an era of vast cities and complex social relations – crimes of violence were said to have been superseded by crimes of fraud. Henry Brougham wrote in the *Edinburgh Review* that prosperous modern societies bred unscrupulous traders 'who pervert their talents to the most dishonest purposes, preferring the illicit gains thus acquired to the fair profits of honourable dealing; and counterworking, by their sinister arts, the general improvement of mankind'. They were called the crimes of 'sophistications', which says it all. The blending of the good and the bad, as in the devious manufacturer of shot silk, stood as a metaphor for the moral condition of the age, but there was no more pertinent example of this than the adulteration of foodstuffs. The ways in which provisioners, brewers and wine merchants maximised their profits by introducing cheap compounds into their goods were not merely fraudulent but endangered people's lives. Vintners would mix wines with oakwood, sawdust, almonds and a tincture of raisins to make 'genuine old port'. Even more fatal were the wiles of quacks, whose medicines included opium, spirits and other dangerous ingredients. Adulteration was one of the crimes of an enlightened society unknown in rude and unrefined times: in the past people killed each other for honour and religion; now they did so to protect their profit margins. Those who practised it were supposedly emblematic of their age: they took the knowledge of the Enlightenment and turned it into a get-rich-quick scheme regardless of the cost to the community.[40]

Hugh Murray wrote that there was a stage in human progress when the vices of ruder times co-existed and thrived with the achievements of civilisation. Britain was said to be going through this painful stage. The rage for luxuries and the devotion to fashion called into being manufacturing towns and busy ports. These towns drew in ever greater numbers of people from the countryside to man the factories and docks and live in wretched slums. Wrenched from the village, from traditional authority and ties of mutual dependence, from the supervision of the Church, the working classes were like abandoned children, traumatised by the upheaval of society. They were impoverished, enfeebled and brutalised by the experience. Therefore, from the highest to the lowest, Britons had moved away from the accustomed ways of life that had existed unchanged for centuries.

Everyone could be said to be artificial in one way or another. The Britons of 'untaught feelings' were a figment of the imagination, the stuff of patriotic fantasy. If they existed, they were quaint relics, powerless against the irresistible march of progress. Britons in the complex nineteenth century, wrote a doctor who examined the psychological implications of modernity, needed to be taught how to live. Compared to their ancestors, and the majority of mankind living in less developed countries, they had become almost a different species, their heads stuffed with new wants, cravings and addictions. Genuine emotions and sentiments were thought to be becoming extinct; refinement had perverted human nature into affected behaviour such as mawkish sentimentality or religious fanaticism. They were the tormented and bewildered reactions of a human born in an unnatural, hyper-advanced society.[41]

It was an age when people could have nothing on their lips but cant phrases: the process of refinement had rendered everything fake and unnatural. The more the question of sincerity was examined, the more people came to doubt that any kind of genuine feeling still existed. Attempts to unburden oneself of the artificiality of modern life made people downright foolish or dangerously fanatical; they felt they had to jump into rose beds or rend their clothing in religious ecstasy. These were just different manifestations of the synthetic behaviour they wanted to escape.

But this was relatively harmless; the no less artificial condition of the lower orders took on a darker character. If the senses had been deranged by refinement, industrialisation and commerce, events in the closing decades of the century showed that turbulent passions had the power to turn society on its head. In 1780 thousands of Londoners rioted when their anti-Catholic resentments were roused by Lord Gordon, himself mentally unstable. The Gordon Riots lasted for days, during which buildings were turned into rubble and the inmates of the capital's gaols were freed to join the orgy of violence; the anarchy only ended when the military was called in. The loss of the American colonies after a disastrous war reminded the British of the fall of the Roman Empire after its people had been made soft and voluptuous by luxury and refinement. The French Revolution – nine years after

London was torn apart – and the Terror that followed was, for British property owners, a horrifying vision of a people perverted by their basest instincts.

Everyone had to struggle with their own tumultuous instincts, or else others had to intervene to restrain them. It was little wonder then that self-government and self-restraint were taking over as moral obligations. Humans must submit to the rules of propriety dictated by society, however unnatural and constraining it felt. The combustible people, in the context of revolution, war and Malthusian anxieties, showed that 'native' simplicity was a national danger, not a national virtue. William Palfrey was undoubtedly in his pristine natural state that day on the canal-side; but he was merely reminding people of what his savage ancestors looked like – degraded and wild. From the late eighteenth century, what Burke called 'the decent draperies of life', the manners that clothed the passions, became *the* moral consideration.[42]

If the eighteenth century was an emotional time, one that prized sincerity and nature, the future seemed to be one of self-restraint and the forcible restraint of others. As many were coming to realise, repressing instincts (particularly sexual instincts) was not hypocritical but noble – a daily Herculean conquest of one's turbulent primordial self. The liberty to indulge instincts, enjoy vulgar pleasures and conduct one's life as one saw fit came to be seen as the freedom for self-destruction and anarchy. 'We love to be at liberty to follow our own inclination, without being subjected to the control of a superior,' Dugald Stewart wrote; 'but this alone is not sufficient to our happiness.' Following 'the force of passion' was really a craven surrender to the weakest and basest aspects of human nature. True independence was the self-possession and dignity 'of being able, at all times, to calm the tumults of passion, and to obey the cool suggestions of duty and honour'.[43] The same could be said for regulating the tendencies of people unable to command themselves; older ideas of liberty that saw preventative police as an enemy of national identity came under pressure from those who prophesied disorder and social upheaval welling up from the cities.

'The first triumph of regulated society', wrote Francis Jeffrey, editor of the *Edinburgh Review*, 'is to be able to protect its members from actual violence; and the first trait of refinement in manners, is to exclude the coarseness and offence of unrestrained and selfish emotions.'[44] But many cleaved to older ideas of what it was to be English or Scottish or Irish. Any suggestion that propriety should triumph over sincerity was taken as an invitation for people to become hypocrites. These people saw the repression of instincts and the desire to control others as a movement towards puritanism. A certain type of morality seemed to be emerging in Britain, an oppressive and unnatural form of manners that hypocritically subjected the lower orders to standards of behaviour and self-denial that were not countenanced by their betters. Charles Dickens wrote of his contemporaries in *Barnaby Rudge*: 'As hollow vessels produce a far more musical sound in falling than those which are substantial, so it will oftentimes be found that sentiments that have nothing in them make the loudest ringing in the world, and are the most relished.'

It was called 'cant' for it was suspected to be a fashion like any other in an age devoid of any sincerity or genuine feeling. People wore their morals like their clothes – à la mode and with finicky attention to trivial detail. But they weren't their own: they were squeezed into corsets or tight breeches; they were obliged to mouth the latest moral sentiment. 'I say *cant*', said Byron, 'because it is a thing of words, without the smallest influence upon human actions; the English being no wiser, no better, and much poorer and more divided amongst themselves, as well as far less moral, than they were before the prevalence of this verbal decorum.'[45]

Many welcomed the reformation of manners and the religious revival, and rejected the charge of insincerity; what others called cant and hypocrisy they saw as the victory of politeness. But for a vocal minority verbal decorum and feigned intolerance of previously forgivable human foibles were attacked as lamentable relapses of the British character. 'As soon as it becomes necessary to appear wiser or better than the mass of mankind . . . the reign of humbug commences,' wrote one commentator, summing up what he saw as the spirit of the age; 'and from that moment the individual . . . labours under a necessity for wearing a mask.'[46]

PART I

Hypochondria
1789–1815

'The character of the English is certainly the most complex of any in Europe . . . They are restless under uncertainty, fearful from contingency, undone from anticipation . . . They submit to phantoms of their own creation, but can bear real misfortune with complacency.'

William Austin, *Letters from London* (1804)[1]

INTRODUCTION TO PART I

Some New World

When tourists arrived in England at the dawn of the nineteenth century they expected to see two things: the overwhelming grandeur of the wealthiest country in the history of the world and the fattest people who had ever walked the earth. The first was the extraordinary achievement of a strange people; the second, the visible results of the victory of commerce and the bounties of empire.

One doctor, William Wadd, wrote that 1810 – George III's Jubilee Year – saw the fattest ox and the fattest human being in the history of mankind. He documented cases of fifty-stone men, who could not be removed from their houses until the walls had been demolished. These phenomena came from 'increasing improvements in the arts of grazing'. Childhood obesity was becoming an object of wonder, and also a cause of adolescent mortality. At the same time, women tortured themselves to be thin, often dangerously so: the fashion was for long flowing gowns, not the constricting corsets of the eighteenth century. Gymnasia and boxing studios were popular for young blades eager to fit into new men's fashions – tighter clothing designed to show off the physique. But for many adult males a generous layer of fat was something to flaunt and a matter of national pride; as a journalist wrote: 'I know what pleasure is felt by one who is congratulated on the portliness of his corporation, and the goodly rubicundity of his visage.'[2]

One of the first things tourists wanted to see was the legendarily fat British waddling along the street. The Franco-American Louis Simond was eager to see 'the original of *Jacques Roast-beef*', the caricature of the rotund Briton known the world over. Benjamin Silliman, who came to London in 1805 as a representative of Yale University, described the scene in Hyde Park on a Sunday: 'Gentry, cockneys, cits are all disgorged, and thousands and tens of thousands are seen going, and returning, in two opposite currents; and such an assemblage of burly corpulent people is probably not to be found in the world beside.' The British middle classes (called 'cits' in London), on their weekly perambulation, appeared to be the most content, well-fed, complacent people on the planet, while people of every class had ruddy and florid faces from the general relish for porter.

But for all their material advantages and the luxuries upon which they gorged – and their unrivalled position in the world – they were not happy. With their new technologies and modern indulgences, the naturally melancholic British had only invented new and more elaborate ways of tormenting themselves. Nikolai Karamzin, the Russian historian who toured Europe in the wake of the French Revolution, summed up the character of the modern Briton: 'He is unhappy from a superabundance of good fortune.' William Austin, an American visitor in 1802, was equally amazed at the melancholy amidst splendour and dismissed the national propensity as a perversion: 'If the Englishman frequently fortifies himself against happiness, and sleeps on thorns in the midst of roses, it is his pleasure, whim, or madness.'[3]

'I find here every thing different from what I had hitherto met with; different houses, streets, men, and food,' Karamzin wrote when he crossed the twenty or so miles to Dover after sampling the major countries of Europe; 'in a word, I fancy myself transported into some new world.' Having arrived on the English coast, tourists' first impressions of Britain were from the coach windows as they travelled to London. In almost every account written by Europeans and Americans alike at this time, the quality of the roads, the neatness of the houses and the conveniences provided for travellers at inns were related with wonder and compared favourably to the backward state of any other country on either side of the Atlantic.[4]

The first sight of London, the centre of world trade, was an event for even the well-travelled visitor. Benjamin Silliman thought he was in the capital when he reached Brentford, so urbanised was that town. But soon the coach entered countryside again, which continued until he suddenly found himself in the great city: 'Hyde Park, with its extended fields, fine forest trees, and promiscuous assemblage of pedestrians, coaches and horsemen, soon came into view on our left; – we whirled rapidly by it, and, at Hyde Park Corner, abruptly entered the Metropolis of the commercial world. We drove through Piccadilly, and were instantly involved in the noise and tumult of London. We were obliged to hold fast as we were driven furiously over rough pavements, while the clattering of the wheels, the sounding of the coachman's horn, and the sharp reverberations of his whip, had there been no other noises, would have drowned out conversation, and left us to admire and wonder in silence, at the splendour of the English capital.'[5]

But for many, including Silliman, the first sight of London was an anti-climax. This was partly because the name London reverberated around the globe as the emporium of world trade and could never live up to its awesome reputation. The first impression was muted also because one was plunged immediately into the midst of the city and could gain no immediate perspective. It was only when Silliman climbed to the top of the Monument that his sense of being in the midst of a stupendous metropolis was reawakened; up high, the noise increased and reached a crescendo, 'so that I was almost deafened with the incessant and confused din of wheels and cries'. Parts of London would be transformed in the 1810s and '20s, giving at least the West End the appearance of a grand and splendid metropolis. At the turn of the nineteenth century it was crude and somewhat shabby. The splendour was superficial, and one French-American visitor soon found himself 'lost in a maze of busy, smoky, dirty streets . . . A sort of uniform dinginess seemed to pervade every thing'. For Louis Simond, the 'inhabitants of London . . . as well as the outside of their houses, [have] a sort of dingy smoky look'. Yet if the streets and the people were gloomy, the shops 'presented . . . appearances and colours most opposite to this; everything there was clean, fresh, and brilliant'. As befitted this commercial people, the glamour and grandeur and unbelievable wealth of London – the envy of the world and the stuff of legend – resided not in public buildings, grand streets, palaces and squares but in its shops.[6]

Robert Southey, in his book *Letters from England*, written under the pseudonym of Don Manuel Alvarez Espriella, wrote of his surprise at the size and unremitting activity of the crowds in the streets: 'I was still more astonished at the opulence and splendour of the shops: drapers, stationers, confectioners, pastry-cooks, seal-cutters, silver-smiths, booksellers, print-sellers, hosiers, fruiterers, china-sellers, – one close to another, without intermission, a shop to every house, street after street, and mile after mile; the articles themselves so beautiful, and so beautifully arranged . . . Nothing which I had seen in the country had prepared me for such a display of splendour.' And according to Southey, the 'finest gentlemen to be seen in the streets of London' were the men who served fashionable women at linen-drapers' and mercers' shops, 'who are to be seen after breakfast at their respective shop-doors, paring their nails and adjusting their cravats'.[7]

'The beauties of commerce surround them [Londoners] on all sides,' wrote Leigh Hunt, 'in shops, in warehouses, in wharfs, by water and by land; in the Babels of exchange, in the shows of my Lord Mayor . . . in the sumptuous dwelling-houses which the merchants enjoy among courtiers and noblemen'; the visitor to London 'can hardly look at a single object without being dazzled by foreign luxury'.[8] The fruits of empire and trade were avidly consumed and added to the comforts of domestic life for every class, but particularly the upper and middle. When the alliance of sovereigns that had defeated Napoleon arrived in Britain in 1814, they asked, 'Where are the people?' The mobs that surrounded their carriages and ogled the assemblage of European royalty looked too well dressed for common folk. But they were 'the people'.

Many Europeans and Americans were fascinated with a country seemingly so advanced in civilisation and so abundantly supplied with modern luxuries. Yet those tourists who recorded their impressions of Britain felt that they could never understand the true nature of its people. They were stiff and formal in public, jealously guarding their real selves and their fabulous wealth in the fortress of their homes; few felt that they had ever penetrated – or ever could – this insuperable barrier. Karamzin enjoyed his visit to England from the point of view of seeing a country at the very pinnacle of civilisation and so-called progress, and of observing the myriad oddities of the people, 'but to live in England for the purpose of enjoying the pleasures of social intercourse – that would be like searching for flowers in a sandy desert'. Most visitors conceded that the British could be pleasant, although they did their best to conceal it from foreigners.[9]

The British were beset with anxieties. Behind the facade of splendour and opulence lurked deep fears and a tendency to moral and medical panics. There was no doubt that the country was wealthy, that many of the people were as plump as the livestock in the fields, and that new luxuries glittered in shop windows. But if tourists wondered how these people could be maudlin, they had allowed themselves to be dazzled by superficial impressions.

Throughout the Revolutionary and Napoleonic wars, some people did very well for short periods, while some thrived one year and suf-

An episode from William Combe and Thomas Rowlandson's *English Dance of Death* series. Tom Higgins, a wealthy businessman, is ground down by *ennui* which he relieves by gorging on tasty morsels and beer. But it is Death himself who takes the most pleasure in satisfying Tom's gargantuan appetite. Obesity was taken to be another symptom of English melancholy, and a price to pay for unbounded wealth

fered the next. Farmers and entrepreneurs involved in war-related manufactures (iron and coal, for example) did very well indeed. The economy fluctuated alarmingly throughout the war: one year there could be a high demand for labour and cheap food; the next there could be near starvation in the countryside and mass unemployment. The outbreak of war with France plunged the economy into recession when the export market to the continent was closed. But between 1796 and 1799 it was recovering in many areas. Good harvests, combined with a vast increase in exports to the West Indies and a greater than ever demand for British manufactures and textiles in the United States, brought back wealth and employment. Disaster shadowed success, however: from 1799 the export market contracted and bad harvests meant a general scarcity of food as the eighteenth turned into the nineteenth century. The next year food prices fell and the textile industry recovered and merchants were hungry for new markets. So hungry, in fact, that in 1808 it was found that even French troops were wearing coats made from West Riding cloth and boots from Northampton.

So it was little wonder that the British seemed like nervous hypochondriacs; prosperity one year could crumble to dearth the next; outrageous self-confidence when times were good drained into despondency when the course of the war deranged the economy. There was nothing gradual about it. In 1808 the good times ended when Napoleon tightened up the blockade of the continent and American tariffs ruined the booming export industry. But the next year even greater prosperity returned: America was open again and Britain's alliance with Spain and Portugal opened up their colonies to British traders for the first time. The new markets lifted trade out of the doldrums, and South America was key to the country's recovery. The peaceable invasion of merchants is remembered in Brazil: the phrase *para inglês ver* ('for the English to see') – meaning to cultivate an artificial outward demeanour – is still in general use.

Britain had never been so rich and powerful, but rarely so timorous, nervous and liable to self-flagellation. The British knew the conspicuous opulence was illusory. 'We are threatened with Invasion; we are loaded with Debts and Taxes; we are divided and weakened by Parties; we are sunk in Doom and Despair,' wrote James Bowdler. In 1795 William Pitt told William Wilberforce that 'My head would be off in six months were I to resign.' 'I see that he expects a civil broil,' Wilberforce wrote in his diary shortly after. 'Never was a time when so loudly called on to prepare for the worst.' The government believed that invasion was imminent, and when it did happen, no one could trust that a hungry and dissatisfied people would rally to the loyalist banner. The next year a thousand French troops of the *Légion noire* landed on the Welsh coast. They were dealt with by local troops, but the 15,000 men under General Hoche were prevented from arriving on the Irish shore only by bad weather. Soon after, the navy at Spithead mutinied. At this time General Cornwallis gloomily asked: 'Torn as we are by faction, without an army, without money, trusting entirely to a navy whom we may not be able to pay, and on whose loyalty, even if we can, no firm reliance is to be placed, how are we to get out of this accursed war without a Revolution?'[10]

The dread of invasion or revolution haunted Britons for years. Even the defeat of the French navy at Trafalgar in 1805 did little to reassure nervous people. In 1809 the 'Fancy' – the 'assemblage of gamblers, sharpers, ruffians and profligates of every degree, from the duke to the chimney sweep' – descended on Hertfordshire to watch two pugilists contest the championship of England. The local inhabitants were ready to flee in terror, convinced that the boxing fans were refugees from a successful French invasion; what else could explain mass migration in this nervous time? Anything out of the ordinary could have this effect; the people were primed for the worst. Sydney Smith playfully wrote that the *Morning Post*, in the manner of an advertiser, 'fixed the invasion sometimes for Monday, sometimes for Tuesday, sometimes (positively for the last time of invading) on Saturday'. In more sombre tones James Stephen wrote that a stroll through the villages outside London demonstrated the wealth of British traders living in their suburban villas and the felicity of the countryside; but in a few years, when Bonaparte ruled from St James's Palace, as he surely would, a walk to these same suburban villages will 'be like an evening visit to a Church yard; presenting nothing but the shadows of impotent ambition and the mouldering records of departed happiness'.[11]

People did as much as possible to ignore the wars and sublimate their fears. Invasion anxieties manifested themselves in other worries: of health and morality and religion. The dawn of the new century added to the sense of unease. Such times do funny things to people, bringing on apocalyptic nightmares and intense self-scrutiny. The country seemed damned by its very success: the richer it became the more vulnerable it was to violent upset and the envy of the others. Those foreigners who mocked the strange contradiction of wealth tinged with gloom perhaps did not fully appreciate the curse that riches brought a country. The more Britain had, the more there was to lose at the hands of Napoleon, the headless mob or the caprice of nature. The attractions of the capital and the inexorable rise of British manufactures (despite periodic setbacks) only served to remind people of the fickleness of fate. 'Often over the contemplation of such scenes', wrote James Stephen, 'have I shuddered at the thought of that sad reverse which may be near at hand. How possible is it that in a few years, aye, in a few months, all this unexampled comfort and happiness may vanish like the painted clouds in a western sky, before the evening tempest!'[12]

People sought reassurance in this unhappy and uncertain world. It was one of those times when religious sects and messianic figures bubbled up, won disciples and evaporated almost as suddenly. This was certainly the case in the 1790s, when bad harvests and military failure brought misery. The words 'fanatic' and 'enthusiast' were repeated again and again throughout the decade as epithets: there were fanatics and enthusiasts in religion, but also in politics, economics, moral philosophy, science and anything and everything else. The final years of the eighteenth century had seen the strange and sad careers of celebrity prophets. Richard Brothers, who called himself Prince and Prophet of the Hebrews and Nephew of the Almighty, attracted attention for a time. He believed that many Britons unwittingly comprised one of the ten lost tribes of Israel. King George would yield the throne to Brothers, who would lead his people on the exodus to Palestine to rebuild Jerusalem. He prophesied the arrival of Satan in London, the modern Babylon. Brothers successfully pleaded with God that London be spared this fate, and it was granted only to spare the prophet. Notwithstanding the hysterical claims, for a short time Brothers attracted a following and he was visited by MPs and ladies of quality.

Even more successful was Joanna Southcott, the prophetess. She began her career in 1792 with predictions about the fate of her friends and family; later she foretold the weather and political events. It is no coincidence that 1792 was the first year of the war. In that turbulent, topsy-turvy, miserable decade, Southcott attracted believers by prophesying poor harvests in 1794, '95, '97, '99 and 1800, and the Spithead mutiny.

The prophetess only asked that people believe her. Hers was a direct, immediate and highly emotional form of Christianity. She expounded the scriptures in simple, homely language and revealed the essence of religion in the recounting of her dreams. Her followers included many well-to-do people and several respectable clergymen. The millennium would not mean the end of the world in a hail of brimstone but the victory of Christ on earth, the advent of a new age of love and plenty: it was to be welcomed by the God-fearing, dreaded only by those who had sealed their hearts against Him. Southcott offered her spiritually malnourished and apprehensive followers the glimpse of the new world for which they ardently longed, one without starvation and threats of invasion. At the age of sixty-five, she informed the world of her pregnancy, which would yield Shiloh, the reincarnation of Christ. There was a long confinement before the promised, but unfulfilled, second birth of the Messiah.

Celebrity preachers thrived in the nervous 1790s and 1800s. Leigh Hunt, in the *Examiner*, said that the 'vulgar' admired tub-thumping preachers 'just as they do violent colours, violent noise, and violent swearing. There must be something to occupy the senses and vent the spleen.' A congregation deluged with the heady rhetoric of a good Calvinistic Methodist preacher was 'seized with demonical convulsions; shrieks and yells were set up by frantic women; men fell as if shot through the heart'. The Old Testament was invoked, and sermons were replete with the language of vengeance, punishment and guilt. It was reminiscent of another nervous time – the millennial excitement of the 1640s and '50s. The shakers, wailers, speakers-in-tongues, Fifth Monarchists and their prophets of doom were back, led by wild-eyed and rabble-rousing preachers. Some made the congregation prostrate themselves on the ground while they drove out their evil spirits. Others conducted 'love feasts'. A Mr Mullinson, of the Magdalene Chapel, Blackfriars Road, had the ability to rouse his congregation, declaiming the most mundane things as if they signified the difference between life and death. 'Hee-hee-oho-he – Here,' Mr Mullinson would say, 'A! A! A! Are you, my brethren, insensible to this? Too-oo-oo-oo he-ee-ee-im, therefore, again, I say, *Too-oo-oo-oo*-Hi-ee-ee-im, address yourselves.'[13]

The hopes and fears of millennialism and the driving force of religious revival were not confined to the poor and ignorant. Spencer Perceval, who served successively as Home Secretary, Chancellor of the Exchequer and Prime Minister, was an evangelical, the great hope of the godly reformers. George III was a pious and God-fearing monarch. Britons could and should be made better; they should be made to live up to the awesome responsibilities bequeathed them by God.

The French Revolution, the Terror and the rise of Napoleon were signs that Evil had been unleashed on the world. In these years hitherto pardonable vice took on a more menacing complexion. The contention that the 1790s and 1800s were decades of unique degeneracy was considered bizarre by those who had memories long enough to recall their youths. Was Britain in 1800 any worse than, say, the 1730s, when there were riots over the price of gin? Perhaps not, the moralisers said, but the world after the French Revolution was radically different. The degeneracy they saw in their own country was far worse in Europe. As they never tired of pointing out, the wrack of the continent was intended by God as a warning to Britain of what happened to vicious and immoral peoples; the British had been spared the full extent of the horror that they might watch, learn and amend.

Political Dreamings! by James Gillray, November 1801. The apocalyptic nightmares of the early 1800s were satirised nowhere better than in Gillray's caricatures. This refers to William Windham's warnings about peace with France (signed in October 1801). Windham is assailed by the phantoms of his imagination: headless French aristocrats beg to be remembered, while guillotined British aristocrats on his left illustrate that the warning has not been heeded. Napoleon has Britannia

in a noose and points to the guillotine, St Paul's Cathedral convulsed by flames and the tricolour flying from the Tower of London. Justice, her scales broken, sits on a chamber pot and weeps. William Pitt guides the pen that signs the Articles of Peace, in reality a death warrant. And at the foot of the bed Charles James Fox as an imp sings a diabolical lullaby. Most disturbingly of all, a revolutionary Death, standing on stilts, tramples emblems of British liberty, including beef and ale

The 'Anarchical Monster' had been rampant since 1789 and had one cause: 'This malignant disease derives its strengths from the moral corruption of society; and it can be effectually resisted only by moral amendment,' wrote John Bowles, one of the most prolific moralisers. In 1800 Lord Auckland said that during the 'paroxysms and convulsions' the world had seen, Britain had survived only because of 'our being a little less irreligious and less immoral than others'; but only less immoral by a whisker. *Reform or Ruin: Take Your Choice!* was the title of a bestselling book by James Bowdler. The British would be wise to follow his advice lest they courted the rapine, violence and anarchy meted out to France by divine providence.[14]

The loss of America, the Terror and the war might have opened old sores and caused people to detect vices that had previously rested dormant or unnoticed. When would God or Providence or the natural order of things call in the debt the nation was accumulating with fate? When would the cycle of history complete its revolution and send the British Empire the way of the Roman?

Natural disaster, food shortages, unprecedented carnage, anarchy, the revolutionary madness of people throughout the world and the very derangement of nature heralded the Apocalypse. The end of the world really was nigh: Prime Minister Perceval predicted it in 1926; for others it was imminent. And Britain stood first in line, damned by its very success: 'If the decline and fall of nations may generally be dated from the period of their highest attainments in arts and luxury, that is also the period of their most heinous offences against God.' It was little wonder that in this context of a war consisting of Good versus Evil there should have been a religious revival. For many, Napoleon was the Beast – a scourge sent to lacerate Britain. 'He has made a league with darkness,' wrote Stephen. 'He has declared war against the mutual intelligence and sympathy, as well as the happiness of mankind.' He seemed irresistible: in 1800 he became Consul, and by the end of the year he had forced Britain's allies out of the war after the battle of Marengo. The news of the French victory at Austerlitz, when it reached Britain in January 1806, was said to have killed William Pitt. 'How I leave my country!' were reported to be his last words.

A code revealed the mark of Evil on Napoleon. The Book of Revelations prophesied that the Beast could be identified by 'the number of his name': 'Let him that hath understanding count the number of the beast.' And the very name of Britain's nemesis contained that number. If the letters of the alphabet are numbered so that the first nine letters represent the numbers one to nine (with A worth one and I worth nine), J is left out and the corresponding numbers then increase in multiples of ten, so K is worth ten, L twenty and Z 160, then the sum of the letters in the Emperor's name totals exactly 666. That it only works if his name is spelt 'Napolean' and the first 'a' in Buonaparte is not counted did not matter. As millenarians stressed, 'Napolean Buonparte' deliberately misspelled his name to conceal the mark of the Beast and confound mankind.

Spencer Perceval believed that the Emperor was the woman in the Book of Revelations, 'the mother of harlots and abominations of the earth . . . drunken with the blood of saints', who rides upon the Beast and visits destruction upon the world. According to the prophecy she committed fornication with the kings of the earth, and 'the inhabitants of the earth have been made drunk with the wine of her fornication'. As a cabinet minister, and eventually Prime Minister, Perceval believed that the war against Napoleon was a war against Evil itself. This was the view of an evangelical, but the Prime Minister's language and terrible vision haunted popular culture and art. Magic-lantern shows terrified people with moving representations of Death personified appearing in many alluring guises before revealing his hideous nature; avenging angels (often blended with caricatures of Napoleon) swooped across the air in the same shows; paintings by Benjamin West, Henry Fuseli and William Blake depicted the Apocalypse, often with all-conquering Death riding a white horse. The nightmarish sense of a disordered world teetering on the brink of convulsion was captured in James Gillray's cartoons, where the motifs of Revelations, the phantasmagoria of the Romantic imagination and ordinary, everyday fears are represented with an almost depraved gusto.

If Perceval was right about the true meaning of the times, the war had to be fought on two fronts. Evil thrived at home. There were many influential voices warning that the vices generated by wealth and modernity would destroy the country. Clergymen, bishops, lords and MPs said that the crime of adultery was becoming ever more common, and God's vengeance would be the result. The Hon. Shute Barrington, Prince Bishop of Durham, stood up in the House of Lords in 1798 to inform the government and the country that the French had a secret weapon more effective than any battalion, mortar or fleet.

> The French rulers [the bishop informed the House], while they despair of making any impression on us by force of arms, attempt a more subtle and alarming warfare, by endeavouring to enforce the influence of their example, in order to taint and undermine the morals of our ingenious youth. They have sent amongst us a number of female dancers, who, by the allurement of the most indecent attitudes, and most wanton theatrical exhibitions, succeed but too effectually in loosening and corrupting the moral feelings of the people.[15]

The Bishop said that unless some action was taken to suppress scantily clad French spies, the men of the country would be enflamed with sexual passion, their wives and daughters corrupted to the level of Frenchwomen, and 'their lordships' time would henceforth be wholly engrossed by causes of divorce'.* Lord Auckland, a great enemy of divorce, concurred – to the cheers of the Bishop of Rochester and others – telling the Lords: 'It certainly is an awful moment, in which it becomes this House to be particularly on its guard against the encouragement in any shape or form, of any circumstances whatever tending to the French immoralities. In my cool and deliberate opinion, those immoralities are the most dangerous mode of attack that the enemy can make. I dread it more than any other kind of invasion.' The French aimed to demoralise Britain in order to win the war: literally divest her of all morals.[16]

It was not just the sexual antics of the great that would bring Britain to the brink. Thomas Malthus warned in his *Principle of Population* in 1798 that the unrestrained vices of the poor, especially their sexual habits, would one day produce a population explosion: the force of nature would turn the world upside down with millions of starved people clamouring for sustenance. 'Famine seems to be the last, the most dreadful resource of nature,' wrote Malthus. 'The power of population is so superior to the power in the earth to produce subsistence for man, that, unless arrested by the preventative check, premature death must in some shape or other visit the human race.'

The population was growing at a rate that would outstrip the resources of the country. Habits of drunkenness and unrestrained sexual gratification in the working people would, if left unchecked, sap the productivity of the nation and stoke population, hastening the Malthusian crisis. Throughout this period this dire warning would act like a nightmare in people's imaginations. Within fifty years the number of people would begin to exceed agriculture's finite resources. The first great crisis

*At this time, and until the mid-nineteenth century, every divorce had to be passed by an act of Parliament.

would then burst upon Britain, and the population would be driven down in a gruesome fashion. Epidemics and plagues, civil war and anarchy would strike first. 'Should success be still incomplete, gigantick inevitable famine stalks in the rear, and, with one mighty blow, levels the population with the food of the world.' And so the cycle would continue for ever, nature's unbreakable law punishing human folly.[17]

The scarcity of food and high unemployment of the war years made this a real, if not immediate, scenario. Death really was astride his white horse; and he came in many guises. Statistical investigation showed that vice of all sorts was thriving. The first census report (1801) revealed that in the midst of vast riches one out of nine lived in 'extreme poverty'. People employed in new manufactures suffered long periods of unemployment. Many agricultural labourers were paid in kind, so were particularly vulnerable to cataclysmic harvest failures. There were 50,000 prostitutes in London alone. The glamour and frivolity of aristocratic life reached ever greater heights of absurdity and extravagance, and corrupted those below them. Dogged by such fears, it was little wonder that the so-called 'Saints', the evangelicals, had a desire to iron out the coarseness of society, whether as bishops or politicians or as vigilante neighbours. 'God has set before me as my object the reformation of manners,' said William Wilberforce, a sentiment shared by many others. When asked what Britain could do to avoid ruin and disaster James Bowdler wrote: 'The answer is plain and short – *We are not reformed. A thorough Reform* would set all right.'[18]

The time was riven by intense passions and deep fears. Outrageous self-confidence was as easily replaced by deep pessimism. Zealous religiosity sat uneasily with boisterous conviviality. Tormented hypochondriacs and heroic soldiers eyed each other with wonder. It was a hard-drinking country, and one where colourful eccentrics were encouraged and feted. While some enjoyed the quiet sobriety of Methodism, many more accepted coarseness, cruelty and the exuberant vulgarity of life as an expression of British liberty. Hazlitt wrote that only in England was the word 'blackguard' considered a compliment and a laudable national characteristic. 'England is a blackguard country,' Lord Erskine told the American envoy Richard Rush.

'A great country,' Rush replied, diplomatically, unaware of the connotations of a word which in any other country would be an insult.

'Yes,' concluded Erskine, 'a great blackguard country; a boxing, fighting country, and don't you call that blackguard!'[19]

I

Sinking, Sinking, Sinking

'If I were desired to define the national character of the English with a single word, I should call them sullen, just as the French are called volatile and the Italians cunning.'

Nikolai Karamzin, *Travels from Moscow* (1803)[1]

He's one of those, as I've heard tell,
Who think it vulgar to be well,
And deem it elegance to sit,
Vap'ring in melancholic fit.

William Combe, *The English Dance of Death*: 'The Hypochondriac'

'I am nervous; I am not ill, but I am nervous; if you would know what is the matter with me, I am nervous.'

George III, during his first spell of derangement, 1788[2]

Scratched on the windowpane of a travellers' inn, among the usual graffiti ('I love pretty Sally Appleby of Chipping Norton'; 'Dam Pitt', etc.), there was the anguished scrawl: 'I am very unhappy. Sam Jenkins.' The gloom that visitors to Britain mocked and cheerfully delineated for their countrymen infuriated the victims of their critiques. 'The English in general do not much care about salad, and garden herbs,' Karamzin informed his readers, diagnosing the national moroseness. 'Roast beef and beef-steaks are their usual food; and hence their blood becomes thick, and themselves phlegmatic, melancholy, and not infrequently self-murderers. To this predisposing cause of the spleen we may add the following: viz. the mists continually arising out of the sea, and the smoke of the pit-coal which hangs like a dense cloud over the towns and villages.'[3]

It was a character type the British were all too willing to acknowledge to themselves, even if they didn't like being told so by Russians, Americans and Frenchmen. Sydney Smith wrote of John Bull: 'His forefathers have been out of spirits for six or seven hundred years, and, seeing nothing but fog and vapour, he is out of spirits too; and when there is no selling or buying, or no business to settle, he prefers being alone and looking at the fire.'

Their attitude to their health and mental state was best summed up in the best-seller of 1806 – and one of the most popular books of the decade – *The Miseries of Human Life*, by the Oxford don James Beresford. It was a two-volume satire on the 'fashionable' maladies of the time. The humour of *The Miseries of Human Life* did not long survive the 1800s, and few today would read it with the delight with which it was received in 1806. But it tapped into an obsession of the time. Reviewing it in the *Edinburgh Review*, Walter Scott said that had there been a book of a similar title published in any other European country, it would be a heartbreaking tale of genuine existential anguish or tortures of the heart. A typical Briton, however, was rendered miserable by the mundane, petty vexations of daily life: a clattering dish, a queue, a traffic jam, an unexpected visit by a friend. 'He knows, indeed, that miseries are necessary to his happiness,' wrote Scott, 'and though perhaps not quite so pleasant at the moment as his other indispensable enjoyments roast beef and beer, would, if taken away, leave just as great a craving in his appetites as would be occasioned by the privation of these national dainties.'[4]

Through the book's two volumes Timothy Testy and his friend Samuel Sensitive compete at length as to who is the most miserable. Every minor inconvenience, slight delay, spillage, unavoidable accident or the sheer business of getting through the day is likely to send the two heroes into agonies of misery; both experience the same worries and vexations; but each claims to feel it on a profounder level than the other. Beresford claimed to be doing a service to the downcast public, for reading about the anguish of Timothy Testy and Samuel Sensitive would be 'an opiate for your fiercest pangs'; every other misery would pale into insignificance after wading through two volumes of his characters' catalogue of woes. Testy and Sensitive had *real* miseries, 'which excruciate the minds and bodies of none more insupportably than of those Heroes in anguish, those writhing Martyrs to the plagues and frenzies of vexation . . .'

'Well, Mr Testy,' asked Mr Sensitive of his friend on the first page of the book, 'and how are things going with you?'

'How! – why just as they always *have* gone,' replied his friend, '– downwards – backwards – crookedly – spirally – any how but upwards, or straight forwards. . .'[5]

Timothy Testy represented the old-fashioned English disease, 'the stately spleen', while Samuel Sensitive was a man of the times, suffering from a more modern and certainly more refined illness, the 'feverish fastidiousness' and 'quivering susceptibilities' of nervous disorders. The spleen was an old English trait, popular in the eighteenth century, a quick and reflexive anger reminiscent of Squire Western in *Tom Jones*. The symptoms of nervous diseases were not so passionate: the sufferer experienced lowness of spirit, feelings of melancholy, sensitivity to light, loss of appetite, indigestion, cravings, dimness of sight, 'confusion of thoughts', 'a wandering mind' and other vague ailments. They were the evils that beset the polished, discriminating and sophisticated. As Sensitive boasted to Testy: 'I, indeed, by the painful privilege of my nature, am as it were ambidexter in misery, being no less exquisitely sensitive to those grosser annoyances, or tangible tribulations, of which you are the victim, than to those subtler and elegant agonies, which is my own particular inheritance.'

Nothing really bad ever happens to Beresford's heroes, but the annoyances of a journey, walking down the street, reading the papers and every other conceivable triviality have a profound effect on their mental state. Many would have seen a reflection of themselves in Samuel Sensitive. The novel did not satirise sensibility (although there is a connection) but the fashion at the turn of the century to treat every feeling or emotion as a medical condition. The renowned and fashionable Dr Thomas Beddoes took 'hypochondria' very seriously, and urged the medical world to do likewise; Samuel Sensitive was a creature to be pitied, not mocked, for he suffered from a debilitating and little understood condition. Beddoes wrote that a genuine sufferer of hypochondriasis finds 'language fail[s] him' when describing his symptoms. He could experience a host of symptoms, including the most common: heartburn, shortness of breath, 'prickings, startings, and most distressing throbbings in the belly', costiveness, tension, feelings of anxiety, memory loss, paranoia, sleeplessness, undefined guilt, palpitations, cramp, ringing in the ears, giddiness, fluctuations of temperature, delusions and so on, ad infinitum. 'In short you see before you, the most miserable wretch upon the face of the earth,' Beddoes commented. It was a profoundly democratic disease: few would fail to experience the myriad symptoms at one time or another. And it was a condition inseparable from the age in which they lived.[6]

Samuel Taylor Coleridge was a real-life Samuel Sensitive, frequently at death's door, always tortured with non-specific diseases and obsessed with self-diagnosis. In 1801 he wrote in anguish to Humphry Davy:

Sinking, sinking, sinking! I feel that I am *sinking*. My medical attendant says that it is irregular Gout with nephritic Symptoms – Gout in a young man of 29!! Swoln [*sic*] knees, and knotty Fingers, a loathy stomach, & a dizzying head – trust me, Friend! I am at times an object of moral Disgust to my own Mind.[7]

Many felt, as Coleridge did, rarely free from a plague of worries. Nervous complaints ('those fashionable tormentors') were the punishment Britain had brought down upon herself for being the most advanced nation in the history of the world; they went hand in glove with progress, the inseparable *gemini* of modernity. Nervous vitiation was the sign of degeneracy and an effeminate, pampered and hedonistic society; William Austin – a hardy American who had nothing but contempt for the state of the present inhabitants of the mother country – wrote of modern Englishmen that 'a thousand nervous afflictions have rendered them women without the spirit of women'. It was a misery no benighted foreigner could know, nor anyone born in the early or mid-eighteenth century, and was known as 'The English Malady'. The Duchess of Bedford claimed to be immune from the disorder because 'she was born before nerves were invented'.[8]

Happy the ignorant and the simple; fortunate the elderly who were immune from modern diseases. The progress of the country – its incredible advances in technologies and trade, its markets stocked with imported food – had created new ways of being ill. 'When wealth and luxury arrive at a certain pitch in any country,' wrote Dr Thomas Trotter, 'mankind cannot remain long stationary in mental qualifications or corporeal strength'; when a people become addicted to spicy food and high living, and when a taste for luxury and vice spreads through the whole community, this is the age when a 'polished society may be said to bring on its own *dotage*, and to dig its own *grave*!'[9]

Trotter published his influential medical textbook, *A View of the Nervous Temperament*, in 1807 as a comprehensive guide to good health for all diseases and all social classes. Part medical treatise, part moral sermon, part historical philosophy, it aimed to diagnose modern society as much as cure physical and mental complaints. For doctors such as Trotter, and for much of the public, the health of society and the health of the individual were inseparable. Analysis had to begin with the moral, political and financial state of the country before one could hope to cure maladies. Doctors should have an intimate knowledge of the minutiae of home life, the prevailing fashions and the prejudices of a people, for it was thence that diseases emerged. The reformer of bodies should also necessarily be a reformer of morals.[10]

Both Trotter and Beddoes were physicians of experience and of high repute. And they had much in common. Born in the same year (1760), they were self-made men who had pulled themselves up from obscurity to affluence and fame. Trotter was the son of a baker from Melrose, and Beddoes the son of a Staffordshire tanner. Although he wrote his *View of the Nervous Temperament* in retirement in Newcastle, Trotter had served with distinction as physician to fleets commanded by the Lords Admiral Howe, Bridport, St Vincent and Cornwallis; he was a member of the Royal Medical Society of Edinburgh, the Medical Society of Aberdeen and a former physician at the Haslar Royal Navy Hospital at Portsmouth. Marked most clearly on his mind, as a grizzled naval doctor returning home, was not the horror of war but the impression that his countrymen on the home front had degenerated into a race of weaklings and pampered fops. They were ill, and there was something deeply wrong with a society that allowed itself to get into this state. He was irritated by the new race of Samuel Sensitives, and compared them unfavourably with the men he was used to treating: 'Hardship, danger, and privation, are the lot of naval service: to brave the weather, the season, and climate, is their delight and duty.' Trotter, it was said, gained his unrivalled knowledge of nervous diseases 'by attendance on some thousands of cases in both sexes, under all the varieties of rank, employment, age, situation, and climate'.[11]

Beddoes had the best education possible at the time, studying at Oxford, London and Edinburgh. He was a scientist first and foremost, burning with the ideals of the Enlightenment. He was a friend of Erasmus Darwin, the Wedgwoods and the Watts, and married into the Edgeworth family, at the centre of the famous Lunar Society. In common with his friends, he burned with radical zeal and had an undying faith in progress. In Bristol in the 1790s he had campaigned for the rights of man with Southey and Coleridge. He believed in the triumph of rationalism and the victory of science over superstition; medicine would follow the breakthroughs in science and philosophy when the medical world underwent a thorough reform – *its* Enlightenment –

and made research and training pre-eminent. He set himself up as the physician to the progressive, wealthy, respectable and ambitious bourgeoisie: he practised in the appropriately named Hope Square in the new suburb of Clifton in commercial Bristol. His colleague Dr Trotter was also in a close position to observe the emergence of an affluent provincial middle class and their attendant medical problems, based as he was in Newcastle. Both physicians wrote to shock the complacent middle classes out of negligence, ignorance and bad habits. As Beddoes admonished his readers, 'our chronic maladies are of our own creating'.[12]

Thomas Trotter admitted that, as a young doctor, he had made some serious blunders, which left him depressed and convinced that he could only make people worse, not better. It was only much experience that taught him that the nervous temperament was the fount of all diseases; indeed, according to him two thirds of all physical maladies were actually nervous diseases. The first step to the cure of any illness was to understand the patient's nervous constitution. The vitiated nervous state was caused by 'this venal age'; the vices of the times led to excessive stimulation of the nerves and agitated the mind, weakening the body and rendering men and women prone to a host of bodily complaints and mental strain quite unknown to humans in a simpler age. 'The more complicated and various the pleasures and business, which man is to pursue in life,' he wrote, 'he will be the more liable to defeat and disappointment: and the more ardent his passions, they will the sooner terminate in exhaustion and disgust. The busy scene, therefore, leads quickest to satiety: the retired circle preserves the longest enjoyment. So that thousands of human beings walk the round of gaiety and dissipation, for the certain reward of nervous debility.'[13]

In early-nineteenth-century Britain, the intensity of living and perpetual competition to keep up with the pace of life jarred the nervous system and left the body susceptible to complete breakdown. The rage to make money, spend money and keep up with fashions, the new wants and needs that nagged at the assurgent middle classes, had combined to push them into the abyss of mental breakdown. A commercial society subject to the caprice of the stock market and the mysterious flows of international trade had 'filled the nation with degenerate fears, apprehensions and hypochondriacism'.[14] People became listless and apathetic, their minds confused and their bodies enfeebled and prone to biliousness, indigestion, gout, cold sweats, asthma, 'weak blood', impotence and sterility; women were especially vulnerable, inviting barrenness or miscarriages, extreme exhaustion, hysteria, fainting fits and premature death. The medical term that described these seemingly unrelated conditions was hypochondria. Illnesses and symptoms had been grievously misdiagnosed; when, for example, someone complained of angina or ague, it was, in reality, the manifestation of a deeply rooted nervous complaint nurtured and encouraged from childhood.[15]

Diagnosis must begin with an exploration of modern British society, so that diseases could be traced to their roots – the way that people lived their lives. Understand that, and the physician could unlock the mysteries of human illness and actually cure his patients. Well-off Britons were assailed from all sides by new needs and wants. Beddoes wrote that a scream pursued one throughout the day: '*Did you see the papers today? Have you read the new play – the new poem – the new pamphlet – the last novel?*' Southey told a story of an eastern tyrant who offered a reward for the invention of a new pleasure; 'in the like manner this nation offers a perpetual reward to those who will discover new wants for them'. Every day there were new must-have inventions advertised in the papers: labour-saving corkscrews, novel candle-snuffers, even a 'hunting razor', so that the busy gentleman, shaving at full gallop, need not miss a second of sport. 'Pocket-toasting forks have been invented, as if it were possible to want a toasting-fork in the Pocket.' It was a particularly British habit to lavish money on gadgets for which they had no conceivable need; they were 'the devices of a people made wanton by prosperity'.[16]

It was the unnaturalness of modern living that alarmed Trotter and Beddoes; mankind had forced itself into a straitjacket and channelled instinctive passions into wholly new and abstracted avenues. Little wonder then that the mind was in a constant state of agitation and the body poisoned; small surprise that myriad new ways of being ill had been invented. 'The Indian paddling his canoe; or the Norwegian sculling his skiff, remain unchanged in their manners; because they return at night to their family, and to intercourse with their kindred.' The outdoor labourer in the countryside improves his bodily strength and inhales the fresh air, and 'a corresponding tone is given to his nervous system: his mind is not debauched by effeminacy; while his temperance and moderation secure him against the disorders which prevail in fashionable life'. His nerves were not ruined, for he had 'no painful emotions for his success in a busy world'. In contrast, the refined and polished gentleman or lady – sitting, as they believe, at the pinnacle of civilisation – 'changes to a different species of being'.[17]

From birth, boys and girls have to submit to the rules and habits of a depraved society. Boys were at least allowed to run around and exercise themselves at a young age, but girls were doomed, left cosseted in overheated rooms dressing dolls. Females were particularly susceptible to nervous derangement; Trotter argued that their education seemed deliberately designed 'to induce a debility of body, from the cradle upwards . . . Their whole tenor of living, and domestic economy, are at variance with health'. Children were nurtured in a sickly, effete and materialistic world, taught to value greed and gain for its own sake. They were pulled further from the natural, their heads and bodies crammed with strange addictions and cravings. A man in the modern world was cast adrift in an unnatural environment:

> He is obliged to undergo a kind of training in how to live . . . Where the savage feels one want, the civilized being has a thousand . . . He is no sooner brought into the world, than he is taught to admire every thing that dazzles, glitters, or makes a noise. His every employment is play; and all his toys are either shining or sonorous . . . Every thing within his view is calculated to prompt his desires and provoke his passions.[18]

Toys and gewgaws might first spark the cravings for commodities and useless fripperies that would be exacerbated with age, but more pernicious passions were inflamed in the nursery. Popular culture was awash with erotic images, lewd prints, dirty songs and salacious novels. Yet the knowing, leering and often comically bawdy attitude to sex was an unsatisfactory introduction to its mysteries; the passions were roused before boys and girls learnt about reproduction. Here was one of the root causes of enervation.[19]

Who could boys and girls ask about sex? For the wealthy, the first friends of children were their servants, 'loose companions' who delighted in telling their young masters and mistresses lewd stories, interlarded with tantalising hints and tall tales. Under the instruction of free-talking and candid footmen and maids, children first saw sex as delightfully naughty and intriguingly seductive. Poorer children also learnt the mysteries of life outside the home, and satisfaction was easier to come by. Francis Place remembered that poor children in London in the late eighteenth century were 'pretty well acquainted with what relates to the union of the sexes. Conversation on these matters was much less reserved than it is now [in the 1820s], books relating to the subject were much more within the reach of boys and girls than they are now, and I had little to learn on any part of the subject.' Nor did many others; salacious images were not hard to find in the metropolis, and all the print dealers, major and minor, displayed them in their windows. Even stationery shops contained hidden delights. Place remembered just such a shop in Russell Court, where Mrs Roach would encourage boys and girls who came to buy penny books and sheets of paper to look at 'pretty pictures', as she called her portfolios of erotica. 'And this was done by many others.'[20]

Doubtless Place was confident on such matters, but the books from which he tells us he learnt about sex were hardly satisfactory. *Aristotle's Compleat Master Piece* was the most popular sex-education book of the eighteenth and early nineteenth centuries, the guide for Place and thousands of his contemporaries. (And, for some, it survived as an antidote to the general silence on matters carnal. In *Ulysses*, Leopold Bloom brings home a copy for Molly.) Richly comic and with all the appearance of candour, *Aristotle's Compleat Master Piece* made sex education fun and represented intercourse as joyous and exciting.

The lesson was to have sex early and have it often: 'it eases and lightens the body, clears the mind, comforts the head and senses, and expels melancholy. Therefore sometimes, thro' the omission of this act, dimness of sight doth ensue, and giddiness; besides, the seed of man, retained above its due time, is convened with some injurious humour.' And prolonged abstention was equally dangerous for girls. From the age of thirteen, with the onset of puberty, 'natural purgations begin to flow' which 'stir up their minds to venery'. Celibacy was dangerous for teenage girls, for they would suffer from chlorosis or the 'green sickness' – respiratory problems, hysteria, loss of appetite or 'an unnatural desire of feeding on chalk, coals, stones, tobacco-pipes, sealing wax, and other things of an hurtful and improper nature' – if their lusts were not sated.[21]

Free from piety, prudery and disapproval it might have been, but accurate it was not; it is hardly surprising if many children were left more confused on reading the lively and graphic descriptions of the body and intercourse. The penis was referred to (rather scarily) as 'the yard', and the full description of its role in intercourse was described in verse:

And thus man's nobler part described we see,
For such the parts of generation be;
And they that carefully survey, will find,
Each part is fitted for the use design'd.
The purest blood we find, if well we heed,
Is in the testicles turn'd into seed.
Which by the most proper channels is transmitted
Into the place by nature for it fitted;
With highest sense of pleasure to excite
In amorous combatants the more delight.
For nature does in this great work design
Profit and pleasure in one act to join.[22]

The essentials of the male and female 'organs of generation', conception and sex itself were all described in rudimentary detail – and in verse. If anyone wondered where babies came from, or what happened between the sheets, *Aristotle's Compleat Master Piece* would answer some questions but beg many more. What, for example, was the enquiring mind to make of this description of sex, told from the male point of view?

Now my infranchis'd hand on every side,
Shall o'er thy naked polish'd iv'ry slide . . .
. . . I shall enjoy thee now, my fairest; come,
And fly with me to love's Elysium.
My rudder with thy bold hand, like a try'd
And skilful pilot, thou shalt steer, and guide,
My bark in love's dark channel, where it shall
Dance as thy bounding waves do rise and fall,
Whilst my tall pinnace in the Cyprian streight
Rides at anchor and unloads the freight.[23]

As a sex guide, *Aristotle's Compleat Master Piece* set out to be ribald, refreshingly open and free from squeamishness. Yet there is coyness, or repression, in the bawdy; the anonymous writer hides behind the humour, using it to deflect more graphic (perhaps more helpful) information. The comedy diffuses the tension and attempts to acquit the writer of the intention of deliberately arousing the readers with erotica disguised as medical writing. It was the most popular sex guide, one people turned to in great numbers: it had run to at least forty-three editions by 1800. For all its failings, misinformation, half-truths and euphemisms, it had an impact on the lives of generations brought up in ignorance of sex. But it was seen as subversive and deliberately arousing. Doctors such as Thomas Beddoes saw this kind of writing as pernicious, for it increased ignorance and indoctrinated young people in vicious habits: early stimulation, masturbation and premature sexual experiences. And this kind of literature ruined the nerves. It meant a 'life of surfeits', which inevitably led – as with all gluttony – to loss of appetite and 'perpetual mawkishness'. Early stimulation would set in train a series of nervous complaints, such as epilepsy and premature aging.[24]

When they grew up, these boys and girls would enter a marriage market, which would prove sexually unrewarding and alien to their natural propensities. Again, for Thomas Trotter the 'savage' in a pristine primitive state is happiest: 'His passion for the sex is temperate, because it meets with no refined allurements, from dress, manners, or fashion, to enflame it beyond bounds.' After all, women's clothes were nothing more than 'a few folds of fine muslin, so loosely put on, that the whole dress appears to be made for the purpose of being thrown aside, in an instant, like a cloak or a shawl'. So, with lust worked up to a pitch by a thousand illicit temptations, the young man was prevented from indulging his instincts. How different from the man who dwelt in peace in a simpler society, who 'is neither perplexed with doubts or fears, nor tantalized by false hopes and promises. The damsel of the forest is a stranger to those airs and duplicities of the coquette and the prude.' Knowing that love had very little to do with marriage, fathers tolerated their sons' philandering: 'the sordid parent winks at the son's indiscretions with the sex, rather than consent that he should marry the woman he loves, without a rich dower'.[25]

Unrequited love and irregular sex with prostitutes 'harassed' the nerves for boys, estranging them further from the inclinations imbued by nature. They were replaced by other false emotions and perverted passions. Young men's health was ruined at the brothel, while women read novels: 'The mind that can amuse itself with the love-sick trash of most modern compositions of this kind, seeks enjoyment beneath the level of a rational being,' wrote Trotter.[26] The heady romance of most novels unleashed passions destructive both to individual health and the state of society; the habitual novel reader would soon experience 'constant uncomfortable feelings, complaints which delicacy declines confessing, disgust in matrimony, the mortification of miscarriages, incompatibility of discharging the first office of the mother, or a state of atrophy if it be attempted'.[27]

Throughout daily life, modern man 'forsakes a mode of life that had been prescribed to him by nature'. It was most conspicuous in the rich and fashionable, but nervous complaints were said to be contagious. They originated with the pampered and hedonistic upper class, but were transmitted to the middling and lower by the example of the richest and their demands for luxuries and services. Beddoes wrote of the lower classes that 'upon *them* bursts the torrent of evil from the crimes and insanity of their superiors, collecting more exterminating rage, as it comes down from a loftier point'. Trade and business made men avaricious and ambitious and weakened the nervous frame. Trotter said that businessmen were all pale, sallow, slender and effeminate, with 'a smallness of voice, that sometimes make[s] their sex doubtful'. And many more who engaged in sedentary work, especially those who benefited from the commercial revolution, such as perfumers, tailors, dressmakers, fruiterers or merchants of all descriptions, suffered their own specific nervous dysfunctions. Their cringing servility to customers was supposedly another cause of the disease. The proliferation of writers, caused by the degenerate tastes of the age, had their own symptoms as well. Trotter had observed that, in writers, 'the muscular power is diminished, the fleshy parts grow soft and flabby, and general debility is the consequence. Few men attached to literary pursuits are active, strong and athletic.' The pressure on their already shattered nerves was further intensified by 'the cold charity' of publishers and booksellers and the precarious nature of their trade.[28]

A contributor to the *Gentleman's Magazine* commented, after reading Trotter's book, that 'The last century, it is generally admitted, has effected a mournful alteration in the constitution of our countrymen: the rigid fibre and rich blood of our ancestors exposed them principally to attacks of the pleuritic and inflammatory kind. They were strangers to the tremors, the palpitations, the sinkings of modern invalids. Their diseases were the diseases of robustness. In the present days, the low lingering morbid symptoms of debility generally prevail.' Timothy Testy's disease was of the older variety; Samuel Sensitive had been contaminated by overexposure to modernity.

And, as Trotter warned, this was only the beginning of national degeneracy. Those habits of luxury and intemperance were only just taking root; after further decades of self-abuse, the British would be weakened beyond all recognition. But how had the hardy ailments that characterised a vigorous people in the eighteenth century been replaced with the insipid maladies of the nineteenth? Surely, in the past, people's nerves had had to put up with far worse than trifles over business and pleasure? The problem, as Trotter and others saw it, was that the nervous state of modern Britain derived from her very strength. She had conquered large portions of the globe, subdued her rivals, and the fruits of her labour could be seen in every market and on everyone's table. Britain had, after such manly exertion, gorged on foreign foods, and the people were suffering a collective hangover from overindulgence.

The toxins had settled in the stomach, which was, for Trotter and many others, the most important part of the body. Jenner called it the 'grand Monarque of the Constitution'. It was inordinately complex and formed 'a *centre* of sympathy between our corporeal and mental parts, of more exquisite qualifications than even the brain itself'. This intricate organ was at the centre of the nervous system; this, said Trotter, was the great secret that unlocked the mystery of human illness. 'Hypochondria' derived from the Greek *hupokhondria*, meaning the belly, which was the seat of melancholy. The intemperate brought dyspepsia upon themselves, the root of all nervous complaints and hence all physical ills; they were racked with disorders of the mind, felt pains everywhere, suffered bad sleep and loss of appetite as the first stage in a complete breakdown. Fevers and fits soon followed when the stomach was damaged. Colonial imports were particularly dangerous: tobacco, for example, 'acts powerfully on the nervous system, destroys the sensibility of the stomach; and it is observed that those who devour it in great quantity, die of apoplexy, palsy, and dropsy'. Smoking it could lead to sudden death.*

Other commodities wrecked the 'vital power of the stomach' in similar ways. Tea, said Trotter, 'excites nausea and vomiting, tremors, cold sweats, vertigo, dimness of sight, and confusion of thought'. It was a narcotic, and the initial high led naturally to alcoholism, because, as Beddoes maintained, tea and coffee produced 'a sense of intoxication, with enfeebled faculties, uncomfortableness and languor afterwards'. In the short term, it corroded the stomach and nurtured illness; Beddoes quoted a Dutch doctor to the effect that tea and coffee provoked 'various nervous complaints, which were *totally*

*An advertisement from America found its way into the British press in 1807: 'Died in Salem, Master James Verry aged twelve, a promising youth, whose early death is supposed to have been brought on by excessive smoking of segars.'

unknown before these liquors were introduced'. Truly then, it was a beverage 'well suited to the taste of an indolent and voluptuous age'. Of all the dangerous foreign imports, cayenne pepper, spices of all sorts, soy, catchup and other seasonings were the worst. They were used in sauces, and so were 'dangerous as being narcotics the most enticing when applied to the taste; and, children that are early accustomed to such poisons, will run the great hazard of ending their career as sots and dram drinkers'.[29]

The consumption of luxurious foods was not confined to the wealthy. Patrick Colquhoun, a police magistrate and observer of the habits of the poor, wrote that all shared the new imports due to thieving from warehouses and ships which fed a thriving black market, so that 'the superabundant circulation of riches, the gains of the low gambler, the swindler, the common prostitute, and the criminal offender, increase as the wealth of the nation is augmenting. It descends even to the lowest classes of society, who indulge in luxuries little known a century ago'. Trotter found that nervous disorders were 'rapidly extending to the poorer classes'.[30]

The first Indian eatery opened in London at this time – a harbinger of a worldwide assault on the poor British digestive system. The previous generation suffered the 'diseases of robustness' because they stuck to plain, simple and manly foodstuffs. Further in the past, people were in a way immune from the nerves and capable of consuming a richer diet because they led healthier lives. 'Robinhood [*sic*] and Little John, the alert and airy inhabitants of the greenwood shade,' wrote Beddoes, 'could take liberties with the bottle, which are very unsafe for us, under our close roofs and between our stuccoed walls.' But the moderns led softer lives and ate richer foods and drank more toxic liquors, so it was essential for doctors to prescribe a diet for John Bull. Cayenne pepper, rum and tea were a noxious cocktail, imbibed from the poisoned chalice of empire.[31]

The tourist Louis Simond observed that Britain and the British had become *addicted* to trade. The small island, poor in natural resources, had built itself up on a mountain of commercial enterprise; once commenced, the momentum and direction could not be changed. Americans did not feel the same urge, nor had they become as abjectly dependent on trade, because they had resources in abundance; they retained therefore their simplicity and virtue. 'The necessity of acquiring, not merely the real necessities and comforts of life, but the means of living in style – a certain inveterate habit of luxury, inexorable activity constitutes the strength of England. Whether it secures private happiness is not so certain. Placed as England is, she must be great and glorious, or perish. The people of the United States may be weak and happy with impunity, and remain so, in spite of themselves, for a century to come.'[32]

The burgeoning health problems pointed to wider moral issues. Crisis was looming because, as was obvious to the medico-moral examiners, Britain was rapidly moving into a particular phase in the historically inevitable march of progress. For Trotter the empire was at once a sign of greatness and a terrible trap. It brought not just poisons but introduced a number of uncomfortable moral questions that had to be addressed. The British were being punished for the evils of the slave trade by being spoon-fed honey-coated poisons. What else were the East and West Indies to Britain but 'a theatre of oppression and slavery, to gorge her with commercial wealth'? Africa had been 'made a field of blood' to supply the slave labour and resources to power the commercial revolution, but 'whose produce only tends to weaken the manly character, and overwhelm her with nervous infirmities!' Beddoes was more proud of his country, saying that, in the history of the world, Britain exceeded the example of Athens in its glory and had 'contended with rivals, as formidable as Sparta'. Britain was famed for its morality, benevolence and unchallenged supremacy. But, one question would dog the conquerors: 'Have we borne our faculties more wisely than the Athenians? . . . Has Britain wasted her vigour in the debauches of glory? Has she bruised her breast by straining to grasp unwieldy masses . . .? Is the multitude exhausted by toil and want, that their superiors may pine under the effects of intemperance or effeminate luxury?'[33]

Thomas Trotter was more certain as to the answer. Britain, he warned, had better think of Rome, where 'power overgrown, and riches unbounded' had ruined the people. The bounteous rewards of colonisation contained within them the seeds for the destruction of an empire. When the Romans had lost 'their moral virtue and dignity, and with these, their physical strength, [they] became a prey to barbarous hordes; who, undebauched by refined pleasures, found the enervated Romans an easy conquest. Let Great Britain look to this example.' But the wars had made prominent the degeneracy of the British. The Martello towers that were built along the coast to defend the shores from invasion betokened a nervous country. Rather than engage the enemy, the navy preferred to blockade enemy ports. Politicians and generals, like nervous patients tormented with imaginary ailments, were wilfully blind to real and present evils. The jumpy people started at shadows and with fevered brains conjured into being a phantasmagoria of terrific visions and apocalyptic signs.[34]

Nervous disorders were the maladies of affluence and sophistication. Who were you – what were you lacking – if you were immune from it? To be beset by the nerves was to parade one's wealth, refinement and sensibility. It was, for some, the hallmark of the civilised, at once a curse and a privilege. It also showed an extraordinary propensity for vanity and self-pitying fantasies in the public: nerves were the diseases of narcissism and obsessive introspection. They were also the manifestation of deeper worries – about commerce, modernity and the war.

It was hardly surprising, then, that nervous disorders swept through the country in the 1790s and 1800s, once they were given legitimacy by respected doctors. In novels, heroines and sensitive young men inevitably suffered from them. Every twinge, headache or hangover was put down to the derangement of the nervous system; as Beddoes admitted, a young girl who reads too many fashionable magazines, novels and medical books and catches a cold 'is therefore persuaded that the cough is *nervous*'. Masters and mistresses became irritated when their servants started complaining of 'the nerves'.

The diagnosis of nervous disorders was suggested by physicians of the stoic tradition alarmed by rampant capitalism. Looking at the phenomenon from a medically sophisticated age, it would seem that 'the nerves' was the name that people gave to hundreds of undiagnosable complaints – from physical ones to serious mental problems. It was perhaps inevitable at a time when superstition was superseded by science, but rationalisation had not been complemented by remedy. They were the same old diseases and maladies, but with a modern explanation applied to them. 'Nerves' became the catch-all expression. This is suggested in *Pride and Prejudice*, where Mrs Bennet ascribes all her aches and pains, and even her emotions, to her nerves: 'When she was discontented she fancied herself nervous.' Like Samuel Sensitive, every feeling could be medicalised and every annoyance was a threat to her health.

'You take delight in vexing me,' she tells Mr Bennet. 'You have no compassion on my poor nerves.'

'They are my old friends', her husband replies, '– I have heard you mention them with consideration these twenty years at least.'

The *Annual Review* said that after doctors such as Beddoes started taking the disease seriously, everyone was popping pills, outdoing one another with exaggerated symptoms and buying an array of spurious medical equipment. One Samuel Jessop took 226,934 pills and 40,000 bottles of medicine between 1791 and his death in 1817 (at a ripe old age, it has to be said). In 1814 alone he swallowed 51,590 pills. All Britons, the *Annual Review* commented, were 'fanatics in physic'.[35]

This spirit was satirised in the monthly London journal *The Scourge* by Hewson Clarke. He has a fictional Mr Valentine Vickers write to the magazine, complaining that his new wife Polly Buxom ('a young lady remarkable for the sprightliness of her temper and the bloom of her countenance') has started reading medical books. As a result, 'her life is now one continued alternation of horrors. She is always afflicted with the disease about which she has been last reading . . . she is now labouring, Sir, under a fashionable complaint called nerves . . . [I] begin to conjecture that reading about a disease may actually produce it.' The ravages of 'the nerves' had turned his English rose into 'a timid, listless, complaining picture of old maidism – [who] is afraid of her every breath of wind, and suspects that there is poison in everything she tastes.'[36]

It was only natural to want a cure, an immediate tonic to save one from the discomfort of nervous afflictions. The dream of a wonder drug or palliative was bewitching to many. Fortunately, there was a medicine on the market, designed with the fashionable in mind. It was a refined cure for a refined people; its inventor said that there had never been a more 'elegant and efficacious' medicine. It could be taken to cure

> weak and shattered constitutions, weakness of sight or memory, hypochondria, tremblings, horrors of the mind, sexual debility, and all other diseases arising from a relaxed state of the nervous system, and often the consequence of intemperance, debauchery, inattention to the necessary cares of healthy luxury.[37]

The Cordial Balm of Gilead offered to cure the diseases highlighted by the medical establishment, but it asked very little of the afflicted. Whereas doctors of the stoic tradition urged individuals (and society) to practise self-denial, the Balm of Gilead offered patients – or customers – a cure which did not impinge on their pursuit of pleasure, self-indulgence and business. After all, most nervous disorders, this particular doctor reassured the public, were caused by 'inattention', not greed, gluttony, culpable negligence or immorality. It salved the conscience and restored the jarred nerves to equilibrium.

Nervous Britons had Dr Samuel Solomon to thank for the invention of a remedy for their reigning malady. They did so with their cash. Dr Solomon was one of the wealthiest men in the country – his business's turnover was £40,000 in 1807 – as well as being a best-selling author and an international name. When Benjamin Silliman arrived from Boston at Liverpool, he passed Gilead House, the doctor's grand country estate, on the road to Manchester. It was one of the sights that every tourist should see. 'I need not inform you', he wrote home, 'that the Doctor is well known in America, for every man who has learning enough to read a newspaper, and eyes enough to peruse double pica letters on an apothecary's door, must have become acquainted with the merits and modesty of Dr Solomon.' And the same could be said for people in Europe, the West Indies and India. At his height, Samuel Solomon's name was one of the most famous in the world.[38]

Solomon sided with the patient. The people suffered under the tyranny of the medical establishment, a clique of self-serving, secretive and greedy physicians. This closed club stifled free enquiry and claimed a monopoly on medical knowledge, only to enrich themselves and keep out competition from pioneers with new, better and therefore unwelcome ideas. Under the dominion of the faculty, medical knowledge had stagnated; there had been few advances since the days of Hippocrates or Galen; there had been no Newton of medical science, the doctor said.

Solomon believed that he, as a free-thinking doctor, was a victim of this outrageous cartel; but the true sufferers were the British public, who were charged exorbitant prices for useless drugs, outdated information or downright lies. Solomon had, he claimed, brought medical knowledge to the people of the world because he was not ashamed to speak through the newspapers. Every year he spent some £5,000 on advertisements. He had been stigmatised for cheapening the science by using them, but Solomon answered that his methods were at once a means of education and a proof of the efficacy of his cures. 'It requires the *strongest* conviction of *intrinsic* worth and *physical* excellence, by *long* and *great experience*, to induce an inventor or proprietor to incur the serious and certain expense of making [his medicines] known by ADVERTISEMENTS.'

For over twenty years, he said, he had taken on corrupt doctors on behalf of the people of Britain, democratising medicine and diffusing knowledge. His advertisements in papers, posters and handbills deluged the English-speaking world and most European countries, and must have been one of the most recognisable features of daily life. Patients who were too embarrassed, or too poor, to consult their local physician could write to Solomon and reveal symptoms and diseases in complete secrecy 'which seldom are fairly submitted for fear of exposure to any other medical men'. His much-revised textbook *A Guide to Health*, first published in 1798, went to sixty-six editions and was said to have sold 120,000 copies. 'I am happy . . . in the reflection that I have not lived in vain,' he wrote in the last edition of *A Guide to Health* (1815); 'as it is with heartfelt pleasure I see the success of my labours, and daily receive the acknowledgements of those who have been benefited by my discoveries.'[39]

It was often claimed that Solomon's *Guide to Health* sat next to the Bible on every household's bookshelf and people held it 'next in veneration to the sacred volume', the one offering life in the next world, the other life in this. When the *Edinburgh Review* devoted an essay to Keats, Byron wrote: 'Why don't they review and praise "Solomon's Guide to Health"? it is better sense, and as much poetry as Johnny Keats.' *The Scourge* quipped that 'No work of modern times, perhaps, has been more read by persons of every rank and description; and no man ever rose from the perusal of it.' Solomon claimed that it owed its success to his candour and willingness to tackle taboo subjects. The worried and ill-informed had nowhere else to turn with embarrassing or shameful questions. A woman, for example, who was worried about menstrual problems, her sexual health, barrenness, sterility or frigidity (symptoms of nervous disorders, of course) could not find satisfactory answers 'without wounding her delicacy by a disclosure of her fears or her apprehensions, to the rude security of PRETENDED FRIENDS'. And there were plenty of other people harassed by similar ignorance and unease: 'YOUTH who have ungardedly [*sic*] plunged themselves into licentious love, and feel the dreadful effects of impure embrace . . . will find a faithful "GUIDE

TO HEALTH", and HAPPINESS too, in the perusal of the present publication . . . Young people of either sex, who have unfortunately given way to a delusive, secret and destructive vice, injured their health, and destroyed their whole animal functions, will meet with a "Balm of Consolation".'[40]

It is one of the most interesting and beguiling books of the first years of the nineteenth century. With its catalogue of infirmities and panoply of nervous symptoms it was well suited to a decade in which one of the favourite works of fiction was *The Miseries of Human Life*. Solomon was a brilliant observer of his times, able to latch on to changing moral attitudes, especially towards sex. He knew, like Beresford, that the British were predisposed towards melancholy and sullenness, and they wanted a cure for *that* national disease more than any other malady. He also understood – far better than Trotter and Beddoes – that the British would never reform their habits, and it was ridiculous to expect them to do so.

However, like the diagnosis of Trotter and Beddoes, Solomon's book could provoke a psychosomatic reaction. If the reader wasn't ill before he or she read it, *A Guide to Health* would transform the heartiest into a whingeing hypochondriac. In the same way as the books already considered in this chapter, the symptoms of nervous disorders are exhaustively described and the same causes identified: the luxuries and inactivity, the stresses and pressures of modern living. But whereas the other doctors suggested that the illness was the fate of the affluent and sedentary, the metropolitan and those employed in new industries, Solomon universalised the phenomenon of nervous complaints to every social class and all ages, to farmers and labourers as much as wilting duchesses and debauched young men. He persuaded his hundreds of thousands of readers that anyone who had ever had a cough, bilious attack, muscular ache or feeling of depression was a sufferer. Even common and grave diseases such as consumption and the ague were included in his diagnosis. He claimed to cure:

Weakness, Flatulence, Palpitations, Watchfulness, Drowsiness after eating, Timidity, Flushes of heat and cold, Numbness, Giddiness, Pains, (especially of the back, head, and loins) Hiccough, Difficulty of Respiration, Dry cough, Debility, Lowness of Spirits, Loss of Appetite, Relaxation, Indigestion, Sickness, Vomiting, Gouty Spasms of the Stomach, Hysterical and Hypochondriacal affectations, Dimness of Sight, Confused Thoughts, Wandering of the Mind, &c.

In other words, no one was immune and everyone needed to take the medicine (as that wonderful '&c' makes clear). The crucial difference from Beddoes and Trotter was that Solomon was a man on the make, someone with a fantastic business mind but no academic qualifications and very little medical knowledge. Most importantly, he had a drug to sell.

Throughout *A Guide to Health*, as the perplexed reader begins to realise that every minor and easily ignored annoyance was in fact a symptom of a deeper malaise, Solomon provides an answer. *A Guide to Health* is tediously repetitive if read from cover to cover. But it has a good index and was obviously intended for the reader to dip into, so that worried hypochondriacs could look up what immediately concerned them. After long descriptions of terrible, frequently undiagnosed diseases and their long-term consequences, the concerned doctor always lists one cure: The Cordial Balm of Gilead. The supposed medical cyclopaedia, for use by a worried mother in the home, was one long, ingenious advertisement for Solomon's wonder drug. In 1800s Britain, the Balm of Gilead was the popular cure for nervous illnesses. But it was easily adaptable: in America it was marketed, to great effect, as a specific for yellow fever.

It was said, probably with some truth, that Samuel Solomon came up with the name and the uses of the drug and began advertising it before he set about 'discovering' it. Its evocative name (which has been used for twenty-first-century drugs) comes from the Old Testament: 'Is there no balm in Gilead; is there no physician there? why then is not the health of the daughter of my people recovered?' (Jeremiah, 8:22). It took many years before the true ingredients were revealed to the world; in the meantime, people had to trust Solomon's claim that the nostrum was 'a most noble medicine composed of some of the choicest balsams in the whole Materia Medica. The process is long and laborious, and requires the most nice and minute attention.' He also claimed that its ingredients originated in the Holy Land itself and the process of developing it cost him £5,000 a year. Descriptions of the medicine sounded enticing, but, beyond the hyperbole, were meaningless:

> . . . besides the nutritious quality of a restorative, it has a fragrant, subtle, oleos principle, which immediately affects the nerves, and gives a kind of friendly motion to the fluids, yielding plenty of animal heat, the true source of firmness and vigour.[41]

The doctor was adept at creating mythologies about his products. But he was an enigmatic personality. Stories about Solomon – one of the celebrities of the 1800s, after all – are many and various, and most are clearly malicious inventions. The attacks were not overtly anti-Semitic (although a few were), concentrating instead on the rapaciousness of all quack doctors, Jewish or not. Few university-educated metropolitan journalists had anything but contempt for quacks and were shocked at his success; they did not stint on denigrating him at every turn. As far as we can tell, he was born in 1768 or '69 in Bristol or Liverpool (his place of origin was disputed even at the time), orphaned early, and found work at the docks in one of these two cities, where he attracted attention on the wharves 'by his amazing volubility, his greediness after gain, and his unfailing impudence'. Thereafter he was able to 'carry on a *roaring* business as a Jew pedlar', as *The Scourge* put it.

Again it was disputed, but it appears that at this stage of his career he was either a boot-blacking salesman in Newcastle or a vendor of hair-curlers in Birmingham – or both. Whatever the true story, he quickly became adept at the salesman's patter and was a gifted businessman. He soon fell in with Dr William Brodum, the most famous quack of the time and a 'hoary poltroon', in the words of *The Scourge*. Brodum had blazed a trail that Solomon was all too eager to follow. The older man had purchased a medical degree from the University of Copenhagen and cashed in on the rage for nervous disorders, selling his nostrum, 'The Nervous Cordial', and a book called *A Guide to Old Age*. He had made a fortune from the British public in the 1780s and '90s. Solomon learnt at the feet of Brodum. He developed the same sales techniques and converted from Judaism to the Church of England, as Brodum had done. However, Solomon desired 'to wind round his own brow the laurels which he designed to tear from the temples of his precursor in the path of impudence and imposition'. And the younger man was destined to far surpass his mentor.[42]

Solomon purchased his MD from Marischal College in 1789, at the tender age of twenty, and in the same year began a publicity tour round the country to demonstrate his miracle-working Balm of Gilead. The tour had two purposes: the first was to demonstrate the medicine to crowds of people; the second, and most important, was to collect testimonies of the nostrum's efficacy from eminent men. In

Birmingham he raised money for advertising in the newspapers and added commendations to his list of grateful and awestruck patients. Within a few years he had collected, he said, accounts of stunning recoveries from a host of diseases from all over Britain, as well as North America, France, Sweden, Germany, Norway, Holland, Jamaica and Russia. It was not until the late 1790s that the elixir really took off, and in 1798 he wrote *A Guide to Health* (much of it plagiarised from his mentor's *Guide to Old Age*), which sent the Balm of Gilead into the first rank of empiric medicines. In 1805 the extent of his fortune and the commercial success of his medicine and book was signalled to the world, and flaunted in the face of university-trained physicians, when he built the palatial Gilead House outside Liverpool, where he retained a staff of richly liveried servants and where, according to one journalist, he 'indulges in every pleasure which can gratify himself'.[43]

Samuel Solomon's success rested on his mastery of provincial newspaper advertising. He knew full well that the unspoken truth of the press was its reliance on advertisements – for revenue and to attract readers, who often bought the papers solely to peruse the classified columns. It was, he thought, better to avoid the hypocrisy of the self-proclaimed incorruptible press and the supposed disassociation between editorial and advertising. He went straight to editors, arranging a mutually beneficial profit-sharing scheme. A typical puff piece comes from the *Salisbury Journal*, an advertisement masquerading as 'news':

> The Printer of this Paper has received information from Mr J Moore of Poole . . . stating that several gentlemen have taken the Cordial Balm of Gilead and have experienced great benefit indeed; the first bottle gave them the most wonderful relief, and a few more affected a complete cure of a deep decline.[44]

Both quack doctor and newspaperman knew well enough that, for all the discredited nostrums and bogus medicines that had had their moment on the market and all the disappointed dreams of recovery, the public still had an appetite for the cure-all; the more outrageous the claims of its miraculous powers, the more audacious the language, the more lurid the stories of sudden recoveries and the greater the cost, the better the medicine would do. People enjoyed reading quack doctors' puffs and promotions; journalists liked writing stories about preposterous recoveries from death's door. And as nervous disorders became highly fashionable, and hypochondriacs were taken seriously, such stories and panaceas could only become more popular.*

It is understandable that people suffering undiagnosed illnesses would turn, often in desperation, to whatever seemed like a plausible salvation from pain. Solomon knew that in lambasting the medical establishment he would attract a ready audience. For many, the local physician would indeed be a remote figure, very expensive, notoriously badly educated and often unable to offer any relief for complicated or little-understood diseases. Most people lived in a world of doubt, scared that a slight ache or an upset stomach could lead to something far worse. It is little wonder that the age saw hysterical diseases, hypochondria and what we would call depression. There were those who 'caught' nervous diseases because they were so widely discussed, but there were many who were seriously ill, mentally or physically, yet could find no one to give them an explanation or succour. He who spoke with the most confidence, therefore, would attract the greatest number of customers and get the best results – at least in the short term.

Solomon, knowing that most of his customers wanted someone to give a plausible diagnosis, asked of them nothing more than their absolute confidence. 'The patient must be comfortable and content to be ruled by his physician,' he wrote in *A Guide to Health*, 'otherwise all his endeavours will come to no good end . . . The body's mischiefs [*sic*], as *Plato* proves, proceed from the soul; and if the mind be not first satisfied, the body can never be cured.' The Cordial Balm of Gilead, he said, would only work if the patient *believed* in it, really believed in it. A contributor to the *Critical Review* pointed out that the whole medical profession was in disarray and did not deserve trust. It was entirely understandable that people would put their faith in the quack because

> medicine is utterly inefficient, except as a palliative, and a very imperfect one too. Numbers are languishing under long, tedious, and painful maladies, and at last die in spite of all that can be done for them by medicine. Multitudes are the perpetual victims of hypochondriacal and nervous diseases . . . Men will not quietly submit

*The *Birmingham Chronicle,* a great supporter of the doctor (especially after he donated money to the Birmingham Dispensary), wrote a poem in his honour: 'And so to thy BALM, that with Gilead's name grac'd/ Has heaped up thy coffers with wealth;/ The good things of this world are, on Thee, not misplac'd,/ Thy Balm keeps the World in good health.'

to suffer. They go from physician to physician, and try drug after drug . . . They must be amused and gratified, and fed with vain hopes and assurances, that will never be realized. Humanity almost demands this concession to poor, weak, frail, and sinking beings. In a word, they must be deceived.[45]

There were many such people who were prepared to put all their faith in Solomon, and it is no surprise that there were many cases of people who swallowed a dose of the Balm of Gilead and rose from their beds after months or years in bed plagued by their own fears. The *Examiner* newspaper satirised this craving for an authority figure: a letter from 'Lazarus', who had worn a patch on his neck all his life and who wrote that he had called Dr Solomon in desperation: 'As he entered the house, I found a perceptible improvement; the sound of his shoes creaking on the stairs healed a wound of eighteen years tenacity; and as he entered the apartment, the patch falling to the ground, I had only to tender his fee, and dismiss him.'[46]

Every fairground charlatan and itinerant huckster relied on his performance and self-confidence to make an audience trust him, at least for as long as it took them to buy his panacea and for him to make a quick exit. But Solomon rarely met a patient, and his medicine was not a one-off fast seller; the good doctor could not simply disappear over the hills to con another village. He relied on repeat sales and knew, because of his prolific advertising and fame, that his reputation was a matter of international discussion. To sell his Balm for over a quarter of a century, communicating only through print, was an act of faith healing that was quite extraordinary.[47]

Solomon's advertisements became ever more daring and exaggerated, caught in an inflation of hyperbole; he had to preserve his authority and retain the faith of his customers, who would otherwise turn to the next quack doctor and another set of stories. The overblown advertisement and puff was a necessary ingredient in the 'cure', as was the high price – half a guinea a bottle. Even the poorest customer would hesitate to buy a cheap medicine, because the cost reflected its curative properties.* Much of Solomon's advice in his book is helpful and sound. He recommended restraint from immoderate drinking, illicit sex and coffee, to be supplanted by exercise, tem-

*Solomon claimed that the Balm of Gilead contained dissolved gold, further enhancing its attraction. One journalist took it as a joke on Solomon's part: 'it cannot be disputed that gold is dissolved or wasted in the purchase of it, and this was doubtless the strict meaning of the artful quack'.

perance, personal and domestic hygiene, sociability and rest, just so long, of course, as it accompanied regular doses of the Balm of Gilead. (It would be no surprise if most patients felt better after this regimen, and the credit, presumably, would go to the Balm of Gilead.) But the image of the benign, anti-establishment doctor could only sell so many phials and books. There had to be another ingredient.

Any quack doctor knew that he had to create illness as much as claim to cure it. There is a much darker side to Samuel Solomon, which destroys any claim that he might have done any good with his nostrums and dubious advice. Solomon would boast of his candour and straight-talking: he would talk of matters stifled in other medical guides or conversation. 'The mind of the patient should be soothed by the consolations of friendship,' he reassured his readers. And there was one subject on which people wanted the advice of a confidant. Solomon called himself 'the "SILENT FRIEND" which . . . [young people] may consult *without exposure*, and with assured confidence of success'. Sex sells, especially when ignorance reigns. But in his profession of trustworthiness and openness, Solomon put forward a new and disturbing explanation for the enervated state of modern Britons. And it played on the darkest of fears.[48]

'Youth in particular rush headlong into the vortex of dissipation and death,' Solomon wrote in the preface to *A Guide to Health*. His aim was to universalise nervous diseases, and he had suggested the British climate as a primary cause of these ailments. It was not a specifically middle-class malady, but bound up with the nation itself. But there was another way of widening the market for remedies for nervous disorders. The many advertisements for the Balm of Gilead contained long lists of the usual symptoms, but also dark hints about one degenerative illness, caused by 'secret venery' committed in youth. This 'foul pollution' was the *true* cause of nervous derangement. In later life, every ache, fever, period of low spirits – indeed, any physical or mental breakdown, including barrenness and frigidity in women – could be attributed to early vicious habits.

There could be nothing better calculated to foster guilt and panic, increase hypochondria and spread alarm among young ignorant people and worried parents. Early self-abuse would weaken every organ in the body and sow the seeds for spasms, fevers, paroxysms and depression in later life. Sex, even illicit sex, was healthy because of 'the mental triumph and exultation, together with the absence of regret and repentance, which accompany the enjoyment of the beautiful or desired object, animate and invigorate the whole frame, give new strength and sprightliness to the circulation of all the humours, and promote the generation of all the animal spirits'. Solitary enjoyments left shame and wasted the 'vital spirit' without the compensation of mutual enjoyment, which would invigorate the circulation and revivify the essential humours. Youthful habits were dangerous because when the thoughtless youth 'carries about him the instruments and incentives of his own guilt, when no accomplice is necessary, when solitude encourages and darkness protects, what can indict the odious propensity . . .?' And the guilty, no matter how much they repented, would carry around the shame and the knowledge that their health was forever ruined. Those confirmed in the habit could be identified because they 'generally find themselves disgusted at all amusements, absent in company, stupid and lifeless every where, and if they think at all feel themselves plunged into deepest melancholy' – a pretty good description of any teenager, guilty or not.[49]

Who could claim to be innocent of this, the foundation of all diseases? Solomon was banking that not many would, or would at least be so confused by his vague language and vulgar hints that they would *imagine* themselves guilty. It must be prevalent, he said. One had only to observe modern Britons: humans had deteriorated through the generations due to the ravages of onanism; look at the muscular and giant Homeric heroes, he said; what had happened to mankind since then? Nothing but self-abuse and secret crime; their descendants had become progressively diminutive and, judging by the puny relics of the nineteenth century, would inevitably continue to degenerate. In due course, humans would become incapable of procreation. But, thanks to him, there was a cure available. Indeed, the Balm of Gilead was designed specifically to combat this horror. 'Youth of either sex, who have practised a secret and destructive vice, and thereby relaxed, weakened, and debilitated the whole nervous system, will find the Cordial Balm of Gilead the most powerful, certain, and effectual restorative.'[50]

Anxiety about masturbation was nothing new, and Solomon cannot be said to have invented it. But his business brain was finely tuned to every prevailing worry and sexual unease – especially those that people dared not talk about. He did not necessarily believe the concern about onanism, nor personally condemn it from a medical or moral point of view. Yet he knew what would sell medicine. Many of his targets were no doubt lonely apprentices and maidservants, people who had no one to turn to and could be made to feel guilty and desperate for some kind of cure. Solomon wanted to spread panic among the ignorant and credulous, the vulnerable young. The greater the anxiety and sense of shame, the greater his returns.

Solomon was criticised for preying on the lonely and ignorant with specious jargon and invidious hints. He wanted nothing more than 'to fill his own pockets, at the expense of the foolishly weak, and the ignorantly superstitious among the community'. But he was savaged because it was felt that he wanted to encourage the vices he claimed to abhor. If he was a truly altruistic doctor, if his Balm really was a miracle cure, everyone would be transported to perfect health and his business would crumble. Many believed that if there was a cure for an odious vice (even if it was spurious), it merely gave licence to the guilty to sin, knowing they could buy easy redemption.

What was to stop young people engaging in horrid practices if they believed that nature's punishment could be arrested for half a guinea? Indeed, books like *A Guide to Health* could be condemned as nothing more than inducements to criminal activity – erotica dressed up as learned medicine. Parts of the book and some of the promised 'cures' could suggest, depending on the reader's ability (or willingness) to read between the lines, that the Balm was an aphrodisiac, a specific against venereal disease or a hangover cure, among many other advertised benefits. Hewson Clarke, writing in *The Scourge* on Solomon's book, said: 'It is more than probable, considering the taste and disposition of the age, that its immoral tendency, and the temptations it holds out to vice may have tended to increase its sale, and to give it the vast degree of vulgar *éclat* which has been attached to it.' Clarke and others believed the book was an initiation into vice and barely disguised pornography. Thus there was a willing complicity between the quack doctor's confidence trick and some sections of his market. The 'case studies' of recovered victims of vice, especially women, could sometimes read like pastiches of *Fanny Hill*: that, many believed, was the real reason for buying *A Guide to Health*.[51]

In an age alive to the threat of the impostor, the quack doctor was the most vivid example. Britain had supposedly reached the peak of civilisation and progress, yet it was becoming increasingly difficult to differentiate the plausible criminal from the polite gentleman or lady – or even, in daily life, the moral from the immoral. Britain was worryingly vulnerable to the skill of the impostor who could inveigle himself into polite society by using his charm and insights into human nature, only to seduce with gilded words as a prelude to fraud and robbery. This was true of a host of polished crooks and rapacious fraudsters, including seducers, courtesans, fanatic preachers, pseudo-scholars, social reformers, poetasters, shady businessmen and myriad others who hid behind a meticulously constructed facade of politeness and sincerity. Their ability to put on a convincing performance, to interlard their remarks with high-sounding jargon, to trumpet their (feigned) morality and beguile an honest audience allowed them to make their way through society, evading detection and making a fortune. Even worse was the artificiality of modern men and women, who were accomplished at hiding their vices and passing for moral people. There was something of the quack or impostor in everyone. It was the real definition of being a hypocrite.

Armed with plausible jargon, adept at beguiling the credulous and disguising his cupidity under a veneer of morality and respectability, the quack represented the perverted culmination of 'refinement'. There were those who had taken all the virtues of progress and turned them into money-making scams or used them to camouflage outrageous vices. Samuel Solomon had made much of his philanthropy, candour, sincerity, morality, knowledge and humanity, all the cardinal virtues of civilisation and part of the impossibly high standards Britons set for each other. Yet, according to his critics, he inverted these. What philanthropist or person imbued with high intelligence (as Solomon undoubtedly was) found it necessary to invent or encourage or foster specious diseases which existed solely in the minds of worried people? His candour was in reality a salacious and unnecessary insight into the seamier side of human weakness.

Under the guise of plain speaking, he manipulated the credulous and titillated the curious; 'candour' was in reality the licence he gave himself to enter unwholesome territory for his customers' sexual gratification and his own profit. In the same way, the parade of morality – his exaggerated horror of 'secret venery' and illicit sex – was both unnecessary and feigned: he hijacked or created moral panic, without any strong or sincere feelings, to fill his pocket, probably the most outrageous of his vices. And what was most shocking was his inexorable rise and rise. This is what contemporaries would have called 'over-refinement', when all the benefits of progress could be learnt, imitated and finally inverted by the unscrupulous impostor.

And the key thing was Gilead House. Here was the reward of a lifetime of imposture, lies and subtle performance. A quack was not an impostor who was hard to spot, yet Solomon had triumphed. His estate was a monument to charlatanism and sharp practice, the visible riches of the most unscrupulous and parasitic member of society.

The quack illuminated another moral truth with his extraordinary and conspicuous wealth. The people *wanted* to be tricked; they craved a palliative, an easy answer to life's problems. 'Castigator', a correspondent who began exposing the machinations of quack doctors for the *Tyne Mercury* in 1812, said that 'nostrum-mongers' like Solomon flourished in Britain because 'the unsuspecting openness of the national character' was combined with ignorance: most people were 'not yet sufficiently enlightened'. The people were simple and touchingly naive, most of them as yet uncorrupted by the downsides of progress; they were thus ill-equipped to resist the patter of the refined, nostrum-mongers chief among them. But, as Thomas Beddoes pointed out, most of the willing victims of quackery were 'the fashionable' who purchased nostrums and listened with believing ears to the 'rude eloquence of their propagators, in gestures, looks, ejaculations and groans'.[52]

Gilead House did not bode well for observers of the moral state of Great Britain. Beddoes and Trotter had pointed out that a faith in men like Solomon and Brodum was in itself the clearest evidence of the nervous vitiation of their countrymen. Men and women would not address their physical, mental and moral problems, individually or collectively. It was considered a sign of the times that people preferred the flashy, jargon-talking doctor to the expert and the quick fix to the harsh regimen of a thorough purgative or a rigorous diet. And if they turned so readily to quacks' nostrums to heal their ills, they would run with no less alacrity to the nostrums of sham reformers and 'quack' politicians with their own specious theories and meretricious cure-alls. Quack doctors and their medicines were vestiges of idolatry, witch doctors and lucky charms: the mind that could believe in the Balm of Gilead could believe in anything.

Quacks and quackery have always been metaphors for self-seeking adventurers who diagnose society's imaginary ills and prescribe panaceas of their own invention. But people in the 1800s saw something of themselves reflected in Samuel Solomon; that is what made him so disturbing a figure. One day everyone would be a Solomon, expert in concealing immorality beneath artfully constructed layers of refinement and verbiage. Such fears haunted Britons; the impostor would trample over simple virtues as 'progress' reached its apogee. The 'age of cant' was heralded by the triumph of the bogus.

It was not until the 1810s that it was finally discovered what Solomon's elixir contained. And it helped explain why so many people who complained that they had been confined with 'low spirits' and 'lack of confidence' suddenly leapt from their beds and claimed to feel immediately better. The primary ingredient was half a pint of brandy, infused with cardamom seeds, lemon peel, tincture of cantharides and perfumed with Sicilian oregano. 'The patient mistakes the frenzy of inebriation for the natural glow of renovated health.' No wonder these people suddenly felt a burst of energy and their nervous disorders melt away. Solomon recommended a course of at least a dozen bottles of the Balm of Gilead. The immediate spark of good spirits was succeeded by an even worse low, so the dose would have to be upped until the patient became an addict.[53]

The popularity of the Balm dropped off during the 1810s. Stories

Death enjoys a profitable apprenticeship with the nostrum-monger

began to appear in the national and local press which chipped away at the confidence needed to sustain the medicine. A favourite story went that a frantic Solomon called a properly trained physician to Gilead House. The visiting doctor could find nothing wrong and dismissed the complaints as a 'trifling matter', but the alarmed quack gasped, 'Trifling, Sir, not so trifling . . . My dear Sir, do not leave me, *for, in mistake, I have swallowed some of my own Balm of Gilead.*' Such stories were an occupational hazard of being a quack, but headlines such as 'Insanity and Death Occasioned by the Administration of Solomon's Balm of Gilead' were another matter. The *Leeds Mercury* reported that a Mr Forster had been found dead clutching an empty phial of the medicine after a few days of madness. 'Castigator' in the *Tyne Mercury* began a campaign of revealing the ingredients of quack nostrums and exposed editors of newspapers who refused to report deaths from the ingestion of such nostrums as 'the servile instruments in the hands of those unprincipled cheats'. His revelations caused the first small decrease in the sale of the Balm of Gilead in the north of England, a portent of what was to come. The local press's realisation that their association with unscrupulous quacks was common knowledge, and that the story was not now miraculous cures but sensational deaths, sounded the death knell for the Balm.[54]

Samuel Solomon himself died in 1819 with much of his fortune intact. The cure and *A Guide to Health* died with the great performer, and he faded from people's memories. In 1840 his extraordinary mausoleum at Mosley Hall in Liverpool – a vast obelisk surrounded by four smaller ones – was cleared away to make way for a railway, a new and more reassuring emblem of progress.

2

Drunk on Liberty

'The enslaved are the fittest to be governed by laws, and free men by custom.'

St John of Antioch

'What two ideas are more inseparable than Beer and Britannia?'

Edinburgh Review[1]

'Reason and experience teach us, that the most dangerous enemy a nation can have, is *itself*; and that when it becomes voluptuous, it will be discordant.'

Jonas Hanway[2]

'There is a political, as well as a bodily hypochondriasis,' Sydney Smith wrote in the first number of the *Edinburgh Review* in 1802, reflecting on nervy panic; 'and there are empirics always on the watch to make their prey, either of the one or the other. Dr Solomon, Dr Brodum, and Mr Bowles, have all commanded their share of the public attention.'[3]

John Bowles, the third member of Smith's triumvirate of ultra-quacks, was a very respectable man. He was a barrister, a government employee, prolific author, sincere churchman, a firm London magistrate and a founding member of the Society for the Suppression of Vice. He took upon his shoulders the reformation of manners and morals amid the Sodom and Gomorrah of nineteenth-century Britain. The difference between him and Samuel Solomon could not, it appeared to the world, be greater.

Bowles was one of the most prominent prophets of national degeneracy at the turn of the century and in the midst of war. In Britain, he wrote, 'the progress of luxury, dissipation, and vice . . . the rage for pleasure and the thirst for gain' would inevitably reduce the great nation to the state of France: 'our career of vice is likely, in a short time, to precipitate us into an abyss of ruin'. Anyone who was middle-aged or older in the 1800s, he said, could 'testify how much habits of luxury, dissipation, and, their natural consequence, a spirit of insubordination, have increased, within the period of his recollection; until, at length, they have become the distinguishing characteristics of the age, and their dominion seems to be fully established in the human breast'.[4]

He was giving vent to a fear that had been growing since 1789. Bowles did not give specific examples of the vice that was eating away at modern Britain. Perhaps he felt it superfluous. There was a generalised impression that the anarchy unleashed in France would one day reach Britain; since the 1790s there had been food riots and the government bruited an imminent revolution. The 'insubordination' Bowles complained of was evident everywhere. The British were rarely quiescent or deferent. William Austin gave the example of the chimney sweep: 'he wraps himself up in his sooty consequence, and all who would pass by him must either hazard the evil of contact, or walk in the mud, until they are out of the reach of his influence'. Servants were said to be sullen from January to November; only as the prospect of the Christmas tip loomed did they begin to behave with the requisite respect. The very lowest could be as proud and haughty as the grandest duke – their show of mock equality.[5]

The people might be contemptuous of authority and allotted an altogether dangerous level of freedom, but that was hardly news. 'The commonality of England certainly have a most ferocious appearance,' Austin wrote, comparing the mass of the people to the comfortable middle class: 'but as far as I have observed, it is only an external habit. We cannot expect the deportment of those, who bear the whole weight of society, should be so engaging, or their countenances so rounded with complacency, or their dispositions so placid, as if they spent their lives without the pressure of daily anxiety.' The very lowest looked like 'outlaws from the community'.[6]

The character of the people was said to derive from the permissiveness of the state and the law. 'The liberties of a free people', wrote William Paley, '. . . permit not those precaution and restraints, that inspection, scrutiny and control, which are exercised with success in arbitrary governments.' Offences against persons and property were punished savagely; riotous pastimes and antisocial behaviour were left to the community and individuals to sort out. William Frankland told Parliament in 1811 that 'actions only slightly inconvenient to the community, ought not to be the object of penal laws, but should be left to the controul of manners and morals'. Policing the people might reduce crimes and allow the respectable to sleep soundly in their beds, but it would alter the national character, making the people servile and the state oppressive. As it was, freedom fostered a 'lofty, fearless, independent spirit, the best fruit of our liberties, and the surest foundation of individual happiness, and of the nation's glory, prosperity and power'.[7]

Not everyone agreed. The nervousness of the higher and middling classes meant that the freedom of the people took on a menacing aspect; the hunt for symptoms of revolutionary urges in the country made hitherto tolerable behaviour seem big with danger. The mind already tormented with apocalyptic imaginings was highly aware that the boundary that divided seeming prosperity and cataclysmic ruin was imperceptible to more sanguine judgements. Such a mind was attuned to the imminence of disaster: every civilisation, every moment of human progress incubated within itself the seeds of its own destruction. Success and degeneracy shadowed each other like malignant twins. 'A people, polished and improved to the utmost, cannot remain long stationary; it must degenerate in body and mind.'[8] Society's self-destructive tendencies and the cruel hand of fortune could be allayed, but only if there was a return to civic virtue and Christian values. The antidote was painful: regeneration could only come through self-denial, frugality and strenuous discipline.

Drunken and disrespectful popular culture was always looked upon with suspicion; now it seemed to presage something worse than a mere nuisance. The common people were frequently described as 'saucy': devoid of respect and outspoken in their rudeness. The diary of John Skinner, the rector of Camerton in Somerset between 1809 and 1836, reveals a man who felt marooned among a drunken, fighting, disobedient people. At the time of the Bath Fair he knew that the village was teetering on the brink of combustion, but, he said, 'I can do nothing, as there is not a single person in the Parish on whom I may depend for assistance in the discharge of my duty, and the preservation of order'.

The Reverend Skinner was a highly strung, nervous man. His journal gives the impression that he was the only vertical man in a village populated by sottish farmers, agricultural labourers and miners; his parishioners drink, dance, fight, gamble, swear and have sex with single-minded determination; death from inebriation recurs with melancholy frequency in the life of the village. Those who showed any inclination for sobriety were, in his view, fanatical Methodists who did not listen to him either. When Skinner gave Sunday service he felt as if he was on the stage of a theatre in front of a chatting, bored and volatile audience. The choir saw itself as a drinking society and demanded money and beer; the church was frequently commandeered by bell-ringers, who also demanded reward for their services and locked Skinner out. His parishioners were a 'perverted people' who would do nothing for their own amendment and treated demands for reformation and sobriety as unwanted busybodydom. He did not endear himself when he tried to get a public house to shut its doors at ten at night. Local customs and the absence of restraint made the people contemptuous of authority. 'At the time of the Revel', Skinner recorded in 1809, 'I thought the behaviour of the people reprehensible, there being a wedding in the morning, and it was conducted with such indecorum I was obliged to tell the young man who was to be married, if he laughed in such a manner again I would stop the service.'[9]

The reverend was not unusual in seeing something threatening in the conduct of the lower orders. The defence for their behaviour was that it was enshrined in custom and long-standing local tradition. At Christmas, singers would parade around villages and towns demanding money. It was an early form of 'trick or treat' – only then it was more like 'vandalism or beer'. On Plough Monday, the first Monday after Twelfth Night, the ploughboys would don harlequin costumes bedecked with brightly coloured ribbons, black their faces as a disguise and pull a plough to the homes of their well-off neighbours. If no money was donated, the householder could expect to have his lawn ploughed up by the next morning. There were many other occasions when the poor would demand 'doles' or 'largesse' – customary gifts in exchange for a song or crude performance. Under the cover of a local or calendar custom, old scores could be settled by a mob disguised in their gaudy costumes. The people cleaved to their customs, holding the rich to ransom. 'This is the day of our fair', Sir Joseph Banks said resignedly at harvest time in 1783, 'when according to immemorial custom I am to feed and make drunk everyone who chooses to come, which will cost me in beef and ale near twenty pounds.'[10]

Such occasions existed to remind the rich of their duties to the poor. It was also a time to mock authority and turn the social order on its head with cruel parody and disrespectful imitation. The poor demanded money, beer and meals as a right, not a gift. Behind every apparently traditional festival lurked violence and the potential for disorder. Such times were moments of fear for respectable people; many gave grudgingly and wished their poorer neighbours would learn better habits of deference. They tolerated them because they had to: the resources to quell popular festivities were feeble and, like John Skinner, they must have felt besieged. Fairs and revels were times when restraint was lifted and strangers descended on normally quiet places. For example, labourers and servants who came to annual hiring fairs to find work for the coming season were intruders who brought vice with them. 'When the market is over', wrote a witness of the aftermath of a hiring fair in Cumberland, 'the girls begin to file off and gently pace the streets, with a view of gaining admirers, whilst the young men with similar designs follow them; and having "eyed the lasses", each picks up a sweetheart, conducts her to a dancing-room, and

Anarchy and misrule: the 'Mayers' of Hitchin in Hertfordshire. Two men, their faces blacked in disguise, take the role of Mad Moll and her husband, the Lord and Lady of a May Day ceremony that shamed unpopular members of the community and extorted beer money from the richer

treats her with punch, wine, and cake.' And where there were young women, young men and alcohol there were fights.[11]

In small communities the disenfranchised and dependent could assert themselves with a repertoire of ceremonies and rituals. So-called 'rough musick' of makeshift drums, trumpets, pots and pans and whatever came to hand could be deployed against unpopular neighbours as a shaming ritual. Husbands who were cruel to their wives, adulterers of both sexes, old men who married very young women, scolding wives, henpecked husbands and everyone who was thought to have deviated from sexual and matrimonial propriety could be subjected to the jeers and music of their neighbours. Or they could be paraded around the streets in person or by proxy on a wooden horse in what was called a 'Skimmington ride'. One person who was subjected to this was John Cooke of Exeter. Cooke, a saddler, was a steadfast royalist and petty official. Throughout the 1790s he made himself conspicuous by putting up notices exhorting the people to be loyal to the King. He was rewarded by being made Captain of the Sheriff of Devon's 'Javelin Men', the twenty-four men who attended the Sheriff at the assizes.

Cooke was just the sort of man who got up the noses of the lower orders. He was obsequious to superiors and meddlesome towards his inferiors. He relished his petty power and the Captain's uniform, which was very grand indeed and included a laced cocked hat: 'to those who saw him enforcing the rules and regulations of the court with all the energy of a veteran disciplinarian, he seemed a greater man for the time than the judge himself'. Cooke made himself even more unpopular at the races in 1815, when he enforced the rules against the rowdy lower orders with punctilious efficiency. He was also active in suppressing other pleasures. The folk of Exeter got their revenge in 1817 when anonymous squibs hinted that for all his puffed-up pompousness and local power he was a henpecked husband. On the appointed day they formed a procession, a cruel parody of Cooke's beloved paraphernalia of office. Four cocklemen bearing flags rode donkeys; next came six boys ringing hand bells and leading a full band. They were followed by eight men with flags and then a troop of twenty-four mock Javelin Men led by their own captain. Then came the main event: someone playing the part of Mrs Cooke as Jezebel beating a proxy of her husband with a broomstick and a ladle. The procession was followed up by twenty-four asses with white ribbons tied to their tails. They marched through Exeter for three hours, drinking and making merry before they arrived at the Cookes' house to serenade the local tinpot tyrant. John Cooke and his wife took the thing in good part; they had to avoid offending the crowd. There were 'a few exhibitions of fun and some polite salutations which were graciously returned from within', and the procession dispersed 'highly delighted with the amusements of the day'. Cooke had been put in his place and ridiculed as an officious busybody; the Captain, for his part, knew that it was a ritual and he too must play his part and submit graciously to the mob.[12]

These kinds of customs and festivities could only exist in small communities where everybody knew each other and there were precedents that were interwoven with local history and the calendar. When in a mob and defended by what they considered inviolable ritual, the people felt empowered by custom, which set aside law for the moment. For the respectable, such occasions could be frightening visions of a world without restraint or deference. Or they could be tolerated as part of local tradition – boisterous saturnalia that reconfirmed the permanence of the hierarchy and which were unthreatening in themselves. Among the 'better sort', many hated such rowdiness; others learnt to live with it; and a few relished it as part and parcel of life.

It was uneconomic too: employers taken with the science of commerce and political economy could not but deplore the waste that such habits fostered in workers. The spirit of conviviality existed in larger towns as much as in the countryside. In London and other cities there was a conspicuous demi-monde of young men and women of all social classes, who frequented the same rowdy haunts and shared their pleasures together. Well-heeled young gentlemen took great delight in venturing into London low life. Henry Angelo, Old Etonian, childhood friend of the Sheridans, the Garricks and the royal dukes of Gloucester and Cumberland, and fencing master to the young bucks (including Byron), threw himself into the fun at places such as the notorious Dog and Duck in St George's Fields, Southwark, which was 'the evening resort of youth of both sexes, for purposes not at all tending to the practice of virtue' or, more bluntly, the 'wholesale receptacle for vice'.

There were also the low pleasure gardens, such as Bagnigge Wells – 'that rendezvous of thoughtless young men, and worthless young women' – and rowdy taverns such as Jacob's Well at the Barbican, which was full of 'spouting, speechifying, singing, drolling, mimicking, and sing-song'. It was open till three or four in the morning, and was the favourite haunt of dandified apprentices, because it was, in Angelo's easily understandable pun, 'the most renowned seminary for forming that strange animal, a *city buck!*' Vauxhall Gardens on the south bank of the Thames was 'more like a bear garden than a rational place of resort'. There, in the late eighteenth century, men and women of the gentry and nobility would rub shoulders with prostitutes, apprentices and shop boys until six o'clock on Sunday morning. The veteran magistrate William Fielding recalled in 1816 how in places such as these, and especially the Dog and Duck, the Temple of Flora and the Apollo, the character of the highwayman was much in vogue; young gents liked to masquerade as devil-may-care celebrity criminals, if only for an evening.

According to Fielding, in the late eighteenth century these pleasure gardens 'were certainly the most dreadful places in or about the Metropolis, they were the resorts of women, not only of the lowest species of Prostitution, but even of the Middle Classes . . . they were the resort as well of apprentices, or every sort of dissolute, profligate and abandoned young man'. The Yale man Benjamin Silliman, on his visit there in 1802, was scandalised to see parties of young men and their sisters or female friends from the gentry class rubbing shoulders and even dancing with common prostitutes with no sense of shame; they put aside, for the moment, the yawning social chasm between them. Popular songs were celebrations of highwaymen and daring criminals or were dirty. Francis Place recalled a respectable gentleman singing 'Sandman Joe' at the Crown and Anchor on the Strand. In it, Joe has been selling his sand around Holborn, calling out 'white sand O!', when he spies 'his flash girl Sally':

> Why blast you, Sall, I loves you!
> And for to prove what I have said,
> This night I'll roundly fuck you.
> Why then says Sall, my heart's at rest
> If what you say you'll stand to.
> His brawny hands, her bubbies prest
> And roaring wild, white sand O![13]

Sall and Joe continued their fun by going to St Giles's to drink gin. 'Sandman Joe' was a favourite, enjoyed by respectable gentlemen at club dinners and by young girls in the street alike. Two female ballad singers chanted it outside St Clements on the Strand, 'amidst roars of laughter'.

Angelo and his aristocratic friends adored the freedom and carefree fun of society like this; there was nothing like it in the higher echelons. Jacob's Well, for example, was a haven for would-be actors and singers, where anyone who felt like it could 'enter the lists' and attempt to amuse the notoriously unforgiving audience. 'There, the amateurs of fun and frolic, might obtain a rich treat, for the accustomed price of a broil, a Welch rabbit, and a glass of wine, or spirits and water; and waste the evening in glorious independence.' In the rule-bound and stilted atmosphere of upper-class society, an evening at such places must have been a joyous release. Truly, the reason for joining low-life sybarites at the Dog and Duck was for a taste of that 'glorious independence'.

Angelo mixed with the young apprentices (many of whom, no doubt, would grow up to become well-to-do, *respectable* City shopkeepers, traders, merchants, maybe even aldermen) in the company of the seventh Earl of Barrymore, who was accomplished at 'seeking life in all its grades' and dedicated to the pursuit of the 'free and easy' life. It was Barrymore, a friend of the Prince of Wales and one of the most outrageous figures in late-eighteenth-century high society, who dragged Angelo to these places. One evening they arrived at Jacob's Well to find it full of 'motley groups, eating, drinking, and smoking'. It was 'a scene of true conviviality', not to be found elsewhere. Barrymore, Angelo and their companions joined the animated apprentices and their lady friends incognito – it would never do to flaunt rank in front of the democratic London pleasure seekers; respect or deference would not be expected, and certainly not given. They would not be included in the fun if their status was discovered.

'This clatter and clanger of knives, forks, glasses, and tankards, is quite exhilarating,' the Earl muttered to Angelo as they took their places; 'I suppose we must do like our neighbours.' Angelo set about getting a good stock of food, drink and pipes. 'The entertainment, as Lord Barrymore often said, was the most prolific of fun, that his lordship, whose very being was to seek frolic, had ever witnessed in all his peregrinations.' Late into the night, or early in the morning, Angelo, 'exhilarated by copious draughts', was persuaded to dress as a barmaid to entertain the drunken crowds, while the Earl sang songs 'with great glee'. But it all came to a sad end when someone entered the pleasure ground to say that there was a coach waiting with an earl's coronet emblazoned on it. This 'put an end to [that] night's frolic', and the company left distraught that their evening had come to a premature close.[14]

Later in the nineteenth century people would look back at the days of their parents and grandparents with a mixture of horror and slight envy. The freedom that people had been allowed in order to carouse and indulge their inclinations was considered amazing. The most prolific of these social historians was Francis Place, who grew up to abhor the waste and profligacy that people showed in his youth; but nonetheless his accounts are tinged with nostalgia for the passing of a world where people were free from restraint, particularly sexual restraint.

Place entered the world in London in 1771, fathered by the dissolute Simon, sometime master baker, bailiff at the Marshalsea prison and keeper of a 'sponging-house' – a private prison lodging house. The Marshalsea was where debtors were imprisoned, and many of the 'respectable' inmates would bribe Simon to provide them with good lodgings in which to serve out their term. Later Simon took over a tavern on the Strand, providing the perfect home for his son to observe 'the very low moral state of society'.[15]

The Places came not from the labouring but from the lower middle class. Yet even so, as an adult Francis took a dim view of the wasteful and immoral habits prevalent among people of his background, the so-called 'better sort'. In the 1820s and '30s he recalled 'the ignorance, the immorality, the grossness, the obscenity[,] the drunkenness, the dirtiness, and depravity of the middling and even of the better sort of tradesmen, the artisans, and the journeymen tradesmen of London in the days of my youth'. He wrote in the 1820s that it 'appears to us sober people of the present day almost incredible' that someone like Simon Place, his father, who was proficient at 'Drinking, Whoring, Gaming, Fishing and Fighting', could have advanced in his career as a baker, become an officer upholding the law, then been trusted with the care of a public house, retained his customers and been fairly affluent.[16] One writer in the 1790s talked of a class of people 'who hold a middle place between the industrious and the rabble; and vibrate betwixt the opposites of restlessness and sloth; – they are a politer sort of mob'.[17]

Place senior would appear to be in this category. He was a popular man and his milieu comprised attorneys, barristers and magistrates;

the Duke of Norfolk and Sir John Fielding, the reforming magistrate and brother of the novelist Henry, were included among his drinking cronies. The balmy days of bribes and backhanders came to an end when Simon's open corruption was outlawed by an act of Parliament in 1779. With plenty of money, he was able to buy the lease of the King's Arms tavern from the Duke of Norfolk. He was a popular landlord, renowned for the quality of his beer; Simon was able to keep up his lifestyle of drinking with companionable professionals and even wayward aristocrats. The tavern was frequented by sailors on shore leave and was occasionally raided by the press gang. It also hosted lottery clubs, punch clubs (as drunk as you liked for a shilling), clubs for apprentices – clubs for anything as long as it involved alcohol and songs.

Francis Place's upbringing could hardly be said to be typical. He grew up among a particular section of the London lower middle classes: publicans, criminal lawyers, shopkeepers and other kinds of people who lived in the inner city. Many of his judgements of life in the eighteenth century were based on these kinds of people, not respectable and industrious middle-class people such as doctors, bankers, manufacturers or prosperous farmers. His account is of urban lower-middle-class families who were relatively prosperous but, crucially, were not property owners and were therefore not 'respectable'. Yet despite this, his autobiography recalls the kinds of unrestrained behaviour characteristic of the time, especially of people who were conspicuous to politicians, churchmen, magistrates and all those who diagnosed the moral state of the country. In the minds of social commentators, a finely graded class system did not exist; the Places and their milieu were indistinguishable from 'the people', 'the mob'. It was noted that among the Gordon rioters in 1780 were many middle-class men, and, as Burke observed, the French Revolution was led by the untrustworthy middling classes. As far as people such as John Bowles were concerned, the country was divided into the rich and the poor: property owners and the rest.

The middle classes in the emerging industrial cities would later earn a reputation for industriousness and morality. But at this time they were suspected of being drunken thugs, very little different from the class they or their parents had emerged from or the people they employed: 'uneducated – of coarse habits – sensual in their enjoyments – partaking of the rude revelry of their dependants – overwhelmed by success – but yet, paradoxical as it may sound, industrious men, and active and far-sighted tradesmen'. Like the Places' sort in London, the industrial middle class supposedly had no need for, or understanding of, propriety: 'drink was their only amusement and occupation'. Master manufacturers, according to caricature, would drink for most of the night, then get a few hours' drunken slumber before being woken by the factory bell. Yet they would get through the business of the day with 'untiring activity and unerring rectitude', though ready 'again to plunge, at the expiration of the hours of labour, into the same vortex of inebriation and riot'.[18]

The effect of private vices on public reputation was not as important as it was to become for the next generation. It was taken for granted that people might have had dubious pasts, and few questions were asked. Unbeknown to Francis and his mother, Simon had married another woman many years before but refused to acknowledge the validity of the union as it was conducted without banns or a licence. Such a history seemed typical of Simon Place, a man without much respect for the decencies of life: 'He was a resolute daring straight forward sort of man, governed almost wholly by his passions and animal sensation both of which were very strong, he was careless of his reputation excepting in some particulars in which he seems to have thought he excelled.' He was good-natured and generous; as late as the 1840s old men remembered Francis's father as an honest and genial man. But Simon was a horribly cruel father, his mode of teaching being 'a word and a blow but blow always first'. The Place children were beaten if they were late, if their shoes were wet, if they had been fighting or swimming, if he met them in the passage, if they asked questions.[19]

People such as Simon Place did not stand out as immoral or profligate among their own class. Many of Francis's boyhood friends were the sons and daughters of middling tradesmen and professionals. Despite their relatively well-off parents, the boys were always dirty from scavenging in the mud, 'coarse and vulgar in their manners' and proficient at petty thieving. Adults were no cleaner, and often not concerned with their external appearance. Place remembered that the wives and daughters of shopkeepers and tradesmen would wear leather stays which were never washed, 'altho worn day by day for years'; these garments were sometimes stained black and held together by dirt by the time they reached the end of their lives. Quilted petticoats would be worn unwashed until they rotted.[20]

Francis and his friends went to print shops to look at erotic prints, as we have seen. Their parents would not have been shocked; free talk and badinage was exchanged at home, and their daughters did not blush. Conversation was 'coarse and vulgar and frequently indecent to an extent scarcely to be credited[:] their language was inaccurate and mean, their habits in respect to cleanliness very inferior to what they are now, and their sense of delicacy remarkably gross, as a reference to the songs sung in their domestic parties will shew. Their children were permitted to run about their filthy streets, to hear all sorts of bad language and to mix with whomsoever they pleased.'[21]

The company with which the Places associated might have been worse than most others, but it was well known that popular culture was characterised by the bawdy and salacious, and that conversation and language were not as guarded as they were to become within the first decades of the next century. At home, some families would perform risqué plays and sing the lewd songs Place alludes to. Much later Place tried to remember these 'flash songs' and consulted some 'of the old fellows whom I have known' – his boyhood friends. They put together some of the popular songs which had entertained them as boys. These were the ones that had been sung in the streets by ballad singers, copies of which were often hung on walls and posts. Children would have heard them, and, like many popular songs, they lodged in the brain – so much so that some could still be remembered thirty or forty years later. The 'blackguard' or 'flash' songs celebrated famous criminals or involved some sort of sexual comedy. They must have added to the image of the lower orders as hopelessly immoral, but none were 'at all objected to' by the people on the streets. The upper class had their dirty songs, the most graphic of which were written by Captain Charles Morris, a companion of the Prince of Wales, and many of which would shock readers even in the twenty-first century. These kinds of songs were probably enjoyed in male company; street culture was not so guarded.[22]

The young girls of Place's acquaintance would have heard women balladeers chanting songs such as 'Sandman Joe' or 'The Morgan Rattler' – the most explicit of all such songs remembered by Place, which celebrated the size of the male member. Many of them lauded male prowess and described violence towards women. The flash song 'Drunk the Other Night' told of a man who was accosted by a prostitute as he was staggering home:

> She suddenly seized me, and swore how she'd please me,
> If I would go with her and give her some gin.
> Her cheeks look'd so rosy, her eyes looked so wanton,
> Her waist so well shap'd and her bubbies so ripe.[23]

The song ends in the drunken man assaulting the woman. Yet other songs put women in a position of dominance or portrayed them as lusty predators. The usual male anxieties, such as impotence, inadequate performance or flighty wives, were cruelly mocked. Such songs gave women a leading and dominant role in sex, something denied them in plebeian comedy of a later era. Girls of Place's age were told that they should seize the initiative and get the pleasure that was their right. Another song recounted how a young man was reduced to extreme exhaustion by the demands of his wife. The last lines went:

> And for which I am sure she'll go to Hell
> For she makes me fuck in church time.[24]

Such an unsqueamish attitude to sex, legitimate and illegitimate, must have fuelled growing anxieties about the profligacy of the poor. Place and his contemporaries in London, avid readers of *Aristotle's Compleat Master Piece*, felt every urge to experiment as soon as possible. Boys and girls enjoyed a game called 'Drop the Handkerchief', a fairly primitive and recognisable initiation rite. The boys and girls would hold hands and form a circle; one girl would throw her handkerchief at a boy, at which point she would leave the ring and try and run around it and regain her place without being caught by the boy of her choice. Often the boy was held down by the girls to allow their friend a head start. From this harmless rough and tumble they graduated to the more advanced 'Kiss in the Ring', where the girls chased the boys. Unsurprisingly, the boys only made a token effort to evade capture, for the 'penalty' was a mock marriage in the centre of the ring, which was consummated with much kissing.[25]

Parents not only tolerated this but enjoyed watching the fun. It seems harmless, but the openness and lack of embarrassment or modesty meant that 'want of chastity in girls was common'. Peter Gaskell wrote in the 1830s that in the previous century pre-marital sex was 'almost universal' in the countryside: 'Many of the sports of the period, amongst the young of both sexes, were obviously intended to facilitate and give opportunities to familiarities of the closest kind.' Sex was common among young couples, but there was 'a tacit understanding . . . that marriage would result'. Demographic study suggests that 40 per cent of marriages among the lower orders occurred when the bride was already pregnant.[26]

Place recalled going 'a palming' every Palm Sunday when he was a bit older. This was the old pre-Reformation custom of travelling out to the environs of London to collect willow branches, a substitute for palm leaves. An old proverb had it that he who did not have a palm on that day would have his hand cut off. In the eighteenth century it was an excuse for something else. The teenagers would ramble around the Surrey villages, starting their walking and drinking early. By lunchtime they were all roaring drunk. Everyone knew what 'palming' involved, but girls were 'then under comparatively little restraint'. Opulent tradesmen smiled indulgently when their daughters were picked up by their 'sweethearts' on Palm Sunday morning to go drinking and . . . Just what Place holds back from telling us.[27]

Much later Place claimed to have been '*comparatively* chaste amidst scenes of excessive debauchery and among remarkably dissolute associates'. What did that 'comparatively' mean? Not much, it seems: Place was, by his own admission, by no means abstemious. His instincts got the better of him when he was head boy of his school. The girls were taught in a separate room, and young Francis was asked to check their sums. As a consequence he was left on his own with them. It was an opportunity not to be missed. Unfortunately, the romance that transpired was too much for Francis's son, who ripped the account from the Place Papers when they were given to the nation, leaving the laconic comment: 'The consequence was bad for both parties giving rise to much licentiousness.' His father might have disagreed: 'Want of Chastity in the girls was common, and was scarcely matter of reproach if in other respects they, as was generally the case, were decent in their general conduct.'[28]

John Bowles talked of the necessity of a 'domestic struggle' that made the war against Napoleon seem trivial. The reformation would be 'truly Herculean; so great are the Augean Stable of modern depravity'. The urban middle classes and the lower orders were coarse, ill-mannered and unrestrained in their pleasures. It was not harmless fun or the lusty expression of the national character. After the French Revolution, the pastimes of the poor, not to say their disrespectful attitude, began to seem like the ingrained habits of a population that had the power to overturn the entire social system. Malthus's warning about an unproductive population and the spiralling costs of maintaining the unemployed during the war fuelled these fears.[29]

One of the most famous investigators of modern Britain was Patrick Colquhoun, a wealthy Scottish magistrate, born the son of a judge in Dumbarton in March 1745. As a young man he left Scotland to seek his fortune as a lawyer in America. He returned to Glasgow during the American Revolution, unwilling to sacrifice his loyalty to the Crown. Throughout the 1770s and '80s he was, to use his own phrase, one of the 'chief springs' of industry in the kingdom. He was able to supply 1,000 soldiers for his sovereign's use in North America, at his own expense – the only man to do so and not insist on being made an officer. During the 1780s he was, successively, a member of the Council of the City of Glasgow, Chief Magistrate for three years and an ambassador for Scottish manufactures; his Scottish career culminated in him being Lord Provost of his adopted city. He left Glasgow in 1789 as the 'highly respected and venerable father of that city', and moved to London. He craved the recognition of the world, the respect of the great men of the kingdom, the thanks of a grateful king. In 1792 Henry Dundas, the Home Secretary, relented to Colquhoun's demands for a public role, and he was appointed a magistrate at the police office in Worship Street, Shoreditch.[30]

Like many who move from business to public life, he immediately saw that nothing worked with the requisite machine-like efficiency: civil servants and legal officials were either amateurs or institutionalised, cut off from the real world and monstrously inefficient. After a few months on the bench, observing the comings and goings at the Worship Street police office, the refractory and ungodly mob, the lowest criminals of the East End and the petty vices of Londoners, he presented his thoughts to Henry Dundas in a long memorandum on the deficiencies in policing the lower orders; it also included a study of the prevailing characteristics of the labouring classes, which had to be understood as a first step in the prevention of crime. But the Home Secretary was not very interested in the advice of an officious and meddlesome businessman. Deeply offended and very surprised that ministers did not take him – the ultra-loyalist and high-achieving business genius – seriously, Colquhoun courted public opinion and published his memorandum as *A Treatise on the Police of the Metropolis*, which went to seven editions by 1806, the year he followed it up with a more detailed study of the morals of the lower orders, *A Treatise on Indigence.*

The books made him famous throughout the world; they were translated across Europe and published in America. Spurned by the government, Colquhoun collected the testimonies of a grateful public, picked up an honorary doctorate, was transferred to the more prestigious Westminster magistrates' court, and a succession of Home Secretaries were obliged to receive him. Most importantly, his books shaped the way that many, including ministers and magistrates, came to see the lower class. He would be quoted by journalists and politicians for decades and cited by foreign writers as the expert on the state of John Bull's morals. Colquhoun came closer than anyone else to being taken seriously as the age's authority on lower-class behaviour, thinking, domestic economy and morality.[31]

Colquhoun transferred his businesslike skill of computing raw data to the world of moral reform. He ransacked folios of statistics and made full use of the new census reports. One journalist wrote of his *Treatise on the Police of the Metropolis*: 'Crimes and criminals, offences and offenders were posted against each other, with the formality of a ledger account. The account ran high.' This skill marked Colquhoun out from other moralisers. The manners of the poor had been described by an earlier generation of magistrates – most notably Henry Fielding – or caricatured in their grotesque magnificence by William Hogarth. Colquhoun's books would have been yet another diatribe on lower-class immorality had they not been endowed with the authority of statistics. And as such, his voice was important at a time when anxiety about the moral breakdown of society was reaching a pitch.[32]

In his book *A Treatise on Indigence*, Colquhoun showed that from a population of eleven million, 1,040,716 men, women and children received £4,267,985 from parish relief and £3,332,035 from private charities. In other words, the million or so who made up the 'phalanx of paupers in the pay of the country' lived on handouts contributed by a mere 700,000 industrious tax payers. Added to these were some 300,000 who 'live[d] chiefly by the labour of others': those who lived on the proceeds of 'unproductive' occupations, such as 'lewd and immoral women', vagabonds, ballad singers, dealers in obscene books and criminals. £700,000 worth of property was stolen annually by petty thieves in London alone, and that was excluding the proceeds of serious house and shop burglaries. The cause and potential cure of the problem was obvious to Colquhoun: 'Vicious habits, idleness, improvidence, and sottishness, prevail in so great a degree, that until a right bias shall have been given to the minds of the vulgar, joined to a greater portion of intelligence in respect to the economy of the poor, one million of indigent will be added to another requiring permanent or partial relief, producing ultimately such a gangrene in the body politic as to threaten its total dissolution.'[33]

Whereas people like John Bowles saw the poor as Jacobins in the making, Colquhoun was most worried by the *cost*. It seemed that the industrious part of the community was bearing the weight of what were now laughably called the 'labouring' classes. He drew a distinction between poverty and indigence. The former was an inevitable and not necessarily shameful rank; the latter was a species of culpable poverty caused by drunkenness, sexual profligacy and 'habits of laziness and sloth'. Colquhoun offered evidence that idleness was the ambition of *all* working people; unless they were regulated, they would be irresistibly drawn to a life of repose, crime or beggary. The reason why so many were dependent on their neighbour's money was because 'the working classes are improvident, careless, unthinking, and dissolute in their manners'; they were poor 'from the habit of frequenting and almost living in alehouses'. Every year, the two million poorest people spent £16,000,000 on alcohol; the duty brought in a fortune to the Treasury, but it was 'a revenue dearly purchased by the state', given that much more was wasted when the source of labour in the country was 'contaminated'. Putting the cost to the country aside, it showed that most working people had no ambition to become comfortable and respectable by thrift and saving, but instead lavished their money on luxuries such as gin. Thus labour, 'the great and essential spring from whence all our comforts, and all our affluence, power and prosperity arise', was poisoned at the source by an increasingly work-shy and uncontrollable population.[34]

During the war the gap between the moderately well-off and the mass of the working poor widened alarmingly. The respectable part of the community asked why this should be so in a modern and wealthy country. Dr Colquhoun and John Bowles provided answers. The people had lost habits of thrift and prudence; they frittered away what little they had without any thought of the next morning. The rich should have very little pity; those that seemed hungry had only themselves to blame. Dangled in front of the people of London and other ports was the bounty of the world. And rather than work hard to earn it, they simply took it. According to Colquhoun, the merchandise was stolen from the docks and distributed through a sophisticated black market to even the poorest-*looking* people. They lived the high life for a fraction of the price that the wealthy and law-abiding paid. These habits would destroy all semblance of decency and civic virtue: 'they are restrained by no principle of morality or religion, (for they know nothing of either,) and only wait for opportunities to plunge into every excess and every crime'. The wholesome character traits of self-restraint and moderation had been eradicated from the working class. Colquhoun informed his readers that there was a network of criminals who operated throughout the kingdom, fencing the pilfered articles from the docks. Crime had become a habitual way of life for a large proportion of the urban labouring class.[35]

No wonder they were poor! Their comforts were transitory; they were rich for the passing minute, bingeing on what they had for all the world like wealthy *bon viveurs*, but they had no thought to save what they got their hands on. Most of the layabouts did not even know how to cook; they dined out every night in alehouses, squandering money that could have been saved by preparing meals at home from cheap ingredients. Colquhoun persuaded himself that a large portion of the lower classes enjoyed the same kind of pleasures as the rich: 'Such is the thoughtless improvidence of this class of labouring people, that they are generally the first who indulge themselves by eating Oysters, Lobsters, and Pickled Salmon, &c, when first in season.' Gorging on a rich stream of luxuries, feckless, immoral and sure that, even if they squandered all their money, the parish would step in to provide money, '*almost universal* profligacy prevails' among the lower classes.[36]

There had always been those who deplored the extravagance of the poor and wanted to reform or restrain them. What was different at the commencement of the nineteenth century was that crime, disorder and indigence were now seen as social problems applying to the 'lower class' as a group, where before they had been dealt with as local or personal issues. There was a growing perception of the urban proletariat as a threat to property and to the social system itself. Traditional authorities, such as the Church, ceased to have day-to-day and face-to-face influence over large swathes of the lower orders. If modernity had made the middle class refined, the urban lower classes had become no less artificial. Modern man was a different species of being, and there had to be means of restoring those moral qualities that had been lost to modernity.

Colquhoun's answer to the moral crisis was to instil the poor with habits of frugality and thrift. They should not be paid more than was necessary for their subsistence so that they weren't tempted to indulge their appetites on things that weren't necessary. Employers should keep a beady eye on the behaviour of their workers, punishing and restraining them where they could. Philanthropists could induce better standards by holding out positive inducements for moral rectitude. Abstention, self-denial and habits of prudence were the pillars of morality and social order; enforce this on the working population and crime, beggary, indigence and political dissatisfaction would dry up. As far as John Bowles was concerned, the conflict was with a severe addiction, against those 'luxurious habits which have gotten such fast hold of us'. The danger was near and serious, but only a few observers were capable of discerning it: 'Although luxury has proved the severest scourge ever known to the human race – although its ravages far exceed those of famine, pestilence, and the sword; nothing is so difficult as to prevail on mankind to regard it as an enemy.' What had made the middle classes fat and nervous had made the poor depraved.[37]

Bowles wrote that discipline, sobriety and decency stood little chance against the heady cocktail of pleasures and temptations to engage in sexual adventures, eat rich food, drink to excess and gamble. Eventually these addictions would become so ingrained, the appetite and desire so heightened, bodies so weakened and the people so jaded that they would seek fresh stimulation from new and more depraved gratifications.

This process 'destroys the nature of man as a social being, by rendering his disposition sensual and selfish . . . Two feelings then engross the soul; an insatiable thirst for pleasure, and equally insatiable desire for wealth.' And when these passions were fuelled by sensuality and vice, when the pursuit of pleasure and frivolity became an end in itself, the national character would be stamped by selfish greed and dishonesty. Unable to tear their faces from the trough of pleasure, lazy to the utmost, addicted to vicious pursuits and broken down with illness, such a people would become utterly selfish and lacking in any patriotic feeling, more likely to hide than fight an enemy. Any invader would be able to saunter over such a sottish population. And that would only be if the British had not already torn themselves to pieces first, having lost all their morals.[38]

Books by Colquhoun and Bowles presented caricatures of the lower classes; they were ill-informed, impressionistic and alarmist. Much later in his life, Francis Place would refute Colquhoun on more or less equal terms and with first-hand evidence. In the 1790s and 1800s, however, the magistrate grabbed the public's attention as unemployment and indigence increased alarmingly during the years of scarcity and economic depression. The concern over the morals of the poor must be read in the context of general alarm and anxiety. What had previously been regarded as pardonable excess were coming to be seen as the seeds of national decline. Crime was a symptom of a wider malaise in the character of the labouring classes. Colquhoun had no evidence of the crime wave he described. It came from deductive reasoning about the corrosive effects of luxury on the poor: in other words, greater temptations would inevitably mean greater crime.

The poor may have been careless and improvident, but this was being conflated with immorality. In the experience of the poor at this time there was very little reason to be frugal and abstemious. In a fluctuating economy it was counterintuitive to save when what little could be amassed could be blown away by a disaster. Miners were regarded as a particularly bad example. They worked very hard and were paid well; they were also better fed and clothed than other manual labourers. But they wasted their decent wages on alcohol and gambling binges. They also had greater debts than others of their class; they were accused of staking future wages on present pleasures. Their behaviour was considered to be so careless because their labour was dangerous and uncertain. They were confined underground and used gunpowder. Their pay could be high, but the conditions of their employment were casual: they could be laid off or they could hit a poor seam and earn nothing. So it was little wonder if they relished what enjoyment they could when they could.[39]

The 'spiritless continuation of daily labour' experienced by most of the lower classes destroyed all sense of futurity and providence. They did not save and were not frugal because they had nothing to put aside and were aware that the caprice of fortune could ruin them overnight. They were not poor because luxury had vitiated the moral obligation to be frugal. 'At the same time that it must be admitted that the poor are not provident,' wrote one sympathetic philanthropist, 'it should be observed in their exculpation that they frequently have not the means of being so.'[40]

Francis Place saw this spirit of intemperance and lack of frugality in the customers at his father's public house, in boyhood friends and later when he found work. Many had a reasonable income and were clever, resourceful people, but they all lived from day to day, without ambition beyond affording the evening's spree. They were professional in their work, but they lacked a professional attitude. Money was easy come, easy go; people knew they could get by and live well enough on what they could get. Any thought for the future, for periods of illness, unemployment, their children or old age could be safely ignored. It was a feature of an economy which was dogged by uncertainty. People were aware of the arbitrariness of fortune; even the most providential family could end up in debtors' gaol through no fault of their own. The volatile economy and the experience of sudden reverses of fate left many feeling powerless against the mysterious forces of the economy.

Place knew about this because he conducted his life in exactly this way. His youth was divided between school and riotous adventures around London. School gave him a lifelong passion for books and critical enquiry, but it did not stop a rage for gambling in his spare time. When he was fourteen he was apprenticed to Joe France, a leather-breeches tailor. France was a thrice-married old tippler and, even by the standards of the time, a dissolute man. He had five children. The eldest daughter was a common prostitute; the second was 'visited by gentlemen'; and the third was the mistress of a naval captain, 'in whose absences she used to amuse herself as such women generally do'. One son was a 'first rate genteel pickpocket' and the second a thief who had enlisted in the army to evade capture and execution. But for all that, Joe France had plenty of savings and was fairly affluent; like Simon Place, he was 'good natured, simple and obliging'.[41]

Francis proved to be good at the job and earned around eight shillings a week, enough to make him 'a great man for [his] age'. He mixed with a group of fifteen to twenty like-minded young men, 'all turbulent unruly fellows' and, like Francis, 'sons of persons of easy circumstances'. These teenagers were all dressed in the latest fashions and were 'fine men' to some of the prostitutes who walked Fleet Street and St Catherine's Lane in the Strand. The boys would spend their money in taverns, often renting rooms for dinner and drinking with their Fleet Street companions. The prostitutes could be good company, and the danger of consorting with them heightened the excitement. They wore low-cut dresses which exposed partially or wholly their breasts. 'Drunkenness was common to them all and at all times when the means of drunkenness could be found. Fighting among themselves as with the men was common and black eyes might be seen on a great many.' When they tired of their boisterous prostitutes, Place and his friends all had their own sweethearts, with whom they 'were as familiar as we could be'.[42]

There was plenty of opportunity for such play: Francis was allowed as much freedom as he wanted, as long as he did the work. Place proved to be an accomplished leather-breeches apprentice. He managed to clear work very quickly and to a high standard. He soon became indispensable to his employer, so much so that he challenged Joe France to a fight if the old drunk so much as gave him an order. Quite soon, though, France's business declined and Place found work with his brother-in-law, James Pain (an addition to the Place family who matched their low standards of decorum), as a journeyman woodcarver.

Once again, Place's abilities propelled him forward in his new trade: in the first week he made eighteen shillings, in the second twenty-five and the next week thirty-two. Then Pain refused to increase the rate, so Francis went back to making leather breeches, this time at a tailor's on the Strand. But he got into trouble wherever he worked. He refused to take orders or accept low pay, and he infuriated his employers by turning up to work when he felt like it. He would spend his evenings at a 'two-penny hop' at 'some blackguard public house' or in a low tap room in the 'Holy Land', the slang for St Giles's, the seamiest area in London. Place would often stay out late and be locked out of his lodgings or turn up to work without having slept. But he had nothing to fear from any employer; whenever he was sacked for irregular hours and sottish behaviour he did not care – with his abilities, another job was always easily available.[43]

If Place had been a clerk he might not have been so free. He would have had his time and work rate set by rules. But Place's teenage experiences of employment were not uncommon for people engaged in traditional trades. For many there was no such thing as a nine-to-five job, and certainly not the kind of discipline associated with regulated work.

Some labourers, journeymen and artisans operated in an economy where as long as they did their work they could set their own hours and working conditions. Others did not have a choice. In some cases work was apportioned by masters, so journeymen could be left for long periods of the week waiting for something to do. Labourers such as building workers, canal diggers or dockers would be employed by the day or for particular projects; work came and went. Agricultural labourers were often not tied to the land but went to hiring fairs to barter their labour season by season. Depending on the cycle of agricultural work throughout the year there would be weeks of inactivity, times of local revels, festivities and fairs. It was little wonder that for all these jobs the uncertainty of continuous employment and the periods of inevitable inactivity led to drinking. A workforce uncontrolled by a structure, discipline or the regulatory aspect of master–worker relations was a principal worry for those who saw Britons slipping into depravity and insubordination.

Independence was jealously guarded by thousands of workers. There was a hatred of authority and control. Relations between masters and workers was one of negotiation, compromise and custom. Journeymen used their independence as a bargaining chip to set wages and regulate their practices. This was before the factory system, which insisted upon set hours and discipline, became a significant employer of working people. In trades where labourers were relatively free, where industry was small in scale and outworking was common, Monday was a day off, whatever employers wanted. This custom – called 'St Monday' by those for whom it was a sacrosanct holiday – was to be enjoyed in the alehouse or in rowdy sports. The first day of the week would be used for checking machinery, running repairs and administration. Productivity was not ruined by this custom: workers fitted six days' worth of work into the remaining five.

St Monday declined throughout the nineteenth century as work discipline was tightened but was retained in more old-fashioned jobs until the twentieth century. The factory or workshop clock was, for many employers, made into a garish reminder of the passing of time and sacredness of order.[44] The practice was indicative of many customs and rites that existed before large-scale industrialisation. In many trades, the provision of beer over and above wages was insisted upon as a customary right. 'There is an opinion with people who perform certain laborious work for good wages, that they must drink beer,' Place told a parliamentary select committee on drunkenness in 1834; 'they have a notion that unless they do drink beer they cannot go through their work; almost all men who do hard work have this notion.' There was a machismo in drinking. As the saying went among manual labourers: 'The hardest drinker is the best man.'[45] During the harvest, agricultural labourers would not work unless they were fed a constant stream of ale. In the 1820s one man who oversaw coopers complained of his workers: 'They will have as much beer as they please; if we only happen to be out of beer for ten minutes all the yard is in a ferment.'[46] Masters might not approve of a refractory, independent and heavy-drinking workforce, but most were incapable of reforming those they relied upon. A conversation was overheard during the harvest in Hertfordshire:

'Master, what horse shall I take to drive cider mill?' asked a labourer.

'D—n the cider and the mill too,' replied the farmer; 'you waste one-half of your time making cider, and other half in drinking it. I wish there was not one apple in the county. You all think of cider, no matter what comes of the plough.'[47]

Drinking was so ingrained in British life because exertion was compensated by inebriation. It was not idleness that led to drinking, but long and hard work. One doctor talked of 'the British forcing system', by which he meant the work ethic. Hard labour, irregular and long hours of work and the complete absence of alternative recreations or sensual pleasures placed the bottle at the centre of people's lives. Colquhoun criticised them for going to alehouses for meals and heavy drinking, but when their dwellings were damp and squalid, their jobs strenuous and there was little opportunity for leisure, then it should be no surprise that '[m]any in all walks of life take refuge in a public house, for want of satisfactory occupations at home'.[48] It was the only thing that enlivened the spirits and the only stimulus in people's lives. 'Put an Englishman "behind a pipe" and a full pot and he will sit on until he cannot stand. . .' wrote William Hone. 'At first he is silent, but as his liquor get towards the bottom he inclines to conversation. As he replenishes, his coldness thaws and he is conversational. The oftener he calls to "fill again" the more talkative he becomes; and when thoroughly liquefied, his loquacity is deluging.'[49]

This was not just true for the poor. Two of the greatest men of the age were believed to have died from intense work relieved only by wine: William Pitt and Charles James Fox both died in 1806 after lives of toil and impressive alcoholic consumption. Francis Place said that it was more surprising that working men were not habitual rather than occasional drunkards. He had run away from work whenever he could, and where else could he meet people his own age than at the public house? The lower classes were miserable and bored and starved of sensual pleasure. 'Drinking is the sole means such men have of getting away from themselves, and the pleasure of drinking to excess is beyond all comparison greater to such men than to any other class of person.'[50]

These were just the kinds of habits that Colquhoun laid down as typical of the lower classes and offered as the cause of crime. The workplace should be where at least some effort was made to bring discipline and subordination into the lives of the poor; instead it was just another forum for dissipation and idleness. 'What', asked one worried commentator, 'can be more worth the attention of the legislature, than the framing of laws which would tend to make several millions of poor labouring people sober, industrious, frugal, temperate, virtuous, and happy, and the state, in consequence of this, the richest and most powerful in the world?'[51]

Masters and trade guilds were supposed to subject their apprentices to strict conditions of behaviour; employers should do the same with their workers. But this was not the case. Colquhoun gave the example of a young apprentice which sounds rather like Place's real-life experiences as a teenager. The boy would look to his employer, grown old in the habits of depravity and a regular tavern-dweller, and copy his vicious habits. First he would pick up a habit which Colquhoun considered the fount of all vice:

> In vulgar life, it is the first ambition of the youth, when approaching towards an adult state, to learn to smoke tobacco. When this accomplishment is acquired, he finds himself qualified to lounge, and waste his time in the tap-room. It is here that his mind receives the first impression of vice. The force of evil example is powerful. He insensibly imitates the detestable propensities of his seniors in point of age, until at length he is initiated in all the mysteries of low gaming, contracting at the same time habits of idleness and dissipation, which render him afterwards *a bad husband, a bad father, and a bad member of society*.[52]

Place wrote that masters and their apprentices would drink together and attend the same clubs, where the 'amusements were drinking – smoaking – swearing – and singing flash songs'. The most notorious were the 'Cock and Hen clubs', to which, as the name suggests, women were welcome to join the singing, drinking, dancing and whatever else. Couples paired off until, by midnight, no one was left. Place and his friends 'would work hard and drink hard', with little concern that they were squandering their money or failing to save for the uncertain future. They were rich young bucks for the moment, and that's what mattered. Place's progress was not hampered by his lifestyle, which probably says much for the low expectations of his masters. At the age of sixteen or seventeen he had become a foreman in charge of fifteen men.[53]

'The poor man is reconciled to *poverty* by the possession of LIBERTY.'[54] Many felt that the poor deserved to enjoy their pleasures in freedom and should not be required to submit to strict moral obligations because their lives were miserable enough. William Austin was puzzled by the way the British idolised freedom and equality under the law, and could only assume it was a hypocritical excuse for the appalling conditions that working people suffered. As it was, in the eighteenth century popular culture was often coarse and bawdy, sometimes violent, and always drunken. The fierce spirit of independence, whether it was shown at work or at leisure, was seen as a national trait that could be effaced with no less ease than changing the colour of the cliffs of Dover. 'Although many inconveniences arise from an excess of liberty in this country,' commented *The Times* in 1785, 'yet they are so greatly advantageous, that we cannot be too careful to preserve a blessing which distinguishes us from all the world.'[55]

Others, however, dissented. An 'excess of liberty' was fool's gold for the benighted poor as well as for the country. The unique circumstances of the nineteenth century demanded regulation and restraint. The lower orders were not capable of the privileges they were given; freedom awakened the basest passions and disordered weak minds. Any custom or holiday or pause in working life gave rise to self-destructive anarchy and misrule. Frugality, self-discipline and civic virtue – the pillars of Protestant ethics and civilisation's only defences against its own degenerating tendency – found no fertile ground in which to take root in such a blasted environment. As Josiah Tucker, Dean of Gloucester, complained, 'Our people are *drunk with the cup of liberty*.'[56]

3

Resolute Debauches

'A secure provision for the indigent is to the philanthropist what a pineapple is to the epicure.'

Jeremy Bentham[1]

'What a shocking idea which brands poverty as a crime! And how false! Here the poor man must languish unpitied, and conceal his indigence. In the midst of abundance, and surrounded with heaps of guineas, he is doomed to feel all the tortures of a Tantalus.'

Nikolai Karamzin[2]

The popularity of books by Bowles, Colquhoun and Malthus suggests that, for some, the fear that the nineteenth century would see the nation threatened by the urban poor was mounting. For these people, reform was critical; its success or failure would decide the fate of Britain in the new century. Others despised this attitude. It was indicative of a new spirit pervading certain sections of society. The desire to interfere and pry into the habits and customs of the people smacked too much of incipient puritanism; give the busybodies a modicum of power and Britain would be on the high road to the days of the joyless Commonwealth and dreary Cromwellian social control. 'Woe to us if we live to see a parliament of Ebenezers, or an association of Ebenezers dictating the laws,' wrote Robert Southey.[3]

It was easy to laugh at people like Patrick Colquhoun or John Bowles for their tendency to see plots in every act of minor delinquency and their hyperbolic prose. The satirical monthly *The Scourge* imagined Colquhoun exercising his magisterial authority to arrest a cobbler 'under whose shed the canine fornicators of the parish had long been accustomed to perform their lascivious evolutions'. The Rev. Sydney Smith mocked Bowles's 'vulgar violence, and the eternal repetition of rabble-rousing words'; he found it impossible to believe that anyone would take seriously the contention that singing after dinner or the thinness of ladies' petticoats was part of a plot to destroy the country or presaged an apocalypse. The *Critical Review* defied anyone to be angered at such palpable nonsense and hypochondriacal bleating, and recommended Bowles's books to insomniacs.[4]

But the lofty Whiggish disdain for such opinions should not obscure the fact that Bowles's call to moral reform was music to the ears of an influential section of the community. Smith's criticisms are valid: Bowles was vague in his terms and rarely gave an example of the vices he considered to be gnawing at the vitals of the community. His excitable prose and empty rhetoric does make him seem like an itchy hypochondriac raving at imaginary ailments. Why, then, do men like him matter? The answer is, in a word, power. Bowles had it as a justice of the peace and later as a zealous member of the Society for the Suppression of Vice. It was the power to impose his moral view on the lower sections of the community.

Bowles might not have been the best writer on the moral condition of Britain, but he was one of the most widely read, especially among reforming philanthropists. There were many people who were thinking what he was thinking, and they were men of importance, albeit often at a parish or county, not a ministerial, level: bishops and clergymen, lords lieutenant, magistrates, constables and other officers of the peace, churchwardens, Poor Law overseers and many other such people who held a considerable degree of influence over people's daily lives. R. Shaw accused Colquhoun of creating 'false alarms in the minds of the timid' and making men and women suspicious of each other, but it has to be said he was not converting hordes of hitherto liberal-minded people: his books only confirmed what they feared already.

In Britain, where 'police' in the hands of the state meant something foreign and something slavish, the ways of regulating and restraining the people was left to private effort. Philanthropy and religion were ways of obviating the need for an interfering police force by providing other means of regulating the masses. Charity was a way of clearing a path for better reception of the word of God. But it also had a fundamental interest in revolutionising society. As one historian has said of philanthropy, 'Few subjects bring out so well the differences between ourselves and our ancestors.'[5] It was not merely voluntary work, a supplement to the state, but the point at which the well-off and the poor met. Most importantly, philanthropic experiments, theorising and the vast literature they generated were the focal point of debate about how society functioned.

Most people were dependent at some time in their life on the benevolence of their betters – for work, medical aid or food and relief in sickness, unemployment or old age. By varying the conditions under which this was given, the philanthropist could change the environment in which the poor had to live and in doing so radically alter and amend the very nature of mankind. The people could be made diligent workers, more abstemious in their appetites, provident in habit and restrained in conduct. In the later years of the eighteenth century this became a duty for evangelicals and also for people motivated by other reasons, most prominently Jeremy Bentham. Revivalist Christianity and secular utilitarianism converged in their aims and methods to remodel modern man.

Traditional forms of charity were based on the assumption that the poor would improve if they were given incentives. Thomas Bernard founded the Society for Bettering the Condition of the Poor in 1797 on the principle that charity meant providing the poor with the means to improve themselves: alleviate their situation and give them the tools to augment their income and they would become moral without the heavy-handed intervention of others. Bernard deplored force in charity: it would only harden the resistance of the poor to new ideas. As he wrote, 'the poor have never yet had a fair trial. Let *useful* and *practical* information be offered to them; give them *time* to understand, and a *choice* of adopting it; and I am mistaken, if they do not shew as much good sense on the subject, as any other class of men in the kingdom.'[6]

Few other peoples lavished so much money on charity as the British. London boasted large and impressive institutions dedicated to the relief of the unfortunate and supported by private money. Prominent among them were endowed schools, public hospitals, refuges for prostitutes and many houses where poor women could give birth; there was the Bethlehem lunatic asylum (Bedlam), Coram's Foundling Hospital, the Magdalene Hospital for prostitutes, the Locke hospital for venereal disease, the Cancer Institution, the London Fever Hospital and the School for the Indigent Blind, among the more famous private charities. It was not lost on the casual observer that many of the most handsomely endowed institutions were dedicated to the relief of the consequences of vice: illegitimate children, prostitution and VD. Perhaps the British were so generous because they had so much to clean up after themselves.

Benevolence was considered one of the national virtues; people of all social classes contributed to help their neighbours. It was an emotion like any other, but it was an ennobling one. The habit of performing good actions developed and strengthened what the Scottish moral philosophers called the 'moral faculty'. Morality was innate in humans, and it was by observing the virtuous actions of others and performing them yourself that you became alive to mankind's essential goodness. It created warm sensations, and these were the proofs of virtue. Men and women of sensibility wept at the performance of charity, a sign of the incorruptible altruistic nature of humanity and evidence that pure emotions survived beneath layers of refinement. If other emotions should be repressed, surely benevolence was one that could be indulged?[7]

'There is a sort of luxury in giving way to the feelings!' Elizabeth Fry wrote in her diary when she was seventeen. 'I love to feel for the sorrows of others, to pour wine and oil into the wounds of the afflicted; there is a luxury in feeling the heart glow, whether it be with joy or sorrow.' Mrs Fry felt the philanthropic impulse deeply. At the age of thirty-three she dedicated herself to the reformation and amelioration of the female prisoners in Newgate prison at a time when even the governor and the warders were afraid to enter the women's side of the gaol. Mrs Fry is justly celebrated to this day as a tireless philanthropist. She was accused in her own time of hypocrisy, self-love and of the 'cant of humanity'. Yet no one doubted her intentions and accused her of ulterior motives more than she herself did. On her work with the women prisoners, she wrote bitterly in her diary: 'They are to my feelings too much like making a show of a good thing.' At other times she worried that she was working only out of habit and prayed for 'a more lively spirit and devoted heart' so that she might accomplish her tasks without hypocrisy. 'Some poor people were here,' she wrote when she helped some needy supplicants; 'I do not think I gave them what I did with a good heart . . . Shameful!'[8]

On the birth of her first child Mrs Fry felt strong and immediate maternal love. She had to struggle with herself 'to overcome these natural feelings'. It was a sense of mistrust and self-doubt she had all her life. Emotions were tyrants that would doom her to self-delusion and take her away from God. She had been born a Quaker, but her family were lukewarm in their devotion; from the moment her religious consciousness was awakened, she believed that she had to justify her faith in every waking moment. It was only when she visited a poor woman in the slums that she gave free vent to her feelings: 'I felt quite in my element serving the poor, and although I was much tired with looking about, it gave me much pleasure, it is an occupation my nature is so fond of . . . it brings satisfaction with it more than most things.' It was the only time she let herself be happy; it was the only time when she could trust herself to surrender to her emotions. Most importantly for her, those feelings were the only ones she could acknowledge as authentic; everything else was a matter of tortuous perplexity.[9]

Philanthropy was so important to those caught up in the religious revival since, as William Wilberforce warned, they knew that they were accused of 'studied hypocrisy' because they were so ostentatiously religious. But the fear of hypocrisy was most potent in their own breasts. The 'Saints' genuinely feared that the strong feelings they experienced might be delusional; there had to be a way to prove to their conscience that their faith was authentic. Christianity, Hannah More wrote, is a 'religion of *motives*'. In other words, merely doing a good act out of habit is useless, as you can't hide from God the spring of action. Most people were afraid of scrutinising their motives and preferred to plunge into charitable work without thought; as Wilberforce wrote, 'we suffer ourselves to believe that internal principles may be dispensed with, if the external action be performed'. The true Christian should be constantly vigilant of inner motives and sincerity of thought. But there was only one way in which these convictions could be justified, to one's self as much as to the world: 'We have every one of us a work to accomplish, wherein our eternal interests are at stake,' Wilberforce wrote. '. . . If we persevere indeed, success is certain; but our efforts must know no remission. There is a call on us for vigorous and continual resolution, self-denial, and activity.' Dedicating one's life to philanthropy and public work was the rational part of evangelicalism, the only way to make sure that religious excitement was not hypocritical or a trick of the mind. It brought the animated heart of the evangelical into harmony with worldly actions.[10]

This obligation of practical charity struck deep into the minds of a generation. Their major achievement was the abolition of the trade in slaves, for which many had dedicated the greater portion of their lives. Wilberforce is remembered as the leading light in that great campaign, but it drew in many more and became the meeting ground for many like-minded philanthropists. Sir Thomas Fowell Buxton, a partner in the Brick Lane brewery Truman, Hanbury & Co., married into the Quaker Gurney family. Influenced by their example, especially by his sister-in-law Elizabeth Fry, and by Wilberforce he joined the anti-slavery movement (he was recognised as Wilberforce's successor as leader of the movement in the 1820s). As with many others, early campaigning to abolish slavery sparked a lifelong need to improve mankind. There is a famous story told of the evening when it finally became clear that an act abolishing the slave trade would pass through Parliament. Wilberforce 'playfully' asked, 'What shall we abolish next?' After a thought, Henry Thornton gravely replied, 'The lottery, I think.'[11] Abolition was never an end in itself but, for many, part of life's work. Fowell Buxton dedicated himself to prison reform and was chairman of the RSPCA. After abolition, many of the anti-slavery campaigners threw themselves into the Bible Society, sending missionaries to India and educating the lower orders in religious principles.

The philanthropic impulse affected people such as William Allen, a prosperous chemical engineer whose factory was in the East End of London. For Allen, after the abolition of slavery the need to bring Christianity and moral reform to the masses was an unavoidable duty. In his private moments, he said, 'the humiliating sense of my own weakness and unworthiness, at times almost wears me down'. It was only in the performance of good works that he found satisfaction in his struggle against spiritual apathy and hypocrisy: in short, 'the potent enemy self'. With his feelings and emotions under strict control in private contemplation, human relationships and daily life, only philanthropy gave him the kind of release everybody needs. An example of this came when he visited the school founded by Joseph Lancaster to teach a thousand poor boys. Allen rejoiced to see so many boys taken from the streets to learn 'habits of subordination' and become intimately acquainted with the Bible: 'The feelings of the spectator while contemplating the results which might take place in this country, and the world in general, by the extension of the system thus brought into practise by this meritorious young man, were overpowering, and found vent in tears of joy.'[12]

For Allen it was a sincere emotion, perhaps the only kind of feeling he acknowledged as genuine. But such feelings could be exceedingly dangerous. All the money that was lavished on VD hospitals and refuges for prostitutes came from people following their benevolent emotions. Did they do any good? As the revenue of charities increased, so did vice. There seemed to be something grievously amiss. The act of giving was enough for such people; what happened with the money was a minor consideration.

Benevolence was only sincere if every intention and consequence was carefully thought through and subject to strict scrutiny. The mind had to be drilled and regulated so that the first flush of a charitable impulse was not really the warm glow of self-love. This was not just true for the serious Christian. Jeremy Bentham was equally afraid that 'false humanity' and sympathy for the plight of the poor would incapacitate his rational mind: 'The stronger my propensity to yield to it, the more strenuous my efforts to subdue it.'[13]

The 'false' emotion of benevolence was, for a vocal minority of philanthropically minded people, one of the major concerns of the day. Malthus said that the benevolent instinct, like the impulse to eat, drink, have sex and all of the other 'natural propensities', had to be strictly governed or it would be fatal to the individual and society.[14] Jane Austen compared the edginess and narcissism of people who had nervous disorders with the competitiveness of charitable work; they both came from the disordered passions engendered by refinement. In *Sanditon* Charlotte described the hypochondriac Parkers: 'Some natural delicacy of Constitution in fact, with an unfortunate turn for Medicine, especially quack Medicine, had given them an early tendency at various times, to various Disorders; – the rest of their symptoms was from Fancy, the love of Distinction & the love of the Wonderful. – They had Charitable hearts & many amiable feelings – but a spirit of restless activity, & the glory of doing more than any body else, had their share in every exertion of Benevolence – and there was vanity in every act they did, as well as in all they endured.' Indiscriminate, self-satisfying charity was worse than no charity at all. Fulfilling the duty of benevolence was, for people like the Parkers, the scratching of an itch or a competitive gesture.

The fear that dogged all reformers and philanthropists was that in attempting to do good they were betrayed by an inner weakness and the power of their emotions into doing something unintentionally evil. As Bentham said, charity was neither a sincere act nor ultimately helpful for mankind: 'It is extorted by painful sensations, not drawn forth by pleasurable ones.' The only answer was to apply rigorous scientific and rational solutions to man's problems, rather than leaving policy to the variety and spontaneity of individual judgement. As the

Philanthropic Society put it, 'a very great proportion of human misery has its origin in the benevolent spirit of man, indulged without sufficient attention to the constitution of the human mind'; relations within society must therefore be refined to a system. The goal was, as the society put it, to harden the heart and do 'efficient good'.[15]

Of all the emotions that had to be diverted and restrained, benevolence was one of the most important. 'Our ancestors, and even many in the present day,' wrote one modern philanthropist, 'seem never to have questioned whether it were possible to direct their charity towards improper objects; but have acted fully up to the letter of the precept of "giving to every one that asketh".' In the nineteenth century the very meaning of charity would be revolutionised. It was so important because it seemed to be the crucial question regarding social policy. The generosity of the British was threatening to destroy their country. Wilberforce said that 'strict scrutiny is no where more necessary, because there is no where more room for the operation of self-deceit'.[16] Well-intentioned benevolence was stoking the flames of vice and criminality. Money bestowed on helping prostitutes and foundlings only encouraged thousands of girls to become prostitutes and have illegitimate children; helping the unemployed and beggars made idleness seem attractive for the worker. The country had to master its emotions and find a form of charity that curbed evil. 'The individual who rectifies some moral malady, and corrects the vices of a fellow-creature, confers a far greater good than he who administers medicine to the sick, or pecuniary assistance to the needy.'[17]

The person who would do good must be on guard against 'false humanity'. The only way to reinvent charity was to anatomise modern man and work from the principles of human nature. Reform, not relief, should be the motive and end of charity. Although philanthropy had always had a reformative aspect, the evangelicals made its policing role more systematic, not to say ruthless. The explanation for why the modern lower classes were so corrupt lay in a recognisably Protestant ethic that was shared alike by Bentham and Wilberforce.

Waste was the great evil as far as Christian philanthropists and the utilitarians were concerned. Wasting time led inevitably to irrational pleasures. 'In the hands of Midas every thing turned to Gold,' said Bentham: 'in the hand of the drunkard every thing turns to drink.'[18] The principles of the Society for Bettering the Condition of the Poor were flawed because they assumed that the people were capable of improving themselves. In reality the poor were radically corrupt: they were lazy and addicted to drink, too foolish to understand where their best interests lay. For the two different types of modern reformers, the religious and the utilitarian, idleness and its related evils had corroded the soul of humankind: the man or woman of the lower orders was left with an inner void thanks to his or her indolence and addiction to strong liquor and vulgar pleasure. Idleness, for Bentham, was utterly repulsive: it was the root of all depravity and inhumanity.

Liberty inculcated lax habits. Employment did not inspire personal discipline and industry nor do much to eradicate humankind's depraved nature. Hard labour and hard drinking went hand in hand. St Monday and all the customs that governed working life allotted so much free time to indulge bad habits. An opportunity to improve people was thus lost. Man was no good governor of himself; he did not know his best interests, but irrationally acted contrary to them. Time not spent in regulated labour was time spent in self-destruction.

A disturbing instance of this was detailed in the newspapers. A constable patrolling the Hampstead Road one evening spotted two men atop a wall next to a lamp post. One of them was six foot tall and the other shorter and stout. The shorter man had tied one end of a neckerchief to the lamp post and the other in a noose around the taller man's neck. When the tall man was pushed off to hang, the constable rushed over to prevent the murder and succeeded in freeing him from the noose. He was shocked when the intended victim struck him, blackened his eyes, broke his nose and tried to remount the wall. The officer had to use his cudgel to prevent the tall man inserting his head in the noose again. Both men were apprehended. When they were brought before the magistrate, it turned out that they were canal workers ('navigators') who, due to the unpredictable nature of their work, had woken to find themselves without a job for the day. Bored, they had been dicing since morning. When James Skeltop, the tall man, had lost all his wages, he bet his clothes (Belcher, the short man, was wearing his friend's jacket and shoes when they were caught). When those ran out, Skeltop had nothing left to offer but his life. That did not stop their spree. The tall man lost for the last time and had no choice but to fulfil the terms of the wager. Skeltop, according to his wife, was a good husband and a conscientious worker. He was shown mercy by the bench and discharged. He submitted to the wager, it was said at the trial, with 'seeming cheerfulness'; he had fought his rescuer because 'it would have been unfair if he had not fully performed the bet'.[19]

Such instances were mercifully rare. It was the worst that could happen when workers were in and out of employment or had loose relationships with their masters. But gambling, drinking, wasteful pleasures and even self-harm were not objectionable in themselves; inactivity affected man at a more profound level. Man was a working animal, put on the world to toil for his bread and his salvation; idleness was a state of being entirely alien to his deepest inclinations and the intentions of God or nature. High wages, the independence allotted to labourers, modern luxuries and the safety net of parish relief had stood on its head what it meant to be human. God's or nature's perfect plan had been deranged and the poor were no longer subject to the pains that punished sloth or the inducements that encouraged industry. In other words, the poor were something other than real human beings; their very nature had been distorted. Brutal recreations prevented them from hearing the word of God; the Poor Laws shielded them from the workings of economics. What was left was the husk of a being, a perverted, artificial creature.

Under nature, humans were governed by firm but fair laws. They were stimulated to work by the pangs of an empty stomach, but this had been deranged by the Poor Laws, which allowed everyone who was out of work enough money or food to keep themselves alive. The Rev. Joseph Townsend, a self-proclaimed 'well-wisher to mankind', compared the instincts of the poor to those of a creature described by William Dampier in his travels to the antipodes. 'Nimble Peter' would strip a tree bare of food and then bask in idleness until it was skin and bones before hauling itself off to find more nourishment. Townsend asked of the poor, 'what cause have they to fear, when they are assured, that if by their indolence and extravagance, by their drunkenness and vices, they should be reduced to want, they shall be abundantly supplied, not only with food and raiment, but with their accustomed luxuries, at the expense of others? The poor know little of the motives which stimulate the higher ranks to action – pride, honour, and ambition. In general it is only hunger which can spur them and goad them on to labour; yet our laws have said, they shall never hunger.' Under the Poor Laws, they were entitled to relief in sickness, old age and unemployment. This humanity deprived them of their human qualities; they had no sense of the future and no interest in thrift. They became a kind of sub-species, incapable of moral judgement and a simmering threat to the state, private property and their own selves. It was little wonder that the streets seemed to be degenerating into scenes of drunkenness and rioting. What had the people to fear from fate or from their bad habits? Why should they ever bother to become industrious and providential? God, working through nature, had provided incentives and punishments for man; the Poor Laws rendered the laws of the world puny.[20]

Frugality and diligence could only exist if the poor were free from the feeble intervention of their sentimental betters. 'The poor laws may, therefore, be said to diminish both the power, and the will, to save, among the common people and thus to weaken one of the strongest incentives to sobriety and industry, and consequently to happiness,' Thomas Malthus wrote. Most worryingly for Malthusians, the Poor Laws provided for the children of labourers, regardless of the behaviour of their parents. Nature taught people a good moral lesson, albeit a severe one: that they must restrain their sexual passions until they were in a position to bring up a family. These natural laws therefore prevented population outstripping the means of production, sparing man the violence and misery predicted by Malthus. The Poor Laws, however, 'afford a direct, constant, and systematical encouragement to marriage, by removing from each individual that heavy responsibility which he would incur by the laws of nature, for bringing beings into the world which he could not support'.[21]

But there could be no return to nature in the modern world. It was beholden on philanthropists, Christian and secular, to restore some of the natural morality lost in the march of progress. Malthusians might have wanted to abolish poor relief altogether, but there was no appetite on the part of legislators to do so. Relations between the rich and the poor should be personal and supervisory, like the paternalism that existed in small communities. The Poor Laws should continue, but reformed so that the industrious were rewarded, the slothful coerced into labour and the lives of the poor regulated by their betters.

Discipline was the only route to salvation. Bentham's greatest allies were evangelicals such as Wilberforce; he was sure to put his arguments in a recognisably Protestant idiom – the work ethic, the morality of discipline and the incontrovertible laws of nature. Self-made businessmen, diligent workers, evangelicals and Quakers like

Colquhoun owed their spiritual and material prosperity to strenuous self-regulation: they had mastered their emotions and directed their efforts toward a higher happiness, beyond instant gratification. This was the only path to redemption, personally and for the nation. Britain could only be reformed if individuals were reformed first. Those who gave in to temptation and indulged their worst instincts were poor; the self-disciplined and restrained inherited the riches of the world. The poor must be taught strict discipline, so that they could command their appetites, turn their backs on irrational pleasures and conform their lives to God or work. Only then could the Malthusian future and the threat of revolution – the spectre that haunted Bentham and Colquhoun equally – be conquered.

For utilitarian and philanthropist alike, work as an end in itself was the foundation of morality and happiness. Hard work and discipline would lead to personal responsibility. In other words, it would foster habits of frugality, which would, as every reader of *A Treatise on the Police of the Metropolis* knew, stem the flow of crime by taming the rage for luxuries. Patrick Colquhoun's solution was to introduce a properly co-ordinated police force to contain the festering immoralities and criminal enterprise of the lower orders. This was Colquhoun's darling project, the reform that would make his name and solve the problems that he had so assiduously detailed in book after book. His treatises describing the depredations of the poor were intended to prepare the public mind and highlight the need for some sort of regulation. Relieving poverty, alleviating its symptoms and punishing hardened criminals was next to useless; prevention was better than cure.

Colquhoun knew all too well that policing in the sense of enforcing laws and investigating private gentlemen was distasteful to the ruling class and the majority of Britons. His police force would have been very different from one which we would recognise; he did not envisage an agency highly skilled at detection and forensic investigation. Rather, the police and the Poor Law would be blended together. Officers would be moral guardians for the poor, not solving crimes but preventing them before they were even conceived in the mind. The two thousand or so 'invalid, ill-paid, drunken watchmen' who were charged with maintaining public order in London would be replaced with an energetic new breed of policemen-cum-inquisitors. The new police would be centralised and superintended by a board under the direct control of the Home Secretary. It would gain its information from parish officials in order to compile a national database, a complete register of paupers detailing their age, trade, the cause of their poverty (whether it was innocent or culpable), the expense they incurred and, most importantly, their 'moral character'.

In other words, it would be a thorough and never-ending inquisition into the habits of the people of England and Wales. The police would use the information to highlight potential troublemakers and prevent 'idleness and loose and immoral conduct', thus nipping in the bud the criminal tendency. And every aspect of lower-class life would be put under iron control. Alehouses would be under constant scrutiny, and police officers would have the summary power to interfere in their business. Not content with this daily scrutiny, Colquhoun further recommended that the officers should enforce the observance of the Sabbath; ensure the poor followed a life of 'providence and economy' and were kept away from 'sloth and idleness, and lounging in alehouses'; children would be made to be dutiful to their parents; women would be observed so that they followed examples of 'frugal housewifery'; adulterers would be rooted out and punished; and, indeed, every waking moment and personal decision would be overseen, including the obligation to eat cheaply. The Home Secretary and his officers would therefore ensure that the workforce was untainted by profligacy and that national productivity was kept high. Labourers would become heavily regulated machines, their every action dedicated to making the country rich.[22]

Malthusians might have wanted to abolish the Poor Laws, but Bentham and Colquhoun's plan was to reform them so that they conformed as closely as possible to the natural ordering of the world. They should discriminate between deserving and undeserving paupers, between the culpable and the merely unfortunate. Once the Laws were made brutally efficient, people would not be rewarded for their laziness and improvidence. Such reforms would not just make claimants of relief more careful; the entire labouring population would know that if ever they fell on hard times they would be judged on their past habits and conduct. If they ever had to make a claim for relief, the indolent and extravagant would be punished for their wasteful existence; the frugal and temperate who had lived simply and saved their money would be treated kindly. If a worker was aware of the invisible but salutary surveillance of Poor Law administrators, the knowledge would meld his manners for the better.

'I do really take it for an indisputable truth, and a truth that is one of the corner stones of political science – the more strictly we are watched, the better we behave.' So wrote Jeremy Bentham. He and Colquhoun shared a belief that the poor had to be broken down and rebuilt as modern men. Supervision and management were the only ways to bring the benighted poor into conformity with their duties as human beings and Christians, for they knew no more of their own good than infants. 'As objects of tenderness and beneficence, they ought to be regarded as children,' wrote Bentham: 'but as instruments ever ripe for mischief they ought to be guarded against as enemies.' Colquhoun advocated policeman-guardians; Bentham's solution was a network of 'Panopticons', pauper prisons where every action of the inmates would be under constant surveillance. It was a solution to the haphazard, expensive and nature-defying Poor Laws. In the Panopticon, the worker would be monitored and regulated at all times, so that idleness and self-indulgence would not creep in and corrupt their souls. Best of all, the institution would be run strictly for profit: food would be kept at subsistence level and the patrons would be rewarded by the labour of the paupers. Children would be put to work as soon as they were able; that is to say, aged four. The new generation, therefore, would be inculcated with internal discipline from the cradle. Mankind would be born anew.

Bentham and Colquhoun's plans were countenanced at the highest level, but were never realised. The moral police and the Panopticon were not as crazy as they might appear; they touched on the principal aspects of modern philanthropy. The government was interested in the schemes, but in general most ministers and MPs were reluctant to involve the state in moral reform. Aspects of utilitarian and evangelical social reform did, however, begin to affect people's lives. Throughout the country the plans were attempted on a relatively small scale. They had to be shown to work in practice rather than theory before they could be widened to the rest of the community.

The Spitalfields Benevolent Society, for example, distributed cheap soup to one third of the local population from a shop on Brick Lane. This was at a time when the East End silk industry had suffered from the restricted wartime economy, and Spitalfields had been hit particularly hard. Many of the local employers and factory owners came from the dissenting and evangelical communities; this time of dearth and distress was ripe for use as a moral experiment. The society was started by Thomas Bernard, Patrick Colquhoun, William Allen and members of the London Quaker community; later it would be supported by the royal family. At first, it just sold subsidised soup made from cheap ingredients in an effort to show the poor how easy and beneficial frugal cookery could be. Soup was the most moral of foods; its very preparation was an object lesson in thrift and efficient domestic management.

Allen and Colquhoun successfully fought against the old-fashioned paternalists to establish an important condition: those who needed the soup during times of scarcity and starvation had to subject themselves to home visits from the worthy Quakers. If the poor of the East End did not live up to the ideals of frugality, sobriety and respectability, and if they were not making every effort to find salvation in Christ, they were banned from buying cheap soup. Feeding the poor was last on the list of the intentions of the members of the society: 'The objects of the Society are, visiting and relieving the poor . . . and affording them Christian instruction (the last, the chief object), and also for our own improvement.'[23]

If they were placed on a comprehensive footing, visiting societies would replicate old-fashioned ideas of paternalism and discriminating benevolence, practical only in small communities. In urban areas, the wealthy and godly would found such societies and use them to extend personal contact to the lives of slum dwellers. They would manage the household economy of the poor, keeping them off the bottle and forcing them into good habits. If the needy did not comply, let them suffer. It was, according to Allen, the most effective kind of policing known to a modern society. 'If this could be carried into effect, I believe the whole face of society would exhibit a great change for the better; instead of crowded gaols and a starving population, we should have little occasion for prisons, our persons and our property would be far more secure, and the enormous sums now spent in the repression of crime, might be employed to relieve *unavoidable* distress.'[24]

This was Colquhoun's police plan in laboratory stage. The gift of food on the condition of personal reform and a commitment to respectability administered by the upright members of the community was a version of Colquhoun's inspectors, who enforced 'frugal housewifery' and restrained drunkenness. Another experiment put into action was the Philanthropic Society, founded with the stated intention of revolutionising the notion of charity itself. It had more than a passing similarity to the principles of Bentham's pauper Panopticon. The society provided three houses – or reformatories – for the sons and daughters of the 'vagrant poor'. Children were taken in at the age of five, when they were too young to have been corrupted by their parents or the evils of the streets, yet old enough to provide labour to pay for their upkeep. The society had little interest in simply providing for needy children. It was another experiment in morality; from this beginning, the whole country could take up the scheme of remaking the vicious poor by taking control of the next generation. 'The society is formed rather on principles of police than of charity,' its founders told the world.[25]

As far as the Philanthropic Society was concerned, the parents of their charges were 'the enemy'. They would only be allowed to visit their children on the strict condition that they wore their best clothes and acted respectably. Contact between the children and their brutal parents would ruin the experiment. The children were expected to do two things to repay the kindness shown them: to earn a profit for their benefactors and to become indoctrinated with habits of discipline. This was the law of God and nature at work: let no one think they could get anything for free or without reimbursing society. If all children learnt this, the pool of labour would become clear and pure, and society would prosper. Charities, like everything else, should be subject to the laws of the market. 'The object in short', said the first report of the society, 'was to unite the spirit of charity with the principles of trade, and to erect a temple to philanthropy on the foundation of virtuous industry.'[26] The greater the profit the children made, the more respectable people were inclined to support the scheme. Vast amounts of money were soaked up by traditional charities; modern philanthropy should be an investment that kept money productive.

One group not consulted on these matters was the poor. The facts of their lives and habits had largely been deduced from general principles or from statistics. The *Quarterly Review* talked of the 'privileged idleness' of the poor, as if they were engaged in one perpetual party and were free from the painful duties of the rich.[27] The evangelical mindset regarded the world as starkly polarised: a human soul was destined for heaven or hell from birth. In a similar way, society was governed by absolute laws. Francis Place, in his writings on the lower orders, provides a reminder of the chaos and messiness of life in an age when absolute values and scientific analysis was beginning to dominate. Most importantly, he used his pen to counter the argument that the working population could be regulated like machines; the human need to seek refuge from drudgery in sensual enjoyment could never be eradicated by all the mechanical laws devised by theorists.

Place saw many of his contemporaries who had 'kept on working steadily but hopelessly more like horses in a mill, or mere machines than human beings, their feelings blunted, poor stultified moving animals, working on yet unable to support their families in any thing like comfort, frequently wanting the common necessities of life, yet never giving up until misery has eaten them to the bone'. If this was the price to pay for self-abnegation and restraint – Colquhoun's recipe for success – it was no wonder that many people turned to drink in desperation, or, more likely, did not bother at all. Better to extract what pleasure was available from the moment than to imitate the discipline of a monastery for the remote chance of entering paradise. The moralists said that failure and poverty were punishments for vice. Poor people, who knew better than their critics, understood something different. The industrious and virtuous were on an equal footing with sots and drunkards as far as earthly rewards were concerned. Yet the hard-working and blameless bore the stigma of failure, with, as Place said, 'all above them, classing them with the dissolute, the profligate and the dishonest, from whom the whole character of the working people is taken'.[28]

Colquhoun, from his position on the magisterial benches at Shoreditch and Westminster, certainly saw the worst of human behaviour. What he seems to have done is to join the dots between isolated incidents of crime and emerge with a picture of widespread depravity and a generalised impression of a whole class. There is and was no evidence that organised crime was as endemic as he suggested or that behind the squalor of the East End or the Borough lurked an Alhambra of booty. Yet there can be small wonder people like Colquhoun saw danger in the surly masses. Francis Place, who had personal experience, said that the poor had been 'made desperate by the oppression under which they groan'. It was hardly surprising if 'they have no character of prudence or reflection to support, and they have nothing of that pride, arising from what is called the decent and respectable appearance a man makes among his neighbours, which should enable them to suppress the first sallies of passion, and the effervescence of a warm constitution'.[29]

There seemed plenty that the stern moral reformers did not understand about the lower classes. They certainly judged them against impossible standards of virtue. They seemed terrified by the appearance of the mob, especially those crammed into London. But what was considered foul immorality and depravity by the godly John Bowles and the thrifty Patrick Colquhoun were acceptable and harmless forms of behaviour to people living in the less salubrious parts of town. They did not wear the outward appearance of decorum and virtue, but that did not necessarily mean they were a danger to the state or a vicious sub-species; the rough exterior did not always betoken a warped mentality. Yet the tendency was to judge virtue and vice by consequences alone: a ragged appearance, coarse manners and misery did seem to be the price people paid for vice. Drunkenness did appear to be the habit of idleness. But, as some tried to remind the moralising writers, sensual relaxation was absolutely indispensable for anyone who worked; this need seemed to have been forgotten in the scientific analysis of mankind. Place wrote of the British labourer: 'Idle he is not, improvident he generally is, to some extent, and it can hardly be otherwise. He must spend an odd six-pence or a shilling now and then, although he had certainly better save it. But as to his idleness – all the work is done that is desired to be done; and there he stands, ready and willing to be engaged in the hardest, the most disgusting, and the most destructive kind of work.'[30]

William Austin wrote that the labouring classes looked terrifying, yet found them characterised by civility and 'far from being destitute of generous feelings, though in appearance, they have not even the outside of humanity'. He compared the lowest Briton with the lowest American. In the United States even a destitute man believed he would one day end up with a farm and a prosperous family; the superabundance of land and resources made this a safe bet. The knowledge kept people going. Britons, however, knew that they came from generations who had never owned a thing; that they could start work on 1 January, work 365 days, and be not a penny to the good by New Year's Eve. Austin was surprised that the lower orders were not much worse than they were: 'Enjoying under the constitution the same degree of liberty with the higher orders, and yet, in reality, detained eternally in a situation from which no docility of nature, and no impulse of ambition, can redeem them, they ought to possess the ferocity of the savage, without his generous sentiments.'

But it was little wonder that the more timorous of the higher orders saw danger in their unruly inferiors. Filled with beer or gin, the labourer probably *was* terrifying. Everyone could attest to the British rage for alcohol. Unlike sophisticated Paris, there weren't many evening entertainments provided for the lower classes in London, few cheap theatres, few places to dance: 'but John Bull is always thirsty, and could not relish such dry amusements'.[31]

The poor, because they knew that their lives were subject to external control – that if they saved money, a spell of illness, a harvest failure, an economic depression or the whim of a master would dash all their hard work in a trice – gave up any thought for the future, choosing to get what they could from the moment and throwing themselves at alcohol with grim abandon. 'They are so sensible of this,' wrote Austin, 'that many . . . with a determined, abandoned sort of principle, consecrate themselves to resolute debauches.'[32]

With much more sympathy for the poor than a Bowles or a Colquhoun, a writer in the *Critical Review* said that it was reasonable to expect that for the average labouring man, with no hope of reward however hard he worked, 'his efforts will proportionally relax, and all his faculties will become torpid and dull'. What else would a person feel who was out of work and forced into the humiliating position of begging from the parish? Was it not natural for a man or woman without hope to seek salvation in the bottle or in sex? Arthur Young responded to people like Colquhoun or Bentham who seemed perplexed that the poor irrationally drank so much and invested so little: 'For whom are they to be sober? For whom are they to save? (Such are their questions.) . . . If I am diligent, shall I have leave to build a cottage? If I am sober, shall I have land for a cow? If I am frugal, will I have half an acre of potatoes? You offer me no motives; you have nothing but a parish officer and a workhouse! – Bring me another pot.'[33]

In such circumstances the 'grosser parts of men' would predominate – or, in other words, the character traits Patrick Colquhoun and others claimed as natural to millions of workers. They claimed that depravity and drunkenness were a cause of poverty and misery and not a consequence of it. This was becoming an idea firmly fixed in the minds of philanthropists and opinion-makers: the poor were to blame for their condition. Thomas Bernard was a lone voice when he said of his own class: 'I see nothing very exemplary in our own conduct, to induce me to doubt but that the poor are as good and as prudent, and as industrious, as we should have been in the same circumstances.'[34]

Francis Place turned his back on his dissolute life at the age of eighteen. He chose a different path because he grew up – and because he fell in love with the girl who served at the next-door pastry shop. Place was bright enough to look around and see what became of people who failed to move on from their youthful high jinks. Joe France, for all his affluence, died in the workhouse. Francis's father, grown old and infirm, worn out by his lifestyle, was taken to the ecclesiastic court by his first, unacknowledged, wife; he lost a lot of money and his tenancy at the King's Arms, and had no labour to offer nor savings to make his old age comfortable. In the end, Simon was ruined by gambling on the lottery. Few of his companions made provision for illness, accident, old age or their own deaths. They bequeathed nothing to their families but endless misery. Place junior resolved to marry his pastry-shop sweetheart, Elizabeth, knowing the dangers; he was not prepared to inflict them on his future wife: 'I was aware of the poverty which awaited us if at any time I should be out of employment but that if she were willing to take her chance with me we should one day be well off in the world.'[35]

Married and with new responsibilities, Place converted to those values of frugality and prudence advocated by Patrick Colquhoun. He abandoned his life of late nights and drinking to build a home for his wife and whatever children they might have. The newlywed Places kept themselves to themselves, and Francis saved his money to buy decent clothes and furniture, the first step, he believed, on the road to respectability and fortune. 'We turned out of bed to work, and turned from our work to bed again,' he recalled of this time of frenetic work when he and Elizabeth toiled eighteen hours a day, seven days a week, and when weeks on end would go by without his leaving his home workshop. 'My hair was black and somewhat curled, my beard was very thick, my whiskers large, and my face somewhat sallow, and upon the whole I must have been a ferocious looking fellow.'[36]

But it was here that he parted company with the thinking of Colquhoun. Though few were possessed of the extraordinary energy and intelligence of Place, he detected changes in the middling and artisan classes and many labourers. And one of the things that propelled the growing respectability and thrift of these people was 'luxury'. The rage for new clothes, decent food, fashionable furniture and education (considered a luxury by most moralisers), which Colquhoun found so revolting and saw as the fountainhead of crime, stimulated people to work harder, save their money and be frugal. It fuelled ambition and decorum rather than spawning idleness and crime. Colquhoun and Bowles wanted people to remain poor and humble, afraid that high wages would corrupt them and muddy the pool of labour. But, said Place, such men 'did not see far enough'; they would not see that a desire for luxury goods and increased purchasing power could make people better, less inclined to blow their wages on gin and beer and encouraged to show greater industry.

This change, this desire to conform to ideas of respectability, according to Place, was going on among the clerical sort, and the better-educated and more ambitious workmen as well. R. Shaw agreed that the poor were more likely than not to strive for small rewards at this time, and said that it was 'not only impolitic but reprehensible, to throw imputations of depravity upon the small indulgences enjoyed by the lower but most useful orders of the people; for they operate as a stimulus to future exertions, at the same time that they contribute to the exigency of the state'. Restrain ambition and the poor would stew in their drunken vices, as many of them evidently did. When Dr Colquhoun was writing his treatises, Place said, he had no idea 'that a material change for the better was going on, among the people, and that getting drunk and quarrelling was gradually declining'.[37]

Colquhoun's observations led him to believe that the whole of the lower orders and a portion of the middling were predisposed to crime and dissolute behaviour; that if they were left unregulated they would slip into depravation or idleness. Place said that at this time there was plenty of theft but most of it wasn't committed by labourers congenitally inclined to criminality. All the work that could be done was done, Place said; the criminal class consisted of a redundant population who were out of work for long periods at a time. The Irish population of St Giles's or Marylebone had to seek work on building projects; the demand for their labour came and went and they could not return to their home parishes to claim relief. In Wapping and Stepney, thousands competed every day for jobs on the docks; they could be idle and destitute for long periods, depending on the fluctuations of world trade and the vicissitudes of the war. Low wages and unemployment were responsible for crimes of necessity being more common than those born of a rage for luxury and laziness. 'Mr Colquhoun, looked at all this [as] men of vulgar understanding always look at these matters, and therefore never see the true reason of poverty and ignorance and consequently the true causes of crime.'[38]

Frugality and thrift did not do much for the Places. At times they almost starved. Throughout the 1790s Francis suffered long periods of unemployment; any savings he and Elizabeth managed to put away were obliterated at the outset of Francis's long spells of enforced idleness. Leather breeches went out of fashion, and he had to turn to tailoring stuff breeches and waistcoats, a terrible and demeaning trade compared to the skilled work of crafting leather garments. Work would dry up for long periods, or else arrive in a glut. Place turned to politics, first organising the London tailors into benefit clubs to insure themselves against periods of unemployment or during strikes, and then joining the political London Corresponding Society. These were bad days, and the Places had to pawn or sell their hard-earned furniture and clothes.

The Places did everything people like Colquhoun said they should, yet every sacrifice was in vain, and they were worse off than the profligate frequenters of Cock and Hen clubs. Indeed, Simon Place had been richer and had had more fun. 'I insisted upon it that I should work myself into a condition to become a master tradesman, and should then be able to maintain myself and my family respectably,' wrote Francis, who refused to be put off by a succession of disasters. He realised that it was pointless waiting for some fairy-tale scenario, for a time when he could open a treasure chest of savings and start a shop.

Possessing capital was not important: a businessman could succeed on his own initiative. Place started out as a freelance tradesman by going to three mercers to buy raw materials and told each proprietor that he was trying out different suppliers. Eager to win the business, and erroneously believing that the smartly dressed Place was rich, the mercers bent over backwards to give him credit. It was a long and slow process to build up a business; Place sold his finished items very cheaply and the profit was miniscule. When he started, he calculated it would take six years of privation, diligence and tortuously slow progress to become an independent tradesman. In the end it took four.

His recipe for success was to live on short credit and never, never let down a lender. In this way, he established a reputation for rectitude and honesty and for having a good business brain. Like all budding successes, Place was a good proposition, or so he made pains to signal to the world.

Place acknowledged that his success, when it came, was as much good fortune as hard graft. In 1799, after surviving the vicissitudes of the tailoring business for a decade, he had saved enough money to join a partnership with one Richard Wild and open a fashionable tailor's shop at number 26, Charing Cross. The shop was stocked entirely on credit. Within a year and a half they were employing thirty-two skilled tailors and were pioneering London fashions, making the fancy waistcoats and pantaloons and the gold braid hitherto favoured by the officer class the ultimate in male civilian design.

It seemed like the Places' fortune was made. But then Wild married a former prostitute who had enough money to outbid the Places and buy the business outright. Elizabeth Place was distraught at this new crisis. 'She was sure we should be turned into the street, industry was of no use to us, integrity would not serve us, honesty would be of no avail, we had worked harder and done more than any body else, and now we were to suffer more than any body else.'[39]

Mrs Place's lament must have been heard in countless homes. Yet she and her husband were luckier. Francis had built up a reputation with his creditors; they trusted him to make a handsome profit and did not want to see him go. Place borrowed enough money to start again, and he and Elizabeth moved to a bigger shop at number 6, Charing Cross, which had possibly the first, and certainly the largest, plate-glass windows in London, the perfect innovation for showing off wares and attracting a crowd. Place did not disappoint; his shop became one of the most successful tailor's shops in London. He was a bad tailor himself but a great manager of skilled ones, a trusted businessman and gifted with the ability to cajole dandified customers. Wild, whose reputation had fallen in value because he had dishonestly forced his partner out, failed as a tailor; Place, the upright businessman, prospered.

Place detested the requirement that, as a tailor, he had to be servile and flatter his foppish customers. 'I had no choice between doing this and being a beggar, and I was resolved not to be a beggar,' he remembered. There was one goal that had driven him in his darkest moments: independence – from cruel masters, from the bleak hopelessness that had sunk so many of his contemporaries, from supercilious customers and from the whole wretched world of grinding, thankless labour. Place worked for another eighteen years, from six in the morning until midnight every day, 'dancing attendance on silly people', submitting to their extravagant, baffling tastes, and yet finding time for three hours of reading a day. Independence cost £20,000. It was more than enough for him not to have to worry again, but most importantly it allowed Place to lead the fight for parliamentary and social reform.[40]

Place's early boisterous behaviour made no difference to his later life. Such is the way of the world, we would say now; that there is no automatic reward for virtue and diligence is a self-evident truth. But had Bowles or Colquhoun read a memoir like Place's, they would draw different conclusions. They would say that by the time people woke up to the virtue of domestic economy, their youthful vices were so deeply ingrained that they would never escape from their consequences; immorality had a habit of exacting its penalty in the end: the collapse of a business or the failure that stalked every industrious journeyman were punishments for youthful indiscretion and early habits of drunkenness. Even if it was not divine retribution, failure later in life was the result of undetectable vices that had penetrated the soul from the start and made people incapable of success. (Place had succeeded; but, the moralists would say, scum rises to the top.) But this scary promise of inevitable punishment would not convince people who had first-hand experience of poverty.

People like Place found it obnoxious that the stern rich should advocate a total ban on the pleasures of their inferiors. There was nothing wrong with juvenile amusements; the somewhat puritanical definition of vice was inadequate when it came to assessing people's worth in society. Place believed that premarital sex was, in many circumstances, healthy and to be encouraged (later in life Place, a committed Malthusian, would recommend contraception). He pointed to his and his friends' teenage girlfriends. No one expected them to be virgins when they got married, and their youthful experiences did not affect their future happiness or morality. Most of Place's girlfriends turned into respectable women and none 'made a bad wife' as a consequence of their teenage frolics. They grew up to mother good families. Many of Place's fellow apprentices in his bachelor days grew up, like him, to become prosperous and well-to-do London tradesmen. Their early 'vices' were teenage high spirits which did not warp their souls. In any case, as he forcibly said, 'Poverty and chastity are incompatible.'[41]

In 1823 Place showed one of his old friends, by then a very respectable family man and wealthy businessman, the portion of his reminiscences which dealt with their rowdy evenings drinking with prostitutes in taverns on Fleet Street. 'God bless my soul!' exclaimed this paragon of domestic economy and business success, '– why yes! – that's true! – Ah! I had forgotten that!'[42]

When Patrick Colquhoun was at the height of his renown as an investigator into the lives of the poor, Francis Place was an unknown and struggling tailor. It would take many years before his kind of defence of the manners and morals of the lower classes attracted any kind of publicity. As it was, Colquhoun's treatises grabbed the public's attention in the 1790s and 1800s. He had his enemies, the most surprising being the monthly magazine *Le Beau Monde*, which informed the upper and upper middle classes of the latest fashions. It called the magistrate's *Treatise on the Police of the Metropolis* a 'slander' on the poor, and accused him of writing little better than a fictional account of the state of the morals and manners of the lower orders. The magazine charged Colquhoun with pandering to the national propensity for gloom, hypochondria and the tendency to see the worst in every situation: 'The fearful catalogue of crimes and delinquencies, and the black muster-roll of criminals and offenders which it exhibits, are admirably calculated to gratify the feelings of the most *sombre* of our countrymen.' People bought Colquhoun's books because they liked reading about the tricks, wiles and adventures of their lower-class neighbours; the treatises read like low-life romances, and the reader was acquitted from prurience because they were dressed up as moral tomes. The public's fascination with low-life depravity and criminal enterprise 'secured his work an easy reception, and the public, lost in astonishment at the mass of turpitude and iniquity which it displayed, acquiesced on its deductions without scrutinizing the data on which it was formed'.[43]

It was doubly dangerous when it was read and believed by people with power over the lives of the poor. 'The justice reads the books concerning pauperty,' the *Monthly Magazine* commented in its review of Colquhoun's *Treatise on Indigence*, 'but he is too lazy himself to undertake the organization of pretended reform; he is too neat to visit the hovel; too much engaged, in shooting or at dinner, to hear the objections of the neighbourhood, every thing is left to his clerk who has all the power but none of the benevolence of his master, and who is indifferent alike to the accommodation of the poor, or to the alleviation of the farmer.'[44]

It was all too easy to believe Colquhoun's assertions without enquiry, with Poor Law contributions growing every year, the fear of revolution or invasion ever present and the threat of a Malthusian crisis seizing imaginations. His style was compelling, his figures seemed correct and the facts truthful. His earliest critic, R. Shaw, said that Colquhoun's books were masterpieces of deceit, carefully constructed to sound shocking and believable. It was this skill as a writer and statistician that made the books deeply troubling: 'Abstract speculations are dangerous when they tend to produce innovations which are not merely useless, but which may prove pernicious to the public body, and be particularly grievous to individuals.'[45]

Colquhoun himself admitted that he deployed numbers to arrest the attention of the public. He must have been delighted when no one provided contradictory figures. Shaw said that because the statistics were deployed 'in order to alarm the timid mind', they should be scrutinised much more closely before people in power took them seriously. The assertion that £700,000 worth of property was pilfered in London each year, for example, came from no more reliable a source than a retired thief, who presumably did not conduct an audit. The fact that stood out most from Colquhoun's *Treatise on the Police* was enough to worry journalists, reformers, magistrates and police officers until the 1830s. It was quoted by writers, including Malthus, years after it was first made. There was, Colquhoun asserted, a growing class of people who roamed about London living from hand to mouth: it was a fact 'that above Twenty Thousand miserable Individuals of various classes, rise every morning without knowing how, or by what means they are to be supported during the passing day; or . . . [where] they are to lodge in the succeeding night'.[46]

There was no evidence for these assertions, although they were imbued with all the authority of statistics and were bold enough to stick in the mind. The idea that London supported such a large population who had no fixed employment and lived on their guile was the stuff of nightmares for all property owners and businessmen. Colquhoun knew what he was doing when he scattered his unreliable figures and tables around; the exact truth did not matter as long as the general impression of the depravity of the lower orders was fixed firmly in the minds of the middle and upper classes. The purpose of his books was more about reforming the attitudes of the wealthy than the manners of the poor.[47]

For all the hopes of the charitable pioneers, the public did not seem to follow them. Most would agree with the *Critical Review* that 'true charity does not enter in to the niceties of calculation. The sight of misery is sufficient to prompt . . . the relief. Its object is to mitigate pain and to alleviate want, and though it neglects not moral considerations, yet even these are not suffered to paralyse the arm that is raised to succour the wretched and the indigent.' Hard-hearted utilitarian calculations, it said, were contrary to true benevolence, which should be spontaneous and unthinking.[48]

He might have been accused of 'cold inhumanity' towards the poor, but Colquhoun dismissed this, saying he waged war on 'false humanity'. He questioned the benevolence of the rich; their pricking conscience might ease their soul, but it corrupted the intended recipients. The well-to-do, politicians, magistrates and jurors should be shocked out of their sentimentality. He believed that 'regulation' and 'amelioration' were one and the same thing; benevolence was a wrong-headed emotional response. Society had to learn to be hard-headed and hard-hearted if it was to stave off the moral diseases of the nineteenth century. Sympathy for the poor was fine and good, but it was storing up disaster. His books were intended to kill sympathy stone dead and encourage a more rational response to Britain's problems. As Malthus wrote of the rich, given the dangers that an unproductive and dependent population could do, charity was irrational:

> Their benevolence to the poor must be either childish play, or hypocrisy; it must be either to amuse themselves, or to pacify the minds of the common people with a mere shew of attention to their wants.[49]

There was only one way to view the poor, and it went against every humane instinct, every liberal feeling. It was still a view held by a minority; many called treatises by Malthus, Colquhoun and others of a similar way of thinking the handbooks of the selfish and unfeeling. They preferred older notions of kindness. But in the turbulence and uncertainty of the war such drastic cures began to seem compelling.

He who would manage the poor, wrote the *Quarterly Review*, 'must divest his nature of all that ennobled feeling and cultivated humanity, which are the best privileges and distinctions of his rank in society; and he must acquire the stern and impassive obduracy which is created in the manner and conversation of those who, as taskmasters or jailors, must hold authoritative intercourse with the basest of mankind'.[50]

4

Reforming Saints

'The prosperity of fools shall destroy them.'
John Bowles[1]

'The English are not fond of a strict police, and would rather be robbed, than watched.'
Nikolai Karamzin[2]

'We have long had our apprehension,' commented the *Anti-Jacobin Review* in 1801, 'that in our laudable anxiety to avoid the *Scylla of licentiousness* we run the risk of falling into the *Charybdis of Puritanism*.' The evangelical desire to reform the people by force was deplored by Tories and radicals alike. It seemed as though the 'enthusiasts' and 'fanatics' and 'godly' were uniting to take over the state by too much interference. Whatever fears Tory writers had of revolution, meddling with the morals of the people was no palliative. The robust national character would turn into milk-and-water piety. The godly, William Cobbett wrote, 'are incessantly labouring to eradicate, fibre by fibre, the last poor remains of the English manners. And, I am sorry to tell you, that they meet with but too many abettors, when they ought to meet with resolute foes.'[3]

A warning of what might happen in Britain could have been found in two popular books about the United States. The English traveller Thomas Ashe contrasted two different settlements on the Ohio. The first, Wheeling in Virginia, was a frontier trading station in 1806 which would have rivalled Pittsburgh, in Ashe's opinion, had the settlers 'attended to worthy commercial pursuits, and industrious and moral dealings, in place of rapine on Indian property, drunkenness, horse-racing, and cock-fighting'. It was the home of fugitives 'from the restraints of moral and political obligations' who had formed their own 'nefarious republic'.

Ashe witnessed savage fights between men in which the participants conducted themselves like 'beasts of prey and . . . carnivorous animals'. The American style of fighting apparently involved eye gouging, biting and kicks to the groin, throat and head. Sundays were conspicuous for race meetings, with attendant bloody fights, drinking bouts, heavy gambling, prostitution and robbery. The population was divided into two types: the 'Eleveners' and the 'Slingers'. The Slingers were so called because they took a swig of spirits mixed with sugar and mint upon rising from bed; the Eleveners were more restrained, waiting until eleven for their first snifter. 'The European learns with astonishment, that the first craving of an American, in the morning, is for ardent spirits,' wrote one observer, perhaps forgetting that many English gentlemen greeted the day with brandy. When the townsfolk of Wheeling and other similar towns were in the mood, the bacchanalia would last for days.*

'The lower classes in this gouging, biting, kicking country', sneered another Englishman and long-term resident in the US, Charles Janson, 'are the most abject that, perhaps, ever peopled a Christian country.' The situation was completely different in Marietta, a flourishing town on the Ohio which was the acme of perfection and rectitude. Here the 'New England regulation of Church and magistracy are all introduced and acted on to the full extent – to a point bordering on an arbitrary exaction'. But there was a price to pay for peace and quiet. American visitors to this town were shocked that their countrymen could impose such restraints on themselves. The Sabbath was rigorously enforced: 'In consequence never was a town more orderly or quiet. No mob, no fighting, no racing, no *rough and tumbling*.' In this and many other places, people were under virtual house arrest on Sundays. Even travellers who ventured through such towns could be forcibly prevented from passing on and compelled to go to church; if they arrived on Saturday evening they might well have to sit in solemn gloom until Monday morning. Ashe got into an argument with a butcher in Marietta, only to be pulled aside and warned that the man was a judge who could impose a summary fine for cursing and swearing: 'Hemmed in on every side,' a chastened Ashe commented, 'I resolved to mend my manners . . .'[4]

The same polarising tendency could be seen emerging in Britain: utterly dissolute habits gaining a hold of some sections of the commu-

*Times change. Wheeling, the capital of Ohio County, West Virginia, had the second lowest crime rate in the US in 2004.

nity, and a rigid, fanatical intolerance in others. 'The Methodists hate pleasure and amusements,' wrote Sydney Smith; 'no theatre, no cards, no dancing, no Punchinello [*Punch and Judy*], no dancing dogs, no blind fiddlers; – all the amusements of the rich and poor must disappear wherever these gloomy people get a footing.'

The godly were not to be put off easily. Evangelicals such as Wilberforce asked that people of influence associate themselves with the efforts of philanthropy. Then would they show the country that the ruling orders were serious about morality. To this end, Wilberforce persuaded George III to issue a proclamation against vice in 1787. The King attacked people of immoral tendencies and ordered that they be shunned by loyal subjects and hounded from society.

Wilberforce's reason for getting the King to issue the proclamation was to encourage members of the nobility and Parliament to involve themselves in a war on vice. He founded the Proclamation Society to prosecute and expose offenders against the moral sense of the nation and do everything within their powers to 'prevent the rapid progress of . . . moral diseases'. In the later seventeenth and early eighteenth centuries the Society for the Reformation of Manners, a private prosecution society, had brought to account some 91,000 immoral people in thirty-three years, from prostitutes and vendors of obscene material to shopkeepers and publicans who traded on Sunday. The society had folded in 1738, and Wilberforce's Proclamation Society wanted to revive the spirit of that God-fearing time.[5]

The King promised that 'Persons of Piety and Virtue' would be rewarded with 'Marks of Royal Favour'. 'We are . . . concerned to observe,' Robert Southey wrote sardonically in 1804, 'that, although the proclamation was issued in the year 1787, such is the lamentable deficiency of piety and virtue among us, no persons of the above description seem to be forthcoming.' The most obvious reason was that individuals who tried to take legal proceedings against their disorderly neighbours would be labelled busybodies, dismissed as puritanical fanatics and become 'a butt for the poisoned arrows of slander, or the scarcely less dreaded shafts of ridicule', as the society was forced to admit. Other countries and societies in the past had set up a powerful and respected magistrate to superintend morality; who in modern Britain would place themselves in 'the censorial chair'?[6]

The Proclamation Society looked formidable. It had the Bishop of London as its president, William Wilberforce as vice-president, and its members comprised two former prime ministers, twenty-seven nobles, thirty-three MPs (including the Speaker), a general and two admirals, Thomas Bowdler (whose name would enter the English language for his censorship of Shakespeare's naughtier passages), the Lord Chief Justice, the two archbishops, eleven bishops and a number of deacons, archdeacons and clergymen. But as the society's annual report of that year admitted, 'its past efforts had been productive of little benefit'; it had neither encouraged others to behave with more decorum nor punished the worst offenders against public morals. It was by intention an exclusive club, restricted to the highest members of society. It promised to hunt down the vicious, but in reality it seemed to be Wilberforce's pressure group to reform the aristocracy by making them at least talk the talk of moral reformation. It failed in that too. In 1800 it had just 149 members; many of its founders were dead, and no effort had been made to fill the ranks.[7]

The Proclamation Society lapsed into its drowsy dotage at just the time when many felt an aggressive crusade against vice was most needed. Its failure was a further sign of national corruption for people like John Bowles, who believed that the upper class had succumbed to 'debilitation, dissipation, and to enervating repose'. Fortunately for the depraved and purblind, there were still enough good people who would join in 'a vigorous contest with vice', men and women who would combat immorality with 'steadiness, perseverance, and unremitting activity'. The country could only defend itself against Napoleon and fight the war on two fronts (against France and against vice) if there was thorough reform, however painful. The few godly people would see to it that the laws were enforced and the dissipated restrained by 'legal coercion'. There was nothing shameful about informing on one's neighbours or engaging in vigilantism; it was a duty imposed on the moral, the patriotic and the benevolent who did not want to see the ruin of their country, their ancient monarchy and their Church.

Banding together into societies in order to enforce a moral code on the corrupted was 'the most meritorious act in which individuals can concur'. The middle classes who were not stained by vice, who were worried by the despicable behaviour of their employees and neighbours and who feared crime should form societies to enforce the laws and see that flagrant immorality did not go unpunished. Such collective action had the advantage that individuals would not be singled out as do-gooders and meddlers, for joining a society meant they could 'take refuge in concealment'. So in 1802 the Society for the Suppression of Vice was founded as an adjunct to the Proclamation Society. Just who was the moving spirit of this movement was hardly a secret: 'Their manifesto is so curious a compound of credulity and folly, that we have little hesitation in ascribing it to Mr John Bowles, whose name stands at the head of the committee list.'[8]

'Our times have witnessed not only the most sanguinary revolution of states, but a most awful revolution of human sentiment,' the SSV declared in its first report, in much the manner of a Bowles rant. Where the older, more aristocratic society had been inactive, the SSV would actively root out the delinquents, whether they openly paraded their vices or concealed them under a facade of politeness, hidden away 'like the poisonous brood of the viper'. Unlike the Proclamation Society, it sought volunteers among all classes (as long as they were members of the established Church and Methodists; dissenters, Catholics and Jews need not apply, howsoever moral they might be), and particularly the people most attracted to the kind of books written by Bowles – the holders of local office. Women were courted not just as members but as volunteers: 'Women are elevated in the scale of society, and that suavity of manners, which distinguishes modern from antient times, may justly be said to be, in operation of female influence.' People of all kinds had to collaborate on this great project, for vice had a protean quality, seeping into every obscure nook and polluting without detection; therefore, the SSV's 'observation will be general and diffusive, and the least shadow of such enormities will scarcely appear undiscovered: the faintest ray may disclose the existence of the evil, and the united efforts of a Society may trace it through all its tortuous windings, and fathom its most covert haunts'.[9]

Here was a case of loyalists going further than the government would. Indeed, the SSV was called into existence to do the work the government had conspicuously failed to accomplish. Bowles said that such private societies had to be set up 'not merely to invigorate the sanction of penal laws, but to assist and facilitate their execution' – a polite way of saying that they needed to do work the government was too indolent or afraid to carry out. In their view, until the late seventeenth century the state and the Church had undertaken their responsibilities to superintend the people's morals, preventing outrages where they could and punishing transgressors when their noisome habits became intolerable. After the Glorious Revolution in 1688 the individual had been granted an unprecedented degree of liberty, civil and religious. The ideals of freedom had become sacrosanct in English politics, the sacred cow of the eighteenth century; governments learnt to restrain themselves, fearing accusations that they were interfering in people's private lives or becoming tyrannical. Allotted a remarkable degree of freedom, the people had only abused it.

'The Laws are good,' said Bishop Watson in a sermon to the SSV; 'but they are eluded by the Lower Classes, and set at nought by the Higher. The Laws are good; but they are fallen into contempt, and require the Zeal, the Activity, the Discretion of such a Society as this to renovate their vigour.' There was, the SSV's members knew, a difference between the moral intent of the law and the licence that the manners of an age gave to certain practices; thus, fashion or habit was permitted to tyrannise over the rules of God and the state, making socially acceptable that which was officially prohibited.

The technique of the SSV was to enact laws which had long fallen into disuse or were used with discretion to avoid making people's lives too hard. Many of them had been drawn up centuries before and had never been repealed, yet these old and useless laws were the society's bread and butter. The members' conception of 'immorality' was anything that their neighbours did to offend their sensibilities. They did not like people idling in public houses, and they could find a law dating back to the early seventeenth century which forbade publicans to permit customers 'to remain or continue drinking or tippling in their Houses', unless they were travellers away from home or workmen, who were allowed an hour at lunchtime. Other rarely enforced laws made swearing, blasphemy, acts of lewdness, drunkenness, gambling, non-attendance of the Sunday service, organising dances and lighting fireworks criminal offences. Francis Place and his friends' youthful exuberance would be criminalised as the streets were swept clean of rowdy, lewd young men and women. As the SSV said, society's main challenge was a lack of obedience to parents, schoolmasters and employers, which undermined obedience to the law and the King. 'Can it then be a cause of wonder, that modern youth are destitute of that decency of deportment and propriety of manner, which we denominate *Respect*?'[10]

These petty crimes and acts of 'minor delinquency' were ignored by magistrates who failed to realise that such acts 'mark the early stages of progressive profligacy'. The SSV believed that if zero tolerance was given to petty criminal activity or antisocial behaviour, the progress of crime would be cut off at its source. In its war against vice, constables and watchmen were to be the foot soldiers of the SSV, whether they wanted to be or not. If they would not actively seek out petty crimes, it was up to members and paid informers to alert the officers. The members of the SSV were alarmed that most officers did not seem to know obscure Jacobean statutes which forbade swearing or tippling. The society printed and distributed *The Constable's Assistant*, a pamphlet that went through many versions over the years and reminded officers of long-forgotten statutes and spelt out their duty to police the morals of the lower classes.[11]

'The common sense and common feeling of mankind, if left to themselves, would silently repeal such laws,' commented Sydney Smith; 'and it is one of the evils of these societies that they render absurdity eternal and ignorance indestructible.' English law contained a plethora of statutes and laws which criminalised petty misdemeanours and minor transgressions. It was expensive to bring a case to court and frowned upon to meddle, so most offences were left unpunished. But both the SSV and Patrick Colquhoun advocated exerting the draconian and often long-buried laws and punishments on every occasion, as if English law were writ on tablets of stone. As R. Shaw wrote in response to Colquhoun's recommendation that people should tolerate a little less and punish a little harder: 'If every trifling offence was to meet with the punishment which the law directs to be put into execution upon every conviction, dreadful would be the state of mankind; as no rank or elevation in life, no prudence or circumspection of conduct, can insure a person from falling into some offences, which without that *compassion to human infirmities* would lead to the most deplorable consequences.' But the SSV and Colquhoun did not believe this was a time for mercy.[12]

At first sight, the SSV looked like a formidable organisation that could replicate the reformation of manners of a century before. Leigh Hunt called it 'the rifle-corps of saints-militant'. The operation of the SSV's moral war was concerted by a General Committee, which met at least once a week to coordinate the efforts of three subcommittees charged with detecting and rooting out the worst evils that were seeping through modern British society. The worst abuses, the SSV's General

Committee admitted, were carried out by those of 'the higher ranks'. They were to blame for invidious female fashions, adultery, outrageous scandal and ruinous gambling; they set the tone for society's morals. But the SSV was not going to direct its efforts against them. The modus operandi of the subcommittees was to encourage 'vigilant' people to gain evidence of turpitude, inform on their criminal neighbours, and then set prosecutions in motion. And the people that the SSV considered the most immoral were dealt with by the three subcommittees. The first dealt with breaches of Sunday-trading laws. The second treated those who preyed on the public with seductive or fraudulent tricks: blasphemers, the purveyors of lewd and obscene books, and traders who used false weights and measures. Disorderly houses, brothels, gaming houses, procurers, lotteries, breaches of the peace and cruelty to animals were the responsibility of the third subcommittee.

The subcommittees were ranked in order of the magnitude of the crimes they were to investigate. The spring of all crimes, all offences against decency, and the great mother of vice was the profanation of the Sabbath. In spite of the commands of God and the laws of the Christian nation, people openly broke these injunctions; the rich caroused on the seventh day more than any other, and kept in employment cooks, footmen, maids, coachmen and the tradesmen who supplied their tables. The weekly promenade at Hyde Park offended against any notion of the sacredness of the day and set a bad example to everyone else in the country. The *Evangelical Magazine* put Sunday newspapers at the top of its list of modern vices and believed that they evinced the triumph of diabolism; they were 'diametrically opposite to the laws of the land', for one thing, and their popularity showed just how far Britain was sunk in vices unknown at other periods of human history. 'The number of these engines of the wicked one have grown of late with most pestilential luxuriance . . . old men and women wear out the last remnant of their sight in poring over their profane pages; and babes, before they have learnt the use of speech, are taught to amuse themselves with their poisonous contents.'[13]

The veneration of the Sabbath came from a mixture of religious anxiety and practical reasons. The flagrant violation of the seventh day was a matter of shame for the pious, an open insult to the Almighty; what would be said of them on the Day of Judgement if they had spent their lives tacitly conniving in their country's descent into blasphemy? Just one person who openly defied the sanctity of the Sabbath ruined it for others more serious in their devotion. The zealous and impassioned had to at least attempt to arrest the progress of atheism to justify their own faith. Indeed, a country that mocked the law of heaven was actively courting the punishment of God. There was a tendency to blame reverses in the war, harvest failures and every national calamity on the lack of reverence for the holy day; the godly had to pay the same penalty as the profane. Less worryingly, those that worked or caroused on Sunday were completely cut off from the word of God; they had no opportunity to confront their peccability and recognise the need for reform or restraint. Bowles said that without the religious obligations of the Sabbath, society would 'otherwise degenerate into sordid ferocity and savage selfishness of spirit'. The one chance they had to comprehend their duties was evaded. The Sabbath, and the way it was treated, was of critical importance to the state of morals generally: if it was not observed, mankind 'will proceed (in aggravated ratio) to the goal of unqualified depravity – to that fatal excess, in which all moral force and influences are lost; and counter-exertion will no more avail, than drops of water sprinkled on a burning city'.[14]

The impulse to defend the seventh day came from a deep attachment to religion. But it was also critical for the reformer for more worldly reasons. If the amendment of the working people could only come about by indirect means, by shutting off the opportunities for vice rather than by persuasion or inducement, then what was or was not permissible on Sunday was of the first importance. As many labouring people worked six days a week and were paid late on Saturday night, after the shops shut, Sunday was the only day to visit a market, have a haircut or find what leisure they could. People who lived in towns and cities would leave for the countryside to visit tea gardens, fish, swim and play games, or engage in the accustomed brutal pastimes of boxing, baiting, bullock hunting or heavy drinking. Alehouses were allowed to open on Sundays, except during the allotted time for divine service, but shopkeepers and market stallholders were forbidden by law to trade. It was therefore obvious that if the Sabbath was rigorously enforced, much lower-class immorality and rowdiness would end simply because there would be no pleasure available on the only full day of free time. As with everything else, the imperative was for suppression, not making people better.

Morals might have improved if Sundays were more, not less, free. The day was gloomy enough in Britain without the SSV intervening to make it worse. Even innocent enjoyments were, strictly speaking, already illegal. A 'sixpenny hop' in a playhouse was forbidden to the people, 'and if they do not dance illegally they cannot dance at all'.[15] The SSV and other sabbatarian movements considered games of skittles in public houses chief among the evils that assailed the seventh day. With no opportunities for rational recreation, the choice that confronted the poor was sitting in austere gloom at home or 'besotting themselves' in alehouses; there was nothing else to do. Again, boredom and existing restraints on leisure hurled the mass of the people towards alcohol and violent sports. Wise magistrates and constables had turned a blind eye to Sunday trading out of compassion for working people who had no other day to buy provisions, and gave latitude to public houses which opened their doors.

The SSV was not so tolerant. Rather than try and persuade the rich to set a better example – which would have been a futile task – the committee persecuted shopkeepers and publicans in London and other towns where it had a following. The first burst of reforming zeal from a society set up to purify the manners and morals of a decadent nation and save the British from ruin was to have 218 publicans, grocers and butchers convicted of Sabbath-breaking in its first year, and 623 between September 1802 and October 1803; a further 2–3,000 were issued with printed warnings and threats of further action if they did not conform. Any attempt to prevent tippling in alehouses, ban gambling or stop fireworks being set off proved impractical without the earnest support of magistrates and constables. Prosecution for trading on a Sunday was an easier task. The success rate of prosecutions was 92 per cent at this time. In the same period, the membership of the SSV limped past the 1,000 mark. It was a healthy number for a public charity, but hardly the union of the respectable that Bowles had hoped for.[16]

The SSV claimed to be on the 'path of *intrepid moderation*'. A butcher or barber hauled up for punishment might have claimed otherwise. The membership might not have been vast, but the branches of the society were spread around the country and among its members were men of considerable influence. It was not one annoyed moralist against an offending butcher but a body of grandees with an unlimited fighting fund. The difference was that a butcher would have to mount an expensive defence on his own, while fighting a court case was an insignificant thing for the SSV, even if it lost. 'The very influence of names must have a considerable weight with the jury,' Sydney Smith wrote in the *Edinburgh Review*. 'Lord Dartmouth, Lord Radstock, and the Bishop of Durham, *versus* a Whitechapel butcher or a publican! Is this a fair contest before a jury?'

In such circumstances, given the influence of the members over juries, judges and constables, the SSV had turned itself into an autonomous 'voluntary magistracy', often acting the part of accuser, prosecutor, judge and jury. After all, it had the instinctive support of its leading members' social equals. Lord Chief Justice Ellenborough praised its efforts: 'It appears to me,' the judge said, 'that they deserve the thanks of all men, and I do not know of one rule of law upon which they have at all trenched.' And it had another mighty advantage: the right name. No one wanted to promote immorality, and to obstruct the SSV might be seen as a way of cheering on vice. The society was, in terms of the letter of the law – if not the spirit of the law – correct. The members said that the SSV was criticised only by those whom 'it deprives of sensual gratification in gin-shops and brothels – by those who delight in the prurient pleasures of a heated imagination'. You were either with them or against them; a friend to the suppressor or an ally of vice.[17]

Unfortunately for the SSV, the punishments that were set in the early seventeenth century for these kinds of offences had not kept pace with the times. A butcher or barber who was caught, tried and found guilty would get a fine of five shillings, and a publican ten: a lot in the seventeenth century, but no stringent penalty in the 1800s. The SSV complained that this amounted to a fairly cheap Sunday trading licence. The guilty could have their goods seized, but, as warrants were not issued on Sundays, this part of the law was nugatory. At best, the campaign was a way of naming and shaming – gibbeting butchers in front of the pious – not a vicious punishment for profaners. The godly members were even more annoyed by the recalcitrant attitude of some magistrates, who believed butchers' denials that selling meat on a Sunday morning before church 'could tend to the violation of public decency or morals'. Among the successful prosecutions there were some failures. In 1808 a keen member called Mr Mortimer, a virtuous Methodist gunsmith, brought several people before the sitting alderman for violating the Lord's Day. The first case to be tried, a barber, was dismissed and the man commended for ensuring that the poor who worked six days a week were clean-shaven on at least one day. The second defendant, a publican in Smithfield who opened his house on Sunday to refresh the drovers who had travelled for the Monday morning livestock market, was let off, and the alderman asked Mortimer if it was not good manners and Christian morality to feed the poor who were compelled to travel all day.[18]

Attempts to manipulate the law were becoming popular with some. In the parish of St Luke's, Shoreditch, a group of Methodists banded into a club like the SSV to prevent their religious sensibilities being injured by the nuisance of public houses opening on a Sunday. The informer told the Worship Street Police Court that he went into a public house on the City Road one Sunday at nine in the evening and – surprise, surprise – had positive sightings of men drinking pots of beer. The magistrate said that the Methodists would have to prove that the people 'were there for the purpose of tippling' rather than 'necessary refreshment'. This magistrate was reluctant to follow the Normans or the Puritans by condoning the vigilantism of a group of outraged killjoys and enforcing a de facto curfew on their less godly neighbours. But many other magistrates were not so good at hair-splitting and had to follow the letter of the law once such cases intruded into their courts. They fined reluctantly. The superannuated William Fielding, the son of Henry and a magistrate of fifty years' standing, said that 'if the same zeal was pursued in prosecuting thieves, more advantage would be derived to society. We have had our office loaded with miserable informations by a society of miserable sectaries, the penalty being only five shillings; and we could do no otherwise than impose the fines.'[19]

Sydney Smith ascribed the emergence of the SSV to the abatement of invasion scares during the short-lived Peace of Amiens. The death of one fear had to be replaced by another: 'What scenes of infamy did the Society for the Suppression of Vice lay open to our astonished eyes: tradesmen's daughters dancing, pots of beer carried out between the first and second lessons; and dark and distant rumours of indecent prints.' During the peace 'every plunderer of the public crawled out of his hole, like slugs, and grubs, and worms, after a shower of rain'.

The founders of the SSV were accused of having little fondness for morality itself, but every enthusiasm for impressing people in power.

Leigh Hunt believed that the vice suppressors set up their society and put on the garb of moral probity only because, 'the complexion of the present reign having given something of fashion to moral profusion and religious observance, they are of course religious and moral'. If the King had not issued his proclamation and been more like Charles II, no doubt they would attract attention by writing dirty, scabrous sonnets and brawling in Fleet Street taverns. *The Scourge* deplored 'the mischiefs that are likely to result from the exertions of men with whom undiscriminating enthusiasm, or the love of notoriety, overpowers every consideration of rational benevolence'. The society was 'a motley assemblage of the idle, the vain, the hypocritical, and the designing'; it was supported by a certain type: 'the lovers of bustle, the parasites of rank, and the proficients in the gossip and tittle tattle of public dinners, are all excited to become the members and directors of an institution in which the officiousness of petty vanity is mistaken for religious zeal, and to profess the enthusiasm of piety is to obtain its honours'.[20]

'I condemn the officious interference of your society,' wrote one anonymous critic in an open letter to a member of the SSV's General Committee. The increasing willingness of people to bully others whose behaviour they disapproved of represented, for many, an increasingly prominent feature of the age. Their meddlesome habits and interference in the pleasures of the people were seen as tyrannical and un-British. Hunt censured the tendency 'to frighten away the innocent enjoyments of the poor by dressing Religion in a beadle's laced hat and praying heaven to bless the ways of informers'. The bullying nature of the SSV and the obsessive veneration of the Sabbath reminded people of the days of Cromwell, 'and the puritanical cant which then and now lost sight of essentials, in its larger desire to remedy imaginary evils'.[21]

'The progress of ascetic fanaticism is deplorable,' Robert Southey wrote of the SSV: 'reason and cheerfulness sicken at its presence: the tongue whines an unintelligible jargon. . .' Many thought that the banner of anti-vice was a covert way of methodising the country. The members of the society and the evangelicals, many believed, both aimed at power, spiritual and temporal, like the saints of another century; both wanted to exert their power over their neighbours; both were backed 'by a vulgar, canting, and illiterate multitude'.[22]

The extent of their persecutory spite was matched only by the uselessness of the campaign, which seemed designed to trumpet *their* moral probity more than a genuine effort to actually reform a single man, woman or child. The whole thing seemed like a vapid set of religious mummeries with zero benefit, either intended or achieved. Sydney Smith said that enforcing conformity was doomed: 'You may drag men into church by main force, and prosecute them for buying a pot of beer, and cut them off from the enjoyment of a leg of mutton; and you may do all this till you make the common people hate Sunday, and the clergy, and religion, and everything which relates to such subjects.' But the SSV probably did not care much whether a rigidly enforced Sabbath made people religious or not. Alehouse frequenters, skittle players, butchers, Sunday promenaders and the like were probably unreformable. Compared with rooting out real vices, chasing butchers was a cheap panacea, requiring little effort. As long as the godly were not offended on their way to chapel by the sight of drunken workmen, the smell of meat roasting or noisy games of skittles, the commonalty could stew in their own vices at home.

The hundreds of butchers and barbers fined five shillings delighted the society but revealed the laughable futility of the campaign. Few of the 'guilty' gave up their Sunday trade; they paid the paltry fine and carried on. The people who might be accused of disregarding the Sabbath were those wealthy people who kept their godly subordinates from going to church by compelling them to work. Did they ever receive so much as an admonitory letter from the society? Of course not. The SSV might have professed otherwise, but its actions spoke louder than words: this was a movement set up to regulate and coerce the poor.[23]

The SSV's other campaigns were harder to criticise on these grounds. The society was on surer ground when it delved into the murky and not much discussed underworld of dirty bookshops and seedy ballad singers. Few would publicly defend obscene prints, erotic literature, the 'flash songs' that Francis Place recalled so clearly, or sex toys, but they were by and large tolerated. In 1802 there were no prosecutions for these kinds of offences, and the whole business was easy to see because no one made any effort to conceal it. It was a soft target; few would risk criticising the SSV, and the task itself was not too onerous. After all, the industry that produced lewd and blasphemous books was a 'powerful engine' which was part of 'a systematic design against the morals of the rising generation'.[24]

There was a sinister band of hawkers, the SSV said, who received cartloads of obscene material from their bosses in London. The filth was disseminated through the country by such pedlars visiting, in particular, girls' schools. When asked how he got in, one 'smiled, and significantly said, he knew how to get in'. It later turned out that the hawkers, many of them women, gained access to the schools by masquerading as second-hand clothes dealers. As was often the case in this kind of moral panic (it had occurred throughout the eighteenth century), neither the material nor the tradesmen originated in Britain; it was another foreign plot to poison the minds and morals of an entire generation of Britons. The danger was so acute that 'it is no longer safe to put any book into the hands of youth' unless it had been thoroughly checked first. The fact that the foreign hawkers were targeting girls' boarding schools was particularly worrying. 'If the female mind be thus easily familiarized to scenes of gross corruption, what security remains for domestic happiness or honour? or for the discharge of conjugal and matrimonial duties?'[25]

When it reported on its activities in 1804, the SSV would not describe the kinds of publications they had discovered in their witch-hunt; suffice to say they were 'the most corrupt device the morbid imagination of voluptuous sensuality ever yet conceived'. The members of the SSV were probably the last people to judge what was obscene. One of its reports quoted a sympathetic magistrate, who said that 'the mischief done to the community by such offences greatly exceeds that done by murder: for, in the latter case, the mischief has some bounds; but no bounds can be set to the pernicious consequences of a crime, which tends to the entire corruption of morals'. It showed a remarkable lack of perspective, added to alarmingly loose criteria for what was unacceptable. One of its descriptions of the kind of material it would hunt down was 'every thing that may tend to enflame the mind, and corrupt the morals, of the rising generation'.

The SSV ransacked circulating libraries, bemoaning that although the diffusion of knowledge might be beneficial, it was destroyed by the filth that found its way into the stock: 'It is a toilsome task to any virtuous and enlightened mind, to wade through the catalogues of these collections, and much more to select such books from them as have only an apparently bad tendency.' But the members protested too much. Trawling for filth was one of their favourite occupations.

During the wars the import market dried up, but the trade survived because there were so many prisoners of war in the country. In 1808 John Birtill of the Bristol branch of the SSV wrote to the General Committee, saying that he had walked out to a prisoners' market in Stapleton, where the captured soldiers and sailors were allowed to sell crafts they had made. Birtill was shocked to find that the prisoners had turned their talents to drawing obscene pictures. The market was at the end of a pleasant country walk, 'the promenade for the youth of both sexes of this city in fine weather, as well as the resort of strangers; so that the mischief is incalculable'. The prisoners, Birtill said, 'wished to obtrude on me a variety of devices, in bone and wood, of the most obscene kind, particularly those representing a crime, which ought not to be named among Christians, which they termed "*the new fashion*". I purchased a few, but they were too bulky for a letter; yet I will forward them if desired.'[26]

Thanks to the zeal of people like Birtill, the SSV had 'a considerable magazine of obscene books, upwards of 1200 obscene prints and drawings'. This treasure trove of immorality was kept secured in a tin chest with three different locks. The keys to this Pandora's box were held by the society's treasurer, its secretary and a member of the committee, 'so that the box can at no time be opened, but, with the concurrence of these three people'. Imagine the excitement of being one of these keyholders – to be aware every minute of the day of the heavy responsibility of being one of the custodians of the filth of the nation. The SSV would have been better keeping its activities secret; the solemn language with which it described its haul of obscenity only drew attention to a rather revealing prurient excitement. These high priests, with their secret meetings and keys, had made a ceremony out of voyeurism. Even the thought of having access, especially a restricted access, must have been a thrill in itself. The benighted schoolgirl would be corrupted by a glimpse of just one of the 1,200 prints; only a trio of vice suppressors in their sanctum could keep a cool head. But why did they need *three* locks? It says much for the power of the images, not to say the weakness of the members, that not even John Bowles could be trusted to be alone with the stockpile.[27]

The SSV's attitude to salacious material was at the heart of objections to the premise of its crusade. If one made a trade of vice hunting, how could one make a reasoned judgement? 'Beginning with the best intentions in the world,' Sydney Smith wrote, 'such societies must in all probability degenerate into a receptacle for every species of tittle-tattle, impertinence, and malice. Men whose trade is rat-catching love to catch rats; the bug-destroyer seizes on his bug with delight; and the suppressor is gratified by finding his vice.' People occupied with the self-imposed task of discovering depravity would quickly see a world of immorality and sin, invisible to the casual observer. Indeed, the very act of volunteering to seek out vice should be enough to disqualify someone as suitable for such a task. As one enemy of the SSV wrote, the idea of a group of people calling themselves 'the Good' was revolting. When they banded together in their meeting, they should adopt as their prayer 'Lord we thank thee we are not like other men.' Believing themselves to be at the pinnacle of human perfection, they were besotted with the idea that they could and should regulate the lives of the weak-minded. The meetings must have been a nauseous spectacle of self-congratulation; among certain people 'there is an excess of goodness, whose zeal assumes a right to persecute and nanny those, who may not have attained to the same degree of perfection'.[28]

It perhaps says a lot for the euphemism-ridden lewd literature and art, and the vagueness of the laws, that the SSV's campaign against the 800 or so people it claimed were disseminating obscenity round the country never really got off the ground. After two years of weekly meetings to coordinate the purge and a rapidly filling tin box, it had only identified seven offences perpetrated by five individuals, which, as one hostile writer put it, was laughable: 'of itself the severest satire upon their proceedings'. What revolted many people was the technique of the SSV: it would provide salacious material to a pedlar, and then have him arrested when he tried to sell it on. Southey believed that the society spent most of its efforts in this regard bullying booksellers who sold *Aristotle's Compleat Master Piece*, if only because it was so well known. Of course, they could have sent their informers to the elite bookshops frequented by the nobility and gentry, whence most dirty books and prints originated, but that would hardly have been in the style of the society.[29]

But if the SSV failed in suppressing the trade in obscene books, it was more successful in destroying the lewd ballad that had been such a feature of street life. Even so, it got to this campaign too late to get the full credit. Throughout the 1790s, in response to an increasingly radical press after the publication of Tom Paine's writings and reformist agitation, the government and loyalist organisations had attempted to wrest control of popular literature and ballads. Hannah More's *Cheap Repository Tracts* on sound moral topics had been distributed gratis, as had other improving pamphlets explaining the glories of the British constitution. The French Revolution had created huge anxiety about the effects of blasphemous, lewd and political propaganda on the minds of the people. Loyal publishers, printers, writers and private societies aimed to monopolise the market by distributing their prints and songs at a cheaper rate than the radicals.

Patrick Colquhoun had hoped that street balladeers would not sing dirty 'flash songs', but rather sing in praise of their king and country. Such a thing was realised, in a way. The popular songs of the late 1790s and 1800s ceased to be laudations of highway robbers and drunken prostitutes; the public taste switched to sea shanties and naval songs in the wake of a series of victories by British fleets. The authorities were no doubt relieved at these lusty patriotic songs, and they assisted the decline of the dirty ditty by giving away free ballads and promising the itinerant singers that they would not be punished for illegal singing if they sang about the *right* subjects. The SSV aided this already established movement from 1802, deploying its informers to report any balladeer who clung on to the dying culture.[30]

A society set up to suppress vice and crime was probably a good thing in theory, but the one the British got in the 1800s was attacked most readily for its 'petty anxieties and frivolous activity' and 'mis-directing their exertions in pursuit of chimerical, unattainable, or secondary objects'. There was plenty of vice and crime and misery that badly wanted correction or amelioration. 'We believe that in the hands of truly honest, intrepid, and above all discreet men, such a society might become a valuable institution,' Sydney Smith wrote. '. . . So many qualities, however, are required to carry it on well, – the temptations to absurdity and impertinence are so very great, – that we ever despair of seeing our wishes on this subject realized.' Robert Southey wrote that any campaign that relied on fear alone was 'the calvinistic scheme of a callous heart'. A society for the promotion of virtue would be the humane alternative: 'One honest labourer preserved in his old age from the poor house, and maintained in decent comfort, because he had laboured industriously, while his strength lasted, would operate as a more efficacious example than ten drunkards in the stocks. Charity is a cheap virtue; the expense of one prosecution would save twenty poor families for a twelvemonth from the sufferings and temptations of poverty.'

Indeed, the SSV promoted vice by employing informers and paying them to pry into people's lives. A person employed to undertake such a loathsome task and court the hostility of the neighbourhood would necessarily be the lowest and most corrupt, or corruptible, wretch. Encouraging common informers would create a nasty society, beset with self-serving, reward-seeking spies, intent on discovering vice for their own profit. Would this create genuine virtue or turn Britain into a nation of pedantic busybodies? 'To suppress vice and immorality is doubtless a desirable thing,' Southey wrote, 'but to attempt their suppression by encouraging a race of informers, is casting out devils by Beelzebub the prince of devils.'[31]

The Scourge was incensed that the SSV persecuted barbers and butchers, the miserable hawkers of mildly obscene books and bathers: 'Why do they not begin with Mother Griffiths of Suffolk-street, proceed to No. 38, Titchfield-street, and finish at the corner of Temple-bar?' It would be an unpleasant tour for the sensitive suppressors of vice, for these were notorious brothels with underage girls on offer. Between Haymarket and the 'Change were some five hundred prostitutes younger than thirteen. There was a difference between the pain of the godly who were bothered by labourers playing skittles on Sunday and 'the immature victims of lust and cruelty', the real sufferers of vice. 'Compared with the scene of depravity here exhibited, every one that has been brought to light by the society fades into insignificance.'[32]

The activities of the SSV and other similar organisations were bringing any reforming ideas into contempt. The combination of bad motives and puritanical zeal put many resolutely on the side of the poor against the meddlers. Indeed, what would happen if the SSV was taken seriously as the saviour of the nation? It would be emboldened to interfere in every aspect of life. Its members were seen as philistines who would wage a war against art and literature if ever they got a toe-hold into government. And the SSV was part of a wider campaign afloat to suppress immorality.

There were many who considered that some kind of centralised police force might be a solution to some of society's ills. But if there was the slightest danger that agents of the state, made up of people like Colquhoun, would have daily control over people and the ability to impose their brand of morality, they would rather take their chances with being mugged in the street or murdered in their beds. It would be like the Society for the Suppression of Vice armed and empowered by the state: the same itch to boss people about and control everything from how they spent their leisure time to whom they had sex with; the same evangelical zeal. People who were sensitive to the boisterous behaviour of the poor should not be put in charge of their morals; as R. Shaw said, '*real* evils may be experienced while attempting to get rid of *imaginary* or *trivial* ones'. If Colquhoun's plan was adopted, the police would become 'another society for the encouragement of puritanism on a large scale, and armed with the mace of overwhelming power'. The *Critical Review* said that 'instead of being made a salutary instrument of moral reform, [it would] be converted into a most dangerous engine of political oppression. We are not for arming ministers, and secretaries of state with more inquisitorial powers than they at present possess.' The traveller Christian Goede was impressed with Colquhoun's proposals and research, but realised that the British would never submit: it would mean the 'introduction of the Parisian system of *espionage* into English politics. No wonder, therefore, if John Bull revolts at the idea of an infringement of his darling liberty; and would rather suffer all other ills, than admit such an enemy to every blessing, public and private.'[33]

'A vexatious magistrate is a public curse,' said the *Monthly Magazine*. As it was, the country was over-regulated by the 'impertinence of pedantic superstitious disciplinarians. The police of the metropolis is already cautious, insulting, gloomy, and oppressive enough: without employing new ferrets to scrub the remaining pleasures out of their skulking-holes.' The magazine told a story of one pious magistrate who objected to boys playing cricket on Sunday, so he had the fields cleared of the nuisance. The boys, deprived of their weekly sport, sloped off to the public house instead. 'And shall such magistrates escape the reproach of being the corrupters of society? Moral intolerance is but too sure a symptom of real inhumanity of heart: and too sure a cause of brutalizing the multitude.'[34]

It was clear that the calls for reform came from certain groups of society motivated by unpopular religious principles and characterised by ignorance of the true condition of the poor and the cause of crimes. A real assault on criminality and vicious sexual practices (which would be a *real* service to the community) 'would require active intrepidity, and they content themselves therefore with attracting public attention to sculptured obscenity and terrifying the poor and industrious into starvation'. The members of the SSV were acting on less than pure motives. They wanted a reputation for virtue on the cheap, the applause of the world earned without much effort. Like so many other sinister or hypocritical people, members of the SSV or advocates of moral reform wore the garb of piety and benevolence either as a convenient way of salving their consciences or for some other ambition. Suppressing vice made up for the void of virtue in their souls.

Throughout the country the officious and nosy spirit of Colquhoun and the SSV was becoming all too real for people powerless to resist. The 'rage for meddling and over-regulating' was becoming a feature of the magistracy and parish officials. And Colquhoun could bask in praise that came from the very top. The Duke of Portland, the Home Secretary, wrote to him, passing on 'the satisfaction with which his Majesty observes your unremitting and zealous attention to all the objects which come within the scope of your official situation, and to the means of a system of morality and good order in the metropolis'. But for other less exalted people the new spirit of bigotry was a growing menace, and Colquhoun and the SSV would cause 'a further diffusion of this prudish political puritanism'.[35]

Patrick Colquhoun and John Bowles were attacked as being nothing more than quacks, great speculators on the marketplace of morality and pedlars of nostrums. Like Dr Solomon, they diagnosed a disease, convinced others that it was deadly and – lo and behold! – they had a cure to make it all better. It was a harsh comparison, but one which had an echo of truth. People like them, the *Examiner* said, were 'abettors of everlasting discord; they need it: the Anti-Jacobin needs war, the Suppressor needs vice; because their harvest can only exist in national corruption, profusion, and abuse'. There was also the feeling that many of the members were not concerned about the ends of the campaign but enjoyed the glow of sanctity they got from being a vice suppressor.

Those who championed moral reform would always be vulnerable to claims of rank hypocrisy, rightly or wrongly; but in the case of Bowles and Colquhoun there was some justification. Both were unashamed loyalists and friends to the government. The charge was that they were whipping up moral panic to enrich themselves and gain favour from the government. The SSV could be a valuable friend of the government, taking on the job of regulating the people. Cobbett said that the government believed that every time people grouped together in pursuit of their pleasures they would inevitably plot revolution and discuss politics; he called the SSV 'Anti-Jacobins, Anti-bull-baiters, Anti-boxers, Anti-revellers, and Anti-dancers, Anti-every thing that is calculated to draw the people together, and to afford them a chance of communicating their ideas; Anti-every thing which does not tend to abject subjection.'[36]

Included in the Home Office Papers at the Public Record Office are letters from both men to the Secretary of State. Had their existence been known at the time, Bowles and Colquhoun might have had reason to blush. The former believed that he had done enough work for the government to merit a plump sinecure. He was already a commissioner of bankrupts, with a salary of £3–400 per annum. In 1795 he wrote modestly to the Home Secretary: 'And though I can reflect with pleasure that motives far different from those of a selfish nature have ever stimulated my public conduct, I am most apprehensive that on that account an Administration like the present, should be the less disposed to honour one with marks of esteem. It is under these impressions, Sir, that I take the liberty of suggesting to you that I should be happy to be favoured with your nomination to the office of Register in Chancery to the Island of Barbadoes [*sic*], which I understand to be vacant.' He was not given the job he sought, but in the same year he was appointed one of five commissioners to manage £3,000,000 worth of Dutch cargo detained in British ports during the war. The fight for moral reform could evidently be a profitable trade.[37]

Patrick Colquhoun always felt neglected by the government. His great proposals were passed over by Home Secretaries and never implemented. He got more favour from the public, and as his status rose as a national figure, ministers began to take him more seriously. Like Bowles, in public he stressed his altruism, but in private he was keen to cash in on his work. In an extraordinary and prolix document he sent to the Home Office (which included pages of helpful appendices, detailing every piece of praise he ever received), he pointed out to the Home Secretary how much the country owed him. Written in the third person, it must be one of the most pompous and egregious statements of self-congratulation it has been the misfortune of any minister to receive.

'For upwards of twenty-five years', the document begins, 'Mr Colquhoun's life had exhibited a series of gratuitous public services.' It continues in much the same vein, telling the ministry of his tireless work, international fame and just why the country should honour him. He had, he constantly pointed out, worked 'without *fee or reward*', which was a pretty broad hint. It concluded by saying that he, Colquhoun, had saved lives and millions of pounds' worth of property, and set the poor on the course of reformation. But no reward was forthcoming. Colquhoun staked his fame on the adoption of his plans. His books magnified both the horrors and the extent of minor crimes for the purpose of making panicked people demand a police force. One journal called him a 'police-monger'; that was his product, and he was determined to find a buyer.[38]

Much of this was suspected but never proved. The members of the SSV were accused of bartering moral reform for public reward, but the confidential documents of the Home Office were not made public. However, in 1809 a scandal erupted that made sense of the extraordinary zeal of John Bowles.

Confronted with £3,000,000, the Dutch commissioners were entrusted with a heavy responsibility, one presumably thought best left to a body which included one of the foremost moral writers in the country. 'They were seated at a rich feast,' wrote William Cobbett, 'and having nobody to carve for them, they were, it appears, not such fools as to forbear from *helping themselves*.' With no auditory body to scrutinise their accounts, Bowles and his four friends acted like merchants in a market rather than government appointees. The Act of Parliament stipulated that the profits deriving from the Dutch cargoes should be invested in the Bank of England. However, the commissioners invested the money in their own banks and earned interest of £133,198 as their unofficial and unsanctioned personal commission.[39]

The fraud came to light in the spring of 1809, during the Mary Anne Clarke furore (see Chapter 6), when anxieties about peculation were running high. The response veered between disgust at Bowles's flagrant hypocrisy and ridicule at this pompous man's spectacular downfall. In Parliament, one MP quoted Bowles's strictures from his *Moral View of Society*: 'Consciousness has now not only lost its power to restrain men from crimes themselves, but even to excite indignation in others; and crimes not formerly tolerated now find advocates in persons laying claim to religious and virtuous characters.'

There were interesting opinions in Bowles's thirty-two pamphlets on the immorality of speculation and the degrading love of lucre. It was little surprise, therefore, that Bowles called people who demanded reform of the 'established order of things' 'traitors' and 'Jacobins' when the 'established order of things' paid such dividends. No wonder he advocated that the poor should, for their own good, remain poor, sacrifice their luxuries for the greater good and gladly watch their country prosper, when he skimmed the national wealth. But as the *Examiner* pointed out, he had no right to dole out savage punishments against poor people who stole to feed their families when he had for fourteen years 'unjustly fingered the Public Money, thereby increasing the overstrained burthens of a distressed people'. In the newspaper's opinion, 'a generation has grown up the educated slaves of the delusion' that vice and political opposition were linked; Bowles had single-handedly blasted that myth.[40]

The early years of the SSV had shown that there was very little appetite for moral reform. The society had given such a campaign a very bad name. It was hypocritical in its attitude to vices belonging to different classes; it mixed cruelty with ludicrousness. In 'English Bards and Scotch Reviewers', Byron mocked the SSV:

> Raise not your scythe, Suppressors of our Vice!
> Reforming Saints! too delicately nice!
> By whose decrees, our sinful souls to save,
> No Sunday tankards foam, no barbers shave;
> And beer undrawn, and beards unmown, display
> Your holy rev'rence for the Sabbath-day.

Most Britons preferred the wildness of popular culture, even if it was occasionally annoying; they liked their bawdy satires and rude jokes. Coarse and sometimes violent they may have been, but the sports and customs of the lower orders were the wild growths of a profuse plant; living in a free country meant taking the rough with the smooth and tolerating others. 'We ought to take care to preserve our national habits, manners, and customs,' said Justice Best. 'From the union of these has arisen our national spirit – our love of independence, of justice, and of our country. The true and only source of all our greatness and all our happiness. Wakes and amusements are amongst the customs, and are the fruits of our liberty. He who would destroy them, would make a change in our manners and habits, the extent of which we cannot see; and for the consequence of which, no good man would choose to answer.' The members might well have been sincere and well-intentioned, but their mode of operating made them seem hypocritical and selfish. The SSV established a connection between philanthropy and cant in the public mind.

There could not be much doubt as to whose vice was most in need of suppressing. After five years chasing Sunday tradesmen while promising a national crusade against immorality, the Society for the Suppression of Vice was in disgrace. A couple of months before Bowles tarnished its reputation, Sydney Smith had launched a blistering attack on its activities and motivation in the *Edinburgh Review*. In it, he had suggested that the members of the SSV had joined 'to hide a bad character' or 'to recommend themselves to their betters by a sedulous and bustling inquisition into the immoralities of the public'. What might have seemed like a hostile overreaction was vindicated when the Bowles scandal rocked the SSV. Its activities would be scaled down over the years, its members by now aware that it had lost whatever public sympathy it might have had. It would take a long time to recover from the disgrace brought upon it by its leading member. Bowles was finally found guilty ten years later, in 1819, the year he died all but forgotten.[41]

'Oh John Bowles! John Bowles!' lamented *The Times* with mock heartbreak when it learnt of the man's crimes and true character. 'Little did we think when we were unwittingly inserting thy paragraphs *against jacobins and levellers*, how much thy loyalty was warmed by considerations like these . . . Oh John Bowles! John Bowles!'[42]

5

Too Strong for Law

'The higher ranks of society are to be considered as the fountain, whence the living manners of the time derive their origin . . . Reformation must begin with the great, or it will never be effectual. Their example is the fountain whence the vulgar draw their habits, actions, and character.'

Philippus Philaretes, *Adultery Analyzed* (1810)[1]

'. . . this earth supports not a more criminal or more detestable race of beings than the whole tribe of seducers; and, surely, the petty thief who dies upon the gallows, is indeed a man of honour compared with them.'

John Scott, sermon on 'The Fatal Consequences of Licentiousness'[2]

'. . . very few husbands love their wives; and I confess, the moment one is obliged to marry any person it is enough to render them hateful.'

Caroline, Princess of Wales[3]

On 6 March 1809 Lady Charlotte Wellesley threw on her cloak and left her home. She was, according to her servants, agitated and nervous; she left in such a hurry that her cloak was inside out. Her overwrought emotions and haste were put down to a fearsome row she had just had with her husband, the Hon. Henry Wellesley MP. She needed to calm her nerves and cool her head; a solitary walk in Green Park would see to that. Lady Charlotte left her maid at the gate and proceeded into the park on her own. The maid waited, but her mistress failed to return.

His wife's sudden disappearance must have shocked Henry Wellesley; but, when it was clear that she would not return, he had no doubt where she had gone. The couple had enjoyed a good enough marriage until recently, and the age gap did not seem to have mattered: he was thirty-eight and she twenty-eight. The row, in any case, concerned an older man, their family friend Henry, Lord Paget, the eldest son of the Earl of Uxbridge. While Wellesley was occupied in the

House of Commons or with his political work, his wife and Paget had begun to spend time together, and their friendship developed into an intense relationship.

It was natural that the Wellesley and Paget families should get on so well. They were among the most talented Tory families in the country, active as soldiers, diplomats and statesmen. Lieutenant-General Lord Paget, a supremely talented soldier and MP, and a renowned dandy, commanded the cavalry in the Peninsular campaign, and his brother Sir Arthur Paget had served as the British ambassador in Vienna and the Ottoman Porte. Henry Wellesley was a politician, and at this point in his career Secretary to the Treasury. His brother, Sir Arthur Wellesley, was one of Britain's foremost generals.

Lady Charlotte had, it seemed, remained faithful to her husband, to whom she appeared to be devoted. But Paget was struggling with temptation. He was married to Lady Caroline, a daughter of the Earl and Countess of Jersey, with whom he had eight children; but as Dallas, his attorney, would say: 'In the midst of all this seeming prosperity, this apparent over-flowing of human happiness, a dreadful attachment was gathering and growing and twining, like a serpent, around his heart.' Lady Charlotte was also falling for her husband's friend. 'The veil, however, was at length removed, and the parties became aware of their true situation. They saw and shuddered at the possibility of approaching guilt, and determined to withdraw themselves, while there was still time, from the impending ruin: their first resolution was never to meet again.' And so they stuck to it; Lady Charlotte devoted herself to her family and religion, but 'they were not sufficient; in the midst of her penitence, in the midst of her adoration, the idea of Lord Paget was ever present in her mind'. Paget had no choice but to throw himself back into his military career, 'quitting the voluptuous pleasures of this luxurious capital' for the front against Napoleon in Spain.

Again, according to his splendidly hyperbolic attorney, Paget was single-minded in trying to efface the memory of Lady Charlotte: 'Careless of his safety, prodigal of his life, he seemed to search for danger wheresoever it was to be found; and to hunt after death in whatever shape it might occur.' He wasn't suicidal, whatever Dallas might have said; he already had the reputation for leading his cavalry from the front. When he returned in triumph to London in 1809, his attractiveness to Lady Charlotte must have been magnified. The soldier's return opened up an old wound between the Wellesleys. Sure enough, Henry Wellesley was correct in his suspicions: after she abandoned her maid, his wife had taken a hackney carriage to Uxbridge House, Paget's family home.

The row between Henry and Charlotte had been brewing for some time, and her flight was premeditated. Paget had expected and feared that the affair would culminate in something like this. It was a decision, however understandable it might seem to us now, which would ruin her for ever: there could be no going back from the moment she left the park. Paget, knowing that it would destroy him too, made an equally difficult decision to protect Lady Charlotte. The press learnt immediately of the affair. The *Examiner* said that Paget deserved 'to be hunted out of society like a wild beast'. That he could have done such a thing was the fault of scandalously lenient laws; if sentences were tougher and men like Paget were punished with prison or the pillory, 'then neither the Peasant, the Peer, nor the Prince, would contrive thus to outrage the best feelings of humanity, and violate the prime source of happiness – domestic tranquillity'.

It was Lady Charlotte's brothers and Paget's family who were most offended by her elopement. Whereas the politician Wellesley bit his lip and remained silent for the moment, Lord Uxbridge threatened to disinherit his son and heir, and Lady Charlotte's brother, Colonel Henry Cadogan, offered to 'sell out of the army in order entirely to devote himself to her protection', if she first agreed to leave Paget. She refused, so he challenged Lord Paget to a duel to 'obtain satisfaction for the injury done myself and my whole family by your conduct to my sister'. Paget's reply, declining the duel, was simple and moving:

March 30 1809

. . . I have nothing to say in justification of my conduct towards your sister, but that it has been produced by an attachment perfectly unconquerable.

She has lost the world upon my account; and the only atonement I can make is to devote myself not to her happiness (which with her feeling mind is, under the circumstances, impossible,) but to endeavour, by every means in my power, to alleviate her suffering. I feel, therefore, that my life is her's [*sic*], not my own . . .

. . . My cause is bad indeed; but my motive for acting thus is good . . .

. . . I have the honour to be, Sir, your obedient servant,

Paget

The letter infuriated Colonel Cadogan. Paget's justification that he had acted out of love was the worst excuse, and his promise to sacrifice everything for Lady Charlotte added insult to injury in the topsy-turvy world of family honour. Cadogan said that Paget had made 'the very injury for which I demanded satisfaction his reason for not meeting me'. Lady Charlotte could not deal with her husband, or even her brother, who was acting on behalf of Wellesley and had offered her the chance to return home. She wrote indirectly, addressing it to Charles Arbuthnot, whom she asked to thank Henry for 'his most kind and generous offer of taking home a wretch who has so much injured him'. She continued: 'degraded and unprincipled as I must appear in the eyes of every body, believe me I am not lost to all sense of honour . . . if you knew all, you would pity more than blame me'. She had, she said, tried to resist 'this criminal, most atrocious attachment', but whereas she enjoyed cordial relations with her husband, she was in love with Paget.

> About my dear, dear children [she continued], I must say one word. Do you think I dare hope, by any remote or indirect means, to hear some times of them; you know how much I love them! You are aware of their merits, and what I must feel at having quitted them; but I have the satisfaction, the inexpressible comfort of knowing they will be taken care of by their father, though their mother has abandoned them. My dear little Henry and Charles – Oh! God bless you!

Wellesley agreed to let Lady Charlotte see her three boys and daughter – on two conditions. The first, that she never have any connection with Paget again; the second, that she return home immediately. Lady Charlotte sacrificed everything to remain with Paget.

Paget eventually relented to the incessant demands for a duel, but only after he had proved that his intentions were honourable by buying Lady Charlotte a house and settling an annuity on her. It was unlikely that they could ever marry in Lady Paget's lifetime; under English law, Parliament could not grant a divorce unless the wife had committed adultery, which was not the case. This time it was another Cadogan, George, aide-de-camp to Sir Arthur Wellesley, who called out Paget. The brother and the lover met at Wimbledon Common on 30 May. Cadogan took aim first but missed his sister's lover. Paget then carelessly fired his pistol, missing Cadogan by some distance. Cadogan accused Paget of further insulting his honour by refusing to shoot him. Paget said 'that nothing would ever induce me to add to the injuries I have already done the family, by firing at the brother of Lady Charlotte Wellesley'. The Cadogan brothers must have been apoplectic with rage at Paget's continued devotion to their sister.

The House of Uxbridge was in disgrace. For all Lord Paget's sense of honour and concern to protect Lady Charlotte, he had made himself one of the most unpopular men in the kingdom. And the family had form. The year before, Paget's younger brother Sir Arthur had eloped with Augusta, Countess of Borringdon (Sir Arthur had previously led a scandalous life in Vienna and eloped with the Duke of Bedford's cook). Lady Borringdon was 'long the envied boast of her own, and the toasted belle among the other sex'; Sir Arthur, a handsome soldier-diplomat, was captivated when he saw her portrait, and the pair began an affair, Bedford's cook now forgotten. When the Earl of Borringdon, himself a philanderer, ordered her to leave her lover and retire to the country, the countess left her husband and her children.

Sir Arthur, like Lord Paget, was a glittering star in high society, having served his country in Europe and Asia. Lord Borringdon, though handsome and intelligent, had opted for a career of less conspicuous duty, first as an MP and a colonel in the military, then as a diligent member of the House of Lords. Sir Arthur's elopement differed from his older brother's, for he actually went to the Borringdons' home and left with the lady in a premeditated flight.[4]

The Paget brothers' behaviour amused and outraged the public at a time when there was a moral panic over the standards of the aristocracy. One of the first consequences of the French Revolution in Britain was to bring the aristocracy flooding into church. The revolutionary menace of the 1790s and the war only made their moral amendment seem more urgent. 'The French Revolution illustrates the connection between good morals and the order and peace of society more than all the eloquence of the pulpit and the dissertations of moral philosophers had done for many centuries,' commented the *Annual Review*. So, if there was nothing new in the abhorrence of divorce and adultery or the vice of the aristocracy, there was now an added urgency for self-reform, not to say a powerful reason for being seen to be virtuous.[5]

'There was needed some reformer of the nation's morals, who should raise his voice in the high places of the land,' wrote Wilberforce's sons; 'and do within the church, and near the throne, what Wesley had accomplished in the meeting, and among the multitude.' Many of the upper class disdained the fervid enthusiasm of Wesleyan Methodists and saw conspicuous piety as something beneath them. Wilberforce, however, was the perfect advocate for reform. He was no wild-eyed enthusiast but a charming and amusing man, good in company and closely associated with the King, William Pitt and the aristocracy. He had a 'hidden seriousness' when in polite society that did not embarrass anyone. 'Mr Wilberforce', remarked Madame de Staël, 'is the best converser I have met with in this country. I have always heard that he was the most religious, but I now find that he is the wittiest man in England.'[6]

'My walk I am sensible is a public one,' Wilberforce said; 'my business is in the world; and I must mix in assemblies of men, or quit the post which Providence seems to have assigned me.' And that task which providence had set him, alongside the abolition of slavery, was the reformation of manners, starting with his class. If the Proclamation Society and the Society for the Suppression of Vice were set up to coerce the poor into something resembling good conduct, the upper class were not without their reformers. The pressure to conform could not be so intrusive, although existing laws were used to restrain their more licentious passions.

From the crisis of the Revolution there was a marked earnestness among many of the upper class, and at least a self-induced pressure to be seen as worthy guardians of the country. Wilberforce's version of moral reform did not suggest that the rich were excluded from heaven, as some revivalists maintained; their wealth and power were ordained by God. Any sacrifice the upper class might make would not trench upon their rank and riches or alter the hierarchy; rather it would augment their power by staving off revolution and checking 'the further progress of a gangrene, which is eating at the vital principles of our social and political existence'. Hannah More, in her *Thoughts on the Importance of the Manners of the Great to General Society*, which was widely popular with 'the great', wrote: 'Reformation must begin with the GREAT, or it will never be effectual. *Their* example is the fountain from whence the vulgar draw their habits, actions and characters. To expect to reform the poor while the opulent are corrupt, is to throw odours into the stream while the springs are poisoned.' They must give the appearance at least of virtue, or the crime would reverberate with increased volume down through society, making more likely that which they dreaded.[7]

Wilberforce, like More, urged members of the upper class to regulate their lives and follow the evangelical example in supporting good works, even if they were not genuinely moved by the religious spirit. Wilberforce said that the punishment of small crimes would be better than attacking greater ones, because the effort of repressing petty flaws would affect the general conduct. There did not have to be a wholehearted conversion. His moral reform started with 'regulating the external conduct', which may not be genuine but it at least removed 'the obtrusiveness of the temptation, that it may not provoke the appetite, which might otherwise be dormant and inactive'. Wilberforce offered the ruling class an easy way to amend their morals, and one which found favour.[8]

Sexual shenanigans were the most obvious way in which the upper class corrupted the morals of their inferiors. In the 1800s there were several papers and journals which attempted to complement Wilberforce and More's carrot of self-reform with a bludgeon. George Manners' *Satirist* and later Hewson Clarke's *Scourge* lifted the lid on the seamy world of upper-class sexual depravity in an attempt to shame the rulers of the country into a semblance at least of morality. Adultery, according to Manners, was 'one of the most flagrant crimes that could be committed by man'. He noted with approval the treatment of adulterers in pre-Christian Poland, who were 'nailed by the offending member to the market place; a razor was placed within their reach, and they were thus compelled either to perish in that situation, or to do justice to themselves'. If few advocated castration, many wanted adulterers to be pilloried or whipped or hounded from society. In the years 1807–9, the number of divorces had reached an unusually high level. An open letter to Parliament advocated stringent measures against the highest of the land: 'A whipping of a *Noble* Lord from Temple Bar to Charing Cross, would let out not only the foul blood in his veins, but would correct the hot blood of those gross sensualists.' Soundly whipped, the offending seducer should then be banished to Botany Bay. Lord Auckland, the foremost enemy of divorce and adultery, told the peers in 1809 that 'the frequency of Divorce Bills in the present session has been to me a subject of much pain and indignation. This frequency is an evil of the first magnitude, affecting the character of the higher ranks of society, and contaminating the morals of every class of the United Kingdom.'[9]

From the late eighteenth century there had been 'solemn calls upon the legislature' from evangelicals and high churchmen alike to change the law. As an anonymous moraliser wrote in an open letter to the

Home Secretary, Spencer Perceval, in 1801 (when the pressure to reform the law was at its height), adultery had been common in past ages, but in the nineteenth century '*deep and general corruption*' had infected the land, made worse because it was concealed by the polish acquired in the 'age of refinement'. When Perceval became Prime Minister in 1809 it was thought that reform of the law would be inevitable. An Adultery Prevention Bill had been passed in the Lords in 1800 but had been thrown out by the Commons. With an evangelical prime minister working with a moralising House of Lords and a pious king, however, the bill could be resurrected and pushed through the Commons. Perceval was likely to agree with Wilberforce, speaking in the Commons on the subject of adultery and divorce: 'I consider this subject of much more importance than any question about peace or war, or any constitutional question . . . [for] if the crime is suffered to go unchecked, nothing could have a greater tendency to destroy the whole fabric of society.'[10]

The best means of curtailing upper-class adultery, it was considered, was to make it illegal for a wife to marry the man who had seduced her. This was what underpinned the Lords' bill. The lords and bishops thought that a woman of their class had an affair only because she believed that she could obtain a divorce and marry the man who had cajoled her away from her husband. The Paget brothers' behaviour seemed to illustrate this point. Lady Charlotte Wellesley and Lady Borringdon might have remained chaste if they thought that their infidelity would utterly ruin them. As it was, many believed that they had indulged their passions because they believed that they would marry a Paget. As the Bishop of London said: 'Many a woman would never consent to the commission of the crime of adultery, were it not for the expectation of afterwards being married to her seducer, and then perhaps being introduced into a gayer situation of life than that in which she was formerly placed.'[11]

The enemies of divorce spoke as if it was the easiest thing in the world for an aristocrat to marry and remarry at will. Auckland called divorce bills 'a code of adultery for a privileged caste'. Passing an act of divorce through Parliament was very expensive and therefore available only to a tiny elite. Whereas other couples had to remain married, the wealthy could cast off their spouses whenever their sexual passions were aroused. But Lord Paget paid a vast price for doing exactly what moral parliamentarians would make illegal. He chose to protect the woman he had seduced and the lengths to which he went to do this were protracted, complicated and ruinously expensive; the only certainty was that Lady Charlotte would be ostracised from polite society and he would have to terminate his glittering career. The easy option would have been to have seduced and abandoned a servant maid. His case was an exception; as Mr John Bastard MP pointed out, if adulterous couples were *compelled* to marry when they were caught, adultery would virtually disappear.[12]

The *crime* of adultery had different meanings and punishments for both the sexes. 'The wound which a woman suffers by her husband's offence is only skin deep; but an unchaste wife, by her adultery, casts an indelible stain in her own offspring; and her society is avoided by the chaste part of her own sex.' Or, as one writer put it, 'Female libertinism, especially of married women, is, beyond controversy, the crying sin of these eventful times.' The law was based on this assumption. The errant wife should lose all privileges, income and rights to see her children, and any property she brought to the marriage would remain with her ex-husband. The last thing people like Auckland or the bench of bishops wanted was for couples to trick the courts or the House of Lords into granting divorces on feeble grounds. They had to be on their guard lest married people colluded to dissolve marriages they were bored with or wanted to end simply to marry someone else. Once divorce became easy and discreet the whole institution of marriage would break down. An absolute divorce could only happen by act of Parliament, and the Lords would only pass such an act after rigorous examination of the circumstances and after other courts had weighed the evidence. The process demanded detailed evidence of adultery on the woman's part.[13]

The first step in the tortuous process of divorce was to get a verdict from the ecclesiastical court. It could grant a verdict *a mensa et thoro*, a separation 'from bed and board'. A woman could only get a divorce if her husband had shown excessive cruelty or deserted her. The most common divorce proceeding was a husband ridding himself of a wife, ostensibly to protect his reputation and estate from the threat of children not his own. Such a verdict often involved collusion, if both man and woman wanted a divorce, because under the rule of recrimination a husband could not separate from a wife if he was also guilty of infidelity. A woman would not present evidence of her husband's infidelity but would allow her name to be blackened so that the separation would be granted. Lady Borringdon, like many women in similar situations, kept tight-lipped about Lord Borringdon's numerous amours for the sake of being granted a separation by the Church. The next step, before the lords could be presented with a divorce bill, was for the wronged husband to sue his wife's lover for 'criminal conversation' (crim. con.). This was a civil suit for damages, compensating cuckolded husbands for the loss of the comforts of matrimonial life. Often a couple remained married after a crim. con. case, having pocketed a large cheque, but it was also a preliminary to divorce proceedings. The verdict established the fact of the wife's adultery before the House of Lords got to consider the case. This stage made collusion less attractive, for the compensation commonly awarded was so outrageous that none but the most ardent lover would voluntarily put himself through it.[14]

Crim. con. trials were one of the most popular subjects for Fleet Street. They were a chance to publish intimate details about the nobility – everything from the tittle-tattle of high-society life to the way in which they conducted their affairs. The editor of the compendium of crim. con. trial reports *The Annals of Gallantry*, who wrote under the barely amusing pseudonym of A. Moore, said that such trials were enjoyed because each one was 'a love story, purified from grossness'. Whether amusing or romantic, crim. con. trials satisfied a prurient craving to learn about goings-on in high society. They were also good reads because the lawyers who represented the nobility were the best of their profession. The euphemistic and flowery language they were forced to adopt for the sake of decency was an art form. Moral legislators were torn between two conflicting requirements. On the one hand, they wanted as much shame and punishment to be heaped on malefactors as possible; on the other, they were concerned to protect public morality. Crim. con. trials certainly embarrassed everyone involved, but in doing so the public was given a full dose of titillation. In reality the incidence of adultery and divorce was relatively low. But as Louis Simond wrote, the indecent testimonies of servant girls in crim. con. trials gave the entire aristocracy a bad name, and the reports of the trials 'calumniate the higher ranks of society, as the celebrated book of Mr Colquhoun calumniates the lower'.[15]

Crim. con. trials were such extraordinary affairs because the damages were set at extravagant levels. An aristocrat who debauched a woman would commonly expect to pay compensation to her husband of between £5,000 and £10,000. The jury took two things into account when they set damages. The first was the loss that a husband had suffered, or, put another way, the cash value of a wife before she was seduced. The second was the punishment due to an errant aristocrat that would serve as a deterrent to other well-heeled rakes. Depending on who debauched one's wife, the rewards for dragging one's affairs through the mud could be well worth the effort. The courtier and novelist Lady Charlotte Bury was amazed at the premise and the frequency of actions crim. con.: 'how can *gold* be a compensation for wounded honour? . . . to take a *price* for an injury is a cowering mean idea, that could obtain currency from its being part of that system of trade upon which hang our law'. As Simond recorded, cuckolds sued regardless of embarrassment: 'The husband pockets this money without shame, because he has the laugh on his side.' When awards could amount to £10,000, it was the seducer who became the object of ridicule for his rash folly.[16]

Both Paget brothers admitted guilt by suffering verdicts by default, sparing the raking up of harmful details. They did not contest the fact of adultery but instructed their attorneys to give as much detail of the affairs as possible in the hope that the jury would not set vast exemplary damages. With so much at stake, crim. con. trials were notorious for the sickening hypocrisy and barefaced lies that the lawyers had to utter. The defendant, if he could not deny that he had seduced the plaintiff's wife, was obliged to present the object of his attentions as a low, debauched, corrupted woman who was worthless to the world, let alone to her sorry husband. The plaintiff, in order to secure a high payout, had to present his marriage as an unending saga of joyous love and his unfaithful wife as the best and most innocent woman in the world before the wicked seducer got his grubby hands on her. Lawyers who specialised in crim. con. were among the best performers in the country, with the ability to present a seedy, broken-down marriage as a festival of conjugal bliss and devotion.

One of the most infamous crim. con. cases in the 1800s was that of *Jesse Gregson v. Thomas Theaker*. Theaker was accused of adultery with Mrs Gregson, the wife of Jesse, a respectable solicitor from Leytonstone, Essex. Mrs Gregson was 'much addicted to liquor' and was well known to have betrayed her husband whenever opportunity allowed; yet her husband valued her charms and comforts, of which Theaker had deprived him, at £10,000. Theaker's lawyer said of Mrs

Gregson that she was of a profligate disposition, and 'in addition to every other failing, she was a drunkard, and though her beauty might surpass even poetic fiction, I would ask, what is the society of such a woman worth? What has the plaintiff lost?' The plaintiff's lawyer, however, was forced to claim that the Gregsons' married life was 'one continued scene of conjugal happiness'. It was clear to everyone that Gregson was in it for the money and did not deserve any compensation for a wounded heart. But what made this case unusual was that the man he hoped to take £10,000 from was not a predatory aristocrat but his coachman.

The trial was enjoyed because, unlike most other crim. con. cases, the plaintiff produced evidence of actual sexual activity rather than the usual guarded circumstantial details. A servant on the staircase had heard Mrs Gregson from a room 'call "Thomas" *in a very low tone of voice*'. The servant then climbed the stairs, where she 'heard the sofa moving, and a soft kind of breathing, for some minutes . . . I am a married woman, and have no doubt but there was a criminal connection between Gregson and the Defendant at that time.' Lord Chief Justice Ellenborough, who was presiding over the trial, interrupted her gratuitous observations: 'I suppose there is not a human being who can have any doubt.'

The defence did not deny that sex had taken place but did deny that Theaker had lured Mrs Gregson 'from the paths of virtue and honour'; she was too far gone in vice to need any encouragement. Ellenborough agreed and said that Mrs Gregson was 'a most abandoned woman . . . influenced by the impulse of unconquerable lust,' and acquitted the coachee of debauching his mistress: 'Seduction could not come from a person whose rank was so unequal to her own.' But Theaker was partly to blame because he had relented to Mrs Gregson's 'profligate desires'. The jury should punish the defendant because servants had a solemn duty to resist 'the licentious and depraved appetites' of their employers and, more than that, actually protect their masters and mistresses from immorality. The jurors, no doubt masters of coachmen themselves, agreed that servants should be better than their employers and able to resist the advances of the ladies of the house, and set compensation for the ruin of the nymphomaniac alcoholic Mrs Gregson at £200. Although small in comparison to most other crim. con. settlements, it would have hit Theaker as hard as the £10,000 an aristocrat would have to pay.[17]

A few weeks later, Jesse Gregson took his friend McTaggart to court for seducing his wife previous to the Theaker incident, and accused him of degrading her to the extent that she would 'submit to the embraces of her coachman'. Sick of Gregson's determination to profit from his wife's moral character, wise to the true value of Mrs Gregson, but legally obliged to compensate the husband, the jury set damages at one shilling.[18]

The Gregson case is an extreme one, but is an example of how these trials worked. In *Massy v. Headfort* (1804) all the contrivances of defence and plaintiff were put on full display. The Rev. Charles Massy and his wife had been married for eight years and lived in Limerick, when the Marquis of Headfort came to visit his mother, who lived near by. Mrs Massy was twenty-three, her husband a little older, and Headfort was fifty. The woman, clearly bored with life in rural Limerick and attracted to London high life, ran off with Headfort when Massy was conducting Sunday service. Charles Massy sued Headfort for £40,000 compensation in what was the first crim. con. trial to be held in Ireland.

The marquis instructed his lawyers to present the Massys' marriage as a sham and Mrs Massy as a depraved harridan. Charles Massy's lawyers had to show that the woman was pure and innocent until the heartless aristocrat stole her from her loving husband. The truth, however, was that at the time of the trial Mrs Massy was living with Headfort, and the Rev. Massy was hungry for a big payout. Headfort allowed himself to be presented as the dupe of a scheming harlot (one, indeed, who was so skilled at her deceptions that they were still living together many years later). Was such a woman worth £40,000? Was not the fact that she was depraved enough to elope proof that she was worthless as a wife and lover? Headfort further accused the reverend of being a complacent husband who let his wife gallivant about Limerick with young soldiers and in the end connived in her flight. Massy should, if he was being honest, have offered to sell his wife in the first place rather than demand retrospective payment.

With £40,000 hanging in the balance, the case attracted the best lawyers in Ireland. The jury was being asked to decide between two equally dubious versions of events, and it would sympathise with whichever side managed to capture its minds and emotions. Fortunately for the Rev. Massy, he had the greatest of Irish orators, John Philpot Curran, summing up his case. Curran agreed with the defence; Mrs

Massy was worth next to nothing now. But that was not the point; the jury had to decide her value 'when she sat basking in a husband's love, with the blessing of heaven on her head, and its purity in her heart'. But the most devastating part of Curran's summing up was his attack on the Marquis of Headfort. 'What are your inducements?' the lawyer spat. 'Is it love, think you? No, – do not give that name to any attraction you can find in the faded refuse of a violated bed. Love is a noble and generous passion, it can be founded only on a pure and ardent friendship.' Headfort had degraded Mrs Massy; she was his 'victim'. By eloping with her, he had rendered her worthless; now she was no better than a prostitute: 'You found her a fair and blushing flower, its beauty and its fragrance bathed in the dews of heaven. Did you so tenderly transplant it, as to preserve that beauty and fragrance unimpaired? Or did you so rudely cut it, as to interrupt its nutriment, to waste its sweetness, to blast its beauty, to bow down its faded and sickly head? And did you at last fling it like "a loathsome weed away"?'

For all Curran's hammy declamations, it was a masterful speech in the circumstances: Mrs Massy was a poor, innocent Irish flower, and Headfort a marauding metropolitan aristocrat intent on despoiling the land. The jury was invited to see Mrs Massy as the representative of all powerless women who might be swept off their feet by dastardly aristocrats: the jurors should think of their wives and daughters. As it was, the jurors were asked to choose between two versions of Mrs Massy. There was no *real* evidence because Mrs Massy was enjoying the company of the marquis far away in England. They would naturally believe the best-painted portrait presented to them in the court. Curran, with all his skills on display, won hands down.

Baron Smith, the trial judge, told the jury that unfortunately they could not punish the fact of adultery and that *no* value could be placed on the loss of a wife. So, in that case, the only thing that could determine the damages was a sum that they felt sufficiently reflected the harm done to public morality. In other words, Mrs Massy's cash value had nothing to do with their verdict, nor did the mitigating factors Headfort claimed render the reverend's case void, despite the fact that that was what the law asked the jury to determine. The jury was there to nail up an adulterer as a public warning. If the jury had scruples about treating the rich and poor differently, it should, Smith said, consider this: 'Virtue is far from being peculiar to the higher ranks; but there is, perhaps, a delicacy of sentiment, and punctilio of honour engendered by the refined habits which belong to opulence and distinction, and which sharpen the sting of such an injury as this.'

The jury did exactly as the judge said they should. It did not agree to Massy's compensation claim – it did not want to reward his negligence – and it did not let Headfort off. The marquis was ordered to pay Massy damages of £10,000; it was intended as a fine for adultery, not compensation or a reflection of Mrs Massy's worth. For the jurors, the facts of the case presented by the defence and the plaintiff did not matter a jot; they wanted to punish a crime. The judge said, and it was accepted by jurors in many other such cases who were willing to act as a kind of moral police, that when it came to fixing compensation juries 'should be liberal, to a degree bordering on prodigality and profusion, for the benefit of public example, and the protection of public morals'.[19]

Lord Paget was thus placed in a difficult position. Other men in similar situations, notably Headfort, by employing lawyers to heap slander on the women they loved had reduced the damages. Paget's lawyers could have attempted to show that Lady Charlotte was depraved, heartless and hence worthless to Henry Wellesley, but Paget would not do that to her. Instead Dallas had to go for a risky strategy. He had to persuade the jury that Paget was an honourable and sincere man who had been overcome by his emotions. His defence was therefore full of rhetoric about how a brave soldier was rendered powerless by love; how hard Paget had struggled with his passion; and the lengths he had gone to in order to avoid Lady Charlotte before she flung herself at his door. From that moment he could not act otherwise, and therefore sacrificed his military career and his marriage to protect the unfortunate female.

'Will it be said that, there was such a blaze of beauty encircling this lady, that he could not resist the flame?' Henry Wellesley's barrister asked. 'This might have had some weight in the case of a very young man: but it will be recollected, that Lord Paget was the father of eight children; that he had a wife of his own, an estimable and valuable woman, to whom all his affections and tenderness ought to have been addressed, and to whom they ought to have been confined.' It was beholden on a nobleman and a general in His Majesty's service more than anyone else to show moral restraint and set a good example to society. The same was true of his brother, Sir Arthur, who had been successfully sued by Lord Borringdon for £10,000.

The jury in Lord Paget's case was not prepared to judge the case on its merits. The power of love was no excuse, and the punishment should reflect the damage he had done to society by failing to restrain his passions. Because he protected Lady Charlotte and because he had acted honourably, the compensation became greater. Clearly, the woman in this case was worth more than a Mrs Massy given the honourable behaviour of Paget. For this he received one of the harshest punishments given by a jury in a civil suit. Wellesley was compensated to the tune of £20,000. For some this was not enough; one writer said that crim. con. cases should be public not private prosecutions and a man as odious as Paget should be punished by something worse than a mere fine.[20]

Paget knew that this would happen from the moment the affair began; it was the price that society demanded for his 'crime'. And he also knew that he could not marry Lady Charlotte. The Borringdons, however, obtained a divorce by act of Parliament on the grounds of the lady's adultery, allowing both parties to remarry; the Countess of Borringdon became Lady Augusta Paget two days after the Bill of Divorce was passed in the Lords. Wellesley divorced Lady Charlotte by the same means, but the House of Lords would not allow the Pagets to divorce, as Lady Paget had not committed adultery and she did not want to relinquish her marriage vows.

There was one outside chance that the affair could turn out right, but it was entirely dependent on Lady Paget's willingness to allow Lady Charlotte to supplant her. As it was, she did not want to see her rival become a countess when Paget inherited the earldom of Uxbridge. When Paget had given up hope, the tale took an unexpected turn. In October 1810 the *Morning Chronicle* reported that 'Lord P and Lady P and Lady AW have all *by pure accident* taken up their residence lately in Scotland', or as a puzzled Louis Simond, who was visiting Edinburgh at the time, wrote: 'Some persons of rank have come here lately on purpose to effect very odd transfers of matrimonial partners.' Under Scottish law, adultery on the part of the husband was enough to obtain a divorce. The Pagets had lived in Edinburgh since April so that Lady Paget could be naturalised a Scotswoman. But there were added complications. Scottish law forbade the marriage of a couple previously guilty of adultery; Paget, in order to get a divorce, had to be 'caught' in bed with someone other than Lady Charlotte if he wanted to marry her after the divorce. Lady Charlotte would not let

Paget near another woman, so she had to disguise herself as a courtesan and allow herself to be witnessed in bed with her lover to satisfy the rigours of Scottish law. The court was told that Paget had been detected in bed with an anonymous woman; he was granted a divorce from Lady Caroline and allowed to marry Lady Charlotte, with whom, as far as the courts knew, he had never slept. Thanks to the morality of the law, Paget was therefore presented as a libidinous wretch, guilty in the eyes of the public of far more crimes than he had actually committed. This absurd legal chicanery completed the farce.

'Such is the consequence of a jaunt to a Scot's *Watering Place*!' commented the *Examiner*. 'Talk of Brighton or Margate, indeed!' The whole thing would never have happened had not the Duke of Argyll 'persuaded the forsaken lady to part with her husband and become a duchess'; until the ducal coronet was dangled in front of her eyes, she was more than happy to punish her husband and Lady Charlotte by refusing to comply with a jaunt north of the border.[21]

Simond was somewhat amazed by this aristocratic wife-swapping holiday. Yet to go through with such a thing and court the gossip and malice of the press was at least one time when an English noblewoman put aside hypocrisy to do an honest act. It showed that she 'could not bear the indelicacy of a double connection', something most women in similar situations put up with. It also meant the sacrifice of social privileges and 'every pleasure in life but one'. Such a penance proved that 'this one must be deemed a passionate attachment'. On top of the vast crim. con. compensation costs, Paget also had to arrange and pay the divorce bill for the Wellesleys, his own divorce and damages to his ex-wife. The first divorce cost £20,000, the second £10,000, and Paget had to provide his ex-wife with £1,000 a year for the rest of her life. The final bill would be in excess of £50,000. All things considered, Paget coolly said, it was 'a good and cheap bargain'.[22]

Whatever the final cost of eloping with their lovers, the Paget brothers' marital decisions hit the house of Uxbridge hard. They were a rich family but not extravagantly so, and the estate was already heavily encumbered. Paget knew that, added to the loss of a vast fortune, he would have to carry on repaying his dues. At the crim. con. trial, Dallas said that Paget desired nothing but 'complete solitude and seclusion': the penance he wanted was to be 'permitted to sink into undisturbed and uninterrupted oblivion'. But it was hardly a voluntary decision. He retired from society with his new wife – knowing they would always be pariahs – gave up his military career and relinquished his seat in the Commons. A divorced woman would be avoided as if she were contagious.

The treatment of divorced women revealed the British at their most hypocritical and vindictive. People who acted honestly and honourably committed the greatest crimes. The punishment that society heaped on divorced women was as cruel as it was capricious. When she was divorced from her husband in 1799, Lady Elizabeth Vassall Webster had found herself deserted by friends and family. Sir Godfrey Webster divorced Lady Elizabeth when he discovered that she had been having an affair with Henry Fox, Baron Holland. Elizabeth Vassall had been betrothed to Webster when she was thirteen and he forty-nine. The marriage was miserable and she was painfully conscious that she had sacrificed her youth and beauty to a cold, distant and neglectful man. Lord Holland was young and a rising Whig politician, the kind of man she would have married had she been given a say in the matter.

Lady Elizabeth Vassall Webster became Lady Holland as soon as her husband divorced her. Could society forgive such a thing? When she was thirteen Harriet Cavendish recorded seeing the new Lady Holland at Astley's Circus shortly after her divorce and remarriage. The puzzled girl was with her aunt, Lady Bessborough, and a group of family friends. 'The first thing that struck our eyes was Lady Holland seated in the box. My aunt moved all her *ten fingers* at once. Mr and Mrs Petersen . . . made signs, Lady Liz twisted her *shawls* with a forbidding glance . . . and I who did not know who she was thought it rather strange that a poor lady looking so demure, and quiet, shld. cause such evident confusion.' And these severe ladies who made such a show of signalling their disapproval of a fallen woman were Lady Holland's *friends*. The bride could only go to public entertainments; fresh from a divorce and remarriage she was humiliatingly forbidden from all private engagements. Lord Holland, on the other hand, could maintain his social life as if nothing had happened, as long as he left his new bride at home. Lady Bessborough wrote about the fate of Lady Holland in a letter to Lord Granville: 'You will hear her very much abus'd, and certainly ye weakness she has been guilty of *always* deserves it in some measure.' The young Harriet Cavendish must have wondered what horrible crime could warrant such severe treatment.[23]

The tourist Christian Goede wrote that although adultery was not punished by law in England, female adulterers were punished by a vindictive public: 'No repentance, no atonement, not even time, can remove the fatal stain; her company is considered contagious.' Paget could have had as many lower-class mistresses as he liked and Lady Charlotte could have entertained lovers to her heart's content as long as they were not caught. In Maria Edgeworth's novel *Belinda* (1804), the eponymous character is drawn into the circle of Lady Delacour, who is married to a drunken rake and leads a life of dissipation and intrigue, fuelled by drink and opium. Belinda's aunt Stella Stanhope encourages her niece's connection with the fashionable peeress, much to Belinda's chagrin; she does not want her reputation ruined by friendship with Lady Delacour. Aunt Stella warns Belinda about the dangers of being thought a 'prude': 'a character more suspected by men of the world, than even that of a coquette'. Besides, continued Aunt Stella, Lady Delacour was unimpeachable in her *public* conduct, even if everyone knew she was not in her private life: 'the world might whisper, but would not speak out'. She was not caught out, that was what mattered. The only arbiter of moral worth or, more to the point, social acceptability was the great goddess fashion: 'Again she raises her wand,' commented *Le Beau Monde*, 'and, now, with its harlequin touch, displays its extraordinary powers, in which she is unrivalled . . . By her aid the Dowager *Belle* of faded beauty, is changed into the blooming nymph with glowing cheeks and flowing ringlets, whilst the frail fair one, by the same spell, shifts the scene as rapidly, and assuming the chaste and graceful veil, with all the other externals of virgin modesty, meets the eye a very vestal in appearance.'[24]

It was an extraordinarily bitter attack from a magazine which was founded on the principles of 'externals', delineating, as it did every month, the latest fashions to the belles and dandies of the *bon ton*. The journal was correcting what it saw as the prevalent vice in the higher echelons of society: the power of fashion to cast a pall of amnesia over immorality. Fashion did not mean just the conjuring trick of using cosmetics and costume to cover up age and defects, but the great blessing of being esteemed popular and therefore beyond reproach. By such a means the female adulterer – 'the frail fair one', as the euphemism went – could put her misdemeanours behind her. Lady Holland faced down the gossips by providing sumptuous entertainments at Holland House. With amazing speed, the magic of fashion made her socially acceptable again.

High society was riddled with failed marriages, adultery and bastard children. Lady Oxford, for example, was notorious for affairs with a series of men, including Sir Francis Burdett and Byron, and had illegitimate children to prove it. But because her husband tolerated her behaviour, did not try to obtain a divorce and therefore have to bring one or more crim. con. actions, Lady Oxford was accepted in polite society. Even when the open secret of her 'amatory adventures' threatened to become public knowledge in a book penned by her brother, she knew she could survive the scandals. This was partly due to Lady Oxford's doughty character: she was a fiery and outspoken radical in politics, both national and marital; a few affairs would not send her quivering into social exile. But she also relied on the complicity of her class. The pithy Lady Charlotte Bury wrote in her diary when the damning book was being mooted: 'We shall break our necks in haste to buy it, of course crying "shameful" all the while; and it is said that Lady O is to be cut, which I cannot absolutely believe. Let her tell two or three old women about town that they are young and handsome, and give some well-timed parties, and she may still keep the society which she has been used to.'[25]

It was almost as if members of the upper class needed scandals like the Pagets' as a scapegoat for their own sins, as an opportunity to express moral indignation. Countess Maria Querini Benzoni, a leader of Venetian society, told Byron that at first she thought the English were ill-natured and spiteful because they were forever retailing malicious gossip about each other. She soon realised that they were not naturally mean, but because 'living in a country like England, where severity of morals punishes so heavily any dereliction from propriety, each individual, to prove personal correctness, was compelled to attack the *sins* of his or her acquaintances, as it furnished an opportunity of expressing their abhorrence by words, instead of proving it by actions, which might cause some self-denial to themselves'.[26]

It was a feature of a society governed by unwritten but nonetheless strict codes. In Britain the upper class conducted their lives in the public eye, submitting to prescribed forms of politeness and decorum. Byron talked of 'the arctic circles, the frozen zones of nobility'. It was a world where people were judged by their reputation, and reputation is dependent on public opinion, not individual moral qualities. It was possible, therefore, to lead a scandalous private life and retain one's good name as long as the private did not intrude upon the public. It created what Byron called 'the cant of virtue', a false moral standard that forced people to follow the fashion in morals as much as in coats and gloves.

'There are certain women of good fashion', wrote Hannah More, 'who practise irregularities not consistent with the strictness of virtue, while their good sense and knowledge of the world makes them at the same time keenly alive to the value of reputation.' When Lady Holland's own 'crime' was forgotten she attacked women who had the temerity to commit adultery. She had the brazen hypocrisy to criticise Charles James Fox, her second husband's uncle, for his 'weakness' in having an affair with Elizabeth Armistead, whom she called 'a pernicious connexion'. And when Lady Caroline Lamb began an affair with her son, she felt obliged to give the married woman a stern lecture. Lady Caroline said that she did not mind being admonished by people with a genuine 'spirit of rectitude of Religion and *strict* undeviating principles', but when people with 'more worldly prudence' tried to play the same game, it was spiteful hypocrisy.[27]

There was a big difference between 'worldly prudence' and real morality. Even women such as Lady Holland, who had suffered at the hands of malicious gossips, had to feign the same type of outrage when others followed their example. 'The world is constrained to pay virtue due homage,' wrote Randle Lewis; 'and it is generally thought necessary to assume the appearance of it at least. It is the universal charm: its shadow is courted, when the substance is wanting. The imitation of it is now an art, and the first study is to learn the speech, and to adopt the manners of candour, gentleness, and humanity.'[28]

This imitative performance of virtue and wilful hypocrisy was welcomed by moralists: the blanket of silence and euphemism at least gave society a good appearance. The necessity for the guilty to live a lie was a suitable punishment for their crime. For others, the strictures of the moral police only exacerbated casual immorality. Cant and humbug, lies and double standards ruled society. Byron had to leave for the continent in 1816 after his messy and public separation from his wife. He was understandably preoccupied with the injustice of society, its thinly veiled hypocrisy and the vindictive punishments it meted out to a select few. He knew why Benzoni might have been appalled by the mores of his countrymen: 'The Italians do not understand the English . . . indeed, how can they? For they (the Italians) are frank, simple, and open, in their natures, following the bent of their inclinations, which they do not believe to be wicked; while the English, to conceal the indulgence of theirs, daily practise hypocrisy, falsehood, and uncharitableness; so that to *one* error is added many crimes.'

There was one notorious woman who refused to play the game and observe the double standards of society. Lady Aldborough, a fearsome old lady who spoke in the coarse and free way more typical of the eighteenth century than the nineteenth, would tell dirty jokes and dropped heavy hints to women about their affairs in a stage whisper which 'wore no mask, and left her hearer very little chance of appearing not to understand them'. When a woman feigned innocence or ignorance as to the old lady's meaning to avoid the anger of her nearby husband or the malicious gossip of her friends, she would get a sharp tap from Lady Aldborough's fan, and a sharper rebuke: 'You understand very well what I mean, my dear.'[29]

Mirza Abul Hassan Khan, who came to London in 1809 as the first Persian ambassador to the English court for two hundred years, was appalled by the artificial and barbarous customs of the nobility. He was asked to record his impressions of the English in a letter to the press. 'I thought', he wrote in Persian, 'I would include among the wonders I have seen – 100-year-old men trying to seduce young girls and 100-year-old ladies flirting with young men at parties so crowded that you cannot move and so hot that you could roast a chicken.' But this is how he phrased it in English for the newspapers: 'Very beautiful lady, she got ugly fellow for husband, that not very good, very shocking. – I ask Sir Gore* why for this. – He says me, perhaps he very good man, not handsome no matter, perhaps he got too much money, perhaps got title – I say I not like that, all very shocking.'[30]

Hassan Khan's letter was relished because he condemned, bluntly and with charming naivety, everything that was tolerated by polite society. When money and status dictated marriage, elderly men would prey on young women, and matrons would flirt with bachelors. Relations between men and women were poisoned by the reserve dictated by social convention. The main reason why the Paget brothers were seen as committing the ultimate crime against morality was because they held up love in their defence. As one journal said, Paget's

*Sir Gore Ouseley, his London mentor.

claim that he loved Lady Charlotte evinced 'some specimens of modern sophistry'. To admit, in cases like these, that passion could overpower duty was to present the affair as more dangerous than a seedy act of sexual gratification. Even if they could not suppress their sexual instincts, better a man or woman have an affair in the deepest secrecy than offend the sanctity of marriage and bleat about the power of love. Love would tear the institution of marriage asunder; it must not be allowed to become a justification for divorce, let alone marriage.

Lord Headfort's lawyer suggested that no rigid legal definition could assess human emotions. His client was accused of seducing a married woman, but should a court of law meddle with the deepest of human emotions? 'Love might be a strong excuse for such conduct, because it is often too strong for law, virtue or morality – it becomes entitled therefore to human consideration.' Such a suggestion was anathema; love was so strong that it *should* be repressed, and defendants should never use it as an apology for inappropriate conduct. With that kind of excuse there would be anarchy in society. Love might be too strong for law; it was also too strong for marriage.[31]

'He who marries from what he fancies is love, is a fool,' one journalist commented; 'because till it is irrecoverable, he knows not what he has done. She who marries for the same motive, is more foolish still; because, deceiving him originally, she has deceived herself now.' Young women had to be guarded against this illusion of 'love'. In 1809 the newspapers reported a story of a victim of passion, a twenty-three-year-old heiress who became pregnant. Her angry father demanded that she name her seducer. The girl replied that it was her maid, Harriett. The suspicious father interrogated the maid to find that Harriett was Harry, a man of scant wealth whom the girl had met, appropriately enough, at a circulating library, no doubt when she had gone to feed her mind with romantic novels. The couple had married in secret and lived together as mistress and maid.[32]

It was a horror story for all fathers. 'To us', Randle Lewis told his male readers, 'love is an amusement; to them it is a capital affair . . . Women, in general, love better than men.' Women had to realise that the idealised love celebrated in novels, plays and poems was a luxury they could not afford; they should know that its presence or absence was not grounds for marriage or divorce. Love was a slippery concept for lawyers and moralisers. If marriage depended on it – if husbands and wives had to see that desires were constantly gratified, and if all the virtues of candour, charity, benevolence, sincerity, compassion and forgiveness had to be practised at every moment – the ecclesiastical courts would be open twenty-four hours a day, seven days a week.[33]

Men knew of the dangers of love and sought to suppress their emotions. The restraint and reserve was undoubtedly regrettable for social intercourse, but even worse was the suspicion it engendered. In *Belinda* the young heroine is sent to stay with her aunt Stella Stanhope in London. Aunt Stella has been the mentor to many a young girl and found them all wealthy, titled husbands. Belinda meets the prosperous and dashing Clarence Hervey, and they are immediately attracted to one another. But good-natured and unaffected Belinda is tainted by her aunt; when Hervey finds out that Belinda is the niece of the notorious matchmaker, he believes that her natural simplicity is a snare: 'but now he suspected her of artifice in every word, look, and action; and even when he felt himself most charmed by her powers of pleasing, he was most inclined to despise her for what he thought such premature proficiency in scientific coquetry'.[34]

The strict rules of courtship and restraint meant that it was scarce exaggeration to say that 'the two sexes are as cautiously separated as if there was a waged and innate war between them; they are as carefully watched and spied as if the one was an article to be stolen, or broken, or eaten up, and the other a thief and spoiler'. A young man and a young woman could not be allowed to be in the same room together without the suspicion that when their parents or guardians returned, they would have long departed for Gretna Green. From this fear, the whole of 'good' society was characterised by suspicion, surveillance and restraint. 'Half the world is employed in watching the other, which is a bad enough occupation; and the other half is watched, which is not a very amiable position. The first half become spies, busy, prying, malevolent – the second learns fraud and cunning . . . The character loses its openness, it is taught to suspect itself, and it soon becomes deserving of suspicion.' Parents watched their daughters; husbands spied on their wives; all were convinced that humankind was too weak to remain chaste for any period of time. The restraint in courtship made marriage nothing more than a lottery and left husbands and wives locked in mutual recrimination: 'There is no happiness under such a system of suspicion.'[35]

There was scant happiness, but a lot of misery. In the 1800s there were plenty of moral worries to add to those of the refractory poor and divorce-mad aristocrats. In 1809 Parliament rejected two laws, one to purify the Sabbath and the other a tightening up of the penal laws for adultery. For some this was a 'mockery of the laws of God'; there had to be strict laws 'for the protection of female innocence against the vile arts and abominable attempts of seducers', according to an outraged correspondent to the *Gentleman's Magazine*. There was a recognition that the position of women was unhappy and unfair. But any plan to make their position better without completely reorganising society would make it worse. 'It is a singular injustice', opined Hannah More, 'which is often exercised towards women, first to give them a very defective Education, and then to expect from them the most undeviating purity of conduct.'

A young, innocent maid was particularly vulnerable to the wiles of polished impostors and intruders. One small slip, and she was ruined for ever, cast out from her family and condemned to a life selling herself to heartless men. 'Is it not most disgraceful and unjust, that, when, from ignorance and inexperience, they are totally unequal to cope with the craft of a designing debauchee, they are left an unprotected prey to any man whose lascivious desires their persons excite?' There was a 'course' or 'progress' of seduction. The plausible young man professes 'the most solemn vows of constancy' and lures the girl from her parents; the couple flee to London, where the man accomplishes his 'infernal purpose of pollution'; he then abandons the poor girl, who can't return to her parents because of 'the recollection of that dagger which she has plunged into their hearts by the disappointment of all their fond hopes'. The girl, with no chance of success in the world now, has no choice but 'to solicit the embraces of any coarse sensualist, of any foul debauchee, that will pay for the enjoyment of her person'; the process of degeneracy continues as she grows older and more desperate; she takes to the bottle and spends time in Bridewell, the prison for prostitutes.[36]

Parliament did not countenance laws against seducers, because, as so often with 'moral' legislation, it was impossible to reconcile liberty with enforced virtue. Criminalising seduction would be like making flirting an offence, as in *The Mikado*. Young maids would be protected no doubt by a system of surveillance and a draconian code of punishments, but it would make social life almost impossible and enforce even further a segregation between the sexes. As it was, the laws against seduction, like the laws of crim. con., allowed wronged parents to sue men for depriving them of the service of their daughters, a straightforward financial transaction. As the contributor to the *Gentleman's Magazine* commented, 'the reproach intended to be cast on us by our Enemy, in calling us a nation of shopkeepers appears most richly merited'. In 1808 the newspapers noted a vast increase in seduction trials at a time when divorces and crim. con. were also becoming more prevalent. Every week brought accounts of young maids being seduced and abandoned.

Among the many lurid stories the papers enjoyed reporting, one stands out as representative of such cases. In 1808 Captain Massey, a married man and an officer in the West York militia, took lodgings at the home of a ship's master and fellow militia officer in Faversham. Every evening the daughter of the house, Elizabeth Banfield, brought the Captain his dinner. Quite soon they were dining together in private; after six weeks in the house, he had seduced Elizabeth and she was pregnant. During the seduction, Elizabeth had complained to her mother that Captain Massey was 'behaving rude to her', but nonetheless her mother encouraged her to go to his rooms for dinner. It was only when Elizabeth became pregnant that her parents sued the Captain for 'distress of mind and anxiety' and for the costs of bringing up his illegitimate child. The defence said that the Banfield family did not deserve any compensation because they had 'afforded every facility to the Defendant to gratify any irregular passions he might cherish'. In other words, poor Captain Massey was the victim, forced as he was to be in the same room with a young woman.

Samuel Shepherd, the Banfields' lawyer, went on the offensive, playing up to the image of the military rake. 'By seducing her', he told the court, 'he had degraded her, and disgraced her in the rank of respectable females, but now he attempted to blacken her reputation to the utmost . . . Such, indeed, was too frequently the course pursued by abandoned libertines; they had too little regard for the seduction of females in the lower ranks.' Servants were frequently thrown into close, unsupervised contact with artful young men: 'The libertine called them "*Fair game*", and thought himself warranted in attacking them with indecent liberties. But the man of honour felt far differently; he felt they were thrown into his way as objects rather of protection than oppression, and from that circumstance alone, would be more guarded than on ordinary occasions.' The courts were careful in these sorts of cases to prevent parents from forcing their daughters on young men for the purposes of suing them later. They had to take a realistic view of such matters. After all, Elizabeth and Massey were consenting adults; if compensation became rewarding, the courts would be bogged down with couples suing each other. There had to be a line drawn between protecting innocent females and rewarding loose women. In this case, Lord Ellenborough ordered Massey to pay Mr Banfield £100, too small a sum to be an inducement for other parents to haul up their daughters' lovers but large enough to signal disapproval. The laws did nothing to help women, only making them less free and making courtship and relations between the sexes more artificial and restrained.[37]

'A woman is too often reduced to this dilemma,' muses Maria Edgeworth's Belinda. '– Either she must marry a man she does not love, or she must be blamed by the world – Either she must sacrifice a portion of her reputation, or the whole of her happiness.' Whatever the motives for banishing passion from marriage, the arrangement invariably meant unhappy marriages and every incentive to seek pleasure or love elsewhere. It made rakes of men and coquettes of women. Forced into an unhappy marriage, couples 'think of nothing but how it may be palliated; and to alleviate their feelings, they solace themselves, one in the arms of a mistress, and the other in those of a gallant'.[38]

As many realised, the manners of courtship and the expectations placed by parents on their daughters made adultery and divorce more likely than not. Lady Anne Hamilton wrote as a note to her satirical poem 'The Epics of the Ton; or The Glories of the Great World' (1807) that elopement and separation had increased in the 1800s.

> Nor ought this to excite and surprise [Lady Anne explained]. That education which teaches the young maid to regard external shew and splendour as the supreme good, and the arts of catching a man of rank and wealth as the only useful acquirements, imparts no real dignity to the character. The female becomes degraded in her own estimation, and is conscious of no meanness where appearances can be saved. But the heart will have its longings as well as the eye; and where a fine coat, and a fine fellow, are fairly balanced against each other, it is ten to one if opportunity does not turn the scale. An education which should inspire religious and moral principles, and impart real dignity to the mind, would be a surer guardian of female virtue, than the watchful dragon of the Hesperian gardens.[39]

Taught to act like a prostitute in the great marriage mart, the noblewoman would act as a prostitute in wedlock. According to the moralisers, young women who came into society were encouraged to behave as courtesans by the pressures of fashion. It was a melancholy thing to see youthful innocence 'exposed to the impudent stare and wanton remarks of the riotous sons of intemperate and noisy intoxication' and to observe 'the natural bloom of beauty exchanged for the meretricious glow of art, and the inexpressibly charming blush of innocence and native modesty, for the bold stare and impudent manners . . . which so remarkably characterise our modern belles'. They were encouraged to be seductive in dress, make-up and demeanour, hoping to excite the lust of the son of some great nobleman. At the same time plays and novels extolled airy notions of love and mocked the 'Darby and Joan' image of staid conjugal bliss. Thus the young girl's attentions were focused on securing a well-bred husband and her head was filled with ideals of love. Nothing could render her less suitable for marriage and more likely to take lovers later on.[40]

The flirtatious habits and meretricious fashions adopted by girls in search of a husband equipped them for promiscuous behaviour later in life. The wife was always to blame, for she set herself as a target for unscrupulous men: 'The light and dissipated manners of our modern females, coupled with the very indecent style of dress which has been the fashion for several years past, gives the first signal, to the unprincipled libertine, of the inward disposition of their minds. Finding his addresses not discouraged, he proceeds, like an experienced engineer, to sap the foundations of virtue, until, at length, he accomplishes the object he has in view. This is the almost uniform progress of the numberless crim. con. affairs which so abound among us.' The Wonderbra of the time was a triangular piece of steel which pushed up and separated the breasts. It was known as 'the divorce' for its tendency to encourage seduction and because both the item of clothing and the legal process were 'designed, most unnaturally, to separate what the hand of their Creator had brought into most graceful union'.[41]

According to the expert in these matters, Randle Lewis, 'men are the principal cause that the fair sex are not better, for the former set the latter daily examples of capriciousness, inconstancy, and dishonour'. So women's adulterous desires could be understood, but they could rarely be tolerated. But they were in a different league from male philandering, which was harmless by comparison. A husband might find opportunities for illicit sex with casual ease in the round of nocturnal pleasures. But a wife, with comparatively little freedom, must use more guile. According to one writer, 'the full completion of the act of adultery requires a combination of time, opportunity, contrivance, and much cool and serious thought, profligate and abandoned in the highest degree must that be, who determines to commit it'.[42]

Any attempt to legislate against adultery was blown apart when Prince George assumed the Regency in 1811 when his father, George III, entered his last, debilitating period of illness. The Regent, a Whig since his youth, incensed the opposition when he defected to the Tories and kept on Spencer Perceval, and, when that premier was assassinated in 1812, accepted the Tory Lord Liverpool as Prime Minister. The radicals were outraged, and in the *Examiner* Leigh Hunt responded to the Tories' oleaginous flattery of the Regent by pointing out that the Prince was, among other things, an unfaithful husband, an energetic adulterer and the companion of rakes who habitually made the marital laws a mockery.

Tried for a libel on the Regent, Leigh and his brother John (the publisher of the *Examiner*) were found guilty. This was thanks in part to the jury, which had been hand-picked, and the judge, Lord Ellenborough, who was a dear friend of the Prince and a declared enemy of the press. In his speech, Ellenborough responded to the claims that Prince George was a companion of philanderers and low women by saying that people in high life deserved privacy. The most obvious target of the Hunts' attack had been the Marquis of Headfort, whose adultery had been proved in a court of law but who had been made a Lord of the Bedchamber in the Regent's new court. Leigh Hunt's charge that the Regent spent his time with adulterers was irrefutable; the judge was therefore obliged to use all his sophistry to prove that writing such things was libellous. Headfort occupied an honourable position, and it was true that he had been sued for adultery; yet, as Ellenborough said, crim. con. suits 'cast a slur' over people, whether they deserved it or not. It was unfair to single Headfort out. Morality had been esteemed very highly in the reign of George III, the judge said, but it could not be claimed that of all the ministers, courtiers and family members who had served the upright monarch, not every one had 'steered clear of a similar misfortune'. And adultery *was* a 'misfortune': 'I chuse to call it by that name,' Ellenborough asserted with stunning bravado; 'for though it may be a vice . . . in some cases, it is not so in all; circumstances may render it venial.'[43]

This cut against the whole system of crim. con., which had been used to restrain the upper class with punitive damages. Ellenborough said that it was unfair to single out unfortunate aristocrats, because crim. con. cases magnified their folly into grave crimes against morality. The trials were worth little more than the paper they were written on, as far as the truth went. That was the implication of Ellenborough's judgement, which suggested that the verdict in Headfort's crim. con. case was neither here nor there.

The Prince had frequently waged war against that meddlesome and pleasure-denying nuisance, crim. con. When Thomas Sheridan, son of Richard Sheridan, had to pay one Peter Campbell, a plantation owner, £5,000 for 'a moment of transitory passion' with Mrs Campbell, high society paid it off with a subscription, to which George contributed £1,000 and the Dukes of Devonshire and Bedford £500 each.[44] Not only did Ellenborough ridicule the truthfulness of crim. con. cases, but he used his authority as Lord Chief Justice to draw their sting and make life happier for his aristocratic friends and his royal master. The vast sums that had been awarded had been intended to encourage husbands to bring to justice the men who seduced their wives. The best way to stop the rush of crim. con. cases and strangle the publicity was to reduce the compensation payments and allow men to bribe their lovers' husbands with a reasonable consideration, thus sparing everyone the embarrassing publicity of a crim. con. trial.

Ellenborough got a reputation for being indulgent towards aristocratic vice and draconian towards the press. In his judgement in the Hunt case, he appeared to have 'given new life to the regions of fashionable pleasure, and restored to animation the adulterous courtiers and licentious matrons who had nearly been shamed into decency by the strong and universal expression of popular indignation'. Whereas courts used to be, or could have been, 'the seats of inquisition on the morals and manners of the *beau monde*', they were now ordered to consider the crimes of a certain privileged few as 'nothing more reprehensible than misfortune'. In any case, shielding the Prince with the libel laws was incompatible with persecuting adulterers. It did not take much to realise that a moral crusade against philanderers could not exist when the courts had the complexion of being laissez-faire on matters carnal: charges of hypocrisy would damage the royal family. Lord Ellenborough, according to the gossip of the legal community in January 1813, 'has professed it to be his object to reduce the damages below what was given in Crim:Con: cases in the time of Lord Kenyon [Ellenborough's predecessor as Lord Chief Justice] . . .'

The Regent's court was notoriously dissolute. Not only was Lord Headfort, the crim. con. veteran, made a Lord of the Bedchamber but so too was Lord Melbourne, who lived in an open marriage; their insights into their jobs were no doubt appreciated. Lord Yarmouth, the stepson of the Marchioness of Hertford, the Regent's plump mistress, was made Vice-Chamberlain. It was no surprise that Leigh Hunt should have attacked such a seedy court. Yet the moraliser was sent to prison for three years while the seducer (the Regent), the adulteress (Lady Hertford), the complicit husband (Lord Hertford) and the stepson who 'serves at home with humble complacency the paramour of his mother' (Yarmouth) were eulogised by Ellenborough's court.

Lord Ellenborough gave immunity to titled people caught in adultery. The moralising tone of Spencer Perceval's administration was over. But mercy would never be extended further than the aristocracy and the cronies of the Prince Regent. Tom Moore imagined the joy of a young lover when he reads of the Lord Chief Justice's indulgence to adulterers. The gentleman proposes a plan to his sweetheart, a married woman:

> Come fly to these arms, nor let beauties so bloomy,
> To one frigid owner be tied;
> Your prudes may revile, and your old ones look gloomy,
> But dearest! we've got Law on our side!*
>
> Oh! think the delight of two lovers congenial,
> Whom no dull decorums divide;
> Their error how sweet, and their raptures how *venial*,
> When once they've got LAW on their side!

The young gentleman had obviously been reading Ellenborough's speech in the Hunt libel trial and believed no jury would inflict damages on him for eloping with his love. The lady was less sanguine:

> Hold, hold, my good Sir! go a little more slowly;
> For, grant me so faithless a bride,
> Such sinners as we, are a little too *lowly*,
> To hope to have LAW on our side.
>
> Had you been a great Prince, to whose star shining o'er 'em
> The People should look to your guide,

*A pun on Ellenborough's full name, Edward Law.

Then your Highness (and welcome!) might kick down
  decorum –
You'd always have LAW on your side.

Were you ev'n an old Marquis, in mischief grown hoary,*
Whose heart, though it long ago died
To the *pleasures* of vice, is alive to its *glory* –
You still would have LAW on your side!

But for *you*, Sir, Crim. Con. is a path full of troubles;
By *my* advice therefore abide,
And leave the pursuit to those Princes and Nobles
Who have *such* a LAW on their side![45]

The public was in favour of punishing men like Paget, as the behaviour of juries in crim. con. cases shows. Yet it was a flawed way of policing morals and one which ultimately frustrated its object by spreading falsehoods and base lies through the rest of society. Certainly, divorce and crim. con. punished the honest and spared the guilty. Louis Simond said that only women who had some 'delicacy' left would expose themselves to public ridicule by leaving their husbands, avoiding the hypocrisy of an open marriage and domestic misery. But the penalty of honesty was ostracism and the reward of brazen hypocrisy was society's indulgence. What were elsewhere considered heinous crimes against decency were in Britain 'varnished with an exterior reserve, and with a semblance of delicacy'.[46]

But it was this hypocrisy that was most ardently advocated by moral reformers. 'We cannot but rejoice in every degree of human virtue which operates favourably on society, whatever be the motive, or whoever be the actor,' wrote Hannah More, '. . . even the good actions of such persons as are too much actuated by a regard for appearances, are not without their beneficial effects.' The aristocracy might strain to show a good example, but the obvious hypocrisy of divorces, crim. con. trials and the capricious judgement on transgressors had a bad effect on the rest of the country. The back-stabbings and cant of the upper echelons were not confined within a small circle but were public knowledge. Manners, if not morals, were derived from the very highest. As a result, society was shot through with the language of hypocrisy and doublespeak. Something like sincerity or

*The Marquis of Headfort, who was referred to as 'hoary' during his crim. con. trial and as such in the press thereafter.

candour was impossibly vulgar. British morality was a joke throughout the world.[47]

In exceptional circumstances, the perverters of public decency could be brought back within the pale. In 1815, by then having inherited the earldom of Uxbridge and lingered for five years in obscurity, Paget was recalled to fight France, Britain needing all the experienced generals it could find. Fittingly for a man of his talents, Uxbridge was made second-in-command and put in charge of the cavalry during the Hundred Days campaign. At Waterloo he personally led the charge of the Heavy Brigade and numerous counter-attacks on the French cavalry; he had nine horses shot under him during the action. He became one of the greatest heroes of the war, ranking with Nelson and Wellington, and was rewarded by being created Marquis of Anglesey and welcomed back to polite society and political life. Not everyone shared the collective amnesia, however.

His commander was the only man better qualified than him, Arthur Wellesley, Duke of Wellington. It was an unexpected, and unwelcome, reunion of the Paget and Wellesley families. Wellington could never forgive Uxbridge for eloping with his brother's wife; only the combined authority of the Regent and the Duke of York induced Wellington to accept General Uxbridge's reinstatement. Relations were cordial. Towards the end of the battle, Uxbridge was hit in the leg by grapeshot as he rode alongside Wellington. 'By God, Sir!' Uxbridge exclaimed. 'I've lost my leg!'

'By God, Sir, so you have!' Wellington replied, with all the concern a Wellesley could be expected to show a Paget.

6

The Glories of the Great

'The highest and the lowest classes approach each other in freedom of manner. The one knows no fear, the other no refinement. Both act much from nature . . . freedom of manners is the principal point at which the high and the low invariably meet: yet from this influence results a logical congenial disposition to despise all restraint.'

A Short Treatise on the Passions . . . by a Lady (1810)[1]

'Old and young, ugly and handsome, all have the rage in England of losing their identity in crowds; and prefer conjugating the verb *ennuyer*, en masse, in heated rooms, to conning it over in privacy in purer atmosphere.'

Byron[2]

Mirza Abul Hassan Khan joined a crowd of some 3,000 people in Cavendish Square one afternoon in May 1810. They were there, high and low, to watch a famous social event. The flower of the aristocracy and the scions of the ruling class were atop expensive and handsomely decorated coaches lined up round the square. The drivers were dressed in sumptuous, distinctive liveries, including blue and yellow striped waistcoats, the whole covered with long coats which reached to their ankles and had mother-of-pearl buttons the size of crown pieces. They behaved like typical coachees: every other word an oath.

Days such as this, the turnout of one of the most exclusive clubs in the country, was, according to Rees Howell Gronow, 'one of the glories of the days of the Regent'. The sight must have confirmed a foreign visitor's impressions of the extraordinary wealth of the British aristocracy: 'The symmetry of the horses, the arrangement of the harness, the plain but well-appointed carriage, the good taste of the liveries, the healthy, sturdy appearance of the coachmen and grooms, formed altogether one of those remarkable spectacles that make a lasting impression upon the memory.' Among the group of wealthy men would have been Lords Barrymore, Sefton, Hawke and Worcester, and Sir John Lade, all of them cronies of the Regent, along with younger men such as Sir Godfrey Vassall Webster. But the fashionable men were not being driven: they were the coachmen.

'Don't tell me about *Gentlemen*, indeed,' said one of the crowd at the first outing of the Four-in-Hand Club in 1808, when he was told that the drivers were members of the ancient nobility: 'why, they are going to fetch home their *masters*: can't you see they are *livery sarvants*?' One journalist wondered if their wives and sisters had a 'Dripping-pan Club' or had formed the 'Cook-maid Club'. 'I was amazed', wrote Hassan Khan, 'that these gentlemen should choose to dress in the livery of carriage-drivers and apparently enjoy driving in the pouring rain!'[3]

Louis Simond, whose journey to Britain overlapped with Hassan Khan's, was equally impressed and appalled by 'the Four-in-Hand Club'. The members vied with each other as to who could display the most splendid equipage and livery, and who could ape best the character and language of a stage or mail coachman. The Earl of Barrymore was often the most conspicuous for his 'four splendid greys, unmatched in symmetry, action and power'; he also trumped the members in other respects: 'If there had been a competitive examination, the prize of which would be given to the most proficient in slang and vulgar phraseology, it would have been safe to back his Lordship as the winner against the most foul-mouthed of costermongers.'

When the members had paraded in front of foreign ambassadors, the ladies and gentlemen of the *bon ton*, the envious middle classes and the perplexed lower orders, they set off. They headed west out of London, 'stopping on the way at several public-houses and gin-shops where stage-coachmen are in the habit of stopping for a dram, and for parcels and passengers; the whole in strict imitation of their models and making use, as much as they can, of their energetic professional idiom'. Nothing, absolutely nothing in the world, could delight a member of the Four-in-Hand Club more and elevate him higher in the eyes of his rivals than to be unwittingly paid by a member of the public for a ride. One member had his front teeth removed so that he could spit exactly like a grizzled coachman ('And calmly did his teeth displace,/ That he might spit with better grace'). If a member was accompanied, his friend would dress as a guard and blow a horn, as was customary on mail coaches. The Club would reconvene at Salthill (a mile from present-day Slough station) and have a 'sumptuous dinner' at Botham's, a watering place for coachmen, 'after which they returned to London, in high spirits, and not infrequently somewhat overcome by the quantity of sound port wine, for which the inn was celebrated'.[4]

In a life bedevilled by stale social occasions, tedious manners and tiresome courtship rituals, dressing up and swearing were perhaps appropriate means of escapism for unimaginative minds. The purpose of the Four-in-Hand Club was partly to have a competition among the members as to who had the most lavish liveries and who could act most like a coachee and partly an opportunity to drink at every coaching inn between Hyde Park and Slough. As far as joy-riding went, the Club was governed by rules which regulated the speed and behaviour of the members. Another similar club, the Whips, rode out to the Black Dog at Bedford in their yellow carriages and also conformed to safe driving. There were other opportunities for joy-riding, which many nobles and dandies indulged on other occasions. Their conduct was frequently a public nuisance, especially that of the younger members, who were often gripped with an 'ungovernable phrenzy' whenever they saw a carriage and had an urge to drive like a Roman charioteer. The men who delighted in racing their carriages were thuggish and contemptuous of lesser mortals. In 1809 Lord Ranelagh was riding along the Uxbridge road with a servant when they passed a Major John Carrington Smith, who was driving his gig. As they passed, the Major cut Ranelagh's servant with his whip. The peer rode back to ask the young man to explain his conduct. 'Who do you think I am?' asked Smith. 'Do you take me for a Cockney riding out on Sunday; I am a Major in his Majesty's service.' He then challenged Ranelagh to a duel. The peer took out a warrant instead and Major Smith was brought before Lord Ellenborough. At the trial, the judge told the young hoodlum that he 'was right in thinking that he might not be mistaken for a Cockney riding out on a Sunday airing. The good citizens of London upon such occasions comported themselves with propriety and decorum, and did not violate the peace by insulting and beating the rest of his Majesty's subjects.'[5]

The *Examiner* called the Four-in-Handers 'the Hopes of the Country'. It is easy to agree with that paper's line; after all, Britain was at war and needed all the hale, adventurous, *natural* leaders that it could find, if only to replace men such as Lord Paget, who had been rusticated for unspeakable crimes. But of course, such men had no intention of joining their contemporaries on the Iberian peninsula,

India, Canada or at sea. The members represented the lowest of the idle aristocracy and gentry, each name a byword for degeneracy. Lord Sefton, for example, was a clever and witty Irish peer (a title that should not have been his: he was, in reality, the illegitimate son of the infamous Hugh Meynell) and a leading Whig MP. He was a man of the times, numbering among his cronies people from the Regent to Dr Samuel Solomon. Like many of his generation, a vast fortune and a glittering array of connections, political and royal, could have been the basis for a useful career as a statesman or soldier; yet he chose to squander it. 'He was a man who filled a considerable space in society,' wrote Charles Greville. '. . . No man probably ever pursued a life of such uninterrupted (and not unsuccessful) pursuit of pleasure. He was possessed of ample fortune, which he endeavoured to convert into a continual source of enjoyment in every mode which fancy, humour and caprice suggested. His natural parts were excessively lively, but his education had been wholly neglected, and he never attempted to repair in after-life the deficiencies occasioned by early neglect.'[6]

'Lord Dashalong' – Lord Sefton in the driving seat, 1801

Sefton was boisterous and amusing, 'stained with no gross immorality', except all-conquering idleness and a tendency to waste his life. The same could not be said for the leading member of the club, Lord Barrymore. This Lord Barrymore, the eighth earl, inherited the title from his brother, the seventh earl, who was so fond of frolicking at London pleasure gardens with the lower orders. The Barrymore family was infamous even among the most depraved aristocracy. The seventh earl was nicknamed 'Hellgate' by the Regent because of the depths of viciousness to which he plunged. The other siblings were named after some of the gates of the City of London: the eighth earl was 'Cripplegate' because he had a club foot; their sister was 'Billingsgate' because she could not utter a sentence without a string of expletives like the notoriously foul-mouthed female fishmongers of Billingsgate Market; and their younger brother, a libidinous clergyman, was called 'Newgate' because he was a frequent inmate at that gaol, and indeed many others throughout the kingdom. 'Cripplegate', the driver, toady-like did Prince George's bidding 'however palpably iniquitous it might be'; it was rumoured that he 'had assisted at the orgies that used to take place at Carlton House [the Prince's London residence]'. Others retailed stories that he had ruined a string of young girls, including a clergyman's daughter, whom he had seduced, degraded and then abandoned to lives of prostitution. In public and private he was a bully, with a notoriously sadistic streak. Barrymore, it seemed, led a life which consisted of little more than the gaming table, the boxing match, the brothel, the palace and driving his coach on tavern crawls to Salthill.

Sefton and Barrymore represented the older generation of the Club: talented but listless, wealthy and bored, privileged but utterly selfish. The pastime of driving carriages fast and recklessly had been a feature of upper-class life for years, and the Regent had, in his youth, raced around in his phaeton. But the habit of driving coaches and masquerading as coachmen was new in the 1800s and 1810s. It had been pioneered at Cambridge between 1806 and 1809 by a generation of bored undergraduates. The hobby was the invention of a younger group of men, 'the Hopes of the Country', not the middle-aged and underemployed aristocracy.

At Cambridge at this time were three quite different men: Byron, Sir Godfrey Vassall Webster (son of Lady Elizabeth Vassall Webster, later Lady Holland, from her first marriage to Sir Godfrey Webster, who committed suicide in 1800) and Hewson Clarke. Few generations of Cambridge undergraduates have distinguished themselves with the idleness and dissolute manners on display at this time. 'They drink a great deal here in general, and appear to be very idle,' wrote a French visitor to the university. 'The professors, who are little known by any literary works, make very feeble attempts to excite the emulation of their pupils; and every degree conferred by the university is obtained by time.' William Wilberforce recalled his first night at the university: 'I was introduced . . . to as licentious a set of men as can well be conceived. They drank hard, and their conversation was worse than their lives.' If he was expecting a sound academic education, he was soon aware that he could only obtain it on his own. If the undergraduates were profligate, the fellows were as bad: 'Their object seemed to be, to make and keep me idle. If ever I appeared studious, they would say to me, "Why in the world should a man of your fortune trouble himself with fagging?"'[7]

Much later the *Quarterly Review* commented that 'the debauchery of this knot of Cantabrigians appears to have been unredeemed by a single feature of elegance: we hear of nothing but what, even in the estimation of the undergraduate world, must have been reckoned low – cock-fighting, boxing matches, and crapulence'. Byron spent his time at Trinity in splendid idleness, bestirring himself to mock authority by entering his bear 'Biron' for a fellowship. He obtained his degree, as the French writer suspected was common, by fulfilling the conditions of nine terms' residence. Byron knew Webster, who was also educated at Harrow, and who preceded him as the lover of Lady Caroline Lamb in 1809–10.[8]

Hewson Clarke was also known to both men. He came from a more humble background. His parents had briefly kept the Red Lion on Gray's Inn Lane before moving to Northumberland. Clarke was employed as an errand boy at a chemist's in Gateshead, but managed to write satires for the *Tyne Mercury*. His talents were spotted and a benefactor paid for him to enter Emmanuel College a year after Byron joined Trinity and in the same year that Webster entered St John's. Unlike his two contemporaries, Clarke was alive to the privileges of university life. Attempting to study alongside the privileged caste, he developed a lasting and fathomless enmity towards the upper class, which saw the university as a kind of finishing school or a haven of indolence; Byron and Webster earned his particular ire. He exposed, first in the Tory *Satirist*, and then in a monthly magazine he himself edited in 1811, *The Scourge*, the dissolute manners of Webster and attacked what he regarded as the mediocre, 'namby-pamby' scrawlings of Byron.

At Cambridge, Sir Godfrey founded the 'Varments', the embryo of the Four-in-Hand and Whip Clubs. (Varment was related to the American 'varmint'; both derive from 'vermin'.) According to Clarke, he represented a new generation of dandies who entered life, after a privileged education at a public school and Cambridge, with the ambition of doing absolutely nothing except pioneering new pleasures and ways to torment the public. The 'life of a dashing Cambridge student', according to Clarke, consisted of waking at 9.30 with a headache. At 10.30, having missed chapel, or spent the service reading *Fanny Hill*, throwing candles at his friends and trying not to vomit, he would be seen parading outside the lecture hall in a shooting jacket. At one, after a ride up and down the Trumpington Road, he ate 'as much pastry as would satisfy a dozen Bond-street loungers'. By four, he would have managed to arrange his cravat, and then it was dinner. After that he would go to a wine party and get 'hellishly cut' as a prelude to roaming the streets looking for trouble with the locals. Then he and his associates would 'break a dozen lamps, wrench off half a dozen knockers, and stagger into college': 'This is the *humdrum* routine of term time.'[9]

The Varments Club was started in the spirit of what Clarke called 'the true style of university buckism'. Cambridge had no shortage of clubs for wealthy undergraduates, all retaining exclusivity by decreeing costly uniforms. The True Blue and the Beefsteak dining clubs were elegant, if drunken, affairs. The Varments rejected smart costumes, preferring the garb of a coachman. Webster 'took care to be seen parading the market place, or driving through the town in his Varment dress, just as the clock announced the hour of attendance at the lecture room'. The Varments were the ones who started to talk in a language which was a hybrid of the patois of highwaymen, thieves, coachmen and public-school boys. There was very little need to join the gallows crowd or enter a low dive in St Giles's: the low-life cant had been collated in a dictionary compiled by Francis Grose.

Saying 'peepers' for eyes, 'lady-bird' for prostitute, 'flash of lightning' for gin and 'blunt' for money might have made them sound like connoisseurs of low life to their contemporaries, but in reality Grose's dictionary was long out of date; street slang was too elusive to be pinned down by a dictionary, and thieves and pickpockets were too clever to allow their slang to be understood and appropriated. The apparently criminal jargon of the Varments was already highly fashionable for young bucks and dandies; Webster and his cronies made it into an art. At Cambridge, Webster and his fellow Varments enjoyed consorting with coachees, copying their phrases, adopting their dress and sitting with them on journeys to London or Stamford, drinking gin, spitting and swearing all the while.[10]

Clarke was not impressed that his social superiors were pretending to come from the class from which he was making pains to escape: 'A ferocious stare, a sluggish negligence of attitude, and an awkwardness of gait, a mincing drawl, or boisterous vehemence of speech, a vulgar phraseology, interlarded with the pickpocket slang from Grose's Dictionary, are eccentricities and acquisitions within the compass of any man's abilities.'[11]

The Varments took pains to be anti-intellectual. The second resolution of their constitution read: 'That we being all jolly, and quite the go being the thing, do resolve that we do not care a *damn* for our tutors.' When Clarke started penning attacks on Webster and the Varments and Byron's poetry in *The Satirist*, he claimed that the Club made their fourth resolution a condemnation of him, because he said 'how that learning and virtue were better than drunkenness and ignoramuses, our said worthy president be desired to call at his rooms and horsewhip him'. In compliance with the rules, Sir Godfrey wrote to Clarke. The letter was later published in *The Scourge* as an example of the style and manners of upper-class 'Jehus'. The spelling mistakes and poverty of grammar in the letter, if it is genuine, would have been intentional, part of the buckish and willingly ignorant posturing of the club. It read:

Sir,

. . . I think really that it will be seen when I declare that your infamous and lieing works, saying as if we were all fools, and being nothing of the kind, you really deserve a horsewhipping. I assure you that you have reason to be afraid, you *little* puppy, for you know that I am two feet higher than any lamp pounder in your college . . .

It only remains to say, that you cannot expect, seeing what you have done, that I shall restrain from exerting my menisses [menaces] wherever I meat you, so would have you prepare yourself, which is only right in a gentleman, and a man of his word, as

I am,
Sir Godfrey Webster

It is little wonder that Clarke nursed a considerable grudge against Cambridge, Webster, Byron and the upper class for the rest of his life. For him, Webster was not just a whip-wielding thug but had polluted Cambridge, then London, with 'vulgar pleasures and joyless debauchery'. For years after, well-heeled undergraduates thought it appropriate to follow the fashions laid down by the Varments. In 1811 a group of aspirant Varments were disciplined with the punishment of saying a sermon on the evils of drunkenness, and the Irish peer Lord Powerscourt, the ringleader and a would-be buck in the mould of Webster, was sent down for drunkenness, raiding shops, riding through the assembled ranks of the local militia and general acts of vandalism.[12]

Byron, Clarke and Webster were all long gone from the university by then. Sir Godfrey had attempted to make himself useful, buying a commission and joining the army in Portugal. In the briefest military career possible, he saw one bit of action, when he, another officer and thirty men attacked a hundred of the enemy, killed twenty and took five prisoners. Quite what Webster contributed in this courageous encounter was not clear. In a waspish letter to Webster's stepfather Lord Holland about other matters, Lord Paget (before his disgrace) summed up the skirmish briefly: ''Twas a most gallant affair,' which is evidently sarcastic, given that 'gallant' had come to mean an amorous venture. In any case, it was not to be repeated. Webster sought a different sort of 'gallant affair' in London with the married Lady Caroline Lamb, and preferred the heroics of the Four-in-Hand and Varment Clubs. He would become a rather supine MP, a negligent husband, and failed to make his mark in any way other than driving a coach.[13]

His brief affair with Lady Caroline was satirised in her novel *Glenarvon* (1816). The main character, Calantha, is Lady Caroline herself, and William Buchanan, a minor character, Calantha's cousin and briefly her lover, was inspired by Sir Godfrey. Calantha is briefly attracted to Buchanan for his 'air of savage wildness'; she soon learns that he is boorish, uncouth and nihilistic, not to say incredibly boring: 'Buchanan consoled himself by talking of his dogs and horses; and having given Calantha a list of the names of each, began enumerating to her the invitations he had received the ensuing week.' He only came alive while driving at top speed through town or conversing with famous pugilists.

'Truly I care not if I am knocked on the head tomorrow,' Buchanan/Webster says at a different time. 'There is nothing worth living for in life: every thing annoys me: I am sick of all society; Love, Sentiment, is my abhorrence.'

'But driving, dearest Buchanan, – riding, – your mother, – your – your cousin,' replied an anguished Calantha.

'Oh d—n it; don't talk about it. It's all a great bore.'[14]

The Four-in-Handers, according to *The Satirist*, were fugitives from the 'minor decorums of society'. The journal meant it sarcastically, but there was much truth in its flippancy. The strict laws of high society, its hypocrisy, the stilted manners of grand routs and levees, the rules of courtship were all worth running away from, if only as far as Slough.[15]

It may have been the age of elegance or the age of refinement, but it was also a time of great boredom and frustrated ambition. Many of the upper class led lives dead to any aspiration beyond a few easily satiated pleasures. The limitedness of the lives of the nobility was a running joke. Lord Onslow was a dedicated driver but was not allowed to join the Four-in-Hand Club because he had a black coach; a famous lampoon on the arid life of this hereditary legislator went:

> What can Tommy Onslow do?
> He can drive a curricle and two.
> Can Tommy Onslow do nothing more?
> Yes, he can drive a curricle and four.[16]

Onslow might have been one nonentity among many bored aristocrats, but the desolate lives of the elite could lead to destructive behaviour. In 1809 Lord Falkland was challenged to a duel by Alexander Powell, a companion of the Duke of Clarence, because Falkland had the temerity to refer to Powell by his nickname, 'Pogey'. The two were evidently 'not perfectly sober' when the incident took place. Falkland paid the price for his audacity, and, according to some papers, died saying, 'I acquit Powell of all blame in this transaction; I alone am culpable.' Falkland's friends denied that he had apologised, and a fresh row broke out in the press. In a jaded world, such trivialities mattered.[17]

The aristocracy felt assailed by vulgar arrivistes: new-money cockneys, upstart politicians rewarded with titles, Nabobs, East and West Indian planters and many other spectacularly wealthy intruders.

Britain had a finely graded hierarchy, but it was fluid. It was not, as in some European countries, legally defined. Anyone who could manage to *look* wealthy could penetrate social barriers at public places. And as most entertainment was public, high society could seem worryingly accessible. The royal court was once the forum where relative status could be established; it was read in clothes and also in personal proximity to the royal family. It was, even in the late eighteenth century, the place where society could see who was in and who was out, played out in ritual and theatre. Courtly politics continued into the reign of George III, who detested the whole thing. But it waned as he became older and more infirm. By the time of the Regency, the court featured but very little in high society, despite the Regent's efforts to revive the days of the Restoration, when the monarchy stood at the summit of fashionable life.

The Regent failed to bring back courtly manners. There were, however, other ways of closing the door. The height of ambition in the social world was to receive an invitation to a ball at Almack's assembly rooms. The club had been founded in 1764 and had not been at all fashionable for the first few decades of its existence; it was, in its early incarnation, a place for gambling and dancing. Later in the eighteenth century gambling ceased and it became a ladies' dancing club. But by the early nineteenth century it was the Everest of fashionable life; conquer it, and all previous vices and slips could be consigned to the waters of Lethe. According to the *New Monthly Magazine*, 'this is selection with a vengeance; the very quintessence of aristocracy. Three fourths of the nobility knock in vain for admission. Into this *sanctum sanctorum*, of course, the sons of commerce never think of entering.'[18]

Captain Rees Howell Gronow described 'the exclusive temple of the *beau monde*; the gates of which were guarded by Lady patronesses, whose smiles and frowns consigned men and women to happiness or despair' for the Victorians, who would have difficulty imagining the world of Almack's. The club was presided over, from 1814, by seven fearsome ladies: Ladies Jersey, Castlereagh, Cowper, Sefton and Willoughby, Princess Esterhazy and Countess Leiven. When one woman was refused an admission ticket, her husband, a captain in the Guards, challenged Lord Jersey to a duel. There was nothing glamorous about the rooms. Indeed, they were drab and the refreshments were unappetising, as if to exaggerate the point that a conspicuous display of even a modicum of wealth was disgustingly vulgar. The conversation was stiff, formal and dull, as if to remind people that interesting conversation was impolite.

The strict rules of the club were designed to force people into conformity and keep out the unfashionable. The patronesses legislated on the exact style in which men and women could dress, when people might or might not come and go, the dances that were permissible and the topics of conversation that were taboo. Aristocratic hegemony was thus retained. Nothing exempted one from the strict observance of the rules, not even defeating Napoleon. The Duke of Wellington was turned away at the door on two occasions, once when he broke the dress code by wearing trousers rather than the prescribed breeches and again when he arrived a couple of minutes late. Rules were rules, and the Duke went away chastened but not offended. Gronow remembered that 'the female government of Almack's was pure despotism, and subject to all the caprices of despotic rule'. As a result, the centre of the constellation of fashionable life was exclusive to a degree bordering on the obsessive.[19]

Edward Lytton Bulwer pointed out in the *Edinburgh Review* many years later that the manners of the early nineteenth century and the period immediately after Waterloo were dictated by the omnipotent deity, fashion. Men and women who were not necessarily distinguished by birth, rank, power or talent sought, and achieved, notoriety by being 'fashionable' or 'singularities' who won popularity from the enervated belles and beaux of high society because they dispelled the gloom of ennui. The whole system was 'the creation of a perverted ambition' that encouraged bored aristocrats to seek glory on a stagecoach or gave celebrity to such people as Beau Brummell or Mary Anne Clarke or even Sir Godfrey Webster. Hugh Murray wrote that people had always sought fame and distinction; in modern society this became harder, for in cities and mass society the individual was, more than ever, 'a drop in the waters of the ocean'. The need to escape from 'this mortifying insignificance' became acute: 'hence men glory even in their vices; anxious to be distinguished for any thing, rather than to remain in obscurity'.[20]

Times were good, said Lytton Bulwer; there was a profusion of wealth and luxury; but amidst the splendour there was little for the monied classes to do. Seats in Parliament cost thousands in the open market of seat-selling, and if one was rich enough to purchase one, the privilege of sitting in Parliament was dubious. After the deaths of Fox and Pitt in 1806, the coalition of Tories had an unassailable majority and the opposition was rendered insignificant. Debates were conducted by a handful of politicians while most MPs, if they bothered to turn up, had little to do but gossip or snooze on the benches. The Commons was, apart from a few periods of intense activity, a rather expensive club.

The drowsiness of political life, the paucity of debate or even of opportunity for advancement allowed 'the wealthier and higher classes an excuse to surrender themselves to a life of ease and pleasure – gave a wonderful impulse to Fashion. Then was Almack's established – and then were "Exclusives" first heard of. In the absence of more energetic and universal excitement – the desire of distinction became prevalent and contagious.' The Four-in-Handers, those who saw an entrée to Almack's as their *raison d'être*, the gossips, the intriguers, the adulterers, the prominence of outlandish dandies and exhibitionists were features of a world deprived of any meaningful opportunity; no wonder that they 'directed their aspirations towards easier roads to notoriety'.[21]

Much of the daily lives of the aristocracy and gentry followed a set routine, often guided by strict rules, which would be enough to frustrate anyone with a modicum of intelligence. Louis Simond described their daylight activities as 'swarming': a member of the fashionable world would never be seen unless among a crowd, in shops, art galleries, print exhibitions, museums, at the park or 'lounging' in Bond Street. At five or six the swarm temporarily dispersed to dress for dinner. 'The streets are then lighted from one end to the other . . . From six to eight the *noise* of wheels increases, it is the dinner hour.' Anyone who ventured into the West End at this time would be caught up in the whirl of rush hour. 'A multitude of carriages, with two eyes of flame staring in the dark before each of them, shake the pavement and the very houses, following and crossing each other at full speed.' For the next two hours all was quiet in the streets of the fashionable quarter as the privileged inhabitants got down to dinner. Their main meal was two hours or so later than dinner time for the middle classes; distinction between the leisured and the monied classes had to be always reiterated.[22]

While many tourists found an English dinner excruciating, a few found company that enlivened it. Hassan Khan was the star feature of society in 1810. His unconventional manners only served to exaggerate British reserve. At the time, his close attendant and translator wrote that the Persian ambassador 'is the great lion of all the Routs, and there is no entertainment given but what he is the principal feature . . . the women are quite mad about him, and make as much interest to get an introduction to him as if he were the Shah in person'. He had considerable charm, a neat turn of phrase, good looks and flowing silk robes which besotted London crowds high and low. The *Morning Herald*, like most other papers, was eager to celebrate the fairy-tale ambassador: 'The Persian Ambassador attracts the particular attention of the *Hyde Park Belles* as an *Equestrian* of singular order, for he rides in silken pantaloons of such wide dimensions, that, being inflated by the wind, make his Excellency appear like flying to a *Turkish Harem*, than riding for the pure air in *Rotten Row*.'

For his part, Hassan Khan enjoyed every moment of his embassy and recorded in his diary with wide-eyed wonder the splendours and foibles of the nobility and royal family; London and the exalted circles with which he mixed seemed impossibly exotic. A much-courted celebrity, he was shown the best that society could offer. On a March evening he dined with a party that included Prince George and his brother the Duke of Clarence, some of the ministers and their wives. This was the first time Hassan Khan had brought his Persian attendants to a dinner party. 'What a unique place this is!' they exclaimed. 'Princes and ministers and high-ranking dignitaries mix happily with sunny-faced women, singing and dancing to banish care! Would that our own country could adopt the customs of the English nobility!'

The Prince ensured that his evening entertainments were relaxed and as unrestrained as possible, something which delighted the ambassador. At a more private party at the Duke of York's residence, a party which included the Duchess, Lord Wellesley and other ministers and ladies, the Prince regaled Hassan Khan with ribald stories. The ambassador recorded in his diary: 'The Prince of Wales was so amusing that I and the other guests could not contain our mirth . . . One of the stories was about the huge size of the penis of one of his Royal brothers – a fact he had discovered one night while riding with him in a carriage. His brother had felt the need to relieve himself: when he did so out of the carriage window, the water flowed as from a fountain and the driver urged the horses forward to escape what he thought was a rainstorm! "This is how I found out," said the Prince, "and I am letting you into his secret too!"'[23]

However, most society was conducted in a way very different from the plain speaking and coarse humour of royalty. Doubtless some enjoyed the odd dirty joke at dinner parties, yet most were restrained before ladies. But if the conversation did not flow untrammelled, the wine always did. It was one of a few antidotes to the monotony of dinner. Gronow said that for his generation all pleasures involved alcohol. It made the unimaginative and never-changing menu at least palatable. Many foreign visitors found the dinner-party custom of toasting the most barbarous thing in British life. The host or a guest would single out another diner and ask him or her to drink a glass with him. Both parties in this ritual would then have to drain their glasses. No one was exempt from the toasts, neither temperate old ladies nor even adolescents. Many visitors to British shores found this ritual akin to a duel. It was a point of honour to accept the 'challenge', and a triumph to walk unaided from the field of combat. 'This is what they here call *being merry*,' wrote Karamzin in disgust after he had been subjected to a tortuous, tedious dinner punctuated with toasts; 'I however, thought otherwise, but perhaps the English drink such large quantities of wine, because it is very dear in England, for they are fond of making an ostentatious display of their wealth; or does their cold blood require such an excitement to make it flow briskly?'[24]

Captain Gronow told his readers in the 1860s that back in his youth a couple of bottles of port might not be an unusual ration for each diner. Simond found that after dinner, when the ladies retired, the men 'make amends, over the bottle, for the restraint necessary before women'. Then the real business of drinking, licentious conversation, talk of mistresses, politics, horses and hunting could begin. 'There were then four, and even five bottlemen,' wrote Gronow; 'and the only thing that saved them was drinking very slowly, and out of very small glasses. I really think that if the good society of 1815 could appear before their moderate descendants in the state they were generally reduced to after dinner, the moderns would pronounce their ancestors fit for nothing but bed.'[25]

But bed was still a long way away. When dinner was accomplished, the party would leave for the theatre or a rout or a ball. The lull in the streets of the West End was brought to a sudden end: 'at ten a *déboulement* comes on. This is the great crisis of dress, of noise, and of rapidity – a universal hubbub; a sort of uniform grinding and shaking, like that experienced in a great mill with fifty pair of stones; and, if I was not afraid of appearing to exaggerate, I should say that it came upon the ear like the fall of Niagara, heard at two miles distance. This crisis continues till twelve or one o'clock.'[26]

Hannah More wrote that fashion had decreed 'that *every body must be acquainted with every body*' and '*every body must also go every where every night*'.[27] At the height of the season, the roads would be crowded with carriages, as people queued for entry to a grand house for a rout; often, the pleasure seekers would spend longer in their carriages than at the party. This was a time to be seen by the crowds and by one's peers, the carriage window thrown open for full publicity. At the door stood the lady of the house, greeting new arrivals as if she knew them. Inside, the crowds and the heat could be intolerable. There would be five hundred people crammed into a few rooms. 'Nobody sits; there is no conversation, no cards, no music; only elbowing, turning, and winding from room to room; then, at the end of the quarter of an hour, escaping to the hall door to wait for the carriage.' Then it would be off for more of the same at another, identical rout. When Hassan Khan held one in March 1810, every street leading to his residence was chock-a-block with carriages and crowds at midnight; many carriages got badly damaged as they were tangled together in the confusion, and the Duchess of Manchester fainted in the press of bodies. It was *the* event of 1810; not to have been invited would have been social death.[28]

In 1810, angry that the ruling class deplored political demonstrations and the tumultuous sports of the lower classes, the *Examiner* compared a *fashionable* rout with an *unfashionable* gathering: 'Five or six hundred persons are assembled together, – in fact a *mob* is created; for the only difference between the mob in doors and the mob out of doors is, that the latter are ill and the former are well dressed. The inconvenience, the heat, the pressure, are equally the same in both cases. You have as much noise and more nonsense; for it is in vain to expect in such a multitude any thing more rational.' Truly, the wise man or woman would avoid such a thing; and they probably would have done had not an absence signalled social suicide, the loss of *status*. In *Glenarvon*, Calantha is introduced into this kind of society: 'every day exhibited a new scene of frivolity and extravagance; – every night was passed in the same vortex of fashionable dissipation.'

A thousand things shocked her at first, which afterwards she not only tolerated, but adopted. There was a want of ease, too, in many societies, to which she could not yet accustom herself; and she knew not exactly what it was which chilled and depressed her when in the presence of many who were, upon a nearer acquaintance, amiable and agreeable. Perhaps too anxious a desire to please, too great a regard for trifles, a sort of selfishness, which never lost sight of its own identity, occasions this coldness among these votaries of fashion.

William Pitt, who was not one for social occasions at the best of times, was once accosted by a duchess who reproached him for not coming to her recent routs. 'Do you talk as much nonsense as ever?' she sneered at the remiss Prime Minister. 'Why, Madam,' Pitt replied, 'I really do not know whether I *talk* as much nonsense as ever, since I have discontinued my attendance at your Grace's Routs. But this I am quite certain of, that I by no means *hear* so much as I used.'[29]

Rule-bound, artificial and stilted, much of aristocratic society did not provide the nutriment for intellectual life; mediocrity, however, flourished. If the aristocracy could not automatically dominate high society by exclusive access to the royal court, it could find new ways to retain its hegemony. Fashion was the way in which it could hold on to its dominance and differentiate insiders from outsiders. One of the most familiar names of the time is George 'Beau' Brummell, the arbiter of fashion and among the leading men of society.

Brummell did not come from the firmament of aristocratic families; his father served Lord North, Prime Minister in the 1770s and early '80s, as his private secretary. He amassed enough emoluments to send the Beau to Eton and leave him £30,000. 'My father was a very superior valet,' said Brummell defensively much later, when Harriette Wilson dropped a broad hint that they should 'cut' grocers and valets who intruded on society; but his parentage did him little harm. At Eton and Oriel he met some of the scions of the nobility and Prince George, and began to cultivate his refinement in dress. At Oxford he became the master of the 'cut', that ability to successfully ignore an unfashionable, unwelcome nonentity, a speck on the horizon of the social world. He was in the army for a brief time but resigned because, some said, officers were obliged to powder their hair, which was going out of fashion in civilian life; the final straw came when he was ordered to accompany his regiment to Manchester, a journey he felt should never be asked of a gentleman. From his coming of age until his exile to Calais in 1816, Brummell retained a hold over the fashionable world, becoming the most famous of all dandies of any age.[30]

There was nothing flamboyant in the style of the dandies of this time. Dandyism was a reaction against the exuberance and perceived effeminacy of eighteenth-century male fashionables, the so-called Macaronis. Charles James Fox had been a Macaroni in his youth, cultivating a foppish ensemble of flowing silks, red shoes with shiny buckles and intoxicating perfumes. He abandoned that style and adopted one that was in part a homage to the American revolutionaries – the blue and buff uniform of George Washington – combined with self-conscious slovenliness that was a celebration of personal liberty. The Beau and his fellow dandies did not modify the essentials of the Whig costume, but they reacted strongly against the dishevelled look of Fox and his Brooks's Club confederates. The dandies of the 1800s competed to perfect every tiny detail. Brummell once said that his 'chief aim was to avoid anything marked; one of his aphorisms being, that the severest mortification a gentleman could incur, was, to attract observation in the street by outward appearance'. The true gentleman could be identified, not by originality nor by imagination, but by his strictly regimented and minutely arranged wardrobe: one deviation from the prescribed uniform was an irrecoverable step beyond the pale.[31]

The length of a neck-cloth or the exact number of buttons on the knees of a pair of pantaloons was raised to the utmost importance; a miniscule variation marked the boundary between success and failure for a dandy. But one thing stood out as the grail of the fashionable. 'To have the best blacked boots in the world, is a worthy object of successful emulation', Southey wrote, describing the driving spirit of the younger male nobility in 1807 '– but to have the second best, is to be Pompey in the Pharsalia of fashion.' Apart from notices for quacks' nostrums, the most common advertisement was for boot blacking. The self-respecting dandy, however, would never be content with buying commercially available blacking, for that would mean one's boots were no better or worse than any Cit or cockney who could afford it. When Gronow went to visit Lord Petersham at Harrington House, 'we found his lordship, one of the chief dandies of the day, employed in making a particular sort of blacking, which he said would eventually supersede every other'. Brummell claimed to get his shine with champagne.

The Caesar of the world of fashionable boots, however, was Captain Kelly, 'the vainest man I ever encountered', according to Gronow: 'He was a thin, emaciated looking dandy, but had all the bearing of the gentleman. He was haughty in the extreme, and very fond of dress.' To the envy of every other man-about-town, he had the shiniest boots in the nation. Kelly was, as it turned out, the martyr in the cause of dandyism. His career at the summit of style was terminated when, in an action no beau would have hesitated to perform, he entered a burning building to rescue his favourite pair of boots. This tragedy sent shockwaves through the fashionable world: 'When the news of his horrible death became known, all the dandies were anxious to secure the services of his valet, who possessed the mystery of the inimitable blacking.'[32]

Brummell always had a 'violent desire to be perfectly correct'. The day uniform for a beau was Hessian boots, pantaloons, a blue coat and a buff waistcoat; in the evenings they would don another blue coat, a white waistcoat, black pantaloons buttoned to the ankles and striped silk stockings. But not everyone could get by simply by wearing this deceptively simple costume. Brummell would spend hours arranging his outfit. He lavished time tying his cravat, so that every fold was correctly placed; Prince George would be an eager spectator at these long ceremonies, hoping to learn something of the Brummell method. Brummell would often delight in sending himself up, but at the same time magnifying his and his fellow dandies' rigid attention to the minutiae of their costume. The careful folds and studied detail were not to be ruffled under any circumstances:

'John!' said Brummell to the waiter when he sat for dinner at his club.

'Yes, Sir.'

'Who is this at my right hand?'

'If you please, sir, it's the Marquis of Headfort.'

'And who is this at my left hand?'

'It's my Lord Yarmouth.'

'Oh, very well!' replied Brummell, who could then begin a conversation with his noble companions, all three bolt rigid, heads unmoved to preserve uncrumpled the fall of their coat, the smooth expanse of the waistcoat and the craft of the virginal cravat.[33]

The Beau was the monarch of the fashionable world partly because he refined his technique with such assiduous attention, partly because he had the patronage of the Prince, but mainly because he was feared. A vain man, Brummell knew that vain people could be terrorised by a disparaging look or a contemptuous word. 'Do you call that *thing* a coat?' was one of his most celebrated 'cuts'. He said it to the Duke of

Bedford, who craved his opinion on a new purchase – a man far above him in the hierarchy, but nonetheless cowed by the judgement of a jumped-up son of a secretary. Capturing the quintessence of Brummell's absolute power over his world, Hazlitt wrote: 'It seems all at once a vulgar prejudice to suppose that a coat is a coat, the commonest of all common things – it is here lifted into an ineffable essence, so that a coat is no longer a *thing*; or that it would take infinite gradations of fashion, taste, and refinement, for a *thing* to aspire to the undefined privileges, and mysterious attributes of a coat . . . What a cut upon a Duke! The beau becomes an emperor among such insects!'[34]

Beau Brummell's much admired repartee, well-timed cuts and affected sarcasm have attracted admirers, but it is the same kind of humour and impulse as a playground bully. The magazine *Le Beau Monde* lectured its privileged readers on their vapid and uncouth behaviour at routs and balls. In the recent past, it said, people went to social occasions and had the etiquette and good manners to talk to everyone regardless of wealth, to be witty and entertaining. 'The modern *Beau* is happily exempt from all these trammels – he now enters the gay circle, not to fascinate with his conversation, or to captivate with his manners, but to see and be seen – his quizzing glass lifted to his eye every minute, as he saunters through the ring.' He would be alive to who was up and who down; which woman was worthy of his attentions; the relative status of everyone was quickly computed in the brain. The 'quizzing glass' – a pair of lorgnettes – was the beau's defence against the importunities of non-elect social *nothings*. The lady who was prominent in another circle the day before but was now, in a more exalted group, a nobody could be safely cut: 'the glass then retains its place, with the *measuring* look of rank, or the more convenient glance of forgetfulness', while the poor woman tries in vain to converse with he whom she rashly counted a friend. Such people would rather leave a party than be seen talking to someone infra dig, incorrectly dressed or unfashionable. The cut was a carefully cultivated attitude and the deadly weapon in a dandy's social repertoire. Brummell and his followers were supreme in laying down the law. For a time, 'no party was complete without him'. His mastery of putting on his clothes, his sharp tongue and his coterie of aristocratic toadies meant that 'he could decide the fate of a young man just launched into the world with a single word'.[35]

'For the dandy', wrote Baudelaire, 'self-control and self-pride were all.' The naturalness of Fox's dishevelment and the emotions of sentimentality were distasteful; restraint and mannered behaviour were the correct mode for the cosmopolitan man. Brummell deplored the 'excessive devotion to stables, dog-kennels, and coachmanship' exhibited by his contemporaries and many of his friends – Sefton and Worcester were members of the Four-in-Hand Club and companions of his. (Brummell enjoyed hunting but gave it up because of what it did to his boots.) Dressing down and acting down to the level of the rude lower sort was contrary to the dandy's first principles. He must be expected on all occasions to subject himself to strict forms of behaviour. It was the victory of propriety over spontaneity; of rules over personal liberty.

The dandies' pared-down, ascetic style was the opposite of the eccentricities and gregariousness of fops and bohemians. In an age when old barriers between classes seemed to be crumbling and it became harder to differentiate between the socially acceptable and the arriviste, the dandy reinvented the exclusivity of the aristocracy for the modern world. The struggle for the absolute perfection of a deceptively simple uniform showed that a man had several hours to tie his cravat and put on his trousers. By the end of his long toilette Brummell would leave a pile of discarded cravats which had failed to satisfy his connoisseur's eye. Such rigorous attention to detail was not permitted of a banker, a merchant or an MP, who were rich of pocket but poor of time. The scrutiny of minute details allowed fashionable society to sort those with the luxury of leisure from those mere mortals who dirtied their hands with business. Those who had an eye for the tiniest detail were therefore the most discriminating, and hence the arbiters of taste. Hazlitt wrote that fashion was like the watermark on a banknote: it is easy to counterfeit the genuine article, but very difficult to replicate the imperceptible mark of authenticity. If a man was insufficiently serious about manners, if he considered a matter of business more important than social convention, it was written on his clothes; it was clear and screamingly obvious to Brummell and his clique, if not the rest of the world, which was too unpolished to tell a genuine dandy from an imitator. That's why they were thrilled if people on the street didn't give them a second glance. Brummell, with his scrupulous formality, took this to the extreme.[36]

The fear that high society would be contaminated by sordid businessmen and people of talent was evinced in the rise of Almack's and the primacy of Beau Brummell. They stood against anarchy in the social world and defended aristocratic values from vulgar meritocracy. The eradication of the court as a setter of trends and regulator of status, the increasing wealth of commercial society and the wars made this competition more fierce. Without the wars it is doubtful that Brummell would have achieved notoriety. Paris, the traditional arbiter of taste and fashion, was closed off from British tourists for decades, with a few short exceptions. Left to their own devices, the British had to develop their own fashions independent of their more sophisticated neighbours. The wars had other implications. Brummell was the leader of a generation of men who were too refined to go to war. They knew their inferiority and compensated for it. Soldiers and adventurers always threatened to undermine established privilege on their return home and upset the primacy of the stay-at-homes. In this period there were rather a lot of heroes to rival Brummell and his friends. Because they did not fight, the dandies and Four-in-Handers had disdain for coarse and muddy soldiers, mere vulgar men of action. And soldiers were equally dismissive of fastidious dandies. 'Damn the fellows,' one Guardsman said of the dandies, 'they're upstarts, fit only for the society of tailors.'[37] Captain Gronow, the principal memorialist of Regency dandy-mania, was one of a few officers allowed into Almack's. Brummell and his praetorians were the heroes of the home front. Their language and conduct was martial in the extreme: they wore uniforms, they inspected their subordinates and they paraded in front of the *bon ton* in Hyde Park. Soldiers and sailors as much as politicians and poets should be kept in their place lest they intrude upon the hallowed ground of fashion. Turning Wellington away from the doors of an assembly room was a nice reminder that a man who had secured his title by merit rather than birth had to submit to aristocratic manners.

Their craving for celebrity was born of a sense of their inferiority; compared to the soldiers and sailors serving around the world, the dandies were nobodies. Yet they carved out a lonely niche in St James's which they ruled with the iron control of a Napoleon. They were a sad bunch of men, bored, repressed and frustrated. Many of them lost vast sums at the gaming table. That was part of the nature of aristocratic stoicism. They could look at the sudden loss of a fortune with equanimity. Who cared about money after all but greedy City speculators? Young noblemen were so far removed from bourgeois values of thrift and prudence that they would stake all on the throw of a dice. Debt was an indicator of class too. Why would a Brummell attend to the clamours of a creditor? He and his friends were too refined to even think about money matters. Paying a debt or sweating over a massive loss were as vulgar as putting on the wrong coat. The dandy craze ran its course and reached its height at the culmination of the war in 1815. It was the year before Brummell had to flee his creditors and begin a long and lonely exile in Calais. Captain Jesse, Beau Brummell's first biographer, and a sympathetic one at that, wrote of his friend and subject: 'Eager for distinction, but conscious that he had not the industry and purpose in any of the useful and honourable paths selected by other men, he chose an easy and amusing mode of arriving at his object.'[38]

*

'Sincerity is a virtue not calculated for promiscuous company,' wrote a clergyman in a guide to etiquette; 'it then becomes impudence . . . a fair and seasonable accommodation of one's self to the various exigencies of the times, is the golden virtue that ought to predominate in a man of life and business.' In *Sense and Sensibility*, Elinor berates Marianne for flirting with Willoughby:

> But I see what you mean [Marianne replies]. I have been too much at my ease, too happy, too frank. I have erred against every common-place notion of decorum; I have been open and sincere where I ought to have been reserved, spiritless, dull, and deceitful.

In all her novels Jane Austen satirises 'sensibility' and praises propriety of conduct, self-mastery and emotional continence. It was a reaction to what she and many of her generation saw as affected and bogus emotional displays – 'the cant of candour'. Marianne's justification that she was 'open and sincere' seems dangerously anarchic, a specious and childlike excuse for defying convention. It harks back to the era of sensibility a generation before. Both Austen and Beau Brummell bear witness to the age's conflicting attitude to the opposing virtues of sincerity and propriety. These two very different people fall firmly on the side of decorum. Austen is concerned with the power of emotions to deceive the weak-minded mortal; for Brummell, sincerity and the hurly-burly of naturalness were vulgar and incongruous with polite society.[39]

'Propriety is the centre in which all the lines of duty and agreeableness meet,' wrote Hannah More. Self-regulation and mannered behaviour were certainly in vogue for the post-revolutionary and wartime upper-class generation. 'The natural tendency of the French Revolution', wrote Tom Moore, 'was to produce in the higher classes of England an increased reserve of manner, and, of course, a proportionate restraint on all within their circle, which have been fatal to conviviality and humour, and not very propitious to wit – subduing both their manners and conversation to a sort of polished level, to rise above which is often thought as vulgar as to sink below it.' There were innumerable examples of this starchiness and formality. Moore gave the example of the way in which men used to call each other Dick (for example, Richard Sheridan), Ned (Edmund Burke), Jack (Townsend) and Tom (Thomas Grenville), 'a mode of address, that brings with it, in its very sound, the notion of conviviality and playfulness'.[40]

Little wonder that men who were constrained in public found outlet elsewhere. It was often with the lower classes that they found a release – at pleasure gardens and taverns, with 'the Fancy' at boxing matches, races, cruel sports and the like. People competed to be what was called 'singular'. Everyone in fashionable life, said *Le Beau Monde*, in 'this singular age', was on a quest for singularity, a desire to break free from the stupefying round of unvariegated entertainments. Everyone wanted to be noted for some eccentricity or as the inventor of a novelty to entertain the privileged portion of the public. One of the English dandies encountered by Captain Gronow at this time was Colonel Dan Mackinnon, famed in his circle for his monkey impressions. He would climb over furniture or whatever obstacle presented itself; he would gleefully take bets to climb to such-and-such a ceiling or a particular roof. During the Peninsular campaign, the Colonel persuaded some Spaniards that he was the Duke of York. The masquerade was kept up throughout a lavish royal reception, Mackinnon only disabusing his hosts by diving head first into an enormous and full punch bowl, leaving his feet waggling in the air. At another time Wellington visited a Portuguese convent during the war. Mackinnon smuggled himself into the nunnery in disguise and was commended by his unwitting commander-in-chief as the comeliest of the order. 'I might say more about Dan's adventures in the convent,' wrote Gronow, 'but have no wish to be scandalous.'[41]

There were many people like Dan Mackinnon in a class where good behaviour was expected on all public occasions. Eccentrics, wits and the 'singular' diminished monotony and set rules at defiance for a while. Men competed in feats of agility for vast bets: cricket matches, walking races (the most popular sport of the time), boxing, racing carriages or rowing. One man achieved 'singularity' by parachuting from church steeples. Success made a gentleman a celebrity, however trivial the achievement might be. Those who could rebelled against narrowing social obligations. One was Princess Charlotte, daughter of the Prince and Princess of Wales (George and Caroline) and second in line to the throne. Though she was deprived of her parents' company for long periods during her childhood (which many would consider a blessing), Charlotte inherited a plain way of speaking, affability and spontaneity from her father, along with her mother's mischievous sense of humour, tomboyishness and hatred of stale convention. 'As soon as she grows intimate with any one,' wrote Lady Charlotte Bury, who was part of Princess Caroline's household, 'she gives way to her natural feelings, and there is an openness and candour in her conversation, which is very captivating. I pity her that she is born to be queen.'[42]

Because she was the daughter of a broken home, neglected by her father and kept from her mother, Princess Charlotte was mercifully free of most of the 'refinement' of her contemporaries. She also knew that she was above the constraints placed on girls her age by the marriage market: a future queen, she would have no trouble finding suitors, who would be lined up in order of diplomatic importance. Living under comparatively little restraint, Charlotte developed contempt for the ennui and affectation of '*good* society'. 'I fear that she is capricious, self-willed, and obstinate,' wrote Lady Charlotte. 'I think she is kind-hearted, clever, and enthusiastic. Her faults have evidently never been checked, nor her virtues fostered.' Yet the naturalness, *joie de vivre* and unaffected manners far outweighed the disadvantages Lady Charlotte detected. During the opening of Parliament in December 1812, the princess sat on the woolsack, laughing and grimacing at her father's speech, 'which did not displease *all* the lords, nor *all* the ladies there'. Charlotte was a thoroughgoing Whig, and made her displeasure at her father's retention of the Tory ministry known. She was one girl who could afford to be sincere.

Lord Glenbervie recorded the Princess's behaviour at a dinner, where she was 'forward, dogmatic, buckish . . . and full of exclamations very like swearing'. After dinner she stretched out her leg and showed her drawers.

'My dear Princess Charlotte,' admonished Lady de Clifford, 'you shew your drawers.'

'I never do, but where I can put myself at my ease,' replied Charlotte.

'Yes, my dear,' replied Lady de Clifford sharply, 'when you get in or out of your carriage.'

'I don't care if I do.'

'Your drawers are too long.'

'I don't think so – the Duchess of Bedford's are much longer, and they are bordered with Brussels lace.'

'O,' said a defeated Lady de Clifford, 'if she is to wear them, she does right to make them handsome.'[43]

Princess Charlotte was lucky. She was able to defy the 'false delicacy', squeamishness, fastidiousness and restrained behaviour that society dictated proper for young girls. The determination not to be cowed by the hypocritical expectations of society, shared by strong-minded women such as Lady Oxford, Lady Holland, Lady Caroline Lamb or Lady Melbourne, only made the contrast with the stilted manners of their contemporaries the more glaring. Showing one's undergarments in public or facing down the accusing stares of disapproving old ladies was an act of defiance against a world dominated by prudes and hypocrites. There is an insight into this in *Belinda*, when the book's heroine questions Lady Delacour:

'"Why will you delight in making yourself appear worse than you are, my dear Lady Delacour," said Belinda, taking her hand.

'"Because I hate to be like other people," said her ladyship, "who delight in making themselves appear better than what they are."'[44]

That is akin to the spirit of the Four-in-Hand Club members and other fugitives from decorum. Restrained conduct in one area will always find an outlet in another. At a time when the manners of the aristocracy were coming under scrutiny and there was a pressure for reform, a minority rebelled against the prudery they detected. It was easier for men to escape the straitjacket of polite society than their wives, sisters and daughters. They pined for the company of strong, witty and fun women, for the kind of company, conversation and relationships that polite society did not permit. 'Whilst frigid unalluring chastity – cold conjugal fidelity, sits moping in neglect and solitude, unable to fix the faithless wanderer,' wrote Elizabeth Taylor, 'the fascinating prostitute waves her wand like a sorceress, draws him within the magic circle of pleasure; and moral duty, domestic affection, with every tie that cements society, is swallowed up in sensual indulgence.'[45]

Christian Goede said that Englishmen were faithful husbands in their own way; but 'they are as fickle in the pursuit of sensual pleasures'. He was amazed that the English should boast of their morals and the sanctity of marriage when there were so many prostitutes on the streets, many of them of fairly high birth, showing that they were forced to ply their trade not from poverty in the first instance but because they were outcasts from society. Nothing showed the hypocrisy or cruelty of the English more: 'in England, *one* false step, is never pardoned: the victim of *one* unguarded moment finds no friendly bosom to receive the tears of penitence and contrition.' Under such circumstances, the man who seduced a woman knew that there was a very high chance he was condemning her to expulsion from her family and a life as a common prostitute. The Poor Laws penalised women who produced bastard children but were more lenient to men. A Gloucester magistrate recorded in 1809 the question put by a woman who was committed to the house of correction for this crime: 'Why the man who had seduced her was not to be imprisoned as well as herself?' 'I could only answer,' the magistrate recalled, '"Because women were not legislators and men were parish officers".'[46]

But if prostitutes were the lowest and most abandoned victims of a hypocritical society and the fickle whims of bored young men, there was a class of professional women who were altogether luckier, cleverer and, to a certain extent, esteemed by society. The 'Cyprian' was the polite word for a kept mistress or courtesan, a woman who was given an establishment, an income and protection by one man (at a time). The Regent's crony George Hanger had nothing but praise for the Cyprian; she was frank, free, gutsy and no less sinful than most fashionable women. She was captivating and, compared to her 'betters', a good deal of fun: 'Ye beauteous fair, to whom all nature yields and bends the knee, whose power the soldier dreads more than hostile foe in battle fierce, strike deep your dagger in my breast; but, oh, in pity heal me with your smiles!'[47]

The courtesans from the 1800s who have lasted for posterity are Harriette Wilson and her sisters Amy and Fanny Dubouchet, as well as Julia Johnstone and Mary Anne Clarke. Wilson and Johnstone published memoirs in 1825 recalling the days of excess in the 1800s and 1810s. Mary Anne Clarke became a household name in 1809 when her financial relationship with Prince Frederick, Duke of York and hereditary Bishop of Osnabrück, erupted into a major political scandal. These, the most famous courtesans of the age, were not all considered beautiful by their contemporaries; one person said that Clarke was not exactly one 'which Phidias would select for a Venus'. Conventional beauty was not a requirement for a courtesan. The Cyprian was not just a sex object; she was there to provide solace, good company and add to the fun of life; indeed, everything that men could not find in stale and loveless marriages or arid social occasions. The Cyprian balls held in the lobbies of the major London theatres were among the most sought-after events for statesmen, soldiers, dandies and aristocratic men. There they could relax and talk freely.

One woman, of respectable background, talked of a reciprocal code observed by mistresses and the honour of the 'open and generous man' who sought a friend and confidante rather than an anonymous one-off encounter. According to Hanger, a good Cyprian was one who could make men happy and keep them in 'a perpetual possession of being well deceived'.[48]

Making sure a man was *well* deceived was the most important thing. The art that such a woman learnt first was to avoid making the relationship seem sordid or mercenary: she should be well paid for her services, but the transaction should be subtle. Her duty was to provide an alternative home for him, complete with both the domestic comforts and sumptuous entertainments that he required for his relaxation from royal, political and military duties. When Mary Anne Clarke told York that the £1,000 he gave her each year was not enough to maintain the establishment he required of her, she remembered the Prince telling her 'that if I was clever, I should never ask for money'; it was a lesson every courtesan should have pinned up on her bedpost. In Mary Anne's case, it was a broad hint to find a new way of benefiting from their connection. Until the relationship went spectacularly wrong, York was to have looked after Mary Anne in other ways, by seeing that her debts were cleared and that she was provided with the furniture and clothes to keep up a good life.

Mary Anne Clarke proved to be as popular with the British public as she was with her male protectors. In 1809 the news emerged that Prince Frederick, the commander-in-chief of the army, was selling commissions below the market rate through his mistress. Frederick and Mary Anne's liaison had begun in 1804 and lasted for two years; during that time the Prince, famously stingy, had become unwilling to pay her debts and the stipulated £1,000 annuity. Mary Anne complained that 'from three to four months his Royal Highness never gave me a guinea, though he was with me every day'; she quickly slipped into debt. Instead, the arrangement was that aspirant officers paid Mary Anne to use her influence with Frederick to have them promoted. Under the regulated prices, a captaincy cost £1,500 and a major would have to pay £2,600. But 'Clarke's prices' were £700 and £900 for those same commissions. It suited all parties: the officers saved hundreds of pounds, Mary Anne got her money without having to bother her paramour, and York managed to pay for his pleasures from public money. The loser was the taxpayer, who was cheated of thousands of pounds in lost revenue.[49]

This happy situation came to an end when the Duke and Mrs

Clarke ended their affair. Stupidly, York also stopped his former lover's annuity and did not pay her debts. News of the Duke's unconventional ways of paying his mistress inevitably leaked out to radical politicians. When Mrs Clarke's new political friends exposed the scandal, the Prince told the government that he was innocent. It was a fatal mistake: the government felt it could investigate the allegations and exonerate the head of the army. Unfortunately for the Prince-Bishop, the investigation revealed details of his private life, his cupidity and the extent of his corruption; although Parliament would not condemn him, he was obliged to resign as commander-in-chief.

The scandal and investigation brought Mary Anne Clarke, hitherto

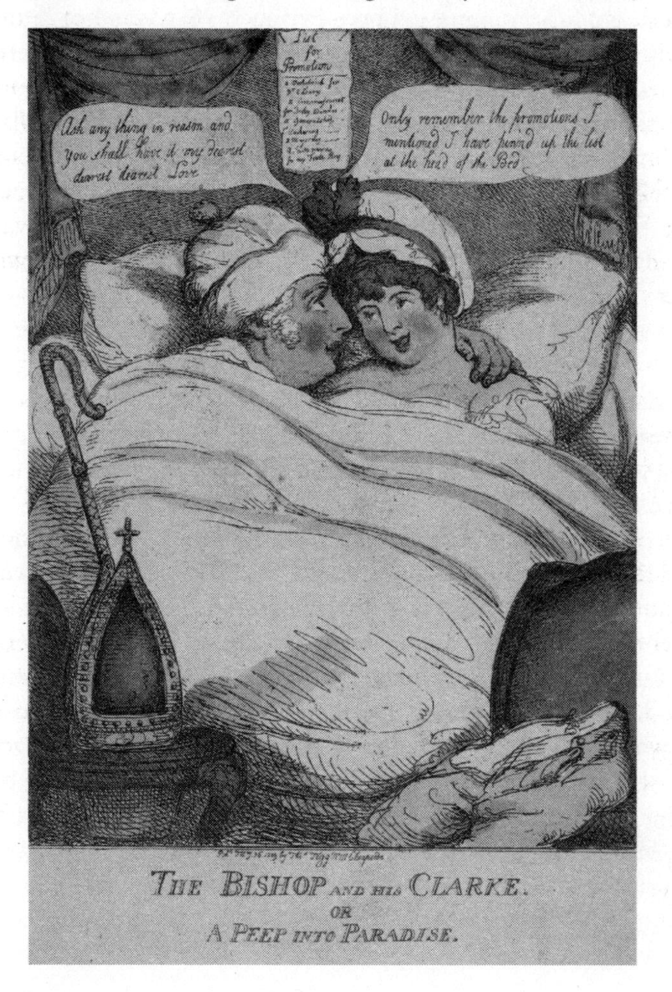

THE BISHOP AND HIS CLARKE. OR A PEEP INTO PARADISE.

well-known only among certain circles, into national prominence. The public demanded details about her life and character, and the biographies and prints began to appear to accompany her public utterances during the House of Commons enquiry. They could not bring themselves to believe that Clarke was not more beautiful than she was, so the prints and cartoons indulged the fantasy and embellished her charms. One of her friends described a woman who, though not 'a perfect beauty', had a pretty oval face, a small nose and fair skin with colour in her cheeks. Her best physical asset, however, was her 'dazzling dark eyes, beaming with the most irresistible archness and captivating intelligence'. One commentator found it strange that such an *ordinary*-looking woman could have gained a hold over so many men (he evidently had not looked into her eyes); it must have been her '*witcheries*', the 'tricks of trade' or her 'meretricious arts' that ensnared and deluded so many for so long. The very things that had attracted her paramours now attracted the British people. She had lived with several men, including her husband, Lord Barrymore ('Cripplegate') briefly, a barrister, a baronet and the Duke of York, 'all of whom complain of her extravagance and artfulness; but admit that she is a most fascinating woman', according to one newspaper. Yet it was the mixture of extravagance, wit, pleasing manners and good conversation that made her so desirable.[50]

As George Hanger advised all Cyprians and would-be Cyprians, the only qualification for a paramour should be the size of his purse: 'the more ignorant and stupid you find him, the better for you'. By these criteria, Mary Anne Clarke had won first prize in the courtesan lottery. One of the things that endeared Mrs Clarke to the public was her gloriously defiant attitude towards Frederick: 'she regarded the Duke of York as a big baby, not out of his leading strings', remembered Gronow. One of Mary Anne's greatest charms was her waspish and pithy repartee; it was delightful to hear, but excruciating to be its target. She wouldn't have been the same woman without the extravagance and free tongue: 'she has . . . great vivacity, not to say impudence, of manner'. It was her power of conversation that kept men enthralled, both her 'protectors' and later the wider public: 'Her wit, which kept the House of Commons during her examination in a continued state of merriment, was piquant and saucy'; there were few women like her.[51]

York eventually became the victim, mocked and traduced by his former mistress in the Commons and the press. Mrs Clarke boasted before she gave evidence that she would make at least half the MPs fall in love with her. And that's what happened. Spencer Perceval was incensed at her 'sarcastic insolence', 'her playful pleasantry' and 'her general cleverness and versatility'. It was a dishonour to Parliament that he wished the House could forget, but to their shame MPs would always remember 'how indulgently they tolerated her jokes, how they seemed to forget her vice in her wit, and be reconciled to her infamy by her manner of displaying it'. Wilberforce, like most men, was in awe of her, saying, 'she was elegantly dressed, consummately impudent, and very clever'. He was disgusted by the response she got from his fellow MPs: 'We are alive to the political offence, but to the moral crime we seem utterly insensible; and the reception which every double entendre meets in the House, must injure our character greatly with all religious minds.' He fretted that the revelations of high society and royal shenanigans would have a dire effect on peasants in remote villages who would learn about them for the first time. It showed the depths of national corruption and dared God's vengeance; 'yet', he wrote, 'there are many righteous, I trust, among us'.[52]

Sir Godfrey Vassall Webster, Beau Brummell, Princess Charlotte and Mary Anne Clarke are a diverse enough bunch of people. Each one in their own way illustrates the pain that strict manners inflicted on individuals. A society that closely scrutinised morals, and one which was ever more anxious that natural behaviour should be straitjacketed, was more than likely to encourage rebellion and loutish behaviour. The petty decorums and fastidious rules that governed social gatherings rendered conversation insipid and friendships artificial. No wonder people sought pleasure elsewhere. Anything to variegate the placid surface of society. The very things that had been invented to safeguard the morals of high society were productive of greater vices. As Brummell's first biographer Captain Jesse said, with its superficial finery and worm-eaten heart, this was 'the gilded not the golden age'.[53]

7

The Theatre of War

> '. . . we all know that a theatre is a place of peculiar excitement; I think [the audience's] applause is enthusiastic, and their dislikes very violently expressed. I do not know anything more terrible than an enraged audience . . .'
>
> Thomas Morton[1]

In September 1808 the Theatre Royal, Covent Garden, burnt to the ground when a piece of wadding fired from a gun during a performance got trapped between some scenery. On 1 December of the same year the Prince of Wales laid the foundation stone of a new theatre. Before the first anniversary of the conflagration, a new building had arisen which 'seemed as the visionary structure of some eastern enchanter'. On Monday 18 September 1809 Londoners of all sorts queued for hours, eager to see a new season's entertainment in a magnificent new theatre. John Kemble, the great actor of the age and the theatre's manager, had an enticing repertoire of plays, starting with Shakespeare's tragedies. *Macbeth* inaugurated the new theatre, and it was to be followed immediately by a farce called *The Quaker* on that first night.

When the doors opened at three in the afternoon, the audience entered through the impressive portico, turned left and climbed a staircase flanked by bronze Grecian lamps on tripods. At the top of the stairs they bought their tickets and continued on up a grand staircase to an anteroom, each side of which was lined with large Ionic pillars with bronze lamps suspended between each; a statue of Shakespeare looked down from one end as the crowd swarmed in for the long-anticipated opening night of the country's favourite theatre. The people passed between eight statues of Greek gods in the main lobby to enter the theatre. The auditorium itself was just as lavish, with gold pillars and a profusion of chandeliers. Everything showed attention to detail and the same classical inspiration. The lower-circle boxes had simple gold Etruscan borders decorated with Grecian honeysuckle.[2]

The management and the crowd were both excited; they had been a year without the great theatre, and its rival, Drury Lane, had also burnt down. It was hoped a dazzling season would make up for their absence. The anticipation was palpable; the audience was overexcited. When the Duke of York took his seat people called out 'Dukey!' and 'My Darling!', in reference to the way Mary Anne Clarke had referred to her lover during their by now public affair. Just before curtain-up, the audience spontaneously broke into 'God Save the King' and 'Rule Britannia'.

No one predicted exactly what happened next. The play started, and when Kemble appeared on the stage he 'was instantly drowned in a torrent of execration'; the superstar actor, who expected to be praised after building a magnificent new theatre for his fans, 'cast around imploring looks for pity' before retiring for a moment to compose himself. When he returned, 'the noise and outcry that followed were continued with an energy truly terrific . . . in one corner of the pit you had a heap of groans, in another a combination of hisses, in a third a choir of yells, in a fourth a doleful ululating moaning, which, mingling with the other sounds reminded one of the infernal regions'.

Upon the Thane's coronation, a man began to bark like 'a huge mastiff'. Macduff was played by Charles Kemble, and when he overcame John Kemble's Macbeth, members of the crowd called out, 'Well done, kill him, Charley.' When Kemble enacted Macbeth's death there was wild cheering, 'as if the spectators congratulated themselves on this temporary demise'. At the end of the night's second play, as the crowd became more vociferous, the actors disappeared, the stage lights were turned down and the trapdoors opened to deter any invaders. Soon, a pumping noise was heard, and the hose of a fire engine appeared through the stage door as a warning to anyone who was thinking of intruding. On Tuesday night, the performance was disturbed by men and women imitating the 'braying of asses, roaring of mastiffs, deep-toned opening of fox hounds, yelping of curs, whiffling of lap-dogs, crowing of cocks, tally-ho's and yo-icks of huntsmen, gee-up of the Four-in-hand gentlemen, and though last not least, the cheering *hear, hear*!' Under such circumstances it was impossible to continue performing, and the theatre was closed on Saturday. The audiences were enraged, and it was put down to the increased ticket prices; but that hardly explained the anger of the protests. At this stage, the extent of the Londoners' rage was hardly grasped. It seemed like ingratitude after so much had been done to provide them with a new theatre. When Kemble appeared on stage, he asked plaintively, 'What do you want?'[3]

The vices of the highest and the lowest were on full display at London theatres. It could often be frightening; it was never dull. While a visitor to London might think that English decencies were observed tolerably well in most circumstances, a visit to the theatre would soon disabuse them of that preconception. Louis Simond described the sailors, footmen, 'low tradesmen' and their wives and mistresses 'who enjoy themselves as they please' in the upper galleries of the Covent Garden Theatre. The catcalls and barking during the disturbances of September 1809 were bad but not unknown during normal times: 'These gods, for so they are called from their elevated situation . . . assume the high privilege of hurling down their thunder on both actors and spectators, in the shape of apples, and orange peel. This innocent amusement has always been considered in England as a sort of exuberance of liberty, of which it is well to have a little too much, to be sure that you have enough.'[4]

John Styles, a zealous Methodist writer, said that if his daughter went to the theatre, 'I should clasp my last child to my bosom, weep at the thought of innocence for ever fled, and mourn the day that made me a parent: – her soul is polluted, and that is the essence of prostitution'. Not only would his daughter rub shoulders with the ferocious crowd, but, if she managed to hear the performance above the noise, her soul would be contaminated by poison. Plays and farces were 'the immoral creature of an immoral audience'; the stage was the mirror that showed the true moral state of society. No wonder adultery, crim. con., seduction and divorce were rife when so many plays mocked marriage and chastity, making light of vows and teasing constant husbands and wives. And the father of the English stage, Shakespeare, was himself one of the 'men of libertine principles', corrupting generations with 'bare-faced obscenities, low vulgarity, and nauseous vice'. The levity and false emotions of the stage made the theatre the 'hot bed of the passions'. The middling tradesman or labourer and their wives learnt their bad habits there, aping the effeminate and lavish habits of libertines and fashionables, imbibing the arts of hypocrisy and sophistry, and allowing their minds to be excited by base passions, low humour and revealing costumes. If Styles's daughter ever entered that pit of depravity, something much worse than the anti-moral creed of plays and acting awaited her: the parallel performance that went on every night at places like the Covent Garden Theatre. The goings-on in the private boxes provided entertainment as fascinating and certainly more corrosive than anything that happened on the stage.[5]

In January 1808 an anonymous correspondent, 'M', wrote to the *Monthly Magazine* saying that he had returned to England after twenty years abroad. M went to the opera with a companion and was appalled to see prostitutes sitting conspicuously in the side boxes. Such women, he wrote, 'used, in my days, to confine themselves to the upper slips, or to the back of the front boxes'. M asked his friend when such a change had occurred; the companion asked M whom he meant. M pointed out some women 'whose bosoms were exposed in a manner that I never saw before, except under the piazzas of Covent Garden of an evening, or in some of the most nocturnal street-walkers'. 'Surely', M said to his friend, 'they are of no other description, unless they are of a higher order of demireps, and kept by men of fashion.' No, they were not common prostitutes, the friend replied, but members of the nobility and women of fashion.[6]

There was plenty on offer for the audiences at the theatre or opera; people were there to see and be seen. People went to the theatre with the 'hope of being mixed up in splendid confusion with the flower of the land', as Hazlitt put it. Fashionable ladies would have a chance to flaunt their dominion over 'the world'; competitors for the laurels could observe and sneer at each other; feuds could be conducted and 'cuts' performed in front of the gaze of a thousand. 'Walking around the theatre,' Hassan Khan recorded in his journal after a visit to Covent Garden in January 1810, 'my companions and I saw beautiful ladies, beautifully dressed, casting flirtatious glances from their boxes.' But the objects of real attention were genuine prostitutes, who openly plied their trade in the pit (as the stalls were called then) and the galleries. It was notorious that there were prostitutes for all ranks and conditions every evening at the theatres, and the Covent Garden Theatre was compared to a brothel. Their behaviour and the men who courted them were an on-going diversion from the acting of Kemble or Sarah Siddons. In December 1808 a Captain B of the navy and a City merchant, Mr C, got into a fistfight: 'The cause of the quarrel was a STRUMPET!' The constables arrived and separated the combatants, who were promptly ejected. Mr C later returned, to find the woman with another man; a further fight broke out. This was not unusual: in the 1800s, the *Examiner* said, 'a riot is as much to be expected as the raising of a curtain'.[7]

The theatre was the true forum of the Cyprian. If the male nobility kept their other lives away from prying eyes, the theatre was a glaring exception. No wonder Styles was determined to keep his pious daughter away. Cyprians came face to face with the wives and connections of their male benefactors at theatres and the opera. The private boxes allowed people to see which beauty was up, which down; who had the favour of Lord So-and-so; which courtesan was the best dressed and most favoured. It was at Covent Garden or Drury Lane or the opera that women such as Mary Anne Clarke or Harriette Wilson were transformed into celebrities. And the men who craved the company of the sisterhood were more than happy to be seen in the exclusive company of a Clarke or a Wilson. When the Duke of York first took Mrs Clarke to the theatre, 'every eye and every lorgnette in the house were directed towards her in the course of an evening', which must have pleased Mary Anne and her 'protector' in equal measure. Years later, at the moment that Spencer Perceval announced the Duke's resignation as commander-in-chief to the House of Commons, Mary Anne was making herself conspicuous in a box at the Haymarket.

'Everybody is talking about you,' Lord Frederick Bentinck told Harriette Wilson when she was at the opera. 'Two men downstairs, have been laying a bet that you are Lady Tavistock. Mrs Orby Hunter says you are the handsomest woman in the house.' In the Round Room at the opera, Harriette would occupy one end, and her sister and chief rival, Amy, the other, both hoping to attract the biggest and most exclusive circle of dandies, beaux, ambassadors, soldiers and noblemen. The desire to be seen in such exalted company got the better of many men. 'Our box was so crowded', wrote Wilson, 'that I was obliged to turn one out as fast as a new face appeared . . . Observing me for a moment, the Duke of Devonshire came into my box, believing that he did me honour'; there could be no doubt, however, who was really being honoured.

The opera was the place for courtesans to establish their status, find new protectors and make mental notes on the comings and goings of society. When Harriette was courting the Duke of Argyle, she was alive to the role she had to play in these circumstances. 'At the opera I learned to be a complete flirt; for there I saw Argyle incessantly with Lady W–, and there it became incumbent on me either to laugh or cry. I let him see me flirt and look tender on Lord Burghersh, one night, on purpose . . .' It was a studied and essential performance, one which could be seen by the parties it was intended for, not to say many others who were doing their best to ignore the background noise of acting. High society was too fashionable to arrive on time. The votaries began to drift in after the first act and ladies of pleasure from the interval. The lowly audience would be reasonably interested in the play until then. But as soon as the courtesans and prostitutes arrived, the general behaviour degenerated into stares, mutters, laughs, shouts and the occasional brawl.

It was little wonder then that in September 1809, when the Covent Garden Theatre was rebuilt with *enclosed* private boxes, the crowd should consider that a significant proportion of pleasure had been stolen from them. The theatre had been rebuilt at a cost of £150,000, of which £50,000 was paid by the insurance company and a further £12,500 a year by offering annual subscriptions for a private box with an annexed private room. The rest of the building programme would be recouped from an increase in the admission price. But although the prices had gone up, the comforts of the pit and the galleries were not improved. Right at the top, in the gods, the audience had to peer between supporting arches, through narrow gaps which were renamed 'pigeon-holes'. The dress circle was banked too steeply, and the view was further obscured by pillars. The boxes, however, had the best view of the stage and every effort had been put in 'to make these secret recesses more luxuriantly magnificent', each one with a boudoir at the back with 'every convenience which luxury and indolence can require'. In the past, the boxes had been open to everyone; even the King's box was let to the public on the nights he wasn't there. Now, the private boxes were let by the year, so they would be left unoccupied on nights when the owner was away rather than opened to the public. These 'snug retreats' were against the spirit of London life and the equality of the theatre; they were intended solely for accommodating people 'too aristocratical to mingle with a British public'.[8]

While such things might be acceptable in Paris or Milan, *The Satirist* commented, 'there is something in them revolting to the British character, and a British audience can never look on them without indignation'. They deprived people of a great deal of amusement; they would sit there knowing that the idle rich were free to conduct affairs and intrigues removed from gossiping servants, 'the impertinent intrusion of an officious landlady' and the curious public. Someone who wrote under the name Thomas Hobbs said that the boxes were pernicious because 'they make too great a distinction in Society, and destroy that grand cement and happy union among Mankind, which has for Ages proved the best and greatest Defender of our GLORIOUS CONSTITUTION'. The new theatre looked superb, but it was clear that the managers had 'consulted little but the accommodation of the higher orders. The people felt this immediately.'[9]

It was said that the people might have accepted the new prices if they felt they were not subsidising social segregation and refuges for aristocratic intrigue. The private boxes became crucial in the so-called O.P. War – O.P. standing for Old Prices. The moans and hisses on the first night were spontaneous signs of disapproval; very soon, however, the movement escalated, becoming one of the most comical, colourful and fiercely contested issues of the 1800s.

In the six days that the theatre remained open, the play became nothing more than a 'dumb show', with men and women standing on the benches, shouting, singing, barking, blowing horns and ringing dustmen's hand bells in the pit. Banners appeared stating 'Old Prices', and throughout the performance people shouted, 'No snug retreats,' 'No extortion,' 'Lower your prices,' 'Damn your pigeon holes.' The lines of *Macbeth* were parodied above the actors' voices:

> When the hurley-burley's done,
> When the battle's lost and won,
> At Covent Garden,
> We'll hail King George, but not King Kemble.

On the third night John Kemble as Richard III 'stared, grinned, threatened, gnashed his teeth in vain'; he could not compete with the shouts and songs, nor with the circling, confused pigeons which were released from the 'pigeon-holes'. When 'King John' Kemble appeared on stage to enquire what the people were doing and what they wanted, he was met with hisses and groans and cries of 'Off, off, off – D–n you, can't you read Old Prices written up?' Kemble made matters worse by speaking 'in the usual frigid way which he mistakes for dignity'. One Mr O'Reilly took the stage after Kemble and, as reported by the *Covent Garden Journal* (which was set up to cover the protest), exhorted the audience 'to look at the private boxes; the sort of company they held (several notorious women were quite conspicuous) and to consider the apartments annexed to them. He did not know that the patent of the managers entitled them to *interfere with other places of accommodation and amusement in town* (laughter and applause).'[10]

Kemble closed the new theatre after the performance on Saturday 23 September, so that he could publish the accounts and justify the new ticket prices. That night a coffin was borne through the pit marking the demise of 'New Prices': 'an ugly child, and base born, who died of the *whooping-cough*, on the 23rd of Sept. 1809 aged six days'. But it was a premature celebration. Kemble and the managers were convinced that they could face down the crowd. But the published accounts only enraged Londoners further. It showed that the theatre made a 12½ per cent return per annum and that Kemble fixed his salary at £6,300, with £1,000 benefits, while five others (including his brother and sister-in-law, Mr and Mrs Charles Kemble, and his sister Sarah Siddons) shared a further £25,175. Quite what the money had been spent on was left unanswered, and doubts were raised about Kemble's probity. The managers were probably in the right, but with their inadequate and somewhat contemptuous response they did little to disabuse the public of its suspicions that money had been wasted by inefficient managers, lavished on the pampered aristocracy or simply embezzled. The price rises were seen as an unfair tax levied by King John on the British public, who were being asked to reward his family and remunerate the extravagance of the theatre's management.[11]

While the Covent Garden Theatre management committee began to look for excuses, the O.P. protest became an organised movement. The coming campaign would be coordinated by a committee, with public meetings and its own press. In the manner of political organisations at this time, there were bibulous public dinners at the Crown and Anchor tavern on the Strand to debate the issue; and like political reform movements the O.P.-ers secured friendly booksellers and publishers. Francis Place, Sir Francis Burdett, the barrister Henry Clifford and the bookseller-publishers William Hone, John Bone and Thomas Tegg attempted to transform the Old Price protest into an adjunct of the parliamentary reform cause, but there was little enthusiasm on the part of the majority to regard it as anything other than about the pleasures of the people. Yet that is not to say that it was without a political aspect. The essence of the O.P. case was that London theatres operated as a monopoly which had been granted under royal licence by Charles II, and from thence had existed under the remote but tacit superintendence of the monarch.

The monopoly was allowed to exist on the understanding that public pleasures should remain affordable for all. As the O.P. leaders said, the 'amusements of the public are in a degree, *the right of the public*'. The management of the theatre were not like merchants in an open market who traded for profit; they held their property under 'a tacit tenure' from the government for the benefit of the public, who, after all, could not seek their pleasures elsewhere, because a free market for pleasure did not exist. A private company might build a bridge, but Parliament had the right and the duty to protect the public by setting the toll. The O.P. protesters fought under the banner of the 1688 revolution, and claimed to be defending the rights of George III against the usurpation of 'King John' and a sinister, profiteering cartel. Papers such as *The Times* agreed, saying that the public had been 'screwed'. Performances were scheduled to resume on 4 October. 'Let the company play to empty benches,' advised *The Times*; 'let the public agree to desert the theatre, and we shall see which can do without the other.'

But the public had different ideas. If they were in open conflict with the management of *their* theatre, they would provide their own entertainment. The principles of the second phase of the O.P. War were to amuse and be amused. When the theatre reopened, the protesters were organised and ready for action: handbills were printed and distributed at the start of every evening; brass medals struck by Francis Place bearing the legend 'O.P.' were worn in men's hats. There was a profusion of banners and placards pinned to the walls and pillars with prearranged slogans: 'Let no monopoly flourish'; 'In an English Theatre all should see and be seen. No Private Boxes'; 'No private performances in private withdrawing rooms in a public Theatre'.[12]

But what made the O.P. War so enthralling was the inventiveness of the customers in the pit. Any thought of coming to see a play was rendered ridiculous. For a few glorious weeks, anyone who wanted to became an actor. People came dressed in outlandish costumes; some men wore drag. Members of the audience outdid each other with new jokes, parodies, renditions of apposite quotations from Shakespeare and specially composed songs; some made speeches and others loudly debated the issue. The pit became an alternative stage for amateur actors and ingenious parodists. Ladies and gentlemen, and the Duke of York on at least one occasion, still took their seats in the boxes. But there was no question that they even thought of coming to see Kemble as Macbeth and Mrs Siddons as Lady Macbeth. There was a far better performance going on below them, and the real stage was relegated to an unnoticed and irrelevant sideshow. On one night, Lord Yarmouth crossed the line of social segregation to soak up the atmosphere in the pit. Other aristocrats acted similarly, including, it was said, Lord Palmerston.[13]

The ladies and gentlemen enjoyed the jokes and autonomous performances from the crowd. And at set times the foot soldiers commenced their *pièce de résistance*, the 'O.P. Dance'. Thomas Hobbs described it for the fashionable inhabitants of Bath, who were unfortunate not to have seen the fun of the dance, 'the effect of which is wonderfully grand: it is performed with great regularity and precision, by lifting up one Foot, and putting down the other – each Performer bawling out O.P in exact time with the movement of the feet!' They did this to the applause of the rest of the audience, until someone shouted out 'Down O.P.'s'; everyone then sat down with their backs to the stage and sang 'Rule Britannia' and 'God Save the King', gave three cheers for John Bull and three groans for John Kemble, then they all ran from the opera to the boxes, falling and jumping over each other in the melee. They would then join in the second O.P. dance, called 'The Rattle-snake Minuet'. The people would form circles and dance around, banging one another's walking sticks. When they weren't dancing, the O.P.-ers sang songs from sheets distributed on handbills. On one night they sang the ditty 'King John was a Manager':

> King John was a Manager mighty and high –
>   Hey populorum jig,
> He built private boxes, the Devil knows why –
>   Hey populorum jig.
> The Lords and gay Madams were shewing their horns,
> But soon the fine gentlemen drew in their horns;
>   With battle 'em rattle 'em,
>   Fiddle dum, diddle dum,
> Spurn him out, turn him out,
> Kemble, O! tremble O!
>   Hey populorum jig.

And on 18 October, the Placarding Committee provided the troops with an anthem:

God save Great JOHNNY BULL,
Long live our Noble Bull;
Send him Victorious,
Loud and Uproarious,
With Lungs like Boreas,
God save JOHN BULL.[14]

Kemble and the managers were not going to back down, even though their theatre was hijacked every night by paying customers. For several weeks, a night at the Covent Garden Theatre followed a set routine. The protest would gather steam, but by the interval they were joined by prizefighters hired by the managers. From that moment, the good-natured and ingenious protest – 'a peaceable tempest of noise' – degenerated into violence. On 15 October Leigh Hunt commented in the *Examiner* that things had taken a nasty turn and 'the Pit has been metamorphosed into a pugilistic arena, where all the blackguards of London, the Jew prize-fighters, Bow-street runners, hackney-coach helpers, and vagabonds returned from transportation, have ranged themselves on the side of the Managers'. And, apparently, there was a play going on somewhere in the background, acted by some of the greatest actors in the history of the British stage; but little could be heard above the songs, shouts, declamations and, after the interval, running battles in the pit: 'Perhaps a finer dumb shew was never witnessed.'[15]

From Hunt's description of the 'blackguards of London' we can gain an impression of the theatre's paid supporters. The audience was joined by professional boxers, many of them Jewish, like the famous Dutch Sam and Daniel Mendoza, doling out punches and thumps to the amateur performers, bell-ringers and horn-blowers. The protesters added a malevolent strain of anti-Semitism to their generally cheery and cheeky defiance of Kemble, with banners reading 'Oppose Shylock and the whole tribe of Israel', as if all Jews were naturally in alliance with underhand managers. The appearance of Mendoza and Dutch Sam allowed the protesters to play on prevalent populist prejudices and unleash their own brooding hatreds. Jews were disproportionately represented in the opposing ranks because they dominated the boxing world and were too poor and precariously placed to refuse paid work like this. Indeed, the whole thing had taken on a more bitter and rancorous aspect as both sides refused to capitulate. Suddenly there were new enemies to be added to the Kemble family and the theatre's managers. In a print drawn by George Cruikshank, the theatre's supporters are depicted as the lowest of the low, while the O.P.-ers are well-dressed and obviously wealthy middle-class men. The O.P. protesters were now on the defensive. The constables who arrived shortly after the fights broke out ignored the 'managerial bravos' and their hired 'corps of terrorism', preferring to round up the real troublemakers, including Mary Austin, a young woman who was caught brandishing a child's rattle.[16]

Miss Austin was sent to Tothill Fields prison, but only after she had made a witty speech in court saying that she would have desisted had she known the heinous nature of her crime. The constables were working at the behest of James Brandon, who was coordinating the anti-O.P. campaign. At Bow Street magistrates court, a young man was accused of whipping up violence by having 'O.P.' written on his hat and singing the national anthem in different keys. A clerk from East India House and his friend were charged with exciting riot 'by running to and fro on the benches, singing and vociferating'. A man who was employed by the excise office was charged 'with unnaturally coughing, sneezing, and howling', although it was unlikely that anyone could find a law specifically mentioning those things. John Ridley was brought to the same court by Brandon. When Brandon was asked whether the prisoner was making a disturbance, he replied, 'Why, Sir, he was sitting in the Pit with his hat on, and wishing to make a disturbance,' added to which he was clapping 'in a way which I pronounce to be very improper'. In his defence Ridley said: 'Sir, I am an Englishman. I was in the Pit with O.P in my hat, and I will go again to the Theatre with O.P in my hat tomorrow night; but if I thought the going there with these letters in my hat was illegal, I should not go.'[17]

Henry Clifford was arrested at the beginning of November and went on the offensive by suing Brandon for wrongful arrest. When he won the case at the King's Bench, he became the hero of the O.P. War. These and similar calls to liberty and freedom of vocal dissent extended the protest out of the theatre into the courts. The defiance was in the same spirit – inventive, humorous and farcical; again, the humble theatre-frequenter became a star for the moment. Ridley, like many others, faced stiff penalties from the magistrates: he had to find bail of £40 and two sureties for his good behaviour at £40 each. When he went back to the theatre, which he did as soon as he was discharged, he was greeted as a returning hero.[18]

The magistrates believed that hissing and booing constituted a riot, while 'employing prize-fighters to thump the public into acquiescence' was acceptable. The boxers rarely had to face a magistrate, and when a blacksmith, who was hired every night to intimidate the audience, was prosecuted by one of his victims, he successfully defended himself on the grounds that he was not punching but holding out his arms to steady himself. The smith was free to go back and 'steady' himself nightly, while people such as Mary Austin languished in gaol. The *Morning Post* labelled the O.P.-ers 'rebels' and saw Jacobinism behind the boos and hoots and songs; the magistrates saw things in the same way. George Mainwaring, a Westminster magistrate and sometime Tory MP, pompously lectured the protesters, saying that while booing was permissible, calling on a business to change its prices 'was a demand neither founded in law, equity or justice'. An audience was not a court of justice and had as much right to complain about admission prices and the layout of the auditorium as they did to set the salaries of the actors, direct the scenes or determine the style of the costume. In other words, there seemed to be a difference between merely complaining and implying in one's complaint that a change should be made.

Moving somewhat away from the case, Mainwaring said that the O.P. protesters represented the unacceptable face of democracy; who would want to live in a dangerously anarchical world where one audience could make a change one night and another repeal the first one's decision the next? There was a difference, however, between magistrates and grand juries. The justices routinely punished anyone connected with the O.P. cause, while grand jurors would only find true bills against people accused of actual violence, but not those who blew horns or waved rattles. Nonetheless, treatment of the Covent Garden Theatre's customers seemed worryingly arbitrary. In future, *The Satirist* said, 'those who frequent puppet shows, had better take care, it seems, how they find fault of the acting of Punch, for the showman may have a constable ready to take them into custody for a grin of disapprobation'.[19]

The O.P. campaigners risked the threat of arrest or broken bones through October, November and most of December, every night, six days a week. At last, just before Christmas and after sixty-seven nights of protest, the theatre capitulated to most of the demands after a meeting held between representatives of the opposing sides at Francis Place's house. At a subsequent public dinner at the Crown and Anchor, the price for admission to the pit was lowered to its 1808 level, James Brandon was sacked, and all but ten boxes had their private rooms taken away. When Kemble later appeared on stage to outline these concessions, a banner was unfurled in the pit reading 'We are satisfied'. The O.P. committee was still not happy, and the number of private boxes was then reduced to just three. In September 1810 there was a brief resumption of chants, horn blowing and singing, not this time in the name of O.P. but 'No P.B.' – no private boxes. Terrified, the managers took out the offending remnants of the dispute. At last, things in the theatre could go back to what passed for normality.[20]

What was the O.P. War about? Most observers were convinced that the slightly higher prices were resented and Kemble's salary considered offensive, but it was the private boxes that provoked people to action. They ruined the ethos of public entertainments by setting up an unwelcome exclusivity in the theatre and, more pertinently, deprived the pit of a good deal of fun by shielding aristocratic vice. At the height of the protest, the *Examiner* said that the prices were not important, but 'a whole circle of the Theatre taken from them [the public] to make privacies for the luxurious great, is a novelty so offensive to the national habits . . . that the Managers . . . deserve to suffer still more for their mercenary and obsequious encouragement of pride and profligacy'. There was an innocent use for the boxes: 'to lounge, and trifle with a jelly, and drawl a little with Mr Sk—e—a—ffington, and talk nonsense instead of hearing it' (Sir Lumley Skeffington was an effeminate dandy and playwright; the reference is to his affected drawl). But everyone knew that the boxes were there because they afforded the easiest 'opportunity for the whole progress of seduction and sensuality'.

The O.P.-ers were not motivated by moral indignation (theatregoers were not renowned for their saintliness) or prurience. Their indignation was ignited because the theatre was one of the few places where people could see and be seen without let or hindrance. Social segregation and privilege were established enough without making portions of the theatre an extension of the club or the great house or the high-class brothel. The *Covent Garden Journal* said that privacy was simply wrong in a place where people go 'for the purpose of forgetting their separation, and where all are united by the same motive, that of rational self-enjoyment'.

One of the slogans read 'No private performances in private withdrawing rooms in a public Theatre'. The people who protested did so because they were determined to protect the notion that theatres were public spaces where everyone – good or bad, entertaining or dull, rich or poor – had to share something face to face and with tolerance. It is notable that the people in the boxes were as eager to see the people in the pit even in less exciting circumstances, but especially when the crowd proved adept entertainers; both afforded their own kind of entertainment. A theatre without the nightly panorama of juxtaposing faces, diverse crowds, showy costumes, farcical sideshows and intrigue would be no theatre at all.[21]

But once the protest started, it took on a life of its own in which the origins became less important. Kemble was jumped-up and arrogant, the management were greedy and violent; the crowd would not cower before a haughty actor (howsoever mesmerising his acting) and his hired thug (James Brandon), nor hand their cash to corrupt businessmen once the response became contemptuous, provocative and then violent. The tussle was as much about pride and honour as money and private boxes by the time the war was into its first few weeks. At all times the public claimed ownership over the few theatres in the West End, as vociferous critics and paying customers. Entertainment was their right and the actors were their servants, not their masters.

Many who joined the ranks, however, were attracted by the fun and theatricality of the nightly protests, perhaps less concerned with the issues than the new source of entertainment. Suddenly everyone could be an actor, rhymester or inventor of a dance or slogan. The publication of books like *The O.P. Songster for 1810* indicates a thriving cadre of amateur composers, parodists and versifiers eager to attract attention and lead the pit in a fresh chant. It was published after the O.P. War was over, so it was a souvenir of those days, to be looked back on with fond memories. Erik Gustaf Geijer, a Swede who was in London at the time, recorded the extraordinary scenes: 'There were hats with O.P. on them. An O.P. medal was struck which was worn on the breast during the struggle. There were O.P. fans, O.P handkerchiefs, O.P. waistcoats and caps.' It was a fashion statement for some, or a protest that became a way of life. The theatre had been commandeered by the public, and the new regime was a meritocracy: only the most accomplished found favour with the crowd of critics, and the dull or mediocre were judged harshly. They must have been exciting days for armchair actors, frustrated thespians, the bored, the raucous and exhibitionists of every kind.[22]

Contemptuous of authority, quick to repay a perceived insult, defensive of their pleasures, inventive, amusing and eccentric, those who joined the crowds at the theatre believed they were the representatives of John Bull, the true custodians of the national character. They were free from the 'false delicacy' and fastidious niceties of uptight members of the Society for the Suppression of Vice and other 'squeamish' people. Their ranks were made up of people who prized their individuality, laughed at conformity and expressed themselves with plain words. Or, at least, that's the point they were eager to press home. The swagger of the crowds and the carnival nature of their protest remains impressive two hundred years later; many at the time saw the whole thing as an expression of irrepressible 'Merry England', another bacchanalian celebration that was an extension of the rumbustiousness seen at annual fairs or tavern entertainments. Charles Lamb (a friend of the Kemble family) said that the mediocre attempts to entertain the pit on the part of overexcited amateur actors was a potent argument for professional actors. Others saw the scenes at the Theatre Royal as yet another example of lower- and middling-class depravity and lawlessness, an unpleasant demonstration of disobedience and rude manners.

Whatever the case, the months of O.P. festivities reveal a slice of early nineteenth-century life; something of the spirit of Londoners erupted in the face of an insult. Many would not be seen dead at the theatre at this time, but the duration of the clash says something of the numbers of the disputants. The cheapest entry price to the theatre was half a shilling, if one paid for admission at the interval. It was not cheap to join the protest. Yet it was maintained night after night from September to December; the same people could not have come every evening, so the ranks must have been augmented by different people on different nights. Every week, tens of participants were arrested and held in gaol; yet the theatre was always packed. The records of those taken before the courts shows the make-up of the O.P.-ers: people of all classes, ages and both sexes; apprentices and labourers as well as fishmongers, merchants, shoe-makers, hatters, barristers, government clerks, stockbrokers, a shipowner and twelve people describing themselves as 'gentlemen'. It has been calculated that of the 161 people arrested, just forty-six were classified as skilled or unskilled workers and a mere ten were apprentices. This is compared to ninety-two who were upper- or middle-class. When they weren't at the theatre, a number of the O.P.-ers reconvened at public dinners to drink, make speeches, debate and propose toasts, just like any other middle-class public campaign. In January, when it was all over, the O.P.-ers had a reunion dinner at the Crown and Anchor tavern, to which Kemble was invited. The campaign could be very genteel when it wanted.[23]

'I hailed it as a new era – as a revival of the golden age of the true British character,' wrote one journalist of the O.P. campaign. A lady who subscribed £1 to a fighting fund for O.P.-ers put on trial said that she 'rejoices to see John Bull assert his independence'. It would be a generalisation to claim that the boisterous and anti-authoritarian behaviour was typical of Britons at this time. But the bizarre and humorous attitude embraced a wide variety of people. The form the protest took was based on long-standing notions of the ways in which public protests should be conducted. The behaviour on display for sixty-seven nights at the Covent Garden Theatre was familiar from the hustings in election campaigns, especially in large London constituencies such as Westminster and Middlesex, when people would dress up, perform, speechify, drink copious amounts of alcohol, compose songs and sometimes fight. Or it could be seen in private theatricals, fairgrounds, tavern societies and sporting events. It was not far different from lower-class Skimmington rides or other shaming rituals. An anonymous lady writing in 1810 said that the gilded manners of society were a paltry act. Go to any place where respectable men were not obliged to wear a mask, especially an election, where one 'may observe how gross, ferocious, brutal, grim, &c gentlemen are; how much they resemble those they despise; in short how like man is to man'. One publication reported an overheard conversation between two outwardly venerable gentlemen walking together in Lincoln's Inn Fields: '. . . I don't frequent the theatre half-a-dozen times in the course of the season, but I'm bl—dy fond of a riot.' 'So am I Jack, by G—d,' replied the other.[24]

There was little to suggest, in the 1800s, that the spirit of moral reform and conspicuous piety had made much headway with Londoners; their manners were as rough and eccentric as ever. It would be sixteen years before the theatre saw anything like it again, and on the second occasion it engulfed playhouses throughout England, Scotland, Ireland and America. The O.P. War was a finale for the John Bull of the old kind. The difference in 1825, both in motivation and the behaviour of the audiences, could not be greater. In the intervening years, there was a change in the attitude of the crowds and the behaviour of the middle classes.

But at the time the O.P.-ers were celebrated as true-born Britons: liberty-loving, humorous, good-natured and independent. They provided a welcome contrast to the sanctimonious rectitude of Methodists and other would-be reformers of the national character. The protest was all about a hatred of high-handedness and officious interference with pleasure. The only reason that the protest could continue for so long was because the government would not send in the army and no London magistrate could find enough constables to quell a disturbance of this kind, as the poor arrest record shows. In a country without a professional police force, such riots were allowed to go unchecked for as long as the government turned a blind eye. If the absence of police allowed John Bull to express his feelings unrestrained by the fear that his excessive displays of liberty would in any way be interfered with, this was a rather elaborate reminder.

When constables did intervene against the protesters in the pit, they were beaten away with sticks by upper-class men sitting in the boxes. When a constable and a patrol tried to stop forty or fifty gentlemen dancing to two fife-players in the street outside the theatre, they found themselves in a fight that only ended when the officers' clothes were torn to shreds by the 'gentlemen'. One night in the theatre, at the height of the war, some elegantly dressed ladies participated from the private boxes, including one who tried to smash a chandelier. In Henry Clifford's trial for wrongful arrest, his lawyer spoke to the court in words that would animate people of all classes: 'I am not in point of law justifying riot and disturbance, but we must take Englishmen as we find them, with all their faults, with all their virtues, and all their vices; and when Englishmen omit to express their sentiments when they have cause to do so, they will cease to have in their veins the blood of Englishmen, they will cease to have that character belonging to them, which has in all times preserved our liberties from usurpation at home, and prevented invasion from abroad.'[25]

Was it a revival in the national character, as some hoped? A more melancholy sign of the times presented itself less than a year later when the economy took a serious downward turn, harvests failed again and Luddite machine-breaking violence broke out in the Midlands. In 1810 the press made much of the fact that a Mr John Bull, a carpenter from King's Langley, was gazetted bankrupt.[26]

PART II

The Arts of Peace 1815–21

'One might have as well counted on fifty Waterloos in succession. If we had been in the excitement of a fever – it could not last for ever.'

Anon, *Quarterly Review*, April 1829

INTRODUCTION TO PART II

Rich and Invincible

Nervous disorders, which had once tyrannised the timorous middle classes, disappeared as surely as knee breeches, periwigs and other formerly dominant fashions. *Blackwood's Edinburgh Magazine* talked of 'a sorely dispersed remnant of "single gentlemen" in lodgings, and single ladies we know not where – a generation afflicted with headaches, tea-drinking, and all the nostalgia of the nerves; people who have never a wholesome taste in their mouths, and are glad to rub their teeth upon any insipid drug that comes their way'.[1]

The *London Magazine* laughed at these lonely hypochondriacs just as much as at those who had managed to recover: 'when nerves were the fashion, every body had the nerves and nervous disorders; and took nervous medicines; and physicians wrote books on nervous complaints; and all the people swallowed castor, camphor, asafoetida, galbanum, musk, valerian, opium, ether, juleps, and heaven knows what more . . . Lo and behold! The nerves have vanished! The whole army of nervous disorders is out of fashion and out of date.'[2]

And well they might be after June 1815, when Britain triumphed over Napoleon. The national mood was understandably jubilant after so many years of conflict, culminating finally at Waterloo. The nightmare of the Apocalypse could be forgotten; those evil passions that had been unleashed on the world had been vanquished. Up in the Lakes, Robert Southey invited Lord and Lady Sunderlin, William and Dorothy Wordsworth, James Boswell junior and 'Messrs Rag, Tag and Bobtail', his lower-class neighbours, to a party atop a fell. 'We roasted beef and boiled plum-puddings there; sang "God Save the King" round the most furious body of flaming tar-barrels that I ever saw; drank a huge wooden bowl of punch; fired cannon at every health with three times three, and rolled huge blazing balls of tow and turpentine down the steep side of the mountain. The effect was grand beyond imagination.' There was an accident with the punch, so the rum had to be drunk neat, with disastrous consequences: 'One fellow was so drunk that his companions placed him upon a horse, with his face to the tail, to bring him down [from the hill-top].'[3]

'Never was any other nation the object of such universal and boundless honour, admiration and benediction,' the *Quarterly Review* recalled in 1822. 'What her population then was, may be gathered from her conduct and achievements. No other than a nation in the highest degree moral, religious, loyal, wise, industrious, and enlightened would thus have rallied round the throne and altar when these *alone* were attacked.' Britain could congratulate herself on feats unprecedented in the history of human endeavour, or so the celebrating masses could be forgiven for believing after Waterloo. The exigencies of war had given Britain a manufacturing base that eclipsed that of any other country. As the Chancellor of the Exchequer, Nicholas Vansittart, told Parliament, the war had created new industries, and public investment had provided London with three new bridges and the country with a network of roads and canals. 'Wealth seemed to spring from expenditure, armies and fleets from the waste of battle, and courage and hope from disaster. She entered the conflict poor and feeble, she came out of it rich and invincible.'[4]

Patrick Colquhoun was not celebrating, however. Amid the national self-congratulation, he published a new book of doom, albeit with an upbeat title, *A Treatise on the Wealth, Power, and Resources of the British Empire*. His previous prophesies of national annihilation had failed to materialise, and he now admitted that Britain had fought a war against larger and more populous nations, and had emerged richer and with her empire undiminished. At the end of the war, Britain had unprecedented wealth and resources, all of which, Colquhoun wrote, 'have given a new feature to the general structure of civil society'. God had forgiven the country all the sins she manifested and granted her the opportunity to make something glorious from the bounty lying at her feet; there was a crying need for redoubled efforts, new measures and a thorough purge of bad habits. The country was rich, but now she needed to concentrate on what Hannah More called 'moral prosperity'. 'It will therefore now become an important desideratum to cultivate the arts of peace,' wrote Colquhoun.[5]

It would be wise, he said, to abandon any idea that the *people* had won the war. National survival and augmentation of wealth had been achieved because the country had the capital and stability to raise vast loans; money had won the war, not the tars of Nelson's navy or Wellington's grizzled veterans. Indeed, the *people* were parasites on the opulence of their country; they were better fed and clothed, and enjoyed more comforts than at any stage in history, 'but their immoral habits have experienced no favourable change'. Soon, the million idle people he had identified in earlier books would be swelled with hundreds of thousands of demobilised soldiers and sailors. The greatest challenge facing a nation that had reached Britain's level of wealth and civilisation was the problem of surplus population. In a few years, the war would seem like halcyon days; the country had become rich because of exceptional circumstances, because world trade was concentrated on her ports. From 1815, for the first time in years, there was serious competition. The population had grown while trade was artificially protected; now the country faced an uncertain and dangerous future. Napoleon was on St Helena; now the enemy was '*a vicious and immoral people*'.[6]

Colquhoun's treatise on the British Empire was a reappraisal of his earlier works. In 1815, however, what he had to say seemed eerily prescient. The good days could not continue in peacetime. The European powers would recover and compete. 'The British people ought to be prepared for such an exigency, by putting forward their whole strength, and by rendering their physical capability as efficient as possible.' Bad times were round the corner if the country was complacent. Imported corn would harm domestic agriculture; continental manufactures would undercut British tradesmen on the world market; a flood of veterans, added to the vastly increased population, would put strain on the Poor Laws and force food prices up. So, if Britons were to weather the storm of peace and become more efficient and energetic, the mass of the people had to be closely watched to make sure they did not slip into vice and sloth and therefore turn the march of progress into a sluggish crawl. Colquhoun, with his mastery of statistics, proposed to use 'political arithmetic' and the practice of 'reasoning by figures' to investigate the population and identify the productive and the unproductive. He would use 'statistical economy' because it 'distinguishes the useful from the noxious members of the body politic, while it shews the relative degree of usefulness or noxious tendency, which applies to all different ranks and degrees of society'.

The figures showed that there was a significant portion of the public who were a 'burden' on the productive, those whose vices rendered them dependent and surplus to the requirements of a modern, industrialised country. 'It is only those who pass their lives in vice and idleness, or who dissipate the surplus labour acquired by inheritance or otherwise in gaming and debauchery, and the idle class of paupers, prostitutes, rogues, vagabonds, vagrants, and persons engaged in criminal pursuits, who are real nuisances in society, – who live upon the land and the labour of the people, without filling any useful station in the body politic, or making the smallest return or compensation to society for what they consume.' Colquhoun was quick to clarify whom he meant by the idle and debauched. It was not the rich; they were the 'master springs in the great machine' who stimulated productivity and industry, even if they were themselves indolent and dissolute. The real enemies of society – vagrants, sots, criminals, prostitutes, beggars and others who made up the vast surplus population that was leeching the lifeblood of the body politic – should be transported to the colonies to cultivate new resources or be compelled to provide for their own maintenance.

Colquhoun attracted a readily believing readership. Despite the high expectations of peace, the years after Waterloo were hard; much of what the magistrate had foretold seemed to materialise. The post-war depression bit hard: unemployment increased; food prices went up and harvests failed after unusually cold winters and wet summers; the veterans returned home to join the growing ranks of unemployed; and for six years there was a revival in political agitation. Victory was indeed a withered fruit. The poor did seem brutal and violent, simmering with discontent and rebellion. 'It is now come to this question,' Robert Southey wrote to a friend, '– Can we educate the people in moral and religious habits, and better the condition of the poor, so as to secure ourselves from a mob-revolution; or has this duty been neglected so long, that the punishment will overtake us before this only remediable means can take effect?'[7]

Southey was greatly influenced by the writings of doom-mongers such as Colquhoun. In his youth, in the 1790s, he had been an ardent republican and utopian; in the 1800s he had had an instinctive sympathy with the poor, defending their pleasures against people like Colquhoun and John Bowles. Yet pessimism had overtaken his zeal. 'There was a time', he wrote in a letter, 'when I believed in the persuadibility of man, and had the mania of man-mending. Experience has taught me better.' His abandoned idealism and loss of sympathy with the poor was by no means unique; many in the country were convinced that Britain was worse morally than she had been at the outset of the war. They feared what was fermenting below the surface of society.[8]

In an essay in the *Quarterly Review*, Southey warned that the urban poor had become brutalised to an extent that was dangerous to the community. Plucked from the ties of kinship known only in rural society, the consolation of the village church and the dignity of outdoor labour, and dumped in cities to work in factories and with no other source of stimulus or solace than the bottle, great bodies of the people had become understandably confused, unhappy and corrupted. As a consequence, the reign of George III had seen a revolution that overshadowed the invention of printing, the discovery of America or the Reformation. The upper and middle classes had benefited, but the effect on the poor was catastrophic. Their morals had become diseased and their danger to the state fathomless. It was, Southey said, 'mournful to contemplate the effects of extreme poverty in the midst of a civilised and flourishing state. The wretched native of Tierra del Fuego, or the northern extremity of America, sees nothing around him which aggravates his own wretchedness by comparison . . . But in a country like ours, there exists a contrast which continually forces itself upon the eye and upon the reflective faculty.'

Southey felt aggrieved that his warnings had been ignored. All that he had discerned in the brutalised people had materialised after Waterloo, as political demonstrations and the popular press became ever more angry. In September 1816 he wrote to a friend, 'Four years ago I wrote in the Q.R to explain the state of Jacobinism in the country, and with the hope of alarming the Government. At present they are alarmed; they want to oppose pen to pen, and I have just been desired to go up to town and confer with Lord Liverpool. God help them, and is it come to this!' The Prime Minister called on Robert Southey because the government considered that the revolutionary menace that the country had been fighting for years had not perished at Waterloo but was alive and well, festering in the slums.[9]

Southey wrote articles in the *Quarterly Review* throughout the 1810s warning of the new danger and advocating a 'radical reform' of the habits and morals of the lower classes. Each issue of the *Quarterly* was selling 12,000 copies, a huge number for the time, and Southey was delighted with his new role: 'this is writing to a large number of readers, and a large proportion of them disposed to believe what they read, however unable they may be to learn, mark, and inwardly digest'. Yet he admitted in private that he rarely left his idyll in the Lakes and had no knowledge of, or taste for, urban living. London gave him a headache and a cough. He knew nothing about the poor but what he read in books by Colquhoun or from studying census reports. 'No inhabitant of this great town could be ignorant that [London's] vast population was mixed up with swindlers and pick-pockets, thieves, vagrants, beggars, and prostitutes,' Southey wrote; 'but Mr Colquhoun enabled us to trace them to their lurking places – he gave to each class a "local habitation"; he brought them to our view in groups amounting to thousands and plunder to millions.'

He believed that the answer was simple: the people would become better if they were prevented from reading radical literature and if they were educated in the principles of the Church of England only. The worst offenders could be kept in check by punishment and coerced into productive labour; there was no need for amelioration. And so Southey became one of the most widely read political journalists, despite being woefully unqualified for the task. Panicked by the threat of revolution, the middle-class public was susceptible to the nightmarish visions of others; Southey said that 'it is a great thing to write for readers who are disposed to assent to every thing you say'.[10]

In 1815 both the Regent and William Wilberforce were summering in Brighton. The two men had been friends for years, but Prince George could hardly be said to have lived up to the injunctions of the evangelicals; what would the two men make of each other? Perhaps surprisingly to many, the royal philanderer sought out the doughty philanthropist at every occasion. The Prince treated the reformer of manners with 'reverence'. 'It is pleasing to see how consistently religion ultimately beats down all hostility,' Hannah More commented. It was also a signal that even if royalty was not entirely sympathetic to their religious principles, it stood four-square with the reforming zeal of the evangelicals.[11]

And indeed, it was noticeable that evangelical schemes were achieving a prominence and respectability as never before. Anna Laetitia Barbauld wrote in 1813 that 'There is certainly at present a great deal of zeal in almost every persuasion . . . Bible Societies, missionary schemes, lectures, schools for the poor are set afoot and spread, not so much from a sense of duty as being the real taste of the times.' Indeed, such philanthropy *was* very fashionable. The British and Foreign Bible Society was the greatest of them all.

The Bible Society signalled the emerging centrality of evangelical morals to national life. Its aim was to distribute Bibles to every home in Britain, and then the world. In 1813 the patrons of the Bible Society were headed by the Princess of Wales, all the royal dukes (except Clarence), nine other dukes, twenty-two earls (including Lord Liverpool, the Prime Minister, and Wellington) and many other aristocrats, politicians, members of the gentry and upper middle class; it was socially exclusive and therefore very fashionable. By 1825 4,252,000 Bibles had been handed out. How many grateful labourers were reclaimed from a life of hard drinking, swearing and profanation of the Sabbath it cannot be said. Whether it was none or millions scarcely mattered. What mattered to the evangelicals was the cachet that their movement now achieved; that the highest members of the royal family and the aristocracy were conspicuous in supporting their version of moral reform was a sweet victory.

'My heart rejoices at the progress of religious society,' wrote Hannah More; '– wide, and more wide the blessed circle spreads in the elevated walks of life.' Those who had been scorned as puritans and 'enthusiasts' were now countenanced as one of the bulwarks of the state. The aristocracy was beginning to realise that it had to be seen as setting the moral tone of society. The projects inspired by evangelicals seemed to be worth their support, even if most were personally lukewarm towards 'vital' religion. Anyone who was opposed to the Bible Society, the *Christian Observer* said menacingly, was 'running counter to the general voice and feeling of mankind'.[12]

Voices of moral certainties, such as Wilberforce and More, were reassuring in this troubled time. The post-war period was one of national self-scrutiny. Parliament began to take seriously the calls for social reform and investigation of the problems highlighted by Colquhoun and others. But on whose terms would it be done?

8

Injudicious Kindness

'Frisk away, let's be gay,
This is Cadgers holiday;
While knaves are thinking,
We are drinking.'

Reputed beggars'
song (1817)

'When war at first assail'd us I quickly left my trade,
Our country was in danger, I flew to lend my aid.
And in my country's service, long, long fatigues I bore,
But now I'm turned adrift to starve upon my native shore.'

'The British Tars', ballad

'The English think very highly of their own humanity; I am willing to admit they are not inhuman . . .'

Louis Simond, *Journal of a Tour and Residence in Great Britain*[1]

The moral country that had prevailed over vicious Europe did not look at all moral. The years after 1815 were hard, and the streets reflected the dislocation of adjusting to peace: many of the veterans of Trafalgar and Waterloo swelled the numbers of beggars; the number of prostitutes was a national disgrace. And the obvious, glaring social problems were met by a grand effort of private and public philanthropy. The sudden rush of philanthropic activity was motivated by a belief that Britain could go on to greater heights. Having conquered Napoleon, she could conquer her own bad habits and build an improved, modern society. The first priority was to clear the streets of the most glaring evils and national embarrassments.

A great effort was made to rehabilitate and redeem the lowest and most depraved, those whom fate had dealt the worst hand. Over the next few years, philanthropic effort would be directed at beggars, gin addicts and poor children from the slums. The philanthropic schemes and social theories developed by evangelicals such as William Wilberforce and William Allen, the Benthamites and Malthusians (discussed in Chapter 3) had never really gripped the public; a way of putting over their view of morality to the millions who made charitable donations became a matter of priority. The post-war years saw a full-scale assault on the habits and inclinations of the public, in part directed by the philanthropists who were emboldened and legitimised after the abolition of slavery. As many acknowledged, these people now had a power in society that was scarcely to be countenanced before. The schemes to reform the lives of the lowest had more to do with reforming the middle classes and all who participated in acts of charity. Changing the way that people gave and making them consider the moral implications of their actions would bring the well-to-do and respectable into conformity with evangelical morality. In this aim, the reformers were remarkably successful.

A start was made with the thousands of miserable streetwalkers – the blight of the great capital. Abandoned women were conspicuous to the compassionate eye; they were the defenceless victims of a cruel world. But they were the cause of society's ills, prostitution being the '*parent and progeny of crime*'; ninety-nine out of every hundred crimes, according to the committee of the Guardian Society, could be traced back to 'illicit association with profligate women'. They were a danger to clean-living youths. An apprentice or clerk who walked the streets of the City or Southwark could not help but see and hear the sirens of vice. Gradually his resistance to such solicitations would be broken down, and against his will and with great reluctance he would be seduced.

'Associations with such women produces an habitual aversion to religious, moral, and parental restraints,' said a petition from the respectable inhabitants of London; '– occasions the lowest degradation of mind – dissipates all benevolent feeling – diminishes and destroys that relative confidence which is the comfort of families – is the parent of deceptions and falsehoods the most flageticious – falsification of accounts – cheating and purloining in all their various modes – forgery – street robbery – juvenile depredations – diseases the most loathsome in their progress and results – pauperism – early deaths – suicides – public executions!' The way that prostitutes would be salvaged would provide the model for what was called a 'moral experiment'.[2]

The problem that kept philanthropists up at night was: how to help depraved people without doing more harm than good by rewarding their vices? The godly philanthropists always felt that their specialised work was being undermined by the mawkish and sentimental. Institutions that helped these poor women were seen as irresponsibly lax and forgiving. William Hale, a writer for the *Evangelical Magazine*, expressed the paradox of charitable relief: if a prostitute was successfully rehabilitated, educated in a useful trade and returned to society a respectable woman, would that not send a message to a servant girl that a few years of prostitution could be effaced and she would actually benefit from her vice? Where was the punishment? Besides, prostitution – like beggary and crime – was voluntary: no one *had* to be a prostitute, Hale reasoned; a sex worker could present herself at the workhouse or house of correction whenever she wanted; only 'delicacy' and false pride prevented her from receiving providence's harsh punishment.[3]

The problem became a matter of impassioned debate. It occupied a group of charitably inclined men and women who formed the Guardian Society in 1813; this was formally launched in 1815 under the patronage of the Dukes of Kent and Sussex. It provided an asylum to receive and reform prostitutes who wanted to better their lives. It was a place of harsh discipline and hard work; the penitent prostitutes had to provide for their upkeep by their own labour. The evangelical Reverend William Bengo Collyer visited the asylum and found that the women had inadequate beds or had to sleep on the floor. This was a good thing: 'I was convinced that no one would have sought a refuge in such an Asylum but those who were truly repentant of their sins . . . hard fare will be acceptable fare, and they will fear no evil but the guilt and punishment of their crimes.'[4]

The Guardian Society's asylum was a dismal failure. When the ladies of the committee visited the Bridewell house of correction, where women convicted of the crime of prostitution were punished, they found that only forty-five out of 130 female prisoners would even talk to them. Of these only twenty-one agreed to be rescued. The ladies said it showed the 'vicious obduracy' of prostitutes, but surely it showed that they realised the society's benevolence really masked coercion. And for all the harsh discipline and enforced penitence, the success rate was poor. Of 394 prostitutes who volunteered for the violent purgation of their sins, 112 had been found jobs in service. Of these only forty-seven could be positively said to be behaving well. Of the rest 120 had been discharged or left, twenty-eight had been forcibly returned to their parishes or sent to the female penitentiary, thirty-seven were still in custody and three had died. The Guardian Society was shocked that so few prostitutes had consented to their brutal regime and put it down to the hardened vice of 'obstreperous Females'. The element of godly punishment was the prime cause of the society's failure. Why would anyone willingly make life worse for themselves? The society could not understand why it was not inundated with women eager for self-laceration. The members wanted prostitutes to be like them, to be pious and submissive.[5]

The zeal to clear the streets was not confined to the Guardian Society. In 1815 two thousand well-to-do Londoners petitioned Parliament to provide better laws to deal with prostitutes. Led by the Lord Mayor, Matthew Wood, the City was on a mission to sweep away the nuisance. The problem was that the existing laws were inadequate. Punishment in Bridewell for a month was no deterrent. Strict property rights did not allow the police to raid even the most notorious brothel. A prostitute would have to be caught in the actual commission of a crime before she could be arrested; this was rare, for few men would come forward as witnesses in such a situation. If a street was cleared, it only made room for more prostitutes. The campaign had failure stamped on it from the very start. There was no better plan than to sweep the problem under the carpet or disguise the trade away. As one critic said, it was like a leper trying to cure his disease by washing away the blotches on his face: 'A quack might do so, but a regular physician would say, and say justly, that that would only be driving the distemper into the constitution.' That's what the Guardian Society and the London Council were trying to do: they were 'labouring to clear its [London's] face of some ugly spots and specks that have appeared upon it, without seeming to be aware that those blemishes are the consequences and symptoms of a mortal distemper which is preying upon its vitals'.[6]

But that is all that Londoners wanted. The challenge was not to *cure* the problem but to sweep it away to 'darkness' so that good, innocent young men would not be sucked into vice against their wills. It was also embarrassing to think that when tourists came to London and saw the shoals of prostitutes, they should mistakenly think that the men of Britain paid for sex. Out of sight and out of mind. Only then would London be 'as distinguished for its public decency and decorum, as it already stands pre-eminent for its extent, its wealth, and its magnificence'.[7]

As with attitudes to other problems, the priority of philanthropy seemed to be to protect the wider community: prostitutes – like beggars, criminals or the insane – should be quarantined so that they did not contaminate society. There was a failure to sympathise with the women and a marked reluctance to confront the real causes of prostitution, not least the willingness of young men to pay for sex, which seemed to have been forgotten. The amount of zeal evinced by the respectable part of the community led one to suppose that London would soon emerge smelling of roses, gleaming with new-found cleanliness and become renowned the world over for its morals. But the wrong-headedness of the crusade made such dreams an impossibility. Few were interested in the real causes of prostitution. Such a campaign would be expensive and would call for the root-and-branch reform of society. It was cheaper to deal with the symptoms.

The attitude that ignored root causes was summed up in an anecdote told by Horne Tooke. A poor and friendless girl applied for relief at the Magdalene Hospital for fallen women, and when she was granted asylum by the board of governors she fell to her knees, exclaiming: 'Thank God thank God! I am saved, I am saved from ruin!'

'What,' cried the Governors in consternation, 'what's that you say of *saved*? Why, you are *ruined*, are you not?'

'Oh no, Gentlemen, I have resisted temptation hitherto, and shall now preserve my virtue, thanks to your goodness.'

'Ah!' replied the Examiners, 'but you cannot be admitted here, if that is the case.'

'And she was accordingly rejected,' concluded Tooke, 'but returned shortly afterwards . . . perfectly qualified.'[8]

The real victims, according to the promoters of this kind of campaign, were the upstanding, generous people, who had their city besmirched by desperadoes and who were imposed upon by the anguished cries of pretended misfortune. The British were famously munificent with their charity: hospitals and asylums were supported by the wealthy, while the poor did not hesitate to relieve their unfortunate neighbours or strangers fallen on hard times. But, as with reclaiming prostitutes, there was a fear that most apparently needy people had brought down misfortune by their vices; charity should not become an inducement to indulge vicious habits. The unfortunate should first prove their worthiness and atone for their sins before the tender-hearted reached into their pockets and wasted money on the culpable and undeserving.

In 1815 there were plenty of reminders that for all the money lavished on charity and the Poor Laws, something was fundamentally wrong. The streets were full of beggars, the victims of the peace. The hospitals and schools were only the tip of British munificence: the most generous givers of money were the poor themselves. Giving money to beggars was the most common form of charity. Encountering a homeless person was the time when the benevolent instinct was easily roused. But were these people, themselves poor and struggling, adding fuel to the fire of social problems and unwittingly making the situation worse, for themselves, the recipient and the economy?

The House of Commons Select Committee on the State of Mendicity and Vagrancy in the Metropolis met a few weeks after Waterloo, on 11 July 1815. The enquiry went to the heart of Colquhoun's most persistent worry: the surplus population which was dependent on the labour of others. The term 'mendicity' embraced many different kinds of indigent people. It included street beggars, vagrants, families who claimed Poor Law relief and 'strangers', those who were far away from their home parishes and ineligible for help.

The tales of poverty were distressing. One of the first witnesses called before the committee, Mr Montague Burgoyne of Mark Hall, Essex, had involved himself with the Irish poor who lived in the Calmel Buildings, Marylebone. Burgoyne had heard that seven hundred Irish were crammed into the buildings, but after he visited for the first time he reckoned that this was a serious underestimate, and that there were three or four families living in each room. He could not determine why there were so many Irish in London: 'you can never believe one word they say; they have so much ingenuity and so much imagination'. One thing was certain however: 'I have been into every room myself,' Burgoyne told the committee, 'and I beg leave to add, that neither in town or country, have I ever met with so many poor among whom there was so much distress, so much profligacy, and so much ignorance.' The inhabitants of the Calmel Buildings, and other Irish communities in London, were 'idle and drunken'. Work came and went, and there was no parish fund to relieve distress. Infant mortality was high, and those children that did survive were 'crippled and crooked, and very unhealthy'. Very often they were sent out to beg, and when Burgoyne told parents they should send their children to school instead, the reply was invariably, 'Aye, Sir, you think of the back, but you ought to think of the belly, we must have something comfortable.'[9]

The rank conditions of the Calmel Buildings and many other similar areas of deepest poverty might have been a good place to start for a committee set up to enquire into the causes and symptoms of indigence. But the committee members passed over the issue. They became obsessed with the idea of the 'sturdy beggar', those people who abandoned honest labour for the *trade* of beggary. The phenomenon was nothing new: statutes going back to Edward III stated that healthy people who begged should be compelled to work. Other reigns had seen similar laws, the most pertinent being an Elizabethan statute that enjoined that fraudulent scholars, gamers, fortune-tellers, minstrels, jugglers and all who begged for money but could support themselves by their own labour should be whipped and sent to the House of Correction and returned to their parish.

The law still stood, but it was not enforced uniformly or rigorously, and if it was, it was laughably useless. Indeed, the public's attitude to beggars was ambivalent. Hostility and suspicion could just as easily be replaced by genuine admiration and sympathy. In popular culture and ancient lore, the beggar was a romantic figure, the last free man. He was an anti-authoritarian symbol who evaded control, cheated fate, lived by his own rules and, unencumbered by responsibilities or demanding employers, pursued pleasure with an unshakeable determination. One of the oldest legends, which went back to the Middle Ages, was the Blind Beggar of Bethnal Green, a wounded soldier who became 'master of his trade', adept at wheedling alms from travellers. He was said to have retired to a large house in east London and to have left his daughter a dowry of £3,000, according to an early-nineteenth-century rendition of the story. A more modern legend was the life of Bampfylde-Moore Carew, a real character, even if his biography was embellished. Carew was born in 1693 in Bickley, near Tiverton, where his father was rector of the village. Young Bampfylde-Moore was educated alongside the gentry and nobility of the West Country, but turned his back on wealth and privilege to join the gypsies. He was attracted to them because they formed an alternative nation-within-a-nation, with their own king, government, laws and values; they had no concept of money, and instead dedicated their efforts to pleasure and good fellowship.

'Their laws are few and simple,' wrote Carew's biographer, 'but exactly and punctually observed: the fundamental of which is, that strong love and mutual regard for each member in particular, and for the whole community in general . . . so that this whole community is connected by stronger bonds of love and harmony, than oftentimes subsists in private families under other governments: this naturally prevents all oppressions, fraud, and over-reaching of one another, so common among other people.' The begging community, according to the Carew legend, convened for joyous celebrations, but dispersed and travelled the country as individuals.

Carew eventually became king of the beggars because he proved himself adept at traversing all social boundaries and being a master of disguise. He tailored his act according to the prejudices of the audience. One day he could pass himself off as a gentleman fallen on hard times; on another he was a cripple; the next he was a burnt-out Oxford scholar in need of funds. He could extract money from the trustees of a private charity by writing a letter full of woe. He once persuaded the Duke of Bolton that he was a nobleman returned from sea penniless, and got clothes, a shave and dinner. The next day he was given money by the Bishop of Salisbury and Lord Arundel on the strength of his connection with the Duke. Then he swapped clothes and got more money from them as a ragged beggar, and then as an out-of-work cobbler. The money was distributed among the fellowship of cadgers and speedily converted into food and drink. Every imposture, lie and act of cunning was deployed to wheedle money from the public; there was never any sympathy for the benefactors, who were rather mocked than thanked. After adventures in Britain, three voyages to America and countless frauds, Bampfylde-Moore Carew abdicated the sovereignty of the begging world, then won a fortune from the lottery and lived out his days a rich and respectable man. He was an example to work-shy cadgers everywhere.

The Blind Beggar of Bethnal Green and Bampfylde-Moore Carew were favourites of folklore; there were innumerable editions about both of them. They were romantic heroes like Robin Hood, exiles from the mundanities and petty cares of normal life. And the popularity of such stories, the glorification of a free and easy life, alarmed the kind of men who were behind the select committee on mendicity. Would not every labouring man thirst after unearned money if he had the chance? In the early nineteenth century there were a number of

'George Dyball, a blind beggar of considerable notoriety, and his dog Nelson'

outlandish and comical beggars who lived up to the romantic ideal. Most people who walked about London knew their habits, tricks and skills; many even knew the names of the street-side supplicants. George Dyball, for example, was 'a fellow of considerable notoriety' who dressed as a sailor, was blind and had to be led by his dog Nelson, 'whose tricks displayed in an extraordinary degree the sagacity and docility of the canine race'. Dyball would cry out '*Pray pity the blind*', upon which Nelson would let out 'an impressive whine, accompanied with uplifted eyes and importunate turn of the head; and when his eyes have not caught those of the spectators, he has been seen to rub the tin box against their knees, to enforce his solicitations. When money was thrown into the box, he immediately put it down, took out the contents with his mouth, and joyfully wagging his tail, carried them to his master.' Nelson had begging pedigree. Dyball got him from Joseph Symmonds, a famous blind fiddler, who got him from another blind beggar, who had trained the dog. Unfortunately, Dyball was deprived of Nelson's money-making skills when the dog was stolen by an itinerant player, 'and he is now obliged to depend on a dog of inferior qualifications'.[10]

The lives and peculiarities of the beggars of the 1810s were preserved by John Thomas Smith in his book of sketches accompanied with prose descriptions, *Vagabondiana* (1817). Smith was Keeper of the Prints at the British Museum and decided to produce his strange book because he realised that the street folk would not last long in the modern world (he did something similar in a book memorialising ancient London buildings about to be demolished in the name of progress). Some of the great artists had used beggars as models and turned them into 'Patriarchs and Prophets' in their works; others had not scrupled to capture the faces and postures of the poor. Smith wanted to do something similar. But he was not going to dignify pauperism like Michelangelo or Rembrandt; as these outlandish creatures would soon be swept from the face of the earth, reading about their habits and wiles 'would not be unamusing to those to whom they have been a pest for several years'.[11]

And amusing many of the famous beggars were to the public. Most

'Charles Wood, a blind man, with an organ and a dancing dog. The real learned French dog, Bob. Money being thrown, Bob picks it up, and puts it into his master's pocket'

of them were either blind or mutilated and either possessed of a talented dog or a flair of their own. Charles Wood, a blind organ player, begged at a pitch on Privy Gardens Wall, Westminster, with 'The real learned French dog, Bob.' Bob was a favourite of ladies and gentlemen and boys and girls because of his virtuosity in making impossible catches. But the crowd would only see the learned canine perform for money: Bob would catch nothing but coins.[12]

Another familiar sight were mutilated beggars who travelled about town on sledges. John MacNally – 'Mac' – from Tyrone was one of the most famous, a feature of Whitehall and the area around Parliament. When he was an apprentice his legs had been crushed by a log, and a life of pulling himself along on his sledge had made him fearsomely strong. 'His head, shoulders, and chest, which are exactly those of Hercules, would prove valuable models for an artist,' commented Smith, a connoisseur of the human form. In later years he employed Boxer and Rover, two dogs, to pull his sledge at great speeds, 'by which contrivance he has increased his income beyond all belief'. So loyal and trusty were the dogs that they knew that when Mac collapsed insensible from drink, they should run at full tilt to their master's lodgings. Tommy Lowe, who became famous as a singer in Marylebone Gardens, raised a public subscription to buy a small dog-chariot pulled by four muzzled mastiffs. He made his money by offering rides to children.[13]

The beggars most richly rewarded by the passing public were the blind, the disabled and black men from the Caribbean, America and British colonies throughout the world, who were popular for their wit and innovation. They were often the best performers on the street. The blind and mutilated excited compassion because they were unable to provide for themselves. West Indians and Africans were pitied because they had been uprooted from their homes by slavery or pressed into the British navy. Wounded, discharged and washed up by circumstances in the British metropolis, they often had no means of support but from the compassionate.

The circumstances of trade and war had made London yet more diverse in its population: there were some 50,000 immigrants living in the capital, from aristocratic French émigrés to Indian Lascars, displaced European people and black sailors. Black and Asian faces were not uncommon in the English crowds. No one can pretend that living in Britain they found a world of opportunity or were welcomed with open arms and without prejudice: they joined the very lowest members of urban society and could expect to stay there, except for a handful who became famous boxers. The best that could be said is that the condition of black people in Britain was better than in West Indian or American plantations. 'It would seem the prejudice against colour is less strong in England than in America,' wrote Benjamin Silliman; 'for, the few negroes found in this country, are in a condition much superior to that of their country [*sic*] any where else . . . An ill dressed and starving negro is never seen in England, and in some instances even alliances are formed between them and white girls of the lower orders of society . . . As there are no slaves in England, perhaps the English have not learnt to regard negroes as a degraded class of men, as we do in the United States, where we have never seen them in any other condition.'[14]

To the casual observer, they might not have starved or worn rags, but a high proportion of beggars were black. Stranded in London, the

'Charles McGee, a notorious black man, whose father died at the age of 108. He usually stood at the Obelisk, at the foot of Ludgate Hill'

degrading profession of minstrelsy was one of the few options open for them; that was the limit of British toleration. Charles McGee, a 'singular' Jamaican, stood at the Obelisk at Ludgate Circus, the busiest crossroads in London. 'Charles is supposed to be worth money,' wrote Thomas Smith. 'His stand is certainly above all others the most popular, many thousands of persons crossing it in a day.' McGee had lost an eye, and his profusion of white hair was tied in a pigtail, with a large tuft at the back; but he was as impeccably dressed as any dandy and wore a smart new coat bought for him by a City pastry cook. McGee might have been among the richest beggars, but two other black men, Billy Waters and Joseph Johnson, were the most famous.[15]

Waters achieved fame in the 1820s, but at the time the mendicity committee sat Johnson was known throughout London and the Home Counties. He had been wounded during the war, but it had happened when he was serving as a merchant seaman so he could not claim relief from the Royal Navy. Finding himself in London, unable to afford a

'Joseph Johnson, a black sailor, with a model of the ship *Nelson* on his cap'

passage home and determined not to fall under the control of the parish beadles, he made money and evaded capture by travelling throughout the capital as 'a Regular Chaunter' of sea shanties. He achieved recognition when he constructed a large and elaborate wooden model of HMS *Nelson* which he placed on his head. 'The man was lame, or, as he himself used to say, damaged in his cock-pit – but in bust, in mien, and with his swarthy, bony face, half concealed by black frizz curls, and crowned by a ship in full sail, he had the bearing of an Atlas.'

He would imitate the motion of the sea with his body as he sang his songs. The effect could be beguiling, especially when the ship appeared, apparently unsupported and tossing on the waves, at a first-floor drawing-room window. Much later, in days when the streets were quieter, the *New Monthly Magazine* recalled with affection Joe's rendition of his best song, 'The Storm': 'he lowered the top gallants, then the stay-sails, and as soon as the time came for the breeze to freshen, Joe was seen to set the braces with a nimbleness and success that would have exhorted praise in the great world of a man of war. Successively you were stunned with the boatswain's bawl and with a raging demon, as he darted from place to place in mimic fury, cutting down masts, casting guns overboard, and gathering all hands to the pump. Here was an improvement on the difficult grace of poetry, making the words an "echo to the sense". Joe acted the song – he passed you through all the perils of the tempest, snatched you from the imminent wreck, without uttering a note. Never shall we forget the shout of satisfaction with which he consigned every bitter remembrance to oblivion, as he fervently cried, "She rights, she rights, boys! wear off shore!"' Johnson would tour villages and towns in the country, singing ballads and shanties, places where he was 'the Incledon of the highways' and 'where he never fails to gain the farmer's penny'. He was a superb entertainer, but one of many similar men, mainly black or Irish, who kept alive the traditions of minstrelsy and street and fairground entertainment. Separated from their families, friends and former lives, they got by as they could. Johnson and his fellow entertainers were among the most familiar sights on London's streets in the 1810s, known and often loved by those who appreciated their antics.[16]

The beggars and performers put on a brave face and were always jolly and entertaining, despite physical disability and poverty; they sought pleasure and comfort despite adversity – that was a main part of their charm. One writer said that beggars were 'our first teachers' in 'the science of humanity'. As unfortunate as the fact of their wretched existence was, they made the yawning gap in society visible so that no one could sweep the realities of life under the carpet; they prevented hearts from hardening and shocked people out of gross selfishness. 'We see them too with gentle interest, because we have always seen them, and were accustomed to relieve them in the spring-time of our days.' Yet everything which endeared beggars and street folk to the people outraged the philanthropists on the mendicity committee. Because they smiled, they seemed to be *enjoying* the carefree life of the streets. And the tender-hearted people were taken in by the trick, and seemed determined to reward indolence, imposture and vice and subsidise the very people who threatened to drag society and the economy down with them. The mendicity committee saw its main task as reversing public opinion, persuading the sentimental crowd that their generosity was, in fact, exacerbating an evil.[17]

Most beggars were not robust blind fiddlers or exotically dressed black immigrants. There were 15,288 people classified as beggars in 1815, five thousand of whom were Irish seeking casual work and six thousand of whom had a right to settlement in an English parish. Over nine thousand were children. Immigrants from outside the British Isles accounted for just 177. The numbers fluctuated, with people coming in and out of distress throughout their lifecycle or during depressions. Matthew Martin, who pioneered a scheme that distributed tickets to beggars which they could exchange for food (rather than buy gin with cash), found that over ten years only a hundred out of 2,000 beggars were still in need of help; the rest had found relief in their parishes, returned to work or died. But from 1815 the number of beggars throughout the country soared as the economy adjusted to peace, the weather became worse and soldiers and sailors tried to find work. The experience of Martin would suggest that few could expect to remain beggars indefinitely; the unusually high number was the result of exigencies caused by the peace. But, as far as the MPs were concerned, there was a new and unprecedented problem emerging as the committee began its work. The members convinced themselves that the great evil was the 'professional beggar', the 'impostor' who aped distress and manipulated the emotions of the crowd.[18]

Alongside the romanticisation of the beggar there has been deep mistrust and revulsion. Yet throughout history they have always been discussed as if they were a problem unique to the particular time. Perhaps it is because they are often taken to symbolise society's wider ills. For John Locke, they represented the breakdown of order, even of civilised society itself. It is almost as if they heralded a general decline in manners and standards; that they stood in the vanguard of society's degeneracy. In 1816 beggars were the detritus of Britain's failures: slavery, Ireland, the parish system and industrialisation. It should be no surprise that they were such a feared and detested group: they were a daily reminder of the country's flaws.

Mendicants could be useful to prove a person's particular theory. Patrick Colquhoun told the committee that the gravest problems came from 'those who beg from inclination', those who flatly refused to submit to the Poor Laws and be carried off to the workhouse, the house of correction or return to their distant home parishes to claim relief.[19] It would seem that taking one's chances on the streets was far too comfortable, and certainly preferable to labour or the workhouse. For such people, mendicity was not a problem of itself but represented everything that was wrong with the entire modern working class. Philip Holdsworth, a senior city marshal and a witness before the committee, said that in Whitechapel there were beggar colonies, with dormitories containing thirty or forty beggars each. The people who rented these lodgings also organised the begging community: 'they are furnished with what is necessary to enable them to beg; they furnish them with children, some who look like twins in a woman's lap. I am informed that at these houses where they take up their quarters, they are certainly very merry in the evening, and in the morning sally forth with all sorts of deceptions; they have different dresses, and have children to put at women's backs; and in eight instances out of ten, I can take upon myself to say they are impositions.' Another witness said that women with babies and infants were richly rewarded; for those childless females, babies were hired out for sixpence a day.[20]

Another witness, Joseph Butterworth MP, confirmed that beggary in London was a centrally coordinated trade with rules and regulations like any other. The central committee would organise 'companies' of beggars and parcel out the 'walks' so that every beggar would have a chance to work the most profitable streets, byways and squares in turn. There were a number of public houses reserved for mendicants, the Weaver's Arms in Whitechapel (renamed The Beggar's Opera) or the Robin Hood and the Maidenhead in Dyott Street in St Giles's. (St Giles's was an appropriate area for the mendicants, for the saint was the patron both of beggars and cripples.)[21]

'I understand', said Butterworth, 'that after the business of the day is over, they frequent these houses and partake their evenings in a very riotous manner; food that is given them by benevolent persons they do not eat, but either throw away or give it to the dogs.' Thomas Smith wrote that one Indian Lascar earned fifteen shillings a day from begging and dined upon roast goose and duck when the day's work was done; witnesses told the committee that many beggars insisted on dressed dinners and the finest liquors. At the Maidenhead tavern, it was said, after a day on the streets the beggars would 'bleed the dragon', or drink in turns from a vast silver tankard filled with punch, for all the world like an association of master tradesmen at a trade club or freemasons. Like Bampfylde-Moore Carew, they set little store by the decorums of society, having no higher ambition than to live for the moment. As one watchhouse keeper said, they lived 'better than any common tradesman: they say it will not do for them to buy fine clothes, for that they spend all their money in eating and drinking; and that fine clothes will not do for them at all'.[22]

The supposed luxury of life on the streets took the committee to the defining issue of the whole enquiry. Beggars would not ask for parish relief, and instead seemed to have worked out their own communal fund or benevolent society to take the place of public charity. Joseph Butterworth said that 'they get more by begging than a great many hard-working industrious men do at their work'. William Dorrell, the Inspector of the Pavement in St Giles's and St George's, complained to the MPs that 'I have said, "Why do not you go out to work?" and they have said to me, "We get more by begging than we do by work".' This contempt for the obligations of society represented the blackest sin against the great god of work and a crime against the people of Britain, as far as the committee was concerned.[23]

What the committee and its expert witnesses refused to understand was why poor people would evade laws set up to relieve their distress. Surely it was a moral duty to conform to the law. But, as a beggar or a prostitute might have said, why would anyone choose to make his or her life worse and submit to oppressive laws that had very little chance of making things better? Under the vagrancy laws, anyone caught begging was to be taken to a gaol for vagrants, before being taken back or given a pass to their home parishes. The system was inhumane, brutalising and inefficient. Sir Nathaniel Conant, the head magistrate of the police office at Bow Street, who had very little time for the credulity of the mendicity committee, told the MPs that 'a poor-house to a pauper, imposed upon him by authority, is a very uncomfortable situation, and they are ready to get out as soon as their hunger is removed'.[24]

Knowing their fate, beggars would do everything possible to avoid falling into the hands of officials, and if they were caught they would fight or fall into a frenzy – anything to avoid being dragged into the horrors of 'the system'. After a spell of between a week and a month in a horrific asylum, beggars would be forced to return to their home parish or last known place of residence. This was the worst moment for the poor and unemployed, even if they weren't beggars to begin with. The interval between applying for relief and it being granted would be excruciating: 'then will be distress and hunger, which will drive the paupers to mendicity', Sir Nathaniel told the committee, describing the vicious circle of poverty. The parishes would not welcome their returning son or daughter with forgiveness and benevolence. Officials would do anything to get out of their obligations. One old man lived on the boundary of two parishes, and neither wanted to pay him out of its poor fund, each claiming that he lived in the other parish. It was determined on enquiry that his house straddled the two parishes. Which parish was responsible for him? The map was consulted and it seemed that the boundary line passed through his bed. With both parishes still in dispute, it was finally determined that the parish in which he rested his head was the one that should look after him.

An unemployed person returning to his original settlement under duress, labelled a beggar and dressed in rags was unlikely to find work in any case. Dragged through the system, a pauper was fit only to beg. The officials would, as Sir Nathaniel said, bribe the beggars with food to stop them claiming relief, and encourage them to return to the street and exhort the mercy of the public. The Poor and Vagrancy Laws were to blame for transforming the casual poor into habitual beggars. A man named James Benjamin was caught begging on Cheapside. He was an unemployed shoemaker who had been four weeks without work and had a sick family. The parish board of St Luke's laughed at him and gave him two shillings to go away. The next day he applied to the parish overseer, who gave him a shilling to buy a broom – which were used by beggars to give them the appearance of doing work. The case was dropped by the Lord Mayor because it was clear that Benjamin had been made a beggar by a parish which wished to minimise its poor rate.[25]

The treatment of most vagrants compelled to seek succour in distant parishes was more brutal. Thomas Davis was paid £300 a year by the county of Middlesex as a contractor responsible for conveying vagrants from London to the next county. He spoke of the rebellious and truculent nature of the people he was obliged to remove: 'they said, they would not be locked in, they had not been thieving, they had fought for their King and Country, and they would not be locked up; they had done no harm'. They would fight and threaten and constantly try to escape, so that Davis was often compelled to call for the constabulary.

Davis was paid to enforce the dictates of the magistrates, who issued passes to vagrants enabling them to return to their home parishes. He would transport them in his cart as far as Egham, where another contractor would take over and supervise their journey to Maidenhead, where another man would supervise the journey on to Hungerford. And so the journey would continue until the vagrants were delivered into the hands of those parish overseers who were legally responsible for them. As soon as this expensive, troublesome and cruel process was complete, the vagrant would be allowed to escape and make his way back to London. Irish migrants were treated worse: they had to be escorted to Liverpool and placed on a ship. Once on board, they could be at sea for days, depending on the weather, all the time without food. Yet the committee members were still mystified as to why beggars did not willingly submit to the legal authorities. They believed that it was the duty of the poor to happily sacrifice themselves under the juggernaut of the parish system. Defiance was seen as an act of treachery and a further example of the beggars' love of illicit luxury and contempt for the laws of the land. One official said that beggars often tried to justify themselves by saying that a life of extreme poverty – among vermin, hunger and cold – was intolerable: 'I have been used to live better,' they would say, 'and cannot bear it.' This was intended to sound shocking – another example of the pride and reluctance to face facts supposedly typical of the lowest – but it sounds like a laudable instinct for self-preservation and desperation for some sort of dignity in a hostile world.[26]

Knowing the indignities and cruelty of the system, the public had an instinctive sympathy with the street folk. Many of the officials who stood before the committee reported with deep regret and alarm that it was becoming almost impossible to arrest a beggar. Few officers would try and arrest one particularly notorious blind beggar with a performing dog who was known to knock out the teeth of anyone who dared such an interference of his liberty. One officer was almost killed. Once, when he was arrested, according to a magistrate's clerk, 'He had the impudence to say, it was his dog begged and not he.' On other occasions, passers-by would crowd round and exclaim, 'What, ill-treat a poor blind man!'[27] And the hostility was common throughout London. John Smith, the beadle of St Giles's, could not wear his beadle's cocked hat in the district because it would have been stolen before he had walked the first street. The inhabitants saw him as a tyrannical petty official who would deprive the unfortunate of their liberty.[28]

Philip Holdsworth lamented that it was easier to get a city police officer to arrest a hardened thief than a beggar: 'the people generally join with the Mendicant, and the officers frequently are ill-used; insomuch so, that one officer, the week before last, in taking up a sailor, whose dog carries his hat, was seriously hurt'. Mobs throughout the city would protect beggars from the authorities with words and blows.[29]

An MP who sat on the mendicity committee met one of his constituents, who asked how he was getting on at the 'Mendacity Committee'.[30] It was a genuine slip, yet it was appropriate. The committee members and most of the witnesses saw their role as, in the first instance, reversing public opinion, not telling the truth. The people helped beggars with their fists, and also with their purses. 'The evil lies with others than with them,' the Rev. William Gurney said of beggars; 'it lies in that which is extremely creditable, the humanity of the population; people cannot bear to pass by distress without relieving it, but in fact they are only adding fuel to the fire.'[31] The committee would do anything to press this home to the public and extinguish the instinct of 'false humanity', even if it meant propagating the myth that well-fed beggars congregated in taverns to eat turkey and goose, drink gin, rum and punch, and laugh at the credulity of their victims. Francis Place was a witness to the committee, but, as he wrote to James Mill, 'I was treated with . . . a hollow politeness beyond anything I expected . . . I told them of their ignorance, and of their absurd legislation.' The tailor's evidence was not what the committee wanted to hear, and it was struck from the record.

Place, who attended every day of the committee's deliberations, believed that Joseph Butterworth, a 'canting methodist', represented the rest of the committee members: 'they would have it inferred that all poverty was wilful, all beggars animals[,] mankind growing worse and worse daily, and no hope of amendment'. The committee was convinced that all beggars were impostors, wretched hypocrites and accomplished actors who committed widespread fraud on the public. Yet in painting this picture, they seemed to contradict or undermine the evidence that suggested that beggars devoted every moment to carousing.[32]

One man elicited pity and money by eating soap and pretending to fall into a raving fever, and a woman by barking like a dog; yet both were apparently – or officially – sane. One of the lowest jobs in Britain was a 'translator of soles', someone who took apparently worn out shoes and converted them into something just about usable for the most desperate. One of these used to scratch and mutilate his feet, so that people would feel sorry for him and donate their old shoes. He would abuse their trust by repairing the shoes and selling them to his poor neighbours for a pittance. A beggar called 'Buckhorse' allowed people to punch him in the face for a shilling; the face, a target for so much frustration and sadistic amusement, 'became at last more like a Good-Friday bun than any thing human'. None of these cases suggest that life on the streets was preferable to a day's work; there is no doubt that these were vulnerable, disturbed and desperate people. Yet the committee and its supporters could only see this kind of behaviour as further evidence that beggars led an easy and luxurious life free from the cares of work. Mutilating one's body, eating soap, barking in public, taking punches were just the easy way out. The real victims were members of the public, who always shed a tear at these performances.

While most of the witnesses told the committee what it wanted to hear, a few flatly denied the lurid stories of excess, luxury and uninterrupted pleasure. Sir Daniel Williams, a Whitechapel magistrate, said that in the course of his career he had come across only two or three genuine impostors.[33] Sir Nathaniel Conant refused to believe the stories about wealthy beggars and nightly feasts; he rarely found a beggar in possession of a shilling or more. Indeed, contrary to the hysteria, there were fewer mendicants on the streets in 1815 than there had been in 1785. The chaplain of Bridewell found it in his heart to pity and explain the noxious habits of the beggars: 'I do not know a more pitiable description of human beings than the poor creatures who are brought into us for a time; the mode of life in which they are living, is reduced to a complete system; they are intoxicated a great part of the day, or they would not be able to support what they have to undergo at night, probably. In fact, their life is such, that it tends to stupefy the understanding and to harden the heart.'[34]

But the newspapers were more likely to recount the stories of jovial beggars using their arts and wiles to afford an evening's carousing. It made good copy. The *Examiner* published portions of the evidence of the committee under the headline 'Begging System', including only the most sensational tales. It was just as the committee intended. John Daughtry, an owner of a carpet warehouse and a volunteer visitor of poor families in Spitalfields, said that the whole problem was caused by people thoughtlessly giving away tiny amounts of money when their sense of humanity was roused: 'the evil of Mendicity may thus derive its chief support from the half-pence of the public'.[35] Stop the mite, and beggars would cease to crowd the streets and the public houses. Many of the witnesses were professionally involved with administering unworkable laws and their hard job was made impossible, as they saw it, by the generous people. The law was flawed, and the resistance of the beggars made it that much harder. Thomas Davis, the Middlesex conveyor, said that beggars escaped as he tried to force them out of London and would always 'get away unless I stood over them with a naked sword'. The implication was that unlimited power would make his job much easier: give him the unsheathed sword and there would be no problem.[36]

And so it was with the beadles, police officers, Poor Law overseers, police officers and magistrates who were charged with administering Elizabethan statutes. Beggars were harmless enough to private people; but as far as petty officialdom went, they were a costly and ungovernable minority. They found themselves chasing about after vagrants, an expensive, time-consuming and futile job: of course they hated beggars. They resented the drunkenness of the street folk and begrudged them every small luxury they got their hands on. Such witnesses were the last people to give beggars any sympathy. Leigh Hunt savagely attacked the politicians and officials who presided over the rickety Poor Laws and participated in the calumny of the poor. It was, he said, disgraceful 'for the movers of this monstrous machine, – the very priests of this destructive idol, to come forward to vilify and defame the helpless victims over which it tramples, for being, what under such dispensation they cannot but be'.[37]

They preferred poor people who chose to half starve themselves. 'As a general fact, the decent poor will struggle to the uttermost, and even perish, rather than turn beggars,' Daughtry told the MPs. These 'decent' and 'respectable' people were the joy and delight of the committee. Better for everyone that they hide the distressing sight of their poverty away from the world and not bother their neighbours with cries for help. Better for the country that they did not ask for money they had not earned; they were to be applauded as good Malthusians who would rather die than make a claim on a finite supply of food.[38]

The poor worth relieving were those who meekly submitted to their betters and complied with the laws, even if those laws were contrary to their interests. Indeed, for Daughtry, the problem of mendicity was not due to the post-war depression but occurred because the poor did not have a decent religious education that instilled into them clean, frugal habits and stoicism. Those who had not been to Sunday School were 'disinclined to submit to the restraints which the discipline of a school imposes'. Submission, restraint and discipline were the three sure ingredients for moral reform and the obliteration of extreme poverty. Those who had been to Sunday School, by way of a comparison that must have been a mouth-watering proposition to politicians and parish officials, did not 'become assuming and impertinent; on the contrary, the order and subjection to which they are trained, and the instruction they receive in their moral and religious duties, excite a more respectful behaviour, and more correct feeling towards their superiors in general'.[39]

The House of Commons select committee on mendicity marked the beginning of the end of the performing mendicants of London, but not of beggary itself. The public came under pressure to withhold their pennies from performers like Joe Johnson and Billy Waters, blind beggars with their ingenious dogs and the miserable poor – the cripples, the discharged sailors and other lost souls. The committee wanted to disabuse the public of the idea that beggars were dignified heroes who pitted their wits against fortune, and foster the impression that they were chancers and fraudsters who mocked their benefactors over roast goose and punch. The words from the enquiry quoted most often in the papers came from Joseph Butterworth: 'I am convinced that begging has a direct tendency to degrade the mind; and that when poor people once find that they can easily get money by begging, they very seldom afterwards have recourse to habits of industry; and I believe from the great number of petitions which I have had occasion to examine, many persons are made beggars from the injudicious kindness of real benevolence.' It was a charge that stuck in the public mind.[40]

When Thomas Smith produced *Vagabondiana* in 1817, it was with the knowledge that the timeless London sight of minstrels, entertainers and mendicants had reached an end. 'It is very obvious', he wrote, 'that since the proceedings of the Committee for enquiring into the state of mendicity, the common beggars have decreased considerably in their numbers.' Like the public, Smith's attitude to beggars was ambivalent. He was fascinated by their tricks and performances, loved their exotic clothes and entertainments, and admired their instinct for survival; yet this was mixed with revulsion at their condition, suspicion about their private behaviour and fear that he was being imposed upon.[41]

Yet who was imposing upon whom? Smith got a handsomely produced and very expensive book out of their lives. Again, like the people who soaked up the stories of deceit and beggarly conviviality from the report of the select committee and the newspapers, he revelled in the romance of the streets. The vagrants were fodder for curiosity and good copy for the papers, affording the public a juicy read. As Charles Lamb wrote, one could project whatever one wanted onto a beggar: had he, like Lear, fallen from great heights to the lowest rank of society? Was he a buccaneer, like Bampfylde-Moore Carew, taking on the laws and conventions of the world? At one moment people could revel in the fantasy of vagrant intrepidity; at others they could lash out at them as impostors and parasites.

Smith unwittingly revealed this hypocrisy when he recounted a story that was intended to shock. He paid a beggar two shillings to sit for a drawing. After ten minutes the poor man grew restless and complained he could make more money at Charing Cross or Hyde Park Corner; he then turned up his nose at a meal of bread and cheese and complained that the veal he had been given was too lean. Smith wanted to illustrate the ingratitude of hardened beggars but instead revealed his own hypocrisy and patronising attitude. Only one man was benefiting from the exchange. The beggar knew it; he took the coins without thanks and said, 'Now that you have draughted [drafted] me off, I suppose you'll make a fine deal of money out of it.'[42]

Smith's disgust at the pride of beggars was manifesting itself throughout the community. People were still generous, but now there was a fear that the people who received their well-meaning charity were professionals engaged in a business. How could people negotiate the treacherous path between humanity and 'false humanity'? Who could one trust in the dangerous modern world, populated by impostors and where nothing was as it seemed? The mendicity committee had warned that indiscriminate alms-giving was the greatest act of folly. No one could tell what sort of character would take the half-penny and what vicious habit he would later indulge. If the committee did not immediately change the law, it certainly got a large and influential section of the community to enforce its recommendations. Better that people withheld the coin so that, even if nine genuine beggars went hungry, one disgusting impostor was punished.

In 1818 the Society for the Suppression of Mendicity was founded under the patronage of HRH the Duke of York and the presidency of the Duke of Northumberland; the rehabilitated and now socially acceptable war hero the Marquis of Anglesey (quondam Lord Paget) was one of the vice-presidents, along with a number of other aristocrats, the Chancellor of the Exchequer Nicholas Vansittart and Matthew Martin. The board of management was a muster roll of modern philanthropists drawn from the utilitarian and evangelical camps, Patrick Colquhoun, William Allen, William Frend, Joseph Hume and David Ricardo chief among them. Supported by generous contributions from the public, the society employed constables to do the work that was neglected by indolent magistrates and stingy parish officers. Beggars were rounded up and subjected to tests. Were they deserving or undeserving? Were they capable of labour? Were they impostors?[43]

In its first year, the Mendicity Society provided 189 beggars with the tools to allow them to resume their trade and 216 were found jobs. But that was set against 1,222 people forcibly returned to their home parish, fifty-four who were repatriated, the 564 adjudged impostors (of which 385 were sent to prison) and 286 who were considered capable of supporting themselves. The society provided sensible and thoughtful relief to a considerable number of unfortunate people. Those who returned to work were genuinely grateful for the revolution in their fortunes. But the society mixed this with brutal coercion against anyone they even suspected of indolence or voluntary mendicity. The public was eagerly doing the work that the government and magistrates refused to carry out.[44]

The Mendicity Society also proposed a better way of relieving distress than simply distributing coins to strangers, the folly of the thoughtless benevolent. For many years Matthew Martin had tried to persuade people to buy tickets to give to beggars, which they could exchange for food and clothes. The secretive world of midnight orgies in low taverns would thus be eradicated, supposing it ever existed. The society reflected the growing anxiety about impostors stalking the streets and sought to allay it. As it implored the public, 'let investigation always precede relief; the circumstances of every case be minutely examined – the character and habits of the party fully inquired into, the relief will then, if deserved, be given in the way most likely to be really serviceable to the object, and most satisfactory to the feelings of the donor'. Beggars had to prove themselves worthy of the help of the high-minded philanthropist, passing a rigorous moral test. If they accepted a ticket instead of a coin, it showed that they were prepared to forgo pleasure; that they were not begging for the sheer joy of it but out of dire need. In short, beggars had to accept their lot; their food must be kept to a set daily ration by a system of tickets, lest the indiscriminate donor unwittingly augment their purse and send a message to the unhappily employed poor that life on the streets was a constant round of pleasure, luxury and dissipation.[45]

Yet habits died hard. Many still gave beggars the benefit of the doubt, and conceded, as Benjamin Silliman wrote, that 'there is reason to believe, that most of them are really the wretches they appear to be, and that the charge of imposture urged against them, is too frequently a refuge of selfishness'; Charles Lamb called the evidence of vagrant feasts 'misers' calumnies'. Street performers were still indulged and cases of distress relieved without the moral inquisition recommended by the Society for the Suppression of Mendicity.[46]

Some asked what was meant by 'impostor'. It could be argued that beggars could not but be impostors of a sort if the word was defined as narrowly as the mendicity committee and Society for the Suppression of Mendicity did. One witness said that a blind and disabled man was begging under false pretences if he could contribute to his upkeep by milling grain with a hand-grinder twelve hours a day, six days a week in a workhouse.[47] Under such a definition, only a deaf, dumb and disabled person could count as genuine, the authentic article. Begging, by its nature, precluded telling the truth. People did not want to hear a life story and learn of a poor person's moral credentials. The exchange was simpler: Joe Johnson would sing and dance for his money, not lament his injuries and inability to work. And indeed, what morality was there in unmasking minor untruths or beginning a minute enquiry before one could bear to part with a piece of small change? Lamb wrote that the 'modern fastidiousness' that motivated such actions was the very opposite of morality, the creed of the selfish and unfeeling.

There was a strong element of social engineering in the Mendicity Society's activities; beggars had to ape the manners and morals of the middle classes before they qualified for help. Was it not an act of hubris to sit in judgement over one's fellows, rejecting one whose habits were noisome and relieving another who passed a subjective test? Lamb advised people '*give, and ask no questions*': 'Shut not thy purse-strings always against painted distress. Act a charity sometimes. When a poor creature (outwardly and visibly such) comes before thee, do not stay to enquire whether the "seven small children" . . . have a veritable existence. Rake not into the bowels of unwelcome truth, to save a halfpenny. It is good to believe him . . . When they come with their counterfeit looks, and mumping tones, think them players. You pay your money to see a comedian feign these things, which, concerning these poor people, thou canst not certainly tell whether they are feigned or not.'[48]

Rejecting beggars on the grounds of imposture and in the name of New Morality had a strong element of sweeping the problem under the carpet. The committee was right that indiscriminate charity encouraged begging; but its case that people should cease giving would only be moral if the state or private philanthropy provided a humane way out of beggary. Thomas Smith celebrated the last of the traditional beggars in *Vagabondiana* because he believed that the street folk would be carried off to a happy life in glittering new workhouses and asylums, where they would be looked after if they were old and disabled or taught a new trade if they were 'sturdy'. People could pretend to themselves that, by withholding the penny or giving a food ticket or supporting the Mendicity Society's efforts to keep the streets clean, they were being cruel to be kind. But there was no evidence that many were successfully rehabilitated. On the contrary, conditions could be worse in the workhouse than on the streets. The Mendicity Society was supported by many who believed that they were doing a moral act, but they did not look closely enough into the motives of the managers, many of whom had a fanatical hatred of the life and colour of the streets.[49]

The word 'cant' derived from the cynical way in which vagabonds extorted money with well-rehearsed whines and pious gibberish. In an age preoccupied with duplicity and imposture, beggars were frequently held up as the ultimate canting hypocrites. Living by lies and performance, they had become something less than human: 'In most cases, idleness and hypocrisy are so wrought into their natures, that they are absolutely inseparable,' one witness told the committee. 'Living by hourly deception, they have less character than even thieves, and are more hopeless to moral reformation.' So there was a kind of justice in imputing cant to the Mendicity Society and its supporters, as many did. They were in thrall to new theories and willing believers of any shred of evidence or biased opinion that supported their prejudices. (A piece of tittle-tattle told to the committee was reported by the members as hard fact: that 'A Negro beggar retired to the West Indies with a fortune, it was supposed, of £1,500.'[50]) They picked up and repeated as truth any piece of jargon that came their way. The supposedly scientific rigour of utilitarianism and political economy and the moral laws of evangelicalism provided a ready-made vocabulary, an ethical justification for hard-heartedness and an easy exit from responsibility.

The enthusiasm for the Society for the Suppression of Mendicity's activities suggested a change in attitudes. The *New Monthly Magazine* published a letter by George Pertinax Growler, a fictional character who represented old English robustness and compassion, which complained about 'New Improvements' that were revolutionising the national character. Simplicity and kindliness were being replaced by cold philanthropy and a bustling, busybody spirit. 'The Society for the Suppression of Mendicity is another boasted institution of these cold-hearted days,' Growler wrote. 'It would annihilate the race of beggars, and remove from the delicate eye the very form and aspect of misery. Strange infatuation! as if an old class of the great family of man might be cut off without harm!' He did not take seriously the charge against beggars that they were impostors and secretly wealthy; and if it was true that they occasionally spent their money on hot food and gin, magnanimity would excuse their excesses: 'If they have even their occasional revellings, and hidden luxuries, we should rather rejoice to believe that happiness has every where its nooks and corners which we do not see; that there is more gladness in the earth than meets the politician's gaze.'

But he admitted that his view was dying out in Britain. The mendicity committee and the debate it sparked showed a country torn by two different emotions. People looked back with fondness at the beggars and minstrels and the kindly and spontaneous generosity they elicited, but they knew that the modern world called for greater restraint and rationality. Growler himself was said to have died in 1818, the year that the Mendicity Society was founded. His physician put it down to a nervous attack brought on by discussing modern society with his progressive neighbour Sir Francis Fluent (the representative of the spirit of the modern age and a keen philanthropist), but his apothecary said it was the result of a typhus infection caught while chatting with a beggar. As it was, there was not much room for the George Pertinax Growlers of the world, with their unfashionable notions of benevolence and susceptibility to nervous disorders.[51]

9

Academies of Vice

'. . . the Pot of Porter is, in every sense of the words, a firm friend of the British Constitution.'

Anon[1]

'The people of England choose to be, in a great measure, without Law and without Police; they have reached a very distinguished point in industry and civilization without them.'

Morning Chronicle

Looking back on his youth, Francis Place was convinced that there had been a revolution in the manners, morals and education of his contemporaries. People were more respectable, sober and ambitious, and enjoyed a better standard of living. Things weren't perfect, but there were signs that the middle and working classes were progressing towards a happier and more enlightened state. There was less drunkenness, cruelty and lewdness seen on the streets of major cities; parents were desperate to send their children to school; the need to save money was firmly ingrained in the mind. The contrast with the London of Place's youth was becoming more marked by the year. Yet this was an age when the Society for the Suppression of Vice beat the drum for moral reform, and conservative journalists wrote of a 'mighty and deplorable change' in the people. Britain had fallen 'from the pre-eminence in intelligence and virtue to so low a point of ignorance and vice' that she stood at the 'abyss of barbarism, guilt and misery'.[2]

The country was modern and advancing; but it seemed that while the middle classes were richer and more seemly, other classes were becoming worse. Indeed, progress gave birth to new crimes: 'The poor are familiar with all the crimes of civilized life without the correspondent improvement of it.'[3] They were more skilful, more *refined* criminals; they had taken the duplicity, artfulness and gloss from the march of progress, leaving the real fruits to rot. Patrick Colquhoun, John Bowles and their followers, and, after 1815, politicians and journalists, were keenly aware of the depravity and degradation of the people.

Never in the history of mankind, commented the *Quarterly Review*, had vice flourished with such barefaced audacity. And what fuelled this decline into barbarism and vicious behaviour? The answer, it was coming to be believed, could be pinned down to two words: gin and beer. Colquhoun, numbers to hand as usual, wrote that the average daily intake of a labouring man was not less than twelve pots of beer. Robert Southey told his readers that while no new churches were being built by the Establishment, alehouses had increased at a ratio ten times greater than population: restraint had been lifted at a time when temptations abounded. According to the census of 1811, there were 49,540 public houses in England, Scotland and Wales, serving a population of 11,956,303; or, put another way, one house in every forty-one was a licensed premises. 'As the establishment of inns is one of the surest proofs of the accomplishments of increasing civilisation,' Southey wrote, 'so the alehouse is not less surely the effect and the cause of an increased and increasing depravity of manners.'[4]

Improved communications created more inns to refresh busy travellers; the multiplication of alehouses betokened a population set simply on drinking on an industrial scale for no other purpose than inebriation. Alehouses, as distinct from inns and taverns, were often private homes open seasonally or occasionally to sell beer. Samuel Bamford described one such place near Bury in 1816, a room lit by two candles in a thatched shack: 'The room was dimmed by tobacco smoke but I . . . could discern . . . eight or ten men seated in various parts of it, some on stools, some on piled bricks, whilst others occupied empty firkins, mugs [barrels] capsized or any other article offering a seat.'[5]

Place said that the moralists diagnosed national malaise at this time because they had ignored the lower classes and the state of morals for so long, had suddenly become concerned at their behaviour and were shocked at what they saw. They had no sense of perspective, he said; Colquhoun, Southey, the SSV and other concerned people had no idea what life was like before they became interested in their neighbours. They were therefore incapable of telling whether things were getting better or worse. Place was delighted when, from 1815, parliamentary select committees began to investigate the condition of the country. For the first time, he believed, the myths propagated by the alarmists that the poor were naturally immoral and that crime and drunkenness were becoming endemic would be revealed for what they were. 'It may be remarked', he said, 'that on no former occasion did committees of the House of Commons push their enquiries to any thing like the extent they were pushed in 1816 and 1817.'[6]

In 1816 the Hon. Henry Grey Bennet MP moved in the House of Commons that a select committee be formed under his chairmanship to investigate the police of the metropolis. The committee sat through the summer of 1816, reconvened in 1817 and again in 1818. It set out to determine the scale and effectiveness of the police and magistracy, whether they were capable of reconciling the liberty of the subject with the protection of life and property, and if they had the means of holding back the tidal wave of immorality predicted by so many. But it became clear that none of these questions could be answered without examining, in minute detail, the relationship between the people and alcohol.

While the mendicity committee made little effort to conceal its bias towards the preoccupations of people such as Colquhoun, the committees on crime were unashamedly on the side of the people against those who would control them. Bennet, a Whig MP, was committed to defending the rights and liberties of the people; Place called him 'an active useful man in unmasking abuses, and promoting good objects'.[7] And when he turned his attention to the moral state of the country, he sought out Place, by now well-known in some circles for his political activism and extensive research into the state of the country. Many years later, the *Monthly Magazine* wrote: 'Francis Place, by his assistant labours and advice given to members of the House of Commons, has produced more effect in that House than any man who was never a member.' Not many knew this at the time, however. But Place was an important figure behind the scenes throughout the long enquiry. 'Few men have done more of the world's work with so little external sign,' wrote the *Spectator* in its obituary of Place in 1854. '. . . He was essentially a public man, but his work usually lay behind the curtain . . . He loved quiet power for the purpose of promoting good ends.'[8]

The direction the committee took when it commenced its vast task was set in part by Place, who focused the enquiry by supplying Bennet with a list of questions to ask the witnesses. He also fed the members of the committee with information about that unknown territory, the state of the people. As he had got richer, he had amassed a massive collection of books; above the tailor's shop was a neat and tidy library stocked with treatises, newspaper clippings, reports and statistics on the changing moral character of the country. 'My library was a sort of gossip shop for such persons as were in any way engaged in public matters having the benefit of the people for their object,' he remembered. Utilitarians, radicals and Whig MPs frequented the library, and it often had the feel of a busy tavern. As far as Bennet was concerned, Place was a hard taskmaster: 'I told Bennet from the first that I should wear him out, and that he would be obliged either to shun me or lead a dog's life with his party. He said, No; I said, Yes. He has done so.' From the summer of 1816 Bennet and Place would guide the committee through the territory that had been subject to so much conjecture, scare-mongering and fear: slums, backstreets, taverns and prisons.[9]

Bennet and Place shared an unshakeable belief that the labouring and artisan classes were improving, marching happily along in step with the progress of the country. Place thought that working men and women were, like him, better behaved and more ambitious. There was, however, a residuum which made up an underclass of depraved, immoral and abandoned people. This small group was confused with the working class by the wealthy and respectable, who took the character of the whole class from police reports in newspapers, from lurid stories retailed by 'police-mongers' like Colquhoun or from their carriage windows. No doubt Place thought back to the time when he looked like a bearded fury; he might have appeared to be the lowest criminal, yet this was when he was exerting every effort to feed his family and build up a business.

The committee's sympathy with the poor and Place's influence on it can be seen in the way some of the witnesses were questioned. The octogenarian magistrate of fifty years experience William Fielding was asked whether the habits and morals of the working people had got better in recent years. Fielding pointed to an increase in gin-drinking and the number of dissolute youths on the streets and said that things were worse. But Bennet and the committee challenged him, using what sounds like Francis Place's personal recollections as evidence against him. They cited the Dog and Duck, the Apollo Gardens and the Temple of Flora, places of drunkenness and sex that Place remembered all too well, all of which had closed down; they said that indecent songs were no longer to be heard on the streets and that bullock hunts, once every apprentice's joy and delight, were extinct.

'Of all these nuisances hardly a vestige remain,' Bennet said; the people of 1816 would no longer tolerate them. Fielding again denied this, and again Bennet betrayed his bias, asking him: 'Does it not appear to you, that upon taking an occasional walk on any Sunday in the year in fine weather, that there is a striking change for the better . . . in the manners, morals, behaviour, and appearance of the lower orders . . . suppose, for instance, a person chose to walk towards Pentonville, and see the beautiful fields in the neighbourhood, filled with thousands of people walking with their families . . . would he not find that the manners and dress of those people very much improved, to what they formerly were?'

Fielding would admit only that there was a 'superficiality of manners' and 'an increase in decency' as far as clothes and outward appearances went. In his notes on the committee's proceedings, Place wrote that the superannuated magistrate was too infirm to have been out and about recently. In this debate on the state of the people, Bennet and Place's optimism was briefly checked by a more old-fashioned view that inner morality could not be measured by the outward garb of decency. Bennet's spat with Fielding showed the principles upon which the committee on policing founded its enquiries.[10]

The committee was well-timed. It coincided with calls for a reform of the policing of the country, and especially of the urban poor. Colquhoun told the committee that at one point the government had been set to introduce his plans for a centralised force but had unaccountably abandoned the plan.[11] There was growing dissatisfaction with things as they were and mounting fear that private property was threatened by the refractory mob. 'The very wealth with which this country abounds', the *Quarterly Review* gloomily commented, 'becomes a snare to its people and a temptation to illegal acts in almost every place and under every form.'[12] Robert Southey, writing in the same publication, continued his lamentation that urbanisation was ruining the people. Lost in horrific hellholes, uprooted from the unchanging security of the village and the health of outdoor labour, they were incapable of looking after their bodies, souls or morals on their own. There were crimes that were specific to London, the largest city in Europe. Yet the problem suggested its own solution: 'Great cities', wrote Southey, 'do not with more certainty generate foul air, and condense contagion, than they assist the propagation of moral diseases. And yet, under a good police, medical and moral, the means, both of prevention and remedy, might be applied there with far greater celerity, and therefore with more likelihood of success, than in places where the population is scattered.'[13]

The first task of the committee was to determine if the panic that was gripping certain sections of society was confirmed by the evidence. Was the current policing adequate, and had morals collapsed to such an extent that a new, more powerful, more professional police force was required? The accounts the witnesses gave of the arrangement of police offices reminded the committee of the local nature of policing. A traveller to London would find 'the metropolis divided and sub-divided into petty jurisdictions, each independent of each other; each having sufficiently distinct interests to engender perpetual jealousies and animosities, and being sufficiently [distinct] from any general control to prevent any intercommunity of information, or any unity of action'.[14]

This apparently chaotic system was fiercely defended. The assumption of policing was that major crimes would be dealt with by a severe code of punishments: the threat of execution, transportation and the pillory would restrain criminally inclined people. In theory, many crimes were punishable by execution; in practice, few people were executed, but the punishment, and its uncertain administration, held out an equal terror to all offenders. Petty crime, riot, labour disputes and disorderly conduct were left to individuals and communities to police and suppress. The people were policed by an insanely bloody code of exemplary justice on the one hand, and a disorganised and frequently lax volunteer police on the other. In such circumstances it was assumed that there had to be – by necessity – tolerance of minor crime and disorder: that was the price to pay for living in a free country. In other words, the middle classes should put up with their poorer neighbours' drunkenness and brutal pleasures; they should turn a blind eye to brothels and learn to live with the casual violence of the streets. An empowered Home Secretary, a policeman on every street and surveillance of any kind were dangers far greater.

Notions of liberty meant that in Britain 'the business of police is chiefly confided to the people themselves'.[15] The system should rest on the cooperation and consent of the people rather than on coercion from above, and on negotiation rather than rigorous enforcement. In theory, order would be kept by the wisdom and liberality of British paternalism: a voluntary constabulary drawn from the respectable members of the local neighbourhood and an enlightened magistracy sensitive to the needs of the community and discretionary in the exercise of the law. In practice, it was arbitrary, cruel and unfair: prisons were sinks of vice and disease; execution was visited on the most trivial offences; officers of the law could be corrupt or partial or lazy; might often trumped right in small communities; and poor victims had few opportunities for redress. But, again, the benefits of minimal state involvement and the privilege of personal responsibility were supposed to make up for the caprice of an antiquated system.

The way that Londoners were policed was a lottery. It comprised 'disjointed bodies of men governed separately, under heterogeneous regulations'.[16] Metropolitan policing was based on the historical development of London. The oldest areas lay under the administration of the Common Council of the City: the Square Mile (population 58,400) and the sixteen parishes (72,000) lying outside the City walls but within its jurisdiction. The City of Westminster (189,400) constituted a separate administrative area which paid for its own watchmen and constabulary. Other parts of London of more recent settlement, such as St Giles's, Bethnal Green and Lambeth – home to 730,700 people, the majority of the capital's population – comprised separate parishes supervised by the county magistrates of Surrey and Middlesex, depending on where the parishes lay. A further five parishes – such as Marylebone and St Pancras – lay outside London's ancient boundaries but were still part of the metropolis, connected by an uninterrupted succession of houses; 224,300 people lived in these parishes.

In the City, the Lord Mayor and the aldermen sat as magistrates and supervised the policing activities of upper- and under-marshals and marshalmen and the lower offices of constables and watchmen who policed the City's twenty-six wards. In the populous districts that lay in Middlesex and Surrey, the parishes were 'separate municipalities' which balloted their respectable male householders to serve as constables and headboroughs in rotation every year. The parishes levied money to employ watchmen and patrols, and the neighbourhood elected a paid beadle to supervise the watch and collect the rates.

It was a system that was trenchantly local and in part voluntary. Most of the 'better sort' picked to serve as officers were too busy or too respectable to fulfil their duties and often paid a substitute. This was deeply unsatisfactory: the substitutes were of low status and augmented their meagre pay by exhorting bribes from publicans, known thieves and brothel-keepers. Those who chose to take up their duties themselves were more often than not men fired by reforming zeal who used their office to suppress nuisances such as Sabbath-breaking or tippling in alehouses. The watch had been notorious for consisting of old and feeble men, but this was now changing. After the notorious Ratcliffe Highway murders in 1811, which exposed the uselessness of the parish system in preventing or detecting psychotic murderers, Parliament discussed a bill to regulate the watch. Even coming in response to horrific murders, this mild reform sparked fears that the state was attempting to impose a police force on the people by the back door and the proposed measure had to be dropped. The parishes resented the increased costs of an improved watch and did not want to surrender their local sovereignty in these matters. Lord Dudley said in the House of Lords that he 'would rather half-a-dozen people's throats were cut in Ratcliffe Highway every three or four years than to be subject to domiciliary visits [and] spies'.

For people at this time 'police' meant the kind of system innovated in Paris: paid agents of the state who informed on their neighbours and interfered in private life. No maintenance of order was worth such a nightmare, and so tolerance of minor misdemeanours and antisocial behaviour was, if not a virtue, a practical necessity. The people hated authority and relished seeing Mr Punch bludgeon the meddling constable. Yet there had been reforms. In 1770 the Bow Street Runners had been formed to police the whole of London outside the City limits. In 1792 the Middlesex Justice Bill had created seven police offices in London, each under the control of three stipendiary magistrates and employing six professional officers.

Sir Nathaniel Conant, the first witness to the select committee, was the magistrate in charge of the most important office in the country, Bow Street. His jurisdiction extended throughout London and even the country; the office was the only one that was open twenty-four hours a day, and so it absorbed a lot of the work of other London magistrates. At his command were eighty-seven Runners who manned foot patrols in London, thirteen conductors of patrols and eight general police officers. This was a lot compared with the seven officers employed by the Union Hall police office, which policed Borough, Southwark, Peckham, Rotherhithe and Deptford, a circumference of forty miles and a population in 1811 of 127,312. The Bow Street mounted patrols had been founded in 1809, and they extended as far as Windsor to the west, into Hertfordshire in the north, Essex in the east and Kent to the south; they had been instrumental in making highway robbery a legend of more lawless days. The Bow Street police office was highly specialised. Its officers were concerned more with cases of fraud and financial chicanery than common crimes. They would investigate dubious City transactions, crimes associated with the Post Office or instances of forgery.[17]

At the time of the 1792 reform Charles James Fox said that the creation of forty-two officers paid by the state was an assault on the liberties of the people, while Sir Samuel Romilly said that such a police force would place the government 'under the miserable and shameful necessity of constantly making an insidious and open war upon the people'. But those in charge of the police were anxious to make sure that did not happen, such was the sensitivity towards the tyrannising potential of professional policing.

At Bow Street, the officers acted independently, unless 'special circumstances may call for general co-operation'. The police did not prevent crimes or detect the perpetrators unless the incident was brought to their attention. The prosecutor had to bear the cost of the investigation and the trial; sometimes poor people had to pawn their possessions to bring out a warrant against someone who had harmed them.[18] The officers were paid two shillings and sixpence a night, but they made their money by claiming rewards from wealthy victims of crime; very often they would devote their time to pursuing a runaway banker's clerk if the remuneration was large, while ignoring more serious but less lucrative crimes. At times the office would be undermanned, when Conant's best officers were employed on freelance work in distant parts of the country or, sometimes, on the continent; even the police-office clerks were private attorneys who only did the job so they could pick up clients and find valuable legal work.[19]

The most famous officer was the dandified James Townsend, an 'eccentric and amusing' man, according to Gronow, who was rarely at Bow Street. He amassed £20,000 as a private detective and as the principal attendant at the royal court from 1792. He stood at royal levees and accompanied Prince George to Brighton every summer. He outlined to the committee his duties as a police officer, which included policing the private lives of the upper class:

> Who has been in more confidence than I have been with the youngest part of society of the highest rank? How often have I gone to brothels, there to talk over a little accident that might happen to A's son or B's son, or my Lord this or the other's

son? . . . [T]he respectable young men, however liberally educated, are very great fools, for they often subject themselves to vast inconveniences through their own misconduct, by committing themselves ridiculously and absurdly, going to brothels and getting into scrapes, and what has been the consequence! the consequence is, 'Townsend, what is to be done?'[20]

Officers such as Townsend were too grand to attend to the ordinary round of plebeian violence, thieving, rape and murder. Order was kept, in the first instance, at parish level. The various police offices and parish bodies in London acted on their own initiative, rarely communicating with each other. They claimed their own powers and resented interference from other authorities. This was said to be good for liberty, as it stopped any one officer or department becoming too powerful. But it also impeded justice. As one critic wrote: 'a watchman, going down one side of the street, does not feel himself obliged to check a delinquency on the other side, provided it is in another parish or ward'. Asked by the committee how common or even notorious criminals could be arrested if officers and magistrates did not talk to each other, most officials replied that they read the newspapers and learnt about the goings-on of the town that way. Conant, the most important police official in the country, would only communicate with the Home Secretary in exceptional circumstances, mainly on matters of national importance.[21]

Sir Nathaniel Conant dismissed the committee's suggestion that a centrally coordinated police would be an improvement on this chaotic and stubbornly independent system of overlapping, secretive and amateur authorities. He also rejected the calls of some for a police that had the authority to impose summary fines and terms of imprisonment on disorderly and antisocial people. If magistrates were obliged to enforce all laws all the time, led by a board of commissioners and in charge of a body of men specifically employed to prevent crime, Conant said, people would be continually harried and pestered for petty offences which were presently tolerated by a benign magistracy. If a reformed police force decided to crack down on the minor misdemeanours and imprudent acts that were part of everyday life, the poor would be the losers; life, magistrates like Conant knew, was rough enough without a constable breathing down one's neck and enforcing outdated or meddlesome laws. The existing system was by no means perfect, but it was cheap and defended personal liberty from the overbearing power of the state or from puritans whose instincts were to regulate others.

Bow Street magistrates' court

The authority that magistrates had to interpret the law on their own initiative was esteemed one of the greatest contributions to freedom. In January 1819, to pick just one example, 'a fashionably dressed young man', a drunk clerk from St Mary Axe, was arrested by the watchman for knocking on doors in Maidenhead Court. The clerk fought the watchman, and when he was finally taken to the watch-house he beat and knocked down the constable. In court, the man defended himself on the grounds that he was drunk and did not know what he was doing. Rather than enforce the law and send the clerk to gaol – which would be excessive and enough to ruin a young man's future prospects – the magistrate suggested that a voluntary donation of two guineas to a charity school in the local ward would be a satisfactory and appropriate punishment.[22]

The committee was interested in asking Conant about the area directly under the nose of the Bow Street office. Everyone in the country, perhaps Europe, knew that the area comprising Covent Garden and St Giles's was the most dangerous and depraved in the country. St Giles's – Rats' Castle or the Holy Land, as it was nicknamed – was so bad because it afforded an opportunity for twenty-four-hour drinking and all the things that went with that – bawdy houses, gambling and

*St Giles's centred on Seven Dials and comprised the area between Shaftesbury Avenue and what is now New Oxford Street.

fighting.* The conditions in the Rats' Castle provided every reason to seek oblivion through alcohol.

There were six thousand poor Irish crammed into this area alone, not to mention other nationalities. Thomas Augustine Finnegan, the master of the St Giles's free school, was asked to describe the manners of the inhabitants. 'Very dissolute, generally,' he replied; 'on Sundays particularly they take their children with them to public-houses, and the children witness the scenes of riot and sanguinary conflict that happen among the parents in the street.' Few would stray into the labyrinth of alleys and courts of the Holy Land. Most physicians would not go in for fear of catching something or being assaulted by the inhabitants. One surgeon who did venture in, William Blair, described what he saw: 'human beings, hogs, and dogs, were associated in the same habitations; and great heaps of dirt, in different quarters, may be found piled up in the streets. Another reason of their ill-health is this, that some of the lower habitations have neither windows nor chimneys nor floors, and were so dark that I can scarcely see there at midday without a candle. I have actually gone into a ground-floor bedroom, and could not find my patient without the light of a candle.'[23]

The Covent Garden and Drury Lane theatres stayed open late, so public houses were permitted to stay open to 'refresh' people whose jobs were connected with the theatre: stage hands, hackney-coachmen and the like. When these alehouses and ginshops closed, coffee houses that illegally sold alcohol under the counter remained open; and before those closed, the houses that served the early-morning market porters opened. There was a notorious house where people who had been drinking and carousing all night, from dissolute rakes to low-life drinkers and prostitutes, would conclude their night's revels. It was called The Finish for this reason, but also because the debauched clientele, clammy from gin and pallid in the early morning light, seemed as ghouls, either raised from or immediately destined for the grave.[24]

That public house had a notoriety that attracted well-heeled debauchees, but the other dives of Covent Garden – so-called flash-houses – served the lowest labourers: coal heavers, dustmen, slaughtermen, market porters, draymen, coachmen, Irish bricklayers and canal workers, women who made matches for a living and other miserable people who did work others would never think of taking. They were also suspected, with very good reason, of being the haunts and bolt holes of professional thieves and prostitutes.

The Finish in Covent Garden in the early hours of the morning

The committee was incredulous that such places could flourish with glorious defiance in the faces of the thousands who went to the theatre, and right on the doorstep of the Bow Street police office. Conant, as a magistrate, had the power to suspend or not renew licences; surely he could stamp out the nuisance if he wanted. But Conant was not as inclined to make assumptions as the committee members. Certainly the taverns *looked* like the headquarters of vice, but it would be an unacceptable act of tyrannical power to close down an alehouse or ginshop just because the customers *looked* like criminals. Public houses were not open for the 'respectable': 'people may be reduced to their last penny, who may want refreshment; they are open for the poor more than the rich, and laborious persons more than any other description'.[25]

As far as Sir Nathaniel was concerned, the poor must have their pleasures – or solaces – and enjoy them free from the crude prejudices of ignorant, 'respectable' people who automatically assumed they were sunk in vice and crime. His chief clerk at the Bow Street office, John Stafford, agreed. Neither officer was going to be pushed into condemning the people of St Giles's out of hand. Bennet asked Stafford if he knew that the streets of Covent Garden were notorious for 'scenes of the greatest debauchery'.

'No,' Stafford replied, 'I do not know it; neither do I think the fact can be established.'

Surprised at the answer, Bennet asked him if he had ever walked the streets. Stafford replied that he had, day and night for years, and, yes, he had seen the public houses to which the committee was alluding. Bennet continued on the theme: 'Is it not a matter of public notoriety that those houses are the receptacles of every species of vice?' – 'No, certainly not.'

Stafford was then asked whether it was the duty of the Bow Street office to clear the streets of 'disorderly people'?

'"Disorderly people" is such a general term,' he replied, 'that I do not know how to answer.' The officers could only act if there was some specific crime being committed; chasing and harassing people who looked poor and depraved would be a grievous mistake, just as locking up inebriated carousers would be an assault on their liberty. Later in the proceedings, a nightwatchman from Covent Garden confirmed that the 'one scene of riot and debauchery' the committee and most of the public believed happened in the area every night was only an occasional occurrence. On most nights the streets were deserted after the theatres closed.

Still disbelieving Stafford's evidence, Bennet asked if he really expected the committee to believe that the houses of Covent Garden were conducted in a correct manner. Maybe not, Stafford replied, if 'correct' was defined by upright magistrates and respectable members of parliamentary select committees; but it had to be said that most licensees made every effort to keep an orderly house. If they occasionally attracted rowdy customers, it was not their fault.[26]

Stafford finished his evidence in an equally surprising manner, but one which must have delighted Bennet and Place. While it might be true that the very poorest inhabitants of Rats' Castle were habitually drunk, there had been an increase in sobriety among the rest of the working classes, especially journeymen, apprentices and mechanics, formerly among the worst-behaved groups in society: 'I have no doubt that the manners of the lower-classes of society are much better than they were ten years ago, those excessive scenes of drunkenness which I have formerly observed are not by any means so frequent.'[27] His opinion was confirmed by the Rev. Charles McCarthy, curate of St Giles's, who reflected on the eleven years he had been in Rats' Castle: 'I think the face of the general appearance of the parish had improved within that time; there is not so great an appearance of vice as there used to be.' The phantom of St Giles's, which had haunted the popular imagination since the days of Hogarth, was open to much revision.

Most magistrates and officers did not want to interfere with the pleasures of the poor or label exuberant or self-indulgent behaviour as vice. In 1814 the Surrey magistrates met to decide what to do with the low public houses in Camberwell and Peckham; they expressed concern at their depravity and vowed to suppress them. But the next year the magistrates reversed their policy and decided that the miserable customers of ginshops should not be persecuted: 'The men who so gallantly fought the battles of their country by sea and land, surely merit a more gratifying welcome on their return to their native land, than to be viewed as objects of horror, to be dreaded as depredators, to be branded as culprits.'[28]

It was better to turn a blind eye to rowdy behaviour than persecute the poorest members of society. Yet there was another reason for their laissez-faire attitude: the flash-house was at the centre of policing. Take away the low tavern, and the police would be deprived of their chief mode of detection; vice and criminality would be pushed from day- or candlelight into a far-off and secret recess. Police officers made no secret of the fact that they drank in the same flash-houses as notorious thieves and listened to the conversations; how else, given the absence of any communication between different offices, would they know what was afoot in Birmingham, Manchester or Liverpool, or even other parishes of London? There were said to be two hundred such places in London, rich pickings for lazy officers who did not relish the work of detection.[29]

John Vickery, a Bow Street officer, thought it self-evidently sensible to conduct the police on these lines: 'It is impossible to prevent these men having their meetings: and suppose they were to meet at each man's private lodging, at different times, we should have no sort of admission to the private lodging-house.' In the past the police would be treated roughly if they entered one of these houses, but in 1816 they mixed with the criminals with a degree of intimacy and conviviality, in keeping with the refinement of the age: 'I am always treated with great civility,' said Vickery. When Sir Nathaniel Conant was asked if it was a good idea for officers to become 'the boon companions' of criminals (until, that was, they came to arrest their friends), he answered that it was 'a part of the mystery, or the art, or the policy, which I can neither understand nor explain'. The mystery or art of policing said much for the complacency of London's criminals, the contempt in which they held the authorities, not to say the laziness of the officers; as the committee said of flash-houses in its report, officers 'go there for their prey, as gentlemen to their preserves for game'.[30]

Henry Grey Bennet's committee learnt very quickly that if it was to fulfil its remit and conduct a root-and-branch investigation into the moral health of the country, the public house stood at the centre of all such considerations. When the committee reconvened in 1817, the chief consideration was beer and gin.

The committee was alerted to the centrality of the public house in all matters of policing in its 1816 session, when disturbing evidence began to emerge of magisterial skulduggery in the East End. The silk-weaving district of Spitalfields, always an East End slum, had expanded out into the countryside, to Bethnal Green and Mile End; the increase in trade had drawn labour to the port district of London – Wapping, St Katharine's Dock and Shadwell. Penetrating this miserable district, the committee brought to light a system of vice, immorality and crime.

The East End contained an extraordinary number of public houses, among them the very worst in the country. In Shadwell, for example, there were eighty-five alehouses, or one for every six houses. No one could imagine that six families could keep a public house in business, unless these people had a phenomenal capacity for drink, a serious problem and deep pockets. The explanation was that a sizeable proportion of the population of the area was transitory. Soldiers and sailors, both of the Royal and merchant navies, spent their leave where their ships docked – in Shadwell, the Isle of Dogs and Wapping. The moral character of the district was affected by the 'Portuguese sailors and Lascars, and people of that description; and where they are, the girls will follow them'; and where there were girls and sailors, there were taverns to take their money.[31]

Publicans were eager to maximise their profits by converting their houses to provide a large room 'for the purpose of having a fiddle and a dance for the sailors and their girls, and going on to a very late hour of the night'. Casten Rohde, a local magistrate, said that Shadwell was so dangerous and depraved because the clientele of the public houses 'consists entirely of foreign sailors, Lascars, Chinese, Greeks, and other dirty filthy people of that description'. The publicans 'get their bread by these sorts of people, and they cannot help admitting them'.

And they got more than just bread; the profits accrued by owning a public house were vast, especially in the lowest ones, where the customers did not confine themselves to sitting at tables over inexpensive pots of porter but stood or danced and drank ruinous amounts of gin. Gin was more profitable than beer, and a corrupt publican could maximise his profits by adulterating the spirits. Not surprisingly, the job of selling alcohol to thirsty sailors and their lady friends was eagerly sought after. People would buy houses at well above the intrinsic value of the property if it was a licensed premises, knowing that the investment was well worth it. The disadvantage was presiding over a rowdy and violent public house, frequented by the worst kinds of people.[32]

The foreigners whom Rohde complained about attracted the same kind of hostility as sailors on shore leave the world over. They were strangers who could behave as they liked, knowing that they would not be judged by their neighbours or become accountable to local authority; they could come, drink, womanise and fight, and then set sail. They brought money, which was something not many local inhabitants had in profusion. The residents of the area were scarcely less drunk, however, even if they were more law-abiding. The 'lower class of the Irish are very industrious', Edmund Wakefield said. They were employed chiefly to unload ships, often those from the north of England carrying coal. The work was fleeting; every morning Irishmen would wake early and walk to the docks to find work; oftentimes they were sent away without employment. Though the men were desperate for work, it was back-breaking and unpleasant, and 'the quantity of beer they drink is proverbial' and necessary to keep them going. In the long, miserable periods of unemployment, '[t]hey walk about and drink. Sometimes they spend their time in a public house, but not generally so.'[33]

Forced to live in one of the bleakest urban parts of the world, working hard without any long-term security, the Irish labourers had an excuse for their drinking. A little to the north, in the disgusting slum of Bethnal Green, the working class found a more destructive way to relax. Many of the labourers here were employed in the laborious textile industries or at the vast Truman-Hanbury-Buxton brewery on Brick Lane. The brewery dominated the East End cityscape. It had been founded by Sir Benjamin Truman, who had died in 1780, leaving a business worth £160,000, a personal fortune of £180,000 and a country estate in Hertfordshire. Truman had gone into partnership with the Hanburys and the Buxton family, of which the famous philanthropist and Wilberforce's right-hand man Thomas Fowell Buxton was a member. The Hanbury family had bought into the business, and they managed it in the 1810s. The brewery stamped its identity on the area: Brick Lane was a succession of alehouses, where the porters, carters, draymen and labourers of the brewery would spend their wages. Anyone engaged in hard labour at this time seemed to need to sustain him- or herself with plenty of drink. John Farrington, a brewery drayman aged sixty-three recorded for posterity in T. L. Busby's illustrated book *Costume of the Lower Orders of London*, worked from four in the morning until seven at night, fuelled by two gallons of porter and a pint and a half of gin consumed during the working day, 'and never felt the worse for it'. He was 'hale and hearty' and, according to Busby, 'he affords a living proof, and recommends as well by precept as example, the excellence of a beverage so much resorted to by all classes of society in London, producing to the Revenue a large sum annually'. Such quantities were hardly unusual. At harvest time, two gallons of beer a day was considered about right for a labourer.[34]

Joshua King, a local clergyman, described the 40,000 inhabitants of Bethnal Green as 'generally of the lowest description of people'. On Sundays, the far east became a place of unbounded riot, with duck hunts, dogfights, gambling and fistfights providing the entertainment. The men of the parish would club together to buy a bullock from one of the drovers bringing cattle to Monday market. They would stuff peas into the ears of the poor animal and pierce its body with pointed iron rods. Infuriated, the creature would charge along the Bethnal Green Road, pursued by 2,000 men and boys. The chief fun of the hunt was watching the damage an enraged and terrified bullock could do. When it was cornered, it would turn on its pursuers, affording new amusement and fresh destruction. The Christmas Day bullock hunt of 1818 was particularly violent. The mob drove the bullock from Mile End and through Bethnal Green, during which a milkmaid and a headborough were tossed by the animal; the maid was reported as being near death a week later. The hunt was enlivened by a running battle between 400 men and twelve special constables, during which the parish officers were seriously wounded by the brickbats and stones wielded by their neighbours. That Christmas hunt was unusual only because the constables intervened; on most weekends, and sometimes Mondays as well, the crowd was left alone 'on account of their being so numerous and so desperate'.[35]

When the Rev. Joshua King complained to the magistrate of Tower Hamlets, Joseph Merceron, the worthy justice replied 'that there was no kind of amusement he was so fond of as bullock-hunting, and that in his younger days he was generally the first in the chase'. Alarmed by the levity of the magistrate, King began to look into the moral state of his parish and the character of Mr Merceron. The magistrate had a vested interest, it seemed, in fostering the vices of the people he was charged with policing. Bethnal Green was rich in disorderly public houses, most notoriously The Sun on Slater Street, which was home to a particularly bad Cock and Hen club, where boys and girls met to 'get drunk and debauch one another'. That house, and twelve others, were owned by Joseph Merceron, who was also manager of the poor rate, a rent collector, licensing magistrate, commissioner of the property tax and a substantial landowner in the district. In 1800 the government had given the area a grant of £12,000 to relieve distress and poverty; Merceron was responsible for its dispersal, but most of it was still unaccounted for in 1816.[36]

Bethnal Green was Merceron's private fiefdom, an area he controlled with his myriad jobs, land holdings and powers of patronage. He arranged and managed local politics because he had an immense power: he was the tax assessor, and so could reward or punish as he saw fit. He had made a fortune from his tyranny over all aspects of the district's life, not least from the profits deriving from his string of public houses. When he died it was found that he was worth a staggering £300,000. The worse the crowd behaved, the fuller his pockets became. Bullock hunts, squalid taverns, juvenile sex and other vicious pursuits were fuelled by the consumption of alcohol, his chief source of income, and were on no account to be discouraged. In case he met a challenge to his dominion, Merceron bribed and encouraged the mob to bully his critics or the candidates that stood against his nominees to parish positions.

Merceron was exposed at the 1816 session of Bennet's committee. He might have seemed at first like a rogue magistrate who had carved out a territory in the badlands, but evidence was emerging that he was just one of a certain type of East End magistrate. The first scent of scandal was suggested by Thomas Barber Beaumont, a witness before the committee and a magistrate based in Whitechapel. He told the MPs that he had had a hundred dwellings and some factories built in Mile End, and believed that his tenants deserved a public house. It seemed like a reasonable proposition; few magistrates would withhold a place of refreshment from the people unless the area was already adequately served with public houses. This was a new settlement with no nearby alehouses to which his tenants could resort for leisure. In an area of Millwall, the ninety-seven people who lived there had the choice of three taverns; the granting of a licence to a *fourth* house was justified by the magistrates on the licensing committee on the grounds that it was unfair to make poor people walk too far for beer on a cold night.

Beaumont was confident that his settlement would easily be judged deserving of a public house if this was the rationale for granting licences. In London and its environs there was one licensed house for every thirty-one private houses, so he could have been justified in asking for three new taverns. In 1813 he took his request to the Tower Hamlets licensing committee, on which he himself sat with Joseph Merceron, Sir Daniel Williams, the Rev. Edward Robson, Casten Rohde and others. To his shock, Beaumont was refused, as he was in 1814 and 1815. He asked other publicans in the Bethnal Green area where he was going wrong, to be told that a licence was easily procured if the landlord donated £100 to the surveyor of the Truman-Hanbury brewery, agreed to sell that brewery's beer and did another deal with a local spirit distillery to sell their gin. What influence did Messrs Hanbury have that a licensing magistrate did not?[37]

The second session of the police committee in 1817 decided to devote itself to answering this question. The licensing of public houses had always been a problematic area of British law. Successive monarchs and parliaments had been alarmed at the nation's relationship with alcohol and had stepped in with varying degrees of failure to counter the problem. Gin created 'a ferociousness that does not occur in the case of intoxication through porter and beer'. The notorious Gin Act of 1736 was intended to suppress the flood of liquor and maximise revenue (the holy grail of parliamentary action on alcohol) by raising the duty and setting licences to sell gin at £50. This would stop its sale by 'hucksters, barrow women and itinerant salesmen' who sold home-distilled gin, which had turned the streets into a scene of continual drunkenness. But revenue fell dramatically and the streets became like Gin Lane; there were also serious gin riots in London. Once licensed gin became too expensive, a plethora of illegally distilled and smuggled spirits supplied the market, depriving the Treasury of money and fuelling the social problem by making alcohol ludicrously inexpensive and universally available. A further act reduced both the cost of licences and the level of duties. It was then thought best to settle the problem by allowing magistrates to police the moral condition of their people by taking into account the requirements of the neighbourhood when issuing licences. They also had to ensure that a licensee had a certificate declaring that he or she was of 'good fame, and sober life' from a clergyman, a churchwarden, a parish overseer or four respectable landowners. By passing this law, Parliament handed the responsibility of regulating the drinking habits of Britons to publicans. If they allowed their customers to drink excessively or encouraged disorderly behaviour, they would lose their good moral character and have their licence taken away by the magistrates.[38]

When the law worked, it worked very well. But by giving discretionary power to magistrates it made the government of public houses worryingly capricious. Given the huge amounts of money involved in the retailing of alcohol, the temptations dangled in front of magistrates were big and hard to refuse. The East End licensing committee seemed excessively fond of the Truman-Hanbury-Buxton brewery, refusing licences for many private applicants without giving a reason and then granting licences for dozens of landlords supported by the Hanbury family without questioning their moral character. Indeed, the brewery appeared to rule the licensing magistrates.

Bennet's committee heard that a clerk employed by Truman-Hanbury-Buxton had boasted that he could get a licence for a coal shed if he wanted.[39] In Hoxton there was a derelict building, a brick shell without a staircase or internal furnishing, that was nonetheless licensed to sell alcohol. The Rev. Joshua King learnt that Joseph Merceron sublet his public houses to the Hanbury brewery, and the magistrate was heard to say 'that Hanbury was a devilish good fellow, that he was always sending him [Merceron] presents, that he supplied his house with beer gratis, and that the week before he had sent him half a barrel of porter'. The Rev. Edward Robson, another licensing magistrate, said that he was more inclined to license landlords supported by Mr Hanbury because he was an important local figure and owner of a vast brewery; therefore, he was eminently respectable and sure to keep his many houses in good order. Robson gave a curious defence of Hanbury to the committee: 'he is a man of so much public spirit in the public charities, and the London Hospital in particular; he has been liberal in a very great degree: I do not know much of Mr Hanbury himself'.[40]

As the saying went in the East End, 'a man is considered a fool who applies for a license through the medium of any person than Messrs Hanbury'.[41] A person would be recommended to the licensing committee if he or she agreed to sell beer produced by the Truman-Hanbury-Buxton brewery and spirits distilled by an allied company. How many magistrates were in the pocket of the great brewer was never determined, but given the influence of the brewery over most of the public houses in Tower Hamlets most of them must have taken Hanbury's shilling. The more houses supported by Truman-Hanbury-Buxton got licences, the more Truman-Hanbury-Buxton beer and gin was sold, the better the brewery and the magistrates did. Therefore, applicants who did not join in league with Hanbury were not the only ones in danger; existing independent landlords who shopped elsewhere for their gin and beer were also threatened. The licensing committee could deprive a publican of his right to trade, and the decision could not be appealed. The discretionary nature of the law meant that a respectable landlord who did not encourage excessive drinking could be judged unfit to retail alcohol, while the lowest, and therefore more profitable, licensee could be deemed reputable enough to retain his house. If a tavern became too notorious for its rowdiness and immorality, the controlling brewery could nominate a new licensee every year to keep the house in business; a disreputable public house could not be shut down if a new landlord took over, it being a proposition of the law that 'stone walls carry no sin'.[42] The tendency of the discretionary power of magistrates, therefore, was to frighten off respectable publicans who would not take bribes or consent to act as a promoter for a particular brewery's wares, and encourage unscrupulous men to take over houses. 'I believe', said one uncorrupted London magistrate, 'that public houses, if there were a fair opportunity for the publicans to get a living uprightly and honestly, might be conducted as well as the shops of other trades with which the poor are connected.'[43]

Henry Grey Bennet and his committee were anxious to combat this noxious abuse. They consulted Robert Henderson, a lawyer specialising in the licensing laws. 'This matter cannot be decided by a reference to abstract principles of morality, applicable only to a pure and perfect stage of society,' he said; 'we must take men as they are, with their present feelings, pursuits, habits and modes of life.' The 'officious interference' of some magistrates and vice suppressors was dangerous and would drive those publicans who had 'a respect for character, morality, decency and respectability' from the trade, while the people would inevitably continue to drink spirits, legally or illegally, amid this 'warfare'. There should be no question of a revival of the prohibition or suppression of strong liquors because the use of them was so widespread: 'if it be a disease, that disease is now deep in the system of society, and rash attempts to cure will only aggravate the disorder'. New laws or duties interfering with the trade in spirits would be worse than ineffectual: 'they would be distilled in secret, and sold pernicious in quality, and more in quantity; only the revenue would be lessened; drunkenness, disorder, and crime would increase'.[44]

The reason why there was a problem was the corruption of magistrates and the monopoly of a handful of brewers. The committee heard how, in many market towns throughout England, the magistrates had allowed big breweries to take over all the public houses. When that happened, the beer was adulterated with burnt sugar, treacle, salt, copperas and extract of liquorice. One butt of beer contained 108 gallons of beer, but brewers would substitute twenty gallons with these illicit ingredients. The beer tasted revolting and the people were left with a choice between undrinkable beer and intoxicating gin. In Wallingford, for example, fourteen out of eighteen public houses belonged to a man who was a magistrate for the county and an alderman of the borough. The standard of beer had declined, and the townsfolk had become addicted to gin. The same had happened in Reading, St Albans, Woking and a few other towns where *all* the public houses were owned by one brewery. In London there were 4,397 publicans, of whom thirty-one brewed their own beer; in the rest of the country 50 per cent did so. This suited the panjandrums of the drink industry: the profit margin on gin, cheap to distil, was much higher than beer. But the public could not always be relied on to drink it; indeed, the consumption of gin had been decreasing throughout the nineteenth century, despite a steady rise in population. This explained the industry's determination to offload as much gin as possible.[45]

According to Henderson's assessment, left to a free market people would drink less gin as a matter of choice. They were not helped by their betters. Even uncorrupted magistrates interfered to the detriment of independent publicans. They preferred, as a rule, to impose a standardised kind of public house on their neighbourhoods. They believed that an ideal house should sell beer and gin at the same counter. But this had the tendency to lump all kinds of people into one house and persuade people to drink more gin rather than wholesome beer. Magistrates also disliked the idea of a comfortable or luxurious public house, as this seemed to encourage people to sit down and drink for long periods of time. But as most publicans knew, standing up to drink increased consumption. Left to market forces, there would be more public houses that served beer only and attracted a more respectable clientele to drink in comfort and peace. Those who wanted to lose themselves in a fug of gin would be allowed to do so, but only in places that catered for it. The sale of spirits, Henderson punningly said, would find a level. It would certainly decrease as more public houses became places of pleasant sociability rather than brutality. But left to the arbitrary control of magistrates and the monopoly of brewers, this would never happen.

The committee reported to the House of Commons in 1817 after two long sessions delving into the lives and habits of the lower classes. It warned Parliament against coercing the people into some kind of moral reform. Such a project, much urged upon Parliament by increasingly vocal groups of people, was doomed to failure. The committee deprecated the abuse of spirituous liquors, but they felt 'it necessary to remark, that however much it may be the inclination of the legislature to check and limit the demand and consumption of these stimulating drugs, yet the experience of every country shows, that some stimulants are necessary for the support and relief of human toil . . . Every nation has recourse to them in different ways; some by the use of opium and various kinds of narcotics, others by strong fermented liquors.'[46]

History showed that consumption of these drugs was lowest where there was a greater freedom of production and sale. Yet it was just as much a part of human nature to try and suppress their use by force. The committee warned the House that measures other than an indirect effort to improve the people by education would be counterproductive. With every attempt at 'positive prohibition', or indirect suppression by adulteration or taxation, 'the constant unvaried effect is not the promotion of more sober and restricted habits, but the driving the people at large into courses more prejudicial to their morals and health'.[47]

The course of action that would most aid the promotion of virtue and the diminution of crime would be legislative action against the flash-houses where young people were 'seduced step by step into vice'. There was no excuse for the 'academies of vice, adapted to both sexes and all ages', the 'legalized haunts' of thieves and prostitutes. In all parts of London that the committee looked at, morals and habits were no worse and often better than the preceding generation's, except in the abandoned areas east of the City – Bethnal Green and the rest of Tower Hamlets.

There was ample reason why this had happened. Bennet left little to the imagination in hinting at a systematic attempt to 'demoralise' the people of the slums. But the committee was no court of law, and the Home Secretary had no right to interfere in the business of magistrates, so corrupt local despots like Joseph Merceron could not be accused of any crime. In any case, magistrates had unlimited powers of discretion in relation to licensing, so it was impossible to unravel their decision-making. It was possible to make an educated guess. 'By what means the firm of Messrs Hanbury and Truman have obtained that weight from the magistracy of the Tower Hamlets division, it is not possible for Your Committee to determine,' the committee members reported to their fellow MPs; 'that they possess it they have no doubt.' As a result, the benighted area was worse than it might have been.[48]

The committee joined Robert Henderson in proposing truly independent, locally accountable public houses as part of the solution. But there was no possibility of this happening while the breweries maintained a pernicious monopoly in parts of London and in towns throughout the country. As soon as the committee reported, Henry Grey Bennet introduced the Ale-houses Licences Regulation Bill to the Commons. He told Parliament that the present system 'deprives the public of the advantage of having a good and wholesome beverage' and that most of the 'vice and immorality' of London could be traced back to it. The act would abolish flash-houses, the known resort of thieves, prohibit brewers from compelling publicans to take a particular beer and abolish the discretionary powers of magistrates.

The last provision was the most important. It was an offence to law and liberty to allow magistrates to ruin a respectable and prosperous businessman overnight in the 'snug and quiet of their licensing room', away from scrutiny and secluded from the voice of the community; cancelling a licence should be the right and free decision of a jury. It was, Bennet said, an attempt 'to ameliorate a system which contains more seeds of corruption and is more fatal to the good habits of the people than any which had yet prevailed in any civilized country'. But as he would have been the first to admit, the bill was doomed. 'Next to his majesty's government, there is scarcely an interest more formidable than the interest of the brewers,' he said later. Many MPs came from or were connected to brewing families. The businesses themselves were immensely wealthy and influential on government. The dominant agricultural interest in the Commons depended on the breweries to take their produce and would not tolerate laws restricting the trade. Few people liked a monopoly, but the brewing monopoly was something else. The bill was dismissed without much discussion.[49]

Bennet and his committee could justly be disappointed at Parliament's reluctance to reform the licensing laws. The central contention of their report was that those who complained of the habits of poor people should stop labelling them profligate wretches and predestined thieves and instead blame magistrates who did not just tolerate vice and disorder but in many cases actively encouraged it. It was hardly surprising that the youth of both sexes were considered 'idle and profligate' when their 'betters' promoted excessive drinking and riot, and when the police officers and magistrates encouraged flash-houses. As it was, the profit-sharing league of magistrates and brewers was a major cause of crime, immorality and misery; throughout the country there was 'a confederacy which is so injurious to the interests of the poor and middling orders of the community'.[50]

It was all too easy to blame the poor for being the authors of their own degradation and unhappiness. But the police committee, unlike the one on mendicity, was suspicious of alarmist parish officials and censorious magistrates. The findings of the MPs could not have been more different from those of the self-professed authority on all matters to do with policing, Dr Colquhoun. Whereas the magistrate had based his findings on conjecture, misleading statistics and unconfirmed reports, the select committee canvassed a multiplicity of different opinions and negotiated between the bluster of panicky officials on one side and the old-fashioned outlook of officers like John Vickery, who believed policing to be a matter of carousing with friendly thieves. In 1818 the committee reported again, citing the evidence 'of persons well qualified to speak on these topics' that 'the general manners and morals of the people seem to have been in a course of gradual improvement'. When they were investigated, it was found that places such as St Giles's and Tower Hamlets were not as scary as some people imagined. When Francis Place's belief in progress was put in the scales with Patrick Colquhoun's vision of growing depravity and general sottishness on the part of the working classes, the Charing Cross tailor's conclusions seemed to have tipped the balance.

The signs of improvement were discerned by another select committee that sat in numerous sessions from 1816. Under the chairmanship of another prominent Whig, Henry Brougham, the committee on education also asked questions about the state of the worst areas in the country, St Giles's and the East End. The committee found that, if the older generation in these benighted areas were poor and wretched, they wanted something better for their children. The war years had seen an increase in charity schools, Sunday schools and cheap penny-a-week subscription schools in the East End and Covent Garden. John Daughtry, who also gave evidence to the mendicity committee, told Brougham's enquiry that the people who lived in the worst part of London, the area around Drury Lane, were all too aware of the danger to their children and the temptations to crime or prostitution on daily display: 'they considered the Sunday school as the best preservation of their children from the surrounding infection; that keeping them as much as they could from the streets, and sending them to the Sunday School, appeared to be the two circumstances on which their hopes were founded'. The master of the St Giles's Free School noted that the poor Irish of the district – famously the lowest and most depraved gin addicts in the capital – 'have all a general disposition to have their children educated, and not only send them but many of the parents, who could not read or write themselves, attend to be taught'.[51]

Other witnesses repeated further stories of ambition on the part of poor children throughout London; some, bred into a life of petty theft and prostitution in Wapping, told a school volunteer that they 'would be very glad to leave it, if any other means were presented by which they might earn their livelihood'. On average, a child who attended a school on Sunday and learnt to read from the Bible might be tolerably literate within three years. The possibilities of a better life were just about apparent to motivate children and parents. Employers such as shopkeepers and keepers of wholesale warehouses and masters who needed servants preferred to take on boys and girls with good manners and at least a rudimentary education. By no means all children went to a Sunday school, but the numbers were impressive; in London 35,460 poor children were taught each week by 4,000 voluntary teachers.[52]

The heads of these and other kinds of schools found the children 'to be more respectful in their behaviour, and cleaner in their persons'. Even their parents were said to benefit; the very fact of having children at school seemed to inspire them to better themselves. The thought that their children could one day earn more money and live in better conditions was in itself a solace and a healthier source of temporary relief than gin in the midst of the despair of Wapping or Bethnal Green. William Crawford pioneered a scheme whereby parents would be visited once a week so they could subscribe a penny to their children's schooling. The money could be collected in other ways, but the visits were intended for a different reason: 'Frequent communications with the poor, on subjects connected with the welfare of their children, have a beneficial tendency on the minds of the parents.' Some of the witnesses were taken up with the utopian possibilities of education: a vicar from Kingsland, just north of the City, said that before the introduction of schools, 'the lower orders in the village were extremely wicked and riotous; the place abounded in bull-fights, men-fights, intoxication, and thieving; and I know from good information: the old inhabitants frequently speak of the remarkable alteration in those respects'.

The emergence of charity schools was the result of an outburst of philanthropic and religious zeal. The positive testimonies were in large part inspired by a faith in redemption through Bible lessons and a belief that the Sabbath could at last be saved by instilling a lifelong reverence for the day in the minds of poor children. Such people, in a warming glow of pious pride, might have overestimated the beneficial effect they were having on the lower orders; but at least an effort was being made, and a desire for improvement was being evinced and reported on. The dark slums, however rat-infested, crime-ridden and hopeless, were not as easy to generalise about as many had imagined.

Henry Grey Bennet's committee was attuned to signs of self-improvement in the poor. It realised that in such circumstances an alarmed attempt to strengthen restraints, increase coercion or impose a moral reformation from above would be counterproductive. The problem was that by even investigating the lower orders and the slums, the committee's report 'tends to make our age and nation *appear* more criminal than, in comparison with others, it really *is*'.[53] Parliament and the public should not be scared into legislative reform.

A solution to the chaos of policing and disorder might have been a centrally organised police force empowered to prevent and detect crime, one which would replace the myriad parish officials and coordinate officers in a unified campaign against crime. 'It is no doubt true, that to prevent crime is better than to punish it,' the committee reported; 'but the difficulty is not the end but the means.' A professional, paid, centralised police force might in theory solve the manifest problems and abuses that the committee had found, but the imposition of one in a free country 'would of necessity be odious and repulsive', and a liberty-loving people would reject it. A reconstituted metropolitan police force 'would make every servant of every house a spy on the actions of his master, and all classes of society spies on each other'. A country enjoying liberty needed only humane laws and an enlightened magistracy to punish daring crimes, not an inquisitorial force charged with enforcing all laws, both petty and serious. While a free people had to pay a price for their personal liberty – 'their property may occasionally be invaded, or their lives endangered by the hands of wicked and desperate individuals' – it was far better than being watched over by a policeman.[54]

The committee was hostile to the very notion of police, and many in Parliament and the country would wholeheartedly agree. They knew from the history of the past twenty-five years what such a system would entail. They had only to look at Patrick Colquhoun's books, John Bowles's aggressive attempts at moral reformation and the quasi-policing activities of the SSV, or more recently the Society for the Suppression of Mendicity, to know that a centralised police force could become the sword of militant puritanism. Such people, given a uniform and the badge of state power, would enforce laws against the petty misdemeanours of all; they would seize the opportunity to effect a moral revolution in their own strict fashion, and the weakest members of society would be the first victims of their social experiment.

As the committee reported to Parliament, a strict line had to be drawn between lower-class pleasures and criminality. The two committees – on mendicity and on policing – illustrated the collision of two ideas of Britain. Those who looked at the problem of vagrancy believed that control and surveillance were indispensable; that systematic action could remake the country and spark moral reformation. Bennet's committee members took a more old-fashioned view. Life was messy, disorganised and complicated; perfection was an impossible dream and the state should have no active role in utopian projects. The members were at war with the cant and hypocrisy of philanthropy, and their view was supported by most in the country. Moral improvement must precede a professional police force, and the first step would necessarily be a reform of the licensing laws. As the committee saw it, there was evil abroad, but it had more to do with the corruption of brewers and magistrates than the absence of policemen. The committee members had heard enough to 'deprecate a severe system of police as inconsistent with the liberties of the people, and they protest against a wanton and meddling interference with the wants and pleasures of the poor'.[55]

10

Slumming It with Tom and Jerry

'... to those venerable noodles who complain that I and my prototype, Pierce, have made this the age of FLASH, I answer – My age is better than the "AGE OF CANT".'

W. J. Moncrieff[1]

'I abominably hate *cant*; I despise *hypocrisy*; I detest *imposition* in any shape,' declares Corinthian Tom in *Life in London*, a book written by Pierce Egan between 1821 and 1822. In it, Tom and his rustic cousin Jerry Hawthorne, often in the company of their bibulous friend 'Oxonian' Bob Logic, pursue pleasure in the form of 'rambles and sprees' in every corner and social setting of London, from routs to brothels and from Carlton House to beggars' clubs in Rats' Castle and ginshops in Wapping. It penetrated all those places and petty crimes highlighted by the parliamentary select committees: the public houses of the East End, Covent Garden flash-houses, ginshops, dogfights and beggars' cellars. Tom and Jerry explore the 'back slums' and 'slum it' with a cast of grotesques and criminals.

By the mid-nineteenth century parts of the book were considered too shocking to bear republication, and the portions that survived for the readers of the 1860s and '70s demonstrated what dissolute lives their grandparents led. Charles Hindley said that Egan's book gave 'every encouragement to those who live under the rule of Queen Victoria to maintain a firm faith in the social progress of the age'.[2] But in 1821 *Life in London* was a sensation: 'It took both town and country by storm.' It was not a novel but rather a succession of urban scenes and vignettes hung together by the somewhat chaotic driftings of Tom and Jerry through high, low and sporting life. The structure was, in part, dictated by the publishing technique. *Life in London* came out between 1821 and 1822, each chapter, published monthly, describing a different metropolitan scenario and each one with a coloured aquatint drawn by the brothers George and Robert Cruikshank. Much of the prose was descriptive of a particular cartoon; indeed, the high quality of the illustrations, drawn by the two best cartoonists in the country, was the biggest draw for the buyer. Egan's name was made.

At the outset of the book, Tom extracts Jerry from the quiet backwater of Hawthorne Hall and introduces him to London, especially those parts of the city where vice, and therefore fun, was most available. The ensuing vignettes of metropolitan excess and insights into the recesses of secret vice, both high and low, made *Life in London* a best-seller. Readers were persuaded that the stories and anecdotes were the fruits of Egan's and the Cruikshanks' experiences. They could enjoy the dangerous thrills and illicit pleasures, Egan wrote, 'without any fear or apprehension of danger either from *fire* or *water*;* avoiding also breaking a limb, receiving a *black* eye, losing a pocket book, and getting into a watch-house; picking up a *Cyprian* and being exposed the next morning before a magistrate for being *disorderly*'. It was as if all these things were compulsory if one was to understand life in London. But fortunately for timorous people, Egan was on hand to run the gamut of urban depravity so that the public could enjoy it by their firesides. The cant and hypocrisy so loudly decried by Egan throughout the commentary was the sin of making moral judgements or striking a virtuous pose without any knowledge or experience of life in all its gory nakedness. The three cardinal sins in his mind were fastidiousness, squeamishness and false delicacy. Only those who explored the good and the bad and did not judge by superficialities were qualified to criticise, condemn or excuse. Knowing the town intimately and confronting its good and bad sides taught people 'not to look down upon their fellow creatures with contempt'.[3]

Corinthian Tom was the perfect guide for the young Jerry Hawthorne. He was a man of independent means, 'a finished gentleman' and a full-time observer of London life: 'pleasure was his idol – novelty his ruling passion – and to gratify this propensity, every avenue was true that led to it'. Tom and Jerry, for all their idleness and wealth, scorned dandies and dandyism and any hint of exclusivity. They were 'swells', men of the world who would carouse with a blacksmith as readily as a marquis, as long as both supplied the requisite entertainment. Tom and Jerry were more at home in a St Giles's flash-house than a fashionable rout; they sought naturalness and candour,

*Fire and water literally – but also the double meaning of spirits mixed with water.

not affectation and stilted politeness. Egan outlined the pedigree of the dandy: 'The DANDY was got by *Vanity* out of *Affectation* – his dam, *Petit-Maitre* or *Maccaroni* – his grandma, *Fribble* – his great-grand-dam, *Bronze* – his great-great-great-grand-dam, *Coxcomb*, and his earliest ancestor, FOP. His uncle *Impudence* – his three brothers *Trick*, *Humbug* and *Fudge*'. (Fribble was an effeminate fop in Garrick's farce *Miss in Her Teens*; fudge was slang for nonsense.) The swell was altogether more manly and robust than the finicky man of fashion. He was not constrained by the rules laid down by Beau Brummell, nor was he obsessed with maintaining status.[4]

Money, rank, birth and breeding were nothing; men and women were divided into the squeamish and the hearty, open-minded and liberal. Variety was crucial: Tom's continual pursuit of pleasure was an antidote to 'will-o'-the-wisp' fashionable dullness. A swell was a man of taste and intelligence, always looking to broaden his mind. Like Byron and other young roustabouts, they would attend Jackson's boxing school to hone their physiques and then mix with the thespians at the Drury Lane Theatre green room. Like the Fancy, they would talk horses at Tattersalls, go to public houses owned by former champions and bet on cockfights. The model for such a character was someone like the politician William Windham, who combined the manners of a refined gentleman and the taste of a classical scholar with a relish for earthy plebeian pastimes, particularly pugilism.

For Egan's swells, attending William Hazlitt's lectures on Shakespeare was as compulsory as drinking with beggars in a cellar in St Giles's or gambling with the aristocracy in St James's. The ideal day for such a man included anything that could satisfy his ranging curiosity: 'A *peep* at the Bow Street Office – a *stroll* through Westminster Abbey – a *lounge* at the Royal Academy – an hour with the Eccentrics – a *strut* through the lobbies of the Theatres, and a *trot* on Sundays in Rotten Row . . .' A visit to admire the Elgin Marbles at the British Museum could be followed by a less salubrious succession of entertainments: 'Washing the *ivory* with a prime *screw* under the *spikes* in Saint George's Fields, or in tossing off, on the sly, some *tape* with a *pal* undergoing a *three months' preparation*.' The friend would be in the King's Bench prison, St George's Southwark, for three months for debt, the fate of many a swell. The *tape*, or gin, would have to be smuggled in, as spirits were banned in prison; for this reason there were more slang words for gin than anything else.[5]

Egan's mastery of street slang was in itself a pun on the spirit of the age. The reader could understand the curious phrases Egan used because he thoughtfully translated the slang in footnotes; he also edited and updated Francis Grose's *Dictionary of the Vulgar Tongue*, so the uninitiated reader had a crib to hand to unpick the mysteries of an alternative language. The anti-authoritarian jargon of beggars and thieves had fascinated people since the sixteenth century, when translations of slang appeared. In the seventeenth century plays such as *The Jovial Crew* gleefully adopted the patois. The public's delight in constantly evolving slang survived until Egan's day, and he was the acknowledged custodian of its secrets.

Beggars were known as the 'canting crew', and their inventive vocabulary found its way to the lips of Cambridge undergraduates, Four-in-Handers and swells through handy dictionaries, books about people like Bampfylde-Moore Carew and theatricals. Grose defined 'canting' as 'a kind of gibberish used by thieves and gypsies, called likewise pedlar's French, the slang, etc'. Cant was also known as the 'flash language', and 'canters' were 'Thieves, beggars, and gypsies, or any other using the canting lingo.'

It was a fleeting language designed to evade and tease authority, to confuse Bow Street officers who might be eavesdropping in the corner of a flash-house. By the time the words found their way to the well-to-do, via the medium of the printed word, most of the slang was out of date, evolving as it did to deny outsiders access. Nonetheless, it was fashionable for people, particularly young and privileged people, to have the backchat of highwaymen, thieves, prostitutes and ne'er-do-well gin swillers constantly on their lips.

There was another meaning of the word. Canting was 'Preaching with a whining, affected tone, perhaps a corruption of chaunting; some derive it from Andrew Cant, a famous Scotch preacher, who used a whining manner of expression.' A canter was 'A hypocrite, a double-tongued, palavering fellow.' Pierce Egan, by writing much of *Life in London* in the 'cant' or 'flash language' of the demi-monde, made a play at what he saw as the cant of the moral reformer, the vice and mendicity suppressor and the philanthropic godly. Swells and low-lifers might conceal their thoughts and intentions in impenetrable jargon, but so too did busybodies, the meddling philanthropist and the conspicuously pious. Egan made use of slang for literary effect, but he played on cant for other reasons. The word was much in use at the time that Egan began to publish *Life in London*. It was associated with the various campaigns for moral rearmament: the Society for the Suppression of Mendicity was in full cry against convivial beggars; the Society for the Suppression of Vice was resurgent after it had weathered the dishonour that John Bowles had brought upon it; and there were plenty of signs that the British public, and especially the middle classes, were becoming less tolerant of deviations from moral rectitude. This was 'the age of cant', writers and journalists said; but Egan aimed to make it an 'age of cant' for another, more amusing reason, by popularising slang.

In *Life in London*, Egan introduced Bill Dash, an acquaintance of Tom and Jerry. Dash was 'a Swell of the first magnitude', who was fond of sport and practical jokes, and his language was 'as coarse as a fisherwoman at Billingsgate' – 'Propriety he laughed at.' He contrasted with the upright citizens of the city of London who, in an effort at mastering the arts of refinement and respectability, had lost the candour and spontaneity of human nature. 'Yet Dash, notwithstanding his eccentricities, has numerous good qualities – he hates *canting* and hypocrisy beyond expression, but he never wants to be asked twice to relieve the really unfortunate, and drops his *blunt* [small change] like a generous fellow.' In this sense of the word, Egan takes cant to mean the rigorous moral tests that people subjected themselves to before they performed the simplest acts of benevolence. As far as beggars or reclaimed prostitutes went, people were required to examine them and take a part in their moral redemption before they gave their mite. This hubris was, as far as people like Egan were concerned, loathsome hypocrisy and cant. *Life in London* wars against the cant of moral reform with another sort of cant.[6]

Pierce Egan was the spokesman for people who detested this perceived conformist and canting spirit. His joy of life and refusal to judge people by appearances came from his exotic family history. His father was a Protestant Irish labourer who moved to London to find work, but the Egans could not be described as coming from the labouring class. His grandfather was a vicar and his uncle, 'Bully' Egan, was an eccentric barrister, later a judge and had been an MP in the pre-Union Irish parliament. One of Bully Egan's sons became inspector general of dairy farming in Hungary, and Pierce's cousins remained substantial landowners in Hungary in the nineteenth century. It was a family of eccentrics, entrepreneurs and adventurers who were upwardly mobile, downwardly mobile, rich and poor. It was the kind of comical chaos that Pierce would bring to his depictions of Regency life and people, a rich world of oddities, unpredictability and opportunity.[7]

Pierce started his career as a compositor in a publishing firm; his use of italics, capitalisation, asterisks and whatever typographical eccentricity he could muster gave his productions a distinct flavour. His extensive reading of everything from gutter ephemera to the classics of English literature at this time informed all his writings. There is a lot of Irish shaggy-dogginess in Egan's writing, presumably transmitted through his father. In 1812 he was employed to put together a history of pugilism. *Boxiana* was first published in 1812 and was embellished and updated in many editions over the next two decades. Egan went from being a compositor to a compiler, but there could be no doubt that he had written much of *Boxiana* transforming second-hand accounts of fights into gripping narratives. Like all his work, it was written in an offhand, chatty style, full of slang and punctuated with jokes, songs, anecdotes and long quotations from diverse sources. He became the 'Plutarch of the Prize Ring'.

His family background and profession as the laureate of boxing made Pierce a decided enemy to those he saw as effeminate, squeamish and fastidious (his favourite terms of abuse). His world was populated by the manly, hearty and unaffected. His mastery of sporting and criminal slang, the fluency with which he recounted fights and the deeds of pugilists and his convivial nature 'soon rendered him eminent beyond all rivalry and competition. He was flattered and petted by pugilists and peers: his patronage and countenance were sought by all who considered the road to a prize-fight the road to reputation and honour.' His writing was praised as 'pregnant with fancy, and overflowing with the most manly sensibilities – everywhere animated with a true British spirit'. As he believed, it would 'outlive all the sneers of the fastidious, and *cant* of the *hyper-critics!!!*'[8]

Yet for such a full-blooded writer he was defensive about his sport, afraid that others believed 'that our feelings might become callous, and acts of brutality be viewed with indifference from the witnessing of these prize combats. We do not war with these writers . . . but are equally afraid in turn that the English character may get too *refined*, and the *thorough-bred* bull-dog, degenerate into the *whining* puppy.' That fear is the key to understanding Egan, the subsequent triumph of

Life in London and his sudden rise to popularity among people similarly scared that moral rectitude, prissiness and prudery were intruding upon traditional pastimes and fundamentally altering Britishness.[9]

The sport was under attack. Magistrates and Lords Lieutenant would forbid and break up contests on the grounds that a meeting was a riotous assembly. Sometimes the boxers and the retinue of thousands of fans would have to travel about the countryside until they found an estate free from supervision. In the 1810s fights increasingly took place at Mousley Hurst because it was near HRH the Duke of Clarence's estate, Bushy Park, and he was able to exert his influence over the local bench. The sport was also under attack from the humane and the 'fastidious writer' who was infected with 'a pretended delicacy of feeling'. But, wrote Egan, more harm had been done to morality by 'superior refinement, graces and politeness' than any boxing match.

What the delicate called 'vulgar sports' upheld the national character, because they taught 'a generous mode of conduct' and 'give generosity to the mind, and humanity to the heart'. The sport was a microcosm of the British way of life. Real boxers fought by the book; they spared a worthy opponent who was injured or exhausted; and they shook hands after. The crowd cheered good sportsmanship and revered a plucky loser as much as a champion. The Englishman would settle an argument with an honest blow and forgive the insult, while the cunning and super-refined Frenchman would duel to the death, an American would kick groins and gouge eyes, and the skulking Dutchman with his snickersnee and the Italian with his stiletto would sneak up on their enemy. No wonder the British, with their armies and navies manned by honest punchers, had bludgeoned their way to dominance over less hearty peoples. If the British enjoyed unparalleled liberty, it was because they were proud and independent, imbued with the virtues of the ring.[10]

Egan claimed that pugilism had made the country what it was: 'the manly art of Boxing, has infused that heroic courage, blended with humanity, into the hearts of Britons, which has made them so renowned, terrific, and triumphant, in all parts of the world'. Unfortunately for Egan and the Fancy, despite the panegyric to British fair play and masculinity, *Boxiana* did little else to refute the charge that boxing was cruel and exploitative; or at least the book showed that the things the Fancy found most delightful and noble in the sport added to the charges against it. Egan gleefully recounted fights that went to sixty rounds of bare-fist onslaught, some of which culminated with ten rounds or more consisting entirely of one pugilist pummelling an exhausted man unable to raise his fists in defence.[11]

Egan told the story of James 'Jem' Belcher, the first boxer to attract a high-society crowd and make boxing fashionable. He fought some thrilling contests with his 'scientific' method and attracted attention for his striking resemblance to the young Napoleon. Unlike most of the boxing fraternity, Jem raised himself above the costermongers and coal heavers in point of manners and gentility, becoming the boon companion of sporting swells. His career came to a premature end when he lost an eye playing rackets in 1803. After two years of morose retirement as the publican of the Jolly Brewer in Soho he came back, only to be defeated in a bloody contest in which his opponent rained blows on his good eye (so much for British boxing's famous integrity).

Jem was not the boxer he once was and could display but little of his former skill; nonetheless, 'his afflicting situation made a deep impression, not only upon his friends, but the company in general, and the involuntary tear was seen silently stealing down the iron cheek of many present for the loss of departing greatness in their favourite hero'.[12] Whether or not Belcher was touched by the tears of his wealthy supporters is not recorded; but it must be said that it was these distraught people's money that had brought about their hero's final humiliating punishment. To be sure, the fight destroyed him: he had bet every penny he had on his success and lost his public house and sold his famous fighting dog – the victor of fifty contests – to Captain Barclay. None of his former friends stepped in to help the redundant pugilist. But then one of the greatest enjoyments in following sport, as it always has been, was the inevitable playing out of the creation and destruction of champions. Pugilists were vivid reminders of the caprice of fortune in their progress from nowhere to the pinnacle of success as a dandified sporting gentleman, and then back, as Egan cheerfully admitted, to 'poverty, wretchedness, and misery'.[13]

Those whom the crowds loved died young: Belcher fell to pieces after his final defeat, going on the rampage and spending four weeks in gaol for disorderly conduct. He died aged thirty, not unusually for one of his profession: the victor of his last fight died at thirty-two. An exception was the fighter John Gulley, champion in 1807/8, who won £40,000 on the horses in two bets, became a coal-dealer and a bookmaker, and then a racecourse owner. Most remarkably, he was returned MP for Pontefract in the reformed Parliament of 1833 and was later presented to Queen Victoria. More typical, however, was the story of Billy 'the Tinman' Hooper, who, like so many others, was the 'plaything of fashion' for a happy season. He was a great favourite of the nobility, and he 'became pampered, insolent and mischievous'. He was patronised and employed as a 'bully', or hired thug, by the seventh Earl of Barrymore ('Hellgate'). Many years later he was found slumped insensible in a doorway in St Giles's and could only reply to someone who asked his name, 'Hoop – Hoop –.' He was recognised as a former champion and 'the miserable remnants of that once powerful pugilistic hero . . . were humanely taken to the work-house, where he immediately expired!'[14]

Boxiana would be just a grim catalogue of destruction, brutality and waste were it not for Pierce Egan's exuberant style; it remains a classic of sporting writing, still popular in the present day. No one captured the spirit of bare-fist boxing in its so-called golden age – with all its swagger and pretensions to nobility – as adeptly as Egan. He understood equally the pugilists, the wealthy men who patronised them and the crowds that swarmed to the bouts to cheer victor and vanquished alike. In *Boxiana* and the *Weekly Dispatch* he charted the rise and fall of the fighters, from their early days to the training camp, and then the bloody combats and, inevitably, the final descent into violence and drink. He dealt with the miseries of human folly and the moments of sporting bravery, knowing that the sport was more than just the hour or two of hard knocks in a ring: it was a way of life, dictated by codes of honour, coarse humour and a kind of mock equality, shared by its hero-victims, the gentlemanly Fancy and the volatile mob alike.

Egan had an ear for the apposite anecdote that brought out a fighter's generosity of spirit or magnanimous character. He knew that it was feats not fights that his readers wanted. As a journalist, he realised that the anatomy of a punch or a dissection of the science of pugilism would be tedious. The fight, as far as connoisseurs were concerned, was a test of endurance, resilience and the ability to soak up punishment. A sixty-round slog, with two fighters almost unable to stand up or raise a fist, lent itself better to the literature of the sport than a hard, fast knockout bout. In his account of Pearce v. Gulley in 1805, Egan was at his best describing the last twenty-four rounds or so. By the thirty-sixth, both fighters were covered in blood, Gulley the worst off with blood pouring from his ears and his head so swollen that no one could see his eyes. By the forty-second round Gulley 'began to appear somewhat shy', according to Egan's account; in the rounds from fifty to fifty-eight 'his brave heart was reluctant to acknowledge superiority'; in the fifty-ninth he had to be dragged from the ring. After one such exhausting slug between Jem Belcher and a giant butcher named Joe Bourke, the latter was boxed into a state of collapse, while Belcher performed somersaults and other exhibitions of agility. If the contest was short, there were other points of interest. When Belcher fought Jack 'the Ruffian' Firby in a mere eleven inconclusive rounds, Jem's exuberance made the fight worthy of Egan's pen. Belcher got the best of the early rounds, and in the ninth showed his contempt for the challenger by hitting him above the eye and then leaping into a mock-defensive posture, saying, 'How do you like that, Johnny?' Firby was enraged and tried to knock the champion out, while 'Belcher smiled, and pointed at him very ironically'.[15]

In recounting such deeds of derring-do and valour, and making heroes of costermongers and butchers, Pierce Egan himself became something of a hero. It was said that his accounts of fights were far better than the ones the crowd had actually seen. Egan perfected a genre of sports writing: the well-written, vibrant account which was as much part of the experience as the event itself. It created a new audience for sport – those who got as much out of the description as others did from the encounter. For some, his coarse style and earthy prose perfectly encapsulated the national character, however brutal it might be. The Tory writers at *Blackwood's* could not get enough of him; he who had not read *Boxiana*, they said, 'is ignorant of the power of the English language'. Egan's writing style was 'rambling . . . quite chitty-chatty and off-hand', but this was entirely appropriate and a much-needed respite from the sickening earnestness of serious journalism and the language of philanthropy and humanity that was dominating public discussion – 'the everlasting ringing of bells, and this taratanta-raraing of trumpets'.[16]

While much writing, particularly of the Whig-reformist school or the evangelicals, was fey, pallid and censorious, Pierce was vigorous, unaffected and combative, and he described life in all its ugliness without veiling it beneath verbiage and mannered language. He was the writer who best encapsulated the vision of Tory Britain: rough and ready, but honest and loyal. 'The pugilists of Britain', Christopher

North, the editor of *Blackwood's*, wrote, 'are part and parcel of her fame, and must, of necessity, be loyal – they must be downright Tories like myself. Every brave and honest man in the kingdom should, in fact, be a Tory; and unless I deceive myself, the valiant heroes of the ring are, to a man, ready to throw a crossbuttock in honour of Church and State . . . No Whigs are pugilists; they have not the heart to shake a fist, or even write a good boxing article.'[17]

For the *London Magazine*, Egan was 'a gentleman who caters more pleasantly for the public mouth than any person now living'. The *London* was not as in thrall to Egan's supposed candour. The reason he was popular was because of the way he softened the brutalities of boxing 'to the taste and timidity of a young gentleman in stays, or a lady at her breakfast table'. Outstanding acts of cruelty and bloodiness were rendered amiable, even funny: 'A pathos – a humour – a gaiety, is thrown into the recital . . . so that a broken jaw comes before the reader under favourable and attractive circumstances'. The slang and cheery tone of the Fancy became another way of evading reality and putting unpleasantness to the back of the mind. In Egan's extraordinary vocabulary of sporting and criminal language, a man punched to the floor 'goes down distressed'; a pugilist was not winded, only 'queered' a little in the 'bellows'; 'dimming the ogles' might sound quaint, but it meant the blinding of a poor fighter. Yet the *London Magazine* saw this as Pierce Egan's greatest strength; no other writer could pull off the trick of turning a brutal sport into a harmless pastime. 'To write faithfully, firmly, and delicately of boxing, requires indeed a pen with a *man* behind it. Mr Egan is altogether, as we learn, a pleasant character. His songs are neatly written, and as full of character as a spirit shop on a Saturday evening; – his voice is clear, easy, and natural; and his management of it betrays any thing but inexperience. He tells a good story, writes a good sentence; and is the most obliging gentleman in the world.'[18]

Egan was adored by the Tories because he seemed to be a man who during the day mixed with the semi-criminal boxers and their managers, shady gamblers, cockfighters and publicans, and in the evening sat down for a long, rowdy dinner with aristocrats and sporting gentlemen. His self-proclaimed ability to travel through all grades of society with ease and grace, everywhere accepted and always popular, made him a legendary figure. The *Blackwood's* writers boasted that when they went to London they would drink with Pierce, 'one of the pleasantest as well as one of the greatest men now extant'. The magazine said that Egan was 'perfectly at home in Tom Cribb's parlour, the Cadger's in the Back Slums, the Condemned Hold at Newgate, or the gin shops in the various regions of the metropolis, in all of which he displays the finished hand of the connoisseur'. He was a member of a club called the Owls, an assemblage of writers, actors, playwrights and the like who met after midnight for hard drinking. Egan exercised his talents for masquerade and impersonations on these occasions. One night his companions put an insensible Pierce into a coach and told the cabby that the reason his passenger was so taciturn was because he was a foreign nobleman. When the coach arrived at Egan's lodgings in Soho, the cabby made a commotion and told the household that the nobleman was home. The lodgers replied that there was no nobleman there, and it was four in the morning. The penny dropped straight away, however, and their eccentric neighbour was found lying at the bottom of the coach, 'rolled up after the manner of a hedgehog at the approach of winter'.[19]

In *Life in London*, Egan played up to his reputation as a man who knew no distinctions in society and seamlessly blended into any environment. People came to believe that the adventures of Tom and Jerry were the real-life experiences of Robert and George Cruikshank, while Bob Logic, older, more worldly, bookish and an expert in urban vice, was Pierce himself.

At the outset of the work, Egan told his readers that the Cruikshanks were his partners in investigation, every bit as familiar with the varieties of life they were to depict with pictures as he was: 'Indeed, I have used all their illustrative touches; and may we be hand and glove together in depicting the richness of nature, which so wantonly, at times, plays off her freaks upon the half-finished bone-rakers and cinder-sifters around the dust-hill, that we may be found, *en passant*, so identified with the scene in question, as almost to form part of the group.' He asked the brothers to '*grapple* with an *Hogarthian* energy in displaying *tout à la mode* the sublime part of creation'. Egan, Robert and George set out to rival and surpass the images of eighteenth-century London that still resonated in the public mind: *Southwark Fair*, *Gin Alley* and *Beer Lane*, *Times of the Day*, *Industry and Idleness*, *The Harlot's Progress* and the other great depictions of street life produced by Hogarth. The Cruikshanks were charged with replicating the energy and comedy of the Hogarthian tradition. They more than obliged. *Life in London* would be nothing without their vibrant and brilliantly comic cartoons.

One of the monthly instalments of *Life in London* broke from the adventures of Tom and Jerry to recount the experiences of Egan himself. He claimed that he had been unable to supply the copy to the printer in time because his research had become too much. He had, he said, been to a party at the Albany with Bob Logic and other gentlemen, where they drank gin ('daffy') mixed with boiling water. 'After a glass or two had been *sluiced* over the *ivories* of the party, which made some of them loudly to *chaff* [talk loudly and lewdly], BOB gave the *wink* to his *slavey* [servant], observing that more hot water was wanted. A large kettle, boiling at the spout, was speedily introduced, but, instead of *water*, read *boiling daffy* . . . "Come, gents," said Bob, "please yourselves, here's plenty of water, now mix away."'

The company unwittingly mixed gin with gin, and they caroused until most had been '*tuck'd* up in their *dabs* [beds], and only the *Roosters* and "Peep-o'-Day-Boys" were out on the prowl for a *spree*'. Eventually Egan had to be escorted to his '*sky-parlour*' (top-storey lodging). No coaches could be found, so they walked through Leicester Fields, where they were 'assailed by some *troublesome customers*, and a *turn up* [fight] was the result. Bob got a *stinker* [black eye], and poor I received a *Chancery-suit* [boxing slang for a rain of blows] upon the *nab* [head]. How I reached the upper-storey [garret], I know not; but on waking, late in the day, I found my pocket book was absent without leave.' The pocketbook contained Egan's notes for the missing chapter of *Life in London*: 'I was in a complete *funk*,' he said; 'I . . . scratched my *moppery* again and again, but could not remember, *accurately*, the substance of my notes. I was sorry for myself; – I was sorry for the public.'

He consulted '*sartain persons*' – his criminal connections – and eventually the pocketbook was returned: 'my *peepers* twinkled again with delight'. The notes came with a letter from a fence:

> You see how I have sent that are *Litter* [literary] Book, which so much *now* has been *kicked* up about amongst us. Vy it an't worth a single tonic [½d]. whose to understand it? vy its full of pot-hooks and hangers [shorthand] – and not a *screen* [£1 note] in it.* . . . If your name had not been chaunted in it, it would have been

*As Egan said: 'An author, indeed, with money in his pocket-book, would be a novelty in Life in London.'

dinged [thrown] into the *dunagan* [privy]. But remember, no *conking* [informing].

From your's, &c.
Tim Hustle

It is impossible to know why the instalment of *Life in London* was not published that month. Whatever the mundane truth, Egan's spirited apology was intended to show his readers that the author trod a dangerous path in his research; that he had a network of thieves and fences at his beck and call; and that his knowledge of slang derived from real sources. It reinforced the perception that *Life in London* was a form of journalism that came fresh from the streets, produced monthly as Egan, Robert and George uncovered more juicy details from the hidden corners and crevices of the metropolis.[20]

The story certainly made Tom and Jerry's forays into the Holy Land and the Back Slums more believable. Corinthian Tom takes his young protégé to Covent Garden for their first spree in low life. They go to a low ginshop (a 'sluicery') after the theatre and meet an unappealing cast of characters who made up the population of St Giles's. All of them are 'as *leaky* as sieves, from turning their money as fast as they get into liquor'. 'Gateway Peg', a prostitute (or 'ladybird'), is onto her ninth glass of blue ruin. Peg is 'an afflicting portrait of the rapid degradations from virtue to vice'. Once this '*lump* of infamy, disease, and wretchedness' was a well-known Cyprian, kept in style by wealthy gentlemen. Gateway Peg is drinking jackey [gin] with the petty thief Mother Brimstone, who has '*toddled* in to have a *flash of lightening* [glass of gin] before she goes home to *roost*'; she feeds gin to stop the crying of an infant she has hired to help her begging. Peg and Brimstone laugh at 'Fat Bet', who is flirting with Tom and telling him with 'pretended *squeamishness*' that she did not drink gin. An urchin, wearing no more than his father's ragged waistcoat, has come in to ask that his parents' butter boat be filled with gin 'to cure his mammy's pain in the stomach'. Swifty Bill, a 'translator of soles', has spent his last tuppence on 'Old Tom' (gin again) and leans against the butt, saying, 'he'll stand by OLD TOM while he has a sole left to support such a good fellow'. Kit Blarney, an Irish fish seller, comes in for a smoke and a drink 'to get rid of the *smell* of fish, which remained in her olfactory nerves'. Egan tells his readers that such a scene is common every night throughout Covent Garden, 'but in much more depraved colours than is here represented'.[21]

Tom & Jerry taking Blue Ruin, after the Spell is broke up.

After the sluicery, Tom and Jerry go to a coffee house, 'drunkenness, beggary, lewdness and carelessness being its prominent features'. The two adventurers immediately eyed up the Cyprians, who in turn were 'throwing their *leering ogles* towards them in hopes of procuring a *Cull* [a dupe to women]'. By now, Tom and Jerry are 'quite *prime* for a *lark*'. The coffee house is brimming with danger and violence, but the heroes are not scared: 'Knowing the use of their *morleys* [fists], fear is out of the question; and coffee or a *turn-up* is equally indifferent to them.' They get both. 'Some of the *kids* [young hoodlums], anxious for a lark, are determined to serve out the *Swells*, as they term Tom and Jerry. . .' It leads to a furious fistfight. 'The Corinthian being no *novice* in these matters, *floored* two or three of the *musty coves* in a twinkling.' The watch is called and the fight continues; eventually Tom and Jerry are '*lugged off* to the Watch House', where they are charged with breaking the peace and bailed. The next day a worldly magistrate orders the two to pay the watchman's expenses and damages, and the matter is settled without recourse to law.[22]

Tom and Jerry won't let the indignity of being arrested go unpunished. A little later they go to a dogfight at the Chaffing Peter in Tothill Fields, where they drink 'claps of thunder' (brandy) interspersed with 'dampers' (porter, a chaser to settle oneself after spirits) with costermongers and dustmen. On the way home, roaring drunk and in the

Drawn & Engraved by I.R. & G. Cruikshank.

Tom & Jerry in Trouble after a Spree.

company of a pair of prostitutes, they rampage through the streets, stopping to revenge themselves on a charley – the watchman at Temple Bar. Of course, this kind of behaviour was merely taking a front-row seat to observe 'life in London'.

Tom continues to escort Jerry Hawthorne through London, going to Hyde Park, fashionable masquerades, Cyprian balls held in the theatre lobby (courtesans such as Harriette Wilson and Julia Johnstone had held highly exclusive parties like these in their heyday, the first decade of the century) and other high-life entertainments. They go to masquerade balls, where the great and the good donned disguises and mixed with the 'impures', similarly anonymous behind their fancy dress. The rake dressed as a Methodist preacher, the pious hid behind the garb of a thief and the prostitute masqueraded as a demure young girl; the protection of a costume bred hypocrisy. But they do not find freedom and enlightenment until they venture to the All-Max Club in the East End.[23]

It was an obvious pun on Almack's Club: 'max' was yet another slang word for gin. When they go to the real, upper-class Almack's, Tom and Jerry have to mind their 'P's and Q's' in front of 'the *imperious* DUCHESS – the *proud* MARCHIONESS – the *stiff* COUNTESS – the *starched-up* LADY – the *consequential* honourable FAIR ONE – the *upstart* MRS – the *contemptuous* BEAUTY – the *pert* COQUETTE

Tom Getting the best of a Charley.

– the *squeamish* MISS, and the *fastidious* PATRONESSES'. They detest it, as they do most upper-class entertainment; the aristocracy and the gentry were bored and listless, compelled to obey rules and invent new ways to stave off ennui. Poor Corinthian Tom has to struggle hard to suppress his sincere ways and free tongue. At the All-Max Club, however, 'a card of admission was not necessary; – no inquiries were made; – and every *cove* that put in an appearance was quite welcome: country or colour considered no obstacle: and *dress* and ADDRESS completely out of the question. *Ceremonies* were not in use.'

The scene at All-Max in the East End is the key moment in *Life in London*. Tom and Jerry's search for unalloyed pleasure and naturalness of behaviour is at last satisfied. They strongly identify with their fellow revellers; no one judges by appearances or baulks at another's eccentricities; no one pretends to be someone they are not; restraint and rules obeyed by lesser men are laughed at. Most importantly, Tom and Jerry and the working-class revellers speak the same language; the world of the swell and the East Ender converge and their slang merges together. Jerry has been to Carlton House, George IV's sumptuous residence, but the grandeur and taste of the King's house 'did not appear to have had more effect upon his feelings, when he entered it, than the group of figures, "all alive O!" at ALL-MAX seemed now to operate on his mind'. Only the working poor, out of the whole of society,

really enjoy themselves and lead a natural life in the city, said Bob Logic: 'They eat with a good appetite, *hunger* being the sauce; they *drink* with a zest, in being *thirsty* from their exertions, and not *nice* in their beverage; and as to *dress*, it is not an object of serious consideration with them. Their minds are daily occupied with work, which they quit with the intention of *enjoying* themselves, and ENJOYMENT is the result; not like the rich, who are out night after night to *kill* TIME, and, what is worse, dissatisfied with almost every thing that crosses their path from the dullness of *repetition*.'

If the sluicery was the Cruikshank brothers' *Gin Lane*, All-Max was their *Beer Street*. For Egan, the clientele of the tavern were the true heroes of the book. Almost everyone else dealt in excuses and evasion, dressing up their pleasures or screening them from the public. There was a dignity and naturalness about the working people of the East End that was worth celebrating. Mr Mace, the publican, did not mix his punch too strong, and he kept his eyes open for signs of excessive drunkenness in his regulars.

Egan reserved the best of his writing to celebrating the club: 'The parties *paired off* according to fancy . . . All was *happiness*, – every body free and easy, and freedom of expression allowed to the very echo. The group motley indeed, – Lascars, blacks, jack tars, coal-heavers, dustmen, women of colour, old and young, and the sprinkling of the remnants of once fine girls, &c, were all *jigging* together . . . *Gloves* might have been laughed at, as dirty hands produced no *squeamishness* on the heroines of the dance, and the scene changed as often as a pantomime, from the continual introduction of new characters. *Heavy wet* [beer] was the cooling beverage, but frequently overtaken by *flashes of lightening*.' Tom, Jerry and Logic are all transfixed by the sight but, as Tom tells Jerry, 'Logic seems determined to *push* his voyage of discovery a point further, at least, than we did'. Bob had spotted a beautiful woman dancing with a coal heaver, and he asked the publican what her name was. The man replied that she was called African Sall ('because she comes from foreign parts'), a woman with a child but no husband; 'but, la! sir', said the publican, musing on her sexual morality, 'it's a poor heart that never rejoices, an't it, sir?' Logic evidently agreed, for he was last seen disappearing into the night with Sally.[24]

On another evening, Tom and Jerry venture to one more social setting where they are shocked by mankind's capacity for hypocrisy and imposture. At the same time, it was one of the jolliest scenes in the series. Towards the end of their adventures, Tom and Jerry don disguises and go to the Noah's Ark – one of the 'Cadgers' Kens', basements where beggars went to enjoy their evening feasts. They have to mind their 'P's and Q's' and obey mysterious rules here as much as they had to when they joined the stilted upper class at Almack's (both contrast with All-Max, where anything goes). Tom tells Jerry that he will see the beggar who writhes around in agony during the day counting over his gains and laughing at the 'flats', gullible people whose feelings he tortured for lucre. The poor mother will have returned the infants back to their real parents, having paid the hire fee. A crippled beggar will be 'the first to propose a dance, after he has cheerfully deposited his stilts, and to join in a *reel*'. The starving wretch who cried that he had not had a meal for weeks, 'although he has a bag full of broken victuals given to him by the charitable cooks, he would not put a bit in his mouth, his *appetite* being so *nice*, may be seen among this diabolical set of IMPOSTORS blowing up the cook for sending in his rumpsteak without the garnish of pickles and horseradish, and selling his bag of *grub* to some really poor and industrious person'.[25] An apparently pregnant girl, who has removed the pillow from her stays, sings:

> There's a difference between a beggar and a queen,
> And the reason I'll tell you why?
> A queen cannot swagger, nor get drunk like a beggar,
> Nor be half so happy as I, as I.

A black beggar, perhaps based on Joe Johnson or Charles McGee, proposes a toast: 'success to FLAT-*catching*'. And as he does so, the drunk and well-fed beggars begin to brawl, over which a 'black one-legged fiddler is *strumming* away to enliven the party; and the peck and booze [food and drink] is lying about that would supply numerous poor families. . .'

Despite the happiness on display, Tom and Jerry are revolted by the scene of hypocrisy and the remorseless conspiracy to impose upon the humane and generous at the expense of others. It sounded like evidence to the parliamentary select committee or propaganda for the Mendicity Society, but before anyone believed Pierce Egan had suddenly become earnest he undermined his high-mindedness. *Life in London* ends with Tom and Jerry visiting Bob Logic in the Fleet prison, where he has been imprisoned for debt. He jokes that he is 'at home' to visitors in the gaol, and no one blames him for his recklessness and prodigality. Indeed, Corinthian Tom advises him to 'gammon the flats' and cheat his creditors. Both Logic and the cadgers, it seems, rely on performance to keep them in drink.[26]

Life in London was a sensation in 1820/1. Egan's fame reached its height, and he was presented to his hero George IV. Much like modern cartoon characters, images of Tom and Jerry were marketed on clothes

Tom flirts with a young beggar, while Jerry (seated, far right) shares a pipe with an apparently blind beggar and the famous Joe Johnson. Billy Waters, the other recognisably real beggar, dances and plays his fiddle in the centre background

and trinkets; the most famous scene of them all, Tom pushing over a watch hut in Temple Bar, was printed on pocket handkerchiefs, fans, tea trays, sweetmeats and snuff boxes. In the US, Tom and Jerry gave their name to a cocktail. In London, Birmingham and Manchester gin-shops were nicknamed 'Tom and Jerry shops' by people who had never read the book or seen the plays. Young men, from apprentices to listless middle-class youths, adopted Tom-and-Jerry styles: tight trousers, high collars and colourful coats and neckcloths. Boxing got a new generation of fans. And, more disturbingly, men started going out on 'sprees', aping the adventures of *Life in London*. No evening was complete if it did not include 'slumming it' in St Giles's or Wapping and – most importantly – overturning a watch hut and punching its attendant. The book bred a generation of 'Tom-and-Jerry gemmen' – surly, destructive and besotted with slang.[27]

The mania for Egan's characters was fuelled by the theatre. From the summer of 1821 and into 1822 five different adaptations were being performed simultaneously in London theatres and there were at least sixty-five pirated or plagiarised versions of Egan's work in book, chapbook, ballad and print form. W. J. Moncrieff, who produced one of the stage versions, wrote: 'This Piece, obtained a popularity, and excited a sensation, totally unprecedented in theatrical history: from the highest to the lowest, all classes were alike anxious to witness its presentation. Dukes and dustmen were equally interested in its performance;* and peers might be seen mobbing it with apprentices to obtain an admission. Seats were sold weeks before they could be occupied; and every theatre in the United Kingdom, and even the United States, enriched its coffers by performing it.'[28]

The public's appetite could not be sated; as the *John Bull* newspaper said, 'instead of being contented with seeing one Tom and Jerry, the town will not be satisfied till they have seen them all'. Just as *Life in London* was not a novel, the stage versions were not plays but part operetta, part variety show, a raucous chaos through which Tom and Jerry thread their way. All the versions consisted of songs, comic turns and elaborate set pieces. The Sadler's Wells version outdid all others by staging a real horse race on a specially constructed racetrack that wound its way round the auditorium. The *Morning Herald* enjoyed

*This was not an exaggeration: many noblemen and women saw one or more of the performances, including HRH the Duke of York.

the plays, and commented that the funniest and most popular scenes were those set in the back slums with the artful beggars. The All-Max scene, with its pantomime and liberal use of slang, 'keeps the whole audience in a roar of laughter for nearly a quarter of an hour'. Harriet Arbuthnot went to the Adelphi version and was shocked at the wild enthusiasm of the audience, who shouted from gallery to pit and threw orange peel about, and 'who seemed to enjoy a representation of scenes, in which, from their appearance, one might infer they frequently shared'.[29]

While Egan's writing was ambivalent, cynical and shy of making moral judgements, the writers of the stage versions were sure to reward virtue and punish vice. Moncrieff gave Tom and Jerry love interests, two girls who test their lovers by masquerading as beggars or gin drinkers or whoever the men are investigating. In the same play, the joyous All-Max imagined by Egan is conflated with the St Giles's sluicery and made bleaker and seedier, with urchins begging for gin and the benign publican Mr Mace transformed into an uncaring extortionist. Tom and Jerry are merely observers who do not participate in what they see, while Logic is punished for his lechery at All-Max. Having learnt his lesson, Corinthian Tom provides the moral of the story, the last words of the operetta before the finale: 'let our experiences teach us to avoid its [London's] quicksand, and make the most of sunshine; – and in that anticipation let us hope our kind friends will pardon Tom, Jerry and Logic, all their sprees and rambles'. It was an apology that Egan would have considered too 'fastidious'. Moncrieff also brought to vulgar life the beggars in the Noah's Ark tavern, but did something Egan would never have done: he included real personalities.

The cast of beggars included a Mr Jenkins, their genteel leader, and representations of two real-life and well-known London beggars, Billy Waters, a minstrel, and Little Jemmy, whose real name was Andrew Whiston. Jemmy was born disabled and travelled through the streets by propelling his little cart with a pair of crutches. He was said to be the most dissipated of all mendicants. Billy was a familiar sight in London at the time. He was not mentioned by name in the original *Life in London*, but the Cruikshanks included him in the print of the Cadgers' Ken, still recognisable even though he has his back to us. Billy was a black American who had been recruited into the British navy during the wars. He had lost his left leg beneath the knee in an accident at sea; some said that it happened during a battle, others that he had fallen down the cockpit stairs fleeing danger, while he maintained that he had fallen from the topsail yard to the quarterdeck of HMS *Ganymede*. He supported his wife and two children by playing the violin throughout the West End.

'Billy is remarkable for good humour and industry,' wrote T. H. Busby, 'for the feathers in his hat, the grin of his countenance, and the sudden turn and kick out of his wooden limb, and his efforts to please are rewarded from the pockets of John Bull.' He was supposedly elected King of the Beggars and wore a military cocked hat, a 'judge's full-bottomed cauliflower wig' and a naval officer's jacket and trousers, 'symbolic of his being the head and arbiter of the naval, military, and judiciary departments of his eleemosynary kingdom'. Moncrieff wrote that 'Billy was an accomplished cadger, a skilful musician, and adroit dancer – doing more on one leg than many others do on two, and possessed of abilities that as an actor would have rendered him a *shining* ornament of the stage'.

Billy Waters became the most recognisable beggar in the country. From the late 1810s he began to appear in satirical cartoons as a bystander whom everyone would recognise from the streets. In 1820 he was celebrated in T. L. Busby's *Costume of the Lower Orders of London*, and in the 1820s Staffordshire potteries made figurines of him. His dancing was represented in puppet shows at fairgrounds. But there are no records of who he was or what he said. We do know that he was an accomplished performer and a popular figure; he was remembered throughout the century by people who saw his dancing, playing and exotic dress in the 1810s and '20s. As was so often the case with such characters, the rest of the world felt free to put words in his mouth and project their own racist fantasies onto him. W. J. Moncrieff spun a story that he was a prince bought from a powerful African kingdom by a Quaker missionary for two axes, a bag of nails and a frying pan. Moncrieff saw Billy as a savage who refused to conform to the 'trammels of civilised society' and the 'mechanical rules of man' and lived on his wits instead; he ruled the beggars because he had an inherent 'princeliness'.[30]

It was Moncrieff who created the character of Billy Waters that captured the public's imagination. His 'operatic extravaganza' of *Life in London* played for more than three hundred nights at the Adelphi Theatre, and the most popular scene was in the back slums, and the favourite character was Billy Waters. Billy enters to drink with Mr

Jenkins, Jemmy, 'Soldier Luke' and 'Creeping Jack': 'Ah, how you do my darley? how you do Massa Jenkins? – I drink wid you. (*Drinks deep: Jenkins takes the pot away.*) – And you Massa Jack, I drink wid you too (*to Creeping Jack.*) – Your helt, – your good helt ladies! (*Jack takes pot away.*)'

The beggars sit around and complain about the Society for the Suppression of Mendicity and its insistence that they should work for a living. Then Little Jemmy pipes up:

Jemmy: 'Gemmen, have you ordered the peck and booze for the evening?'
Soldier Luke: 'Aye, aye, I've taken care of that – shoulder of veal and garnish – Turkey and appendages – Parmesan – Filberds – Port and Madery [Madeira].'
Billy Waters: 'Dat dam goot, me like the Madery – Landlord, here you give this bag of broken wittals, vot I had give me to-day, to some genteel dog vot pass your door: and you make haste wid de supper, you curse devil you!'
. . . *Enter landlord with supper.*
Landlord: 'Now your honours, here's the rum peck, here's the supper.'
Billy: (*takes candle and looks at the supper*) 'Vy, what him call dis?'
Landlord: 'Why the turkey and pie, to be sure.'
Billy: 'De turkey and de pie! I tink you said de turkey and de pie! – what! de turkey widout de sassinger [sausages]! him shock – him wouldn't give pin for turkey widout them . . .'
Landlord: 'I'm very sorry, Mr Waters, but –'
Billy: 'You sorry! – I sorry for my supper, you damn dog.'
Mr Jenkins: (*to landlord*) 'Vhat! sarve up a turkey without sassiges – you're a nice man I don't think.'
Jack: (*to landlord*) 'I tell you vhat, young man, when you talk to gemmen, larn to take off your hat.'
Jemmy: 'Vy, there's no lemon to the weal, nor hoyster saase to the rump steaks. – It's shocking, infamous neglect, that's vot it is.'

Billy Waters became an updated version of Bampfylde-Moore Carew: anti-authoritarian, resourceful and addicted to the good things in life. Egan and Moncrieff do not seem to have been particularly unsympathetic to beggars like Waters or Little Jemmy, yet they both knew that the public was still fond of the comedy of ragged beggars who were secretly wealthy. There was a lot of mileage in depicting beggars as cunning impostors and secret epicures. But by making Billy Waters and his kind comic characters, Egan and Moncrieff were playing into the hands of the Mendicity Society, a body they would not have supported.

Life in London was popular as a satirical book, and later a series of plays, operettas and pantomimes, because people liked thinking of their city as a labyrinth of hidden recesses and impenetrable lives – people, like Egan, who delved into the secret parallel universe of flash-houses and cadger's cellars, as much as the equally mysterious Almack's Assembly Rooms or Cyprian masquerade balls. It is significant that the middling classes are hardly mentioned in *Life in London*, and when they are, they are rather praised than mocked. The book and plays were fantasies of escape from the mundane jobs, routine and petty decorums that were the curse of the clerical kind.

Egan's London is the London that these kinds of people would never dream of visiting; he deliberately chose the poles of the town: Almack's is paired with All-Max and the Cyprians' masquerade ball with the masquerading beggars. The high and the low are played off against each other as if there was no middle class at all. London is either grand and hypocritical or deprived and joyous. Throughout the book, distressing scenes or revolting vices are brushed off and excused as being merely 'Life in London', as if that spares us the need to make a moral judgement. It is unabashed voyeurism, which Egan knew people would enjoy reading as if it was a guidebook to the backstreets and the exclusive salons from which they were debarred. The slang seemed to make the book and the plays seem private and exclusive; but Egan, Moncrieff and their followers were clever enough to make the slang easily decipherable and therefore inclusive. *Life in London* was like a kind of initiation ritual into a secret London that lurked below the surface, obeyed its own laws and spoke a different language. Reading the book or seeing the plays gave the audience the frisson of danger: a sneaky insight into the world that eluded their own. It was like shuddering at a ghost story. Suppose it existed? the polite audience thought; it made the walk home from the theatre a little more exciting, a whit more daring.

Egan knew his audience all too well – their desire to escape restrictions and hypocrisy, if only in their minds. For he was not a swell like Corinthian Tom, an Oxonian gentleman like Bob Logic or a ginshop habitué. He was none of these things: he lived with his wife and large family in St Pancras. He was a suburban family man who, like others, fantasised about shedding his responsibilities and turning his back on the constant pressure to make money to become a fancy-free buck or a low-life playboy. His heroes and heroines are tough survivors – like a boxer still standing and smiling a toothless grin after sixty rounds of punishment – or cheeky ne'er-do-wells who take on the world and win. Certainly, he was a hard drinker at tavern dinners and boxing events and a regular at sporting occasions, but his rural and urban adventures were forays, not a lifestyle.

Life in London looks modern and sounds like reportage. In the use of slang, dialect and accents it anticipates Dickens. The Cruikshanks put the characters in the latest fashions and depicted new buildings, while Egan threw in topical references. Yet it is an illusion: the themes and settings are reworkings of eighteenth-century literature and art. The tale of gentlemen donning disguises and masquerading as petty criminals, highwaymen and layabouts had been around for centuries. Ned Ward's *London Spy* (1699–1700) lifted the lid on urban vice, supposedly as a warning to the unwary, but really an exercise in scandal-mongering. Such books were popular throughout the eighteenth century, and the idea of crossing social boundaries was a staple of literature and art. And if many people believed that it was part of city life, it was only confirmed by the real-life accounts of eccentrics such as the Barrymore brothers, George Hanger, the antics of coach-mad aristocrats and the nightly displays of convivial riot at places like Vauxhall Gardens.

The author of *Real Life in London*, another book written in Egan's style, claimed that 'Honest George' Hanger (the Regent's seedy companion) was the real inspiration for books that described young men who traversed social boundaries. 'I was early introduced into life, and often kept good and bad company,' Hanger boasted of his adventures; 'associated with men both good and bad, and with lewd women, and women not lewd, wicked and not wicked; – in short, with men and women of every description, and of every rank, from the highest to the lowest, from St James's to St Giles's; in palaces and night cellars; and from the drawing-room to the dust-cart.' The same author hinted that Hanger was the inspiration for Pierce's Corinthian Tom and all those caricatures of swells that followed: 'He can drink, swear, tell stories, cudgel, box, and smoke with anyone; having by his intercourse with society fitted himself for all companies.' The seventh Earl of Barrymore ('Hellgate') had been famous for donning a succession of disguises and alter egos; he was notorious for his part as a member of the Botherers Club, which involved playing cruel and destructive practical jokes on members of the public. His noble brother, the eighth Lord Barrymore ('Cripplegate'), was also an important inspiration, having dedicated great portions of his life to chasing 'wenches' and servant girls in the less salubrious districts of town, driving coaches and attending boxing contests and dogfights.[31]

The antics of Tom, Jerry and Logic were familiar to audiences in the early 1820s, but they were old-fashioned. The Four-in-Hand Club was defunct from 1815, when most of its founding members were dead or too old to manage a coach-and-four; George Hanger was also too geriatric to carouse with gypsies or drink in the Holy Land any more; and the next generation considered themselves above such plebeian amusements. *Life in London* smacks more of the war years. Masquerades, Cyprian balls at the theatre and Jackson's boxing school were features of the apogee of Regency excess in the days of Brummell, Byron, Harriette Wilson and Julia Johnstone. None of these were still on the scene, and the world they inhabited was dying out, not thriving as Egan would have it. Pierce Egan retold and refashioned these upper-class diversions for a new generation and a new class. The brief Tom-and-Jerry-mania attracted bored or rebellious young men of the middle class who wanted to flout rules, shock convention and imitate aristocratic buckism.

Egan's descriptions of high society were adequate as pieces of satire, but even his friends at *Blackwood's* gently advised him to stop writing about places like Almack's or Carlton House when it was obvious he knew nothing about such things. If the upper-class sections of the book were badly out of date, what are we to make of the scenes that purport to be reportage from the streets, the bits contemporaries found most believable? Egan was alive to the comedic possibilities of the lower orders. Anyone who read the minutes of evidence of the select committees of the House of Commons would learn of a world of devious imposture, resourcefulness, hard drinking, brutal pastimes, dingy public houses and squalid pleasures. The official folios were a rich mine of anecdotes and tales from Rats' Castle and the East End, most of which could be rewritten as slapstick and comedy.

Was it necessary for Egan to go to a Wapping tavern? Perhaps he really did; but there is little in his accounts of the ginshop or the Noah's Ark that could not have been recreated from spending a few days in the reading room of the British Museum with the official folio of parliamentary sessions papers. In describing All-Max, Egan was eager to defend poor people from the censorious views of meddlers and busybodies; his poor drink and dance as a respite from unimaginable toil in the shipyards, breweries, warehouses or dust heaps.

Coming from Ireland, India, the West Indies and Africa, they have forged a new, urban version of 'Merry England' that deserved to be shielded from the lies, scare-mongering and control of modern puritans. (Or that's the gloss Egan put on it; it was a better story to tell than one of hopeless poverty, disease, alcoholism and misery.)

As far as the very lowest went, however, Egan was not going to demolish any myths. The report of the select committee on mendicity was too good to be true; even if Pierce and Moncrieff did not have any moral antipathy to street minstrels and beggars, the rumours of midnight orgies and ingenious tricks were gifts for comic writers. These scenes were the most popular and eagerly received in the stage productions.

Billy Waters knew how these scenes were received: 'The fickle British public refused to be as liberal as they had been, which he attributed to the production of "*Tom and Jerry*".' The thousands of people who read and saw the adventures of Tom and Jerry believed that they had discovered the truth. Billy had a good life, dined better than they and was ungrateful; would he miss their ha'penny? The fictional Billy and the real Billy who played his fiddle all day to keep his family alive, and who lived in the warren of St Giles's, were conflated, and it was fatal for Waters. Egan and Moncrieff had unwittingly added to the cant they claimed to abhor. Throughout the three hundred and more nights that he was caricatured on the stage of the Adelphi, Billy found that the public's affection turned to hostility. First he was forced to pawn his violin, and then he was sent to the workhouse, where he became ill. At exactly the time that *Tom and Jerry* ended its long run at the Adelphi, Waters died. His last words were said to be an anathema on what he knew to be the cause of his fall and death: 'Cuss him, dam Tom-mee-Tom-ee Jerry.'[32]

PART III

Rich and Respectable 1821–37

'The cry is up – and the cant is up.'
Byron

INTRODUCTION TO PART III

Bubbles Light as Air

Writing in 1822, Robert Southey believed that Britain was poised between the old and the new. For someone who had been so unfailingly and congenitally pessimistic about modern life, and so nostalgic for a utopian past, it is a surprise to read him admitting that he had a 'disposition to be satisfied with things as they are'. The face of the country was altered beyond recognition in this revolutionary decade. Macadamised roads, improved coaches, railways, steamships and the telegraph made the world seem smaller and put mankind (or, more accurately, Britons) at the apogee of civilisation. Enclosures in the country increased the efficiency of agriculture and created a new class of gentrified farmers. Building projects throughout the country gave cities and towns the sheen of modernity. The mechanisation and improvements in printing reaffirmed the modern feel of the age, the illustrated books and newspapers of 1820 making the efforts of 1800 look shoddy, backward and with all the appearance of belonging to a less advanced society. It was a country humming with prosperity, innovation and intellectual activity. The economic dislocation of the post-war period seemed like a blip on the road to the future; misery gave way to better times in the 1820s, and many enjoyed the upsurge of wealth and progress. Britons were self-confident and complacent as never before.[1]

Throughout the war and the difficult years after 1815 the Tory press had predicted the imminent collapse of religion, law, monarchy and morality. Yet things had improved; progress had occurred under an unreformed Tory government. In *Blackwood's*, Horatio Townsend asked what emigrant returning to his homeland after many years 'will hesitate to acknowledge the decided superiority of the Empress of the Ocean, the free and happy Island? . . . Where can he hope to behold such wealth, spirit, intelligence, generosity, and enterprise, as are centred in that vast and respectable body composing the mercantile interest of Great Britain? . . . Years, not days, would suffice to make a person acquainted with the immense extent and variety of her arts, her manufactures, her literary attainments, her cultivated lands, and her commercial cities . . . All the rest of the world . . . never could boast such a throne, such a senate, such a country, and such a people!'[2]

The manners and morals of the people were said to have experienced a comparable revolution. The improvements had been going on gradually and undetected for years; it was only now that they had become apparent. To many minds, economic prosperity in the opening decades of the century had called into being a class of upwardly mobile families, who were swelling the ranks of the middling. Their wealth and number, not to say their economic importance, would revolutionise politics and society and profoundly alter culture. General education was far more common for children of all classes and the rage for learning and knowledge among adults was changing the face of publishing. Where a few journals catered for the curious intellectual in the 1800s, by the third decade of the century the market was crowded with magazines eager to educate the willing masses. 'Booksellers and printsellers find it worth their while to publish for a grade of customers which they deemed ten years ago beneath their consideration.' The 'march of mind' was the slogan of the day, used alike by radicals, Tories, utilitarians and clergymen.[3]

Edward Lytton Bulwer wrote in 1833 that 'The English of the present day are not the English of twenty years ago.' Much of the coarseness and eccentricity of the previous century had been ironed out; from fashion to standards of decorum, conformity took over from the individualistic exuberance of the previous generation. In proportion to the advance in industry, education and wealth, the people were better behaved and less drunk, or so it was said. For many the visible and invisible improvements in the country and its people betokened a golden age of opportunity and freedom. Economic and political power was passing into the hands of the middle class; the radical movement invested all its energy and hopes in the power of education to drag the people up to the level of the ruling class. Other countries had revolutions; autodidactic Britons would remake the world from the classroom and the lecture hall and the pages of improving magazines. (Sometimes the self-congratulatory fervour of this time can get too much.) Nostalgic and conservative writers and politicians looked on this kind of utopian rhetoric with derision. It was deeply disquieting for people like Lytton Bulwer, who already saw 'the removal of timeworn landmarks, and the breaking up of the hereditary elements of society – old opinions, feelings – ancestral customs and institutions crumbling away . . .'[4]

For a few years in the 1820s the excitement and confidence of the press and politicians was every bit as visionary and fervid as the voices warning of destruction and anarchy had been at the beginning of the century. Those who trumpeted the glorious future made it almost heresy to deny or criticise the brave new world. The very notion of 'progress' was intoxicating. The country seemed to be more intolerant in its attitudes to certain groups and people – intolerant of those who offended against the spirit of progress, material, moral and religious. The age – and Britain's unique position in the history of civilisation – demanded greater respect. The punishment for those deemed to be insufficiently attuned to the modern world and its values – from Lord Byron and Edmund Kean to travelling actors and itinerant musicians – could be vindictive, and it was certainly capricious.

The excitement generated by the machine age and the fast pace of improvements made people – or at least the people who were at the forefront of the advance – arrogant and proud. 'Pavilioned in the glittering pride of our superficial accomplishments and upstart pretensions,' said Hazlitt, 'we fancy that every thing beyond that magic circle is prejudice and error; and all, before the present enlightened period, but a dull and useless blank in the great map of time.'[5] And it wasn't just the past that was derided as musty and backward: the relics of the unseemly recent past lived on among the glittering features of the modern paradise. Clownish yokels, drunken labourers, bawdy poets, adulterous actors, gambling-mad aristocrats, Tom-and-Jerry delinquents, travelling minstrels and mountebank doctors existed to remind people of an older, semi-barbarous Britain. There were commentators such as Thomas Love Peacock who saw epic poetry as a revolt against reason; it was almost, he said, as if the poet had not heard of modern inventions, machines, chemistry, political economy, astronomy or the new morality: 'The march of his intellect is like that of a crab, backward. The brighter the light diffused around him by the progress of reason, the thicker is the darkness of antiquated barbarism, in which he buries himself like a mole. . .' In terms of ideas, morality and modernity, poetry was in the wrong century: it was 'the rant of unregulated passion, the whining of exaggerated feeling, and the cant of factitious sentiment'. How unlike the pioneers of modernity – the scientists, economists and utilitarians – 'who have built into the upper air of intelligence a pyramid, from the summit of which they see the modern Parnassus beneath them'.[6]

In 1825, to great offence, Thomas McLean published an elaborate cartoon, *The Progress of Cant* by Thomas Hood, mocking this fervour and earnestness and faith. It savaged all the 'speculations and topics upon which at this time it pleases mankind to twaddle and cant', from the stock exchange to religion and philanthropy. An assemblage of

grotesques parade their morality and list their anxieties under the banners of middle-class causes. It is moral Middle England on the march. Among the slogans are 'The Preservation of Public Morals', 'No Life in London', 'March of Mind', 'Knowledge Is Power', 'Let Every Child Have Its Bible', 'United Schools', 'London University', 'No Pugilism', 'Subscription for Putting Down Bartlemy [Bartholomew] Fair', 'The Caledonian Chapel', 'No Theatre', 'Freedom for Blacks'.

It is a bleak and joyless world. A crippled beggar has been issued

with a Mendicity Ticket to exchange for food. A barber dares not shave customers while his neighbours are in church; the magistrates would close him down if he did anything so profane. (The sign is damaged and reads: 'Nobody to be S-aved during Divine Service'.) The Peruvian Mining Company is based in a tumbledown garret, while the only new buildings are a church and a boarding school for young ladies: a modern city is grafted onto a hopelessly old-fashioned one. A beadle, dressed with all the pomp and grandeur of a field marshal, lazily oversees his neighbours' morals, empowered by the Vagrant Act, reminded of his duties by a yapping dog marked 'office'. Crammed into the print are a mass of symbols, slogans and meanings, seemingly unrelated. What are they doing together?

The Progress of Cant mocks the hollowness and hypocrisy of improvement and modernity. Under the cover of philanthropy and virtue, the ragtag people take the opportunity to kiss, flirt, fight and steal unobserved. A Quaker in a bonnet wears a dress made by the female prisoners in Newgate; she is parading her philanthropic desire to reform fallen women and her support for Elizabeth Fry, but she herself is half housewife, half hussy, clearly out on the streets to catch the eye of a man. She looks like the gaudy figurehead of a ship. The beadle is trying to conceal an erection. A fat boy is about to buy a pie with the money he has been collecting for charity. A jockey beating his broken-down nag proclaims 'Martin for Ever' in celebration of the man who founded the Society for the Prevention of Cruelty to Animals.

They are bad characters, but their conspicuous morality and ardent support for the reclamation of prostitutes, the Mendicity Society and other worthy causes, as well as their evangelicalism, gives them an air of plausibility. The smart girls' boarding school rises above the squalor, but it's a monument to snobbery and fake gentility: parents wanted to refine their daughters, but really the institution teaches them how to flirt and idle their lives away. Down below, the scene is not supposed to represent a typical street but modern Britain. It wants to be good and moral and civilised, but the same old vices, dirt, bad habits and bad health cannot be effaced by mere slogans.

But the crying sin of the age, for Hood, is speculation. The sign for the Peruvian Mining Company in the battered old building provides the clue. Britain had prospered in the early 1820s from low interest rates and a surplus of money. There were two booms: in foreign investment and in trade. Merchants and manufacturers, encouraged by the availability of credit, speculated and profited; in 1824 alone a staggering £372,000,000 was invested in 624 new joint-stock companies (including the Peruvian Mining Company) by eager shareholders promised an easy fortune. From the autumn of 1824 there was a giddy rush of speculation. Money poured out of Britain to fund foreign ventures. The middle classes borrowed to invest in the booming economy. Banks kept up with the demand for cash, issuing more banknotes. As money left the country, banks (including the venerable Bank of England itself) were drained of gold to support its issues of paper money.[7]

Late in 1825 the bubble burst. On 12 December the London bank Pole, Thornton and & Co. crashed, dragging down forty-three provincial banks. There followed a week of headless panic. Banks found it impossible to supply the demand for gold currency; the Bank of England came close to running out of its reserves on several occasions, but was saved when millions of pounds' worth of forgotten sovereigns were fortuitously discovered in some crates in the cellars, and also thanks to the efforts of Nathan Rothschild, who propped up the bank with his own gold reserves. Prices began to rise, and the new ventures crashed to the ground, ruining many eager speculators and importers. During the 'bubble-mania' people were encouraged to invest in visionary schemes – the construction of railways, canals and mines in countries all over the world. Many of these high-tech, modern dreams drew in investors who were besotted with the idea that 'the present had gained a fresh triumph over the past'.

The visionary companies were the ones that fell furthest. It was suspected that they were conducted by conmen who fleeced the middle class with magical promises of the victory of progress and British entrepreneurial brilliance. A list of 'respectable' directors – maybe some with titles or seats in Parliament – completed the honeytrap. Credulous investors would be reassured by the gilt of respectability and gentility and seduced by puffing newspaper articles. But for all the high-sounding words and affectation of gentility, some suspected that the companies were based in seedy garrets, not bright new offices.

The Peruvian Mining Company was the most notorious of these speculations. It had issued a prospectus stating that it had bought a lease of land in Peru cluttered with silver mines that would provide an infinite fund of money. In the Commons, John Cam Hobhouse said that the prospectus talked of 'the prospect of unbounded wealth which opened itself up to the shareholder. The framers of that prospectus evidently proceeded upon the supposition that there was an infinite fund of gullibility in the dupes to whom they addressed themselves.' And so they might. Fifty gentlemen bought 200 shares at £5 a share. When they were issued on the market, the value of a share was £16. From that moment, the directors were in profit if they sold just sixty-six shares. At the height of the bubble frenzy, the value of a share peaked at £700. It made a fortune for the directors (who, of course, had never put any of their own money into the scheme), but there was very little evidence, at the time, that the mines would ever return a profit. Some called the bubble a tax on stupidity.[8]

The 1825–6 crash and the depression that followed wasn't quite Britain's equivalent of the Wall Street Crash. Depressions then tended to be short and sharp. All the same, it had a profound impact on the British imagination, and especially on young men who had been caught up in the breathless excitement in 1824–5. Disraeli was intoxicated by the vision of an easy fortune, investing his money and writing puff pieces to inflate the price of shares he had invested in. He went into his own depression when it all went wrong, and got his revenge on a cruel world by writing acerbic novels mercilessly satirising the hyperbole of the bubble, the gullibility of the people and the jargon of political economists. Many shared his anger. The bursting of the bubble seemed to be God's retribution on a greedy and hedonistic country. It was punishment for the vices of speculation and greed that national wealth fostered. The director of a joint-stock company was, for moralists, the modern version of Samuel Solomon: polished, smooth-talking and plausible, but really duplicitous and greedy. For such people respectability was a commodity, not a mark of virtue. They drew humble investors into their net with smooth words and polished manners: 'Every respectable man can become a director,' wrote one journalist, mocking the way in which words had been twisted and notions of social worth turned on their head. '. . . It is quite clear that respectable men cannot lose, and must gain. The loss falls upon persons not respectable who have little to lose, and who therefore ought to lose that little.'[9]

The 1825 bubble crash was supposedly a tale for the times. The country had become addicted to gambling and drunk on notions of progress. In its greed and self-confidence, it had lost the capacity to distinguish between cant and the truth. Not all joint-stock companies were shady, but they were all treated as such by the ministry and the Tory press. Those middle-class people ruined in the crash had lost their morals and minds, intoxicated by the rage for self-improvement and status. They were willing dupes of visionary get-rich-quick schemes and they deserved all they got. This was the view of old-fashioned Tories, who were uneasy with the moral implications of progress and speculation. The crisis revived the apocalyptic language of the war; however high a country rose (in material success and its own estimation), it was no less vulnerable than it was in darker ages to the levelling hand of fortune or the vengeance of divine providence that punished false pride, gluttony and idolatry.

In *The Progress of Cant* the Peruvian Mining Company fits uneasily, it seems, with the seemingly unrelated charitable projects. But charity could be a speculative scheme as well. In the year of the bubbles, 1824, Elizabeth Fry and other Quaker philanthropists established their own joint-stock company. The Equitable Loan Company had the charitable intent of keeping the poor away from pawnbrokers by loaning the needy small sums. The shareholders would be rewarded with a handsome return: the interest on the loan was 20 per cent. But this profiteering was minor compared to the speculative aspect of one of London's most respectable charities.

The honorary secretary of the Mendicity Society was a very ambitious young man named William Henry Bodkin. In 1821 *The Times* accused him of trying to endear himself to the government by ordering the employees of the society to the Covent Garden Theatre to cheer the King (who was at the nadir of his relationship with the people), so that the loyalist newspapers could report on the people's love for their king. In 1824 Bodkin was in trouble again. He had employed his brother-in-law as auditor of the accounts to cover up the fact that he had embezzled £500 a year of the charity's money. Indeed, the society had received £3,612 in 1823 and could account for only £1,595.[10]

The Times said that 'the bustlers and jobbers are at work' with their 'schemes of wealth and aggrandizement'. Moreover, the society existed, as it said, 'to prevent the artful and fraudulent from participating in funds intended for the relief of genuine misery'; the only thing that differentiated the directors of the charity from hypocritical and imposing beggars, it seemed now, was 'respectability'. The committee of the Mendicity Society defended Bodkin and his friends from the charges by saying that the society was not a charity; it did not exist to give beggars money but to return them to work, so to say that Bodkin had picked the pockets of the poor was simply wrong. The society investigated itself and found that Bodkin was justified in taking the money. Others could be forgiven for seeing this as monstrous hypocrisy. William Bodkin seemed to be pretending to care for the very poor, when really he did so to fill his bank account and win the favour of men in power. Bodkin, said *The Times*, was 'a mere mercenary in disguise, endeavouring to sail by a side wind, and false colours, into Sinecure Harbour'. The scandal is pointed out in *The Progress of Cant*. The disabled beggar has a badge reading 'crippled by an injury from a Bear Bodkin'.

The characters in the print appear to be members of dissenting or Methodist congregations. The ideas of regulating and restricting the habits and recreations of the poor and unconventional had been derided in the 1800s, when the Society for the Suppression of Vice was a risible pressure group and Methodism a dirty word. Things had changed. John Bowles died in 1819 and Patrick Colquhoun in 1820, but the policing theories of the latter had their disciples, while there were many magistrates as stern and unforgiving as the former. The vice suppressors were applauded for their energy in pursuing obscenity and atheism. '"Methodist",' one journalist noted, 'which a few years ago was used as a reproach, has been adopted as an honourable distinction to those to whom it was applied.'[11]

The religion was praised by the kinds of people who had derided it as fanatical, subversive and bigoted a decade before. A Tory writer deplored the tenets of Methodism, but said that 'it almost always amends the life, and renders essential service to public morals'. Britain allotted a vast degree of liberty to its people; therefore, a self-regulating society had to take the place of strict laws. It was an entirely beneficial thing that neighbourhood opinion should operate as a check on unseemly behaviour; Methodism accomplished this task of surveillance and admonishment. 'They provide a vast additional number of religious teachers and places of worship, their discipline jealously watches over the moral conduct of every member, and punishes the most trifling irregularities of life, and they operate principally among the lower classes, over which the regular clergy have the least influence.'[12]

Methodism and evangelicalism had not just prevailed over their critics and won respectability but had become a force in national life. The popularity of Methodism forced the Church of England to compete as an energetic and active religion. When Edward Irving began preaching at the Caledonian Chapel in Holborn in 1823, his congregation was joined by the Prime Minister and members of the cabinet, fashionable members of society and the royal family. This would have been inconceivable in the 1790s; the high-bred congregation would have been stigmatised as fanatics and enemies of the established Church had they been to hear a hectoring preacher. Yet now the Caledonian Chapel was a fashionable venue: 'This obscure spot is now crowded by all the sight-hunters of London, men of fashion, and blue-stockings, the peerage, and the cabinet; scholars and scribblers, all who have eyes to see, and ears to be captivated, crowd to the dingy walls of this ancient receptacle of cobwebs and crabbed Theology.'

The titled and powerful came to hear their lifestyles, politics and morals savaged by Irving. The Marchioness of Conyngham, one of the King's long line of mistresses, joined the godly throng. Irving lambasted 'the sensual incontinence of these times' and the superficial semblance of morality that characterised the people in the modern age. 'He does not spare their politicians, their rulers, their moralists, their poets, their players, their critics, their reviewers, their magazine-writers; he levels their resorts of business, their places of amusement, at a blow.' The preacher praised the grave and zealous soldiers and statesmen of the Commonwealth who advocated a theocracy: '[then] Christians were in this island the Princes of human intellect, the Lights of the world, the Salt of the political and social state', Irving preached to the elite of the country. His style and theology split the press. *The Times* (liberal) and *John Bull* (Tory) called him a quack and canting puritan; the *New Times* (ultra-Tory) and the *Morning Chronicle* (Whig) cheered him on.

Edward Irving stands prominently in *The Progress of Cant* under the banner 'No Theatre'. It is meant sarcastically. William Hazlitt believed that no one would have gone to hear Irving had he been five feet high, ugly and softly spoken. As it was, he looked like a cross between a prizefighter and a Patagonian, according to Hazlitt, with a handsome face and the oratorical flourishes of an actor. People came to see the wondrous performance, even while Irving 'brow-beats their prejudices, and bullies them out of their senses'. Hazlitt said that the fashionable congregation came to enjoy a wild and brilliant performance, to quail for a moment at Irving's blistering attacks just as they might relish a *frisson* of dread during a chilling play.

'Surely, surely it cannot be long before this bubble bursts!' said *The Times*.[13] After a brief spell at the summit of fame, the glitterati got bored of the celebrity preacher; the novelty wore off and the fashion subsided. He illuminated another truth about the age: people adopted the externals of religious observance, made sure they were seen at church once or twice a week, but were they as sincere as the grandees who made sure that they were seen at Irving's weekly sermons? Whether it was in the company of dukes and statesmen at the Caledonian Chapel or with their neighbours at the local church, people wanted to keep up appearances and parade their piety – or that was what some believed.

The charge was grossly unfair. Irving's fickle congregation, like the William Bodkin scandal, were extreme examples of obvious hypocrisy. There were many genuinely devout people who sought a spiritual life in many different ways, some quietly, others with more noise and show. Evangelicalism did seem to many to be a solution to life's problems, both personally and as a cure for society's ills. The people could be dissuaded from their bad habits, or coerced into better behaviour, by religion. An advanced country should give thanks to God and be a standard-bearer of Christianity; or what else was Britain to do with her wealth and prestige?

To invert the title of the cartoon, it was the cant of progress that was objected to most. There had always been a tendency for national self-confidence, even in the depths of war. Victory in 1815 followed a few years later by a booming economy seemed like the blessing of providence; Britain was once more leading the world. It truly seemed that she stood at the dawn of a new epoch in the history of civilisation. The language of self-belief and arrogance was insufferable. New laws of capitalism would govern and direct modern man. Universal education would rescue the masses from ignorance and superstition. Progress would be exponential. And so it went on – few times have been so optimistic or have invested so greatly in the future. At times like the stock-market crash, confidence receded, and that which had besotted the richer classes seemed no more than hot air and cant. But belief in the destiny of Britain never disappeared for long. Millions parroted the latest theory without thought and looked upon less effusive people as hopelessly old-fashioned. The idea of progress had become a great idol to be worshipped by a blessed people.

This brave new world demanded better standards of behaviour. People felt they should live up to the age in which they lived. Placed by God in the vanguard of human progress and at the head of a growing empire, Britons should give thanks in prayer and exhibit to the world the manners of a nation at the apogee of civilisation. From lower-class Methodists to middling-class families to aristocratic grandees, there was a noticeable change in manners. People were judged more than ever by their outward behaviour. Commentators noted in the 1820s that a greater emphasis was placed on maintaining one's reputation. Like the people in the cartoon, but to a less ludicrous extent, they needed to keep up appearances. Righteousness, it seemed, came with this new faith in national destiny. They were mocked for their efforts to seem better than they were. Byron railed at the 'verbal decorum' which forced language into a straitjacket of vapid niceties and strained euphemism.

Morality, it seemed, had become a thing of words – easy, cheap words – not actions. Edward Lytton Bulwer told a story of a man who advertised for a governess who could teach his daughters how to dance, sing and speak French. A former opera singer applied for the post but was turned down. She asked what she was lacking, given her ample qualifications for the job. The father replied that she was in all respects perfect, but he could not employ an opera singer to teach his daughters, the profession having a very low reputation as far as morals went. 'Oh!' replied the woman, 'if that be all, *I can change my name*!'[14]

11

Byroned

> 'I shall end by making him [Don Juan] turn Methodist; this will please the English, and be an *amende honorable* for his sins and mine.'
>
> Byron[1]

In 1828 Pierce Egan killed Corinthian Tom at the end of a two-volume *mea culpa* for the damage he had done and the offence he had caused by introducing Tom and Jerry to the public. It is extraordinary that Egan, the hero of the Fancy and the enemy to prissy manners, should be the author of *The Finish to the Adventures of Tom, Jerry, and Logic*. There is an uncomfortable and obviously affected moral earnestness in this book, and very little slang.

In one scene, the heroes go to the prison hulks at Chatham docks to witness a chain gang. Among the convicts is 'Splendid Jem', a former member of high society who dissipated his fortune and became a sharper and swindler. This would have been an opportunity for some jokes in *Life in London*; the sequel was less cynical. 'But it is never too late to *mend*,' says Jem piously; 'and should Providence enable me to outlive my *sentence*, I hope to return to society an altered and better man; and, by my future good conduct, repair the numerous errors of my early life.' A new po-faced Corinthian Tom draws a moral and a feeble justification for the voyeurism of observing life in London from Jem's pitiful fall: 'it is one of the advantages of witnessing the effects of extravagant Life in London; and the awful lesson which Splendid Jem's career affords to many thoughtless young men upon the town, ought be turned to a good account'. The rest of the book continues with such high-mindedness, a few dreadful warnings of vice and little of the humour, high spirits and energy of the original. It smacked a little too much of the cant that Egan had set himself to destroy.

The Finish of Tom and Jerry's adventures was intended as a tour through the circles of the hell of London to show those who would imitate Tom and Jerry the pits and snares that awaited them. Prostitutes are no longer fair and frolicsome but sirens who lure thoughtless men to the gallows and spread disease. Low-life drinkers were once life-affirming and worthy of emulation; now they are wrecks of human beings whom no one could envy. Such things were not fit material for jokes in 1828. 'Half-quartern Luce', for example, was raised a lady, but is now a bloated drunk who sold her raddled body so she could afford her accustomed thirty-six half-quarterns of gin a day. The town is riddled with addictions, exploitation and disease. In one incident, Jerry gets drunk and awakes in a brothel without a memory of the night before. In the original version, Tom and Logic would mock Jerry, and it would just be a jolly adventure. Now, however, Egan could not let this go without a moral lecture. The scene has none of the *joie de vivre* of before; it is a nightmare. Jerry finds that he has been robbed of everything, including the clothes he was wearing. In 1820 Egan would have excused such youthful exuberance as merely being an inevitable aspect of 'Life in London', his shorthand for the blessings of experience; by 1828 'Life in London' is by no means wholesome – it is seedy and not at all funny. It is a chilling scene; all Jerry can think about is the ravages of venereal disease: he is justly punished for his vices. Shamed and enlightened as to the ways of the flesh, Jerry now 'filled up his time in the most rational manner'.

But he very nearly falls a second time when he is picked up by a prostitute in Temple Bar and taken to a 'hotel'. Before the transaction can take place, a fire breaks out, and Jerry risks his life to rescue the prostitute, Ellen Prettyflower. He feeds and clothes her, and finds her shelter. His generosity makes Ellen reconsider her life and she promises to go to the female penitentiary. In turn, Jerry vows to mend his ways and tells Ellen that he will pay for her to undergo a thorough reformation in an institution (of course, he does not need such radical treatment for *his* vices). She calls Jerry her 'beloved brother, who has stood forward in the hour of affliction', even though a few hours before he was ready to pay to have sex with her. She begins to praise him as a hero and good samaritan, but 'Ellen could not proceed any further with her remarks, occasioned by a violent overflow of tears; and Jerry also blubbered out like a great boy, so much were his feelings overcome by the sentimental, yet pointed language of the unfortunate girl'. Jerry becomes a prig and hypocrite and a good example to schoolboys everywhere, and Egan merely proved the point that the strength of his writing rested solely on the ruthless, cynical tone and liberal use of slang that had made him famous.

The chastened Pierce Egan had been a victim of one of the British public's periodic fits of morality. Ever since the publication of *Life in London*, he had stood accused of teaching the youth of Britain how to sin, glorifying violence and shocking ladies with horrid scenes of sex and drinking. Young men punched watchmen; they flocked to boxing matches and racked up the gins in the Holy Land. 'All this is Pierce's fault,' commented *Town Talk* more in sadness than in anger in 1822; 'it is really a pity that a decent man like Pierce should have done so much mischief.' When *Tom and Jerry* came to the end of its first long run at the Adelphi, a broadside was printed showing the charlies – the watchmen – dancing and rejoicing that they would be spared the assaults of young bucks; they chorus:

> Dusty Bob and Black Sall may grieve
> Because Tom and Jerry are undone;
> But we'll swear if much longer they'd liv'd,
> They'd kill all the charlies in London.

The *New Monthly Magazine* talked of a breed of 'pseudo-gentlemen', better known as Corinthians, who were 'unprincipled, unmannered, uncredited, unwitted'. A Corinthian was a bully, a boaster and a liar. He would talk of intrigues with women he had never met and crimes he was too cowardly to commit: 'His mind is a chaos of confused vices and vanities.' The theatre and the taverns were full of them, and anyone who could afford the clothes could be a Corinthian, including, as the *New Monthly* sniffily said, city apprentices, attorneys' clerks and journeymen tailors. The nuisance continued throughout the 1820s, and in 1828, when *Tom and Jerry* was revived at Vauxhall, watchmen's boxes were overturned by 'young bloods' and 'Tom and Jerry cockney ruffians' in quiet suburban districts like Kennington.[2]

Egan was forced to write *The Finish to the Adventures of Tom, Jerry, and Logic* in the same year that the operetta returned, as Moncrieff said, 'to vindicate the characters of the author and the artist from the unmerited aspersions of having attempted, by the joint efforts of real tales, original anecdotes, and animated sketches, to demoralize the rising generation; and likewise to refute the charge of having turned the heads of older folks towards the acts of folly and intemperance'.[3] The book is Jerry's journey to redemption. He finds that London is not the scene of fun and frolic and the crucible of *life* as the original book had suggested. He retires to the country, back to Hawthorne Hall, where he marries a local girl, hunts, shoots, fishes and talks to his stolid yeomen neighbours. Tom comes to visit, and dies in a hunting accident, with scarce a word of remorse from Jerry or the author. It was a dire warning to anyone who would emulate the swells that their behaviour was the high road to misery and premature death. There is little joy in reading it; there cannot have been much in writing it. When Egan's alter ego Bob Logic is dying in the concluding volume, he says: 'You must perceive that the *comical* part of my career is at an end, and you are well aware that I was always a merry fellow; but . . . I shall be found a *grave* man to-morrow.'

The treatment of Pierce Egan was mild compared to that of other offenders against public decency. He voluntarily killed Tom and turned Jerry into a blubbering do-gooder because he lived on his writing; he had to recant in order to retain the favour of the reading public and continue to sell books. The reaction to two of the greatest talents of the age, the actor Edmund Kean and Lord Byron, demonstrated British moral disapproval – what the *Examiner* called 'this wretched cant of decorum' – at full force.[4]

In 1821 Byron wrote a letter to his publisher John Murray, which was published, on the subject of the Rev. William Bowles's edition of the life and writings of Alexander Pope. In it, the reverend had censured Pope's 'grossest licentiousness', which was hinted at in one of the poet's letters to Martha Blount. The evidence that Pope was a bad man consisted of a rumoured liaison with Blount, a flirtation with Lady Mary Wortley Montagu, gossip that came from Colley Cibber and some coarse allusions in his poems. '*Who* could come forth cleaner from an invidious inquest on a life of fifty-six years?' Byron asked. Indeed, 'Where is the unmarried Englishman of a certain rank of life, who . . . has not to reproach himself between the ages of sixteen and thirty with far more licentiousness than has ever yet been traced to Pope?' Few were entirely innocent, and indeed, although Byron had heard that the Rev. Bowles himself had been less than chaste at university, he was willing to 'believe him a good man, almost as good as Pope, but no better'.[5]

Byron could see 'no worse sign for the taste of the times' than the prurient tut-tutting over silly rumours about Pope and this tendency to hunt down minor indiscretions in order to gossip about them. His anger at these modern verdicts on greatness and all they implied led him to a furious condemnation of the modern English character:

> The truth is, the grand '*primum mobile*' of England is *cant*; cant political, cant poetical, cant religious; but always cant, multiplied through all the varieties of life. It is the fashion, and while it lasts will be too powerful for those who can only exist by taking the tone of the time. I say *cant*, because it is a thing of words, without the smallest influence upon human actions; the English being no wiser, no better, and much poorer and more divided amongst themselves, as well as far less moral, than they were before the prevalence of this verbal decorum.

Most 'men of the world who know what life is' would laugh at the feigned horror over the 'libertine sort of love' imputed to Alexander Pope by Bowles. Wiser men would regard people like Bowles as fanatics or hypocrites, or both: 'The two are sometimes compounded in a happy mixture.'[6]

And Byron knew what it was like to face the ire of an offended British public. Between 1812 and the end of 1815 he was at the height of his popularity. 'I know, from experience,' he said, 'we end by disliking those we flatter: it is the mode we take to avenge ourselves for stooping to the humiliation of flattering them.' When he left his wife in 1816, he knew the press, the gossips and the public would begin a hue and cry against him and wisely left the country. When he left for the continent, he was lucky to get away without a confrontation with the mob. There were rumours of incest with his half-sister and hints of his bisexuality. He was compared to Nero, Apicius, Epicurus, Caligula, Heliogabalus, Henry VIII and Satan: 'I was looked upon as the worst of husbands, the most abandoned and wicked of men, and my wife as a suffering angel – an incarnation of all the virtues and perfections of the sex.'[7]

The public did not know much about the circumstances of the separation, but ignorance did not stop it condemning; as Byron told Lady Blessington, 'there is no story too improbable for the craving appetites of our slander-loving countrymen'. He had always been confused with his misanthropic creation Childe Harold, a brooding, restless figure. From 1816, in the public mind he, like the Childe Harold of the third canto, became cruel, heartless and too wild to be constrained by morality. Both were despisers of domesticity. 'I was accused of every monstrous vice by public rumour and private rancour: my name . . .

was tainted. I felt that, if what was whispered, and muttered, and rumoured was true, I was unfit for England; if false, England was unfit for me.' It was little wonder therefore that Byron's favourite subject in exile was 'decrying hypocrisy and cant' and 'the false delicacy of the English'.[8]

It was often said that Byron's critics were disappointed to find that he and his poems were not worse than they were. It could also be said that Byron was hypersensitive to criticism and was a little too assiduous in his inquisition on hypocrisy and weakness. Nonetheless, rumours kept people busy with tales of the poet's diabolical lifestyle in Venice and Ravenna – of orgies, carousing and debauchery. Some of it was true, some was grossly exaggerated, but the tittle-tattle, added to poems that dated from this time, the last canto of *Childe Harold*, *Beppo* and *Don Juan* seemed to confirm the worst impressions back in London and Edinburgh. Byron, for his part, did not deny that he had wandered from the path of strict morality – but no more than most other people. Indeed, he had probably done English moralists a service by giving a warning for writers to pin on their walls, actors on their mirrors and schoolboys on their poetry books: 'beware of being Byroned'.[9]

'Don Juan was published yesterday,' John Murray wrote to Byron on 16 July 1819 from his retreat in Wimbledon, 'and having fired the bomb – here I am out of the way of the explosion.' Despite the boast to Byron, the publisher had sent forth the first two cantos with neither his name nor Byron's anywhere on it. However brave he pretended to be, Murray knew that his writer's favour with the British public, harmed by his private life, would never recover. The first two cantos were the best of Byron's work, and everyone knew it. But the frank language that described women as capable of the same kind of sexual demands and pleasures as men, the bawdy vocabulary and explicit humour were something new. Byron's female admirers, the mainstay of his public, deserted him in droves in the summer of 1819. A clergyman told Hannah More that he had bought Byron's complete poems, but had burnt the volume containing *Don Juan*. More was shocked; no one should read Byron at all once he had stepped beyond the pale. Many agreed with her that even the innocent poems were now untouchable. Murray wished that he could have cut out some twenty or so stanzas; then his work might have been allowed to sit on ladies' worktables without the reader being accused of being a sexual libertine.[10]

Byron would never censor his own work; *Don Juan* was an attack on the hypocrisy, squeamishness and double standards of his country, and he would not compromise with the prudish. 'You seem in fright, and doubtless with cause,' he wrote to Murray. 'Come what may, I never will flatter the million's canting in any shape: circumstances may or may not have placed me at times in a situation to lead the public opinion, but the public opinion never led, nor ever shall lead, me.'[11]

He could hardly have been surprised by the uproar and the sudden loss of popularity but, as he admitted in October 1819, 'the outcry has frightened me'. It was brutal and rancorous; Byron could be forgiven for being alarmed at what was happening to his countrymen. The furore set friend against friend, writer against editor and parented a spew of articles, books and pamphlets. Most importantly, the treatment of the greatest of English poets, whom many were grateful they shared their time on earth with, exemplified – even created – the spirit of the age for his friends and enemies alike. 'He who balances the profit accruing from [Byron's] influence on our literature against the loss proceeding from its effects on our morals', commented a reviewer, 'will find it hard to determine whether Byron should have lived in another age, or not have lived at all.'[12]

An evangelical critic thought Byron a 'towering genius', and few would dissent. Therein lay his danger, especially to young misses in boarding schools and hot-blooded teenage boys. *Don Juan* undermined marriage because its hero had an affair with Donna Julia, the wife of his mother's lover, and offended Christian morality by turning the famous shipwreck scene into a comic incident. In later cantos, Juan has the pleasure of living in drag in a harem, attends a siege where elderly spinsters complain when they are not ravished by the marauding troops, is seduced by Catherine the Great and is spared having an affair with an English noblewoman in a stately home only because the poem was left incomplete on Byron's death. Byron was never gross in his writing like Fielding or Swift. Yet this was even worse than out-and-out licentiousness: Byron was 'strewing flowers over the *boundary* which separates virtue from vice, so that the mind wanders over it unconsciously'.[13]

Another critic, the Rev. William Bengo Collyer, believed Byron to be 'a libertine of the most dangerous description' because he deliberately lured young people with the greatness of his poetry, and then gradually and artfully sapped their morals with irresistible humour, before blasting their ethical sense to atoms. He set up serious and affecting moral topics, only to make them absurd. The shipwreck in *Don Juan*, where the sailors turn to cannibalism, was a theme from Christian literature (Collyer was thinking of the grandeur of Dante and the Biblical rendition of Noah's Ark) which Byron mocked with double rhymes, sneers and ludicrous language.

> They grieved for those who perished in the cutter,
> And also for the biscuit, casks, and butter.

It was 'revolting to humanity', according to Collyer, and 'disgusting merriment' and 'odious sarcasm' in the view of a vindictive review in *Blackwood's* by John Wilson.[14]

Wilson believed Byron's new cantos to be 'the very suicide of genius' and the 'demon of his depravity'. The publication of *Don Juan* in 1819 was considered to be many times more shocking and worthy of castigation than his crimes three years earlier. When he abandoned his marriage, he hurt only his wife and daughter and his closest intimates; with *Don Juan* he offended the sensibilities of the English-speaking world and commenced a siege on the morals of a generation. No one denied that it was a poem of the highest order; Sir Egerton Brydges said that Byron's poetic qualities 'raise our involuntary admiration'. But it was genius hired by Satan and talent perverted for the purpose of systematic moral vitiation. Many journals and papers refused to review *Don Juan* because they knew the difficulty of reconciling a brilliant poem with its immoral intent; Byron was luring them into a mess of contradictions, with praise and blame uneasily jostling together. He would have the dubious honour of 'remaining to all ages a perpetual monument of the exalted intellect, and the depraved heart, of one of the most remarkable men to whom [Britain] has had the honour and the disgrace of giving birth'.[15]

It was not personal animosity towards Byron or dislike of his poetry that sparked this extraordinary language. He was feared because people knew he wielded a terrifying weapon. A great living poet, Francis Jeffrey wrote in the *Edinburgh Review*, was not like a distant volcano or an occasional tempest but 'a volcano in the heart of our land, and a cloud that hangs over our dwellings'. Poetry had the power to awaken and animate the passions like nothing else in art; a painter could depict a tiger, but only a great poet had the power to imbue a man with the features of a ferocious tiger while making him 'interesting and attractive'. Poetry was explosive and awesome in its hold over the passions: 'it is the object of poetry to make us feel for distant and imaginary occurrences nearly as strongly as if they were present and real'.[16]

Jeffrey wrote that as society became more refined, it subdued and buried the tumultuous passions that had been indispensable in ruder ages. Back then, capacious appetites for food, drink and carnality, a veneration for honour, liberty and family pride and a contempt for danger made for hardy peoples who could defend their homes and kin, compete for food and conquer the harsh elements. Close to nature, our ancestors were controlled by their feelings and instincts. The civilising process took mankind away from this natural state, substituting reason for brute instinct. Repressing desires and instincts was not without its disadvantages, not least the restlessness and ennui it brought, the hankering for great and glorious events and heroic deeds. Religious and political fanaticism became substitutes for this. But poetry had the greatest power to reawaken the latent passions. Modern poets satisfied the craving for excitement and strong feelings by drawing on the age of heroism: Scott wrote of chivalry and Southey of American Indians and East Indian deities. There was little in the modern world that could inspire epic poetry. Byron, Jeffrey wrote, was 'haunted almost perpetually with the image of a being feeding and being fed upon the violent passions, and the recollections of the catastrophes they have occasioned'. It was dangerous because the poets combined modern knowledge, art and science with the powerful emotions that had been repressed. It was a heady cocktail that would disorder the controlled and regulated modern mind. When Byron experimented with the deepest human passions, it was not merely an error in taste but 'perversions of morality'.[17]

Byron was not on the margins or a lonely, forgettable exile but central to national life; he had forced his way into the minds of a generation. Therefore, he was not to be judged like mere men. Bequeathed genius by divinity and possessed of a voice that could never be silenced, the poet had a higher responsibility. Like it or not, he was 'necessarily a Moral Teacher' who could broadcast his lesson a thousand times more effectively than any other authority. Consequently, Byron was 'peculiarly liable to the censures reserved for those who turn the means of improvement to purposes of corruption'. In other words, the public had an ownership over poets and the right to insist that they tailor their work to the prevailing national taste. Brydges wrote that Byron arrogantly believed that he had a 'dominion' over the public mind; but the only way he could demonstrate the fullness of that power was by using his poetry 'to trample down morality'.[18]

With this view of poetry as central to human experience, it was little wonder that Jeffrey could talk of Byron's 'demonical sublimity, not without some traits of the ruined Archangel'. There were some who believed that he was in some sort of alliance with the Beast; when they encountered him in Rome, Lady Liddell told her daughter: 'Don't look at him, he is dangerous to look at.' Southey, not to be outdone, said that Byron was leader of 'the Satanic School' of poetry, a group who 'breath the spirit of Belial in their lascivious parts and the spirit of Moloch in those loathsome images of atrocities and horrors'. *Blackwood's* went further, accusing Byron of making a Faustian pact to wreak havoc on the world – charging him, in short, with being beyond the pale of humanity:

> It appears . . . as if this miserable man, having exhausted every species of sensual gratification – having drained the cup of sin even to its bitterest dregs, were resolved to shew us that he is no longer a human being, even in his frailties; – but a cool, unconcerned fiend, laughing with a detestable glee over the whole of the better and worse elements of which human life is composed – treating with nigh well equal derision the most pure of virtues, and the most odious of vices – dead alike to the beauty of the one and the deformity of the other – a mere heartless despiser of that frail but noble humanity, whose type was never exhibited in a shape of more deplorable degradation than in his own contemptuously distinct delineation of himself.[19]

'So now all things are damned, one feels at ease,' Byron wrote in the sixth stanza.

One critic might have affirmed that *Don Juan* 'is a sealed book to the ladies of our time', but it wasn't entirely true. 'No work of modern days has been so cried out against as immoral and indecent as *Don Juan*,' the *Examiner* commented in 1822; 'and you see the consequence: – the critics, one and all, shake their heads at it; grave old gentlemen turn up their eyes and sigh in lamentation over the depravity of the age; all ladies of character *blush* at its very mention; no writer has yet been found hardy enough to *hint* a word in defence or palliation, – yet, nonsense to relate, every body reads it!'[20]

From John Murray – the pious publisher who would not put his name to the obscene, blasphemous, seditious work – to the thousands who bought it while deploring the diabolism of the poet, the same hypocrisy was at work. They felt, as Brydges said in his criticism of Byron's poetry, that however good the writing was, the 'licentious' verses 'renders it dangerous to praise it very much'. Or they accepted Southey's contention that anyone who bought or took a copy into their homes 'becomes an aider and abettor of the crime'. It was safer to join the voices of indignation but enjoy the volumes in the seclusion of the study. Some wished that extracts made up of the less immoral verses would be published to make it suitable family reading, or at least safe enough to allow a volume to be left out without the fear that a wife or daughter might flick through it. As Byron admitted in the fourth canto:

> Through needles' eyes it easier for the camel is
> To pass than those two cantos into families.

Prince Pückler-Muskau despised the English for their need to disavow their greatest poet in public: 'Many of them cross themselves (inwardly) when they mention him; and even the women, though their cheeks glow with enthusiasm when they read him, in public take part vehemently against their secret favourite.'[21]

The implication in all the moral objections to *Don Juan* was always that it was fine for reviewers and critics and educated men to read the cantos, for they could study them without being enflamed, but it was highly dangerous to allow the poem to get into the wrong hands. Even John Gibson Lockhart, a regular contributor to *Blackwood's* and one of Byron's few defenders in that journal, wrote that the poet had 'acted most unwisely and imprudently' by offending 'the feelings of his age'; in doing so he had estranged himself from the sensibilities of his contemporaries and was 'no longer a popular author'. The publishers who pirated the work and John Hunt, who took over publication after Murray ceased to publish Byron, might have disagreed, but few would *admit* to being one of the myriad readers. Byron was, after all, in Southey's words, 'pander-general to the youth of Great Britain'.[22]

It might have surprised those who swallowed all this press indignation that the son of Belial said that he had 'done more real good in any one given year, since [he] was twenty, than Mr Southey in the whole course of his shifting and turncoat existence'. Byron could no doubt point to individual acts of goodness, but the point was that *Don Juan* served a moral purpose. The primary charge against *Childe Harold* and *Don Juan* was that miscreants were spared punishment for their sins and were instead glamorised. As Francis Jeffrey said, most poets had created peccable heroes, but they served as vehicles to show the inevitable consequences of vice; few poets had sided so unequivocally with their flawed heroes, or sought to exculpate them as Byron had. Brydges stated the rule that 'the consequences of . . . ill qualities or ill deeds must be unhappiness'. Alexander Pope wrote:

> Vice is a monster of so frightful mien,
> As to be hated need but to be seen.

Poetry should reveal that great truth. But as Byron and his supporters pointed out, it wasn't true. Vice was actually quite pleasant on first taste. 'There are a set of prudish and very suspicious moralists who endeavour to make vice appear to inexperienced eyes much more hurtful than it really is,' the *Examiner* said. 'They would correct Nature – and they always overreach themselves.' They were crying wolf, and it was dangerous because young people would be brought up to expect vice to appear in its monstrous garb. The damage would be done when they found that vice appeared attractive and alluring and they leapt at temptation, blind to the consequences. Byron told the truth in his poems, making accurate points about human motives and passions; he did not turn his cantos into moral lectures by introducing contrived punishments for his characters, just in case young men wanted to emulate his hero. Writing that did not include wickedness, depravity and the seamy side of human nature was immoral because it distorted reality, teaching youth a fallacious lesson about the world they would enter. The same was true of Byron's verse play *Cain*, which added blasphemy and atheism to the list of crimes being drawn up by his enemies. He was accused of glorifying Satan, just as he had celebrated adultery in *Don Juan*. But as Byron said, in riposte to his pious censors: 'I could not have made Lucifer expound the Thirty-nine Articles, nor talk as divines do: they would never have suited his purpose – no, nor one would think theirs. They ought to be grateful to him for giving them a subject to write about. What would they do without evil in the Prince of Evil?'[23]

How could a poet paint a true picture of human experience without experiencing all kinds of life? Could one moralise without becoming a hypocrite? 'People may suppose, that I respect not morals, because unfortunately I have sometimes violated them,' Byron railed to Lady Blessington; 'perhaps from this very circumstance I respect them the more, as we never value riches until our prodigality has made us feel their loss; and a lesson of prudence coming from him who had squandered thousands, would have more weight than whole pages written by one who had not personal experience: so I maintain that persons who have *erred* are most competent to point out errors. It is my respect for morals that makes me so indignant against its vile substitute *cant*, with which I wage war, and this good-natured world chooses to consider as a sign of my wickedness.' Or, as he put it less decorously to Douglas Kinnaird: 'As to "Don Juan", confess, confess – you dog and be candid – that it is the sublime of *that there* sort of writing – it may be bawdy but is it not good English? It may be profligate but is it not *life*, is it not *the thing*? Could any man have written it who has not lived in the world? – and tooled in a post-chaise? – in a hackney coach? – in a gondola? – against a wall? – in a court carriage? – in a vis à vis? – on a table? – and under it?'[24]

What offended Byron and his supporters was that most of the outraged moralists had done some or all these things, yet put on the censorious mask to tick the poet off. Most would be lucky enough not to have their juvenile adventures and adult indiscretions raked over in public. An exception was one of Byron's severest critics and an advocate of militant censorship by the Society for the Suppression of Vice, a well-known evangelical and chaplain of the Guardian Society, the Rev. William Bengo Collyer. In 1823 his sex life became a matter of controversy. Collyer worked as a philanthropic doctor to the poor in south London and liked conducting his examination of naked male patients in the Addington Street bathhouse. Two workmen complained that the reverend doctor had committed sexual assaults during one of these consultations. Collyer was defended in some sections of the press and sheltered by 'a phalanx of ladies' as the evangelical community closed ranks, but mercilessly pursued by *The Lancet*.[25]

It was a tawdry case, and the truth was never discovered in the poisoned atmosphere of homophobia on one side and blatant perjury on the other. It was a sorry reminder, if one were needed, that those who complained the loudest about the sordid intention of *Don Juan* enjoyed their own illicit and exotic sex lives free, in most cases, from observation. Shouting and making a fuss about *Don Juan* did not automatically make Britain a more moral place or the 1820s a saintly decade. The same vices and passions existed as they always had, lurking below the surface, and they could not be excused by making Byron a sacrificial victim to atone for the sins of the age. The scandal demonstrated the hypocrisy that informed the entire debate.

Byron's offence was against the niceties and manners of the age, not nature or morality. *Don Juan* was an attack on the prevailing hypocrisy and self-interest of the time; an attack on cant. Don Juan has an affair with Julia, who has been forced into a marriage with an older man. Whose fault is it if she falls in love with a younger man? The immoral act was society's tolerance of mismatches and marriage for money and rank; the act of adultery was natural in comparison and Byron's justifications at least understandable. Besides, Julia is punished by being sent to a convent; Don Juan is separated from her and almost dies in a horrific shipwreck; Haidée (Juan's second love), when she sees her lover wounded and sold into slavery, goes mad. Some reward for vice! What severe penalties did critics want before they ceased accusing Byron of glorifying depravity? At least Juan, Julia and the other characters had experienced life and made their own mistakes. The poet was not the Professor of Moral Philosophy, and he should not be regarded as such, alone among writers in the history of literature.

His critics seemed to scour his work for double meanings and reacted to his jokes as if they were in a sermon, not a humorous poem. Some said that the literati had not been hard enough on Byron; their timorous criticisms had somehow given the impression that the poem was desirable reading. Yet it is hard to see how much harsher they could have been. As it was, the pitch of the reviews and personal attacks were such that *Don Juan* took on an unwarranted notoriety. If someone wanted a dirty poem or craved a thrill, they would be persuaded that Byron's work was the worst that had ever been published. Thanks to the moral majority, *Don Juan* earned a kind of vulgar repute that increased its sales beyond all predictions, and it took on a much worse aspect than it ever had in reality. The 'filth' existed more in the minds of critics than it did in the poem itself.[26]

'Where is this wretched cant to end?' asked the *Examiner*. 'What are we to gain by this affectation as to *names*, while the *things* thrive among us more than ever?'[27] The extraordinary response to *Don Juan* was a telling and uncomfortable insight into modern society. Few other issues stirred up similar passions. Byron wrote in the fourth canto, published in 1821:

> I once had great alacrity in wielding
> My pen and liked poetic war to wage
> And recollect the time when all this cant
> Would have provoked remarks, which now it shan't.

No discussion of the poet was complete, it seemed, without the word 'cant', since Byron used it in the work itself (from the first stanza of the first canto) and in his discussion of William Bowles's prurient deliberations over the extent of Alexander Pope's sex life. There was little doubt that the attacks were motivated by personal spite, deliberate misreading of the poem, insincerity and feigned shows of morality; it was no wonder that 'cant' was applied to Byron's enemies. In 1822 the *Examiner* followed Byron's general line and said that self-appointed censors of his works 'pander to [the] degrading appetite by pointing out all the sources of depraved gratification' – few critics forbore from quoting the passages they adjudged atrocious and disgusting, and quoted them out of context, making them *seem* worse than they were. The paper, paraphrasing Byron, deplored the 'verbal decorum' that 'the puritans and the hypocrites' were trying to impose on society. Byron was their scapegoat, whom they lacerated while ignoring worse examples from literature. Whenever their arguments were countered by those who held up the likes of Chaucer, Shakespeare, Ariosto, Milton, the Restoration writers, Pope, Swift, Fielding, Smollett and Sterne, the critics countered by saying that none of these writers had the education that His Lordship had received, nor did they live in the moral, refined and *polite* nineteenth century. They had an excuse, while Byron was deliberately and wickedly combining the rudeness of more barbarous ages with the sublime poetry of the modern age.[28]

In any case, Thomas Bowdler had already made a start at pruning the indelicacies of the past with his *Family Shakespeare*, which censored the bard's unnecessarily bawdy passages. (There were those who argued that a genius of Shakespeare's calibre could not have written such licentiousness; that that which sullied his page had been inserted by unscrupulous theatre managers and actors playing for laughs.) Francis Jeffrey was glad that the 'cankers' and 'weeds' that grew among the flowers of Shakespeare had been uprooted – *bowdlerised* – because of the 'extreme awkwardness, and even distress' that prevented a father reading the plays to his children or a gentleman to his lady; such things 'cannot be spoken, and ought not to have been written'. This prudishness was ripe for humorous denunciation; the *London Weekly Review* joked that Bowdler was embarking on his next task: rendering the Bible fit for dainty ladies and respectable families to read at last. Nonetheless, such views were becoming ever more acceptable. In 1822 John Rogers Pitman, the Duchess of Kent's chaplain, bowdlerised Bowdler's *Family Shakespeare*, which he considered insufficiently pure. 'The rising generation must be rigidly guarded from the knowledge of profligacy or impurity,' commented the *Examiner* in a mordant mood. '. . .What a delectable state of things – what a Puritanical paradise!'[29]

A society that was becoming increasingly frightened of talking about sex was in trouble. It was not that people talked about the facts of life at home, but literature and popular culture provided early lessons. Boys read *Aristotle's Compleat Master Piece* and other titillating or bawdy street literature, as Francis Place and many other middling-class boys had done; young gentlemen at public schools had their fill of Ovid and Catullus. But if 'adult' topics were to be judged by the effect they might have on adolescents, then a blanket must necessarily be thrown over most of literature, art and drama. Place's favourite sex guide was removed from the shelves, and public schools confined themselves to expurgated Latin texts. This brought a host of new problems for an increasingly intolerant society. As a child, poor young Juan is forbidden to read anything that might inflame him:

> . . . not a hint of any thing that's loose
> Or hints continuation of the species
> Was ever suffered, lest he should grow vicious.

And so began his problems. When puberty and nature asserted themselves and he and Julia fell in love, he was 'Tormented with a wound he could not know'; he slips into his first crime because his schoolboy reading was bowdlerised.

What was happening to Britain? The public seemed to be becoming dangerously capricious in its moral judgements; the great of one day could become the pariahs of the next. Byron was hauled over the coals, but he was strong enough to survive the ordeal and, in any case, he was living in a less demanding society. Neither William Hazlitt nor Walter Scott relished the hue and cry, but they said that Byron only wrote as he did because, as a lord living in exile, he lived under few of the restraints of ordinary mortals. No one else was as free to break rules. Scott believed that Byron despised hypocrisy so much that he felt he had to continually push and test the boundaries of taste to distance himself from the prudish: 'being of no party/ I shall offend all parties'. No doubt that was true, but Byron was one of many who were hounded by the moralising mob. He was not alone among the talented as someone whose deviation from strict moral propriety rendered his genius something rank. The greatest actor of the time was all but destroyed by mobs armed with a sense of moral righteousness in England, Scotland, Ireland and the United States.[30]

Edmund Kean's Shylock in 1814 was a sensation. It marked the sudden arrival of an hitherto unknown and struggling actor. Thomas Barnes, as theatre critic of the *Examiner*, wrote that Kean's performance was 'the union of great powers with a fine sensibility': 'It was this that gave fire to his eye, energy to his tones, and such a variety and expressiveness to all his gestures, that one might almost say "his body thought".' The critics and public who saw his first run as Shakespeare's villains were certain that they had witnessed the beginning of a revolution in acting and, almost as certainly, the greatest actor in the history of the stage; Coleridge said that witnessing Kean's acting was 'like reading Shakespeare by flashes of lightening'. He rejected the formal and static declamations of classical acting, and brought naturalness and emotional intensity to the plays; 'Mr Kean's appearance was the first gleam of genius breaking athwart the gloom of the stage,' in the opinion of Hazlitt. Barnes, who sat spellbound through Kean's first season, declared that the acting was too good for the public.

'That obscene little personage' was how *The Times* referred to Kean in January 1825; it advised the 'respectable' part of the public to drive him from the stage, howsoever sublime his acting might be. The editor of the paper, Thomas Barnes, began an unprecedented campaign of vilification against his one-time hero and incited audiences throughout the country to punish a man who dared stand before the people despite being a known adulterer. After eleven years watching Kean's magnificent performances Barnes's period of rapture was over when he found out that the star slept with women to whom he wasn't married.[31]

Edmund Kean as Sir Giles Overreach in *A New Way to Pay Old Debts* by Philip Massinger, 1820. The emotional intensity of Kean's acting mesmerised and alarmed audiences, a quality this portrait captures. George Henry Lewes wrote of Kean: 'his instinct taught him what few actors are taught – that a stirring emotion, after discharging itself in one massive current, continues for a time expressing itself in feebler currents. The waves are not stilled when the storm has passed. There remains the ground-swell troubling the deeps. Watching Kean's quivering muscles and altered tones you felt the subsidence of passion. The voice might be calm, but there was a tremor in it; the face might be quiet, but there were vanishing traces of the recent agitation'

After his first triumph and the adulation of the press and the public, Edmund Kean knew he was the best, and he liked it. He leapt to immortality literally overnight, and he made the most of his fame and wealth. He wore flamboyant clothes and kept a pet lion on a leash; the animal would sit with its master as they glided on a boat down the Thames in full view of the star-struck British public. Unlike John Kemble, who was a bourgeois businessman and respectable patriarch of the theatre, superstardom did not make Kean eager to be accepted by polite society. On the contrary, it brought out the spoilt child and untameable rebel in him; elevated to the height of the profession, he refused to accept other people's standards of decency.

Even in the good days, Kean thrived on feeling rejected, flaunting the fact that his mother, Nance, had been a prostitute and strolling player. At other times he made out that he was the illegitimate son of the Duke of Norfolk (his guardian, Charlotte Tidswell, had been the

Duke's mistress at one time); it was another way of affirming that he was born beyond the pale of respectable society, an outsider from conception. He cultivated an image of the outcast genius in a very public private life that consisted of carousing with pugilists and other low cronies, hard-drinking binges, brawls and orgies with prostitutes. His club, The Wolves, was notorious. In the interval of a play, and sometimes between scenes, he would have sex with a prostitute, sometimes two or three.

His looks and his acting faded from as early as 1817 as a result of these antics, and his popularity was on the wane. Given his reputation, few could have been surprised when in 1824 he was named in a crim. con. case as the lover of Charlotte Cox, the wife of Alderman Robert Albion Cox, a member of the Drury Lane Theatre General Committee. Mrs Cox was older than Kean, a compulsive theatregoer and sexually predatory; Kean fell in love. To her irritation, the playboy actor – the rebellious and devil-may-care Edmund Kean – refused to acknowledge their love; rather, he was nervy, indecisive and too scared to risk whatever was left of his reputation. After a farcical relationship lasting a few years, Charlotte Cox got her revenge on both the men in her life by eloping with her husband's clerk, leaving behind Kean's saccharine love letters, which also contained some rather embarrassing details of their love-making. Alderman Cox, short of money and minus a wife, decided to sue Kean for damages, even though he had known about the affair for some time.

The case did not bother Kean, and he relished his new role as a love rat. The press feigned shock at some of the details contained in the love letters, which were read to the court; here was another instance of a public man parading his sordid life to the world, even if Kean had not chosen to have his embarrassing letters read out. As the trial reached its inevitable conclusion on 17 January 1825, he signed a contract to reprise his tragic roles in a season at Drury Lane for £50 a night, making him the highest-paid actor in the history of the stage.

A libertine actor was hardly new, but *The Times* was outraged; it accused the theatre of giving an adulterer publicity. The thought of an audience *applauding* a sexual deviant was too much for that moral paper: 'It is of little consequence whether the character of *King Richard* or *Othello* be well or ill acted; but it is of importance that public feeling be not shocked, and public decency be not outraged.' As with Byron, the moral feelings of the public far outweighed any claims to genius. Better that men or women of supreme talent be suppressed or ignored than they offend the righteous.[32]

For days, *The Times* kept up a barrage of personal insults interlarded with heavy pronouncements on morality. Barnes ensured that the appearance of Kean on stage would be some sort of test of morality. It threatened to be like the O.P. War of 1809 all over again, except this time it would be fought on entirely different grounds. As the first night of the season approached, the Home Secretary, Robert Peel, sent the head magistrate of Bow Street, Sir Richard Birnie, to Robert William Elliston (the impresario known as the Napoleon of the Stage after he bought the lease of the Drury Lane Theatre) to suggest that the season be postponed until enough time elapsed to dissipate the threat of disorder. Elliston found Kean at a tavern in Croydon, where he had taken up temporary residence to prepare himself for the season. The manager offered the actor a postponement of the season so that he could collect himself after the humiliating trial and perfect his lines. Kean heard him out, sitting with a glass of brandy in his hand while a tumbler vaulted over the furniture and a prostitute sang. He refused the gift of time. 'In the meantime, observe how quietly I am living here.'[33]

When it learnt that the season was going ahead, *The Times* fumed that it was 'nothing less than an indecent and scandalous exposure' of a disgraced man; Kean and Elliston would be quickly disabused if they thought that audiences would tolerate his appearance on the stage 'merely because he is a man of talent'. Some might say that delicate people could stay away if they could not bear to see an adulterer, but *The Times* reminded people that the theatre was a monopoly and was obliged 'to furnish means of entertainment suitable to the taste and habits of the moral and decent part of the community'. Publicans who encouraged 'disgusting nuisances' had their licence forfeited; the same should be true of the theatre. The upright Barnes had to balance his admiration for the greatest modern actor with his love of morals, and he said that 'we would rather lose his talents than forfeit our respect for these decencies which ornament, ay, dignify life'. It was one thing, it seemed, to appear every day as a leader of public opinion as editor of *The Times*, and another to act upon a stage. Actors and journalists were no strangers to adultery. Thomas Barnes, the very moral lover of the theatre who deprived himself of the talents of one of the greatest men of his generation because he could not bear to see a philanderer on stage, lived with another man's wife.[34]

Barnes's behaviour was distressing to those who admired his brilliant career. He had effortlessly achieved a first-class degree at Pembroke Hall, Cambridge, in 1808 despite a life of dissipation and idleness, a skill he imported to London, where he speedily conquered the heights of journalism and gained a reputation as a 'complete voluptuary'. Between 1811 and 1817 he won a name as a star journalist on the *Examiner*, *Champion*, *Reflector* and *The Times*. The springtime of his career coincided with the arrival of Edmund Kean, and they had much in common: they both possessed easy talent, and they both had capacious appetites for the pleasures of life, licit and illicit, and had quickly squandered their youthful good looks as a result.

Barnes became editor of *The Times* in 1817, when Kean was at the apogee of his fame. Thomas Barnes was irrefutably the greatest newspaper editor of the age; he transformed *The Times*, making it the acknowledged voice of public opinion, a proudly independent paper and a power in the state: 'Why, Barnes is the most powerful man in the country,' said Wellington. He was liberal in politics, a champion of the poor and oppressed, a hater of bigotry and cant; he himself was a bohemian and bon viveur who cared little for the fussy rules of society. He never married but lived with Mrs Dinah Mary Mondet, who was tactfully referred to as 'Mrs Barnes' in polite society. Given his love of great acting, his generous mind and unconventional lifestyle, it is hard to understand his decision to persecute Kean. One explanation was that he was making *The Times* the organ of 'moral and decent' middle-class opinion, which shone out in contrast to murky upper-class venality and vice. It seems that Barnes was articulating, or thought that he was, the moral sense of his readers. Whatever motivated him, it was obvious that he was depriving the actor of the forgiveness that generous people granted 'Mr and Mrs Barnes'.

The hypocrisy of Barnes and the provocative words of his paper ensured that the opening play of the season – *Richard III* – was an event. Some of the audience came to see a play, but the majority in the pit had come for other reasons. A large proportion had come to protest against the deplorable cant of the paper, and as many at least to hiss an adulterer from the stage. There was as much chance of hearing the play as there had been in 1809 at the Covent Garden Theatre. As with the furore over Byron, Kean symbolised, according to taste, either opposition to puritanical cant or an unacceptable representative of degeneracy. On Kean's side, if *The Times* is to be believed, were caddies, pugilists and prostitutes, and when their hero made his appearance as Richard III, 'a more disgusting scene never met the eye of moralist or libertine'.[35]

Barnes accused Kean of mobilising the Wolves Club. Throughout the season, these people kept up a barrage of shouting and singing. On 29 January a fat prostitute called attention to herself by shouting 'Bravo' and applauding her idol all night without cease. It was clear that many of the caddies and boxers were in a theatre for the first time and were not bothered by what was happening, or was supposed to be happening, on the stage. Just what kinds of people supported the moral crusade, *The Times* did not report. Yet it was clear that this re-emergence of sustained warfare in the theatre was entirely due to that newspaper, which had first made Kean's acting an issue of public decency and then *invited* Londoners to express their opinions. The result was conflict.

Night after night people on the pro and anti sides obeyed *The Times*' call to tell the world what they thought of Kean. Some of the actor's supporters were less concerned with his personal fate and more worried about the deeper issues that this cause célèbre stood for. As in the O.P. War, there was a forest of banners in the pit:

> 'English liberty; and no cant.'
> 'No cant! – No hypocrisy! – Kean forever!'
> 'What Kean wrote, the newspapers published. Which is worse?'
> 'Let not animosity reign in the bosoms of Englishmen.'

The reference to hypocrisy, cant and the spirit of petty vindictiveness had clear references to the debate about Byron and *Don Juan*.[36]

On 28 January, after he had played Othello, Kean came onto the stage to confront his opponents and rally his supporters. 'Ladies and Gentlemen,' he said, '– If you expect from me a vindication of my own private conduct, I am certainly unable to satisfy you . . . I stand before you as the representative of Shakespeare's heroes . . . The errors I have committed have been heard before a public tribunal; and . . . [words drowned out by shouts of applause and disapprobation] . . . It appears at this moment that I am a *professional* victim [laughter]. If this is the work of a hostile press, I shall endeavour to withstand it; but if it proceeds from your verdict and decision, I will at once bow to it, and shall retire with deep regret, and with a grateful sense of all favours which your patronage has hitherto conferred on me.'[37]

He threw down the gauntlet to *The Times*, challenging the paper to allow the public to decide the matter. The conflict continued for another week, and then, on 5 February, Barnes gave up. It was clear that Kean's supporters were not just delinquents from the Wolves Club but ordinary people. The disturbances began to abate as soon as the venerable newspaper abandoned its tirades; Kean's supporters began to outnumber the moral crusaders, and by 17 February the Drury Lane Theatre was back to normal.

On 29 March the run came to its end with *Othello*. At the end of the play, Kean came back onto the stage to thank Londoners for 'the shield of liberality which is characteristic of the England nation'. 'To an England audience am I indebted for my first and only support,' Kean told his clamorous supporters; 'and by their protection have I been enabled to combat against one of the most malignant attacks that was ever made on any individual . . . Without adverting to past circumstances, I cannot but feel that a most powerful engine was placed for my destruction [loud cries from the audience of "*The Times*, *The Times*, ay, *The Times*"].' The London crowd would forgive Kean anything, but in truth he could hardly speak. He was worn out by the rancour of the preceding months, the rigours of acting all Shakespeare's tragedies and several farces and comedies during that time, not to mention the vast quantities he had drunk and the three prostitutes that he had enjoyed during that night's interval.[38]

But it was not over; it never would be. Kean embarked for a provincial tour which saw rioting in Edinburgh reminiscent of the opening night in London. Even in theatres where he was not booed or pelted, Kean found that the public was at best cool towards him. He got a better reception in Dublin and Liverpool, but it was clear that *The Times* had won; Kean would always be tainted. Some sections of the press were still after his blood as the tour continued. *Blackwood's* said he should be pelted with rotten fruit for the audacity of shocking paying audiences: 'The appearance of the little beast was a gross insult to human nature; and, since he persisted in going through his part, he should have been made to do so tarred and feathered.'[39]

It was almost as if Kean was corralling people into the theatre and *forcing* them to watch him against their will. That was certainly the attitude of the press. In Scotland, *Blackwood's* and the *Scotsman* did the work of the now muzzled *Times*; the latter said: 'We are enemies to every thing like prudery in morals. We disapprove of all inquisition after private vices . . . but Mr Kean's vices have been thrust upon the public.' He should retire from Scotland, because the 'moral public of Edinburgh' would make an effort 'for the sake of decency' to express their disapproval. As others pointed out, Kean's 'crimes' had been 'thrust upon the public' by the crim. con. case and the press. Many were named in crim. con. suits and were allowed to remain physicians or carpenters or politicians, say, or journalists; only Kean was asked to retire from public life in shame. Everyone should be treated the same, said others, whether it was the editor of *The Times* or a high-living thespian. As the actor told the audience in Manchester: 'if the press of this country was allowed to visit the public characters of professional men with the punishment due to their private ones, the arts and sciences would very soon sink into insignificance'.[40]

The tour must have convinced Edmund Kean that he was not wanted in Britain; no act of atonement would ever be enough. The victory in London was pyrrhic. The sheer effort of battling hostile audiences or trying to entertain prudish ones, not to mention the onslaught from the press, had taken its toll. Kean was exhausted and his spirit was entirely broken by the vilification and spite of the English, Scottish and Irish peoples. He resolved to tour America. The playwright Thomas Colley Grattan recalled his last meeting with Kean before exile: 'I never saw a man so changed; he had all the air of desperation about him. He looked bloated with rage and brandy; his nose was red, his cheeks blotched, his eyes bloodshot; I really pitied him . . . I could not repress a sentiment of sorrow at the wreck he presented of genius, fame and wealth. At this period I believe he had not one hundred pounds left of the many thousands he had received. His mind seemed shattered; he was an outcast on the world.'[41]

As he embarked at Liverpool, he said that he had been driven from England 'by the machinations of scoundrels, by a combination of ruffians who seem determined to destroy me'. He wrote ahead to New York, telling the press and the people that 'the spirit of ambition is extinct, and I merely ask a shelter in which to close my professional and mortal career'.[42]

But that combination existed on the other side of the Atlantic, even though the crim. con. trial had been held many months before and on another continent. Kean could not be accused of corrupting public morals in the United States, as *The Times* and others said was the case in England. It seemed fine at first. New York theatregoers gave him a tremendous reception, and 'not a murmur of disapprobation' was heard at a packed theatre in Albany. Kean was grateful if rather pathetic, saying that 'the American people have revived, resuscitated, and invigorated the spirit of a poor heart-broken man' and that 'the last palpitation of his heart would beat warmly for New York'. But it was a false dawn. Kean was pelted with apples and rotten eggs in Boston and forced to flee the stage. There was opposition elsewhere, including Philadelphia, and Kean had to admit defeat again in the face of moral indignation. He returned to England, where his last performances were horrible reminders of an extinct talent. He died despised and all but forgotten in 1832.[43]

Great men were raised into the icons of the age by awestruck critics and the fiat of public opinion. But what happened when those heroes let the public down? Byron's great crime, it was said, as far as his enemies were concerned, was that he lived in the same age as them. The past and posterity acquitted him of grossness: if he had been a historical figure, John Wilson, Robert Southey, Francis Jeffrey and all the offended clergymen would have ranked him with Shakespeare; people in the future could appreciate the poetry without having to fret about the example a *living* Byron was setting their children. His contemporaries felt they shared the stigma he had brought upon the early nineteenth century by squandering his vast genius on filth. Their time was supposed to be one of progress, material and moral. Byron, if he was an icon, stood out as a glaring exception that threatened to tarnish the age; he had to be punished for daring to be celebrated. While most writing would be forgotten, they knew that *Don Juan* would hold a permanent place in literary history and future generations would refer to it to understand their times. He should have conformed with the spirit of the age, as he joked to Lady Blessington: 'I shall end by making him [Don Juan] turn Methodist; this will please the English, and be an *amende honorable* for his sins and mine.'

The adulation and the persecution of Byron showed a nasty development in the national character. Hazlitt talked of 'the rage of virtue in the British public', and it always was a *rage*, rarely a friendly call for self-reform. John Gibson Lockhart pointed out the hypocrisy of the public. They had, in a way, created Byron the poet by craving his innermost thoughts and demanding that he dissect his heart for their gratification. Byron was first tempted, then tortured by the public. The moment he deviated from what they approved of, 'we turn around with all the bitterness of spleen, and reproach him with the unmanliness of entertaining the public with his feelings in regard to his separation from his wife. This was truly the conduct of a fair and liberal public!' In a similar way, the great passions, appetites and wildness of Kean, which made him a great actor, also rendered him unacceptable to the moral sensitivities of the public. Byron's career exemplified this; he brought into focus 'the crying sin of the age – *humbug*!'[44]

When Byron died in Greece in 1824, many, including his closest associates, did their best to efface the memory of the poet. There was to be no commemoration in Poets' Corner in Westminster Abbey until well into the twentieth century. The return of his body to London and the procession to Newstead was ignored by literary and fashionable society, but the remorseful crowd flocked to see the cortège. Shortly after, Lockhart wrote: 'A whole chorus resounds in your ears, that Byron was at all events, a perfect villain – the lewdest, the basest, the most unprincipled of men – and that, *ergo*, the subject ought to be dropped.' In some sections of society, his very name was taboo. In the press the vitriol flowed as before. At Albemarle Street, John Murray and an assemblage of Byron's friends burnt his private papers and biographical notes to suppress knowledge of Byron's homosexuality. Not knowing the content of the papers, one journalist ascribed the destruction to 'puritanical squeamishness' designed to spare the blushes of the living, not the reputation of Byron. Whatever the reason, it was counterproductive: 'It has surrendered his fame and that of many of his contemporaries, to his enemies . . . he himself, his nearest relations, and his most distant acquaintances, are now all and equally liable to any and every foul aspersion which calumny may now invent, and credulity swallow.' The controversy would rumble on, fuelled by new myths and familiar partisan rancour.[45]

If this was the price to pay for teasing the public by satirising their hypocrisy and toying with their squeamishness, many would 'beware of being Byroned' and exercise self-censorship. It cannot be said that Pierce Egan approached Byron or Kean in terms of talent and genius, but he did cater to a vast public. The course his career took shows how writers and artists had to tame their words and sentiments. His craven apology came from exactly this fear of offending tender sensibilities and being summoned to the dock of public opinion to stand accused of corrupting youth and encouraging vice. Unlike Byron and Kean,

Egan could not risk defying his public; he had to make a living, and became a trimmer to retain his popularity. When he tried to get Robert Elliston to put on a play he had written, he asked that his authorship be kept secret for the sake of the show. He knew that the public were prejudiced against him as the author of *Life in London*: 'I know that I have to move from my shoulders *almost a mountain*.' The punishment wrought on other, greater men as much as on errant Grub Street publishers in the 1820s must have convinced him that Tom and Jerry could no longer go on sprees and rambles; if they were to exist as fictional characters, they must be used to communicate a moral lesson. If Don Juan never caught up with the tenor of times by becoming a Methodist, Jerry at least transmogrified into a do-gooding prig and hypocrite to appease the public.[46]

The best-selling novel of 1825, the year after Byron's death, was *Tremaine, or the Man of Refinement* by Robert Ward. The eponymous hero was a Byronic figure in the early parts of the novel: restless, misanthropic, cynical and frustrated; a heavy drinker and a rake. Tremaine is Lord Byron: 'his manners, figure, and features, – in all which there was a certain loftiness; his very *finery* . . . had made him a person of no small consideration among the ladies'. He is a heartbreaker (although there is no overt mention of licentiousness). Satiated with metropolitan pleasures (he has 'a splenetic mind in a body sick with refinement'), disgusted by the hypocrisy of the upper-class marriage market and heavy with ennui, he retires to a country estate.

So far, so Byronic. But unlike Byron in exile, Tremaine begins a long conversion to the moral life and discovers the virtues of *worthiness*. The editor of the novel said primly that it was 'a treatise on moral philosophy, not a novel'. A reviewer called it 'half novel and half sermon'. And that was the key to its popularity: it tried to be *Childe Harold* or *Don Juan*, but the naughtiness was replaced with long moral lectures and, at the end, the conversion many might have wished for Juan, or Byron himself, occurs. The reader got the enjoyment of reading about high society without the immorality. *Blackwood's* commended it as an 'ultra-popular' novel that owed its success to its 'admirable moral tendency throughout'. *Tremaine*, commented the *New Monthly*, was 'neither more nor less than a portion of human life in the nineteenth century – with nothing exaggerated, either in the events or the mode of relating them – nothing extraordinary in the characters introduced

– nothing overstrained in the sentiments expressed'. It did not make readers uneasy or their daughters excited with the heady ride of romantic passions and outrageous sentiments. It was safe. Most importantly, it was improving.[47]

With the advent of popular novels like *Tremaine*, Pierce Egan might well have given up. But Egan had to feed his large family. Jerry without Tom was a fit figure for the later 1820s: pious, conspicuously moral and intolerant of urban vice. There was an unattractive strain of hypocrisy and prurience evident in the country. In *Tremaine* Ward was prone to overreacting to petty deviations from propriety: he 'throws off his points of virtue by prancing, and snorting, and kicking, and plunging away, in a manner by no means seemly'.[48] The public was similarly inclined. Whatever Thomas Barnes really thought about Kean, he felt that he was doing his duty as spokesman for the middle classes by responding to new expectations of morality. He was probably right that some parts of the public felt like this, but his ill-conceived little campaign only went to show how two-faced, spiteful and intolerant public opinion could be when its capricious sense of morality was roused.

It did not bode well for a society when it launched witch-hunts against famous transgressors. Goethe was amazed that the English should treat a great poet in this way, and believed that their petty complaints would fade as they came to understand his genius. Prince Pückler-Muskau could not help laughing at the English and their 'pitiful cockney judgements' which meant they could not reconcile themselves to the poet 'because he ridiculed their pedantry, because he could not adapt himself to the manners and usages of their little nook nor share in their cold superstition; because their insipidity was sickening to him, and because he denounced their arrogance and hypocrisy'.[49]

Many in England felt that debates about Byron or Kean exposed an embarrassing and nasty national characteristic. 'I am always lenient to crimes that have brought their own punishment,' said Byron, 'while I am a little disposed to pity those who think they atone for their own sins by exposing those of others, and add cant and hypocrisy to the catalogue of their vices.'[50]

12

Progress

'Were we required to characterise this age of ours by any single epithet, we should be tempted to call it, not an Heroical, Devotional, Philosophical, or Moral Age, but, above all others, the Mechanical Age.'

Thomas Carlyle[1]

'Respectable means rich, and decent means poor. I should die if I heard my family called decent.'

Lady Clarinda, in *Crotchet Castle* by Thomas Love Peacock

In 1821 *The Times* carried an advertisement under the following slogan:

This is the age of cant

The advertisement was for the New Wine Company, and it quoted Byron because its directors wished to answer their rivals, who said they were 'imposing' upon the public. Other wine merchants said that the company's wine was so cheap because it was adulterated. The gentlemen proprietors of the New Wine Company were 'so impressed with benevolent designs – so alive to the public interest – so anxious to protect the public health, the public morals and the public purse, that they erect themselves into a Society for the Suppression of Adulteration'; they were motivated by 'the most "unadulterated" philanthropy' and 'the highest tone of moral sensibility'. They felt they had to defend themselves because 'Canting has descended from "the cant moral, cant religious, cant political [*sic*]", denounced by the poet to even the ordinary trading occupations of society'.[2]

It was a somewhat ingenious use of 'the age of cant' and the jargon of moral reform, adopted specifically to denounce the imputations of rival wine importers. In a culture supposedly poisoned with cant and hypocrisy, it was only natural to expect the same spirit to infect the world of business. The merchants satirised the preoccupations and set phrases and jargon of the day – benevolence, philanthropy, fear of imposition and concern over adulterated alcohol – to publicise their imported colonial wine and fledgling company. By parodying the language and high-mindedness of the Society for the Suppression of Vice, they poked fun at the way in which people seemed to have to bend over backwards in order to stress their moral probity and pure intentions for even the most mundane transaction. There was a ring of truth in the advertisement in an age when men who had become incredibly wealthy as gin-dealers and brewers stressed their abhorrence of spirituous liquor and excessive consumption of beer and signed up to the temperance movement. They wept crocodile tears over the fate of their benighted customers and talked the talk of philanthropy; it was the cant of businessmen ashamed, if not of their success, then of the stigma it brought.

The language used in the advertisement resonated with the generation of Britons who were in their thirties and forties. These people had lived with intermittent threats of bloody revolution and foreign invasion; war, severe economic depressions, food scarcity and riot had dominated their adolescence and adulthood. They grew up when Malthus's books alarmed the world and when unemployment, hunger and crime seemed to eerily prefigure the prophesied crisis. And even this generation was relatively aged: by the mid-1820s 60 per cent of the population had been born no earlier than 1801. A majority of the country had known nothing but war and its miserable aftermath. Their times were dogged by anxiety and moral panic emanating from Parliament, the press and the pulpit. Much more than their parents, they were receptive to new philosophical and economic ideas and to religious revivalism. Their lifetime had been dominated by urgent calls for moral reform. Every literate person was aware of the evidence presented by people like Colquhoun that immorality had seeped into the soul of modern man. Embrace it or reject it, the moralistic language of the advertisement was familiar to readers of *The Times*, who had read the real thing all their lives.

'In no period of our domestic history has so universal a change in the manners and habits of the people generally, taken place, as with the last half century,' Henry Angelo wrote in 1828, comparing the convivial riot at places like Jacob's Well in the eighteenth century with modern recreations; '. . . we may be said to be no longer the same people. Whether the aggregate of moral feeling may be greater or less at the present epoch, is a question which I leave for the moral philosopher to decide; but, doubtless, the manners of the middle class, in their evening amusements at least, are marked by a mighty change, in favour of general decorum.'[3]

The makers of manners were this sizeable young generation. Looking back at his upbringing, Francis Place was less shocked at the depravity of the generation above him than amazed at the progress made by his contemporaries. He and his friends looked back with horror at 'the conduct of those then barbarous people', his parents and their friends who were dirty, drunk, rude and ignorant; by contrast their own children were 'well informed, honest, candid and industrious'. In the course of his adult life, Place noted that people of all classes below the very rich had fought and struggled 'to give their children a much better education than they had themselves received' and remarked with pride on 'the consequent elevation all these matters have produced on the manners and morals of the whole community'. In the 1820s even prostitutes would chase away a balladeer who attempted to sing the kinds of dirty songs so popular in his youth. A sign of progress was evinced in the behaviour of the people of St Giles's: rather than fight in the streets on Sundays, they would betake themselves to the countryside, tactfully out of sight. Even this, it appeared, was to be added to the catalogue of the progress of manners.[4]

In the 1820s the pace of change was dizzying. In retrospect, the Industrial Revolution was a gradual process, but for people living through this time every new advance seemed revolutionary. Railways and steamboats appeared; the Thames was tunnelled; factories mushroomed; improvements gave parts of west London the grandeur of an imperial metropolis. The sky had been conquered with balloons and parachutes; 'the electric fire of heaven' had been captured without mankind suffering the punishment of Prometheus. Man had plunged to the bottom of the ocean in diving bells and tunnelled further into the earth with the use of Davy's lamp ('more wonderful than Aladdin's'). New engines meant that 'we can impel ponderous vessels through the waves, even against wind and tide, with the velocity of a thunderbolt'. Words could be transmitted hundreds of miles within only a few hours thanks to the telegraph. Anything seemed possible: people wondered how long it would be before a Briton set foot on the moon, formed a joint-stock company, sold shares and set about laying Macadamised roads, and it was only half a joke.[5]

To say that it was an age of boundless optimism would be an understatement. In terms of the average age of the population, this was a young country, hungry for change and opportunity. One writer mordantly commented upon the language of self-congratulation and the arrogant belief that Britain had reached the apogee of civilisation. Once upon a time, he wrote, the wide world held mysteries and challenges, 'but we have penetrated into all its secrets, analysed its composition, sifted, weighed, decompounded, exhausted, used it up, and conquered it, and have nothing left, but, like so many Alexanders, to sit down and blubber for a new one'.[6]

Yet such cynicism only reinforces the fact that people at the time were excited by a radically different world. 'In houses, dress, furniture, horses, roads, conveyances, and every thing which can minister to the ease and gratification of mind or body; in the number and refinement of the sources of amusement; and in all the articles of domestic luxury and convenience; the progress that has lately been made is unprecedented either for extent or rapidity,' commented a writer in the *Quarterly Review*. This change was evident throughout Europe, but 'In England, above all, this alteration is conspicuous.' Even in remote corners of the country, the comforts of life had improved beyond anything anywhere else in the world. There was a revolution under way; the diffusion of luxury goods, newspapers, education and other things once confined to an elite was due to improved roads, canals and, in some places by the end of the decade, railways. 'Though few in number and simple in operation,' wrote the contributor to the *Quarterly*, 'they have yet done more to change the face and multiply the comforts of society, than all the inventions which have taken place from the earliest to the present day.'[7]

Prince Pückler-Muskau, a German who visited Britain in 1826, wrote that the new Thames tunnel was 'a gigantic work, practicable nowhere but here, where people don't know what to do with their money'. The Prince visited a year after the great stock-market crash; even so, confidence seemed to have been hardly diminished. If foreign visitors were staggered by the opulence and advancement of Britain at the dawn of the century, it was nothing to what a new generation of travellers found a quarter of a century later. Pückler-Muskau had visited ten years previously, and on his second visit he found that 'Now, for the first time, [London] has the air of a seat of Government, and not of an immeasurable metropolis of "shopkeepers", to use Napoleon's expression.'[8]

The House of Commons might still resemble 'a dirty coffee house' and the City, as always, was grimy and clogged with traffic, but much of the town had been transformed into something befitting the wealthiest capital in the world. Waterloo Bridge had been constructed and the view from it – if the fog ever lifted – revealed a cityscape of London that had hitherto been concealed from the pedestrian at street level by a tangle of streets and alleys. Tourists would not have to debate whether St James's was a palace or a workhouse after it had been renovated. The sweep from Piccadilly to Marylebone had been transformed by the elegance of Regent Street, Portland Place and Regent's Park. The park had 'a design worthy of one of the capitals of the world'; it was superbly landscaped and was 'surrounded by an enclosure of magnificent houses a league in circuit'.[9]

Robert Southey visited London in 1822, the first time for two years, and found that in that short time a new city had grown up over the old: 'A stranger might imagine that our shopkeepers were like the merchants of Tyre, and lived in palaces.' When Pückler-Muskau left Britain, he found Paris 'somewhat dead, miserable, and dirty, after the rolling torrent of business, the splendour and the neatness of England'. In Britain, the hotels were sumptuous and the service exemplary, the roads smooth and fast and the coaches comfortable; when the traveller crossed the Channel back to Europe, 'you think you are transferred a thousand miles in a dream'.[10]

John Miller, writing in the *Quarterly*, said that the middle classes had reached 'a degree of happiness unknown, to the same extent, in any other country in the world'. The expansion in their numbers and wealth was shown in the ownership of private vehicles:

1804: number of four-wheeled carriages: 13,250
of two-wheeled carriages: 20,147
1824: number of four-wheeled carriages: 26,799
of two-wheeled carriages: 45,856

'The increased wealth of the middle classes is so obvious that we can neither walk the fields, visit the shops, nor examine the workshops and store-houses, without being deeply impressed with the changes which a few years have produced.'[11] The fact of a respectable middling class was no new thing. But in the 1820s, after decades of upward social mobility during which many more joined the middle classes, their importance to the economy and politics became a matter of serious discussion. What effect would they have on society and culture?

Francis Place invested much of his time as a social historian investigating the proposition that Britons had been on an onward march of progress from a ruder age to one of refinement, superabundance and morality. The middle classes had become ambitious to share in the advances in wealth, hygiene, health, luxury and material comfort; there had also, many said, been a simultaneous improvement in respectability, gentility and manners. Britain and the British were better; country and people, it seemed, were fast approaching the heights of perfection. 'The progress made in refinement of manners and morals seems to have gone on simultaneously with the improvements in Arts, Manufactures and Commerce,' he wrote. 'The impulse was given about sixty years ago, it moved slowly at first but has been constantly increasing its velocity.'[12]

And things seemed better. The habits of hard drinking and rowdy singing on the part of traders, shopkeepers, merchants and other middle-class businessmen – and even their apprentices – which people remembered from their childhoods were far less common. The radical journalist John Thelwall believed that up until the 1790s there was very little for people to do in the evening – no books, few affordable newspapers and pamphlets, no recourse to rational and improving entertainment. In the 1820s all this had changed and there was plenty to occupy the idle hour: 'as for the clubs, the lodges, and the stupid smoking-rooms, – the Bucks, and the Sols, and the Odd Fellows, and the Cousins, and the Comical Codgers, with all the orgies of "Bacchus and his noisy revelries" that used to make such uproar in our taverns! what has become of them? They have fled before the rising sun of a far diffusing intellect.' The rage for knowledge – gained at lectures and in books and magazines – was a fashion like any other; but it was potent and had worked miracles on the moral complexion of the times. Greater professionalism and higher expectations of private reputation made the middle classes sober and upright. 'People thus informed', wrote Place, 'will struggle still further to improve their condition, and harder still to prevent degradation.'[13]

The middle and artisan classes and the better sort of labourer might seem better, but there were those who lamented the price that society paid for all this improvement. What sort of morality had they accepted as 'respectable'? In his lectures on the English comic writers, William Hazlitt said that until recently the clash of different kinds of people in an old-fashioned coach travelling over pre-Macadamised roads and the consequent accidents and ludicrous situations that people were thrown into had made a journey an adventure full of comic and good-natured incidents: 'Modern manners may be compared to a modern stage coach; our limbs may be a little cramped with the confinement, and we may grow drowsy, but we arrive safely, without any very amusing or very sad amusements at our journey's end.'[14]

'We have no longer any genuine quizzes or odd fellows,' lamented Horace Smith; '– society has shaken us together in its bag until all our original characters and impressions have been rubbed out, and we are left as smooth and polished as old shillings.' If the coarseness of the eighteenth century had been refined into politeness, some of the better and most interesting features of that society were being eradicated. Signs of the times were everywhere. If coaches were more comfortable and faster, and the steam engine promised further possibilities of progress, the crowd in the streets was much altered. Gone were the wigs, pigtails, cocked hats, silks, satins and embroidered velvets and gold lace. As recently as the beginning of the century trades and professions had their own fashions: doctors liked their flowing wigs and gold-topped canes, for example. Now distinguishing a man was like picking out a particular bee from the hive. It would not do to deviate from the practical, workaday clothes now adopted by men of all classes. If it was not for the continued colour and variety of female fashions, said one, 'we might be set down for a nation of Quakers'.[15]

The streets presented 'a monotonous modification of broad-cloth – a homogenous mass of bipeds'. Yet for others it was a sign of progress. As the country became wealthier and the people improved in manners, education and prosperity, it became harder to distinguish different classes by externals alone. People took pride in their appearance and, if the tendency was towards homogeneity, it signalled a destruction of former barriers. 'Persons placed far apart in wealth and station often approach each other so nearly in air and demeanour,' wrote a contributor to the *Quarterly Review*; people had learnt to deport themselves 'with ease and propriety' and there was a 'universal polish' throughout society. Even writers, apparently, 'wear good coats and look like gentlemen'.[16]

Manners and politeness were the province of all who lived up to the standard, no matter their status – and it could be read in one's clothes, the badge of respectability. All who were above rags, it was said, were equals. No more would the outrageous eccentric be accepted with equanimity; no one should stand out. The art of Thomas Rowlandson, for example, depended on the clash of opposites, the juxtaposition of oddballs and bohemians who enlivened the street and the tavern. Rowlandson's England is one of comic vulgarity; the streets are alive with bumps, clashes, crashes and accidents; popular culture is rowdy and lusty; the people are all characters who present their originality to the world. It is difficult to imagine him achieving the same effect in an age of conformity. The trend was for the modern phenomenon of uniformity in style and the anonymity of the streets and public places, which is so much part of our world. Did it betoken a drabber world? Some certainly thought so. If clothes represented the individual character, they projected sobriety and asceticism. One contributor to the *New Monthly* detested 'such a conjunction of duplicates as our streets present – such a mass of dittos – such an accumulation of *facsimiles* – such a civil regiment'.[17]

How were people supposed to dress, behave and express themselves in an anonymous, commercial world? Appearances and behaviour became all important. Businessmen, shopkeepers, manufacturers and farmers owed their wealth to their own exertions, but they were vulnerable to economic fluctuations and so, according to Edward Gibbon Wakefield, 'are troubled, perplexed, uneasy, always on the verge of bankruptcy'. The 1825–6 crash and the depression that followed was another reminder of the unforgiving caprice of the market and the transience of prosperity. Coming after a period of intense self-congratulation and a widespread faith in 'progress', it was even more traumatic. In Britain, where there was a finely graded hierarchy and where notions of respectability were tied to income and financial success, anxiety about status ran high. Fear of its loss was the middle-class bugbear. As Gibbon Wakefield put it, they were the 'uneasy classes'.[18]

The New Wine Company might have mocked the exaggerated language of respectability – called cant by some – but reputation was something people strove to maintain at all costs. Francis Place believed that he and people like him who had clawed their way to affluence and security had done so because the image they presented to the world was one of trustworthiness and scrupulous morals. Who could refuse them credit or withhold their custom? In many ways, ostentatious propriety was an appropriate mode of conduct for anonymous businessmen trading with strangers; how else could trust be earned?

Booming towns such as Manchester, Birmingham and Leeds forced together incomers who were not previously tied by kinship or shared background. The population of London had passed the million mark, and as it did so new suburbs multiplied. As the outlying districts were built over with new houses, the population of the City itself declined. The trading, mercantile, speculating and shopkeeping classes were transformed into commuters who travelled to their former neighbourhood solely for business; the face-to-face culture of the old City was becoming a thing of the past. In the modern world, signifiers such as clothing, manners and formal politeness made public inner intentions that could not be communicated in any other way to strangers or associates. It ensured respect between equals and deference from employees. More importantly, the pursuit of 'respectability' imposed a set of rules, an etiquette for a commercial society, upon which reputation was dependent.

Such a lesson was the foundation of William Cobbett's *Advice to Young Men and (Incidentally) Young Women in the Middle and Higher Ranks of Life*. Anyone could be talented and good at his or her work, but there must be more: 'there must be industry: there must be perseverance: there must be, before the eyes of the nation, proofs of extraordinary exertion: people must say to themselves, "What wise conduct there must have been in the employment in the time of this man! How sober, how sparing in diet, how early a riser, how little expensive, he must have been!"'[19]

Cobbett's *Advice* was a staple of middle-class reading; editions continued to be published every few years in Britain until the 1930s to instil into young men a sense of duty and discipline, and it was translated into many languages, including Tamil (in 1951). 'Quick at *meals*, quick at *work*,' he enjoined ambitious young men. For what was life but a race against the unforgiving hour? The real man would invest every moment in cultivating his business, carving out his independence and securing his family from misfortune and the indignity of poverty. Like the well-run business, the happy family should be provident and efficient; domestic economy should be as well regulated and cost-effective as a shopkeeper's account book. This was true because the hearth reflected the tradesman's aptitude for business. If he was extravagant at home, at the table or in the tavern, what kind of mess would his business be in? Professionalism was learnt at home, and it sent a potent message to the world regarding a man's abilities and virtues – in the first instance to colleagues, customers and creditors.[20]

The need to defend income against fluctuations and businesses against false accusation was a way of regulating and setting standards of behaviour. In 1824 Joseph Brasbridge, a retired Fleet Street silversmith, published his memoirs. It was at once a reminder of the recent past and a dire warning. As a young businessman Brasbridge had determined to be a 'jolly fellow' even while he was building up his business. 'I divided my time between the tavern club, the card party, the hunt, the fight – and left my shop to be looked after by others, whilst I decided on the respective merits of Humphries and Mendoza, Johnson and Big Ben [pugilists]. Every idle sight, in short, was sure to have me for a spectator.' He shared 'the stupidest kind of debauchery' in the Globe tavern with a group of men who were by no means unsuccessful: a surgeon, a printer, a parliamentary reporter, a Treasury clerk and the keeper of Newgate prison, 'who always remained till daylight'.

While he was out carousing, his apprentice systematically defrauded him, spending the business's cash on old hock, in clubs and keeping 'an expensive lady'. Brasbridge only rebuilt his livelihood and became a reputable silversmith when he forsook his jollification, took control of his business and established his good name. The fortunes of his four boon companions depended on their willingness to reform: one became Lord Mayor, two went bankrupt and the last matured to lead a City patrol.

According to Cobbett, moderation did not necessarily mean self-denial; 'sobriety of conduct' or reputation implied 'steadiness, seriousness, carefulness, scrupulous propriety of conduct'. It was a statement of intent, but it could never be established if one attended the club. Brasbridge, at the height of his convivial lifestyle in the last quarter of the previous century, was vice-president of the Free and Easy club at the Horn Tavern (the president was the marshal of the High Court of Admiralty). The thousand members were all City tradesmen who had no great commitment to their counting house: 'Our great fault was sitting too late; in this respect, according to the principle of Franklin, that "time is money", we were indeed most unwary spendthrifts.' This kind of behaviour would be career suicide for an ambitious businessman in the 1820s; few masters would be seen at something as low and dissolute as a tavern club.[21]

'Drinking clubs, smoking clubs, singing clubs, clubs of Odd-fellows, whist clubs, sotting clubs,' Cobbett fumed; 'these are inexcusable, they are censurable, they are at once foolish and wicked . . . there are *quarrels*; there is the vicious habit of loose and filthy talk; there are slanders and backbitings; there are the admiration of contemptible wit, and there are scoffings at all that is sober and serious.' They were dying out by the time Cobbett wrote; Place said that the Cock and Hen clubs that were once frequented by prosperous men were by the 1820s confined to 'the lowest and most disreputable neighbourhoods, and are attended by none but disreputable people mostly young thieves'. And if respectable businessmen now avoided them, ambitious apprentices were keen to prove that they were diligent and sober-minded. This kind of indulgence was dangerous as well as immoral: 'Suffering is the natural and just punishment of idleness, drunkenness, squandering, and an indulgence in the society of prostitutes,' wrote Cobbett. The crying sin of heavy drinking and conviviality was not that it was immoral in itself but that it was *expensive* and therefore contrary to any kind of work ethic. That's when the punishment came: 'we may, and often do, admire the talents of lazy and even dissipated men, but we do not trust them with the care of our interests'.[22]

What Cobbett was hoping for in the moral reform of the people was a distinctively middle-class culture and morality that would put profligate aristocrats to shame. The diligence, moral sense and professionalism of the respectable middling classes should contrast with the decadence and greed of high society, thus proving that the disenfranchised middle-class man was worthy of respect, a voice and a vote. Francis Place believed that the progress of the middle class had mirrored his own life story. He had put aside hard drinking and whoring to afford the good things in life. As incomes had increased, families had learnt the lesson that forbearance and frugality meant that they could purchase luxury goods; they also realised that respectability and reputation were indispensable for retaining their business.

Progress – and all the good things that came with it – had made them moral. Place recalled: 'my resolution was taken to avoid as much as possible, every thing, the tendency of which was at all likely to debase me, or to disqualify me for the acquirements and enjoyments I contemplated'. Greater inducements to good behaviour had made Place and many of his contemporaries advocates of self-help and self-restraint. A 'greater love of distinction' caused the moral amendment of his generation; they took pride in their achievements and in their domestic comforts and strove to live up to their improved situation. 'Moderate clothing, moderate houses, the power of receiving friends, the power of purchasing books and particularly the power of supporting a family, will always remain subjects of rational desire among the majority of mankind,' wrote Malthus. For Place, it was stolidly middle-class values that had driven the moral revolution that had been going on and was apparent in the 1820s.[23]

People like Place and Cobbett were worried that the growing middle classes would be seduced into the kind of luxurious and immoral lifestyles of the rich. That was why they emphasised the unique achievement of self-made families. But is decorum and propriety a characteristic solely of the bourgeoisie? It resembles the values of restraint and reputation which were such salient features of upper-class manners. In the early decades of the century the nobility and gentry had been bywords for depravity. But that was a noisy minority made up of scapegraces like the Barrymores, the Four-in-Hand Club and the Regent's set; their families and friends had been at pains to show the world their morals and they were conspicuous subscribers to the myriad philanthropic projects. The aristocracy tailored their behaviour to the expectations of their public sphere and a Brummell-esque code of unwritten rules and minute signifiers; the self-made businessman and his family were no less subject to scrutiny and judgement. The stock exchange, the market, the shop, the street were as much stages for mutual scrutiny as the rout, Hyde Park or Almack's assembly rooms. As Southey wrote, 'morals, as well as manners, follow the mode, and decorum, at least, is in fashion'.[24]

In his book *England and the English*, Edward Lytton Bulwer wrote that British society was a compound of the aristocratic and the commercial. He talked of a society that was permeated with aristocratic values but enriched by mercantile and manufacturing wealth. The man who had made his money from scratch was dependent on the acceptance of those who were above him in the social scale if not in income. In society, fashion was the omnipotent arbiter of taste and acceptability; people without rank or even money could, in theory, gain access to the upper echelons of society, provided they slavishly kept up with the latest fashions in dress, opinion and manners. It was a peculiarity of Britain, which, unlike other aristocratic societies and monarchies, did not have a class system that was rooted in a royal court and based on an unchanging and static hierarchy. In Britain, the nobility had expanded at a fast pace, drawing in men whose backgrounds were in the professions, manufacturing or military service; in 1700 there were 173 peers, 267 in 1800 and by mid-century there were 399. Baronets and knights increased at an even greater rate in the patronage-happy late eighteenth century. The expansion of the peerage drew in fresh blood and also connected many people to the aristocracy by ties of family and friendship. Fashion and the possibility of social mobility stamped society of all kinds with an aristocratic complexion: 'These mystic, shifting, and various shades of graduation; these shot-silk colours of society produce this effect.'[25]

It was, however, a delusion that rank was open to all, but the impression that it was obtainable by following the fashion and obeying rules of etiquette persisted. Even if middle-class people did not believe they could rub shoulders with the nobility, the same competition for status and rank existed at every level of the social hierarchy. 'Hence, in the first place, that external vying with each other; that spirit of show; that lust of imitation which characterize our countrymen and countrywomen,' wrote Lytton Bulwer. No one, not least the 'uneasy classes', wanted to be seen as poor or unpolished; the need to keep up with one's neighbours (even if they weren't aristocratic), with the latest fashion, the latest opinion, the latest phrase was acute. The older aristocracy felt under threat from so-called 'cockneys', who were so good at copying their clothes, style, conversation and recreations and who flocked to resorts such as Bath, Tunbridge Wells and Brighton. The *bon ton* had to keep moving fast to keep fashion a step ahead of the middle class. 'To what Libyan desert, what rocky island in the watery waste, is high life now to retreat?' asked the *New Monthly Magazine*. It could be a stifling and degrading system of emulation: 'hence, each person imitates his fellow, and hopes to purchase the respectful opinion of others by renouncing the independence of opinion for himself'.[26]

As the life of Brummell showed only too well, the only way to survive in an aggressively competitive and rulebound society was by suppressing outward displays of emotion and submitting to manners. Transgressors against the code become outsiders who would destabilise the equilibrium of a social system based on tacit conventions. Conduct was thus more of a virtue than embarrassing and anarchic sincerity; propriety and etiquette were more conducive to polite society than candour. 'Perfect freedom of manners has been reconciled with perfect decorum,' Joseph Farrington wrote, summing up the major change in British life in the nineteenth century. In commercial society there was an equally pressing need to be restrained by manners. Personal opinions, eccentricity of deportment or speech, grossness, coarse behaviour or sensuality were dangerous because they could alienate one and place a businessman at a disadvantage. As Isaac Taylor asserted: 'Reputation is power.'[27]

Tact and reserve concealed these tics and prevented one from offending or putting off a potentially rewarding connection; conformity prevented the middle-class man and woman from unwittingly stepping beyond the pale of 'respectable' society. This was manifested in the decline of the convivial tavern club and the rise of societies associated with particular careers. The growth of a professional ethos and identity called for a more formal social setting. Manners and politeness were more appropriate than the unrestrained drinking, singing and joking seen at Chair Clubs and the like that Brasbridge, Place and thousands of traders of the previous generation enjoyed. Samuel Taylor wrote that the need to conform to society's expectations was not debatable: 'To speak incorrectly, shows a want of culture; to enter a room boorishly, will give the idea of low life; vulgarity of manners will strongly insinuate the notion of vulgarity of station, company, and sentiment.' The world might be mistaken in believing an uncouth person was inevitably untrustworthy, but that was not the world's fault. Not every polite person was intrinsically good, Taylor said, but every good person was polite. Sincerity and frankness were not the virtues they appeared to be; such openness could offend and alienate and ruin someone's chances in the world.[28]

Those virtues of 'decorum', 'restraint' and 'propriety', and all the vocabulary of mannered society that had been seen as part of an aristocratic, courtly culture, were being applied more than ever to the middle class. And it was not always meant as a compliment. The middle class as a whole were seen as stepping out of their natural sphere, motivated by envy and snobbishness, becoming artificial and insincere as they did so. They were debased by humiliating emulation. Many years before this became a major talking point in the 1820s, Hannah More had warned of the dangers of the middle classes mistaking aristocratic or fashionable manners for virtue. In particular she warned of the fashionable cant term 'accomplishment', which was the word people of the *bon ton* used to describe the graces of socially acceptable young women, regardless of their merits. 'This phrenzy of accomplishment, unhappily, is no longer restricted within the usual limits of rank and fortune; the middle orders have caught the contagion, and it rages downward with increasing and destructive violence, from the elegantly dressed but slenderly portioned curate's daughter, to the equally fashionable daughter of the little tradesman, and of the more opulent but not more judicious farmer.'[29]

Hannah More called it a 'revolution' in the manners of the middling, and a melancholy one at that. It was born of worship of rank and a false conception of what 'refinement' and 'civilisation' meant. Popular authors who taught the middling the riddle of manners and conduct had 'established a fantastic code of artificial manners. They have refined elegance into insipidity, frittered down delicacy into frivolousness, and reduced manner into *minauderie*.' The middle classes, who were conscious of leading Britain's march of progress, wanted to live up to their new position of power. Progress meant 'refinement', and refined behaviour was aristocratic or gentlemanly. But in the gentleman's code there was something shameful in 'trade' and earned wealth. Consequently it became a middle-class virtue to emphasise a sense of duty and piety and a commitment to public charity; it was a self-effacing and genteel answer to the perceived indignity of new money. The luxury of leisure time and conspicuous consumption, or the funds and time to spend on politics, was an aristocratic privilege. Only very successful industrialists, bankers and traders could afford to separate themselves entirely from their work, employing managers to run the daily concerns of a business, which allowed them to lead lives of leisure or public service.

This was an option available only to the very rich, but there were ways that less wealthy families could replicate the gentlemanly life. Middle-class people separated their working lives from the domestic: no more living above the shop or next to the factory or in the commercial districts of towns. It was undignified for the wives and daughters of successful men to help with the family business or pursue any productive occupation. The home was also divided between the domestic and the formal; entertainment was conducted in drawing and dining rooms, away from private rooms and kitchens – the aristocratic house in miniature. To obtain this kind of genteel lifestyle where leisure and domesticity were rigidly divided from the productive and professional was to live respectably.

Added to this was another social prejudice. Firmly implanted in the British mentality was the unbreakable connection between personal worth and personal wealth. It was a Protestant way of thinking, but it was given an urgency by the new piety. In Britain, Lytton Bulwer said, poverty was 'associated with something disreputable': 'In other countries poverty is a misfortune – with us it is a crime.'[30]

The first question one Briton asked of another was: what is he worth? The word 'virtue' had no real meaning when this was the way people were judged; 'the undue regard for wealth produces a false moral standard'. A person was esteemed respectable according to how rich he or she was. Had not hundreds of evangelical and utilitarian writers said that poverty was the price to pay for lack of restraint and the absence of frugal instincts; in short, the punishment for some inner and revolting moral flaw? On the other hand, wealth was the visible blessing of God. Lytton Bulwer was entirely correct in linking poverty to shame and affluence to praiseworthiness in the British mindset. 'The favourite word is "respectability",' he wrote, '– and the current meaning of "respectability" may certainly exclude virtue, but never a decent sufficiency of wealth: no wonder then that every man strives to be rich.' 'Respectability' was totally unconnected with moral worth or even respect; it was a term of universal praise for those who had the appearances of status and wealth. Audiences must have laughed during an 1827 version of *Punch and Judy* when the hero tries to flatter the devil by asking after his 'respectable family'.[31]

It was not merely having wealth that was important; it was the *appearance* of having wealth that was an overriding concern. People went to extravagant lengths to keep up appearances, and this meant being seen to be affluent and successful in the world. It was no wonder then that people looked up to those higher in the social scale for an example of how rich people behaved. The popularity of 'silver fork' novels, as Hazlitt called them, evinced this. This kind of literature provided a crash course in high-life manners: what to have for dinner and how to eat it; how to dress; what furniture and ornaments were in vogue; how to converse with polish and gentility. What the market demanded of booksellers and novelists was a template of a way of life that reconciled the possession of money (even new money) with gentlemanly conduct – the eternal mystery of English life. 'Such has been the rapidity of the general advancement,' commented the *New Monthly*, 'that there is some little confusion in the respective boundaries, and each is put to the contrivances of its pride to distinguish itself from the grade beneath. Hence the servility to superiors, and the stiff-necked repulsive reserve, not to say arrogance towards inferiors or equals, which form the marked and besetting sins of English society.'[32]

A middle-class family fallen on hard times was said to be 'embarrassed'. And well they might be, when morality and earthly riches were such boon companions. They could not afford the carriage, the dinner party or any of the trappings of the respectable life. The fear of loss of status was, according to Gibbon Wakefield, the cause of middle-class uneasiness and 'a new state of things'. Understand this, he said, and you would understand the problems of British society. It explained, for one thing, the sexual squeamishness and hypocrisy of the middle ranks. In Britain, where the middle classes boasted of their 'moral restraint', you could not walk a mile in any town or city without meeting hundreds of prostitutes. 'That demand is occasioned principally by a custom now prevalent amongst the English middle classes; the custom of abstaining from marriage, the custom of celibacy, vulgarly speaking; of "moral restraint", in the language of political economists.'[33]

Thomas Malthus talked of 'moral restraint' as the way of avoiding population growth caused by early marriage and sexual profligacy. The middle classes had appropriated the phrase and used it as an ethical justification for something selfish. Ambitious young men who enjoyed the trappings of the gentlemanly life had a 'dread' of marriage because it was expensive and likely to result in their 'embarrassment'. They therefore put it off until they had made enough money, claiming that they were practising 'moral restraint'. 'Hence, immorality without a parallel in any other country. This is the cause of that exuberant prostitution which shocks an American.' Many middle-class women, on the other hand, were doomed to celibacy. 'One may well say doomed. Custom forbids them to practise that sort of "moral restraint" to which their brothers resort without disgrace; and custom is stronger than walls or bars.' Daughters had to be shielded from temptation lest they present the world with a bastard child, bring shame on their families and great cost to their fathers.[34]

The 'uneasy classes' were behaving like the nobility, where younger sons and daughters had to sacrifice themselves to family pride. This sexual anxiety was said to be new among the middle classes. The fear of losing wealth by imprudent marriage and respectability by having an unchaste daughter ran high. Francis Place's adolescent adventures were unthinkable for the next generation. There was no 'kiss-in-the-ring'; there were no dirty songs, coarse jokes or ribald badinage; nothing, in short, that might arouse teenage passions. When fear of sex gnawed at the respectable, it was little wonder that *Don Juan* should be so loudly decried and excluded from teenage bookshelves. Concern about juvenile sex was not new, but the reasons for tabooing it had changed and the punishments for transgressors were more stringent. It was an unforgivable crime in middle-class families, a stain that could never be effaced. For sex was the only passion strong enough to undo self-abnegation, deferred gratification and the holy grail of respectability. Unchaste behaviour in the eighteenth century 'did not necessarily imply that the girl was an abandoned person as she would be now and it was not therefore then as now an insurmountable obstacle to her being settled completely in the world'.[35]

By the 1820s it would be a deathblow to respectability for a young woman to be thought either clever or sexually inquisitive, unless she fancied a life off the guest list and on the shelf. 'Thus society is crowded with the insipid and beset with the insincere.' The middle class, high and low, rich and not rich, had their marriage markets as surely as the upper class, and it cast its pall over every aspect of social relations. It made people even more reserved and cold and *diplomatic* towards each other whenever and wherever the sexes came into contact. 'Before marriage,' wrote John Wade, 'the shrewdness and superior tact of the London women superinduce a great strictness and reserve . . . Indelicacies in conversation . . . are never tolerated, and an innuendo which would pass in a country circle as a mere *plaisanterie*, would give serious offence in London. But though not in words so pure, the country dames, we suspect, are more chaste in deeds, and examples of infidelity, and illicit intercourse of rarer occurrence.'[36]

There was a story that people told themselves about the period since the French Revolution. The great events of the 1780s and '90s had generated an appetite for reading and discussion, and the generation that had been born in the closing decades of the century had benefited most from this climate. Unlike their parents, who had supposedly been ignorant and therefore cruder in their leisure activities, this generation had their eyes open to the state of the world. They looked at their benighted neighbours and wished to reclaim them from vice and squalor. They regarded their debauched ruling class with wary eyes. In response, the aristocracy had converted to middle-class philanthropic ideas, hoping to retain their position by joining the humanitarian schemes pioneered by middle-class dissenters. During these thirty or forty years, the middle classes had been in the vanguard of progress and were the self-conscious guardians of public and private virtue. Leaving aside the veracity of this triumphant narrative, it was a historical view that was widely accepted. The pressure to live up to the role that history had bequeathed the middle classes (the chosen class in a chosen land, as some would have it) was intense.

John Stuart Mill wrote that 'the virtues of the middle class are those that conduce to getting rich – integrity, economy, and enterprise – along with family affection, inoffensive conduct between man and man, and a disposition to assist one another, whenever no commercial rivalry intervenes'. Money-making and social advancement were reconciled with gentility and respectability. Whatever pangs of guilt that their assurgency came at others' expense or at the cost of their own happiness were assuaged by the two predominant and converging strains of economic and religious thought at this time – evangelicalism and the science of political economy. The conjunction of business ethic and religious morality was expressed with crystal clarity by Archibald Allison in *Blackwood's*. Why, Allison asked, were the middle classes individually and collectively wealthy? The answer was 'because they put a bridle on their licentious appetites; because they restrain present desire, from a sense of future benefit; because they sacrifice sensual gratifications on the altar of domestic duty'. Middle-class ambitions and economic activity were elevated to things of religious worth; they were rewarded by God for their forbearance and resistance to temptation.[37]

When Cobbett talked of 'just punishment' for drunkenness and whoring, the need for private as well as public rectitude and salvation through work, he was articulating a moral philosophy resonant in Protestant history. There is more than a glancing similarity to the religious sensibilities of Wilberforce, Fry or Allen – people Cobbett detested and called hypocritical zealots. The virtues of deferred gratification, individualism, competitiveness, discipline and thrift – things that many successful people had taught themselves – had more than an echo in evangelicalism. Cobbett's gruff puritanism, Bentham's fervid belief in work and the driving forces of 'vital religion' shared a vocabulary and a sense of mission. This is not to say that the religion of Wesley or Wilberforce was universally accepted and followed. But evangelicalism became the moral backbone for many self-made and successful people.

Having no less of an impact on the middle classes was the power of the science of political economy. It was put across with the same urgent, proselytising force as evangelicalism. For its devotees, it was the most portentous discovery ever made: 'it must transcend any thing to which the name of science has hitherto been given among men'. Political economy taught how industry and trade could be made most efficient, employing the least amount of labour for the greatest output; the subsequent augmentation in wealth would provide the population as a whole with greater comforts and luxuries. But it did much more than that: it was the means of radically transforming man and his environment.

The world, political economy taught, was governed by invisible rules and a universal law decreed by nature; hitherto, humans had failed to deduce these, and the story of their history had been one of wars, dearth, disease, blundering incompetence, uncontrollable population and exploitation. When a person understood the science, its advocates said, he would perceive his standing within the economic system and his relationship to the market; he would then see, with absolute clarity, where his interests lay; he would become happy, rational, productive and pacific. The laws of a free market dictated human behaviour; left to its own devices, it would provide food and employment and teach civilised values and morality.

In such a situation, without artificial things like tariffs, regulations, the Poor Law, charity and so on, a man would ultimately learn his own best interests by conforming to the universal laws. A human's passions, needs, wants and inducements could be analysed, dissected, examined and amended by the science, as if he was a machine. The unfettered market would satisfy all his wants, while the demand for labour would provide him with continual, useful employment immune from man-made fluctuations and depressions. Thomas de Quincey said that it was only by studying David Ricardo that his opium-induced hallucinations evaporated and he could see the world clearly. For others it was indistinguishable from Christianity. Some who heard Dugald Stewart lecture on political economy said it was like a revelation from heaven. Lord Althorp wrote: 'My two lines of reading are divinity and political economy: the first to do myself good: the other to enable me to do good to others.'[38]

The political economist's argument for free trade was like the evangelical's conception of God's government of the world. The free market swept away mankind's pathetic and purblind efforts to intervene in the world's affairs. It restored the law of nature, that is to say God's laws. Providence taught moral restraint to prevent population explosion; it rewarded the frugal, industrious and prudent and savagely punished the feckless; and it provided food and work for the millions who laboured and saved their wages. Progress and civilisation were the outcome of this. Political economists stressed the sad futility of indiscriminate charity, benevolence and humanitarian relief as zealously as any evangelical. 'Political Economy', wrote the Rev. Thomas Chalmers, 'is but one grand exemplification of the alliance, which a God of righteousness hath established, between prudence and moral principle on the one hand, and physical comfort on the other.' In the 1820s many believed that the principles of political economy, backed by evangelical religion, would come to govern the world.[39]

Political economy was not just academic study in the 1820s but staple reading for the literate. The founders of the *Edinburgh Review* had studied under Dugald Stewart at Edinburgh University and had attempted to educate the public on the principles of political economy. But it was only in the mid-1820s, when another of Stewart's pupils, J. R. McCulloch, began a series of lectures on the science, that it became so central to public debate. His lectures in 1824 were attended by cabinet ministers, MPs, economists and archbishops, and his *Discourse on the Rise, Progress, Peculiar Objects, and Importance of Political Economy* was a best-seller. 'So great and absorbing is the interest which the present discussions excite that all men are become political economists and financiers, and everybody is obliged to have an opinion.' Books, tracts and newspaper and magazine articles articulated the theory for the middle-class and artisan readership. Its advocates stressed the advantages of a deep understanding of the science. Middle-class readers had better read up on it or they would be left creeping along at a sluggish pace in the race of progress; as Francis Jeffrey wrote of political economy in the *Edinburgh Review*, 'it is certain that it is at the same time the best nurse of all elegance and refinement, the surest guarantee for justice, order and freedom, and the only safe basis for every species of moral and intellectual improvement'.[40]

Throughout the 1820s the opportunities to learn were greatly expanded. Mechanics institutes provided lectures and loaned books to the lower classes; schools were set up everywhere; Brougham's Society for the Diffusion of Useful Knowledge printed cheap books on a variety of topics, from literature and history to science and mathematics; cheap magazines catered for the hunger for instruction. London University provided a modern education for the middle classes and all those who were excluded from Oxford and Cambridge: dissenters, Jews, Catholics and atheists. For some, the accessibility of ideas and books was so much cant: the diffusion of cheap half-truths and what Peacock called 'Steam Intellect' – the platitudes of the machine age. These people deplored the smattering of superficial knowledge which cheapened intellectual attainment and would level literature to a smooth plain of mediocrity. People learnt facts but were incapable of judging the value of knowledge. For others, however, it was the gleam of enlightenment breaking out for classes who had been born in ignorance. In the House of Commons, Frederick Robinson said: 'when we find that in every class of the community the spread of knowledge is going on in a manner which half a century ago, I believe, would have been deemed impossible, are we, who sit here, some of us Ministers of the Crown . . . are we to be behind hand with our countrymen, or rather ought it not be our endeavour to be foremost in the race?'[41]

For self-made people, these economic and religious ideas chimed with their own experiences and helped explain the world. The doctrines of political economy and evangelicalism said that wealth creation, discipline and competition were not just good in themselves but religious and moral duties. For those uneasy people worried about the personal disadvantage of suppressing their emotions, the exploitation of others in a fierce capitalist economy or the social stigma of new money, it offered immediate reassurance that what they were doing was natural, perhaps even a noble thing, and certainly the inevitable consequence of progress. It reassured people as consumers as well, for conspicuous consumption of luxuries was a stimulus to the economy. The successful deserved their riches by natural right; by the same token, the benighted poor merited their own position.

In the world of the evangelical and the political economist, self-help and personal responsibility were cardinal virtues. The self was firmly at the centre of their world view. 'Self-instruction, self-command, self-acting energy, will be absolutely necessary to render the best education effectual, and will carry every advantage to its highest degree,' wrote Isaac Taylor in his book *Self-Cultivation*. Going out into the world to subdue the forces of the market and carve out independence was supposedly a masculine virtue. No less manly was the subjugation of emotions. Every successful man had to get over his youthful thoughts and fancies. The passions, wrote Taylor, were sources 'of pleasure or of torment all through life'. Early mastery of them by habits of industry and restraint would pay dividends later in life in the form of wealth, security and happiness: 'They will be curbed in their violence; – happy effect! they will be trained to proper action; – what a source of comfort to the man's self, and to all around him! The main source of miseries of human life is ungoverned passions.'[42]

Science, social theory and religion gave solid backing to middle-class habits and decisions. Emotional continence was an indispensable character trait, and it had a lot in common with the suppression of instincts that evangelicals preached and practised. When political economists and evangelicals persuaded people to desist from giving money to beggars, it was more than just clearing the streets. It was the first object lesson in both evangelical morality and political economy. It taught people to master their benevolent instincts in the pursuit of a higher goal. It taught them to weigh every motive, scrutinise their intentions and assess the likely consequence. And it had worked: people, and especially the middle classes in towns and cities throughout the country, had imbibed the religious and economic arguments. 'I remember the time', wrote Brougham in 1825, 'when money given to beggars was supposed to be well bestowed – a notion now exploded.'[43] Anti-mendicity propaganda stressed that one small coin conferred on an unworthy beggar was a crime against natural law, fuel to the fire of unproductive labour and an encouragement to a surplus population.

This was a microcosm of the new morality. Apparently small acts had to be seen as significant in themselves: they should be judged in light of their economic and moral implications. People should scrutinise their own – and other people's – motives and actions. Candid conversation, a tendency to drunkenness, hints of sexual incontinence, wastefulness, extravagance and profligacy could all suggest that a person was untrustworthy and a bad member of society. The domestic sphere was raised to prominence; behaviour in the home was the way that people were judged. Were they frugal? Were they virtuous and sober? As never before, domesticity and private habits became signifiers of a person's worth.

Stockbrokers, barristers and shipowners who joined the rioters in the Covent Garden Theatre in 1809 knew that their unrestrained private conduct could be indulged without affecting their public standing at the Exchange, the shop or the office. This was less acceptable for their sons and daughters. Decades of evangelical moralising and utilitarian reasoning had had their effect. People were judged by how they behaved at home or in their leisure hours; by their conformity to manners and points of etiquette. The British boasted of their 'superior morality', said Thomas Carlyle, but it was really the 'Argus eyes' of public opinion forcing people to mug the characteristics of respectability: 'Wonderful "Face of Public Opinion!" We must act and walk in all points as it prescribes; follow the traffic it bids us, realize the sum of money, the degree of "influence" it expects of us, *or* we shall be lightly esteemed.'[44]

The very things that had made Britain prosperous and successful, Prince Pückler-Muskau said, had created unhappiness and anxiety. The middle classes had grown rich on routine, efficiency and discipline, and this had 'given birth to the dullness, the contracted views, the *routine* habits of thought as well as of action, the inveterate prejudices, the unbounded desire for, and deference to, wealth, which characterize the mass of Englishmen'. Commercial prosperity and extraordinary wealth exacted a penalty; the British were victims of outrageous success; it had brought out 'an ill-humour and moroseness innate in the nation, and a cold stony self-love'. Reviewing Pückler-Muskau's book in the *Edinburgh Review*, William Empson agreed, saying that improved communications and the rapid circulation of ideas had this effect: 'The originality and diversity of individual humour, for which the English nation was at one time distinguished, have been reduced of late, we believe, within much narrower bounds . . . The growing tendency to sameness and artificialness, no reasonable Englishman will deny.'[45]

Fashions and morals were both dictated, as Empson said, by the same 'imitative uniformity'. The change was shown in the way middle-class people spent their leisure time. Throughout the 1820s they were accused of turning their backs on their accustomed simple pleasures out of fear of what others might say. They were desperate not to be classed with the swinish multitude, and the only way to do this was to avoid anything unsophisticated and 'vulgar'. Below them, the middle classes believed, was a brutish and degrading popular culture of irrational pleasures and profligate behaviour. Many of them knew this all too well, for they had emerged from the stew of lower-class life. Anything that was not rational or improving was a waste of time. These ideas became sacrosanct in middle-class mentalities as they sought at any cost to distance themselves from the labouring classes. Anyone who claimed to enjoy simple rustic amusements 'incur[red] the heaviest penalty of ridicule' and was accused of 'vulgarity and affectation'.

In the 1810s there were eighty-six fair days held in and around London between Easter and October each year.[46] The people used to relish their bawdy and rowdy humour once in a while: 'They are then like a school-boy let loose from school, or like a dog that has slipped his collar,' wrote Hazlitt. There was an outburst of jollity and coarseness that was so different from the normal characteristics of the British, so 'that [they] may return to serious business with more cheerfulness'. No one could pretend that popular entertainments were refined or improving. But for all that, they were once events enjoyed by many precisely because they were crude and boisterous. Nowhere else other than at fairs was 'the artificial garb which society imposes so entirely doffed'. *Blackwood's* described ancient Bartholomew Fair in 1824:

> What a convocation of jugglers and gingerbread bakers there are! and what a collection of knaves and ninnies to admire them! They are fine things, past question, these shows . . . The eye becomes unsteady amid a variety of objects; and has not time to pause for a second upon one before it is caught up, willy-nilly, by another. In front, we see a company of comedians; behind, a troop of horse-riders: there, a grotesque fellow dances upon a rope; there, a motley ruffian curvets upon a wire. Then, the roar – the shout – the deafening, incessant, unrelaxing din, of twice ten thousand keys! of ravings, male and female – howlings, human and animal – whoopings, joyous and angry – besides noises *non descript* . . . There are fruit-sellers, showmen, ballad-mongers, and pie-projectors; dealers in toys, strong waters, porter and pastry; fiddlers scrape, ginger-beer corks pop, children weep, and nurse-maids giggle! Then comes the yelling of wild beasts – the swearing of their keepers – the creaking of wheels – the crashing of roundabouts – the ringing of bells – the blowing of horns – the whirling of rattles – and the cries of 'Take care of your pockets'.

There was 'mirth and freedom without restraint, bruises without apologies, impudence without shame, [and] maids without virginity'.

You might hear an old drunken woman courting a ragged dustman by singing, 'Vould you this wirgin-heart forsake?' – it was all part of the fun of the 'convivial riot'.[47]

In 1825 William Hone toured the stalls and booths of the fair. There were stalls selling chapbooks, Bible prints, wicker baskets, toys and hardware; long tables covered in cloths served all kinds of food and drink – the fair-goer could dine 'handsomely for threepence and sumptuously for fourpence'. There was space for dancing. The showmen exhibited biblical and historical scenes, puppet shows, menageries (lions, tigers, elephants), plays and farces, human freaks (cannibals, dwarves, giants, incredibly fat people, etc.); there were tightrope-walkers, jugglers, clowns, conjurers, fortune-telling pigs,* mind-reading horses, mermaids and many more. The plays and comedies were variable in quality and probably in decline since the days when a young Edmund Kean acted in a booth at the fair. Back in 1811 *The Scourge* mocked those who objected to such fairs: it was terrible for some sensitive people 'that the youth of both sexes visit these scenes of gaiety for no other purpose than to laugh and dance and make love; that many of them have the unheard-of insolence to titter in the presence of their superiors; and that multitudes gorge themselves on these occasions with sweetmeats, or gratify a vain passion for dress, by the purchase of trinkets and finery'.[48]

One magistrate complained that the scenes of drunkenness were not confined to boorish labourers: 'Nay, even the better part of the company resorting to these fairs, under the influence of an extraordinary elevation of spirits, seem to consider themselves released from the ties of decorum, which on all other occasions, they regard as indispensable.' The historian James Malcolm observed in the 1800s a cart crammed with everyone, from the 'dregs' of society to servants and the daughters of respectable London tradesmen, going to a fair at Edmonton. But this was coming to an end; the 'better part' of society was reluctant to attend.[49]

*Learned, or sapient, pigs – universally known as Toby – were always popular. An advertisement for one read: 'He will spell, read, and cast accounts, tell the points of the sun's rising and setting, discover the four grand divisions of the Earth, kneel at command, perform blindfold with 20 handkerchiefs over his eyes, tell the hour by a minute by a watch, tell a card, and the age of any party. He is in colour the most beautiful of his race, in symmetry the most perfect, in temper the most docile.'

A writer in the *New Monthly Magazine* deplored the extinction of popular festivals which had once drawn the people together. 'Within the last half century our national character has experienced a manifest and violent change.' And if such a change could be measured at all, it was by looking at old customs and forms of recreation. The middle classes now considered rubbing shoulders with their poorer neighbours to be vulgar and unbecoming of their sense of dignity. Festivals and fairs that had once been sources 'of a wide-spread and genuine pleasure' were fading away; by the 1820s fairs that used to be held at Stepney, Bow and Hampstead had been banned, and those at Peckham, Camberwell and Greenwich Park had dwindled because of lack of enthusiasm from some sections of the community or languished 'under the strait-waistcoat of police'. In the past all had revelled in such boisterous carnivals together, but notions of refinement and respectability held back the middle class.[50]

In December 1817 Leigh Hunt wrote of the 'Death of Merry England', which had been replaced by her great-granddaughter, who 'is very bustling, very talkative, and, as the phrase is, very successful in the world; but somehow or other, she is not happy'. She was rich, but she was melancholy. She was too enlightened and upright to condescend to participate in the simple pleasures of her youth.[51]

In the recent past at Christmas, London was bedecked with boughs and mistletoe, 'as if a rural city had started up in the midst of winter'. By the late 1810s, however, the festive season had become dreary and withdrawn, and 'an air of constraint and business is thrown over every thing'; the holiday was 'rather honoured than enjoyed'. People hardly sang carols any more, and printed collections of them were rare; they were a dying folk custom said not to belong to the advanced and refined nineteenth century. Writing in 1823, P. G. Patmore wrote that the Christmas festival – from 24 December until Twelfth Night – was once the time when 'all that restraint, stiffness, and formality, which are the sins of English society' were forgotten in a round of dinner parties with rich meat dishes, puddings, cakes, pies, fruits and dainties and enlivened with songs, glees, toasts and boisterous games.[52] 'The stiff manners and fastidious taste of the present race of English, have nearly exploded this,' Patmore explained. Another wrote of the winter festival: 'The middle classes make it a sorry business of a pudding or so extra, and a game at cards.' Hunt said that the English (i.e. not the British) had an 'habitual indisposition to enjoyment', but ascribed the reason for the new joylessness to 'the commercial and jobbing spirit' that kept people at their desks or counting houses and 'that habit of trying every thing by the test of common sense and utility'. The new rectitude of comportment and sobriety of manners was augmented by the 'melancholy disease of taking merriment for vice'.[53]

Holidays such as Christmas had customarily been a time of giving 'doles' to poorer neighbours in the form of money, beer and food. In recent memory, on Christmas Day or Boxing Day the parish beadle would don his gold-laced hat, full greatcoat and carry his vast gold-topped staff of office on a parade through the parish asking for contributions 'for cheering the abode of the needy at this cheerful season'. In towns and villages, 'wassailers', 'mummers' and carol-singers would parade from house to house demanding gifts. William Hone believed that of the old customs 'the few that remain are rapidly declining . . . without such feelings, the few occasions which enable us to show a hospitable disposition, or from whence we can obtain unconstrained cheerfulness, will pass away, and be remembered only as having been'.[54]

There was always, as we have seen, a context of threat and violence in these customs which had hitherto been tolerated. But there were very good Malthusian reasons for withholding this customary generosity. It was just another relic of dark, ignorant ages when the good-natured unwittingly weaned the poor away from good working practices and habits of self-reliance. In most places, according to the *Mirror of the Month*, 'the unfeeling and mercenary urge "false pretences" with the vain hope of concealing their private reasons for refusing charity'. People feared, or claimed to fear, that a gift of charity at Christmas would debauch their idle neighbours and teach them to be parasites the rest of the year.

Whatever economic theory they cited, the respectable were no longer prepared to tolerate festive high spirits, their rowdy neighbours menacing them and the prodigious waste of time and money involved. Christmas was inimical to the good ordering of society and the values of modern Britain. The lord of the manor of Princes Risborough took a case before the Charity Commission to ask whether his Christmas dole of mutton and beef was a voluntary custom or an obligation under common law. The behaviour of the poor was enough to suggest its abolition: 'The practice . . . seemed to have been productive of much intoxication and riot: the poor are said to have paraded the town during the whole night preceding the distribution with an incessant clamour, effectually banishing all repose . . . On the door being opened, they rushed to the feast prepared for them with so little decorum and forbearance, that often in their zeal for priority they inflicted wounds on one another with their knives. The whole of the remaining portion of Christmas Day is also stated to have been spent by many of them in public houses.'[55]

It was considered better to ignore Christmas altogether than allow it to turn into twelve nights of idleness, drinking and cadging. (It would only become popular later in the century, when it had been sanitised, sentimentalised and shorn of plebeian drunkenness.) The new virtues of respectability and deportment made the middle classes targets for much mockery. They were too serious and much too nice to condescend to participate in simple entertainments, far too superior to their parents to lower their dignity, and fearful of their reputation if they did. Patmore wrote that there were still 'a few days which the common people, the mere vulgar (always wiser than their betters) still persist in squandering on happiness, instead of seriously attending to their respective duties of getting their daily bread'.[56]

Leigh Hunt wrote in 1825 that the new manners had come about because old English vulgarity and plain-speaking had been conquered by the 'pretended politeness and reasoning spirit' of French manners. This was combined with the cold calculations of business and mercantile reasoning and the revival of dour puritanism: 'Our dancing was now to be confined, like a sickly person, to its apartment. We might have as much gallantry as we pleased in a private way . . . none in a more open and innocent one . . . we were to show our refinement by being superior to every rustic impulse; and do nothing but doubt, and be gentlemanly, and afraid of committing ourselves. Men of all parties, opinions and characters, united to substitute this false politeness and quiescence to the higher spirit of old English activity. The trader was too busy for pastime; the dissenter too serious; the sceptic too philosophical; the gentleman too high-bred; – and, like master like man, apprentices became too busy, like their employers; the dissenter must stop the dancing of the village; . . . and the footman must be as genteel as his master, and have a spirit above clownish gambols.'[57]

In *The English Spy* by 'Bernard Blackmantle' (a pseudonym for Charles Westmacott), the Marigold family are supposedly typical of the aspirant metropolitan middle classes. Mr Marigold has dragged himself up to become a wealthy merchant and a City alderman. Reluctantly, Mr Marigold has been uprooted from his beloved City by his socially ambitious wife and daughter and forced to live in fashionable Tavistock Square in Bloomsbury. He pines for his accustomed entertainments: *Punch and Judy*, boisterous clubs and fairs.

One Sunday he paid a shilling for an entertainer to perform *Punch and Judy* in the street outside, to the outrage of his overeducated, fancy and self-conscious daughter Biddy. 'La, mama,' whined Miss Biddy Marigold when the performer came back the next week, 'I declare, it's that filthy fellow Punch coming afore our vindow with his imperence; I prognosticated how it vould be, ven the alderman patronised him last veek by throwing away a whole shilling upon his fooleries.' But, for all her airs and graces and fastidiousness and clever words, Biddy can't deny her heritage (just as she can't hide her cockney accent); she enjoys the show despite herself.

'Plague take your drives in Hyde Park and promenades in Kensington Gardens!' Mr Marigold tells his snobbish wife and daughter. 'Give me the society where I can eat, drink, laugh, joke, and smoke as I like, without being obliged to watch every word and action, as if my tongue was a traitor to my head, and my stomach a tyrant of self-destruction.'[58]

13

Merry England

'The people of England have so much good temper that they could be easily led; but they have so much high spirit, that the attempt to drive them would be as impractical as it would be unjust.'

Colonel Thomas Wood MP[1]

'A general spirit of selfishness has diffused itself among those lilies of society, that neither toil nor spin,' wrote a contributor to the *New Monthly Magazine*; 'and with a pharisaic morality, which is the offspring equally of blindness of understanding and hardness of heart, they have lopped away, one by one, nearly all those holiday relics which the poor hailed with eagerness and enjoyed with delight. Whatsoever was imaginative and poetical in the life of the lower classes, has faded away.'[2]

If the respectable sections of society turned their noses up at 'vulgar' entertainments and discontinued their visits to the fair or dance, that was their business. It was another matter, however, to actively seek to suppress what little opportunity for fun and frolic existed for the labouring classes. Many of the old customs of lower-class life – the rural festivals, the rowdy holiday rituals, Skimmington rides, St Monday and other lusty pastimes – were driven out in the name of order and economics. The drunken and brutal customs of the lower orders had always been disapproved of by many; in the 1820s these people found the self-confidence, backing and ability to purge them from society.

There was an intolerant spirit abroad which sought to drive away noise, carnivalesque rowdiness, perceived nuisances and unconventional behaviour. The word 'unproductive' sparked a Pavlovian response in people who had reached adulthood in the early nineteenth century. Unproductive labour and pastimes were dangerous to the individual, the community and the country. They had intimations of Malthusian horrors, spiralling crime rates and economic disaster. Anything unproductive and wasteful should be suppressed. This did not come from above, from parliamentary pressure; the impulse welled up from public opinion and from private effort. The streets should, these vocal and increasingly influential people believed, reflect the morals of a godly and grave civilisation. But whose morals were they? By the mid-1820s young couples would be arrested by zealous officers for the heinous crime of kissing in public.

In the 1820s there was what can fairly be described as moral panic and the pervasive belief that Britain was in the grip of a crime wave. If 'the people' at the beginning of this period were regarded as brooding revolutionaries, that fear had been replaced by something new. George Mainwaring wrote that it was impossible to differentiate the poor 'from the barbarous hordes which traverse an uncivilised land'. In 1806 there had been 4,346 committals for criminal trials in England and Wales; by 1826 this had rocketed to 16,147. Prisons were overflowing. There were, as we shall see, plenty of reasons other than a massive increase in criminality why this should be the case, but it did not stop people imagining that lawlessness was rampant. Some believed that the law was lax and supposed deterrents were mild. Transportation to New South Wales was seen as the privilege of being sent to a balmy clime; prison was soft; and fewer criminals were being executed. The Surrey bench of magistrates said that the streets had become even more dangerous and unwholesome than they had been during the war years: 'the female part are constantly on the alert for enticement of the unwary; while the males are earnestly watchful for the means of pilfering and robbery'. These years had seen increases too in ginshops and unlicensed wine shops and other breeding grounds of depravity. The 'fair-frequenting' parts of society were another danger; they were at the forefront of social evils. 'Thieves, prostitutes, and sharpers – loose, idle, and disorderly persons of every description, flock thither as to their harvest,' one magistrate wrote to *The Times*. Fairs showed the 'growing depravity of the times', particularly the 'awfully increased band of juvenile delinquents'.[3]

Alcohol and fairgrounds: these were the chief aspects of popular culture that had to be curbed. But how were centuries of plebeian entertainments to be effaced? The followers of the late Patrick Colquhoun continued to demand a police force to grapple with the burgeoning social crisis. Mainwaring wanted a strong system of policing that would 'so change the manners and habits of the people, upon whom it is to act, as to drive them to the pursuit of industry'. He spoke for many who wanted a system of surveillance to keep a close eye on lower-class immorality and provide a strong arm to restrain it. But there was little indication until the late 1820s that Parliament would commit what they saw as liberticide and reform the police.

Afraid of the unpopular step of introducing a centralised police force, the problem was dealt with by legislative reform instead. Until Robert Peel's reforms, many petty crimes were capital offences. Not wanting to have a wayward neighbour killed for a trivial transgression, many victims refrained from prosecuting. Downgrading scores of crimes meant that criminals were now pursued and sent to prison. The apparent rise in committals and convictions reflected this change in the law. A seemingly merciful reform in the law in fact meant a more draconian system, especially for petty offences. Thanks to the work of Elizabeth Fry, her Quaker and evangelical allies, and a parliamentary committee chaired by Henry Grey Bennet, the horrendous conditions of prisons had become a matter of notoriety. There were more of them, and they were built and maintained on better sanitary principles than before. A judge and jury now had no compunction about sending more people – even young boys – to gaol, in the belief that they would be treated well there, or at least not abused and infected with disease. The better prisons were perceived to be, the lower the stock of mercy fell.

'The humanity of this country, in criminal law, seems to have taken a very perverse turn,' commented the *Globe* newspaper. Some of the French papers expressed shock that the English were now sending boys to prison 'for robbing a clergyman's garden of some apples'. But judges and juries did not see such an offence as a footling matter or the sentence as an inappropriately heavy-handed response; there was now a faith that prison worked. Confinement behind bars was a means of social engineering: it had the possibility of reforming and renewing criminals and nipping the tendency to thieve in the bud as far as juvenile delinquents were concerned. Petty acts of delinquency weren't nuisances but the root of all crime. In practice, zero tolerance had the effect of inventing a whole host of new crimes, particularly juvenile offences; things that had hitherto been tolerated or considered youthful high jinks were now seen as the first step in a life of crime. There had not been a greater increase in crime proportional to population, but there had been an increase in punishable offences. Society was inclined to forgive less and condemn a lot more. The new language of humanity was expressed by the chairman of the Middlesex Sessions in 1828. 'I'll give these boys another chance,' he said when indicting a collection of ragged young boys, including a homeless and starving twelve-year-old boy, for stealing two buns and eight biscuits, '– let them be confined for three months, and be twice well whipped.'[4]

Crime might not have been rising in a greater degree than before, but expectations were. Lucas Benjamin Allen, a magistrate at Union Hall in Southwark, wrote in 1821 that the problem with superintending the populace, in the absence of a rigorous police force, was that the law did not allow officers to apprehend idle and disorderly people. A known pickpocket, for example, could not be carted off to prison unless he was caught actually committing a crime. Similarly, it would be fanciful to suppose that one could suppress the trade of prostitution completely, but at the same time it was shocking that the authorities could not oblige prostitutes 'to adopt an outward decency of demeanour, and prevent them from shocking the eyes and ears of every decent person who may meet them'. There had to be summary punishment for all kinds of people, not just prostitutes, who disrupted the smooth surface of society. 'Decent' people needed special protection, it seemed. There did not necessarily have to be a change in the law but, as Mainwaring said, 'restraint which works by moral influence rather than legal power' instead.[5]

People who needed to be forced into a better mode of life usually fell under the category of 'incorrigible rogues', according to the vagrancy laws. This bundle of ancient statutes lumped together the detritus of succeeding ages: from the archaic nuisance of tumblers and minstrels to the perennial annoyance of prostitutes and drunks. In 1821 the MP George Chetwynd chaired yet another House of Commons select committee, this time examining the laws relating to vagrants. The evidence presented was identical to that examined by the mendicity committee of 1815: the same accounts of people choosing to become beggars for the thrills and spills and largesse of life on the streets and lanes.

As was to be expected, the committee, and all but one of the witnesses called, emphasised the joys of a life of vagrancy and the numberless pleasures of prison. Most of it was exaggeration and misrepresentation, but, as members of committees now knew, the more alarming the evidence could be made to sound, the more likely action would be taken. In 1822 Chetwynd introduced the Vagrant

Acts Amendment Bill, which would consolidate centuries' worth of defunct laws 'to adapt them to the present state of society', toughen up the penalties for vagrancy and give magistrates greater summary powers. Those classed as vagrants could be arrested without a warrant and held in a watchhouse before going before the bench. The rules of evidence were shifted in favour of the testimony of officers; magistrates did not need any other corroborating evidence. The right of trial by jury was taken away and discretionary power placed in the hands of the magistracy. A beggar would be given up to three months' hard labour and perhaps a salutary whipping on apprehension, and 'incorrigible rogues' would get up to a year.

But the bill would do more than that. Perhaps dazzled by the depravity listed by the select committee, Parliament passed an act some of its members would later come to regret. It gave magistrates almost unlimited powers to clear the streets, fairgrounds and fields of any kind of undesirable – not just beggars. That was certainly the intention of Chetwynd and his followers. According to the vague language of the act, anyone in the kingdom could at some point be defined as a 'vagrant': anyone who was drunk, travelling without purpose, without visible means of support or unable to give a good account of him- or herself could be classed as such. Many more harmless, unconventional or, at worst, rowdy people would count as 'incorrigible rogues'. Vagrancy laws had been introduced in the sixteenth and seventeenth centuries to combat the then very real threat of armed gangs who roamed the countryside. But years of change in society meant that many of the rigorous laws could be used against the merely annoying – 'negligent workmen, idle apprentices, and even truant schoolboys looking for birds' nests' – not genuinely dangerous criminals.

Some MPs knew at the time that the new Vagrant Act of 1824 could be used to destroy popular entertainments. Colonel Thomas Wood told the House that he 'knew that some persons fear that a very entertaining personage called Mr Punch will no longer be allowed to amuse the public': itinerant performers were listed in the definition of vagrants from the sixteenth century. Another MP 'hoped that my friend Mr Punch, as well as the persons who carry wild beasts for show, will not be included in the list of vagrants by this law, as they are subject of great and general amusement'. Chetwynd admitted that the act would threaten old customs: 'I have heard that some persons, particularly ladies, complain that by the Bill the minstrels who perambulate the streets will be prevented from serenading them.' But he had little sympathy. Strolling players and fairs were already subject to the law, albeit law that had been lax for decades. His act would accomplish what had always been intended by the vagrancy laws: the moral reformation of the people.[6]

The word 'vagrant' was a misnomer; or, at least, it should not be confused with mendicity. One writer spoke of a 'vagrant spirit' which characterised the lower orders. Like the hated beggars, they were habitually drunk, lazy and given to impostures, and oscillated between plunder and charity as sources of maintenance. So it came as no surprise that the new act would be deployed against people whom Parliament had not intended to be included when it passed the legislation – people who were not, strictly speaking, vagrants. The laws allowed the police to deal with beggars, but after 1822 they were equipped to raid so-called 'Hells' – low gambling dens – and other places of bad repute that had flourished with impunity. Soon after it became law, constables used the Vagrant Act to raid theatres in north London and arrest the actors and the audience under their interpretation of the definition of vagrant. Magistrates dismissed the ridiculous charges, but not until numbers of 'young people in all stations of life' had spent a night in the watchhouse with prostitutes and thieves: a fine way to purify the morals of the youth of the capital.[7]

At the same time, other acts of Parliament increased the regulatory powers of magistrates. They were aimed at scenes of popular entertainment. New laws gave the bench powers to interfere in the hours of public houses and suppress fairs. Justices of the Peace in Middlesex used their discretionary powers to decide that eleven o'clock at night marked the boundary between early and late, and insisted that the public houses in their jurisdiction closed at that early hour. Fairs within ten miles of Temple Bar were effectively destroyed when it was decreed that they should close at the same time as alehouses. With the new laws to hand, the authorities could arrest people who lingered in public houses, publicans, fair-goers and players as vagabonds if any of these regulations were broken.

John Adolphus, a barrister and critic of the new laws, was appalled at this draconian spirit: 'Whatever desire may exist any where to suppress the supposed licentiousness of the fair-frequenting class of the community, it will not easily be imagined that such severe penalties can have been deliberately affixed to such small transgressions. Forty-shillings for staying in an alehouse till his pot of beer is out, or not quitting the puppet show . . . is the penalty to be exacted from the labourer who earns perhaps twelve shillings a week, or the servant girl whose wages are six guineas a year.' The act disproved 'the propriety and possibility of restraining excesses and curbing licentiousness, without ruthlessly destroying some of the best and most cherished popular amusements'.

The act was harsh on what Albany Fonblanque, editor of the *Examiner*, called the 'little pleasures of the poor'. 'To delight the ears of the poor is an act of vagrancy,' he wrote, parodying a stern magistrate. 'What indeed, have the ears of the poor to do with the sounds sweet to them? – the use of their ears is to hear commands.' When two musicians played in Jermyn Street, half the residents enjoyed the performance and crowded round the fiddlers, while the other half complained of the nuisance. The two were classed as minstrels and arrested under the act. The objection was to the disturbance the players caused, but who ever heard of magistrates raiding a lord's house and arresting Paganini because the street outside was congested with carriages? 'An obstruction occasioned by a fiddler in the street is associated with the ideas of dirty shirts, corduroy breeches, worsted stockings, working jackets, and fusty, frouzy smells.' Legislators and magistrates could not believe that 'the unwashed can have enjoyments entitled to sympathy and respect, far less to encouragement and cultivation'. The tendency was to dismiss popular entertainments as 'vulgar', and to conflate vulgarity with criminality.[8]

Some said that the claret- and madeira-drinking class was tyrannising the beer-drinking classes. The *London Magazine* went further and said: 'We are a people crossed, not only in liquor, but in laughter.' When the magistracy believed that popular amusements were criminal, it put 'a *veto* on any piece or custom which does not exactly square with its idea of what is right. So many magistrates, so many sentiments. One dislikes this, another finds something amiss in that.' The godly Surrey magistrates, for example, objected to fireworks going off at Vauxhall Pleasure Gardens at eleven o'clock; like their fellow justices north of the river, they did not like the idea of clerks staying up too late. They also disliked public dancing, and ordered Frederick Gye, the manager, to put up notices saying that only professional dancing was permitted and that the bands should revert to a slow march if anyone defied the order. Gye told the bench that 'when half a dozen or a dozen parties commenced dancing, at the same time, and where some 3000 or 4000 persons were assembled, they would be likely to take the case in their own hands'. One magistrate, a Mr Jackson, said that 'if Mr Gye declined undertaking to prevent all dancing except professional dancing, he [Jackson] should press his motion for excluding dancing altogether'. The worthy bench would not back down in the face of licentious pleasure; to do so would, they said hysterically, be to hand power to the depraved: 'The question now was, whether the magistrates were to rule Vauxhall Gardens, or Vauxhall Gardens to rule the magistrates?' The *London Magazine* said that the magistrates should be combated with ridicule: laughter was 'a wholesome corrective to these officious whimsies'. It was laughable, but nonetheless they 'were cruelly oppressive in their efforts'.[9]

Such nuisances were easier to suppress. An act of 1822 allowed magistrates to put down unauthorised fairs. When William Hone went to the Whitsuntide fair at Greenwich in 1825 to conduct research for his *Every-Day Book*, he found a sad affair. It had been one of the favourite festivals for Londoners. 'At the entrance in all the streets of Greenwich, notices from the magistrates were posted, that they were determined to put down the fair; and accordingly not a show was to be seen in the place wherein the fair had of late been held.' The vicar, churchwardens and parish overseers had petitioned the magistrates in April, saying that the fair held out 'incentives to licentiousness' to the middle class, offended 'Christian morality' and harmed the trade of local shopkeepers. The magistrates empowered the special constables to pull down any stall they saw. Voltaire had relished his visit to this fair many years before and had depicted the merrymaking of the subordinate classes, but now, apparently, it was the pit of depravity. But accounts differ in the 1820s: some said it was disgusting, others that it was innocent and joyous. In 1814 *The Times* said that Greenwich Fair had never been more orderly in thirty years.

When Hone went, there were booths for dancing and refreshment at night, but there were no plays or shows, no gingerbread stalls, no learned pig, no dwarves or giants and no exhibitions or entertainments of any kind except for swings set up for children. No drinking was allowed in the park. It was the result of a long campaign to suppress the accustomed 'boisterous rudeness'. By then many of the London fairs had been 'crushed by the police, that "stern rugged nurse" of national morality'. Yet people had flocked out from London to Greenwich as they always did at Whit; except this time there was only a pale shadow of a fair. With drinking and amusement banned, the people had few options but to resort to public houses and drink the day – and night – away.[10]

The same fate awaited other suburban fairs; Peckham and Camberwell Fairs were attacked by the local magistracy. But the great London saturnalia was ancient Bartholomew Fair, held at Smithfield every September since 1133. It had always been considered an 'intolerable nuisance' by City authorities, and there had been attempts to suppress it throughout the seventeenth and eighteenth centuries; in 1798 the council had recommended total abolition. In the 1820s the Lord Mayor talked of 'the necessity of doing everything to reform the morals of the people'. However, Bartholomew Fair was protected by ancient charter, so it was not as easy to attack as Greenwich or Camberwell Fairs. In 1823 *The Times* believed that abolition was unnecessary in any case; the fair would die a natural death within two years. But it was not so. After the 1825 fair, Alderman Joshua Jonathan Smith noted that it had swollen to occupy St John Street to the north and Old Bailey to the south, and expressed his determination to 'lessen the criminal extension which had arisen, if not abolish the degrading scene altogether'. Hone was equally concerned that the fair should be banned: 'The well-being of . . . apprentices and servants and the young and illiterate, require protection from the annual scene of debauchery, which contributes nothing to the city funds, and nothing to the city's character but a shameful stain.' The long-held dream of abolishing three days' annual drinking in the centre of the City 'may be contemplated as near at hand'.[11]

Had the fair suddenly become worse, enough to warrant its immediate abolition? Not a bit of it: Hone noted that the 1825 fair was the most orderly and well-conducted in living memory. But the complexion of the fair-goers was different: 'No person of respectability now visits it, but as a curious spectator of an annual congregation of ignorance and depravity.' A member of the City's Common Council said: 'No one would suspect me of the wish to take away the amusements or lessen the enjoyments of the humbler classes. The question is, do they derive real pleasure and amusement from the delights of Bartholomew fair? I rather think they do not.'

The definition of fun should rest with the grave and respectable Common Councillors. The fair lingered on until its final abolition in

1854, but every year it faded a little more; 1825 could be said to have been the last of the glory days. If the council could not ban it until then, it could make life harder for the showmen. Rents for spaces for stalls went up from 1826 and instances of arrests for petty offences – such as selling gingerbread on a Sunday – became more common. The zeal to ban the nuisance and the vigilance of the council and respectable people were awakened from the 1820s. What had changed was not the character of the fair but what the middle class, typified by Hone, was prepared to tolerate. That which they had enjoyed throughout their lives was now disgusting and disgraceful and in need of control.[12]

Adolphus wrote that MPs had no idea 'of the extensive means of tyranny and extortion they have put into the hands of those who never were, and never will be, sparing in the use of them'. Such powers were as a dream come true for the Society for the Suppression of Vice and its supporters. They had argued for over two decades that petty crimes and coarse pleasures should be stamped out, and the poor regulated and coerced into a better semblance of moral rectitude. Now, with the new laws, magistrates, if they shared the SSV's sentiments, could enforce the ancient regulations that they found in Elizabethan and Jacobean statute books. And not just magistrates. The act was a boon to 'village reformers', busybodies who objected to the exuberance of their neighbours' amusements. It gave 'every old woman's whim the force of law'. The possibilities of clearing the streets ranged from suppressing drunken excess to trivial annoyances. Hone noted the absence of London barrow-women: 'They are quite "gone out", or, rather, they have been "put down", and by many they are not even missed.' But it was not ever thus. In Hone's youth, the barrow-woman was the joy and delight of many city folk. Throughout the summer she brought seasonal fruit to town; she carried whatever was ready, 'but cherry-time was the meridian of her glory'. As she walked the streets she sang:

> Round and sound,
> Two-pence a pound,
> Cherries! rare ripe cherries!

At other times, gooseberries, amberberries or currants would replace cherries. Customers would stand at their doors, waiting with basins and salivating at the prospect of ripe, succulent fruits. But in their last years 'the poor things were cruelly used'. For some they represented another nuisance that cluttered the streets. If they stopped for a moment, 'street-keepers, authorized by orders unauthorized by law, drove them off, or beadles overthrew their fruit into the road'. It smacked too much of vagrancy.[13]

As *The Times* commented when the Vagrant Act was a year old, the puritanism of some magistrates was bringing the whole law into contempt and had seen the creation of crimes unheard of before. In Kent alone some 1,061 destitute people were reclassified as vagrants and sent to prison for the new 'crime' of being homeless and helpless: it was a lot cheaper than providing for them under the provisions of the Poor Law.[14]

Adolphus wrote that the excesses of some magistrates typified 'the political and religious punctiliousness of the day'. There was a clear connection between unmerciful use of the act and religious zeal. 'The reform of the common people seems to be a favourable project in these times, and, as, in every reform, one must see something of the temper, habits, and propensity of the reformers, so I observe, with regret, in these attempts a manifestation of a gloomy, austere, and unsocial temper, an inclination to break up the accustomed forms of popular intercourse, to render difficult, if not impossible, the enjoyment of ordinary indulgences, and to enforce, in appearance at least, a rigid, formal, inflexible piety, and an unintermitting attention to the externals of exact religious observance.'[15]

A magistrate who lived in a village on the outskirts of London was very godly and liked to go to chapel from six until after eight every Sunday evening; unfortunately for him, not all the local inhabitants were so inclined. The thought that others could be enjoying a pot of porter while he was engaged in solemn devotion was too much. The pious magistrate acted as judge, jury, prosecutor and witness and had the publicans severely punished for selling beer when *he* was at divine service; it was no concern to him if the locals 'were at least as much incommoded as he was edified'.

It was in the same spirit as the derisive Society for the Suppression of Vice, only now sabbatarianism was a respectable and well-supported campaign, especially among the middle classes. Throughout the 1820s calls for better observance of the seventh day got ever louder. Under proposed new laws, public houses, tea gardens and most forms of transport would be banned on the Sabbath. In Newcastle in 1832 an outbreak of cholera was put down to the punishment God inflicted on Sabbath-breakers; others warned that if Parliament did not outlaw Sunday pleasures, 'the tide of immorality . . . will then burst forth with all the insolence of triumph, and deluge the whole country'. But others pointed out that God was unlikely to unleash his vengeance, given that the Sabbath was a human creation. The Sabbath of the Old Testament was strict and joyless, but Christ had relaxed the rigours of the day. It was possible to go to church and then seek pleasurable recreation without committing sacrilege; the whole day did not have to be engulfed in Stygian gloom. Nonetheless, the sabbatarians talked of its sacredness and warned of divine retribution. For others, it was a never-changing debate: the ulterior motive for all this piety was to ban all pleasure on the only working-class holiday. 'So then, at last, the people are to be humbugged into obedience to the law of the land, and to the performance of their duty,' wrote an enemy to the 'junto of puritans' he saw dictating to the population. 'This in good keeping with this age of cant and humbug. A pious fraud is to be practised to keep the people in order!'[16]

Parliament was reluctant to acquiesce in purging Sundays of pleasure, but the Vagrant Act could be used to accomplish some of the reforms dreamed of by the sabbatarians. The act was most keenly felt in districts where Methodists or evangelicals held a monopoly of public office. In January 1824 a young man took a young lady to the theatre, and then to dinner at his father's house in Southwark. When they parted on the doorstep at midnight he kissed her 'as was usual with him, and he supposed with every other young man in such circumstances'. But as they did so, a watchman emerged from the shadows. 'I see what you are about,' he declared, 'you are indecently exposing yourself, and I have a mind to take you off to the watch-house.' And so he did.

The young couple were released by L. B. Allen, the magistrate in attendance at Union Hall, after a night locked in the watchhouse. But it was an indication of the ways in which zealous people could manipulate the act. A provision of the law was to prevent vagrants indecently exposing themselves. Yet like so much of the ill-conceived law, it was so inadequately defined that it was left up to individual taste to decide what constituted an indecent act. The newly founded journal of medical record, *The Lancet*, took great exception to the act. The laws gave watchmen and officers 'a power as *unprecedented* as *unjust* – and not more *unjust* than *unconstitutional*'. The couple arrested for kissing at midnight were lucky that L. B. Allen was presiding at Union Hall police office the morning following their chaste kiss. *The Lancet* pointed out that another magistrate at the office, Maurice Swabey, had very little tolerance for public displays of affection. Another young couple in the area were brought before him after being caught holding hands by the patrol. The officer claimed that they were about something more lascivious than that. In court, the couple and friends swore that they were respectable people and were not causing any offence by holding hands in public. 'All your observations will not controvert the statement of the patrol,' Swabey told the defendants and their friends; 'he has sworn you were in that situation, and *I believe him*; but for this once I discharge you.'[17]

The Southwark watchmen and patrols were eager to apprehend canoodling couples because they knew that puritanical magistrates like Swabey were inclined to cleanse the streets of what they considered unacceptable behaviour. For each easily achieved conviction, the arresting officer would pick up a reward of five shillings. On another occasion one Mr Hook, who had been drinking with his friend's wife, Mary Merrit, stopped on the Borough Road to relieve himself. Both Hook and Merrit were arrested and sent to the House of Correction by Swabey. In the same way, bathers and swimmers and, indeed, anyone who took their clothes off for any reason, were courting magisterial displeasure. The act could also be used to criminalise adultery. A provision of the act classed 'persons threatening to run away and leave their wives and children chargeable to the parish' as vagrants. This badly worded line seemed to refer exclusively to a certain class of person – the very poor man who knew that the Poor Laws would provide more money for his children if he abandoned them than if they stayed together as a family. Yet, read another way, magistrates could punish whomsoever they considered *likely* to run away. John Adolphus said that this was one of the most vindictive aspects of the law; it left any man vulnerable 'to the assertion of any discontented or spiteful individual' – especially bitter wives or jilted mistresses. And exactly this happened to 'a good-for-nothing sort of fellow' who had a dirty weekend with a neighbour's wife, between whom 'it had long been suspected there existed a sneaking kindness'. The prisoner said that the brief affair 'was only a foolish freak of his' and he never intended to leave his wife permanently.[18]

There were frequent cases of couples detained for kissing in public. It was by no means common throughout the kingdom, but it did show that the act, when placed in the hands of aggressively puritanical people, could be used as a weapon of moral reformation. When the House of Commons heard how their legislation was being used, many MPs were incensed that magistrates and peace officers were using the law for their own personal moral crusades. The act had given the magistracy an unprecedented and unconstitutional power over the individual, which, some said, usurped Parliament. Joseph Hume told the Commons about one William Lotcho, a labourer from Whitechapel, who was arrested in the East End late one night and condemned to hard labour 'for violating the decency of the place'. He was, he claimed, guilty of nothing more than giving a woman directions to Brick Lane. The magistrate believed the watchman – the only witness – and decreed that the lost woman was a notorious prostitute and the couple 'were guilty of as open an exposure of their persons as could be imagined'.[19]

It was not a trivial case: Lotcho lost his reputation for good and had to undergo a course of hard labour in prison. And this was all on the say-so of just one watchman. Was he a vindictive witness? Was he motivated by religious zeal to set an example for his neighbourhood? The point was that the liberty of the subject was susceptible to the dictates of a watchman and the whim of a magistrate. 'I would ask,' Hume said to the Commons, 'in going through the streets of London, crowded as they are with females, whether one of ourselves might not be placed in the same situation as this individual? If any of us were asked by a woman on the road, he would not be much of a gentleman if he refused that act of politeness.'[20]

William Lotcho had to spend a month in the House of Correction, and his days would be occupied by the most modern and progressive of reformatory punishments. After centuries of wondering what to do with idle and incorrigible rogues, this enlightened age had come up with a solution that was both salutary and cost-effective. The Vagrant Act was intended to round up the lazy and unproductive; their punishment should teach them better habits of industry. Above all, the punishment would be wholly useless if it was as unproductive and as burdensome to the taxpayer as the prisoner's usual mode of life. The treadmill gave magistrates the perfect punishment now that they had a free hand to correct the idle habits of vagrants.

The tread- or discipline-mill consisted of two long cylinders some twelve feet high which opposed each other; the revolution of the two cylinders would turn a cog, move the planes and grind corn. Each cylinder had a number of tread boards running along its length and arranged like a watermill or paddle wheel, so that up to forty prisoners could surmount the wheel and turn it with the tread of their feet, like a hamster in a cage or a dog on a turnspit. The prisoner's movement was twofold: he would step up and down and shuffle sideways. He or she would mount the cylinder at one end, while another stepped down for a short rest at the other. The cylinder never had to stop during the working day. Best of all, the grain from the mill paid for the prisoners' upkeep. What could be more appropriate in the machine age?[21]

Such a punishment augmented the new powers given to magistrates; a prisoner, without ever facing a jury and with no possibility of appeal, could be subjected to months of hard labour at the discretion of a magistrate. In the past, they might not have committed too many petty criminals to gaol because a large prison population cost the county a lot of money. This restraining factor was removed now. *The Times* went into ecstasies over 'the absolute perfection of the treadmill'. The machine was cheap, it did not have any complicated components that could be worn down, it could turn all day without interruption and no instruction was needed for its operatives. No other age or society had yet discovered a punishment that made money *and* produced a moral and religious effect on the prisoner. Whereas prisons were 'theatres of profligate indulgence' and altogether too comfortable, a prison yard with a treadmill broke 'the stubborn spirit' of the inmate, taught him or her the value of labour for the first time and relieved the taxpayer of having to support criminals in luxurious idleness. Most importantly, the mill and the use of corporal punishment, according to Robert Peel, 'produced a salutary terror' in the rest of the community.[22]

When people complained of the inhumanity of the treadmill, they were accused of simpering milk-and-water sentimentality; the mill had been introduced to huge popularity in 1822. It seemed as if all the failures of penal servitude and punishment had been solved; it was a badge of progress – 'a miraculous combination of mercantile speculation and moral improvement'. The enthusiasm on the part of magistrates, MPs and the law-abiding part of the community for the 'felons' wheel' was endless, as Sir J. P. Acland wrote: 'The Tread-wheel is so much sanctioned by popular opinion as a new mode of punishment that the philanthropy of the day does not recoil at it, and it is to be carried on throughout the prisons without consideration.' But Acland had a warning for all those who believed that modern Britain had perfected a way of ending crime and reclaiming abandoned criminals: 'presently, we shall find the impropriety of it appealed against, and voted cruel and dangerous, and the like; and it will be ordered to be laid aside as disgusting and unsuited to the age we live in, and the humanity due to prisoners'.[23]

The ideological principles of the mill bound together the ideas of reformers of all hues. Prisons were objected to because of the horrendous conditions, but what was worse was the policy of non-interference with prisoners. Brought to the attention of the state, incorrigible rogues, lawless types and squalid wretches were left alone to wallow in their depravity. In the prison hulks the hatches were bolted and guarded; down below the prisoners drank, fought and engaged in acts of sodomy. In gaols, the inmates gambled, got drunk, boxed and treated the places like brothels with no exit. They meted out their own rough justice in mock trials and laughed at authority. There was no idea that criminals should or even could be reformed or coerced into better behaviour; this was, as far as the reformers were concerned, the greatest evil of penal servitude. When members of the 'dangerous class' were captive audiences, the state passed on the one opportunity when they could be exposed to the word of God and taught wholesome discipline. 'Let the evil-doer in prison, be as in a school, learning the nature of his offence, and the danger which attends it, with respect to his soul as well as his body; and whether he is to die or not, he will, by degrees, be convinced of his crimes.' This was the humane view of one reformer. But, like policing, the state delegated authority to the discretion of governors and magistrates, sticking firmly to the idea that it had neither the right nor the duty to interfere.[24]

Evangelicals and Benthamite utilitarians believed that with the right kind of regime, prisoners could be reclaimed. The old discretionary theory was inherently wrong because it left punishment to the whim of individual governors and warders; a centralised and scientific *system* of punishment was the only answer. A penitentiary, as opposed to gaol, should be run according to strict regulations: prisoners should be kept in solitary confinement and fed on a subsistence diet; the chapel and hard labour would dominate the prisoner's life. Reduced to silence and mechanical, routine work, the prisoner would be forced to confront his or her punishment in a way that was inconceivable in the lax environment of a traditional prison. Such a system might appear cruel, but it 'is pregnant with the salutary effects of pure humanity and sound religion'. Religious and secular reformers might disagree as to the outcome, but they shared an absolute faith in the means. The prisoner would, if treated this way, awake to the nature of sin (as far as evangelicals were concerned) or realise that crime was directly opposed to his interests (for utilitarians). Inmates would be ground down, born anew and returned to the community conscious that self-discipline and work were rational and the route to salvation.[25]

The great experimental penitentiary built at Millbank between 1812 and 1816, where this utopian system would have been unveiled to the world, was a failure. It was massively expensive, and, rather than become quiescent human machines, the inmates, although kept in better conditions than ever before, broke into frenzies of rage caused by sensory deprivation and loneliness. However, the treadmill preserved many of the virtues of the penitentiary. It had been invented by Samuel Cubitt, magistrate of Ipswich, and earnestly advocated by the Society for the Improvement of Prison Discipline, an association dominated by religious reformers and utilitarians. The labour was mechanical, repetitive and, best of all, silent and solitary. For hours every day prisoners would be forced to contemplate their sin and wretchedness. For once in their life they would learn what discipline meant.

Years before, Jeremy Bentham had proposed a whipping machine. The problem with corporal punishment was that it depended upon the strength and enthusiasm of whichever warder was administering it; severity of punishment varied from prison yard to prison yard from day to day. No two whippings were the same, and this offended against utilitarian notions of consistency, strict justice and scientific principle. The mill was an adequate substitute; every day thousands of prisoners in every part of the kingdom would share an identical, unvarying experience uncontaminated by the contingency of human discretion. The mill was the answer to evangelical and utilitarian prayers. It transformed prisons from places of binge-drinking and sex to one of quiet and routine labour. As a system for rebuilding modern man, the treadmill stood as the proud symbol of the predominant religious, economic and sociological ideas of the time. Nothing else so eloquently expresses the thinking of the philanthropists, and the popular enthusiasm for the scheme showed the extent to which they had influenced society.

The economic and mechanical efficiency of the wheel was the proudest boast of its fond parents. But, under investigation, it was not quite the mighty modern engine it seemed. An icon of modernity it might have been, but it more closely resembled a juggernaut. Prisoners were obliged to spend ten hours a day at work. During that long day, the prisoner stepping up and down would cover a distance equivalent to just two and a quarter miles. John Ivatt Briscoe, the only magistrate in the whole of Surrey to object to the wheel, said that the machine exhibited the novel 'spectacle of Englishmen subjected to torture . . . in the garb of labour'. The great movers of the mill made 'a series of slow, and regular, and successive steps, by which they climb, as it were, an endless flight of steps'. That is to say, the effort put into turning the mill bore no relation to the output; an industrialist would reject the whole thing as uneconomical and cumbersome if someone wanted him to place it in his factory. And, although the prisoners covered such a pitiful distance in their endless upward climbs, the cost to their bodies was horrendous.[26]

The treadmill was accused of being hostile to the British constitution – both politically and bodily. John Mason Good was a surgeon who took it upon himself to investigate the health benefits of the mill. He wrote: 'From the tortuous attitude and uneasy motion manifestly displayed in mounting the endless hill of this mighty cylinder, on the toes alone, with the hands fixed rigidly on the horizontal bar, and the body bent forward to lay hold of it, I could not but conclude, not only that the prisoner is hereby deprived of all the healthful advantage of athletic exercise, but must be fatigued from the very outset, and perpetually *in danger* . . . of cramp, breaking the Achilles' tendon, and forming aneurismal and varicose swellings in the legs.' After a few minutes on the mill, prisoners suffered from stiffness, ruptures, numbness, stress to the joints, extreme thirst and respiratory problems. Many men complained of swelling in 'the private parts'. The shaft of the wheel frequently broke, throwing the treaders twelve feet to the hard floor.[27]

While hard labour might be good for some prisoners, said Good, '*morbid* labour' was entirely different. In the House of Correction in

Reading, conditions were so bad that the men mutinied and refused to go on the mill until they were given adequate food and shoes; they were forced back onto the machine by keepers armed with muskets and bludgeons. At Coldbath Fields prison, at the very time that the mill was brought in, the daily diet was reduced to one pint of thin water-gruel and a pound of bread. It was a ration worked out as being the cheapest possible to sustain the workers of the machine; it was thought wise to factor in the cost of fuel to the economics of the process. A woman at the same gaol suffered a miscarriage on the mill. Another woman at Guildford was found suckling her illegitimate baby – the reason why she was condemned to the wheel – while stepping up and down for hours on end. Men in gaols in Aylesbury, Swaffham and Leicester were thrown to the ground and killed. One boy was reduced to spitting blood. 'I was aware how readily such people are to complain, in order to get free of labour,' said the surgeon who attended the youth; 'I purposely passed him over.'[28]

The treadmill was supposed to cure people of criminal inclination and return them to the community as good, moral citizens imbued with habits of industry. John Cam Hobhouse doubted that twelve months on a wheel ever made anyone a better person; as he said in Parliament: 'no man could ever look upon himself as a man was entitled to do, after being made to run around like a dog in a wheel, for the amusement of those who might choose to stand and gaze at him'. In a thunderous article in the *Edinburgh Review*, Sydney Smith wrote: 'The labour of the tread-mill is irksome, dull, monotonous, and disgusting to the last degree. A man does not know what he is doing, what progress he is making; there is no room for art, contrivance, ingenuity and superior skill – all of which are the cheering aspects of human labour.' A husbandman might watch his crops grow, a smith watches with satisfaction the transmogrification of iron on his anvil, a weaver has some indication of what she is doing; in most cases labour had a definite purpose, and the knowledge of the result of the work brought some dignity. Not so the man on the mill who had to take for granted that his endless climb was productive of something, anything: he 'is turned at once from a rational being, by a justice of the peace, into a *primum mobile*, and put upon a level with a rush of water or a puff of steam'.[29]

Upon release, the miscreant would have a pretty dismal concept of the benefit of labour and would have learnt no better trade than walking up a staircase. In many cases, several months on the mill rendered sturdy workmen useless for any kind of manual work. The blessed mill was uneconomic, a poor moral teacher and contradictory to the best interests of society. But few would acknowledge these evident truths. Briscoe presented his investigations to his fellow Surrey magistrates. He included the testimonies of prisoners who had served long stints on the wheel at Coldbath Fields and Brixton prisons:

> I was very well in health on coming here. I have been used to as hard work as any man in England of my age. I never found any so fatiguing as this.
>
> William Hensley, 18, twelve months on the wheel

> I was quite well on coming in. I have now a great pain in the back part of my legs, my loins, and left side. I get weaker every day. I can hardly stand upright. I know not how I shall be able to do a day's work. I have nothing to depend upon but my labour.
>
> Robert Warner, 20, four months on the wheel

> I fell off from dizziness in the head, right through the trapdoor, and was seriously hurt . . . I was worn to a shadow, and till I could work no more . . . It had like to have cost me my life.
>
> Michael McCave, 49, six months on the wheel

Briscoe cited these and other abuses and called the treadmill 'an engine of torture'. He called on his fellow magistrates to investigate the uses and efficacy of the mill, and found himself in a minority of one. He was accused of fermenting hatred of the magistracy. Indeed, the bench (which had not investigated the treadmill) had its own opinion. 'A month's labour was sure to remove members of diseases; and those who had to undergo a long spell of discipline, were sure to leave the prison in a most enviable state of health.' A petition to the Commons got similar treatment. The treadmill, said *The Times*, made prisoners happy.[30]

The treadmill was defended with such eagerness in the face of facts because its chief attraction was its cheapness. When people complained that it was inhumane and opposed to the principles of British justice, Sir Thomas Lethbridge MP said that the only 'hardship' and 'injustice' felt was by landowners who had hitherto been obliged to pay for criminal prosecutions and the costs of detention through tax. Yet even the economic justification was suspect: treadmills frequently ground nothing but clean air when there was no demand for grain.[31]

Albany Fonblanque commented that increased discipline and theories of reclaiming criminals might be grand and meritorious, but they were widely off mark. The Vagrant Act 'sweeps the highways and byways of every creature convicted of being houseless and penniless, and supposed therefore likely to be criminally disposed: while shoals of notorious thieves are suffered to swarm the streets of London'.[32]

The changes of the 1820s ripped up many of the themes of popular literature. In November 1822 *The Times* complained about 'the shop-boys and apprentices, who nightly disturb the quiet of the streets by their imitations of *Bob Logic* and *Corinthian Tom* – irritations which have consigned many aspiring young gentlemen to the "tread-mill", and ought to have consigned a great many more'. The Vagrant Act and treadmill allowed the authorities to deal more effectively with the delinquency and rowdiness that had plagued the streets – nuisances which had to be tolerated or reluctantly ignored just a few years before.[33]

Pierce Egan's *Life in London* was well timed in that it was written on the eve of the Vagrant Act and the introduction of the treadmill: Bob, Tom and Jerry could not have got away with their rambles and sprees with impunity if the watch had been armed with such power. And so it turned out for Egan's imitators and the pirates who leeched off his work. In a farce of 1822 or '23, *The Tread Mill, or Tom and Jerry at Brixton: A serio, comic, operatic, milldramatic* [sic] *farcical moral burletta*, Old Pringle, a country squire, and his son Jack venture to London, the father to relive his youth and Jack to imitate what he has read in his 'Jerry Book'. As they leave, the rustic servants ruminate on the 'canty Lunnunners' who are obsessed with improvements, reforms and everything likely to threaten the good old ways. They know things have changed, but the Pringles are determined to explore the illicit joys of urban life. It is, however, a sad relic of its former glory; the capital is seedy and dangerous. After the usual Egan-esque London adventures, father and son are arrested in a 'hell'. When they complain that they are gentlemen, they are told: 'When gemmen mixes along with pickpockets and gamblers, they must be taken for what they seem, and not what they is.' That was what the new Vagrant Act had decreed: if you mixed with ne'er-do-wells, your choice of company reflected on you. The Pringles are spared the treadmill by a sympathetic magistrate, but other would-be bucks would henceforth be punished as vagrants.

*

MPs were adept at playing on the idea of 'cant', using that word and all its connotations to attack what they regarded as puritanical meddling. There were three issues that allowed them to speak up for the common folk of the nation: beer, the Sabbath and cruelty to animals. While they gave interfering magistrates new summary powers with one hand, they attempted to halt the decline of rowdy pastimes with another.

Every year from 1822 Richard Martin, MP for Galway, introduced a bill for the better treatment of domestic animals, such as cattle and horses, and animals used for lower-class sport – badgers, bulls, bears, cocks and dogs. Humanity Dick, as George IV nicknamed Martin, enlisted the help of notable philanthropists, including Thomas Fowell Buxton, and in 1824 they founded the Society for Prevention of Cruelty to Animals (later to become the RSPCA). 'A society might here be formed productive of effects equally calculated to alter the moral feeling throughout the land,' Fowell Buxton said at the first meeting. The SPCA would join the two other primary evangelical organisations, the Bible Society and the Prison Discipline Society, which had, according to Fowell Buxton, already 'changed the whole face of the country'. A society that prosecuted cruel people (in the manner of the SSV) would effectively relegate bad old popular culture to oblivion.[34]

The House of Commons enjoyed Humanity Dick's annual bills, if only because they allowed some of the more facetious orators to knock down an unpopular measure in the name of the people. When he presented a bill in 1824 to outlaw bull-baiting, bear-baiting and cockfighting and other cruel sports, Martin wearily said that he was prepared to be answered with witticisms by the House, not reasoned debate. He was used to ill-treatment by his fellow MPs, from the fox-hunting, pheasant-shooting and fishing Tory squirearchy to Whig libertarians and radicals. He had to explain that his bill was aimed against butchers' boys and porters: 'Those who sport in their own manors, or fish in their own streams, are a very different sort of man.'[35]

Poor Martin was mocked and reviled by all sides of the House. One MP said that the poor were already oppressed enough and Parliament had already curtailed too many popular pastimes; the House should not sanction 'such a petty trumpery'. The House knew that for most members of the SPCA (although not Martin, who was a sincere animal lover), the bills were about evangelical man-making and vice suppression, not cruelty to animals. Martin could be cast as an insincere reformer who talked about animals in pain but really wanted to subjugate his fellow man. Whenever Martin introduced one of his bills, MPs dared him to include fox-hunting, fishing and shooting in the sports he wanted to see banned; only then would he be free from the charges of hypocrisy and partiality and of bullying the lower orders.

Robert Peel, the reforming Home Secretary and the man who would later bring in the Metropolitan Police, traditionally used the occasion to stress to the Tory backbenchers and the country at large that he was not a meddlesome and intrusive Secretary of State. 'After the toils of the day,' he told the House, 'it is proper that there should be some places of relaxation – some species of amusement for the lower orders.' Even if much of popular culture was cruel and violent, it was better to tolerate it than to impose 'one rigid system of undeviating morality'. These words and sentiments distanced Peel further from the evangelical morality of Wilberforce, Fowell Buxton, Allen and the other religious revivalists, even though he was instinctively on their side.

Martin's bill was a suitable occasion on which to do this because the stakes were so low. Peel could also signal his hostility to a reformed police force, even though that is what he was secretly planning. The bill, if it ever became law, would necessitate the creation of a new police force to coordinate the investigation and prevention of cruel sports. Like many other things, there was a difference between what things ought to be like and what they were; improvement was all very well, but the cost of reform was high. A vigilant nationwide police force might cut crime, 'but I have no hesitation in saying I like the existing system better: I prefer England as it is, to what it might be under such an alteration of her police. I like even the wild luxuriance of the plant; and would be the last to cut and trim it down to the prime precise standard which the hon. gentleman's proposition would go to establish.'

Give Martin a concession on cruel sports, Peel said, and he 'would come to the House, session after session, now with some tale about a cock, and now with one about a bull'. The Attorney-General punned about taking the bull by the horns, and many other MPs turned comedian for the hour. George Lamb stated the views of many when he said that 'while there are persons who like to be amused in this way, I would rather see them so amused, than not amused at all'.

Richard Martin was swatted away session after session, as MPs and ministers queued up to show how much they were concerned to defend the pleasures and liberties of the people against meddling zealots. On the many occasions when the evangelical lobby attempted to enforce the Sabbath, MPs could again establish their intolerance for cant and religious interference. In 1824 some pious fishmongers petitioned Parliament to repeal a law passed in the 1690s permitting the sale of mackerel on Sundays. Most MPs found this kind of thing amusing and easily dispatched; one said that 'a more ridiculous, absurd and, I would add, canting petition has never been presented to the House'. In 1832 Parliament received a great number of petitions from pious members of the middle class begging for more stringent laws to enforce the sanctity of the seventh day. One MP was 'of the opinion that cant, humbug, and hypocrisy was the characteristic of many of the petitions which have been presented on the subject. If ever the bill should proceed so far as to get into committee, I shall certainly move as an amendment that it be entitled "a bill to promote cant".'

'Cant' became a parliamentary buzzword; MPs knew its resonance with the public and were content to manipulate it when it suited them. They used language that appeared to put them on the side of the people against prim reformers. There was no better occasion for this than when dealing with a subject dear to the heart of every Briton: beer. Licensing and the price of alcohol bedevilled every discussion of public morals and order, and had never been solved satisfactorily. In political orthodoxy, beer and British liberty went hand in hand. 'The best mode of encouraging the consumption of beer by the people in general ought to be steadily kept in view by the legislature,' the Chancellor of the Exchequer William Huskisson told the House in 1822.

Beer was a wholesome drink, the perfect beverage for the busy labourer. People, and especially British people, needed some 'exhilarating beverage'; it was their right. But, due to the adulteration and price-fixing monopolies exposed by Henry Grey Bennet's select committee, this indispensable drink was in poor condition. 'Unless the poor are to be deprived of every enjoyment, and made to subsist, like felons, on bread and water, what can we expect, under the existing laws, but that gin-drinking should increase?' Thomas Macaulay asked.

Either that or they would be reduced to drinking tea, as the newly founded temperance movement wanted. 'It is notorious,' wrote William Cobbett in an angry mood, 'that tea has no *useful strength* in it; that it contains nothing *nutritious*; that it, besides being *good* for nothing, has *badness* in it, because it is well known to produce want of sleep in many cases, and in all cases to shake and weaken the nerves. It is, in fact, a weaker kind of laudanum.' It was no wonder that children of the labouring poor were so raggedly dressed and their parents so emaciated. Cobbett worked out that tea cost a family £11 a year if consumed every morning and deprived a woman of 365 potentially productive hours a year preparing the foul brew (this was the equivalent of thirty working days). If a working man had home-brewed beer at breakfast he would be hearty and blooming with health, but as it is 'he makes his miserable progress towards death' – a demise hastened by the ravages of tea. The reason that the labouring poor did not drink beer at breakfast any more was because high duties on hops and malt had made domestic brewing impossible. The government and magistrates could deprive the people of beer if they wanted to by raising prices and restricting licences, but history showed that they could never get rid of spirits. They would always be produced, legally or illegally, and sold cheaply. As it was, in 1830, a pint of beer cost between 3½ and 4d, while a quartern of gin cost 2½d and a pint just 10d. 'The people do not prefer gin', commented Macaulay, '– they are driven to it.'[36]

A solution was suggested by the Whigs Henry Grey Bennet and Henry Brougham and the Tory Chancellor of the Exchequer William Huskisson. Reform was put in a language that was irrefutably distinct from the tortuous logic of philanthropy. The supporters of beer self-consciously put themselves forward as men of the world who could cut a swathe through the bluster and insincere talk of wordy moral reform and provide simple, workable answers to mankind's problems. Bennet suggested that Parliament should 'allow every individual to sell beer as they might bread'. Freely available beer would improve the morals of the people, for they would naturally choose beer over spirituous liquor. Throughout the 1820s Brougham and Bennet and later the Chancellor of the Exchequer presented bills aimed at reducing beer duties and creating a completely free market in the retail of alcohol.

No reform made the people more sober or perceptibly more moral. In 1830 the laws were liberalised even further in a two-pronged approach: tax on beer was taken off and the licensing regulations were relaxed to the extent that anyone might turn their house into a beer shop. This disempowered the baneful influence of the magistrates and would make beer more available and cheap enough to compete with gin (and tea). Most importantly, the vast and hitherto omnipotent breweries and publicans would have to compete with the minnows of the trade and brew better quality, unadulterated beer. It was the culmination of a long attack on the licensing system, which had been highlighted by Bennet's committee in 1817. Support for the Beer Bill was presented as an attack on 'cant' itself. It was an answer to the specious arguments that brewers had made to protect their interests: that magisterial control over the public house and high prices safeguarded the morals of the people. 'Cant, hypocrisy, and affectation having past into our Acts of Parliament . . . had interested so many people in their favour by pretending a regard for the morals of the poor, that they could be only overthrown by repeated assaults,' *The Times* commented, explaining why reform had taken so long.[37]

MPs who supported the bill did so for economic reasons, but also because they realised that so much had been stripped from popular culture in recent years. They also wanted to give the people personal responsibility to decide how much they drank. 'I have on more than one occasion observed too great a disposition upon the part of gentlemen to interfere with the amusements and gratifications of the people,' said one MP. 'The poor have a right to procure their Beer where they like: if they do wrong they might be punished; but certainly it is not fair or right to anticipate evil.'[38]

MPs were sensitive to what they saw as the cant of philanthropy and the systematic regulation of the poor. The MPs' frustration came from the belief that these things had triumphed in Britain. The freedom to drink was one of the few things left to the lowest members of society. As one MP said to the do-gooders who blamed the poor for an apparent depravation of morals: 'there are many causes that have produced the present state of the poor, among them the taking away of common rights, enclosing lands, stopping footpaths, and a variety of measures interfering with them in every way, so that they have no other resource for amusement, and dissipating idle thoughts, than tippling'.[39]

When in 1831 the bishops in the House of Lords launched an attack on the Beer Act in the name of morality, many members of the lower House were incensed. The prelates wanted to enforce the Sabbath and bring back restraints on alehouses. 'Now, I will say,' thundered Joseph Hume in the Commons, 'that if ever cant and hypocrisy were signally manifested in this country, it is observable here. [Hear, hear.]' Daniel O'Connell said that if a bishop entered a St James's club to lecture the noble drinkers on their habits, he would be laughed out: 'But if a poor man has an extra pint of beer, there is an immediate outcry about morality. [Hear, hear.] I therefore agree with my hon. friend [Hume], that there is, in such proceedings, crass cant and hypocrisy.'[40]

Members of Parliament of all hues – Tories, 'advanced Whigs', radicals and independents – were concerned that reforms were depriving the poor of their pleasures and liberties. They were prepared to stick up for the lower orders against their would-be controllers, and the word that came most readily to hand was 'cant'. But while more power was given to the magistracy that waged war on fairs and such like, the right to abuse animals was fiercely defended. MPs were scared of being classed with the meddlesome and puritanical, but this fear pushed them into a mistrust of any kind of social reform and a suspicion of the intentions of philanthropists. While the best aspects of popular culture came under attack, the very worst were passionately defended by people terrified of being classed with the 'canters'.

14

No Cant

'. . . if posterity should have reason to rue the present generation, they would have reason also to laugh at it.'

Anon, 1822[1]

'We desire to be delivered from any suspicion of a wish to check the "march of improvement"; but the "march of quackery" seems to be running just now very strongly side by side with it.'

The Times, 29 January 1828

'A hypocrite seems to be the only perfect character – since it embraces the extremes of what human nature *is*, and of what it *would be thought*.'

William Hazlitt[2]

'Yesterday I wandered into Regent's Park and saw how the people amuse themselves on a Sunday. Of eating, drinking, singing, music, dancing, not a trace – they walk up and down and lie on the grass, which is growing bare and yellow.'[3]

So wrote a German visitor in 1835. The old gregarious and boisterous behaviour – the culture of defiance symbolised by Mr Punch and remarked upon by earlier generations of tourists – had died away, suppressed by a greater attachment to public rectitude on the one hand and by force and law on the other. 'I miss the cheerful cries of London,' wrote a nostalgic journalist, 'the music, and the ballad singers – the buzz and stirring murmur of the streets.'[4] The generation that was passing into old age in the 1830s and '40s had seen rough and ready Britain, where bawdiness, low-level violence and drunkenness were tolerated and often celebrated, transform into a policed and more regulated country.

The old manners and customs slipped into oblivion very quickly. Bartholomew Fair was finally abolished in 1854 by the Common Council of London. The way that ancient festival was eradicated replicated the way the country had changed: 'In its humours we have seen the humour of the nation blended with the riot of the mob. Yet when the nation had outgrown it, a Municipal Court with the help of but a few policemen put it quietly away.' And the same happened with other leisure activities, with no more fuss. The 'golden age' of ferocious pugilism ended when the magistrates in the district of Mousley Hurst, the last remaining spot for championship bouts, got tougher, despite the local influence of the Duke of Clarence (later William IV), a boxing fan. Bull-baiting and other cruel sports were all banned by 1850.[5]

George Sala visited Pierce Egan in 1848 and called the old man 'a highly curious' relic of a departed age. Two decades had wrought great changes since Egan was at the height of his fame. 'He descanted on the cock-fighting, the bull-baiting, the badger-drawing, the ratting and fighting he had seen in the brave days of old,' Sala remembered of their conversation, '. . . he was the abstract and chronicle of the manners of an age which had vanished, and which, it is most devoutly to be wished, will never repeat itself on the sublunary sphere again.'[6]

Egan was dead within a year of that meeting, but his books lived on, republished several times in Victoria's reign with some of the more offensive passages censored. Thackeray remembered that when *Life in London* came out in 1820, 'we firmly believed the three heroes . . . to be types of the most elegant fashionable young fellows the town afforded, and thought their occupations and amusements were those of all highbred English gentlemen'. But when they were republished he wrote that 'the style of the writing I own was not pleasing to me; I even thought it a little vulgar . . . and as a description of the sports and amusements of London in the ancient times, more curious than amusing'. And that was how his contemporaries saw Egan's work, as curiosity pieces that seemed to belong to a long-lost and dimly remembered world. Society, like Thackeray, had grown up and turned its back on its immature predilections.

Many of the 'blackguard amusements' had disappeared: the rudeness of Plough Monday in the countryside and St Monday in towns lingered on, but the violence and drunkenness were contained by parish officers and police constables armed with the Vagrant Act, the New Poor Law and the threat of the treadmill. The festivals that spat in the face of authority – the Skimmington rides and Lords of Misrule – were rarely seen or tamed into harmless folk festivals. Such outbursts of lower-class defiance could not exist when the rich insisted on deference and respect as conditions of employment and public relief. 'The times, and the spirit of the times are changed,' wrote a historian of rural customs in 1838, the year of Victoria's coronation: 'we are become a sober people. England is no longer Merry England, but busy England; England full of wealth and poverty – extravagance and care.' There were those who lamented the changes that had leavened the coarseness and pined for the good old days: 'They might as well attempt to bring back jousts and tourneys, popery and government without representation . . . The better qualities of the old English character I trust we fully retain, but the more juvenile fantastic ones are irrevocably destroyed in the shock of the most momentous convulsions.'[7]

Looking back at the recent past, the customs and behaviour of Britain seemed anarchic and a little too close to nature. The park is a symbol of bourgeois values, a more decorous and respectable forum for tranquil recreation. The heyday of the park, the botanical garden and recreation ground was the physical symbol of the changes that had assailed British society in the first flush of industrialisation. Until the 1820s Londoners of all descriptions used to pour out of the capital to the suburbs on Sundays. The very meaning of suburban life itself was transforming. From the first intimation of spring until the end of autumn the people went to famous 'resorts': the tea gardens, theatres, taverns and 'ordinaries' (houses that provided a menu) among the fields, groves and streams in suburban districts like Islington, Highbury, Hampstead, Camberwell, Peckham and St John's Wood. In the misnamed tea gardens, up to four thousand people would sit around tables and drink beer, gin and punch and smoke pipes. An eyewitness, a fierce sabbatarian who wanted to ban such things, said that, apart from the obvious sacrilege, 'there was no breach of order; they were quiet, excepting noisy and talkative'. After a week in the City, a walk and a meal, a drink and some entertainment offered a rare opportunity to enjoy rural life. The New River, especially where it ran through Islington, was popular for fishing and idling; in fields and meadows people would watch or play sport or take walks. For some members of the lower orders, a Sunday in the suburbs involved boxing contests, fights to settle scores, hunting, bull-baiting or dogfights. And the ring of countryside was within strolling distance of St Paul's.

In the first decades of the century, the fields and groves were built over as the population of the capital became uncontainable. The population of the ancient City had declined sharply; it was becoming a place of commerce, not residence. People no longer wanted to live over the shop or next to the factory, and certainly not cheek by jowl with the lower orders. Modern cities were polluting, and the contagion came no less from the effluence of the industrial process than from human immorality. Birmingham had the pleasant district of Edgbaston to house its genteel inhabitants, and other booming towns were parcelled into quarters so that the nice and the rude were safely segregated.

'The precincts of London have more the appearance of a newly-discovered colony than the suburbs of an ancient city.' This was to use the word suburb in an archaic form, meaning villages, fields and pleasure gardens; the modern use was entirely different. There were terraced houses stretching from the City to Kentish Town to Hampstead Heath; Bayswater-fields had become a new town nicknamed Moscow; the 'rustic and primeval meadows' of Kilburn had gone; Camberwell Grove (whence there used to be 'the finest burst of scenery' anywhere near London) had become brickfields and modern housing. Islington, the oldest and most popular area of recreation – a village of spas, river-bank tea gardens, taverns and fields – was built over. The date when Hampstead Heath would fall victim to the demand for housing was 'a secret in the bosom of speculators and builders'. The fields and woods, with their tea gardens and recreational spots, were swallowed up by terraced housing, roads and factories.[8]

It was inevitable that the privileged circle of fields would have to give way to the needs of the city. Their disappearance was a subject of mourning for many Londoners. It fundamentally changed the nature of urban living. The centre was sealed off for good, and the suburbs became what we now understand to be suburbs. They were no longer places of semi-rustic resort and leisure. The process was not new: the middle classes had been leaving the cramped and claustrophobic city for new districts for years, and poor housing sprawled out to the east and the south to accommodate the growing population of workers. In the 1820s this change became a subject of discussion for people who realised that the old ways had gone for ever. It symbolised wider changes. Some writers of the 'old school' wondered how people found their way at night to their identikit homes in indistinguishable streets. The new art of suburban living had its own needs and requirements. Suburban/rural tea gardens, taverns, gravel pits and streams, with all the disorganised, rowdy and sometimes brutal pleasures they afforded, were replaced with the more sedate park. The old way of leisure disappeared and many of the pleasures faded away simply because there was nowhere to conduct them any more.

The changed landscape was a manifestation of the march of progress, and society had changed radically in other ways. Uniformed policemen were on the streets of London from 1829 after years of agonising and stiff resistance to the very notion of preventative policing. The New Poor Law, introduced in 1834, enlarged and standardised workhouses to manage and segregate the 'unproductive' and 'undeserving' poor on sound Malthusian and utilitarian principles. It took away the right of outdoor relief, making pauperism pretty much a crime lest it be seen as attractive. What more could philanthropists and social reformers like Patrick Colquhoun, marginalised, ignored and insulted in his lifetime, have wanted? Traditional paternalistic and laissez-faire ideals of government that restrained the hand of active intervention and allowed people an extraordinary degree of liberty were gone for ever. The state had a right and a duty to police (in all its senses) the people. In such an altered world, the old ways of life – of work, leisure, custom and culture – were dead.

There could not but be a change in social expectations and the very definition of manners and morality. For domestic and foreign commentators alike, Britain was the prototype of what society would be like in the age of machines, industry and capitalism. Depending on the prejudices of the commentator, it was an inspiring or a doleful example of what awaited other peoples and nations. Here was how an industrial workforce would have to be regulated; how legislatures should react to change; what manners and modes of behaviour would take over when the old features of a face-to-face and hierarchical society became extinct.

Britain looked modern and pioneering, but the forces of progress were believed to have altered the character of the people. One of the great advances had been in education and the availability of books and newspapers to a wide public. Yet with this advance was supposed to have come a degradation of culture and a future which would be characterised by mediocrity and an absence of genius as people were elevated – or reduced – to the same standard. 'It is the substitution of mere knowledge for the power of saying and doing that which is fit,' one critic wrote of the 'march of mind' in the 1820s, 'which, more than anything besides, contributes to stamp this the age of moderate men, and to render the existing state of society so unfavourable to every sort of extraordinary excellence.'[9] Cant, hypocrisy and imposture were the inevitable effects of progress; people in the coming world of mass society, public opinion, capitalism and democracy would neither rise above nor sink below a fixed line of standardised values. The censorious press and public opinion, according to Francis Jeffrey, would have 'a sensibility for small faults, and an incapacity to great merits'.[10]

'Among such busy elements there is little of stagnant life; every one being intent upon some object of ambition, profit or deception,' wrote John Wade of modern British cities. 'The magnitude of the place, and consequent ignorance of individuals of many by whom they are necessarily surrounded, precludes all nice scrutiny into motives and purposes; even the distribution of wealth and rank are lost in the crowd; and all that can be relied upon are certain external indications and appearances which may be genuine or counterfeit.'[11]

'Ambition', 'profit', 'deception': these were the daily concerns of modern man; it could not be otherwise. What were once esteemed virtuous – the genuine and sincere – were lost and gone for ever, supposing they ever existed; everyone was an actor on a stage, an accomplished and refined actor, adept at 'counterfeit'. Place wrote that 'we are told that what we have gained in polish, we have lost in honest simplicity, that . . . cant has taken the place of sincerity'.[12]

Debate in the 1820s – in the press, criticism, poetry, Parliament and common parlance – resounded with that word. 'Cant' appears over and again with competing or overlapping meaning, ever greater intensity and increasing ferocity wherever one looks. For a society alive to the vice of hypocrisy it was a word charged with a power that escapes us today. We do not acknowledge hypocrisy as the greatest sin; the word 'cant' has been disarmed and certainly does not have the implications it had then. It was deployed as an all-embracing term of abuse that was meant to strike deep into the heart; an exposure of the malignity that lurked in the human soul. Candour and sincerity had lost their meaning; it was impossible to trust anyone any more in this mechanical age. There brooded in everyone the tendency for duplicity, imposture and dishonesty; motives were therefore likely to be base and deeply suspicious. 'The age of cant' became the phrase that seemed to sum up all the changes that had happened within so short a time.

It was a poisonous and rancorous way of looking at the world; it hunted down and interrogated motives. If human relations become an ever-lasting inquisition into intentions, then trust becomes impossible. 'Never since the beginning of time, was there, that we hear or read of, so intensely self-conscious a Society,' wrote Thomas Carlyle. 'Our whole relations to the Universe and to our fellow man have become an Inquiry, a Doubt.'[13]

'The age of cant' was, many believed, an inevitable stage of modernity. John Stuart Mill wrote that 'plausible pretence' was the characteristic of many people, and it had been forced upon them by the demands of civilisation. In a mass society, where individuals increasingly blended into a crowd, where universal rules of deportment took over from individualism and when competition became ever more fierce, it was to be expected that there would be a prevalence of 'quackery' and 'puffing'. It was the unavoidable consequence 'of a state of society where any voice, not pitched in an exaggerated key, is lost in the hubbub. Success, in so crowded a field, depends not upon what a person is, but upon what he seems: mere marketable qualities become the object instead of substantial ones, and a man's labour and capital are expended less in *doing* than in persuading other men that he has done it.'[14]

In the past 'quackery' implied the complete absence of anything laudable or genuine; now it was a condition of existing as a businessman or trader: 'It is our own age which has seen the honest dealer driven to quackery by hard necessity, and the certainty of being undersold by the dishonest. For the first time, arts for attracting public attention form a necessary part of the qualifications even of the deserving; and skill in these, goes further than any other quality towards ensuring success.'[15] Like it or not, and in spite of themselves, everyone was a version of Samuel Solomon, obliged, in the manner of the late doctor, to project the attributes of gentility and trustworthiness to a cynical world. The honest and the unscrupulous were reduced to the same necessity of straining their language and conduct to be heard in the clamour. Whether this was so new an addition to the human condition or universally prevalent in British society in the 1820s and '30s is questionable. What is certain, however, and just as important, is that this was how an increasing number of people saw their society and their age. When these doubts were mooted, who could you trust?

There were no people, it seemed, whose good works entitled them to the claim of sincerity and disinterestedness of motive. Those most actively involved in easing the condition of their fellows were accused of concealing the blackest soul. Philanthropy was a byword for hard-heartedness. It was an efficient means of self-aggrandisement that opened the door to government patronage. When the scrutinising language of cant and hypocrisy took over, nothing was what it seemed. There was no heartfelt humanity, just 'false humanity'; there were no genuine feelings, only mawkish sentimentality; the language of benevolence was 'canting hypocrisy' designed to make the patron feel a glow of self-satisfaction and extend his or her control over powerless groups. When 'cant' was used in this sense, it was a way of describing the alleged victory of the meddling and fastidious, who had ruthlessly manipulated and spun the language and adopted the garb of morality to propel themselves to power and impose their narrow views to alter fundamentally the national character. Like businessmen who adopted the clichés and cant of the age to advertise their wares, the philanthropist filched the vocabulary of humanity to conceal his real motives. The thoughtless people were guilty of 'cant' because they followed what was fashionable in morals as assiduously as what was fashionable in boots. They picked up and slavishly repeated the current jargon, so as not to stand out or be thought amoral.

The combination of religious zeal and social control gave philanthropy a bad name among people of all hues: philosophical radicals, Tory squires, old-fashioned people who remembered a less high-minded age, metropolitan journalists, cosmopolitan young men and women and, not least, the poor themselves, who really felt its hard edge. When the New Poor Law imposed Union workhouses ('Pauper Prisons') on the neediest members of society under the name of philanthropy and science, there were those who were old-fashioned enough to believe that the very concept of 'philanthropy' had been mangled: 'if it be the product of Philanthropy, may Philanthropy be sunk to the bottom of the sea!'[16] The charge of false motives and insincerity was applied to every scheme; the best way to attack an opponent was to accuse him or her of imposture, ulterior motives, hypocrisy or unthinkingly following the herd.

This was expressed most clearly in the campaign to emancipate the West Indian slaves. The wealthy, influential and noisy plantation lobby could be expected to lacerate the likes of Wilberforce and Fowell

Buxton and accuse them of acting out of low, hypocritical or misguided motives. At a meeting of the merchant shipowners and other people whose interests were bound up with slavery in 1833, the Earl of Harewood articulated an all too familiar argument when he said that philanthropists were self-interested and the public was carried away by the heat of conscience and pangs of humanity that disarmed its rational faculties. 'Cant' was the magic word for the merchants. A supporter of Harewood lambasted the 'cant' of the abolitionists – 'this morbid and theatrical philanthropy', 'this fallacy', this 'cheap liberality'. The evangelicals and liberals were 'respectable', to be sure, but they were blinded to the realities of the world by feelings which 'ought not to govern a nation'. They worked themselves up about the condition of the slave without considering the damage that emancipation would wreak on the colonies and the empire. At a time of deep cynicism about mankind's motives and the hollowness of benevolence, the language of cant and hypocrisy was a weapon that was easy to wield. The abolitionists were hotheads and zealots. The public who supported the abolitionists could be presented as dupes who luxuriated in the pleasurable emotions of humanity without ever examining the facts. It was a vocabulary that resounded with men who prided themselves on plain speaking, common sense and hard-headed rationality. The spokesman for the plantation owners 'trusted the colonial empire would not be frittered away for cant and sentiment'.[17]

It might be expected that plantation owners, shipowners, importers and everyone whose livelihood was bound up with colonial slavery would be compelled to use this kind of language as they saw their world being swept away by a tide of humanity. But it is sad to hear it from other lips. William Cobbett passed on few opportunities to attack the 'canters' and 'the philanthropic ruffians'. Their 'canting' was their 'madness for the blacks'. The abolitionists could be divided into two sorts: 'the *thoughtless* and the *foolish*' and 'the *hypocrites* and the knaves'. 'The latter use the former as their tools in this work, the objects of which are, first, to get for themselves a character for *justice*, *mercy* and *humanity*; and next, under that character, to get for themselves *power*, or *public money*, or both.'[18]

There was no motive base enough to explain the soppy and sentimental concern for slaves, as far as Cobbett was concerned. As far back as 1792, when he heard an anti-slavery speech, he vowed never to take sugar or coffee or anything produced by slave labour again. It was only when he went to live in the US that he refined his opinions. His heroes, Presidents Washington, Jefferson, Madison and Monroe, had all kept slaves. There was no question that these patriots and democrats were infinitely better and more virtuous men than the whining 'canters' of the British abolition movement: Wilberforce, Allen, Fowell Buxton, Hannah More, Brougham, Zachary Macaulay, George Stephen and Thomas Babbington. But he kept up his personal boycott of slave produce, although for different reasons. He had 'always disliked to have any thing to do with beings, who my eyes, ears, nose, and reason, told me were *a race different from and inferior to, that to which I belonged*'. Freed slaves, he believed and frequently repeated, were temperamentally unsuited to the kind of free labour that white people did to better themselves; they would impoverish themselves and the land once coercion was taken away. Emancipation would also destroy Britain. It would ruin the colonies because freed slaves had no work ethic; before long the islands, impoverished by freedom, would revert to another power, probably the US, which would re-enslave the black population and treat them worse than benevolent British owners.[19] 'I trust', Cobbett thundered, 'the country is not again to be cajoled; and that the humanity for which it is so justly famed, is not to be so perverted by base and artful men as to make it conducive to its own disgrace and ruin.'[20]

Cobbett's obnoxious racism combined with an almost fanatical mistrust of philanthropy. His response shows how deeply these ideas of cant had penetrated. The very idea of charity and benevolence had become associated with bad intention and selfishness. The people were taught to sing 'Britons never will be slaves', 'while barracks, and new jails, and tread-mills, and *gendarmerie* were being established all over the kingdom'.[21] At the same time the common people were being deprived of wholesome beer (by corrupt brewers) and their entertainments (by policemen). And it did not take much to realise who was using philanthropy to subjugate and regulate the British people. William Wilberforce, Thomas Fowell Buxton, William Allen, Hannah More and their allies all stood high on the list of supporters of prison discipline, repressive laws, conditional relief, the reform of the police and every other thing that was calculated to degrade the poor.

In a pamphlet, Wilberforce said that he wanted to raise the condition of the black population of the Caribbean to that of the British working class. Nothing could be better calculated to raise the ire of

William Cobbett to apoplectic levels. He wrote an open letter to Wilberforce: 'There is a great deal of canting trash; a great deal of lying; a good deal of that cool impudent falsehood for which the Quakers are famed; a monstrous quantity of hypocrisy is there evident in these seventy-seven pages of yours.' To suggest that a Briton was better off than a slave was offensive when supposedly free labourers were attacked by the army (as at Peterloo, August 1819), shackled by the Poor Laws, subjected to the brutality of the Vagrant Act and paid little above subsistence level. For Cobbett it was 'nonsense too beastly to be used by any one but a son of cant'.[22]

To promise the miserable existence of a British labourer to a black slave was a false and disingenuous offer, the equivalent of fool's gold, a quack's nostrum or adulterated beer. Wilberforce should look at the emaciated British working class and then 'at your fat and laughing and singing and dancing negroes and negresses; and then believe, if you can; flatter yourself, if you are able, that we shall think you a man of humanity, making, as you do, such a bawling about the imaginary sufferings of the former, who are your own country-people, who are living under your very nose, and with whose miseries and degradation you must be acquainted'.

Wilberforce was 'the most mischievous man that ever lived in England'. He and his friend Hannah More had gained their reputation for humanity by concentrating on foreign slaves and ignoring the sufferings of British people. Indeed, they had spent their money and time distributing religious tracts to the miserable poor and giving practical help only on conditions of deference, and for what? 'To teach the people to *starve without making a noise*! To teach them to die *quietly*!'[23] It was as if emancipation and the improvement of the working classes were incompatible; as if there was some interconnected plot to free black Africans and enslave white Britons. In reality, as most knew, this was nonsense. It was Cobbett's ignorance combined with a pervasive belief that *all* philanthropy, *all* legislation was designed specifically to aggrandise one group and degrade another.

Accusing the evangelicals, Quakers and other philanthropists of 'canting hypocrisy' did not work. For a start it was not true. You could accuse Wilberforce of being insensitive to the poor, and many of the philanthropists could be wrong and heavy-handed. But the very last thing they were was insincere. When it came to slavery, most people were on the side of Wilberforce and the Saints, not Cobbett.

The word 'cant' was a four-letter political expletive that was becoming an all-embracing term of abuse. The publication of Lady Blessington's *Conversations of Lord Byron* in 1834 only served to fuel this language of cynicism and mistrust. In her recollections of Byron's musings, the word 'cant' crops up unremittingly. He had named his lifetime as the age of cant and humbug; Blessington's Byron is made to repeat the charge in a variety of forms. 'He on all occasions professed a detestation of what he calls *cant*; says that it will banish from England all that is pure and good; and that while people are looking after the shadow, they lose the substance of goodness; he says, that the best mode left for conquering it, is to expose it to *ridicule*, the only *weapon*, added he, that the English climate cannot rust.' He made it fashionable to see the world in these terms, to disparage professed virtue or any discussion of morality as affected and bogus.[24]

It was a cynicism that both Sydney Smith and William Hazlitt understood all too well and brought to the attention of the readers of the *Edinburgh Review*. One of the prevailing views of the age was that humanitarianism was fake; that it was the preserve of the fanatic and enthusiast or the designing and hypocritical. It was not just Cobbett's rants; from Egan's spitting and cussing Corinthian Tom ('I abominably hate *cant*; I despise *hypocrisy*') to Tory paternalists to disillusioned radicals there was the same suspicion of 'good works' – renamed 'meddling', 'busybodydom' and 'canting'. Many journalists and MPs were terrified of being thought to be joining the ranks of the evangelical do-gooders. They objected to Richard Martin's anti-cruelty measures on these grounds. Like Cobbett, they became blind to what was good in philanthropic projects, rejecting the whole thing as soppy sentimentality and hypocritical cant. In 1830 the MP Sir Charles Wethrell felt that he had to constrain his language when discussing a bill to repeal capital punishment in cases of forgery. Like so many others, he felt that any expression of humanity might be taken as pretended religious zealousness and 'false humanity': 'I will venture to say,' said Wethrell, 'though not a Quaker, that I feel as warmly, and as deeply for the sufferings of my fellow creatures as any theoretical sentimentalist of them all. But mine is no bastard inconsistent sympathy; I am for no pseudo-morality – no small-beer relaxation of the sternness of criminal jurisprudence.'[25]

It was as if the pious had a monopoly on morality – or so suggested Sir Charles's apology. He and many others effectively disarmed their vocabulary, making themselves sound amoral. They left the field clear for the kinds of philanthropy they detested. As Hazlitt wrote, society should be on guard not against excessive zeal but against excessive indifference. 'We are aware that there is a cant of humanity, and a cant of liberality . . . and sorry we should be to learn that this cant was quite exploded; for when there is no longer any cant about a thing, we may be sure the thing is pretty well out of fashion; cant, in reality, being nothing but the overacting of pretenders to popular merits.'[26]

Byron had led the way in suggesting that cant was the worst aspect of the British character and a cloak for immorality. But was it as bad as he suggested? Cant might not be attractive, but it is better than the deceit of hypocrisy. There are, after all, worse things in the world than straining to be good. 'Cant is the voluntary overcharging or prolongation of a real sentiment,' wrote William Hazlitt; 'hypocrisy is the setting up a pretension to a feeling you never had and have no wish for.' We like to be thought better than we are, or at least to keep up with popular sentiments and give praise for what is good and express horror at the abominable; sometimes the gap between what we feel and what we are capable of expressing is so great that we have to exaggerate our responses and borrow society's jargon and clichés. 'Indeed, some degree of affectation is as necessary to the mind as dress is to the body; we must overact our part in some measure, in order to produce any effect at all.'[27]

It was better to be sneered at for being overly humane and accused of 'canting' than to cynically mistrust any philanthropic project and treat such things with 'hard-hearted irony'. If cant was no more than the froth that rose to the top of an argument, or the clichés that attached themselves to any campaign, it was a small thing to put up with. In 1775 the then Solicitor-General, acting on behalf of the slavers, had said that 'he was not to be put down by a false cry of pretended humanity' when he justified his clients' decision to throw slaves overboard on the grounds that human cargo was private property and as such freely disposable. This was the swagger of a plain-talking lawyer who had conquered his emotions and taken an equitable view of the world; or that's how he had intended to seem. But it was impossible to say these things in the 1820s 'because, on that question at least, the cant of humanity has in the end triumphed over the loathsome jargon opposed to it'.[28]

Edward Lytton Bulwer said of Members of Parliament that as they took their seats every afternoon in the Commons, 'they write upon their minds the motto, "No cant"'. That cynicism, Sydney Smith wrote, came from 'disgust excited by false humanity, canting hypocrisy and silly enthusiasm'.[29] The MPs, and the many people who shared their feelings, were victims of a delusion. They had rendered their arguments powerless by closing their ears to the moral feeling of the respectable portion of society. The enemies of hard-hearted and cruel social policies had a point, but they made themselves seem unprincipled and uncaring. The feeling of the country was running fast in the opposite direction. For most of the 'respectable' middle-class public, the idea that cant was an evil was meaningless. High-mindedness was in fashion. 'Hypocrisy and cant are rife,' wrote Cyrus Redding. But this was a distraction: 'The order and decencies observed in society, the ornaments and luxuries of life, exceed what the most imaginative persons of old could have dreamed possible. Refinement is not more superior to barbarism than is our present state to that of our forefathers. It is the ignorant and wilfully blind who do not see this, as well as those who prefer the past from mere feverishness, because they have determined that nothing in modern days is, or can be, as they wish it.'[30]

Those who said it was the age of cant were out of step with the temper of the times. If they regretted the changes that had taken place in these years and wished to oppose them, they failed to appreciate one very important thing. The problem was not that people were insincere. In attitudes to poverty, immorality, philanthropy and politeness they were all too sincere. In most cases the desire to change the world for the better came from deep-held religious and moral obligations. The trouble was that their good works did look like self-interest and hypocrisy. Lucy Aikin commented in a letter to a friend that it was all too easy to write evangelicals off as joyless suppressors: 'With much of the Puritanical rigour, in such points as the observance of public amusements, they are certainly a better set – indefatigable superintendents of schools, munificent patrons of Bible societies and missions, and incessant visitants of the sick and poor. Of course there must be many self-interested hypocrites among them, and not a few sour and censorious fanatics . . . but I think that many of them are . . . exemplarily good and . . . sincerely pious.'[31]

Those who conformed to the new morality genuinely believed they were doing right. They had been brought up at a time when evangelicalism, utilitarianism and the science of political economy were dominating public discussion. Born into a world seemingly menaced by perpetual war, anarchy, famine and disease, the hard truths of revivalist religion and political science held out the promise of certainty and, above everything else, reassurance. Their values became the values of the age; the truths they seemed to tell about the way society worked – from the management of the poor to the laws of the market – dominated public discussion and, under the Whigs in the 1830s, government policy. They became orthodox. It would have been hard to resist them. 'At present,' Carlyle wrote in 1850, 'and for a long while past, whatsoever young soul awoke in England with some disposition towards generosity and social heroism, or at least with some intimation of the beauty of such a disposition, – he, in whom the poor world might have looked for a Reformer, and valiant mender of its foul ways, was almost sure to become a Philanthropist.'[32]

By the 1820s fewer than four out of ten people had been born in the eighteenth century and fewer still had memories of a time before the war, cyclical economic depression and the writings of Malthus. At the same time, and in spite of apocalyptic terror and despairing gloom, Britain seemed to have prevailed over anarchy, Napoleon and nature itself. Religion and political economy helped explain the general trend of progress. The people who did well in the first decades of the new century were told that they were in the vanguard of a new era in the history of mankind. Thomas Love Peacock satirised the power of these views on the public, making his character in *Crotchet Castle* Mr Mac Quedy (based on J. R. McCulloch) list the Scottish contributions to civilisation: 'Morals and metaphysics, politics and political economy, the way to make the most of the modifications of smoke; steam, gas and paper currency; you have all these to learn from us; in short, all the arts and sciences. We are the modern Athenians.'[33]

Accusations of excessive zeal and itchy enthusiasm were potent before the 1810s. Philanthropists were like John Bowles: hysterical, fanatical and corrupt to the marrow of their bones. A couple of decades later this way of looking at good works and moral reform was less satisfying. It was an eighteenth-century view of things, one that disparaged enthusiasm, deplored heavy-handed meddling and accused those who evinced these characteristics of self-deceit and ulterior motives. The editor of the *Examiner*, Albany Fonblanque, argued that the very notion of cant was counterproductive in a time of self-confident earnestness. 'From our experience of the world we should say, that the charge of cant is far more questionably bandied than that of hypocrisy. There is a vast deal of cant, undoubtedly, in the world; but there is also much of excellent benevolent purpose, which, unintelligible to the minds of grovelling worldlings, is scoffed at under the name of cant.' He preferred to describe the religiosity and controlling aspect of the times as 'Pharisaic Morality'. In the Bible, the Pharisee was punctilious in his observance of the externals of religion and a stickler for enforcing them in the community. His bustling activity and controlling instinct came from an anxiety about the sincerity of his faith; he needed to prove it by his energy. The phrase 'Pharisaic Morality' encapsulated the spiritual pride that characterised many, but which was quite different from hypocrisy.

Fonblanque did not question the sincerity of the philanthropists' motives, but he did object to the form it took. If any group had the right to call it the age of cant, it was the poor. The rage for philanthropy was directed at them, and it was they who were placed under the most stringent obligations. As most of the examples of philanthropic activity cited in this book have shown, the aim of most charitably inclined people was to save the poor from themselves by encouraging sobriety, respect, deference and habits of industry. Science and religion suggested that this kind of controlling guidance was the only solution. The great numbers of the middle classes who joined these kinds of campaign really believed that there was no other option. But for the poor it appeared hypocritical and puritanical and just another way of subjugating them. They might have agreed with Engels in *The Condition of the Working Classes*:

> Englishmen are shocked if anyone suggests that they neglect their duty towards the poor. Have they not subscribed to the erection of more institutions for the relief of the poor than are to be found anywhere else in the world? Yes, indeed – welfare institutions! The vampire middle classes first suck the wretched workers dry so that afterwards they can, with consummate hypocrisy, throw a few miserable crumbs of charity at their feet.

In London a soup kitchen and house for temporary relief suspected that some of the supplicants were not deserving of its charity. Its 'allowance was too attractive' and was thus inducing poor people to give up work and wallow in idleness. When they reduced the ration to bread and water and replaced bedding with straw they found that fewer people applied for help. This seems (and seemed to some at the time) to be horribly cruel and a downright wrong conclusion to draw. But the benevolent were convinced that they were being cruel to be kind: the former recipients of soup did not come for stale bread and rancid water because they had been spurred to productive labour.[34]

Many have agreed that the middle classes only wanted to control, that their mouths were full of cant phrases and do-me-good jargon. That they were motivated by a desire to control and a fear of a hungry mob might be true, but such a view should not obscure the fact that they believed they were doing God's work. Few knew, or would have cared if they did, that their good works looked like the worst kind of religious bigotry and spiritual pride. Continuing her description of the genuine desire of the evangelicals to improve the country, Lucy Aikin wrote: 'I think, however, that their moral influence on the whole, and particularly amongst the lower class, is in many points unfavourable. They make religion exceedingly repulsive to the young and the cheerful, by setting themselves against all the sports and diversions of the common people, and surfeiting them with preaching, praying and tutoring.'[35]

Being wrong does not make one hypocritical, even if that's what it looks like. The poor were caught in an uncomfortable situation. If they wanted their children to receive an education or their families to get medical care and food in hard times they were forced to conform. If they had learnt anything at all from the great changes in the nature of benevolence, it was that the philanthropist demanded something in return for his or her gift. Members of the working class knew that they were expected to live up to expectations of respectability and frugality. The hard-nosed aspect of philanthropy rewarded the decent poor but punished the slothful and inebriated – the culpable poor – in the workhouse and on the treadmill. In his *Rural Rides*, Cobbett wrote of the Hampshire landowner Sir Thomas Baring and his wife, of whom he had heard 'that they are very kind and compassionate to their poor neighbours; but that they tack a sort of *condition* to this charity; that they insist upon the objects of it adopting their notions with regard to *religion*; or, at least, that, where the people are not what they deem *pious*, they are not objects of their benevolence'. On this occasion Cobbett did not question the sincerity of the Barings, but he said that their method would make one man or woman good while it created a hundred hypocrites.[36]

Uriah Heep was born whenever a condition was placed on benevolence: the person who was humble, grateful and adept at talking about self-reform was best placed to receive work and help. Practical philanthropy and the high standards it set actively fostered habits of hypocrisy in the poor. One manufacturer set out his criteria for choosing a worker: 'if he can read and write, the next question is, where do you come from? and what are you? and can you produce a character? Unless he conforms with these enquiries, I cannot employ him.' There was an easy way round that, and it was to act whatever part the employer wanted.[37]

Treated as abject failures, inveterate drunks and irresponsible louts, and judged on unashamed double standards, it was little wonder that a great many of the poor felt even more alienated. Why should they comply willingly with efforts to reform their manners and foster respect? What was supposedly aimed at improving their manners appeared to be ways of suppressing their amusements and small pleasures. They had a right to complain of the hypocrisy. When the Metropolitan Police was formed in 1829, it was intended to mete out justice equally to all classes. In practice, police constables devoted much of their time to clearing the streets of nuisances: most of the arrests in the police's early years were for drunkenness, petty disorder, violations of the Sunday trading laws, antisocial behaviour and that conveniently vague criminal offence, vagrancy. The whole thing stank of class bias and subjugation for those whose behaviour was objectionable to the respectable. This was not the intention of the police reforms, and in time the police would go out of their way to stress its impartiality. But the rancour uniformed bobbies provoked was undiminished.

The people who responded to all kinds of calls for reform or good works with 'No cant' effectively rendered themselves silent. They were afraid of being classed with evangelical zealots if they even talked about humanity. 'I have been afraid of too much caution, as tending to produce cold heartedness,' Francis Place wrote to James Mill in 1837.[38] He soldiered on as a social reformer, despite having to sit in uneasy and often junior partnership with people whose aims he despised. In his work with schools and charities and on the parliamentary select committees he found that the people with the money, enthusiasm and, above all, the moral credibility were evangelical philanthropists. With their absolute and politically conservative values, they won support from the royal family, the government, the aristocracy and much of the middle class. Their kind of 'improvements', Place wrote, 'were solely aimed at the comfort – the honour – the honesty – and the intelligence of the working people, towards whom a fiendlike disposition was shewn by the Saints and Hypocrites, in their proposed enactments to make them as wretched, as gloomy, as perverse and ignorant, as the anti-social want of human feelings could devise'.[39]

Place carried on, and so did many other middle-class people who were motivated by a genuine desire to help the most deprived and miserable of their neighbours. But they had to accept the lead of the evangelicals. Many gave up, alarmed at the cold-heartedness and puritanism of modern charity and the values associated with it. It was the absence of any alternative that gave room for what we recognise as Victorian morality – the rigour and hard-heartedness of employment, philanthropy and the law. Those who advocated old-fashioned views of benevolence and unconditional charity or objected to the Pharisaic character of the age were sidelined and marginalised because of their cynical and snarling view that all talk of good works was consummate hypocrisy.

Accusations of cant should be used sparingly. Those who see hypocrisy everywhere and impute it indiscriminately to their opponents place themselves on shaky ground. If cant was so endemic, then what put them in the privileged position of being honest and candid? Those who detested the temper of the age and wanted to be seen to be free of hypocrisy and affectation all too often resorted to overacting their part. Despising decorum, they became boorish. Their contempt of prudery made them gratuitously obscene. Because some charitably inclined people were excessively fanatical, they became hard-hearted or apathetic. Writing of Lord Byron and Charles Churchill, Sir Walter Scott said that 'Both carried their hatred of hypocrisy beyond the verge of prudence, and indulged their vein of satire to the borders of licentiousness.' Something similar was true of other people in the 1820s and 1830s – from journalists to bored young gentlemen to labourers. It partly explains the brief rage for acting the part of Tom and Jerry: it was a rebellion against the manners of the day. It ranged from the loutish to the ridiculous: *The Times* reported on the foundation of a Society for the Encouragement of Vice in Brighton, which was clearly a derisive jest aimed at the SSV, although the pious paper of record seemed to believe that such a club had been instituted and reacted with requisite outrage.[40] These kinds of malcontents had in the front of their minds a checklist of prejudices: 'Nothing modern can be good. Every recent improvement is an unwarranted innovation upon the sacred system of the past. Every scheme projected for the public benefit, every new invention, is the butt for censure and the object of a sneer.'[41]

This is the spirit of Thomas Love Peacock's *Crotchet Castle* (1831). In the novel, Peacock brings together a cast of characters who represent the predominant, fashionable strains of thought: there are caricatures of J. R. McCulloch, James Mill, Robert Owen, Robert Southey, S. T. Coleridge, Leigh Hunt, Tom Moore and every other representative of modern theories. Together they babble the latest stock phrases, fashionable clichés and flashy jargon in futile and never-ending discussions. When the local clergyman gently criticises the host's propriety in displaying some nude Venuses when unmarried women were present, Mr Crotchet replies:

> Sir, ancient sculpture is the true school of modesty. But where the Greeks had modesty, we have cant; where they had poetry, we have cant; where they had patriotism, we have cant; where they had anything that exalts, delights, or adorns humanity, we have nothing but cant, cant, cant.

This outburst showed frustration at all the insincere and unthinking platitudes that were being spouted during the house party at the castle. Mr Crotchet goes on to say that he has purchased the statues for a reason: 'to show my contempt for cant in all its shapes, I have adorned my house with the Greek Venus, in all her shapes'.[42]

Mr Crotchet is typical of those who deplored the fastidiousness of the age. He does not buy art sincerely, because he likes it, but in order to show that he is not a prude. Such people preferred provocation and sneers to reasoned argument, and bandied the word 'cant' like a talisman. Because their squeamish opponents hated drunkenness, cruel sports, pugilism and all the other rough aspects of popular culture, they felt compelled to indulge and defend them to an exaggerated degree. Because their opponents were conspicuously pious, they had to deride all religion as fanaticism. It made them look immoral, but it also meant that their arguments rebounded on them. Based on their own definitions, they were as affected and insincere as the people they mocked. Scott wrote that such people would 'do well to remember that the cant of imputing to hypocrisy all pretensions to a severer scale of morals, or a more vivid sense of religion, is as offensive to sound reason and Christian philosophy, as that which attaches a charge of guilt to matters of indifference, or to the ordinary amusements of life'. Those who start to root out hypocrisy and throw the charge of cant about without reflection will soon find that there is nothing but cant and hypocrisy in the world. They will sink into apathy, leaving the field clear for those whose sense of righteousness and moral certainty gives them nothing to fear from the accusation.[43]

Indeed, there was some honour in being accused of cant by the malcontents. The Bishop of London complained that if he and the bench of bishops remained silent on issues such as drunkenness, they were accused of torpor and indifference; if they vented the moral feeling of the Church, they were charged with canting hypocrisy. In response Lord Chancellor Brougham said: 'I am quite ready to share with the right rev. Prelate . . . the charge of cant, which I treat with proper contempt, because, since I have come into public life, I have observed, that men who have no principle themselves cry out against the canting folks, as they term those who promote the good of their fellow creatures. These persons, have, at least the merit of candour. They do not pretend to principle themselves – they do not render the homage of hypocrisy, which Vice is said to pay to Virtue.'[44]

In Brougham's words we can see how much attitudes had changed since the eighteenth century. If he did not quite accept the charge of cant with pleasure, he was making a powerful statement that if there was a choice between apathy and enthusiasm, he was on the side of what the world disparagingly called cant. The word, and the concepts it expressed, were meaningless because they had been overused and abused. Those who opposed the tenor of the age would find themselves like Mr Chainmail, the hero of *Crotchet Castle*, who rejects modernity in favour of a romantic fantasy of the communal values, conviviality and honour of twelfth-century Merry England. With no place for him in 1830s Britain and no resources to suggest an alternative to the manners of the time, he insulates himself from the tyranny of utilitarianism and political economy, the din of machinery and the cant of verbal decorum in his baronial hall, where he can indulge his nostalgic dreams. It is his private 'fortress of beef and ale', where simple manners, manly virtues, true benevolence and good old-fashioned fun can be enjoyed.

But it is those who leave their fortress and engage with the world who make the manners of their age. In his speech, Brougham also articulated a view that was shared by many others, if not expressed so outspokenly. He acknowledged the triumph of propriety of conduct over simplicity of manners. Hypocrisy *was* the homage that vice paid to virtue, and it was an entirely appropriate mode of behaviour in the 1830s. Hypocrisy and pretence had been the greatest of vices for the generation before, for whom the open display of emotions and feelings was natural and honest. Their children and grandchildren had learnt to master their emotions. In the same way, they had accepted that society had the duty to impose restraints on the customs and manners of the people. In the previous century the French slang 'talking English' meant being frank to the point of being offensive. In the nineteenth century 'English' was still a colloquialism on the continent, although it stood for something different. In Germany it was slang for 'what we should call puritanism in language and excess of delicacy in matters of physical love'.[45]

There were those who preferred the coarse manners of the older culture: at least you knew where you were with people who were not polished by refinement; for all their crudity and occasional deviations from strict propriety they did not bury deep vices by concealing petty ones. Vice remained unconquered, indeed stronger now that so many arts had been perfected for its concealment. Sir Walter Scott had a dim opinion of those who boasted of the triumph of progress and the reformation of morals: 'We are not now, perhaps, more moral in our conduct than men of fifty years since; but modern vice pays a tax to appearances, and is contented to wear a mask of decorum.' John Wade was similarly mistrustful of the sincerity of the middle classes: 'But though the age has improved in appearance, there is none, we fear, in sentiments.'[46]

'This is a gross error,' Francis Place wrote angrily in his notes in response to these two opinions. 'Some say we have refined away all our simplicity and have become artificial, hypocritical, and upon the whole worse than we were half a century ago,' he wrote at another time. 'This is a common belief but it is a false one, we are much better people now than we were then, better instructed, more sincere and kind hearted, less gross and brutal, and have few of the concomitant vices of a less civilized state.'[47]

It was as if politeness and decorum were bad things, as if courtesy and consideration in the public sphere were signs of internal corruption. For people like Place who had pulled themselves up from poverty and had altered their mode of conduct to serve their ends, the excessive concern for the death of sincerity and simplicity was wrong-headed and ridiculous. If, as Walter Scott and others said, people avoided vice because they were following fashion or for appearance's sake, it was hard to see what the problem was: vicious actions would be avoided and bad habits would be consequently weakened and eroded. Decorum and good behaviour were learnt by example and imitation, and it was absurd to wish people were spiritually cleansed from the inside as well. For example, obscene print shops had been driven out of the West End and Fleet Street 'not by prosecutions, but from want of customers'; whether or not the former clientele were genuinely better people or were too ashamed to be seen poring over erotica was inconsequential; the point was the effect was good and the whole of society improved regardless of whether manners were motivated by good or bad intentions.[48]

What could be wrong with that? Society's demands should override individual scruples about what was genuine or counterfeit. Place urged people to embrace the artificiality of modern life. If people mourned the loss of *naturalness*, this was an error: the natural state of man was brutal and degraded. People had to learn how to live; how to reconcile their brutish instincts with the needs of society; how to pursue their best interests without being diverted by their emotions and passions. Interrogating the sincerity or otherwise of someone's intention was a futile and deluded thing to do. The point was that people, mainly of the middle and artisan classes, were richer, more secure, more sober and more dignified than the generation before. If eighteenth-century notions of personal freedom meant giving licence to coarse, cruel and destructive instincts, they were better left in the history books. Some said that the people and society itself had become artificial – 'but', riposted Place, 'this is so far from being a subject for complaint [that it] should be a subject for congratulation'.[49]

If their parents and grandparents had regarded burying passions and acting a part as the vices of the dissembler, the next generation was inclined to see those things differently. For example, when Harriette Wilson published her memoirs of high-life sex scandals in 1825, it showed how publicity could harm the upper class. In the reformist agitation of the 1830s it was believed that unless they cleaned up their act, the House of Lords had only a few years left before it was abolished altogether. There were fewer young noblemen who arrogantly paraded their vices, as their fathers and uncles had done; the vices survived, of course, but hidden away from view. 'Our men of rank', commented the *Morning Chronicle* in 1827, 'may occasionally *assume* a virtue which they have not, they may sometimes be greater hypocrites than their forefathers were, but hypocrisy is, at all events, an homage offered to public opinion, and supposes the existence of a fear of the people.' Indeed, it was only to be regretted that every patron of prostitutes, every dram-drinker and swearer, even of the lower orders, did not have his Miss Wilson to expose him to his wife and neighbours. Her *Memoirs* at least heralded a world where those who openly shunned the manners of the age were gibbeted for execration. Some called it 'newspaper morality', but, for all that, it confined unappealing behaviour behind closed doors.[50]

It could be said that people in the 1830s, on the eve of Victorianism, were more relaxed about hypocrisy, as the *Morning Chronicle* seemed to suggest. Sir T. Charles Morgan wrote that modern society had decreed 'that not to be a hypocrite is to lack common decency; and to call "things by their right names" is to unsettle the foundations of the world's repose'. Most would not have admitted it in so many words. What had changed was that their definition of hypocrisy was less exacting. It shaded into politeness. Lady Blessington rejected Byron's tendency to see cant as the greatest British sin: 'what he calls hypocrisy is but the respect to public opinion that induces people, who have not courage to correct their errors, at least to endeavour to conceal them'. If it was hypocritical to mask bad passions and unappealing instincts, then so be it; it was a hallmark of being civilised to master one's emotions. Repression and abstinence were good qualities. The generation that had grown up during the wars had had that drilled into them, and it was a sacrifice they made willingly. 'He who is no hypocrite, knows nothing of life, nothing of its enjoyments, nothing of its amenities . . .' wrote Morgan. 'That there can be any vice in practice so universal, so respected, and so serviceable to mankind, seems eminently impossible.'[51]

This generation did not acknowledge that the way they behaved was hypocritical. They could say that their parents were no less hypocritical. Although people in the eighteenth century talked of candour and naturalness and affected to hate hypocrisy, it was an illusion. They were governed by their animal instincts; it did not make them any more free or honest. Those who had mastered their emotions were the liberated. It is a reasonable argument: every age is more or less hypocritical in its own way, after all. But the difference was that hypocrisy was no longer considered the 'vice of vices', the source of all other crime. This shift in opinion made people more comfortable with the behaviour and morality that we associate with Victorianism – studied rectitude of conduct, squeamishness about the mention of sex and the body, high-minded philanthropy, sense of duty, subdued emotions and all the other meanings the term has for us. It was no doubt a more respectable time, but the morality that made appearances and conduct a priority allowed double standards to exist without being condemned as hypocritical – the definition of Victorianism for many now.

Verbal decorum, which many congratulated themselves on, consciously buried unsavoury topics and prevented honest discussion. The existence of vice itself was denied; any talk of it would add fuel to the flames. And so vice and crime flourished. Once the traditional popular culture of bawdy images and smutty jokes was tabooed, and mildly erotic cartoons were banished from mainstream print shops, pornography was invented. It can scarcely be denied that prostitution soared in the Victorian era. As Cobbett wrote, while people strained to prove their 'excessive modesty and delicacy', while women blushed at the mention of underwear or chicken breasts and explicit language, but while there were shoals of prostitutes on the streets and bastard babies abandoned in asylums, 'it becomes us, at any rate, to be silent about purity of mind, improvement of manners, and the increase of refinement and *delicacy*'.[52]

The changes that had occurred in Britain seemed to have happened with great speed; that is why the Regency seemed so distant and alien to people a couple of decades later. But had the British really changed all that much in so short a time? 'Surely,' said the *Literary Gazette*, 'if we have not become more virtuous, we have become more decorous; in language and outward appearance at least, we are improved, and perhaps that is all, for human nature is pretty much the same in all ages.'[53] There was something recognisably British in the form the reformation of manners took. Macaulay famously wrote of the periodic fits of morality that broke out in the public. History showed an oscillation between puritanism and sensuality: they pushed both to excess – as individuals and as a people. The dour and fanatical age of

Cromwell gave way to the hedonism of the Restoration, which was itself succeeded by another period of moral restraint. In all cases there was the same bossiness and competitive spirit, the same preference for the compulsory over the voluntary. The British loved exposing the foibles of their celebrities and neighbours with prurient malice.

William Hazlitt saw no difference between the British of the late eighteenth century and their supposedly sedate children and grandchildren. The moral war against Byron and Edmund Kean exhibited 'the rage of virtue in the British public'. Yet this moralistic attitude was the modern version of the spite, malice, violence and love of tumult that had always been a British trait. The public held a 'moral grudge'. It was in the same spirit as the O.P. War; the people relished rows and fights – only the form they took changed. In all campaigns for moral reform, be it reform of the poor, self-reform or the scrutiny of the moralising press, there was the same dependence on force, compulsion and surveillance: 'with us, where there is always an eye to the beadle and the treadmill, nothing but appeal to brute force tames the natural rudeness of our characters, or appeases the *moral* grudge, that rankles like a heart-burn or a liver-complaint in our bosoms. We always aim to arrive at the agreeable through the disagreeable.'[54]

The literature and journalism of the 1820s and '30s expresses an awareness that Britain had changed for ever. The most successful *Life in London* rip-off was *The English Spy*, written by Bernard Blackmantle and illustrated with characteristic skill by Robert Cruikshank alone, his brother George having married, sobered up and rejected the coarse humour that had made him famous. It was serialised in 1825, but whereas Pierce Egan's *Life in London* was up to date and supposedly modern, *The English Spy* had no more materials to hand than scandals conducted at least a decade earlier. Vice had grown old; the modern world did not have colour enough to sustain a book of this sort.

While Egan wrote in the present tense, Blackmantle used the past. *The English Spy* is a nostalgic look back on a world of conviviality and gentlemanly riot now lost for ever. Life in London, in the way Egan, George Hanger, Henry Angelo and the Barrymore brothers envisaged it, was impossible by the time *The English Spy* was published; it is strange to think that just four years separates it from the romps of Tom and Jerry. The 'low coffee shops' which were once integral to a 'spree' in 'conquest of the Holy Land' (as Tom and Jerry found) were no longer there. The severity of the magistracy since 1822 had seen to that. Other things had changed the character of the district. 'The general introduction of gas throws too clear a *light* upon many *dark* transactions and midnight frolics to allow the repetition of the scenes of former times.' Truly then it was an enlightened age, inimical to 'the *spreeish* and the *sprightly*' and 'the eminent, the eccentric, and the notorious' who used to flock there.

When Blackmantle ventures into Covent Garden, he tries to recreate the old ways but finds that the place is tinged with gloom, and what pleasure remains cowers in fear of Bow Street officers empowered by the Vagrant Act. Blackmantle and a number of aging swells remember how the piazza at Covent Garden was once full of Cyprians, the 'first beauties of the land'. But now they were cleared away, and the Cyprian Balls, once the most exclusive and entertaining events in the capital, were defunct. Back then, bucks, dandies, MPs, actors and writers used to consort with the courtesans in grand brothels presided over by 'Her Majesty the Queen of Bohemia' and Mother Butler. 'How many jovial nights have I passed and jolly fellows have I met in the snug sanctum sanctorum! a little *crib*, as the *flashmongers* would call it, with an entrance through the bar, and into which none were ever permitted to enter without a formal introduction, and gracious permission of the hostess.'

But now the notorious public house kept by Mother Butler, The Finish, was finished, its licence suspended by vigilant magistrates. The 'mad pranks' and sprees of the bucks were over, and Covent Garden was seedier and more depraved than before. One aging rake lamented the passing of the old: 'I remember when a gentleman might have reeled around the environs of Covent Garden, *in* and *out* of every establishment, from the Bedford to Mother Butler's, without having his pleasures broken in upon by the irruptions of Bow-street mohawks, or his person endangered by any association he chose to mix with; but we are returning to the times of the *Roundheads* and the *Puritans*; *cant* has bitten the ear of authority, and the great officers of state are infected with the jesuitical mania.'

The English Spy can be trusted as much, or as little, as an insight into real life as Egan's work: Covent Garden was never quite the glittering pleasure ground imagined by Blackmantle. Yet both books reflect the mood of the time. It was impossible to imitate Egan in 1825 because legislative reforms, the increased surveillance of the authorities and the propriety of the reading public rendered the incidents of *Life in London* history. The possibility of crossing social boundaries was gone, as the aging rake quoted above acknowledged, because associating with petty criminals and beggars would be enough to have one arrested as a vagrant.

When Pierce Egan returned to bury Tom and Jerry in 1828, he was constrained by the moral temper of the time, and also by the changed face of London. In *The Finish to the Adventures of Tom, Jerry, and Logic* it would no longer do to have two young men defying the puritans and the police; such a thing would expose Egan to the charge of encouraging imitators. Instead, he invented a new character to be his foot soldier in his war on cant. Sir John Blubber was known 'as the uncommonly big gentleman': he was old, fat and comical. No one would think of emulating such a mound of flesh and eccentricity, so he can mouth Egan's sentiments yet shield the author from the charge of corrupting youth by glamorising vice.

Sir John was a cockney orphan made good, rising from poverty to affluence and achieving status as an alderman and an MP. He was a throwback to an earlier generation, and his values contrasted with the spirit of the age: he was 'a most facetious, jolly, good-natured soul; one of that class of persons deemed independent; and his property enabled him to "care for nobody"'. He did not have to keep up with the pretended values and fashionable cant of the middling classes; his money was made and he could afford to look down on the pretentiousness of earnest and strait-laced men and women. Unlike most other successful people, he did not treat less prosperous people with contempt, as culpable for their status, especially not 'those characters whose circumstances in life reduced them to the appellation of being called – POOR'.

Indeed, Sir John atones for the sins that Egan had committed when he took a hard line towards beggars in the first instalment of Tom and Jerry's adventures. Blubber is a decided enemy to the Society for the Suppression of Mendicity's cant: 'His purse was never closed against the real object of unavoidable misfortune and distress; indeed, it was much better to be duped at times, than to let a deserving man or woman, in need of charity, be "sent empty away", as a token of revenge on the plausible wretch and sanctified hypocrite.' Nothing could be more old-fashioned or further from the spirit of Britain in 1828. Egan had changed his tune since his Mendicity Society propaganda in the first book. Perhaps he felt pangs of guilt about his hand in Billy Waters' death.

Throughout the book, as Tom and Jerry become more staid and serious, Blubber is the last voice of merriment and joviality, a relic of another age. In an incident entitled 'A Burning Shame', Sir John single-handedly takes on the restraints of the modern world. Tom and Jerry come across the portly gent fighting an 'Old Scout' (a watchman) at the door of a brothel; Blubber wins easily, but notwithstanding 'was puffing and blowing like a broken-winded horse'. Tom and Jerry laugh at their elderly friend's antics.

'You are wrong, Jerry, very wrong,' says Sir John, '– this is above a joke; and I am determined to have satisfaction for the insult put upon me by this rascally watchman.'

'It is too bad, indeed,' Tom replies, 'to *baulk* any gentleman's pursuits, either private or public; and I was very glad to see you punish the varlet for his impertinence.'

The 'burning shame' was the new technique used by parishes and the Society for the Suppression of Vice to drive brothels out of neighbourhoods. They would put illuminated banners outside the place reading 'Beware of a Bad House', just in case someone accidentally wandered in and was absent-minded enough to be seduced. They also

THE BURNING SHAME! – TOM *and* JERRY *laughing at the turn up between the uncommonly big-Gentleman and the Hero of the Roundy-ken under suspicious circumstances.*

affixed lanterns on poles to indicate a house of ill repute. A 'burning shame' meant something that ought to be put out and 'extinguished' for good. It was hoped that such a public display would shame the pimps and bawds and prostitutes and their clientele, who would be driven from the neighbourhood by the glaring light of truth. It did not work quite like that: as a barrister said in a prosecution brought by the SSV, 'Those who had gone before continued to go still; and those who had not gone before found their way more easily.'[55]

'This is a "*burning shame*" with a vengeance to it,' observed Sir John. '. . . Is the liberty of the subject thus to be trampled upon? . . . Shame I say, on the laws that would give such a low fellow the power to insult his betters under the disguise of morality! Away with such cant and hypocrisy!'

Sir John Blubber spoke for an older generation, whose moral sentiments belonged in the last century. The old knight represents the rough-edged and unpolished eighteenth century coming into unhappy collision with the prim and prurient nineteenth, the watchmen representing society's new-found vigour for investigating what was previously considered strictly private. Egan wrote for those who pined for that world free of exaggerated high-mindedness, when Britons spoke with freedom and acted as they saw fit and were not afraid of their feelings. He was describing, with his customary boisterous humour, what the somewhat more serious Thomas Carlyle called the 'grand characteristic of the age': the 'undue cultivation of the outward'. The 'superior morality' that was dinned into people's ears was really created 'by greater perfection of Police; and of that far subtler and stronger Police, called Public Opinion'.[56]

But this more subdued and regulated world was generally welcomed. For the generation that had been brought up during the dark days of the 1790s, when apocalyptic nightmares and nervous disorders raged, and during the no less anxiety-ridden years after the wars, the absolute values and rigorous morality that dominated public discussion offered reassurance. They bequeathed their children, 'the Victorians', a veneration of respectability, gentility and public duty. A country that appeared to be destined for greatness as the head of a vast empire and as a commercial superpower demanded an appropriate morality to justify its position in the world. Those who benefited from stability and the heyday of empire in the later nineteenth century had grown up in unsettled times: rural unrest in the 1830s, political agitation in the 1840s and famine in Ireland were no less nightmarish than the problems that faced the preceding generation. They knew the chaos and disorder out of which their prosperity had emerged, they knew how vulnerable society was to *fortuna*, and they would resist any degeneracy in public morality or civic values – anything that threatened a return to the turbulence of another age.

And if we know that the Victorians had their peccadilloes, secret vices and bolted closets, there is no doubt they considered that their best interests lay in conformity to public expectations. It is also clear that as never before private morality came under the scrutiny of society and the law (a situation that was challenged by the Wolfenden Report in 1957[57]). This book has taken a street-level view of aspects of the commercial revolution that were noted by political theorists, most notably Benjamin Constant, Alexis de Tocqueville and John Stuart Mill: principally that society had overpowered the individual. Compared to the previous generation, wrote Mill in *On Liberty*, when different classes, neighbourhoods, professions and so on contributed to the rich diversity of life, people in the modern world 'read the same things, listen to the same things, use the same things, go to the same places, have their hopes and fears directed to the same objects'.[58] One of the themes of this book has been the change in the people, from producers of their amusements to consumers; they became passive observers of the world rather than active participants. This *sameness* is what concerned Mill in the 1850s. The atmosphere of social freedom, the individuality and spontaneity prized in a previous age had nurtured the soil in which genius had thrived amid the wide and wild variety of a tolerant and permissive society. For, according to Mill, individuality can grow only when there is an atmosphere of social freedom; and for this good end freedom is worth having, even if it permits the offensive, the outrageous, the impious and the plain annoying to flourish as well. 'Eccentricity has always abounded when and where strength of character has abounded . . . That so few now dare to be eccentric marks the chief danger of the time.'[59] *On Liberty* could fairly have been entitled 'On Cant'. One of many in a society that levels everyone to the same standard of mediocrity and sees quirks as antisocial, Mill's modern individual has lost the power of original thought and independent morality. His or her thoughts are the thoughts of society; common beliefs – even convenient untruths – are maintained because 'people feel sure, not so much that their opinions are true, as that they should not know what to do without them'.[60]

When the Great Exhibition of 1851 was being planned, the realists predicted that the crowds would come, they would see the great wealth laid out in front of their eyes and, like the European revolutionaries of 1848, they would be worked up into a jealous rage. At the very least, they would drink and brawl and disport themselves in the customary disorderly manner. In the event they came, they saw the rich panoply of modern luxuries and consumer goods, and they were decent, sober and respectable. There can be no doubt that it was a more peaceable society. Mill, and many other voices heard in this book, joined those who celebrated the progress of the country; but they emphasised that society had paid dearly for its security. Britons seemed better behaved, but can he who governs himself in conformity to social expectations be said to be an autonomous moral being? In the same way, a country that needed a police force had seemingly turned its back on personal or communal moral responsibility; not wanting to commit crimes because there is a bobby on the beat is obviously very different from refraining voluntarily. 'We have lost in imagination what we have gained in knowledge,' wrote Constant; 'as a result, we are even incapable of lasting emotion; the ancients were in the full youth of their moral life, we are in its maturity, perhaps in its old age.'[61] The human in this new world would enjoy a cosy enough existence, to be sure, but he or she would be emotionally stunted, intellectually timid, morally neutral and ambitious of little more originality than parroting stock phrases and reheated opinions.

The difficulty of reliably distinguishing independent thought from the thought of your society, generation or profession – or how it is inwardly digested and outwardly expressed – seems to me to be inevitable and equally true whether one lives in a small village or as an anonymous member of a labyrinthine city; in a pre- or post-industrial age. Indeed, there is as much or more reason to be afraid of bigotry, narrow-mindedness and capricious censure in a village than in a large and complex society. It is worth noting that those who complained of a present or impending 'age of cant' never thought that *their* minds would become less independent – it was always directed at opponents and, principally, down the social scale. If large numbers of people babbling clichés, reading the latest half-baked theory and gorging on the seamiest gossip is the price to pay for wider education, greater literacy, the rage for instruction at mechanics institutes, cheap newspapers and a free press – advantages the Victorians enjoyed over their parents – it

'Life is but a Masquerade'. If life had become bogus and artificial, one thing was inevitable. While the guests at the masquerade ball try to hide their identities behind their masks, Death reveals himself without shame, mocking feeble human attempts to dissemble their natures and cheat fate

was one worth paying. A better educated reading public did not become wholly artificial automata incapable of independent thought or authentic emotions; literature and science were not made less pure by greater diffusion (even if mankind did have to put up with a greater number of sub-mediocre books). But it is not surprising that in the earnest and moralistic atmosphere of the 1820s and the early years of Victoria's reign, when the idea that men could be remodelled and directed by their moral and religious superiors was thriving, many saw these powers over the individual growing and beheld a future of onerous social control and stultifying conformity.[62]

Despite such fears, the British did not quite lose all their eccentricity or independence of mind – even if the surface of society became more placid and society itself more homogenous. The beleaguered human soul could survive even the pressure to conform to the 'tyranny of the majority' and the brain-numbing cant of 'newspaper morality'. Many Victorians dreaded the self-righteousness and staidness of their time – even if they outwardly conformed – and looked back with nostalgia to the carefree days of the eighteenth century and the Regency. The reaction against 'Victorianism' was strong; we still feel it today, when many equate moralism with Victorianism, and hence repression and hypocrisy. There is something in the human spirit that will rebel against what is perceived to be artificial and constraining. As the great German philosopher rightly said, 'Out of the crooked timber of humanity, nothing straight was ever fashioned.'

Acknowledgements

I am grateful for the invaluable help and support of Ian Bahrami, Clare Conville, Walter Donohue, Scott Moyers, Lucy Owen, Zoë Pagnamenta, Rebecca Smith, Inigo Thomas and Marney Wilson.

Notes

Abbreviations

Add. MS: British Library Additional Manuscripts
BL: British Library
ER: *Edinburgh Review*
Hansard1: *Hansard's Political Debates*, first series
Hansard2: *Hansard's Political Debates*, new series
Hansard3: *Hansard's Political Debates*, third series
HO: Home Office Papers (Public Record Office)
ODNB: *Oxford Dictionary of National Biography*
OED: *Oxford English Dictionary*
Parl. Hist: *Cobbett's History of Parliament*
PP: Parliamentary Papers
QR: *Quarterly Review*
SBCP: Society for Bettering the Condition of the Poor
SSV: Society for the Suppression of Vice

Introduction: Untaught Feelings

1 Hazlitt, *Works*, vol. XX, p. 284.
2 *Times*, 1 Oct. 1817 and 29 Oct. 1818.
3 *Hansard1*, vol. XXI, 1815, pp. 568–70, 614–6, 690–2; *Times*, 2 June 1815.
4 *Times*, 29 Aug. 1803; 27 Aug. 1805; 29 Jan. 1816; 20 July 1816.
5 [SSV], *Appeal to Common Decency*, pp. 3, 4, 5, 7–12; *Times*, 23 March 1809.
6 Brown, *Fathers*, pp. 439–40.
7 Lennox, *Life*, vol. II, p. 292; Barbauld in *Monthly Review*, LXXI, 1813, p. 210.
8 *Scourge*, II, 1811, pp. 202ff.
9 Cobbett, *Advice*, para. 239; Byron, *Letters*, 26 Oct. 1819.
10 As Cyrus Redding defined it in his article 'Cant', *New Monthly*, II, 1821, p. 301.
11 OED: entries for 'cant', 'canter' and 'canting'. William Paley wrote in 1790: 'There is such a thing as a peculiar word or phrase cleaving, as it were, to the memory of the writer or speaker and presenting itself to his utterance at every turn. When we observe this we call it a cant word or a cant phrase' (*Horae Paulinae* [1840 edn], p. 395).
12 *New Monthly*, II, 1821, p. 301, and vol. XI, 1824, p. 302; McCutcheon, 'A Note on Cant', p. 30.

13 Blessington, *Conversations*, p. 12.
14 Byron, *Letter to* **** ****** [*John Murray*], p. 16.
15 Langford, *Englishness Identified*, pp. 90–1.
16 Boyer, *Dictionnaire Royal.*
17 Walter Scott, *Miscellaneous Prose*, vol. III, pp. 520–1.
18 Anon, *Short Treatise on the Passions . . . By a Lady*, vol. I, p. 79.
19 Pückler-Muskau, vol. II, p. 131; Collier, *Tragical Comedy*, *passim.*
20 Anon, *Essay on Trade and Commerce*, p. 92.
21 *Hansard1*, vol. XIX, 1811, pp. 631, 647–8.
22 *Cobbett's Monthly Religious Tracts*, 1 March 1821, p. 1.
23 Arendt, *On Revolution*, pp. 100–1.
24 Godwin, *Enquiry*, vol. I, p. 276.
25 Burke, *Reflections*, pp. 86–7.
26 Lord Erskine, Introductory letter to Charles James Fox's *Speeches* (1815); Hazlitt, 'Character of Fox', in *Eloquence of the British Senate* (1807).
27 Horace Walpole, *Correspondence*, vol. XI, p. 263; Crane, 'Suggestions Toward a Genealogy of the "Man of Feeling",' pp. 205–6.
28 Tompkins, *Popular Novel*, pp. 92, 103; Stewart, *Outline*, p. 145.
29 Godwin, *Enquiry*, vol. I, pp. 278–9.
30 Vickers, Introduction to *The Man of Feeling*, p. viii; Anon, *Short Treatise on the Passions . . . By a Lady*, vol. I, p. 118.
31 Hazlitt, 'Pleasure of Hating'; Adam Smith wrote: 'The man who skips and dances about with that intemperate and senseless joy which we cannot accompany him in, is the object of our contempt and indignation' (*Theory of Moral Sentiments*, vol. I, p. 97).
32 Arendt, pp. 95ff; Shklar, 'Let Us Not Be Hypocritical', *passim*; Trilling, *Sincerity*, *passim.*
33 Wilberforce, *Practical View*, pp. 47, 56–9, 168–9.
34 Fellowes, *Religion Without Cant*, pp. 4–7, 27, 133; Wilberforce, *Practical View*, p. 47.
35 *Satirist*, II, March 1808, pp. 18–20.
36 Southey, *Espirilla's Letters from England*, vol. III, p. 290; Murray, *Enquiries*, pp. 17–18 and *passim.*
37 Smith, *Theory of Moral Sentiments*, vol. II, p. 146.
38 *Examiner*, 12 Dec. 1819.
39 *New Monthly*, X, 1824, p. 43; Gibbon Wakefield, *England*, p. 82; Corry, *English Metropolis* (1820), pp. 188–9.
40 *ER*, XXXIII, Jan. 1820, pp. 131–8; Accum, *Treatise*, *passim.*
41 Trotter, *View of the Nervous Temperament*, pp. 225–6 (see Chapter 1 of this book: 'Sinking, Sinking, Sinking').
42 Wilberforce, *Life*, vol. I, p. 98, vol. IV, pp. 343–4.
43 Stewart, *Outlines*, pp. 93–4.
44 *ER*, XXIII, April 1814, p. 199.
45 Byron, *Letter to* **** ****** [*John Murray*], pp. 16–17.
46 *New Monthly*, XI, 1824, p. 302.

Introduction to Part I: Some New World

1 Austin, *Letters*, p. 84.
2 Wadd, *Cursory Remarks*, pp. 3–6, 45; *New Monthly*, X, 1824, p. 181.
3 Simond, *Journal*, p. 22; Silliman, *Journey*, vol. I, p. 307, vol. II, p. 211; Karamzin, *Travels*, vol. III, p. 313; Austin, *Letters*, p. 271.
4 Karamzin, vol. III, pp. 202–3.
5 Silliman, vol. I, p. 126.
6 Silliman, vol. I, p. 126; Simond, p. 22.
7 Southey, *Espirilla's Letters from England*, vol. I, pp. 75, 119–20.
8 *Examiner*, 13 Nov. 1808.
9 Karamzin, vol. III, p. 315.
10 Bowdler, *Reform or Ruin*, p. 4; Wilberforce, *Life*, vol. II, p. 114; Rose, *Life of William Pitt*, vol. II, p. 299.
11 Aikin, *Correspondence*, p. 306; *Examiner*, 15 May 1808; Sydney Smith, *Peter Plymley*; Stephen, *Dangers*, p. 35.
12 Stephen, *Dangers*, pp. 33–4.
13 *Examiner*, 22 May 1808; Southey, *Espirilla's Letters from England*, vol. III, pp. 2–3; *Scourge*, Sept. 1811, p. 247.
14 Bowles, *Reflections*, pp. 3–4, 25, 74; Bowles, *Dispassionate Inquiry*, pp. 29–30; *Parl. Hist.*, vol. XXXIV, 1798–1800, p. 1,560.
15 *Parl. Hist.*, vol. XXXIII, 1798, p. 1,307.
16 *Ibid.*, p. 1,306.
17 Malthus, *Essay on Population* (1803), pp. 6–7, 12–13, 350.
18 *Satirist*, Sept. 1809, pp. 265–6; Wilberforce, *Life*, vol. I, p. 130 (cf. p. 149); Bowdler, *Reform or Ruin*, pp. 4–5.
19 Rush, *Memoranda* (second series), p. 352.

Chapter 1: Sinking, Sinking, Sinking

1 Karamzin, vol. III, p. 315.
2 Burney, *Diary*, vol. IV, p. 237.
3 *Le Beau Monde*, I, Jan. 1807, p. 158; Karamzin, vol. III, pp. 208–9.
4 *ER*, IX, Oct. 1806, pp. 184–5.
5 Beresford, *Miseries of Human Life*, vol. I, dedication and pp. 1–2.
6 Beddoes, *Hygëia*, Essay VIII, pp. 76–9.
7 Coleridge, *Letters*, no. 397, 4 May 1801, p. 726.
8 *Satirist*, July 1810, p. 29; *ER*, IX, p. 186; Austin, p. 116.
9 Trotter, *View of the Nervous Temperament*, p. 168.
10 Beddoes, Essay II, pp. 72–3; Essay III, pp. 8–9, 78.
11 *Gentleman's Magazine*, vol. 78, 1808, pp. 318–9; Trotter, p. viii.
12 Beddoes, Essay VII, p. 98.
13 Trotter, pp. 226–7.
14 *Ibid.*, p. 149.
15 *Ibid.*, pp. 182–3, 189–90.
16 Beddoes, Essay IX, p. 163; Southey, *Espirilla's Letters from England*, vol. I, pp. 180–2, 185–6.

17 Trotter, pp. 19–32.
18 *Ibid.*, pp. 49–51, 225–6.
19 Beddoes, Essay IV, p. 61.
20 *Ibid.*, pp. 37–9; Place, *Autobiography*, p. 45; BL Add. MS 36,625, f. 8.
21 Aristotle, *The Works*, p. 62; Solomon, *Guide to Health*, pp. 112–3.
22 Aristotle, *The Works*, pp. 12–13, 15–16.
23 *Ibid.*, p. 42.
24 Beddoes, Essay IV, p. 62
25 Trotter, pp. 29, 35, 79.
26 *Ibid.*, p. 90.
27 Beddoes, Essay III, p. 82.
28 Trotter, pp. 38–41.
29 Beddoes, Essay III, pp. 31–4.
30 Colquhoun, *Treatise on the Police of the Metropolis*, *passim*; Colquhoun, *Treatise on Indigence*, p.34; Trotter, p. xvii.
31 Beddoes, Essay IV, pp. 94–5.
32 Simond, vol. I, pp. 253–4
33 Beddoes, Essay III, pp. 4–7.
34 Trotter, pp. 149, 164–5, 223–4.
35 Beddoes, Essay IX, p. 10; Hone, *Every-Day Book*, vol. I, p. 661; *Annual Review 1803*, pp. 738–43.
36 *Scourge*, Vol. II, July 1811, pp. 52–3.
37 Anon, 'A Collection of Advertisements', number 70: Samuel Solomon, *Balm of Gilead* (ad, n.d. *c.*1800).
38 Silliman, vol. 1, pp. 66–7. See also, Janson, *Stranger in America*, p. 349.
39 BL c.142.a.176, number 74: S. Solomon, *The Following Are a Few of the Numerous Cures Performed by that Most Inestimable Medicine the Cordial Balm of Gilead* (ad, n.d, *c.*1800); Solomon, *Guide to Health*, pp. iv, xiii–iv, xix–xxii.
40 Beddoes, Essay II, pp. 17–18; *Scourge*, II, Oct. 1811, p. 296; Leigh Hunt, *Lord Byron*, letter dated 18 Nov. 1820; Anon, 'A Collection of Advertisements', number 69: ad. for Solomon's Anti-Impetigines (n.d., *c.*1800).
41 Anon, 'A Collection of Advertisements', number 70: Samuel Solomon, *The Balm of Gilead* (ad, *c.*1800)
42 *Scourge*, I, Jan. 1811, pp. 35–6 and Oct. 1811, II, pp. 287–90. ODNB: Samuel Solomon.
43 Anon, 'A Collection of Advertisements', number 73: Samuel Solomon, *An Account of that Most Excellent Medicine, the Cordial Balm of Gilead* (1801?); *Scourge*, II, Oct. 1811, p. 302.
44 *Salisbury Journal*, 22 Aug. 1798 (quoted in *A Guide to Health*, p. 105).
45 *Critical Review*, third series, vol. XIX, 1810, p. 192.
46 *Examiner*, 1 Nov. 1812.
47 Solomon, *Guide to Health*, pp. 46–7.
48 *Ibid.*, pp. xiii, 47.
49 *Ibid.*, pp. xiii, 189–202, 225.

50 *Ibid.*, pp. 189–90; Anon, 'A Collection of Advertisements', numbers 70, 71 and 79.
51 *Scourge*, vol. II, Oct. 1811, pp. 295–6.
52 Beddoes, Essay II, p. 91; Castigator's article reprinted in the *Examiner*, 29 Nov. 1812.
53 Paris, *Analysis*; *Scourge*, vol. IV, Nov. 1812; *The Book of Health* (1829) p. 105.
54 *Scourge*, II, Oct. 1811, p. 299, and IV, July 1812, pp. 43–4; *Examiner*, 29 Nov. 1812.

Chapter 2: Drunk on Liberty

1 *ER*, XXXVIII, Feb. 1823, p. 87.
2 Hanway, *New Year's Gift*, p. 132.
3 *ER*, I, Oct. 1802, pp. 94–5.
4 Bowles, *Reflections*, p. 75; Bowles, *View of the Moral State of Society*, p. 67.
5 Austin, pp. 12–13; *General Evening Post*, 26 Dec. 1809.
6 Austin, pp. 176–7.
7 Paley, pp. 541–2; *Hansard1*, vol. XIX, 1811, pp. 626, 647–8.
8 Trotter, p. 227.
9 Skinner, *Journal*, pp. 29, 42, 183, 206, 231–2, 238.
10 Malcomson, *Popular Recreations*, p. 69.
11 Hone, *Every-day Book*, vol. II, pp. 668–9.
12 Radford, 'The Loyal Saddler of Exeter', pp. 227–35.
13 Add. MS 27,825, f. 154.
14 Henry Angelo, *Reminiscences*, vol. I, pp. 283–5, vol. II, pp. 1–2.
15 Place, *Autobiography*, pp. 20–3, 34–6.
16 *Ibid.*, pp. 20–4, 27–8, 34–9.
17 Wahrman, *Imagining*, pp. 149–50.
18 Gaskell, *Manufacturing Population*, pp. 55–63.
19 Place, *Autobiography*, pp. 34–40.
20 *Ibid.*, p. 51; Ad MSS 27,827, ff. 50–2.
21 Place, *Autobiography*, pp. 49–51, 57, 58–9.
22 Add. MS 27,825, ff 143 (part B), 144–165; Morris, *Festival of Anacreon*, esp. pp. 22ff.
23 Add. MS 27,825, f. 157.
24 *Ibid.*, f. 147.
25 Place, *Autobiography*, p. 56; Add. MS 27,832, ff. 228–9; Hone, *Every-day Book*, vol. II, pp. 665–6.
26 Gaskell, *Manufacturing Population*, pp. 27–30.
27 Place, *Autobiography*, p. 55; Add. MS 35,144, ff. 175, 176; Hone, *Every-Day Book*, vol. I, pp. 396–7.
28 Place, *Autobiography*, pp. 45, 56, 56n, 61, 73.
29 Bowles, *Dispassionate Inquiry*, pp. 29–30; Bowles, *View of the Moral State of Society*, p. 79.

30 Place, *Autobiography*, pp. 20–4; Iatros, *Biographical Sketch*, pp. 5–8, 14–16; PRO HO/42/66.
31 Iatros, *Biographical Sketch*, pp. 16–23; PRO HO/42/66; for the use of Colquhoun's *Treatise* in books about England see, for example, Goede, vol. I, pp. 117, 140–2.
32 *Beau Monde*, I, April 1807, pp. 325–6.
33 Colquhoun, *Treatise on Indigence*, pp. 37–43, 59, 60, 62–3.
34 *Ibid.*, pp. 234–6.
35 Colquhoun, *Treatise on Police*, pp. 313–4.
36 *Ibid.*, pp. 312–3n.
37 Bowles, *Dispassionate Inquiry*, pp. 29–30.
38 *Ibid.*, pp. 31–4, 38–40, 49; Bowles, *View of the Moral State of Society*, pp. 22–3, 41.
39 SBCP, *Reports*, 1805, vol. I, pp. 272–6, 351ff.
40 *Ibid.*, vol. I, pp. 106, vol. II, pp. 5, 14.
41 Place, *Autobiography*, pp. 71–2.
42 *Ibid.*, pp. 74–6; Add. MS. 27,828, f. 119.
43 Place, *Autobiography*, pp. 77–8, 78n, 81–2, 93–5.
44 Thompson, *Customs in Common*.
45 PP. 1834, vol. VIII, pp. 5, 175.
46 John Rule, 'Against Innovation? Custom and Resistance in the Workplace, 1700–1850', in Harris (Ed.), *Popular Culture*, p. 173.
47 Bushaway, *By Rite*, p. 120.
48 SBCP, *Reports*, 1805, vol. II, pp. 437ff.
49 Wardroper, *World*, p. 196.
50 Place, *Improvement of the Working People*, p. 12.
51 *An Essay on Trade and Commerce*, p. 71.
52 Colquhoun, *Treatise on Indigence*, p. 285.
53 Place, *Autobiography*, pp. 77–8, 78n, 81–2, 93–5.
54 SBCP, *Reports*, 1805, vol. II, pp. 437ff.
55 *Universal Daily Register* (as *The Times* was then known), 1 July 1785.
56 Thompson, *Customs*, p. 383.

Chapter 3: Resolute Debauches

1 Poynter, *Society*, p. 140.
2 Karamzin, *Travels from Moscow*, vol. III, p. 309.
3 *The Annual Review ... for 1804*, vol. III, pp. 230–1.
4 *ER*, I, Oct. 1802, pp. 95, 97; *Critical Review*, New [second] Series, 1801, XXXI, p. 216.
5 F. K. Prochaska, 'Philanthropy', in F. M. L. Thompson (Ed.), *Cambridge Social History*, vol. III.
6 SBCP, *Reports*, 1805, vol. I, introduction.
7 Smith, *Theory of Moral Sentiments*, vol. I, p. 391; Stewart, *Outlines*, pp. 99–103, 118–22, 246–7, 251; Stewart, *Philosophy of the Active and Moral Powers of Man*, vol. I, pp. 270, 274–6, vol. II, pp. 269, 277–8, 444–7, 458–9.

8 Fry, *Memoir*, vol. I, pp. 18, 345.
9 *Ibid.*, vol. I, pp. 106–7, 116–17, 409, 410–11.
10 Wilberforce, *Practical View*, pp. 47, 59–9, 60–1, 168–9.
11 Z. Macaulay, *Life and Letters*, pp. 268–9.
12 Allen, *Life*, vol. I, pp. 25, 41, 95.
13 Bahmueller, p. 146.
14 Malthus, *Essay* (1803), p. 558.
15 Bahmueller, p. 83; Philanthropic Society, *First Report*, pp. 2–3, 24.
16 Wilberforce, *Practical View*, p. 175.
17 Bichenco, *Inquiry*, pp. 10, 57ff.
18 Bahmueller, pp. 48–9.
19 *Examiner*, 19 April and 20 Sept. 1812.
20 Townsend, *Dissertation*, pp. 13, 24–5.
21 Malthus, *Essay* (1803), pp. 410–11, 523.
22 Colquhoun, *Treatise on Indigence*, pp. 89–91, 94–9, 99, 104; Colquhoun, *State of Indigence*, pp. 26–7.
23 Brown, *Fathers*, pp. 153–4.
24 Allen, *Life*, vol. I, p. 339.
25 Philanthropic Society, *First Report*, p. 2.
26 *Ibid.*, pp. 13ff.
27 *QR*, vol. XVIII, Jan. 1818, p. 267.
28 Place, *Autobiography*, pp. 127–8.
29 Place, *Illustrations*, pp. 162–3.
30 *Ibid.*, pp. 154–5.
31 Austin, *Letters*, vol. I, pp. 12–13, 83, 87, 90–1, 176–7; Goede, *Stranger*, vol. II, pp. 115–17.
32 Austin, *Letters*, vol. I, pp. 275–6.
33 Young quoted in Poynter, *Society*, p. 103.
34 SBCP, *Reports* II, pp. 12–13.
35 Place, *Autobiography*, pp. 87, 93, 96, 100–1, 104–6.
36 Wallas, *Place*, p. 16.
37 [R. Shaw] *Observations*, p. 23; Add. MSS 27,826, ff. 168–170, 27,287, ff. 47–8.
38 Add. MS 27,826, ff. 168–70.
39 Place, *Autobiography*, pp. 201–2, 205, 208–9, 210, 211–2.
40 *Ibid.*, pp. 216–8.
41 Add MS 27,827, f. 193.
42 Place, *Autobiography*, pp. 74–6, 81–2.
43 *Beau Monde*, I, April 1807, pp. 325–6.
44 *Monthly Magazine*, XXVI, part II, no. 175.
45 [R. Shaw], *Observations*, p. iv.
46 Colquhoun, *Treatise on the Police*, pp. 313–4n.
47 [R. Shaw], *Observations*, pp. ii–iv, 21–2, 70–1.
48 *Critical Review*, 3rd series, 1809, XVI, pp. 220–1.
49 Malthus, *Essay on Population*, p. 511.
50 *QR*, XVIII, Jan. 1818, pp. 281–2.

Chapter 4: Reforming Saints

1 Bowles, *Moral State of Society*, p. 76.
2 Karamzin, vol. III, p. 295.
3 *Cobbett's Annual Register*, 1802, pp. 20–7.
4 Ashe, *Travels in America*, pp. 28, 94–102, 105–110, 122–4, 191; Janson, pp. 100–1, 299, 302–5; *ER*, XV, Jan. 1810, pp. 442ff.
5 *Report of the Proclamation Society* (1799), pp. 5–6.
6 *Ibid.*, pp. 4–8, 19–21, 22.
7 *Ibid.*, pp. 25–35.
8 Bowles, *Dispassionate Inquiry*, pp. 98–100; *The Annual Review . . . for 1804*, p. 225.
9 SSV, *Address*, part 1, pp. 31, 34, 36, 39n, 49–50.
10 SSV, *Constable's Assistant* (1808), *passim*; SSV, *Address*, part I, pp. 92–3.
11 SSV, *Constable's Assistant*, pp. 5, 10, 28–30, 30–1n.
12 *ER*, XIII, Jan. 1809; Shaw, *Observations*, pp. 75–9.
13 *ER*, XI, Jan. 1808, p. 257; *Evangelical Magazine*, 1808, pp. 204–5.
14 *Address of the Society for Promoting the Observance of the Christian Sabbath* (1806), pp. 5–6.
15 Southey, *Espirilla's Letters from England*, vol. III, pp. 216–9.
16 SSV, *Address*, part 2, pp. 5–7, 9, 11–13; John Scott, *Account of Societies for the Reformation of Manners*, p. 8.
17 Scott, *Account*, pp. 18, 19; *ER*, XIII, Jan. 1809.
18 *Examiner*, 17 April and 7 Aug. 1808.
19 *Ibid.*, 1 Jan. 1809; *Minutes of Evidence taken before a Select Committee appointed by the House of Commons to inquire into the state of the police of the metropolis* (1816), p. 240.
20 *Examiner*, 11 Nov. 1809; *Scourge*, I, June 1811, p. 313 and III, July 1812, pp. 24, 29.
21 Anon, *Letter to a Member of the Society for the Suppression of Vice*, pp. 10–11, 34; *Examiner*, Prospectus, 1 Jan. 1808.
22 *Satirist*, V, Sept. 1809, pp. 265–6.
23 Anon, *A Letter to a Member of the Society for the Suppression of Vice*, p. 33.
24 SSV, untitled report, 1825, pp. 29–30.
25 SSV, *Address*, part 1, p. 43; part 2, pp. 16–18, 18n, 20–1, 25–7; SSV, untitled report, 1825, p. 30.
26 SSV, untitled report, 1825, pp. 31–3.
27 *Ibid.*, pp. 34–6, 41.
28 Anon, *A Letter to a Member of the Society for the Suppression of Vice*, pp. 7, 9.
29 *Ibid.*, pp. 49–50.
30 Add. MS 27,825, ff. 144–5.
31 *Scourge*, III, July 1812, p. 24; *ER*, Jan. 1809; *Annual Review . . . for 1804*, pp. 226–7, 230–1.
32 *Scourge*, I, June 1811, pp. 313–5.
33 Shaw, *Observations*, p. v; *Critical Review*, 3rd series, vol. XII, 1807, pp. 267–8; Goede, pp. 140–3.

34 *Monthly Magazine*, XXVI, no. 175, 1808, part II, pp. 111–2.
35 *Ibid.*; Iatros, *A Biographical Sketch*, p. 24.
36 *Cobbett's Political Register*, 22 April 1809, p. 611.
37 HO/42/27, f. 836.
38 HO/42/66; Shaw, *Observations*, p. 73; *Monthly Magazine*, XXVI, no. 175, 1808, part II, pp. 111–2.
39 *Cobbett's Political Register*, 22 April 1809, pp. 606–7; *Times*, 18 April 1809; *Examiner*, 7 May 1809.
40 *Examiner*, 23 April and 21 May 1809, and 11 Nov. 1810.
41 *ER*, XIII, Jan. 1809.
42 *Times*, 18 April 1809.

Chapter 5: Too Strong for Law

1 Philippus Philaretes, *Adultery Analyzed*, pp. 26–8.
2 *Evangelical Magazine*, July 1810, p. 283.
3 Bury, *Diary*, vol. I, p. 24.
4 Crim. Con., *Trial of . . . Lord Paget, for Criminal Conversation*, pp. 23–7; Crim. Con., *Trial of Sir Arthur Paget*; A. Moore, *Annals of Gallantry*, vol. I, pp. 226ff, 322ff; *Examiner*, 22 May, 24 July 1808; 12 March, 21 May, 4 June 1809.
5 *Annual Register* (1798), p. 229.
6 Wilberforce, *Life*, vol. I, p. 130, vol. II, p. 162, vol. IV, p. 167.
7 *Ibid.*, p. 187; Wilberforce, *Practical View*, pp. 261 ff; More, *Thoughts*, p. 95.
8 Wilberforce, *Life*, vol. I, p. 131.
9 *Examiner*, 14 Aug. 1808; *Hansard*, vol. XIII, 18–30 March 1809, p. 1; Randle Lewis, *Reflection*, pp. 140–1.
10 Anon, *A Letter to the Hon. Spencer Perceval*, pp. 28–9; *Parl. Hist.*, vol. XXXV, 1800, pp. 321–2.
11 *Parl. Hist.*, vol. XXXV, 1800, p. 283.
12 Auckland, *Substance of the Speech*, p. 30
13 Randle Lewis, pp. 39–40; Philaretes, *Adultery*, p. 202.
14 Randle Lewis, pp. 64–5, 90–5, 131, 140–1.
15 Simond, vol. I, p. 35.
16 Bury, *Diary*, vol. I, pp. 253–4; Simond, vol. I, pp. 34–5.
17 Crim. Con., *Crim. Con. between coachee and his mistress.*
18 *Examiner*, 31 July 1808; A. Moore, *The Annals of Gallantry*, vol. III, pp. 283ff.
19 Crim. Con., *A Report of the Trial on an Action for Damages, brought by the Reverend Charles Massy against the most noble the Marquis of Headfort, for criminal conversation with plaintiff's wife.*
20 Crim. Con., *Trial of . . . Lord Paget*; Anon, *Hints to the Public and the Legislature, on the prevalence of vice*, pp. 17–19.
21 *Morning Chronicle*; *Examiner*, 21 Oct. 1810; Simond, vol. II, pp. 44–7.
22 Simond, vol. II, pp. 46–7; ODNB.
23 Keppel, *Sovereign Lady*, pp. 70, 89

24 Goede, vol. II, pp. 92–3; Edgeworth, *Belinda*, vol. I, p. 15; *Le Beau Monde*, I, 1807, p. 353.
25 [Lady Charlotte Bury], *Diary*, vol. I, pp. 111–2; cf. More, *Strictures*, vol. I, pp. 58–9, vol. II, pp. 92–3.
26 Randle Lewis, p. 52; Blessington, *Conversations*, p. 37.
27 Holland, *Journal*, vol. I, pp. 149–50; Keppel, *Sovereign Lady*, pp. 178–9.
28 Randle Lewis, p. 52.
29 Gronow, *Reminiscences*, pp. 167–8.
30 Khan, *A Persian at the Court of King George*, pp. 236, 246.
31 *Sporting Magazine*, vol. 34, May 1809, p. 83.
32 *Examiner*, 9 April 1809. ('The old gentleman, however, is now reconciled to the loving couple.')
33 Randle Lewis, pp. 25–6, 27, 56, 58–9; *London Magazine*, new series, IV, 1826, p. 43; Crim. Con., *Report of the Trial . . . brought by the Rev Charles Massy against . . . the Marquis of Headfort*, p. 59.
34 Edgeworth, *Belinda*, pp. 13–14.
35 *London Magazine*, new series, IV, 1826, pp. 38–40.
36 *Gentleman's Magazine*, Jan. 1810; More, *Strictures*, vol. I, p. ix.
37 *Examiner*, 14 Aug. 1808.
38 Edgeworth, *Belinda*, vol. II, pp. 18–19.
39 [Lady Anne Hamilton], 'The Epics of the Ton', pp. 80–1n.
40 Philaretes, *Adultery*, pp. 84–5, 89, 93–5, 98–101.
41 Randle Lewis, pp. 36–7, 39–40; Philaretes, *Adultery*, pp. 200, 203–4, 206–7; Anon, *Mirror of the Graces*, pp. 100–1.
42 Randle Lewis, p. 43; Philaretes, *Adultery*, p. 206.
43 Ellenborough's address to the jury in *Examiner*, 20 Dec. 1812.
44 A. Moore, *Annals*, vol. I, p. 193; *Examiner*, 19 March 1809.
45 Thomas Brown, the younger (pseud., Tom Moore), *Intercepted Letters*, pp. 85–6.
46 Simond, vol. II, pp. 46–7; Anon, *A Letter to the Hon. Spencer Perceval*, pp. 28–30.
47 More, *Thoughts*, pp. 8–9.

Chapter 6: The Glories of the Great

1 Anon, *Short Treatise on the Passions . . . By a Lady*, vol. I, p. 79.
2 Blessington, *Conversations*, p. 210.
3 *Morning* Post, 9 June 1808; *Sporting Magazine*, XXXII, June 1808, p. 147, July 1808, *passim*, XXXIII, Jan. 1809, p. 197, June 1809, pp. 142–3; Khan, *A Persian at the Court of King George*, p. 235; Gronow, *Reminiscences*, p. 85; *Morning Post*, 9 June 1808; *Examiner*, 12 June 1808; *Satirist*, II, July 1808, pp. 488ff.
4 Gronow, *Reminiscences*, pp. 85, 245; Simond, vol. I, pp. 99–100, 129–30; *Sporting Magazine*, XXXIII, Aug. 1809, p. 247; Combe and Rowlandson, *English Dance of Death*, vol. II, p. 57.
5 *Sporting Magazine*, XXXIII, Jan. 1809, pp. 197–8; *Examiner*, 26 Feb. 1809.

6 Greville, *Memoirs*, vol. IV, pp. 100–2; Glenbervie, *Journals*, p. 157.
7 *Tableau de la Grande Bretagne* (1800); quoted in *Critical Review*, new series, XXXI, 1801, p. 535; Wilberforce, *Life*, vol. I, pp. 10–11.
8 *QR*, XLIV, p. 178.
9 *Satirist*, II, May 1808, pp. 218–9, III, Aug. 1808, pp. 20ff, 78ff, Sept. 1808, pp. 123–4; *Scourge*, Feb. 1811, pp. 85ff.
10 *Satirist*, III, Dec. 1808, pp. 476–7.
11 *Scourge*, Feb. 1811, p. 92.
12 *Ibid.*, Feb. 1811, pp. 90–1; *Examiner*, 1 July 1810.
13 Keppel, *Sovereign Lady*, p. 162.
14 Lamb, *Glenarvon*, vol. I, pp. 228, 230, 253–6.
15 *Satirist*, V, Oct. 1809, pp. 345–8.
16 Gronow, p. 245.
17 *Examiner*, 5 March 1809; *Sporting Magazine*, XXXIII, March 1809, pp. 309–10.
18 *New Monthly*, X, 1824, pp. 291–2; Gronow, pp. 70–1.
19 Gronow, pp. 70–1.
20 Murray, *Enquiries*, pp. 22–5.
21 *ER*, LXV, July 1837, pp. 115–6.
22 Simond, vol. I, p. 26.
23 Khan, *A Persian at the Court of King George*, pp. 151–2, 168–9.
24 Karamzin, vol. III, p. 229.
25 Simond, vol. I, p. 48; Gronow, pp. 72–3.
26 Simond, vol. I, pp. 26–7.
27 More, *Strictures*, vol. II, p. 140.
28 Simond, vol. I, p. 28; Khan, *A Persian at the Court of King George*, p. 171.
29 *Examiner*, 29 April 1810; Lamb, *Glenarvon*, vol. I, pp. 203, 267.
30 For an account of Brummell's early life and the Brummell family history see Captain Jesse, *The Life of George Brummell*, and Kelly, *Brummell*.
31 Jesse, *Brummell*, vol. I, pp. 57–9, 60.
32 Southey, *Espirilla's Letters from England*, vol. III, pp. 303–4; Gronow, pp. 104, 109.
33 Jesse, vol. I, pp. 60–3.
34 *Ibid.*, vol. I, p. 63; Hazlitt, *Works*, vol. XX, pp. 152ff.
35 *Le Beau Monde*, I, pp. 351–2; Stanhope, *Chesterfield Burlesqued*, pp. 7–8; Jesse, vol. I, pp. 98, 106–7; Raikes, *Portion of the Journal*, vol. II, p. 218.
36 Hazlitt, *Works*, vol. XVII, p. 53.
37 Kelly, *Brummell*, pp. 246–7.
38 Jesse, vol. II, pp. 355–6.
39 Trusler, *System of Etiquette*, p. 17.
40 Moore, *Life of Sheridan*, vol. I, pp. 297–8.
41 More, *Strictures*, vol. I, p. 6; *Le Beau Monde*, vol. III, p. 290; Gronow, pp. 96–7.
42 Bury, *Diary*, vol. I, p. 33.
43 *Ibid.*, vol. I, pp. 61, 162–3; Glenbervie, *Journals*, p. 153.
44 Edgeworth, *Belinda*, vol. I, p. 167.

45 Taylor, *Authentic Memoirs*, pp. 1–2.
46 Goede, vol. I, p. 129; Thompson, *Customs*, p. 503.
47 Hanger, vol. I, pp. 130–1.
48 Anon, *Observations and Strictures on the Conduct of Mrs Clarke, by a lady*, pp. 14–5; Hanger, vol. I, p. 153.
49 Clarke, *Authentic and Impartial Life*, p. 19; *Examiner*, 12 Feb. 1809; Hanger, vol. I, pp. 145–6.
50 Clarke, *Authentic and Impartial Life*, pp. 2–9; *Examiner*, 5 Jan. 1809; Taylor, *Authentic Memoirs*, pp. 23–33; Anon, *A Letter to Mrs Clarke*, pp. 2, 52.
51 Hanger, vol. I, pp. 162–3; Clarke, *Authentic and Impartial Life*, p. 97; Gronow, p. 115.
52 Wilberforce, *Life*, vol. III, pp. 402–3, 405.
53 Jesse, vol. II, pp. 359, 366.

Chapter 7: The Theatre of War

1 PP. 1831–2, vol. VII, p. 219.
2 *The Covent Garden Journal* (2 vols, 1810), vol. I, pp. 33–4, 45, 49, 58; *Examiner*, 17 and 24 Sept. 1809.
3 *Examiner*, 24 Sept. 1809; *Satirist*, vol. V, Oct. 1809, pp. 403–5; Bull, *Remarks*, pp. 7, 10–15; *The Covent Garden Journal*, vol. I, pp. 148–50, 151; Gibbs, *The Speech*, *passim*.
4 Simond, p. 90.
5 Styles, *Essay on . . . the Stage*, pp. 6–8, 13–15, 22, 24, 28–9, 33–6, 45–6, 47–9, 52–4, 71–3, 107–8.
6 *Monthly Magazine*, 1 Jan. 1808, pp. 547–8.
7 Hazlitt, *Works*, vol. XX, p. 287; Khan, *A Persian at the Court of King George*, p. 92; *Examiner*, 1 Jan. 1808.
8 *Satirist*, V, Oct. 1809, pp. 403–5; Bull, *Remarks*, pp. 4, 8–10.
9 *Satirist*, V, Oct. 1809, p. 406, Nov. 1809, p. 459; Hobbs, *Short Sketch*, p. 6.
10 Bull, *Remarks*, pp. 10–16, 18–20, 33; *Examiner*, 24 Sept. 1809; *The Covent Garden Journal*, vol. I, p. 175.
11 Bull, *Remarks*, p. 35.
12 *Examiner*, 15 Oct. 1809.
13 Bull, *Remarks*, pp. 4–5; *The Covent Garden Journal*, vol. I, pp. 185, 189, 191.
14 Hobbs, *Short Sketch*, pp. 7–8; Anon, *The O.P. Songster*, p. 4; Anon, *National Air*; *Covent Garden Journal*, vol. I, *passim*, vol. II, p. 536.
15 *Covent Garden Journal*, vol. I, p. 150.
16 *Satirist*, V, Oct. 1809, p. 405; *Examiner*, 15 and 22 Oct. 1809; *Covent Garden Journal*, vol. I, pp. 107, 183.
17 *Times*, 29 Nov., 30 Nov., 2 Dec. 1809.
18 *Examiner*, 29 Oct. and 5 Nov. 1809.
19 *Satirist*, V, Nov. 1809, pp. 510–1.
20 *Examiner*, 24 Dec. 1809, 16 Sept. 1810 and 23 Sept. 1810.

21 *Ibid.*, 19 Nov. 1809; Hobbs, *Short Sketch*, p. 6; Bull, *Remarks*, p. 3; *The Covent Garden Journal*, pp. 71–2.
22 Geijer, *Impressions*, pp. 97–8.
23 The classification of protesters comes from Baer, *Theatre and Disorder*, p. 142.
24 *Political Review*, 4 Nov. 1809; *Times*, 8 Nov. 1809; Anon, *Short Treatise . . . By a Lady*, vol. I, pp. 65–6.
25 *Covent Garden Journal*, pp. 255, 306–7, 373–4; *Whole Proceedings on the Trial of an Action Brought by Henry Clifford* (1809), pp. 12–13.
26 *Examiner*, 22 July 1810.

Introduction to Part II: Rich and Invincible

1 *Blackwood's*, V, 1819, pp. 640–1.
2 *London Magazine*, new series, III, 1825, pp. 178–9.
3 *Life and Correspondence of . . . Southey*, vol. IV, pp. 121–3.
4 *QR*, XXVIII, Oct. 1822, pp. 197–8.
5 Colquhoun, *Treatise on the Wealth, Power, and Resources of the British Empire*, pp. viii, ix, 48–50; More, *Moral Sketches*, p. 91.
6 *QR*, XIX, July 1818, p. 543.
7 Southey, *Life*, vol. IV, p. 247.
8 *Ibid.*, vol. III, p. 5; cf. vol. IV, p. 200.
9 *Ibid.*, vol. IV, pp. 201, 202, 205, 208.
10 *Ibid.*, vol. IV, pp. 218–9; Southey, *New Letters*, vol. I, p. 470, vol. II, pp. 51, 180, 104–5; Southey, *Essays*, vol. I, p. 163.
11 More, *Life*, vol. III, pp. 444–5.
12 *Ibid.*, vol. III, p. 145; *Christian Observer*, 1816, pp. 727–31.

Chapter 8: Injudicious Kindness

1 Simond, vol. II, p. 72.
2 Guardian Society, *Report* (1816), pp. 8–9, 14–15, 26; *Report* (1817), pp. 10, 13, 32–3.
3 Hale, *Address*, *passim*.
4 Guardian Society, *Report* (1816), p. 37.
5 *Ibid.*, pp. 24–5; *Report* (1817), pp. 23–4; *Report* (1827), p. 12.
6 PP. 1816, vol. V, Appendix 12, pp. 368ff.; S.T., *Address*, p. 8.
7 Guardian Society, *Report* (1817), p. 35.
8 Quoted in Fonblanque, vol. I, pp. 71–2.
9 PP. 1814–1815, vol. III, pp. 10–12.
10 Smith, *Vagabondiana*, pp. 25–8.
11 PP. 1814–1815, vol. III, pp. v–vii.
12 *Ibid.*, pp. 29–30.
13 *Ibid.*, pp. 38–9.
14 Silliman, vol. I, pp. 209–10; Austin, pp. 170–1.
15 Smith, pp. 33–4.
16 *Ibid.*, p. 33; *New Monthly*, XIII, 1825, pp. 543–4.
17 *New Monthly*, I, 1821, p. 103.

18 PP. 1814–1815, vol. III, pp. 5–10.
19 *Ibid.*, p. 54.
20 *Ibid.*, pp. 21–2.
21 *Ibid.*, p. 48.
22 *Ibid.*, p. 48; Smith, p. 36.
23 PP. 1814–1815, vol. III, pp. 48–50, 65–6.
24 *Ibid.*, p. 40.
25 *Times*, 28 Jan. 1824.
26 PP. 1814–1815, vol. III, pp. 59ff.
27 *Ibid.*, p. 16.
28 *Ibid.*, p. 64. cf. *Times*, 29 Aug. 1822. An apparently healthy beggar was defended by a large crowd when officers came to arrest him, 'as might be expected'. The Lord Mayor said in response to the incident that it was 'quite the fashion' to interfere with the police and it came from the 'foolish humanity' of taking the part of 'sturdy beggars'.
29 PP. 1814–1815, vol. III, pp. 21–2.
30 *QR*, XIV, Oct. 1815, p. 120.
31 PP. 1814–1815, vol. III, p. 29.
32 Add MS 27,826, ff. 255–60.
33 PP. 1814–1815, vol. III, p. 46.
34 *Ibid.*, pp. 37–41, 45.
35 *Ibid.*, pp. 73ff.
36 *Ibid.*, pp. 59ff.
37 *Examiner*, 23 March 1817.
38 PP. 1814–1815, vol. III, p. 74.
39 *Ibid.*, pp. 74–6.
40 *Ibid.*, p. 48.
41 Smith, *Vagabondiana*, p. 51.
42 *Ibid.*, pp. 31–2.
43 Society for the Suppression of Mendicity, *First Report* (1819); *Times*, 25 Feb. 1819.
44 Society for the Suppression of Mendicity, *First Report*, pp. 14–15.
45 PP. 1814–1815, vol. III, pp. 5ff; Society for the Suppression of Mendicity, *First Report*, p. 13.
46 Silliman, vol. I, p. 233; Lamb, 'Complaint of the Decay of Beggars in the Metropolis'.
47 PP. 1814–1815, vol. III, p. 16.
48 Lamb, 'Complaint'.
49 Smith, *Vagabondiana*, pp. 51–2.
50 PP. 1816, vol. V, p. 3; PP. 1814–1815, vol. III, p. 50.
51 *New Monthly*, I, 1, pp. 100–5.

Chapter 9: Academies of Vice

1 Anon, *Letter to a Member of the SSV*, p. 48.
2 *QR*, XXVIII, Oct. 1822, pp. 198–9.

3 Bichenco, *Inquiry*, pp. 2–5.
4 *QR*, XIX, April 1818, pp. 82–3.
5 Clark, *English Alehouse*, p. 278.
6 Add MSS, 27,826, ff. 192–4.
7 Add MS 27,809, f. 26.
8 *Monthly Magazine*, May 1835; *Spectator*, 7 Jan. 1854.
9 Wallas, p. 177; Add MS 27,837, f. 172.
10 *Minutes of Evidence taken before the select committee* (1816), pp. 234, 237–9.
11 *Ibid.*, p. 54.
12 *QR*, vol. XXIV, Oct. 1820, p. 241.
13 Southey, *Essays*, vol. II, pp. 134–5.
14 *London Review*, I, 1829, pp. 253–4.
15 Wade, *Treatise*, pp. 2–3.
16 *London Review*, I, 1829, p. 252.
17 *Minutes of Evidence*, pp. 1ff.
18 *Ibid.*, p. 110.
19 *Minutes of Evidence*, pp. 10–11; PP. 1822, vol. IV, pp. 21, 25–6, 32.
20 *Minutes of Evidence*, pp. 262–3.
21 *Ibid.*, pp. 10–11, 29–30; Wade, *Treatise*, pp. 91–2.
22 *Examiner*, 3 Jan. 1819.
23 PP. 1816, vol. IV, pp. 1–2, 18–19, 254–5.
24 *Minutes of Evidence*, p. 78.
25 *Ibid.*, pp. 22–5.
26 *Ibid.*, pp. 69, 70, 275–7.
27 *Minutes of Evidence*, pp. 73–4.
28 Edwards, *Letter to the Lord Lieutenant*, pp. 33–4.
29 *Minutes of Evidence*, p. 271; *Hansard1*, vol. XXXVI, pp. 911–2.
30 *Minutes of Evidence*, pp. 27, 334–6; PP. 1817, vol. III, p. 17.
31 PP. 1817, vol. III, p. 51.
32 *Ibid.*, pp. 25–28, 40, 43, 49, 51, 195.
33 PP. 1816, vol. IV, pp. 52–3.
34 Busby, 'John Farrington'.
35 *Minutes of Evidence*, pp. 477–81; *Examiner*, 3 Jan. 1819.
36 *Ibid.*, pp. 278, 281–4, 349ff.
37 *Ibid.*, pp. 122–34.
38 9GeoIIch23; 26GeoIIch31; PP 1817, vol. III, pp 3–7; PP 1828, vol. VI, p. 134.
39 *Minutes of Evidence*, p. 339.
40 *Ibid.*, p. 297
41 *Ibid.*, p. 284.
42 *Ibid.*, pp. 22–3.
43 PP. 1817, vol. III, pp. 231–2.
44 *Ibid.*, pp. 58–9, 60, 62–5
45 Wade, *Treatise*, pp. 311–12.
46 PP. 1817, vol. III, p. 11.
47 *Ibid.*, p. 11.
48 *Ibid.*, p. 15.

49 *Hansard2*, vol. VII, 1820, pp. 327–33, 560–2, 737, 1,397–9.
50 PP. 1817, vol. III, pp. 13, 18–19; *Hansard1*, vol. XXXVI, 1817, pp. 910ff., 1,298–9.
51 PP. 1816, vol. IV, pp. 1–2, 13, 18–19, 55–6, 77.
52 *Ibid.*, pp.55–6, 76, 78–9.
53 *ER*, XXXV, July 1821, p. 330.
54 PP. 1818, vol. III, pp. 32–3.
55 PP. 1817, vol. III, pp. 16–17.

Chapter 10: Slumming It with Tom and Jerry

1 Moncrieff, introduction to Egan, *Finish* (1869 edn), p. 21.
2 Hindley, *True History*, p. iv.
3 Egan, *Life in London*, pp. 19, 38.
4 *Ibid.*, p. 42n.
5 *Ibid.*, pp. 24, 31, 32, 34.
6 Egan, *Life in London*, pp. 160–1.
7 Reid, *Bucks*, pp. 1–5.
8 *Blackwood's*, VII, 1820, p. 60; *Boxiana*, pp. iii-iv; Hotten, *Tom and Jerry*, p. 18.
9 *Boxiana*, p. 4
10 *Ibid.*, p. 14.
11 *Ibid.*, p. 3.
12 *Ibid.*, pp. 124–5.
13 *Ibid.*, p. 5.
14 *Ibid.*, pp. 5–6n, 120–7, 141–2, 144, 166, 169.
15 *Ibid.*, pp. 138–9, 163–5.
16 *Blackwood's*, VI, 1820, pp. 611–12.
17 *Ibid.*, VIII, 1821, pp. 671–77.
18 *London Magazine*, II, 1820, pp. 155–6.
19 *Blackwood's*, XIV, 1823, p. 21, and XV, 1824, p. 334; Hotten, *Tom and Jerry*, pp. 18, 21, 23–5.
20 Egan, *Life in London*, pp. 275–80.
21 *Ibid.*, pp. 178–80.
22 *Ibid.*, pp. 181ff.
23 *Ibid.*, pp. 292ff.
24 *Ibid.*, pp. 286–91.
25 Many of these details come from the House of Commons Select Committee on Mendicity (1815); the story of the beggar giving his donated food away, preferring a sumptuous cooked meal, for example, is lifted directly from PP. 1814–1815, vol. III, p. 26.
26 Egan, *Life in London*, pp. 342–9.
27 Moncrieff, introduction to Egan, *Finish* (1869 edn), pp. 1–3; PP. 1834, vol. VIII, p. 53; Cruikshank, *Sunday in London*, p. 59; Gaskell, *Manufacturing Population*, p. 350.
28 Moncrieff, introduction to Egan, *Finish* (1869 edn), p. 7n.
29 *Ibid.*, pp. 27–9; Francis Bamford and the Duke of Wellington (Eds), *The*

Journal of Mrs Arbuthnot, vol. I, p. 144.

30 Hindley, *True History*, frontispiece and pp. 103–8; Catnach, *Black Billy*, p. 4; Busby, 'Billy Waters'.

31 Anon, *Real Life*, pp. 25–8; Hanger, *Life and Adventures*, vol. I, pp. 10–11.

32 Hindley, *True History*, frontispiece.

Introduction to Part III: Bubbles Light as Air

1 Southey, *Life and Correspondence*, vol. V, pp. 115–7.

2 Blackwood's, XV, 1824, pp. 1ff.

3 Southey, *Life and Correspondence*, vol. VI, pp. 39–40.

4 Lytton Bulwer, *England*, vol. I, pp. 4–5, vol. II, p. 166.

5 Hazlitt, *Lectures, Chiefly on the Dramatic Literature of the Age of Elizabeth*, p. 5.

6 Thomas Love Peacock, 'The Four Ages of Poetry', *Olliers Literary Miscellany in Prose and Verse*, no. 1, 1820, pp. 183–200.

7 *ER*, XLIV, June 1826, pp. 87–8.

8 *Hansard2*, vol. XII, pp. 1,048–57.

9 *London Magazine*, new series, I, 1825, pp. 241–6.

10 *Times*, 25 and 28 July 1821; 20, 30 Jan. and 9 Feb. 1824.

11 *New Monthly*, VII, 1823, p. 187.

12 *Blackwood's*, XV, 1825, pp. 395–9.

13 *Times*, 15 July 1823.

14 Lytton Bulwer, *England*, vol. I, pp. 364–5.

Chapter 11: Byroned

1 Blessington, *Conversations*, p. 206.

2 *New Monthly*, II, 1821, pp. 303–7; *London Magazine*, new series, IV, 1826, p. 45; Vizetelly, *Glances*, pp. 12–13.

3 Moncrieff, introduction to Egan, *Finish* (1869 edn), pp. 1–2.

4 *Examiner*, 10 Nov. 1822.

5 Byron, *Letter to* **** ****** [John Murray], pp. 12–13, 15–16.

6 *Ibid.*, pp. 16–17, 52; cf. Barbauld in *Monthly Review*, LXXI, June 1813, p. 210.

7 Medwin, *Journal*, p. 47.

8 Moore, *Life of Byron*, vol. II, pp. 361–4; Blessington, *Conversations*, p. 38.

9 Blessington, *Conversations*, p. 260.

10 Roberts, *Memoirs*, IV, pp. 181–2.

11 Byron, *Letters*, 1 Aug. 1819.

12 *London Magazine*, X, 1824, p. 462.

13 *Spirit and Manners of the Age*, I, 25 Feb. 1826, p. 117.

14 *Investigator*, V, Oct. 1822, pp. 335–6, 337–40, 355.

15 Brydges, *Letters*, pp. 123–5; *Blackwood's*, V, 1819, pp. 512, 517, 522.

16 *ER*, XXVII, Dec. 1816, pp. 280–1.

17 *ER*, XXIII, April 1814, pp. 199–204, XXVII, Dec. 1816, pp. 280–1. See also Thomas Love Peacock, 'The Four Ages of Poetry', *Olliers Literary Miscellany in Prose and Verse*, no. 1, 1820, pp. 183–200.

18 *ER*, XXVII, Dec. 1816, p. 280; Brydges, pp. 4–5.
19 MacCarthy, *Byron*, p. 327; Southey, *Essays*, vol. II, pp. 185–6; *Blackwood's*, V, 1819, p. 513.
20 *Blackwood's*, XIV, 1823, p. 283; *Examiner*, 10 Nov. 1822.
21 Brydges, p. 185; Southey, *Essays*, vol. II, pp. 183ff; Pückler-Muskau, vol. I, p. 201.
22 *Blackwood's*, XIV, 1823, p. 283.
23 *Examiner*, 1 Oct. 1819; Medwin, *Journal*, pp. 127–9.
24 Blessington, *Conversations*, pp. 298–9; Byron, *Letters*, 26 Oct. 1819.
25 *Times*, 25 Aug., 1 Sept., 12 Sept., 15 Oct. 1823; W. B. Collyer, *Interesting Letter*, *passim*.
26 Medwin, *Journal*, pp. 154–5.
27 *Examiner*, 24 Nov. 1822.
28 *Examiner*, 10 Nov., 22 Dec. 1822.
29 *ER*, XXXVI, Oct. 1821, pp. 52–3; *Examiner*, 10 Nov. 1822
30 Walter Scott, *Miscellaneous Prose*, vol. IV, pp. 395–6, 451–2.
31 *Times*, 29 Jan. 1825.
32 *Times*, 18 Jan. 1825.
33 FitzSimons, p. 194.
34 *Times*, 20, 28, 29 Jan. 1825.
35 *Times*, 25 Jan. 1825
36 *Times*, 25, 29 Jan., 1, 3, 5 Feb. 1825.
37 *Times*, 29 Jan. 1825.
38 *Times*, 29 March 1825.
39 *Blackwood's*, XVII, 1825, p. 372.
40 *London Magazine*, new series, II, p. 88; Hawkins, *Kean*, vol. II, p. 248.
41 Hawkins, *Edmund Kean*, vol. II, p. 245.
42 *Ibid.*, pp. 248–9.
43 *Times*, 21 Dec. 1825, 21, 24 Jan. and 8 Feb. 1826; *New York Commercial Advertiser*, 7 Dec. 1825.
44 Hazlitt, *Works*, vol. XX, p. 285; *Blackwood's*, XVII, 1825, pp. 136–7; Brydges, pp. 308–9.
45 *London Magazine*, X, 1824, p. 449; *Blackwood's*, XV, 1824, pp. 530–1, and XVII, p. 132.
46 Reid, *Bucks*, pp. 151–3.
47 Ward, *Tremaine*, editor's preface, p. xii; *QR*, XXXIII, March 1826, pp. 479, 482; *Blackwood's*, XVII, 1825, pp. 518–19; *New Monthly*, XIII, 1825, pp. 320–1, 328–9; *London Magazine*, new series, I, pp. 534–5.
48 *London Magazine*, new series, I, pp. 534–5.
49 Pückler-Muskau, vol. I, p. 201.
50 Blessington, *Conversations*, pp. 299–300.

Chapter 12: Progress

1 *ER*, XLIX, June 1829, pp. 441–2.
2 *Times*, 29 Nov. and 13 Dec. 1821.

3 Angelo, *Reminiscences*, vol. I, pp. 283–4.
4 Add MS 27,825, f. 50.
5 *New Monthly*, X, 1824, pp. 24–6.
6 Wrigley and Schofield, *Population*, pp. 217, 529; *New Monthly*, X, 1824, p. 24.
7 *QR*, XXXIX, April 1829, pp. 492, 499,
8 Pückler-Muskau, vol. III, p. 45; vol. IV, p. 97.
9 *Ibid.*, pp. 45, 47–8, 53, 59–61, vol. IV, pp. 44–5; *London Magazine*, new series, II, 1825, p. 445.
10 Southey, *Life*, vol. V, p. 115; Pückler-Muskau, vol. II, pp. 248–9.
11 *QR*, XXXII, June 1825, pp. 186–7, 189, 190; cf. Graham, *Corn and Currency*, p. 9.
12 Place, *Autobiography*, p. 82.
13 *Panoramic Miscellany*, I, no. 1, 31 Jan. 1826, pp. 1–3; Add MS 27,825, f. 53.
14 Hazlitt, *Lectures on the English Comic Writers*, p. 307.
15 *New Monthly*, V, 1822, pp. 243–4, and XIV, 1825, p. 258.
16 *Ibid.*, pp. 243–3, and X, 1824, p. 345; *QR*, XXXIX, April 1829, pp. 501–2; Wade, *Treatise*, p. 148.
17 *New Monthly*, V, 1822, pp. 243–4, and XI, p. 464–5.
18 Gibbon Wakefield, *England and America*, pp. 82–4, 103–4.
19 Cobbett, *Advice*, para. 6.
20 *Ibid.*, paras 20–8, 30, 104, 106.
21 Brasbridge, pp. 5, 10–11, 32–5, 41–5, 50–1, 67–9.
22 Cobbett, *Advice*, paras. 28, 40, 170–1.
23 Place, *Autobiography*, p. 12; Add MS 27,825, ff. 51–3.
24 *QR*, VIII, Dec. 1812, p. 339.
25 Lytton Bulwer, *England*, vol. I, pp. 26–34.
26 *Ibid.*, p. 29; *New Monthly*, X, 1824, p. 291.
27 Taylor, *Self-cultivation*, p. 137.
28 *Ibid.*, pp. 107–8.
29 More, *Strictures on Female Education*, vol. I, pp. 69–74.
30 Lytton Bulwer, *England*, vol. I, pp. 33, 35.
31 *Ibid.*, pp. 33–4, 57; Collier, *Tragical Comedy*.
32 *New Monthly*, XI, p. 465.
33 Gibbon Wakefield, pp. 76–7, 105.
34 *Ibid.*, pp. 103–4.
35 Place, *Autobiography*, pp. 81–2.
36 Lytton Bulwer, *England*, vol. I, pp. 137–9; Wade, *Treatise*, pp. 150–1.
37 *Westminster Review*, XXV, 1836, p. 15; *Blackwood's*, XLVIII, Sept. 1839, pp. 295, 300.
38 McCulloch, *Discourse*, *passim*; *ER*, XLIII, 85, Nov. 1825, pp. 1ff.; Althorp in Hilton, *Age of Atonement*, p. 240.
39 Chalmers, *Power, Wisdom and Goodness*, vol. II, p. 49.
40 Greville, *Memoirs*, 20 Feb. 1826; *ER*, XLIII, 85, Nov. 1825, p. 2.
41 Robinson in the Commons, 14 March 1826; quoted by Place, Add MS 27,827, f. 85.

42 Taylor, *Self-Cultivation*, pp. 7–8.
43 Brougham, *Practical Observations on Popular Education*, pp. 33ff.
44 *ER*, XLIX, June 1829, p. 457.
45 Pückler-Muskau, vol. III, pp. 113–4; vol. IV, p. 371; *ER*, LIV, Dec. 1831, p. 396.
46 *New Monthly*, IV, 1822, p. 554; *Times*, 20 Aug. 1819.
47 *Blackwood's*, XIV, 1823, pp. 359–60; *New Monthly*, XIV, 1825, p. 557; *Scourge*, X, Oct. 1815, pp. 280–1.
48 Hone, *Every-day Book*, vol. I, pp. 1,168ff.; *Scourge*, vol. II, Sept. 1811, p. 208.
49 *Times*, 20 Aug. 1819; Malcolm, *Anecdotes*, vol. I, p. 361.
50 *New Monthly*, IV, 1822, pp. 554–58.
51 *Examiner*, 21 Dec. 1817.
52 *Ibid.*; Patmore, *Letters*, vol. II, pp. 177–80.
53 Hone, *Every-Day Book*, vol. I, p. 1623; Patmore, *Letters*, vol. II, pp. 175–6; *Examiner*, 21 Dec. 1817.
54 Hone, *Every-Day Book*, vol. I, p. 44.
55 Quoted in Bushaway, *By Rite*, p. 24.
56 Patmore, *Letters*, vol. II, pp. 172–3.
57 *New Monthly*, XIII, 1825, pp. 459ff.
58 Blackmantle, vol. II, pp. 67–8, 105–7.

Chapter 13: Merry England

1 *Hansard2*, vol. VIII, 1823, p. 367.
2 *New Monthly*, IV, 1822, p. 556.
3 Jackson, *Considerations*, pp. 8, 11–12, 16–17.
4 *Morning Chronicle*, 8 Aug. 1826 and 17 Sept. 1828; Add MSS 27,826, ff. 206–8.
5 Allen, *Considerations*, pp. 19–22; Mainwaring, *Observations*, pp. 7, 55–6, 101.
6 *Hansard2*, vol. VI, 1822, pp. 1,047–8, 1,382–3.
7 Adolphus, pp. 8–9.
8 Fonblanque, vol. II, pp. 118–25.
9 *London Magazine*, new series, III, pp. 370–4.
10 Hone, *Every-day Book*, I, p. 441; Longhurst, 'Greenwich Fair', pp. 200 ff.; *Times*, 14 April 1814 and 25 May 1825.
11 *Times*, 5 Sept. 1823, 29 July and 7 Sept. 1825, 22 Aug. and 7 Sept. 1826.
12 Hone, *Every-day Book*, vol. I, pp. 1,251–2; *Times*, 29 July and 7 Sept. 1825, 7 Sept. 1826.
13 Adolphus, p. 14
14 *Times*, 3 Oct. 1823 and 26 Nov. 1824.
15 Adolphus, pp. 54–6, 66–7.
16 Anon, *An Affectionate Address*, pp. 3–4; Anon, *Sabbath-Breaker's Monitor*, pp. 22–3; Anon, *Observations on a Bill now pending in the House of Commons*, pp. 2, 9; Higgins, *Horae Sabbatica*, pp. vii–viii.

17 *Lancet*, I, 2 Nov. 1823, pp. 166–72; *Times*, 30 Jan. 1824.
18 *Times*, 25 Oct. 1823; Adolphus, p. 4.
19 *Hansard2*, vol. X, 1824, pp. 106–8, 111–12.
20 *Ibid.*, p. 118.
21 *Times*, 21 Aug. 1822; Briscoe, *Letter*, *passim*; Good, *Letter*, *passim*; *Mirror*, I, pp. 1–3; Society for the Improvement of Prison Discipline, *Report* (1819).
22 *Times*, 21 May 1823; *Hansard2*, vol. XI, p. 1,085.
23 Briscoe, *Letter*, p. 31.
24 Hanway, *New Year's Gift*, p. 18.
25 *Ibid.*, p. 10.
26 Briscoe, *Letter*, p. 20.
27 Good, *Letter*, pp. 4, 7–9; Briscoe, *Letter*, p. 62.
28 Good, *Letter*, pp. 27, 29; *Times*, 27 Nov. 1822; *Examiner*, 10 March 1822; *John Bull*, 23 March 1823; Briscoe, *Letter*, p. 126.
29 *Hansard2*, vol. XI, 1825, pp. 509–12; *ER*, XXXIX, Jan. 1824, pp. 299ff.
30 Briscoe, *Letter*, pp. 41, 60, 62, 72; *Times*, 21 May 1823, 15 Jan. 1824, 7 Feb. 1824.
31 *Hansard2*, vol. X, 1824, p. 243; *Morning Chronicle*, 8 Aug. 1826; Add MSS 27,826, ff. 206–8.
32 Fonblanque, vol. I, pp. 70–1.
33 *Times*, 8 Nov. 1822.
34 *Times*, 17 June 1824.
35 *Hansard2*, vol. X, 1824, pp. 486–8.
36 *ER*, L, Jan. 1830, pp. 486–7, 493–4; Cobbett, *Cottage Economy*, paras 11–21; PP. 1828, vol. VI, p. 7; PP 1830, vol. X, p. 37.
37 *Times*, 15 May 1830.
38 *Hansard2*, vol. XXIV, 1830, p. 410; vol. XXV, p. 865.
39 *Hansard3*, vol. XXII, 1834, p. 1,163.
40 *Times*, 25 Aug. 1831. This account differs from *Hansard3*, vol. VI, 24 Aug. 1831, p. 542 (which truncates parts of the speeches), Hume's and O'Connell's words presumably deemed unparliamentary and the cheers of the backbenchers unseemly.

Chapter 14: No Cant

1 *Times*, 19 Jan. 1822.
2 Hazlitt, *Works*, vol. XX, p. 127.
3 von Raumer, vol. II, p. 263.
4 *London Magazine*, new series, II, p. 68.
5 Morley, *Memoirs of Bartholomew Fair*, p. 390.
6 Sala, pp. 200–2.
7 Howitt, *Rural Life*, vol. II, pp. 142–3, 274.
8 Hone, *Everyday-book*, vol. I, pp. 634, 858–63; Wilson, *Laughter of Triumph*, pp. 358–62.
9 *QR*, XXXIX, April 1829, pp. 496–8. The review has been attributed to

Southey, although he denied it. The author's enthusiasm for the Reformation, an event Southey detested, makes it unlikely that he wrote it, although he would have concurred with most of the opinions. Cf. Francis Jeffrey, *ER*, XXI, Feb. 1813, pp. 17–21: 'Men learn, instead of reasoning. Instead of meditating, they remember; and, in place of the glow of inventive genius, or the warmth of a generous admiration, nothing is to be met with in society, but timidity on the one hand, and fastidiousness on the other – a paltry accuracy and a more paltry derision – a sensibility for small faults, and an incapacity to great merits – a disposition to exaggerate the value of knowledge that is not used, and to underestimate the importance of powers that have ceased to exist' (p. 21).

10 *ER*, XXI, Feb. 1813, p. 21.
11 Wade, *Treatise*, p. 7.
12 Add MS 27,827, f. 115.
13 *ER*, LIV, Dec. 1831, p. 366.
14 *London and Westminster Review*, XXV/III, 1836, pp. 15, 18.
15 *Ibid.*, p. 15.
16 Howitt, *Rural Life*, vol. II, p. 131.
17 *Times*, 28 May 1833.
18 *Political Register*, vol. LXIX, no. 21, May 1830, p. 710.
19 *Ibid.*, no. 26, June 1830, pp. 815–21.
20 *Ibid.*, vol. XLVIII, no. 11, 1823, p. 843.
21 *Ibid.*, vol. LXIX, no. 24, June 1830, p. 770.
22 *Ibid.*, vol. XLVII, no. 9, Aug. 1823, pp. 514–15, 520–1.
23 *Ibid.*, vol. XXXIX, April 1821, pp. 13–14.
24 Blessington, *Conversations*, p. 12.
25 *Hansard3*, vol. XXV, 1830, pp. 65–6.
26 *ER*, XXXV, July 1821, p. 315.
27 Hazlitt, *Works*, vol. XVII, pp. 353–4.
28 Fonblanque, vol. II, pp. 172–80; *ER*, XXXV, July 1821, p. 315.
29 Lytton Bulwer, *England*, vol. I, p. 325; *ER*, XXXV, July 1821, pp. 286–7.
30 *New Monthly*, VIII, 1823, pp. 431–2; this article – 'The Good Old Times' by Cyrus Redding – was a counterblast to recent articles published in the magazine deploring the new morality and pining for older notions of benevolence and sincerity by such contributors as Horace Smith, Leigh Hunt, W. C. Graham and Thomas Noon Talfourd.
31 Aikin, *Correspondence*, p. 29.
32 Carlyle, *Later Day Pamphlets*, no. II, 1 March 1850.
33 J. S. Mill in *Westminster Review*, July 1825, pp. 88ff.; Peacock, *Crotchet Castle*.
34 Anon, *Extracts, &c, Concerning the Prevalence of Vagrancy in Some of the Western Counties of England*, pp. 6, 12.
35 Aikin, *Correspondence*, pp. 29–30.
36 Cobbett, *Rural Rides*, pp. 15–16.
37 Add MS 27,827, f. 133.
38 Add MS 27,816, f. 258.

39 Add MS 27,828, ff. 77–8. See also Add MS 27,823, ff. 96–7.
40 *Times*, 31 Dec. 1824. When a man was proved to have fathered a bastard, the parish could charge him for the costs of maintaining the child; this society was apparently a common fund to defray the damages that its members might become liable for if their private lives got out of hand.
41 Walter Scott, *Miscellaneous Prose*, vol. III, p. 523; *New Monthly*, VIII, 1823, p. 428 ['The Good Old Times' by Cyrus Redding].
42 Peacock, *Crotchet Castle*, chap. 7.
43 Walter Scott, *Miscellaneous Prose*, vol. IV, pp. 451–2; Shklar, 'Let Us Not Be Hypocritical', *passim*. Cf. *Letter to the Right Hon Lord Byron by John Bull*, pp. 7–9.
44 *Hansard3*, vol. XXV, 1830, pp. 756–7.
45 Langford, *Englishness Identified*, p. 159.
46 Walter Scott, *Miscellaneous Prose*, vol. III, p. 516; Wade, *Treatise*, p. 150.
47 Add MS 27,828, ff. 53–4; Place, *Autobiography*, p. 82.
48 Add MS 27,825, ff. 100–1; 27,828, ff. 53–4.
49 Add MS 27,827, f. 205.
50 *London Magazine*, new series, I, 1825, pp. 626ff.; *Morning Chronicle*, 1 Oct. 1827.
51 *New Monthly*, XI, 1824, pp. 302–4; Blessington, p. 39.
52 Cobbett, *Advice*, para. 241.
53 *Literary Gazette*, 20 May 1824, p. 177.
54 *Atlas*, 4 Oct. 1829, in Hazlitt, *Works*, vol. XX, pp. 283ff.
55 *Times*, 25 July 1821.
56 *ER*, June 1829, pp. 452, 456.
57 'The law's function is to preserve public order and decency, to protect the citizen from what is offensive or injurious, and to provide sufficient safeguards against exploitation and corruption of others . . . [But] It is not, in our view, the function of the law to intervene in the private life of citizens, or to seek to enforce any particular pattern of behaviour.' (Report of the Committee on Homosexual Offences and Prostitution [1957].)
58 Mill, *On Liberty*, p. 70.
59 *Ibid.*, pp. 64–5. 'In this age, the mere example of non-conformity, the mere refusal to bend the knee to custom is itself a service.'
60 *Ibid.*, p. 23.
61 Constant, *Political Works*, pp. 104–5.
62 Mill, *On Liberty*, p. 17. 'The disposition of mankind, whether as rulers or as fellow-citizens, to impose their own opinions and inclinations as a rule of conduct on others, is so energetically supported by some of the best and by some of the worst feelings incident to human nature, that it is hardly ever kept under restraint by anything but want of power; and as the power is not declining, but growing, unless a strong barrier of moral conviction can be raised against the mischief, we must expect, in the present circumstances of the world, to see it increase.'

Bibliography

Place of publication for all published material is London, unless otherwise stated.

Journals and newspapers

Annual Register
Annual Review and History of Literature
Anti-Jacobin Review; or Weekly Examiner
Le Beau Monde, or Literary and Fashionable Magazine
Bell's Life in London
Black Dwarf
Blackwood's Edinburgh Magazine
Boxiana
Christian Observer
Cobbett's Political Register
Covent Garden Journal (1810)
Critical Review: or, Annals of Literature
Eclectic Review
Edinburgh Review
Evangelical Magazine
Examiner
Gentleman's Magazine
Investigator; or Quarterly Magazine
John Bull
Lancet
Leeds Mercury
London Magazine
London Review
London Weekly Review
Monthly Magazine
Monthly Review
Morning Chronicle
Morning Herald
Morning Post
New Monthly Magazine
Notes and Queries
Observer
Punch in London
Quarterly Review

Satirist, or, Monthly Meteor
Scotsman
Scourge, or, Monthly Monitor
Spirit and Manners of the Age
Sporting Magazine
The Times (also cited by its original name, *The Universal Daily Register*)
Tyne Mercury
Westminster Review (merged with the *London Review* in 1836 to become the *London and Westminster Review*)

Parliamentary Papers

Cobbett's Parliamentary History
Hansard's Parliamentary Debates
Sessions Papers:

I. Reports and Minutes of Evidence from the Select Committees of the House of Commons:

1. *On the State of Mendicity and Vagrancy in the Metropolis and its Neighbourhood* (evidence to the select committee): 1814–1815, vol. III. *Report of the Committee*: 1816, vol. V.
2. *On the Police of the Metropolis*: 1816, vol. X (reprinted as *Minutes of Evidence Taken Before a Select Committee Appointed by the House of Commons to Inquire into the State of the Police of the Metropolis*: 1816); 1817, vol. III; 1818, vol. III; 1822, vol. IV; 1828, vol. VI.
3. *On the Education of the Lower Orders in the Metropolis*: 1816, vol. IV.
4. *On the Existing Laws Relating to Vagrants*: 1821, vol. IV.
5. *On The Retail of Beer*: 1830, vol. X.
6. *On the Observation of the Sabbath*: 1831–2, vol. VII.
7. *On Dramatic Literature*: 1831–2, vol. VII.
8. *On Drunkenness*: 1834, vol. VIII.

II. Acts and Bills:

A Bill (As Amended on Recommittal) for Consolidating into one Act, and Amending the Laws Relating to Rogues, Vagabonds, Vagrants, and Idle and Disorderly Persons: Parliamentary Papers 1822, vol. I.

III. Proceedings of the Common Council, of the City of London, in Sessions Papers, 1816, vol. X.

Primary Printed Material

Accum, Frederich, *A Treatise on Adulterations of Food and Culinary Poisons, Exhibiting the Fraudulent Sophistications of Bread, Beer, Wine and Other Articles Employed in Domestic Economy and Methods of Detecting Them* (1820).
Adolphus, John, *Observations on the Vagrant Act, and Some Other Statutes and on the Powers and Duties of Justices of the Peace* (1824).
Aikin, Lucy, *Correspondence of William Ellery Channing, D. D., and Lucy*

Aikin, from 1826 to 1842 (Ed. Anna Laetitia Le Breton, 1874).
Allen, Lucas Benjamin, *Brief Consideration on the Present State of the Police of the Metropolis; with a Few Suggestions Towards its Improvement* (1821).
Allen, William, *Life of William Allen, with Selections from His Correspondence* (3 vols, 1846).
Angelo, Henry, *Reminiscences of Henry Angelo, with Memoirs of His Late Father and Friends* (2 vols, 1828–30).
Anon, *Advice to the Million, by a Friend to the People: or, How to Live and Enjoy Vigorous Health on Sixpence per Day* (1830?).
– *An Affectionate Address to the Inhabitants of Newcastle and Gateshead, and Their Vicinity, on the Present Alarming Visitation of Divine Providence in the Fatal Ravages of the Spasmodic Cholera, Intended as a Warning Voice Especially to Persons in the Habits of Intemperance, Sabbath-breaking and Lewdness* (Newcastle, 1832).
– *The Book of Health; a Compendium of Domestic Health* (1828).
– 'A Collection of Advertisements of Patent and Proprietary Medicines, c. 1790–1810', British Library pressmark c.142.a.17.
– *Cursory Remarks on a Recent Publication Addressed to the Public, upon the Tendency of the London Female Penitentiary* (1809).
– *A Defence of the Principal Doctrines of Evangelical Religion in a Letter to 'a Barrister'* (1808).
– *An Essay on Trade and Commerce: Containing Observations on Taxes: Together with Some Reflections on Our Trade to America* (1770).
– *Extracts Concerning the Prevalence of Vagrancy in Some of the Western Counties* (Shaftesbury, 1827).
– *A Few Words on the Licensing System, and the Proposed Unlimited Increase of Public Houses* (1830).
– *Hints to the Public and the Legislature on the Prevalence of Vice, and on the Dangerous Effects of Seduction* (1810).
– *The History of the Blind Beggar of Bethnal Green* (Newcastle, c.1800).
– *A Letter to a Member of the Society for the Suppression of Vice: in Which Its Principles and Proceedings Are Examined and Considered* (n.d.).
– *A Letter to Mrs Clarke* (1809).
– *A Letter to the Hon. Spencer Perceval, in Consequence of the Notice Given by Him that He Would Forward a Bill for the Punishment of Adultery* (1801).
– *The Mendicity Society Unmasked in a Letter to the Managers Wherein Is Shown the Real Character of this Pretended Benevolent Society, as Developed in the Proceedings of Its Begging Letter Committee* (1825).
– *The Mirror of Graces; or, the English Lady's Costume, with Useful Advice on Female Accomplishments, Politeness, and Manners. By a Lady of Distinction* (1811).
– *National Air. Humbly Submitted to the Placarding Committee* (1809?).
– *Observations on the Bill Now Pending in the House of Commons for the Better Observance of the Lord's Day* (1833).
– *The OP Songster for 1810* (1810).

– *Real Life in London; or, the Rambles and Adventures of Bob Tallyho esq. and His Cousin the Hon Tom Dashall Through the Metropolis* (1821–2).
– *The Rebellion* (1809).
– *Sabbath-Breaker's Monitor* (1831).
– *A Short Treatise on the Passions, Illustrative of the Human Mind. By a Lady* (2 vols, 1810).
– *The Tread Mill, or Tom and Jerry at Brixton: A Serio, Comic, Operatic, Milldramatic, Farcical, Moral Bulletta in Two Acts* (1822?).
– *The Vagrant Act, in Relation to the Liberty of the Subject. By a Barrister* (2nd edn, 1824).
– *Whole Proceedings on the Trial of an Action Brought by Henry Clifford, Esquire, against Mr James Brandon, for an Assault and False Imprisonment* (1809).
Arbuthnot, Harriet, *The Journal of Mrs Arbuthnot* (Eds Francis Bamford and the Duke of Wellington, 2 vols, 1950).
Aristotle (pseud.), *The Works of Aristotle, Complete in Four Parts. Containing I The Complete Master Piece. To Which Is Added The Family Physician. II His Complete and Experienced Midwife. III His Book of Problems. IV His Last Legacy* (1776).
Ashe, Thomas, *Travels in America, Performed in 1806, for the Purpose of Exploring the Rivers Allegheny, Monongahela, Ohio, and Mississippi* (1808).
Ashton, John, *Modern Street Ballads* (1868).
Auckland, Lord, *Substance of the Speech . . . in the House of Lords . . . in Support of the Bill for the Punishment and More Effectual Prevention of the Crime of Adultery* (1800).
Austin, William, *Letters from London: Written During the Years 1802 and 1803* (Boston, MA, 1804).
Barrington (pseud.), *Barrington's New London Spy for 1809* (1809).
Beddoes, Thomas, *Hygëia: or Essays Moral and Medical, on the Causes Affecting the Personal State of Our Middling and Affluent Classes* (3 vols, Bristol, 1802–3).
Bee, Jon, *A Living Picture of London for 1828, and Stranger's Guide Through the Streets of the Metropolis* (1828).
Beresford, James, *The Miseries of Human Life, or the Last Groans of Samuel Sensitive and Timothy Testy, with a Few Supplementary Sighs from Mrs Testy* (6th edn; 2 vols, 1807).
Bernard, Sir Thomas, *The Barrington School* (1812).
Bichenco, J. E., *An Inquiry into the Nature of Benevolence, Chiefly with a View to Elucidate the Principles of the Poor Laws, and Show Their Immoral Tendency* (1817).
Blackmantle, Bernard (pseud.), *The English Spy* (2 vols, 1825–6).
Blessington, Marguerite Gardiner, Countess of, *Conversations of Byron with the Countess of Blessington* (1834).
Blizard, William, *Desultory Reflections on Police* (1785).
Bowdler, John, *Reform or Ruin: Take Your Choice!* (12th edn, 1798).
Bowdler, Rev. Thomas, *The Family Shakespeare* (1821).

Bowles, John, *A Dispassionate Inquiry into the Best Means of National Safety* (1806).
– *Reflections at the Conclusion of the War* (1801) .
– *Remarks on Modern Female Manners* (1802).
– *A View of the Moral State of Society* (1804).
Bowles, William L., *Observations on the Poetical Character of Pope* (1820).
Boyer, A., *Dictionnaire Royal François–Anglois et Anglois–François, Tiré des Meilleurs Auteurs Qui Ont Écrit dans Ces Deux Langues* (2 vols, Lyons, 1780).
Brand, John, *Observations on Popular Antiquities: Chiefly Illustrating the Origin of Our Vulgar Customs, Ceremonies and Superstitions* (2 vols, Ed. Henry Ellis, 1813).
Brasbridge, Joseph, *The Fruits of Experience; or, Memoir of Joseph Brasbridge, Written in His 80th Year* (1824).
Briscoe, John Ivatt, *A Letter on the Nature and Effects of the Tread-wheel, as an Instrument of Prison Labour and Punishment, Addressed to the Right Hon. Robert Peel MP* (1824).
Brodum, William, *A Guide to Old Age, or a Cure for the Indiscretions of Youth* (2 vols, 1795).
Brome, Richard, *A Jovial Crew* (Ed. Ann Haaker; Nebraska, 1968).
Brougham, Henry, *Practical Observations on Popular Education* (1825).
Brownlow, Lady Emma Sophia, *The Eve of Victorianism* (1840).
Brydges, Sir Egerton, *Letters on the Character and Poetical Genius of Lord Byron* (1825).
Buckingham, James Silk, *Autobiography* (2 vols, 1855).
Bull, John (pseud.), *Letter to the Right Hon. Lord Byron* (1821).
Bull, John (pseud.), *Remarks on the Cause of the Dispute between the Public and the Managers of the Theatre Royal, Covent Garden* (1809).
Bulwer, Edward Lytton, *England and the English* (2 vols, 1833).
Burke, Edmund, *Reflections on the Revolution in France* (Oxford, 1993).
Burney, Fanny, *Diary and Letters of Madame d'Arbley* (4 vols, 1842).
Bury, Lady Charlotte, *Diary Illustrative of the Times of George the Fourth* (4 vols, 1838).
– *The Diary of a Lady in Waiting* (Ed. A Francis Stewart; 2 vols, New York, 1908).
Busby, T. L., *Costume of the Lower Orders of London* (1820).
Buxton, Thomas Fowell, *An Inquiry, Whether Crime and Misery Are Produced or Prevented, by Our Present System of Prison Discipline* (1818).
Byron, George Gordon, Lord, *Childe Harold* (1812–18) .
– *Don Juan* (1819–24).
– *English Bards and Scotch Reviewers* (1809).
– *Letter to **** ****** [John Murray], on the Rev. W. L. Bowles' Strictures on the Life and Writing of Pope* (1821).
– *Letters and Journals* (Ed. Leslie A. Marchand; 13 vols, 1973–1994).
Carew, Bampfylde-Moore, *The Life and Adventures of Bampfylde-Moore Carew, Commonly Called the King of the Beggars, to Which Is Added a*

Dictionary of the Cant Language Used by the Mendicants (Bath, 1802).
Carlile, R., *Every Woman's Book; or, What Is Love?* (4th edn, 1826).
Carlyle, Thomas, *Latter Day Pamphlets* (1850).
Catnach, James, *The Death, Last Will and Funeral of 'Black Billy': also, the Tears of London for the Death of Tom and Jerry* (1823).
[Cavendish, Harriet], *Letters of Harriet Cavendish, Countess of Granville, 1810–1845* (Ed. F. Leveson Gower; 2 vols, 1894).
Chalmers, Thomas, *The Christian and Civic Economy of Large Towns* (3 vols, Glasgow, 1821).
– *On Political Economy in Connexion with the Moral State and Prospects of Society* (Glasgow, 1832).
– *On the Power, Wisdom and Goodness of God* (Glasgow, 1833).
Clarke, A., *The Authentic and Impartial Life of Mrs Mary Anne Clarke . . .* (2nd edn, 1809).
Clarke, Rev. Thomas, *A Letter to the Proclamation Society and the Society for the Suppression of Vice* (1812).
Cobbett, William, *Advice to Young Men, and (Incidentally) to Young Women, in the Middle and Higher Ranks of Life, in a Series of Letters Addressed to a Youth, a Bachelor, a Lover, a Husband, a Father, a Citizen or a Subject* (1829).
– *Cobbett's Monthly Religious Tracts* (1821).
– *Cottage Economy; Containing Information Relative to the Brewing of Beer, Making of Bread, Keeping of Cows, Pigs, Bees, Ewes, Goats, Poultry* (1821–2).
– *Rural Rides* (Ed. Ian Dyck, 2001) .
– *A Year's Residence in the United States* (3rd edn, 1822).
Coleridge, Samuel Taylor, *Collected Letters of Samuel Taylor Coleridge* (Ed. Earl Leslie Gredds, 6 vols, Oxford University Press, 1956-71).
Collier, J. P., *The Tragical Comedy and Comical Tragedy of Punch and Judy* (1828 & 1870).
Collyer, William Bengo, *W. B. C.'s Interesting Letter in Vindication of His Own Conduct, from the Calumnious Reports Circulated Against Him* (1823).
Colquhoun, Patrick, *The State of Indigence, and the Situation of the Casual Poor in the Metropolis Explained* (1799).
– *A Treatise on Indigence; Exhibiting a General View of the National Resources for Productive Labour; with Propositions for Ameliorating the Condition of the Poor* (1806).
– *A Treatise on the Wealth, Power, and Resources, of the British Empire in Every Quarter of the World* (1814).
– *A Treatise on the Police of the Metropolis* (1797).
Combe, William, and Rowlandson, Thomas, *The English Dance of Death* (2 vols, 1815).
Constant, Benjamin, *Political Writings* (translated and edited by Biancamaria Fontana, Cambridge, 2000).
Corry, John, *The English Metropolis, or London in the Year 1820* (1820).
– *A Satirical View of London at the Commencement of the Nineteenth Century* (1801).

[Crim. con. cases], *Crim. Con. Between Coachee and his Mistress. Fairburn's Edition of the Trial between Jesse Gregson, Esq and Tho. Theaker, His Coachman* (1808).

– *A Report of the Trial on an Action for Damages, Brought by the Reverend Charles Massy Against the Most Noble Marquis of Headfort, for Criminal Conversation with Plaintiff's Wife* (Dublin, 1804).

– *The Trial of Sir Arthur Paget, KB, Late Ambassador to the Courts of Vienna and Constantinople, for Criminal Conversation with Countess Borringdon* (1808).

– *The Trial of the Right Honourable Lord Paget, for Criminal Conversation with Lady Charlotte Wellesley* (1809).

Cruikshank, George, and Wight, George, *Sunday in London* (1833).

Davenport, Allen, *Life and Literary Pursuits* (1845).

Davis, William, *Hints to Philanthropists; or, a View of Practical Means for Improving the Condition of the Poor and Labouring Classes of Society* (Bath, 1821).

Donne, William, *Law and Justice Against Repression!* (1809).

Douglas, Sylvester, Baron Glenbervie, *The Glenbervie Journals* (Ed. Walter Sickel, 1910).

Edgeworth, Maria, *Belinda* (2 vols, Dublin, 1801).

Edwards, Thomas, *A Letter to the Lord Lieutenant of the County of Surrey, on the Misconduct of Licensing Magistrates, and the Consequent Degradation of the Magistracy* (1825).

Egan, Pierce, *Life in London; or, the Day and Night Scenes of Jerry Hawthorn, Esq, and Corinthian Tom. With Thirty-Six Scenes from Real Life, Designed and Etched by I. R. & G. Cruikshank* (1821).

– *The Finish to the Adventures of Tom, Jerry, and Logic, in Their Pursuit Through Life in and out of London* (1828).

– *Boxiana, or, Sketches of Ancient and Modern Pugilism . . . by One of the Fancy* (1812; 1818–24).

– *The Pilgrims of the Thames in Search of the National* (1838).

Fellowes, Robert, *Religion Without Cant* (1801).

Fonblanque, Albany, *England Under Seven Administrations* (3 vols, 1837).

Fox, Charles, *The Speeches of the Rt. Hon. C. J. F., in the House of Commons* (Ed. J. Wright, introduced by Lord Erskine, 1815).

Fry, Elizabeth, *Memoir of the Life of Elizabeth Fry, with Extracts from her Journal and Letters* (Eds Katherine Fry and Rachel E. Cresswell; 2 vols, 1847).

Gaskell, Peter, *The Manufacturing Population of England, Its Moral, Social, and Physical Conditions, and the Changes Which Have Arisen from the Use of Steam Machinery* (1833).

Geijer, Erik Gustaf, *Impressions of England 1809–1810. Compiled from His Letters and Diaries* (trans. Elizabeth Sprigge and Claude Napier, 1932).

Gibbs, Sir Vicary, *The Speech of Sir Vicary Gibbs, Knt, His Majesty's Attorney General . . . on Moving for a Rule to Shew Cause Why a Criminal Information Should Not Be Filed Against Henry Clifford Esq and Others* (1809).

Godwin, William, *An Enquiry Concerning Political Justice and Its Influence on General Virtue and Happiness* (2 vols, 1793).
Goede, Christian August Gottlieb, *The Stranger in England; or, Travels in Great Britain* (3 vols, 1807).
Good, John Mason, *Letter to Sir John Cox Hippisley, Bart., on the Mischiefs Incident to the Tread-wheel, as an Instrument of Prison Discipline* (1824).
Graham, Sir James, *Corn and Currency: in an Address to the Land Owners* (1826).
Granville, Countess of, *Letters of Harriet Countess Granville 1810–1845* (Ed. Hon. F. Leveson-Gore, 2 vols).
Greville, Charles, *The Greville Memoirs* (Eds Lytton Strachey and Roger Fulford, 1938).
Grimaldi, Joseph, *Memoirs* (Ed. Charles Dickens, 1838).
Gronow, Rees Howell, *Reminiscences of Regency and Victorian Life 1810–60* (Ed. Christopher Hibbert, 1991).
Guardian Society, *Report of the Provisional Committee* (1816).
– *Reports* (1817–27).
Hale, William, *An Address to the Public upon the Dangerous Tendency of the London Female Penitentiary* (1809).
Hamilton, Lady Anne, *The Epics of the Ton* (2nd edn, 1807).
Hanger, Col. George, *The Life, Adventures and Opinions of Col. George Hanger. Written by Himself* (2 vols, 1801?).
Hanway, Jonas, *A New Year's Gift to the People of Great Britain, Pleading for the Necessity of a More Vigorous and Consistent Police* (1784).
Hawkins, F. W., *The Life of Edmund Kean from Published and Original Sources* (2 vols, 1869).
Hazlitt, William, *Complete Works* (Ed. P. P. Howe; 21 vols, 1930–34).
– *The Eloquence of the British Senate* (2 vols, 1808).
– *Lectures, Chiefly on the Dramatic Literature of the Age of Elizabeth* (1820).
– *Lectures on the English Comic Writers* (1819).
– *The Plain Speaker* (1826).
– *The Spirit of the Age* (1825).
Headlam, John, *A Letter to the Right Honourable Robert Peel . . . on Prison Labour* (1823).
Higgins, Godfrey, *Horae Sabbaticae* (1833).
Hindley, Charles, *The True History of Tom and Jerry* (1888).
– *Curiosities of Street Literature* (1871).
– *The Life and Times of James Catnach* (1878).
Hobbs, Thomas, *A Short Sketch . . . of the 'Row' at the Theatre Royal* (Bath, 1809).
Hodson, G., *The Remonstrant* (1809).
Holland, Elizabeth Vassal, Baroness, *The Journal* (Ed. Earl of Illchester, 1908).
Hone, William, *Every-day Book, or Calendar of Popular Amusements* (2 vols, 1825–6).
– *Table Book* (1827).
– *Year Book of Daily Recreations* (1832).

Hotten, John Camden, Introduction to Egan's *Life in London* (1870).
Howitt, William, *The Rural Life of England* (2 vols, 1838).
Hunt, Leigh, *Lord Byron and Some of his Contemporaries* (1828).
Hurstone, J. P., *The Piccadilly Ambulator; or, Old Q* (2 vols, 1808).
Iatros, *A Biographical Sketch of the Life and Writings of Patrick Colquhoun, Esq, LLD* (1818).
Irving, Rev. Edward, *The Last Days: a Discourse on the Evil Character of These Our Times, Proving Them to Be the 'Perilous Times' of the 'Last Days'* (1828).
Jackson, Randle, *Considerations on the Increase of Crime* (1828).
Janson, Charles William, *The Stranger in America: Containing Observations on the Genius, Manners and Customs of the People of the United States; with Biographical Particulars of Public Characters* (1807).
Jefferson, Thomas, *Notes on the State of Virginia* (Paris, 1782).
Jesse, Captain, *The Life of George Brummell, Esq., Commonly Called Beau Brummell* (2 vols, 1844).
Johnstone, Julia, *Confessions of Julia Johnstone. In Contradiction to the Fables of Harriette Wilson* (1825).
Karamzin, Nikolai Mikhailovich, *Travels from Moscow, through Prussia, Germany, Switzerland, France, and England* (3 vols, 1803).
Kelly, Thomas, *Thoughts on the Marriages of the Labouring Poor* (1806).
Khan, Mirza Abul Hassan, *A Persian at the Court of King George: the Journal of Mirza Abul Hassan Khan, 1809–10* (Ed. and trans. Margaret Morris Cloake, 1988).
[Lamb, Lady Caroline], *Glenarvon* (3 vols, 1816).
Lennox, Lady Sarah, *Life and Letters* (Eds Countess of Ilchester and Lord Stavondale; 2 vols, 1901).
Lewis, Randle, *Reflections on the Causes of Unhappy Marriages* (1805) .
Macaulay, Zachary, *Life and Letters* (Ed. Margaret Jean Holland, Viscountess Knutsford, 1900).
Mainwaring, George, *Observations on the Present State of the Police of the Metropolis* (1821).
Malcolm, James Peller, *Anecdotes of the Manner and Customs of London during the Eighteenth Century . . . With a Review of Society in 1807* (2 vols, 1810).
Malthus, T. R., *An Essay on the Principle of Population, as It Affects the Future Improvement of Society; with Remarks on the Speculations of W. Godwin and M. Condorcet and Other Writers* (1803).
Martin, Matthew, *Letter to the Right Hon Lord Pelham, on the State of Mendicity in the Metropolis* (1804).
Martineau, Harriet, *Illustrations of Political Economy* (1832–3).
— *Poor Laws and Paupers* (1833–4).
McCulloch, J. R., *A Discourse on the Rise, Progress, Peculiar Objects, and Importance of Political Economy* (Edinburgh, 1825).
Medwin, Thomas, *Journal of the Conversations of Lord Byron* (1824).
Merle, W. H., *Odds and Ends* (1831).
Mill, John Stuart, *On Liberty* (Everyman's Library, 1992).

Moncrieff, W. T., *Tom and Jerry; or Life in London. An Operatic Extravaganza, in Three Acts* (1828?).
Montagu, Basil, *Thoughts on Laughter* (1830).
Moore, A. (pseud.), *The Annals of Gallantry* (3 vols, 1814).
Moore, Thomas, *Intercepted Letters; or the Two-Penny Post-Bag* (1813).
– *Letters and Journals of Lord Byron: with Notices of His Life* (2 vols, 1830).
– *Life of Sheridan* (2 vols, 1825).
More, Hannah, *Cheap Repository Tracts*, from the BL collection, pressmark 3130.m.11.
– *Moral Sketches of Prevailing Opinions and Manners* (1819).
– *Sketches for Persons of the Middle Ranks* (1835).
– *Strictures on the Modern System of Female Education* (5th edn, 2 vols, 1799).
– *Thoughts on the Importance of the Manners of the Great to General Society* (1788).
Morris, Captain Charles, *The Festival of Anacreon: Being a Complete Collection of Songs by Captain Morris* (9th edn; n.d.).
Murray, Hugh, *Enquiries Historical and Moral Respecting the Characters of Nations and the Progress of Society* (Edinburgh, 1807).
Nolan, Michael, *Speech . . . on Moving Leave to Bring in a Bill to Alter and Amend the Law for the Relief of the Poor* (1822).
Paley, William, *The Horae Paulinae of William Paley Carried Out and Illustrated in a Continuous History of the Apostolic Labours and Writings of St Paul* (1840).
– *The Principles of Moral and Political Philosophy* (1785).
Paris, Ayrton, *Analysis of the Most Celebrated Quack Medicines* (1812).
Patmore, P. G., *Letters on England. By Victoire Count de Soligny* (2 vols, 1823).
Peacock, Thomas Love, *Crotchet Castle* (Penguin, 1969).
– 'The Four Ages of Poetry,' *Olliers Literary Miscellany in Prose and Verse*, no. 1 (1820).
Philanthropic Society, *To the Public* (1788).
– *Reports* (1789–1830).
Philaretes, Philippus, *Adultery Analysed; an Inquiry into the Causes of the Prevalence of That Vice in These Kingdoms in the Present Days* (1810).
Pitman, John Rogers, *The School-Shakespeare* (1822).
Place, Francis, *Autobiography* (Ed. Mary Thrale, Cambridge, 1972).
– *Illustrations and Proofs of the Principle of Population: Including an Examination of the Proposed Remedies of Mr Malthus, and a Reply to the Objections of Mr Godwin and Others* (1822).
– *Improvement of the Working People* (1834).
Porter, R., *Progress of the Nation* (1836).
Pückler-Muskau, H. L. H. von, *Tour in England, Ireland and France, in the Years 1828 and 1829 . . . by a German Prince* (1832).
Raikes, Thomas, *Portion of the Journal Kept by T. Raikes Esq, from 1831 to 1847* (4 vols, 1856).
Raumer, Frederick von, *England in 1835: Being a Series of Letters Written to*

Friends in Germany During a Residence in London and Excursions into the Provinces (3 vols, 1836).
Roberts, William, *Memoirs of the Life and Correspondence of Hannah More* (4 vols, 1834).
Rush, Richard, *Memoranda of a Residence at the Court of London* (Philadelphia, 1833 (first series) and 1845 (second series)).
Russell, Lord John, *Essays and Sketches of Life and Character* (1820).
Sala, George Augustus, *The Life and Adventures of George Augustus Sala* (1898).
Scott, John (editor of the *Champion*), *A Visit to Paris in 1814* (rev. 4th edn, 1816).
Scott, John (minister, Hull), *An Account of Societies for the Reformation of Manners, and the Suppression of Vice; with Answers to Objections Against Them* (Hull, 1810?).
– *The Fatal Consequences of Licentiousness* (Hull, 1810).
– *Relaxation of Discipline the Source of Corrupted Morals* (Hull, 1827).
Scott, Sir Walter, *Miscellaneous Prose Works* (3 vols, 1829).
[Sedgwick, James], *Hints to the Public and the Legislature on the Effects of Evangelical Preaching. By a Barrister* (two parts, 1808).
Serres, Olive, *Observations and Strictures on the Conduct of Mrs Clarke by A Lady* (1809).
[Shaw, R.], *Observations on a Late Publication: Intituled, A Treatise on the Police of the Metropolis, by P. Colquhoun, Esq., by a Citizen of London: But No Magistrate* (1800).
Silliman, Benjamin, *A Journal of Travels in England, Holland, and Scotland, and of Two Passages over the Atlantic, in the Years 1805 and 1806* (2nd edn, 2 vols, Boston, MA, 1812).
Simond, *Journal of a Tour and Residence in Great Britain* (2 vols, 1815).
Skinner, John, *Journal of a Somerset Rector, 1803-1834: Parochial Affairs at the Parish of Camerton* (Eds Howard and Peter Coombs, rev. edn 1971).
Smiles, Samuel, *Self-Help* (introduced by Keith Joseph, 1986).
Smith, Adam, *The Theory of Moral Sentiments* (2 vols, Edinburgh, 1808 edn).
Smith, John Thomas, *Vagabondiana; or, Anecdotes of Mendicant Wanderers Through the Streets of London* (1817).
Smith, Mary, *Observations on Seduction, and the Evil Consequences Attending It* (1808).
Society for Bettering the Condition and Increasing the Comforts of the Poor, *Reports* (1797–1817).
Society for Carrying into Effect His Majesty's Proclamation Against Vice and Immorality, *Reports* (1788–1800).
Society for the Improvement of Prison Discipline and the Reformation of Juvenile Offenders, *Description of the Tread Mill Invented by Mr W. Cubbitt for the Employment of Prisoners, as Recommended by the Society* (1822).
Society for Promoting the Observance of the Christian Sabbath Conformably with Divine Command, *Address of the Society* (1809).
Society for the Suppression of Mendicity, *Reports* (1819–1830).

Society for the Suppression of Vice, *Address to the Public from the Society for the Suppression of Vice, Instituted in London, 1801* (1803).
– *An Appeal to Common Decency and the Law of the Land, Against the Practice of bathing* (1818).
– *The Constable's Assistant* (1808).
– *Report for 1825* (BL pressmark, 8276.e.62.1).
Solomon, Samuel, *A Guide to Health; or, Advice to Both Sexes, in Nervous and Consumptive Complaints, Scurvy, Leprosy, and Scrofula; Also, on a Certain Disease and Sexual Debility. To Which Is Added an Address to Boys, Young Men and Guardians of Youth with Observations on Watering Places, Hot and Cold Bathing* (1815 edn).
– See also: 'A Collection of Advertisements of Patent and Proprietary Medicines, c. 1790–1810', BL c.142.a.17.
Southey, Robert, *Essays, Moral and Political* (2 vols, 1832).
– *Letters from England: by Don Juan Manuel Alvarez Espriella* (3 vols, 1807).
– *Life and Correspondence* (Ed. Rev. Charles Southey, 1849).
– *New Letters* (Ed. Kenneth Curry, 1965) .
– *Sir Thomas More; or, Colloquies on the Progress and Prospects of Society* (1829).
Stael-Holstein, Augustus de, *Letters on England* (1825).
Stanhope (pseud.), *Chesterfield Burlesqued, or School for Modern Manners* (1811).
[Stephen, James], *Dangers of the Country* (1807).
Stephen, James Fitzjames, *Liberty, Equality, Fraternity* (1874).
Stephen, Leslie, 'Social Macadamisation', *Fraser's Magazine*, new series, vol. VI, no. XXXII, August 1872.
Stewart, Dugald, *Outlines of Moral Philosophy. For the Use of the Students of the University of Edinburgh* (2nd edn, Edinburgh, 1801).
– *The Philosophy of the Active and Moral Powers of Man* (2 vols, Edinburgh, 1828).
Stewart, Rev. J. Haldane, *The Pastor's Duty and Encouragement in the Present Times.* (1832).
Strutt, J., *The Sports and Pastimes of the People of England* (Ed. William Hone, 1830).
Styles, John, *An Essay on the Character and Influence of the Stage on Morals and Happiness* (2nd edn, 1807).
– *Strictures on Two Critiques in the Edinburgh Review, on the Subject of Methodism and Missions* (1808).
T., S. (as signature), *Address to the Guardian Society* (1817).
Taylor, Elizabeth, *Authentic Memoirs of Mrs [Mary Anne] Clarke* (2nd edn, 1809).
Taylor, Isaac, *Self-Cultivation Recommended; or Hints to a Youth Leaving School* (1817).
Thom, W., *Pedestrianism; or an Account of the Performances of Celebrated Pedestrians during the Last and Present Century* (Aberdeen, 1813).
Townsend, Joseph, *A Dissertation on the Poor Laws. By a Well-Wisher to Mankind* (1817).
Trotter, Thomas, *A View of the Nervous Temperament* (2nd edn, 1807).

Trusler, Rev. Dr John, *Principles of Politeness* (1777) .
— *A System of Etiquette* (1805).
— *The Way to be Rich and Respectable* (1796).
Vaughan, Robert, *The Age of Great Cities, or Modern Society Viewed in Relation to Intelligence, Morals and Religion* (1843).
Vaux, James Hardy, *Memoirs of J. H. V. Written by Himself* (1819).
Vizetelly, Henry, *Glances Back Through Fifty Years* (2 vols, 1893).
Wadd, William, *Cursory Remarks on Corpulence* (3rd edn, 1816).
Wade, John, *Treatise on the Police and Crimes of the Metropolis* (1829).
Wakefield, Edward Gibbon, *England and America: a Comparison of the Social and Political State of the Nations* (2 vols, 1833).
Walpole, Horace, *The Yale Edition of Horace Walpole's Correspondence* (Ed. W. S. Lewis, New Haven, Yale University Press, 1937–).
Ward, Robert Plumer, *Tremaine, or the Man of Refinement* (1825).
West, William, *Brief Inquiry Concerning Institutions for Relief of Poor Travellers* (1831).
Weyland, John Jr, *Observations on Mr Whitbread's Poor Bill* (1807).
Whyte, Robert, *Observations on the Nature, Causes, and Cure of Those Disorders Which Have Been Commonly Called Nervous, Hypochondriacal, or Hysteric* (Edinburgh, 1765).
Wilberforce, Robert Isaac and Samuel, *Life of William Wilberforce* (5 vols, 1838).
Wilberforce, William, *A Practical View of the Prevailing Religious System of Professed Christians, in the Higher and Middle Class of This Country, Contrasted with Real Christianity* (1797).
Wilson, Harriette, *Memoirs of a Lady of Pleasure* (1825).

Secondary Material

Aldridge, A. O., 'The Pleasures of Pity', *ELH*, vol. 16, no. 1, March 1949.
Altick, Richard, *The English Common Reader: a Social History of the Mass Reading public, 1800–1900* (Chicago University Press, 1957).
— *The Shows of London* (Cambridge, MA, Belknap Press, 1978).
Anderson, Digby (Ed.), *The Loss of Virtue: Moral Confusion and Social Disorder in Britain and America* (Social Affairs Unit, 1992).
— *Gentility Recalled: Mere Manners and the Making of Social Order* (Social Affairs Unit, 1996).
Anderson, Patricia, *The Printed Image and the Transformation of Popular Culture, 1790-1860* (Oxford, Clarendon Press, 1991).
Andrew, Donna, *Philanthropy and Police: London Charity in the Eighteenth Century* (Princeton University Press, 1989).
Arendt, Hannah, *On Revolution* (New York, Harmondsworth, Penguin, 1973).
Augstein, Hannah Franziska (Ed.), *Race: the Origins of an Idea, 1760–1850* (Bristol, Thoemmes, 1996).
Baer, Marc, *The Theatre and Disorder in Late Georgian London* (Oxford, Clarendon Press, 1992).

Bahmueller, Charles, *The National Charity Company: Bentham's Silent Revolution* (Berkeley, University of California Press, 1981).
Bailey, Victor (Ed.), *Policing and Punishment in Nineteenth-Century Britain* (Croom Helm, 1981).
Barker-Benfield, G. J., *The Culture of Sensibility: Sex and Society in Eighteenth Century Britain* (Chicago University Press, 1992).
Barrell, John, *The Birth of Pandora and the Division of Knowledge* (Basingstoke, Macmillan, 1990).
– *The Dark Side of the Landscape: the Rural Poor in English Paintings, 1730–1840* (Cambridge University Press, 1980).
– *The Idea of Landscape and the Sense of Place, 1730–1840: an Approach to the Poetry of John Clare* (Cambridge University Press, 1980).
Barry, Jonathon and Brooks, Christopher (Eds), *The Middling Sort of People: Culture, Society and Politics in England, 1550–1800* (Basingstoke, Macmillan, 1994).
Beier, A. L., Cannadine, David and Rosenstein, James M., *The First Modern Society: Essays in English History in Honour of Lawrence Stone* (Cambridge University Press, 1989).
Bold, Alan (Ed.), *Drink to Me Only: the Prose (and Cons) of Drinking* (Robin Clark, 1982).
Bordua, David Joseph, *The Police: Six Sociological Essays* (New York, Wiley, 1967).
Boulton, William B., *The Amusements of Old London* (John C. Nimmo, 1901).
Boyer, George, *An Economic History of the Poor Law, 1750-1850* (Cambridge University Press, 1990).
Bradley, Ian C., *The Call to Seriousness: the Evangelical Impact on the Victorians* (Cape, 1976).
Brailsford, Dennis, *Bareknuckles: a Social History of Prize-Fighting* (Cambridge, Lutterworth, 1988).
Brewer, John, *Pleasures of the Imagination: English Culture in the Eighteenth Century* (Harper Collins, 1997).
Bristow, Edward, *Vice and Vigilance: Purity Movements in Britain since 1700* (Dublin, Gill and Macmillan, 1977).
Brown, Ford Keeler, *Fathers of the Victorians* (Cambridge University Press, 1961).
Brundage, Anthony, *The Making of the New Poor Law: the Politics of Inquiry, Enactment and Implementation, 1832–39* (Hutchinson, 1978).
Bushaway, Bob, *By Rite: Custom, Ceremony and Community in England, 1700–1880* (Junction, 1982).
Campbell, Colin, *The Romantic Ethic and the Spirit of Modern Consumerism* (Oxford, Basil Blackwell, 1989).
Carwardine, Richard, *Transatlantic Revivalism: Popular Evangelism in Britain and America, 1790–1865* (Westport, CN, Greenwood Press, 1978).
Castle, Terry, *Masquerade and Civilization: the Carnivalesque in Eighteenth Century English Culture and Fiction* (Methuen, 1986).
Chancellor, E. Beresford, *The Lives of the Rakes* (6 vols, Philip Allan, 1925).

– *Life in Regency and Early Victorian Times* (1926).
Clark, Kitson, *The Making of Victorian Britain* (Methuen, 1962).
Clark, Peter, *The English Alehouse, a Social History, 1200–1830* (Longman, 1983).
Colley, Linda, *Britons Forging the Nation* (Yale University Press, 1992).
– 'Whose Nation?' *Past & Present*, 113, 1986.
Corfield, Penelope, *Power and the Professions in Britain, 1700–1850* (Routledge, 1995).
Crane, Robert, 'Suggestions Toward a Genealogy of the "Man of Feeling"', *ELH*, vol. 1, no. 3, December 1934.
Daunton, Martin (Ed.), *Charity, Self Interest and Welfare in the English Past* (University College London Press, 1996).
Daunton, Martin, *Progress and Poverty, an Economic and Social History of Britain, 1700–1850* (Oxford University Press, 1995).
Davidoff, Leonore and Hall, Catherine, *Family Fortunes: Men and Women of the English Middle-Class, 1780–1850* (Hutchinson, 1987).
Digby, Anne, *Pauper Palaces* (Routledge and Kegan Paul, 1978).
Donajgrodzki, A. P. (Ed.), *Social Control in Nineteenth Century Britain* (Croom Helm, 1977).
Dyer, Gary, *British Satire and the Politics of Style, 1789–1832* (Cambridge University Press, 1997).
Emsley, C., *British Society and the French Wars, 1793–1815* (Macmillan, 1979).
– *Crime and Society in England, 1750–1900* (Longman, 1987).
– *The English Police: a Political and Social History* (Harvester and Wheatsheaf, 1991).
– *Policing and its Context, 1750–1870* (Macmillan, 1983).
FitzSimons, Raymond, *Edmund Kean: Fire from Heaven* (Hamilton, 1976).
Fontana, Biancamaria, *Rethinking the Politics of Commercial Society: the* Edinburgh Review *1802–1832* (Cambridge University Press, 1985).
Ford, John, *Prizefighting: the Art of Regency Boximania* (Newton Abbot, David and Charles, 1971).
Gammon, V., 'Song, Sex and Society in England 1600–1850', *Folk Music Journal* 4/3(1982).
Gash, Norman, *Mr Secretary Peel: the Life of Sir Robert Peel to 1830* (Longmans, 1961).
Gatrell, V. A. C., *The Hanging Tree: Execution and the English People, 1770–1868* (Oxford University Press, 1994).
Gatrell, V. A. C., Lenman, Bruce and Parker, Geoffrey (Eds), *Crime and the Law: the Social History of Crime in Western Europe* (Europa, 1980).
Gill, Frederick, *The Romantic Movement and Methodism: a Study of English Romanticism and the Evangelical Revival* (Epworth Press, 1937).
Golby, J. M. and Purdue, A.W., *The Civilization of the Crowd: Popular Culture 1750–1900* (Batsford, 1984).
Graham, Peter, *Don Juan and Regency England* (Charlottesville, University Press of Virginia, 1990).
Gray, Denis, *Spencer Perceval: the Evangelical Prime Minister* (Manchester University Press, 1963).

Harris, Tim (Ed.), *Popular Culture in England, c1500–1850* (Macmillan, 1995).
Harrison, J. F. C., *The Second Coming: Popular Millenarianism, 1780–1850* (Routledge and Kegan Paul, 1979).
Hay, Douglas and Snyder, Francis (Eds), *Policing and Prosecution in Britain 1750–1850* (Oxford, 1989).
Hellmuth, Eckhart (Ed.), *The Transformation of Political Culture: England and Germany in the Late Eighteenth-Century* (Oxford University Press, 1990).
Hilton, Boyd, *The Age of Atonement* (Oxford University Press, 1988).
– *Corn, Cash, Commerce: the Economic Policies of the Tory Governments, 1815–1830* (Oxford University Press, 1977).
– *A Mad, Bad, and Dangerous People?* (Oxford University Press, 2006).
Himmelfarb, Gertrude, *The De-Moralization of Society: from Victorian Virtues to Modern Values* (New York, Alfred Knopf, 1995).
– *One Nation, Two Cultures* (New York, Alfred Knopf, 1999).
Horn, Pamela, *Life and Labour in Rural England, 1760–1850* (Basingstoke, Macmillan, 1987).
Ignatieff, Michael, *A Just Measure of Pain: the Penitentiary in the Industrial Revolution, 1750–1850* (Macmillan, 1978).
Ingrams, Richard, *The Life and Adventures of William Cobbett* (Harper Collins, 2005).
Jaeger, Muriel, *Before Victoria: Changing Standards of Behaviour, 1787–1837* (Penguin Books, 1967).
Kelly, Ian, *Beau Brummell: the Ultimate Dandy* (Hodder and Stoughton, 2005).
Keppel, Sonia, *The Sovereign Lady: a Life of Elizabeth Vassall, Third Lady Holland, and Her Family* (Hamilton, 1974).
Langford, Paul, *Englishness Identified: Manners and Character, 1650–1850* (Oxford University Press, 2000).
Laver, James, *The Age of Illusion: Manners and Morals, 1750–1848* (Weidenfeld and Nicolson, 1972).
Leach, Robert, *The Punch and Judy Show: History, Tradition and Meaning* (Batsford, 1985).
Longhurst, Ronald, 'Greenwich Fair', *Transactions of the Greenwich and Lewisham Antiquarian Society*, VII, 4, 1970.
Malcolmson, Robert, *Popular Recreations in English Society, 1700–1850* (Cambridge University Press, 1973).
MacCarthy, Fiona, *Byron: Life and Legend* (John Murray, 2003).
Mason, Michael, *The Making of Victorian Sexual Attitudes* (Oxford University Press, 1994).
McCutcheon, Roger P., 'A Note on Cant', *Modern Language Notes*, vol. 36, no. 1, January 1921.
McGowen, R., 'Terror, the Prison, and Humanitarian Reform', *Journal of British Studies*, XXV, 1986.
Miles, Dudley, *Francis Place: the Life of a Remarkable Radical* (Brighton, Harvester, 1988).
Moers, Ellen, *The Dandy. Brummell to Beerbohm* (Secker and Warburg, 1960).

Morgan, Marjorie, *Manners, Morals and Class in England, 1774–1858* (Basingstoke, Macmillan, 1994).
Morley, Henry, *Memoirs of Bartholomew Fair* (1859).
Morris, R. J., *Class and Class Consciousness in the Industrial Revolution* (Macmillan, 1979).
– *Class, Sect and Party: the Making of the Middle Class, Leeds 1820–1850* (Manchester University Press, 1990) .
– 'Voluntary Societies and British Urban Elites', *History Journal*, XXVI, 1983.
Nash, S., 'Prostitution and Charity', *Journal of Social History*, XVII, 1984.
Paley, Ruth, '"An Imperfect, Inadequate and Wretched System"? Policing London before Peel', *Criminal Justice History*, X, 1989.
Perkin, Harold, *The Origins of Modern British Society* (Routledge and Kegan Paul, 1969).
Pocock, J. G. A., *Virtue, Commerce and History: Essays on Political Thought and History, Chiefly in the Eighteenth Century* (Cambridge University Press, 1985).
Porter, Roy, *Disease, Medicine and Society in England, 1550–1860* (Basingstoke, Macmillan, 1993).
– *Quacks, Fakers and Charlatans in English Medicine* (Stroud, Tempus, 2000).
Poynter, J. R., *Society and Pauperism: English Ideas on Poor Relief, 1795–1834* (Routledge and Kegan Paul, 1969).
Quinault, Roland and Stevenson, John, *Popular Protest and Public Order. Six Studies in British History, 1790–1920* (George Allen and Unwin, 1974).
Quinlan, Maurice, *Victorian Prelude: a History of English Manners, 1700–1839* (New York, Columbia University Press, 1941).
Radford, Peter, *The Celebrated Captain Barclay: Sport, Gambling and Adventure in Regency England* (Headline, 2002).
Radford, Ursula, 'The Loyal Saddler of Exeter', *Transactions of the Devonshire Association for the Advancement of Science, Literature, and Art*, vol. LXV, 1933.
Radner, J. B., 'The Youthful Harlot's Curse: the prostitute as symbol of the city', *Eighteenth Century Life*, vol. II, 1976.
Radzinowicz, Leon, *A History of the Criminal Law and its administration from 1750* (Stevens & Sons, 1948).
Rashid, S., 'Dugald Stewart, Baconian Methodology and Political Economy', *Journal of the History of Ideas*, XLVI, 1985.
Rawson, Claude, *Satire and Sentiment* (Yale, 2000).
Reid, John, *Bucks and Bruisers: Pierce Egan and Regency England* (Routledge and Kegan Paul, 1971).
Reiman, D., *The Romantics Reviewed* (5 vols, 1972).
Rose, John Holland, *The Life of William Pitt* (2 vols, G. Bull & Sons, 1911).
Rose, Michael Edward, *The English Poor Law, 1750–1830* (Newton Abbot, David and Charles, 1971).
Rosenfeld, Sybil, *The Theatre of the London Fairs in the Eighteenth Century* (Cambridge, 1960).
Rudé, George, *The Crowd in History: a Study of Popular Disturbances in France and England, 1730–1848* (John Wiley and Sons, 1964).

Rule, J., *Albion's People: English Society, 1714–1815* (Longman, 1992).
Semple, Janet, *Jeremy Bentham's Panopticon Prison* (University of London, 1993).
Sennett, Richard, *The Fall of Public Man* (Cambridge University Press, 1977).
Shklar, Judith, 'Let Us Not Be Hypocritical', *Daedalus*, CVIII, 3 (summer, 1979).
Shyllon, Folarin, *Black People in Britain* (Oxford University Press, 1977).
Sigsworth, Eric M. (Ed.), *In Search of Victorian Values* (Manchester University Press, 1988).
Smout, T. C. (Ed.), *Victorian Values: Proceedings of the British Academy*, LXXVIII (1992).
Storch, Robert (Ed.), *Popular Culture and Custom in Nineteenth Century England* (Croom Helm, 1982).
Taylor, David, *The New Police in Nineteenth Century England: Crime, Conflict and Class* (Manchester University Press, 1997).
Thomas, Donald, *A Long Time Burning: the History of Literary Censorship in England* (Routledge and Kegan Paul, 1969).
Thompson, E. P., *Customs in Common* (Merlin Press, 1991).
– *The Making of the English Working Class* (Victor Gollancz, 1963).
Thompson, F. M. L., *The Cambridge Social History of Britain* (3 vols, Cambridge University Press, 1990).
Todd, Janet, *Sensibility: an Introduction* (Methuen, 1986).
Tompkins, Joyce, *The Popular Novel in England 1770–1800* (Constable, 1932).
Trilling, Lionel, *Sincerity and Authenticity* (Oxford, 1974).
Vickers, Brian, Introduction to Henry Mackenzie's *The Man of Feeling* (Oxford, 1987).
Wagner, P., *Eros Revived: Erotica of the Enlightenment in England and America* (Secker and Warburg, 1986).
Wahrman, Dror, *Imagining the Middle Class: the Political Representation of Class in Britain, c1780–1840* (Cambridge University Press, 1995).
Walford, Cornelius, *Fairs Past and Present* (Elliot Stock, 1883).
Wallas, Graham, *The Life of Francis Place, 1771–1854* (Longman & Co., 1898).
Walvin, James, *The Black Presence: a Documentary History of the Negro in England, 1555–1860* (Orbach and Chambers, 1971).
– *Black and White: the Negro and English Society, 1555–1945* (Allen Lane, 1973).
Wardroper, John, *The World of William Hone: a New Look at the Romantic Age in Words and Pictures of the Day* (Shelfmark, 1997).
Wilson, Ben, *The Laughter of Triumph: William Hone and the Fight for the Free Press* (Faber and Faber, 2005).
Wiltshire, J., *Jane Austen and the Body: the Picture of Health* (Cambridge University Press, 1992).
Wrigley, E. A. and Schofield, R. S., *Population History of England, 1541–1871* (Edward Arnold, 1981).

Index

Figures in italics indicate captions.